RAOUL WALSH

Screen Classics

Screen Classics is a series of critical biographies, film histories, and analytical studies focusing on neglected filmmakers and important screen artists and subjects, from the era of silent cinema to the golden age of Hollywood to the international generation of today. Books in the Screen Classics series are intended for scholars and general readers alike. The contributing authors are established figures in their respective fields. This series also serves the purpose of advancing scholarship on film personalities and themes with ties to Kentucky.

SERIES EDITOR
Patrick McGilligan

BOOKS IN THE SERIES

Hedy Lamarr: The Most Beautiful Woman in Film
Ruth Barton

Von Sternberg
John Baxter

The Marxist and the Movies: A Biography of Paul Jarrico
Larry Ceplair

Warren Oates: A Wild Life
Susan Compo

Being Hal Ashby: Life of a Hollywood Rebel
Nick Dawson

Some Like It Wilder: The Life and Controversial Films of Billy Wilder
Gene D. Phillips

Arthur Penn: American Director
Nat Segaloff

Claude Rains: An Actor's Voice
David J. Skal with Jessica Rains

Buzz: The Life and Art of Busby Berkeley
Jeffrey Spivak

RAOUL WALSH

THE TRUE ADVENTURES OF HOLLYWOOD'S LEGENDARY DIRECTOR

Marilyn Ann Moss

THE UNIVERSITY PRESS OF KENTUCKY

Copyright © 2011 by The University Press of Kentucky

Scholarly publisher for the Commonwealth,
serving Bellarmine University, Berea College, Centre
College of Kentucky, Eastern Kentucky University,
The Filson Historical Society, Georgetown College,
Kentucky Historical Society, Kentucky State University,
Morehead State University, Murray State University,
Northern Kentucky University, Transylvania University,
University of Kentucky, University of Louisville,
and Western Kentucky University.
All rights reserved.

Editorial and Sales Offices: The University Press of Kentucky
663 South Limestone Street, Lexington, Kentucky 40508-4008
www.kentuckypress.com

15 14 13 12 11   5 4 3 2 1

Library of Congress Cataloging-in-Publication Data

Moss, Marilyn Ann.
 Raoul Walsh : the true adventures of Hollywood's legendary director / Marilyn
Ann Moss.
     p.   cm. — (Screen classics)
 Includes bibliographical references and index.
 ISBN 978-0-8131-3393-5 (hardcover : alk. paper) —
 ISBN 978-0-8131-3394-2 (ebook)
 1. Walsh, Raoul, 1887–1980. 2. Motion picture producers and directors—
United States—Biography. I. Title.
 PN1998.3.W35M58 2011
 791.4302'32092—dc22
 [B]
                              2011008580

This book is printed on acid-free paper meeting
the requirements of the American National Standard
for Permanence in Paper for Printed Library Materials.

Manufactured in the United States of America.

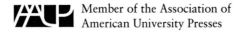 Member of the Association of
American University Presses

For my father, Louis Moss,
gone far too soon.

In the best films of Raoul Walsh, you can see the way he can put people into action . . . where they don't act but move and express, indirectly, subconsciously, their experience of life.

What makes something happen?

The placement of the camera.

The angle.

The lens.

The distance of the camera from the scene.

The physical execution.

—Pierre Rissient

Contents

Illustrations follow page 242

Acknowledgments

American cinema's original iconoclast, Raoul Walsh gave the movies some of their greatest action films as well as some of their most beautifully etched heroes and heroines caught either on their way up to a romance or on the downside of a doomed adventure. Walsh knew cinematic archetypes like the back of his hand: he had helped create them. He gave them fictional frames that were singularly his—the streets of teeming, sorrowful cities and the large western vistas in which a lone rider travels, casting his shadow against the side of a great mountain range. He took moviegoers onto the prairies, into the hubbub of New York's Bowery, and out onto the billowing seas, all the while helping transform the Hollywood studio yarn into a breathless art form. With a career that spanned over half a century, from the era of one- and two-reel silents to the tumultuous 1960s, Walsh belongs to that generation of filmmakers who learned to make movies on a dime in a fledgling industry at the start of the twentieth century and who invented a Hollywood picture that made storytelling bigger than life itself.

But, when he wasn't near a movie camera, Walsh wanted to escape into the narratives he put on the screen—and into stories of himself he chose to present to the public. For that reason, he was a challenge, unconsciously daring this biographer to understand him in the complex way he deserved. Getting to know the deeply evasive and enigmatic Raoul Walsh took some doing, and, toward this end, I found the help of many who knew him, worked with him, talked with him, or simply admired him. I am indebted to the circle of scholars, film aficionados, and colleagues, both Walsh's and my own, who gathered around to offer their experiences with Walsh and with his movies, all of which added much-needed breadth and depth to this biography. Walsh's life and career were so extensive and complex, his artistry so layered, that I was happy to benefit from their help. I hope that I have emerged from the life with a book that understands the man in a deeply truthful way.

Some thanks are in order. I could not have gathered the large collection of Walsh materials I needed without the help of Ned Comstock, whom again I have to call the *brilliant overachiever* running the Cinematic Arts Library at the University of Southern California. Ned should probably be listed as the coauthor of almost every film-related book that sees publication these days: he's a gifted researcher and archivist and a stickler for detail who is forever hunting down, photocopying, and generally manifesting indispensable materials for those of us who simply write and look at him with awe. I am, as always, indebted to him.

Luckily for this book, Walsh's nephew on Mary Walsh's side, Hank Kilgore, and his wife, Sue, gave unselfishly of their time to help me understand the personal side of Walsh. The Kilgores generously opened the doors of Walsh's home to me, searching through Raoul and Mary Walsh's photographs, letters, and personal documents, laying them out before me so that I could get to know Walsh the family man. They also put me in touch with the wonderful Hisayo Graham, Walsh's secretary in the 1960s and later his good friend, who traveled a good distance to meet with me and let me interview her. I also thank George Walsh Jr., Walsh's nephew, who spoke with me patiently on the phone several times about his uncle and his father, George, Raoul Walsh's younger brother.

I am also indebted to Kevin Brownlow, the film historian, scholar, and film preservationist extraordinaire, who likewise researched, photocopied, and generally shopped in his own amazing archives for me so that I could understand the richness of Walsh's silent film career. Kevin has a direct pipeline to every film, filmmaker, and performer who graced the silent screen, and I have benefited enormously from his generosity.

Walsh was, if anything, an endearing and much-loved friend to many people in his long life. Luckily for me, when he was already in his eighties, he met the literary agent Bob Bookman, then a student at Yale, whom Walsh came to love as a son and in fact called his "Number One Son" in the numerous letters he wrote to him that Bob shared with me—along with Walsh's original manuscripts for his novels and autobiography and a painting or two that Walsh, ever the diligent artist, gave him.

I am very grateful to Sandra Joy Lee and Jonathan Auxier, curators of the Warner Bros. Archives at the University of Southern California's School of Cinematic Arts. This amazing archive formed the basis of most of my research, not only because Walsh worked for Jack Warner for thirty years, but also because under Jack's thumb the studio set in place the golden rule to write everything down on paper—every thought, every word ever uttered by an actor, a writer, a director, a producer, or a crew member. For that reason, Warners has an enormously rich archive to offer film scholars and historians, one that overlaps the Twentieth Century–Fox Papers held at the University of California, Los Angeles, which offers fewer materials.

My deep thanks go out to dear friends and colleagues who kept me sitting upright during those long days and nights of uncertainty when Walsh's body of work loomed large and larger before me: To Harley Lond, my great friend and the best editor of my work. To Fred Lombardi, with whom I developed a good friendship during the course of writing this book; his emails kept me going as I worked on the West Coast and he sat in New Jersey writing the biography of Walsh's good friend, Allan Dwan. To Paul Lynch, who accompanied me on so many of the interviews conducted for this book and who constantly egged me on to finish. To Sandra Kumamoto Stanley, Gayle (G.G.) Golden, Virginia Crane, Eunice Lederman, and my film compadre, Linda Civitello, a scholar, a foodie, and a talented film historian—you are all my clan. I am so grateful to Ross Williams, who helped me track down information on Walsh's second wife, Lorraine Walker, and offered so much support; we're still looking for her.

A nod to my two biography heroes, Joe McBride, a brilliant biographer and a wonderful friend, and Patrick McGilligan, who was this book's first reader and who offered suggestions that transformed an early, unruly manuscript into a readable text.

My good thanks go to Rudy Behlmer, the go-to mensch for anything Warners, who sat with me at Musso and Frank's (at Sergio's station!) early into this project and talked Walsh for hours; to the Walsh aficionado Pierre Rissient, Walsh's good friend in France, who put up with four interviews with me and gave me my first inclination of who the man Raoul Walsh really was; to Bertrand Tavernier, also a Walsh aficionado, who kindly put me in touch with Pierre Rissient. Many thanks to Michael Henry Wilson, whose book on Walsh inspired me early on and who opened his home to an interview with me. A nod also to Toni D'Angeli in Rome, whose book on Walsh is a brilliant piece of critical analysis. Toni's web magazine, *La furia umana,* published an early draft of my work on Walsh's *They Drive by Night.*

I owe a great debt to Walsh's colleagues who agreed to interviews and who shared their memories of the man: to my hero, the awe-inspiring Olivia de Havilland, who graciously spoke to me by fax from her home in France (and to the wonderful Robert Osborne, TCM's great host, who first put me in touch with Miss de Havilland); to the beautiful, indomitable Jane Russell, who invited me to her home more than once to talk about Walsh and about her own colorful career; to Sir Ken Adam, the brilliant art director, who corresponded with me from his home in England and sent some wonderful photographs; to Bryan Forbes, the formidable writer-director and a close friend of Walsh's; to the ever-entertaining Richard Erdman, Hugh O'Brian (who also offered an evening of splendid magic tricks), and Harry (Dobe) Carey Jr.; to Kirk Douglas, who patiently emailed me with answers to my questions; to Walter and Susan Doniger, who also showed such patience with my many questions; to Jack Larsen, who has great stories to share; to Peter Newbrook, the cameraman who gave me some of the funniest stories about Walsh during the early 1950s; to Joan Leslie, who provided me with a vivid portrait of Walsh on the set of *High Sierra;* and to Tommy Cook, who also talked to me about working with Walsh.

A very special thanks to essential film scholars for me: Peter Bog-danovich and Richard Schickel, both of whom took great care to talk to me about their friend Raoul Walsh. The generous John Gallagher, who selflessly shared with me some essential interviews he conducted with Walsh's colleagues, also made this book richer and sent me Walsh movies I wouldn't have otherwise seen. I admire John's scholarship to no end. I also thank the D. W. Griffith scholar Tom Gunning and the USC scholar Nicholas Cull, who shared with me information about Walsh's fiasco with Warner Bros. over the production of the film *PT 109* in the 1960s. I also thank George Stevens Jr. for his emails to me concerning that episode and Connie Martinson, the wife of the director Leslie A. Martinson, who directed me to Nicholas Cull's work on the subject. My thanks also to Christa Fuller for talking to me about the friendship between her husband, Sam Fuller, and Walsh; and to Jeanine Basinger for an early and enlightening phone conversation about her friend Walsh. My gratitude goes to Gregorio Rocha, whose documentary on the lost footage of Walsh's early work on Pancho Villa was illuminating, as was my brief correspondence with him. Also, I thank my friend and fellow writer Alan K. Rode.

I give thanks many times over to my friends at the Margaret Herrick Library at the Academy of Motion Picture Arts and Sciences in Beverly Hills: the research archivists Barbara Hall and Jenny Romero as well as the always diligent photographic archivist Faye Thompson. To my long-time friend at the UCLA Arts Library Special Collections, Lauren Buisson, who pulled Twentieth Century–Fox production files in a jiffy when I needed them. Also at UCLA, thanks to the archivist Julie Graham, and a special thank you to Mark Quigley at the Film and Television Archive, who made available to me so many of Walsh's early silent films. At the Museum of Modern Art, I thank Charles Silver, curator of the Film Department, who arranged a screening of Walsh's *The Loves of Carmen* for me and who pulled files and offered up some great Walsh stories.

I also thank Joan Miller, the archivist at Wesleyan University's Cinema Archives, who gave me unlimited access to the papers of Raoul Walsh that the library holds. Along those lines, I cannot thank enough my indispensable and consistently sharp archival research assistant, Karl Ljungquist, who put in order so many Walsh documents and helped enormously with assembling Walsh's intricate filmography and this book's index. I also thank Leith Johnson, a former archivist at the Wesleyan University Cinema Archives, the very helpful Emma Furderer and Kathleen Dickson at the British Film Institute, and Jared Case, the film cataloger at the George Eastman House in Rochester, New York. I am also grateful to Elizabeth Anthony for providing information about the actress Alida Valli's involvement with Walsh's film *The World in His Arms* and to Theresa Schwartzman, who so long ago alerted me to Gregorio Rocha's documentary *The Lost Reels of Pancho Villa*. Thank you, also, Claire Brandt, the matriarch at the indispensable Eddie Brandt's Saturday Matinee in North Hollywood, California, which has videos, photographs, and DVDs that exist nowhere else on the planet. Thanks also go out to researchers at the Harry Ransom Library at the University of Texas at Austin and at the George Bancroft Library at the University of California, Berkeley. I also salute my talented copyeditor, Joseph Brown, and, at the University Press of Kentucky, my creative and very patient editor, David Cobb. Thanks also go to the equally patient Anne Dean Watkins, acquisitions editor at the University Press of Kentucky.

This book would be missing a good part of Walsh's life were it not for the generosity of two special people. First is Bonnie Coles, senior search examiner at the Library of Congress, who searched endlessly through Miriam Cooper's papers housed there and who photocopied enormous amounts of material and conducted her own research at the library on my behalf. Finally, and with unending gratitude, I thank the wonderful actor-director L. Q. Jones, whose anecdotes about Raoul Walsh, a man he admired greatly, gave this book the greatest kick in the pants it could have gotten.

To my wonderful and supportive family, you have all my gratitude and my love. And to my brave and very creative daughter, Lizzie: you are my heart. Thank you yet again for putting up with all those black-and-white movies, some with sound, some without, that I suspect you never would have searched out on your own! And, of course, for Sol.

And, finally, to Anne Francis, who, despite her own health problems, unselfishly returned phone calls, and even initiated phone calls, to talk with me about working with Walsh in the 1950s. Sadly, she did not live to see the publication of this book, but her generosity and her spirit are here.

After this long journey to the land of Raoul Walsh, I honestly can understand what all the others have been saying to me all along: "I sure miss that man!"

Prologue
A Wild Ride

When Raoul Walsh was fifteen years old, he awoke one night from a dream that left him shaking. He trembled as much from dread as from a half-formed sense of excitement. In a sleep that seemed as much nightmare as fantasy, he saw that his beloved mother, Elizabeth, had suddenly died. He could make no sense of it and could no longer reach out to touch her. An overwhelming sadness took over. But at the same time he had a sense of something startling: he now stood on the brink of a fabulous journey, a great adventure that offered escape from the hole he felt had just been shot through the middle of his heart.

The dread that touched the young Walsh that night was no fiction. Just two days earlier, his beautiful and much-beloved mother, Elizabeth Walsh, had died of cancer at the age of forty-two, leaving behind a devoted husband, three children, and a household she had filled with endless storytelling and fanciful flights of imagination. For Raoul Walsh, the grief was almost unbearable. As he wrote in his autobiography more than seventy years later, "I was quite unprepared for the sudden blow that left me motherless at fifteen. . . . Mother passed away in the big master bedroom into which I used to steal and beg for one of her stories about an earlier America. . . . Where before I had loved it, the place became unbearable. . . . The terrible thing was that she was gone and I was only half a person."[1]

Not only did the stories cease; so did Elizabeth and Thomas Walsh's renowned dinner parties, where the Walsh children sat at the table infatuated while listening to the ramblings of a Lionel Barrymore or a John L. Sullivan in the time it took to finish one course and move on to another.

1

So adrift was young Walsh that he could not understand his life now or what lay in store. His only recourse lay in creating another kind of dream that encapsulated a great adventure, one that, perhaps unknown to him then, began the moment his mother died: it would last a lifetime. He jumped so quickly into fantasy that he may even have imagined the adventure that lay before him. The line between what was true and what was fantasy became blurred—but either way he embarked on a wild ride.

The fantasy came quickly: Walsh's father, Thomas, seeing how Elizabeth's death devastated his oldest son, encouraged the boy to travel so as to escape. Thomas's brother, Matthew, was about to set off on the high seas for Cuba, and Thomas made certain that his son was on board when Matthew's schooner, the *Enniskillen,* sailed out of Peck's Slip in New York City in one week's time. From now on, only the *telling* mattered.

In this moment, Raoul Walsh created the fundamental subject of his life—and of his art to come. He knew how to escape great sadness by dreaming, then creating, an adventure of his own making, one shaped by his own design. His escape was forged from a schism in his psyche that he would come to articulate in storytelling, that he would come to count on. The pervasive mourning that had left a hole in his soul responded easily to the sense of imagination and fantasy that leaped up to fill it. Adventure and fantasy offered the only viable means of escape from the grief that, ironically, he never would escape. These two—grief and adventure—locked themselves together in his mind. It would be ironic that the grief he felt at the loss of his mother gave his art great range; he escaped repeatedly because he had to. Now only "half a person," Walsh had to fill in the other half of himself, and he would do it through adventure and storytelling.

Forced to make friends with sadness, Walsh, unconsciously, perhaps, took that sadness with him into stories he told himself. As he got older, his great sense of storytelling served him well when, on the cusp of his twenties, he found his way into the fledgling movie industry, where storytelling could fill huge movie screens. Telling stories to others, he found fictional characters persistently embarking on an adventure of some kind. His film art would depict great action that, emotionally and physically, drove his characters forward—their sense of duty more often than not triggered by a sadness, a mistake, that they leave behind. As it did in Walsh's early life, sadness haunts the tragic outsiders Roy Earle and his girlfriend, Marie, in *High Sierra;* while they make plans to evade the police, their actions stem from a desperate need to save their own lives. In Walsh's first Warner Bros. outing, *The Roaring Twenties,* although Jimmy Cagney's Eddie Bartlett returns home from the war with great expectations, his life spirals downward as he makes one mistake after another in trying simply to make a legitimate living. A sense of sadness also underscores *White Heat's* Oedipally deranged Cody Jarrett as he unintentionally maps out his climb to chaos, ending in his fiery demise in Walsh and Cagney's hugely iconic 1949 outing.

Even earlier than these postwar films, darkness defines the society Walsh paints in his silent films *Regeneration, The Honor System,* and *What Price Glory?* just as it manipulates his soldiers' and renegades' adventures later on in the 1950s films and wreaks havoc in the lives of his 1950s women, especially Mamie Stover and the four women holed up at a ranch in *The King and Four Queens.* Walsh's darkness is more often than not driven underground in his characters' psyches. They look to be moving forward, yet a tinge of world-weariness shows on their faces, in the way they move, in the choices they make.

Throughout the 1910s and 1920s, Walsh wrote and directed at a fever pitch. He took a huge chance and traveled through seven states to film the achingly difficult *The Big Trail,* a financial gamble that didn't pay off and that instead sent him reeling for the next decade until he rebounded when he landed at Warner Bros., the studio that oversaw his golden period of storytelling. During this time of great success, Walsh never appeared to challenge the system he worked within. If anything, he looked to be its best yes-man, taking work when, as he liked to say, the studio dropped off a script on his front lawn the morning after he had just finished shooting the previous one. He said yes because he lived in a much deeper psychological place; he lived in his filmic adventures and kept them as a great protection. While the social world around him saw tragic events envelop other directors' art—responses to two world wars, for one, and the Great Depression, for another—Walsh kept moving at lightning speed, his pictures seeming unscathed by that real world and existing instead in a dream state, the state induced by making movies. He escaped that far more dangerous world and stayed inside his own fictional intentions.

This seeming doubleness—existing in one world (looking like a yes-man) but more authentically living in another—made Walsh a maverick in the truest sense. He directed pictures that gathered audiences and momentum: they could be humorous, ribald, gutsy. But always they were technically agile and at the same time displayed a broad understanding of American types, American landscapes. His stories hinged on a swift movement and rhythm that became his signature. Yet the maverick psyche lay elsewhere—hidden, untouched.

The need for escape from sadness never abated. On the first page of his autobiography, *Each Man in His Time,* written when he was in his mideighties and nearing the end of his life, sadness is the first feeling Walsh recalls and wants his reader to see. He writes about his "marvelous childhood" yet begins with an image of a man grieving: "One of my earliest memories: the sadness of Edwin Booth's face, when he came to visit my father at our brownstone house on Forty-eighth Street in New York. . . . 'Why does Mr. Booth look so unhappy,' I asked my mother, adding in six-year-old wonder, 'Didn't he have a good dinner?' Mother tactfully explained that our tragic guest's brother, John Wilkes Booth, was the man who shot President Lincoln. She shook her head. 'Poor Edwin!'"

Walsh talks about Edwin Booth but really refers to himself and to the characters to come who live in front of his camera—people who long to be safe and long to redeem themselves, even if the longing is only half formed in their consciousness. His dream held within itself the seeds of adventure, mystery, and romance. Yet, at its core, it contains a kind of grief that drives his psychology to those imaginary places. Walsh never acknowledged, and perhaps only half knew, that the actor who eventually played John Wilkes Booth, the maverick, emotionally veiled director he became, was the true subject of his own adventures.

Grief, adventure, spiritedness—all these meshed together as Walsh traversed his long career. He was a man extremely conscious of how Hollywood viewed him, and he did all he could to help shape that view. In his early career, when movie directors were seen both as gods and as odd curiosities, he began giving interviews to the press. He quickly gained a reputation for being wild; reporters painted him as a handsome, restless man, often flailing his hands in the air, jumping up and down on the set to get the performance he wanted out of his actors. With his blue eyes and wavy brown hair, he had movie-star good looks and a personality that strutted. Underneath that persona, however, Walsh was a serious soul, determined to get a picture wrapped on time and on budget. He never fudged on that goal in his fifty-plus years in the business.

As Walsh grew older, the press saw him not so much as a wild spirit as a humorous man whose life spilled out onto the public through endless anecdotes; he told crazy stories about his antics with Errol Flynn, Jimmy Cagney, and Humphrey Bogart. He quipped endlessly about prostitutes he had known, about cowboys and bandits he had run with, about getting drunk with the legends who visited his set, with the crew he adored more than any other bunch.

But these were stories, part of the adventure, part of the fiction he learned to wrap around himself so that he would not really be seen. "Let's get the hell out of here!" he often yelled out on the set when a scene wrapped. Part humorous, part serious, the quip is the essential Walsh—the man half in but at the same time half out the door, perpetually ready to bolt, to leap and walk quickly away, and to disappear into the dark corners of a soundstage where no one could find him but where everyone always knew he was just the same.

1

Becoming Raoul Walsh

> There was things which he stretched, but mainly he told the
> truth.
>   That is nothing. I never seen anybody but lied, one time or
> another. . . .
> —Mark Twain, *Adventures of Huckleberry Finn*

When Albert Edward Walsh was born on March 11, 1887, in New York
City, the moving-picture business was little more than a flicker in the
country's collective consciousness. George Eastman would not produce
or market celluloid film for another year, and the earliest known film
on record, W. K. L. Dickson's *Fred Ott's Sneeze,* was still four years
away. So was Thomas Edison's move to file patents for the Kinetograph
and Kinetoscope, neither of which would be displayed until the Chicago
World's Fair in 1893. By the time the first nickelodeon opened in Pitts-
burgh in 1905, Walsh would be eighteen years old, having left home for
the adventures he so craved—the fantasies movies are made of.

Yet the stories that the soon-to-be renamed "Raoul" Walsh would
write and direct were already taking shape around him. In New York
City, the Bowery that he later put on film was already a sprawling tenement full of lower-class concert halls, brothels, and flophouses, an area
Walsh soon relished as a childhood hangout. The ships and schooners
that he spent hours sniffing out as a kid and that billowed into huge
proportions in his films *Captain Horatio Hornblower* and *Blackbeard
the Pirate* already stirred his imagination—there they were, docked at
New York's Peck's Slip, a romantic neck of the city that Walsh and his
younger brother, George, loitered in regularly. Even the gangs on the
Lower East Side were taking over Hell's Kitchen and adjacent neighborhoods that Walsh later re-created on the "New York" streets of Warner
Bros. for *The Roaring Twenties,* his Cagney-Bogart gangster picture.

Out West, mythic heroes had already made a place for themselves somewhere in Walsh's imagination. Just seven years before his birth, Wyatt Earp, whom Walsh later claimed to have met on a Hollywood back lot, had just joined his brothers at the OK Corral and gunned down the Clanton boys. Buffalo Bill Cody, whom Walsh said used to stop by his family's brownstone when he was a kid to sample his father's fine wines, had just set up his first traveling show in 1883. Sitting Bull had surrendered his rifle to General Alfred Terry, who five years earlier had directed the campaign that ended in the Lakota chief's victory over General George Custer at Little Big Horn—a battle no one would reimagine as romantically as Walsh did when he later directed *They Died with Their Boots On* at Warner Bros. studios.

Fiction and myth followed Walsh so closely throughout his life that it almost seemed as if he'd forged himself *from* them. If he was not creating a story for the big screen, he was creating one for his own life—a way to explain himself to himself and to others so as to weave his life inexplicably into legend. The line between what was fiction and what was fact would always be blurred in his imagination; he would be the last one to find a distinction between them. Speaking to reporters and to his myriad of film-buff followers, Walsh loved to tell a good story; no one ever knew whether it was truth or embellishment. Although it was well-known that he was raised in New York City, Walsh thought nothing of changing that story for dramatic effect. Sometimes he was born in Montana, at other times in Texas. Even better than the "stretchers" that escaped the lips of Huck Finn—in a novel published, serendipitously, just two years before Walsh's birth—Walsh's stories could be taller and wider. No one loved a stretcher more than he did.

"I'm not a Mortimer," Cary Grant yelps to a cabbie at the end of Frank Capra's *Arsenic and Old Lace*, "I'm the son of a sea captain!" "I'm not a cab driver," the cabbie yelps back, "I'm a coffeepot!" Walsh could have easily joined the choir, himself yelping, "I'm not just the son of a man named Thomas Walsh of New York City; I'm a fiction of my own making, and I've slipped off the page, off the screen, and into the public eye." This might be the defining quip about Raoul Walsh's life; the stories constantly changed, the identity tipped slightly to the left or to the right. One layer of self slipped away in the telling to reveal a new one. These are very much like his fictions that hit the movie screen: one character is a gangster, another a cowboy, a third a Navajo Indian. They are in his blood; they coalesce into the narratives that Walsh unleashed during his years in Hollywood and that he gathered for his well-received autobiography, *Each Man in His Time,* published in 1974, when Walsh was eighty-seven years old. The stories amaze. Did Walsh's father really get wind that Samuel Clemens was on his deathbed and take his young son to meet the dying author? Is it fact that, later on, when Walsh was a well-respected Hollywood director, the gangster Bugsy Siegel asked him to take a suitcase full of money to his friend William Randolph Hearst, to bribe the publisher to stop trying to scotch Siegel's plan to open a dog-racing park in Culver City? Did Walsh truly look Siegel in the face, say, "Nothing doing," and walk out the door without even looking back? For Walsh, all these things happened the minute he voiced them.

Lost in History

The truth is that fiction may always be on Walsh's side when it comes to knowing the details of his early life. Walsh will always have the last word on the way the story plays out simply because very little of what he concocted in interviews and in his autobiography can be proved or disproved. There is scarce historical record to shed light on his ancestors before they landed in the United States or to allow us to know how many arrived and created new lives once they came to the United States. Walsh's version of his ancestors' arrival, told in his autobiography, will always reside in the fortunate province of myth—that imaginary narrative that takes over when historical fact recedes or becomes lost. The landscape of his past lay wide open and waiting for him to walk into and fill with his own stories by the horse load.

"In the late 1870s," Walsh wrote in his autobiography, "Thomas Walsh, my father, emigrated with three brothers from their native Ireland, bound for America by way of Spain. The roundabout route was necessary because the four, in company with my grandfather, had staged a breakout from a Dublin jail, where the British had sent the senior Walsh for subversive activities; a Spanish ship was the only available means for their reluctant flight from the old sod. As my uncle Matthew told it, Grandfather was the rebel and his sons, using a stolen laundry van, contrived to release the old man from jail after shooting it out with the guards. He was wounded during the escape and died at sea before the ship reached Spain. . . . According to Uncle Matthew, the ship's Spanish captain, Don Raul Almendariz, took a liking to my father, and my first name (somehow or other with an added 'o') was one of the results of this remembered friendship."[1]

This narrative, sounding not unlike one of Walsh's 1950s sea pictures, is easy to like and difficult to dispute, even if Walsh's first wife, the D. W. Griffith ingénue Miriam Cooper, refuted one part of it: the way Walsh picked up the name Raoul. According to Cooper, while Walsh was working as an actor on the New York stage during his early twenties, his friend Paul Armstrong thought the name Albert could be improved on. The two men came up with Raoul, thinking it sounded more romantic.[2] The truth is slippery.

A few facts about Walsh's ancestors are known. His paternal grandfather, George Walsh, was born in County Waterford, Ireland, probably in the 1820s. The family soon moved to Sheffield, England, where George grew up, meeting and marrying Walsh's grandmother, Elizabeth Shortland, around the year 1850. George became a journeyman blacksmith (as written on his son's birth certificate)—or, according to family legend, a master tailor for the British army. In his autobiography, Raoul Walsh claims that there were four sons born to his grandfather. But Walsh's brother, George, later said that there were, in fact, three.[3] Walsh's father, Thomas, was born in Sheffield in 1856. In a 1900 New York City census, he indicated that he arrived in the United States in 1870; he would have been fourteen years old.

Raoul Walsh's Irish ancestry seems just as likely linked to his mother, Elizabeth Brough, as to his father. That same 1900 census indicates that Elizabeth's parents were both born in Ireland, although their whereabouts is untraceable after that. Walsh's story that Elizabeth's family arrived in the United States well before the American Revolution seems untrue. The story he gives of her grandmother being a staunch member of the Daughters of the American Revolution also seems unlikely. Yet it is fact that Elizabeth's father's surname was Brough. An 1870 New York census has thirteen-year-old Elizabeth Brough and her ten-year-old sister, Briedget, living in New York City with an Anne and James Scanlon, both approximately ten years older than Elizabeth. Most likely they were family members since George Walsh, Raoul's brother, often used the last name Scanlon when he first followed his older brother into the movie business. It may also be true, as her sons later claimed, that, when she was a young girl in New York City, Elizabeth was considered by many men to be the belle of the ball.

When Walsh's father, Thomas, arrived in New York, he found work in a men's clothing store. Not long after that he found employment at the prestigious firm of Brooks Bros., where he carved out a successful career. Family hearsay has it that Thomas was a driving force in the design department of Brooks Bros. and almost single-handedly put the company on the map in the years he worked there, helping design military uniforms for famous clients such as General George Custer and, much later on, Teddy Roosevelt's Rough Riders.

Thomas married Elizabeth Brough in 1886 in a ceremony at St. Patrick's Cathedral. One year later their first child, Albert Edward, was born. His brother, George, was born in 1889, and a sister, Alice, was born two years later.

It Was an Enchanted Childhood

Walsh always recalled his childhood as being a magical time. "All of us adored our mother," he wrote in his autobiography, "though we stood in awe of Father's muscular six foot two frame."[4] He looked back at his parents through a romantic gaze, bathed in nostalgia. In fact, the children *had* lived an enchanted childhood, even as Walsh recalled (with great affection) the way Thomas and Elizabeth handled his unfortunate years as a student. First, he and George were deposited in the rough New York City public school system; then Walsh lived through a short stint at Seton Hall Preparatory School in New Jersey. His stay at Seton Hall was brief as he was soon expelled. This suited Walsh fine as he had little interest in any kind of classroom education. George, on the other hand, was blessed with a voracious appetite for knowledge and soaked up as many books as he could. Walsh was always more rough-and-tumble and daring than George. In complete contrast, George attended Fordham University in the Bronx and, later on, Georgetown University, intending to become an attorney. He also developed into a world-class athlete and later made a stab at entering the Olympics. He was disqualified, however, after accepting money for sports exhibitions. "This was either ignorance or shortsightedness on his part," his son, George Jr., later said, "and it was a shame, because the only man who ever outran him was Jim Thorpe—and it was just by a couple of inches."⁵ Mythmaking ran in the family.

When the children were still quite young, Thomas went into partnership with Carl Lange, a German Jew, and the firm of Walsh and Lange was born, giving young Walsh a worldview that the Jews and the Irish were clearly in synch, simpatico. Later, when he worked for Warner, Walsh always banked on the combination of Warner's Jewishness and his own Irish roots to be the glue that held them together through a thirty-year friendship and successful business relationship. Whenever Walsh wanted to borrow money or get an advance from the studio, he wrote Warner a memo peppered with misspelled Yiddish phrases that he hoped would show his boss his warm affection for him. "The Jews and the Irish carry the troubles of the world on their backs," he told Warner repeatedly.

Walsh and Lange opened its wholesale garment business at 596 Broadway in New York and became successful with little trouble. Following the example of his brother, Matthew, who, as Walsh claimed, ended up in South Dakota defending the rights of the Sioux Indians, Thomas became an impassioned supporter of the tribe after a visit to the state, and at one point Walsh and Lange were supplying the Sioux with the warm clothing he thought they desperately needed and that the U.S. government shamefully failed to supply. Thomas's philanthropic vein marched on, and later, when Walsh was still a young boy, Thomas and Lange became active in aiding Jewish families wishing to leave Canada for the United States. The firm would finance their passage and help them settle and find employment. As gratitude for this kindness, the Jewish community gave Thomas a gold medal with the Star of David engraved on it.⁶

Walsh recalled that, when he turned eleven, the war with Spain broke out, and Walsh and Lange, "already busy with their long list of customers, received a windfall in the guise of a government contract to make uniforms for the U.S. Army." Later, Walsh also recalled, "It was Father who designed the outfits for Teddy Roosevelt's Rough Riders, cocked hat and all." This fact is true, as Walsh's nephew later corroborated, although Walsh did give the story a Hollywood western sheen by injecting, "A lot of his uniforms went up San Juan Hill and some of them stayed there."[7] Walsh wrote that Roosevelt himself pulled some important strings to make certain his Rough Riders were outfitted with khaki uniforms designed exclusively for them by Brooks Brothers (Walsh no doubt confused the time Thomas worked for the firm and the time he opened his own).

Dinner parties were likely a frequent event in the Walsh household, even if Walsh's eighty-four-year-old imagination embellished them somewhat for his autobiography. Guests included Edwin Booth (the brother of John Wilkes Booth), John L. Sullivan, and the Barrymore clan (the only documented guests), who lived across the street. When Walsh was a teenager, the family moved to larger quarters on Riverside Drive, a very posh part of the city (the address was actually 141 W. Ninety-Fifth St.). Walsh remembered a guest list that grew in his imagination: "I remember 'Buffalo Bill' Cody stopping by to sample the champagne of which he had become a connoisseur during his stay in England." He also recalled a great singer: "I was not sure what line of work Enrico Caruso was in until he threw back his head and hit high C to my sister Elizabeth's accompaniment. Fresh from her first piano recital at Carnegie Hall, Liz had the grace to blush when the great tenor dropped to his knees in the middle of our parlor carpet and crossed himself while humbly thanking God for giving him a voice."[8] No sister named Elizabeth ever existed, of course. She was born only in the pages of Walsh's autobiography—no family member ever recalled her.

As Walsh grew older, the parties and the guests arrived more often—at least in Walsh's mind. "'Diamond Jim' Brady brought Lillian Russell and I fell madly in love." The list of guests grew to embrace Frederic Remington, Theodore Roosevelt, and President McKinley. Walsh fantasized that Roosevelt talked politics with Thomas Walsh and felt much better about the world when he left their house. As Walsh also says, no doubt unaware of the irony, memory, like luck, can be a fickle jade.[9]

Walsh spent his days wandering around New York City with boundless energy, visiting his favorite haunt, Peck Slip, where he would watch steam tugs berth the clippers and square-riggers. He dreamed that he was in the China Sea repelling pirates. There were many other experiences that stayed with him. Wandering around the Bowery provided him with memories that would influence his expression of the area's atmosphere and flavor when he later directed, for one, *The Bowery* for Twentieth Century Pictures in 1933.

Walsh and his younger brother were handsome young men, Walsh the more slender of the two, just under six feet, with wavy, almost curly brown hair, and George, more solidly built, just slightly taller, with a heavier face and dark brown hair that looked almost black. Both were athletic and more than willing to take advantage of any sporting activity their father taught them. Thomas Walsh had a great love of horses and often raced Thoroughbreds, and he took Walsh to the tracks and to horse auctions. He told his son that there was only one good horse in every three hundred. The equestrian life was easily had, given the family's wealth and upper-middle-class lifestyle in New York City. Both boys were born riders.

Walsh obviously listened to his father about horses—and looked for that one good horse, triggering a family story passed down for decades. By the time he was ten years old, so the story goes, Walsh had saved enough money to buy an old horse along with a Mexican saddle and bridle. His parents thought he was crazy. One morning he saddled up, took the ferry across the Hudson, and took off. But he got only as far as Virginia when the horse went lame. Walsh sold the animal and returned home. This adventure was never substantiated but, nonetheless, still lives in the imagination of Walsh's family.[10]

But all Raoul Walsh's childhood fantasies, real or imagined, came crashing to a halt in 1902, when he was fifteen years old, and his mother, Elizabeth, only forty-two years old, died of cancer. "Life up to now had been reckless and exciting. . . . So I was quite unprepared for the sudden blow that left me motherless at fifteen. . . . We were all stunned, desolated by the slowly growing awareness of our loss."[11]

Thomas Walsh's reaction to his wife's death was to appear as if his life changed little for him. But he froze Elizabeth in time to keep her with him permanently. He stayed in the family home for the rest of his life and kept his wife's room exactly as she left it the day she died. Her silk dresses still hung in her closet, her shoes stayed on their racks, and her cut-glass perfume bottles and silver toilet articles remained on her dresser until Thomas Walsh gave them to Miriam Cooper some years later. The maid cleaned and aired the room every week, but the rest of the time Thomas allowed no one to enter it but himself.

Elizabeth's death left the young Raoul devastated. Years later he wrote, "The terrible thing was she had gone and I was only half a person."[12] It would make sense, then, that Walsh would create a sister named Elizabeth as a replacement for his mother. This is something a child would do as a way to hold on to a lost parent. He could have left home after his mother's death, although this cannot be substantiated. But Elizabeth Walsh unwittingly left her son a legacy that would mold his personality and urge him toward becoming a storyteller in the century's grandest public arena—the movies. The way to survive his loss, and the way to hold on to the mother he loved, the only way he knew how, was to replicate her being by becoming a storyteller himself. He would occupy the landscape of his mother's soul by leaping into the greatest escape he could mount: stories of adventure and romance designed to be rendered as perfectly as she would have told them. He might then relive the moments he had with her and the Americana she gave him. Where Elizabeth ended, he began.

The Stuff That Dreams Are Made Of

"My family moved to Texas [around Del Rio, near the Mexican border] soon after I was born," Walsh told the British journalist James Child in 1971. "Was brought up down there, went to several schools, and lasted a couple of weeks in each." He added:

Then my family finally sent me up to that Jesuit school at Seton Hall.

Incidentally, that's where I met Jack and Lionel Barrymore. When the three of us got together, we were out in a week. . . . I was soon back in Texas. Postgraduate course. So I never graduated from college. Christ! I never even graduated from grammar school. I stayed on the family ranch, grew up on a ranch. Worked part of the time in Montana, then I went back to Texas and got a job with the government breaking horses: "topping" horses. The government was out buying horses for the cavalry and the ranchers were supposed to run in horses that were broken. Every now and then they'd send in a bronc to sell. When the colonel overseeing the operation saw a horse that looked a little like an outlaw, we'd top it. I got twenty-five cents for topping a horse.[13]

Walsh told a similar story to Kevin Brownlow a few years earlier, not long after talking about his childhood with other journalists as well. Miriam Cooper read one of these stories in the paper and responded in her autobiography, "He'd tell the wildest tales. He never bored you with the truth. Though we'd been divorced for forty-five angry years, I couldn't help chuckling when I read an article on him in *The Los Angeles Examiner* early in 1972 . . . how he'd grown up on a ranch in Montana [*sic*] and tested broncos for the United States Cavalry. I'd never heard that one before. Oh, that Raoul!"[14]

The stories about a Texas or Montana childhood fall into the soup of Walsh's grand gestures of fiction making—small oddities in the larger pot of stories Walsh concocted and circulated for years about different periods of his life. The story changes, or the family names change, but in the end the details come together to create a necessary fiction for Walsh. In fact, none of the stories that he told about the period from his mother's death until he landed in Texas at the age of twenty can be documented or substantiated. They are partly truth, partly fiction—and they add up to a tale not unlike the heavily fictionalized truth telling about General George Custer that Walsh directed and partly concocted in 1942's *They Died with Their Boots On*.

For example, Walsh claims in his autobiography that, after his mother's death, his father gave his consent for him to sail with his uncle Matthew on the *Enniskillen* and that the two soon headed for Havana. There are numerous versions even of this story, however. He told Peter Bogdanovich in the early 1970s that he headed off without his "family's" consent and wrote to them once he and Matthew reached their destination. Still other versions have fifteen-year-old Raoul running away from home, not to return for at least a decade, or even not at all.

These stories reached their zenith in the early 1970s when Walsh attended retrospectives and students and historians looked up at him, taking in his wild tales. Also at this time Walsh was writing his autobiography and working on two novels. One would be published in France; the other he envisioned as a movie that he himself might direct. One is a love story, the other an adventure yarn. In his mind, there could hardly be a difference between either of these texts. Either could have become the other.

Walsh was looking back over his life, stirring up memories of his mother's death, and reliving the adventures he either took or imagined. It is clear, then, that he thought again about his bereavement over his mother's death. His escape from that grief was to run away and travel— throughout the United States (the landscape of the tales his mother told him) and even beyond, around the globe. Sooner or later, even in the pages of his autobiography and in the stories he gave to the press, Walsh would have to land. But every story he told, no matter how altered and retold, nonetheless contains a kernel of truth, if not more, and should be viewed as the truth. The stories had meaning for him, and by that token they are true—even if the characters and events are fiction.

His grief was a fact of his life and often shaped and determined the avenues Walsh took. That grief would follow him in some fashion not just on his adventures but even later as he created characters on the big screen. There would be no adventure Walsh would create on the screen where a character did not attempt a grand, dangerous escape, did not attempt to right a wrong from the past, or did not try to do it all for love of a woman (or a woman as his country). The past would be ominous, the future unclear.

Walsh penned many of the one and two reelers he directed under D. W. Griffith's instruction at Biograph Studios in the early 1910s and throughout the 1920s at Fox Studios. But the story of his schooner ride to Havana, where he and Matthew were subsequently shipwrecked, which eventually was extended to travels in Mexico, the Southwest, and other U.S. environs, is, in a necessary and fundamental way, one of his earliest and finest fictions. All the fictional conceits he would eventually commit to film—from high seas adventures in *Captain Horatio Hornblower* and *The Sea Devils* to espionage tales and Western yarns—are foreshadowed in the romantic narrative he concocts to extricate himself from his motherless childhood and the grief he thought he might leave behind him. If his adventure story were a psyche wrapped in a narrative,

Walsh would look like a kid imagining and cooking up the grandest tale he could possibly find.

On the Road

In Walsh's predominant narrative of his teenage years, he and his uncle Matthew headed out on the *Enniskillen* and reached Havana in eight days. Walsh's joy in being at sea was profound, and he could hardly take in enough of the sea air. But, while on a shipping lane between Havana and the coast of Mexico, horrific weather damaged the schooner. The ship's repair took a long time, and, while on land waiting to sail, Walsh began to grow despondent and wondered why he did not ask his uncle to put him back on a ship bound for New York. But he remembered, "I had no home now that Mother was dead. My family were [*sic*] little more than grieving shadows among the memories she had left with us. No, I would go on."[15] These stabs of grief grew smaller and less frequent as Walsh grew into manhood, but they also took on a different guise, lodging themselves in the movies he would direct. Often, they took shape as one of his characters' poignantly sad moments, say, the moment Roy Earle realizes he will never have Velma for his own or, just as poignant, the moment in *Silver River* when Plato (Thomas Mitchell) realizes that Mike McComb (Errol Flynn) set up Georgia's (Ann Sheridan) husband and caused his death at the hands of the Indians. At this young age, however, those expressions lay far off in the future.

Walsh found great excitement in the days following the grand shipwreck. The *Enniskillen* was towed into San Juan de Ulua "hard up the Vera Cruz harbor."[16] It would be five months before the ship could be repaired. Walsh wrote in his autobiography that he had just turned seventeen when they pulled into Vera Cruz. Somehow he lost two years in his narrative. But, whatever his age at the time, he recalled that he could not fathom staying in one place that long a time. Luckily, he met a horse trader named Ramirez who changed the course of his life when he taught Walsh the art of rope twirling and horsemanship. Walsh practiced both nonstop and believed he had hit on his first passion.

An attentive student at last, Walsh quickly learned to jump inside his own loop of the rope and catch a running steer by either its front or its back legs, this despite getting one good throw from a steer that left him dazed but resolved to continue. When Uncle Matthew decided to sail on to Galveston, Texas, once the *Enniskillen* was repaired, Walsh declined to accompany him and jumped at the chance to join a cattle drive to the Rio Grande. Though the experience was a good one and, if it truly did happen, gave him the psychological muscle to direct westerns later on, the drive also taught him the difference between the romantic notions of the West he had learned from reading westerns and the harshness of the drive itself: "I also found that, although I could fork a horse, throw a rope, roll a cigarette with one hand, and cuss with the best [these actions could easily describe Walsh on the set of all his movies; it is hard to know which came first, the actual experience or its recall after a lifetime behind the camera], I knew nothing about trail-driving. Knowledge came the hard way. . . . In addition to keeping the herd moving, there was scouting ahead to find water and graze, side trips into towns along the way to haggle over supplies. . . . Looking back on that drive, I still wonder why more cowmen did not lose their reason." But, by the time he saw the Rio Grande, Walsh considered himself a seasoned cowhand who could hold his own with the best riders. He could "ride anything with hair on it."[17]

Walsh stayed on for a while in South Texas, among other adventures getting mixed up with a Mexican woman who betrayed him early on in their romance; he found himself in this episode hightailing it out of town after being accused of cattle rustling. The year, said Walsh, was 1904, and South Texas was a tough place that had not moved out of the rough-and-tumble years of the Old West. He saw a man killed for the first time just before he joined up with another man named Hans Cotton (a liar, Walsh said, which bothered him very little) to help ship a couple of carloads of horses to Butte, Montana. Walsh found himself one of three men who had to handle, water, and feed sixty head of half-broken horses overland by train. Horse wrangling was not for him.

Though Walsh planned on heading back to South Texas after the gig, his fortunes changed once again when he hired on to break horses for a six-foot-five Kerry man named "Colonel" Sarsfield Scanlon who ran a livery stable and owned an undertaking parlor. Scanlon was an even bigger liar than his last boss, but Walsh did not realize it right away. Scanlon put him to work breaking horses and also put him in charge of two Cree Indians and appointed him head gravedigger for his business. Money was scarce, and Scanlon "often cut the overhead still further by dressing the deceased in shirt and coat but no pants. The mourners, when there were any, never knew the difference."[18]

After working for Scanlon for a while, Walsh shifted gears and became a driver and then the anesthetist—no training necessary—for the area's new doctor, a Frenchman named René Echinelle (Walsh switches the story, sometimes saying the doctor had the same first name as he—Raoul—an interesting fact of storytelling that could suggest how close Walsh's characters are to himself). He noted how interesting it was that, while the good doctor was performing surgery on his patients, ashes from his cigar often fell into the body on the table. Walsh seemed to have great affection for the doctor and felt sad when he died of lung disease not long after his tenure with him. Walsh then decided he had had enough of Butte and pulled out, heading back to San Antonio. Once there, he found a notice at the local post office issued by the U.S. Cavalry Remount Service that the federal government was looking for "thoroughly broken four- to six-year-old brown or bay geldings." The government also needed "toppers," experienced riders "to gentle any fractious ones." Walsh found the U.S. government to be a generous employer and was satisfied with the job, until a mishap occurred one day in an area called Kerrville. Walsh got on top of a "bad buckskin" at one of the ranches, the horse reared backward, and Walsh fell off before he could get out of the saddle.[19] By that time, the horse had rolled over him and broken his right leg. Walsh landed in a San Antonio hospital to mend. He found a room at a cheap motel for a few days, once again not knowing the turn his life was about to take.

Showbiz

It was 1907, and Walsh was about to turn twenty. Sitting on the porch of the Lone Star Hotel in San Antonio, his good leg displayed, his injured one hidden for no good reason except that it was the most comfortable way to sit, serendipity visited Walsh and changed the course of his life. A stranger happened to walk by and see the good-looking Walsh sitting, sporting a cowboy hat. "Do you want a job, cowboy?" the man yelled up to him, telling him to show up at the town's theater that evening if he was interested. He was, and later on he limped over to the theater. But he was using a cane and caught the man by surprise, who asked Walsh how in the world he was going to ride a horse with that bad leg. Walsh just asked where he could find the horse. When he found it, he climbed on a chair, then climbed on the horse. After that, he was asked to ride a treadmill. He did, and from here on out we see the true events in Raoul Walsh's life unfolding, no matter how much he tried to embellish them.

Walsh got the job, which turned out to be for a traveling show of *The Clansman,* a popular play just adapted for the stage by Thomas Dixon from his novel that was published that same year. The book, *The Clansman: A Historical Romance of the Ku Klux Klan,* was the second volume in Dixon's Reconstruction trilogy, a piece of out-and-out racism that called for the maintenance of white supremacy in America. While this view of racial inequality was prevalent in America in the first decade of the twentieth century, it still managed to cause controversy, but not enough to dampen the popularity of the play, which toured the country in 1905.

The play's racism and inherent message to northerners was plain and clear: racial segregation should be maintained because blacks turned savage when freed from slavery. The message seemed to have escaped Walsh during the time he performed in *The Clansman* (and, later, during his involvement with D. W. Griffith's adaptation of part of Dixon's original novel for *The Birth of a Nation*). It never occurred to him to question any of Dixon's belief system; at the time, that system was firmly entrenched in the nation's popular consciousness.

Walsh learned that he had been hired because, ironically, the cowboy originally scheduled to perform busted a leg (or broke his neck) and could not go on. Walsh was handed a Ku Klux Klan outfit and, after getting on his horse, was also handed a cross on fire. Stagehands pulled him and the horse across the stage while the audience whistled and cheered. That was when he got the stage bug, he said years later. He stayed with the show until it reached St. Louis.

The play's leading man, Franklin Ritchie, tried to find more for Walsh to do in the play and told him to study everyone's part so that he could go on at a moment's notice should anything happen to one of the actors. No one became ill, however, and Walsh never got his chance. But a fellow character actor took notice of him: Walsh sincerely enjoyed act-

ing. The friend was about to head off to New York to try to find an agent
and asked Walsh to join him. The two men went back East, and Walsh
made the rounds, signing with at least five agencies. He considered himself an actor now and managed to get one job in a show with the director
Al Parker. He went off to Chicago with the show, even though it lasted
only a brief time, and then he was back in New York looking for work.

The young Walsh was especially happy to see his family again as
he took up residence in the big house on Riverside Drive. "I proudly
told [Father] that I was an actor and played the part of the leader of
the Ku Klux Klan, and that I rode a horse across the stage, carrying a
fiery cross," Walsh wrote later in his autobiography. "My father said,
'You should not feel proud of portraying the part of an infamous bigot,
whose organization is anti-Catholic, anti-Jew, and anti-Negro. But as
sure as there is a God above us, these hatemongers will one day fade
away like leaves falling from trees in autumn.'"[20] The statement serves
Walsh the writer in multiple ways in the autobiography—as a comment
made to heroicize his father in his nostalgic look back at him; possibly
a statement to let himself off the hook for what in old age he may have
perceived as a slip in conscience. It could also have been a nod to his
readers to acknowledge a sensitive subject at the time his autobiography
was published, 1974. He could firm up a fact that he believed of himself:
he had been a lifelong defender of Native Americans in this country.
Whatever meaning it has, the memory (created in the moment of writing
or not) carried great import for Walsh.

Now calling himself Raoul, Walsh slept in his childhood bed and
came to terms with more memories of his mother. He sought solace in
the world and got on with the business of finding acting work. He truly
believed at this juncture in his life that being on stage was his destiny,
and he put all his energies into pushing the dream forward. In his view,
fate intervened at this very moment. One day, he entered the office of the
agent Bill Gregory. Though Gregory was out at the time, his secretary
took notice of Walsh and asked whether he would mind acting in the
movies—something most actors she encountered refused to do, considering it more demeaning work. But Walsh said no he wouldn't, and she
sent him across the river on the ferry to Union City, New Jersey, to meet
two brothers by the name of Pathé. They could speak only bad English
but through an interpreter embarked on the rocky road of communicat-

ing with Walsh. They asked him whether he could ride a horse, he said yes, and just like that he was a movie actor—at least in his eyes.

The Pathé Frères (Bros.) company was founded in France in 1896 by the four Pathé brothers—Charles, Emile, Theophile, and Jacques—as an adjunct to Charles's Paris gramophone shop and factory. They first began to make film equipment and then branched out into making films, exporting them to New York, where they were shown in the Vitascope Theater. By 1904, when the Pathé Company opened in New York, it owned a catalog of twelve thousand titles, and between 1905 and 1908 it accounted for about one-third of the films distributed in the United States.

Walsh said he began working for Charles and Emile Pathé late in 1909 and stayed with them until early 1910. But, in the narrative of his days with Pathé, he may have mixed them up with the Melies brothers, both of whom were in America, while only one of the Pathé brothers, Charles, was actually in the United States during the time of Walsh's account. As Kevin Brownlow has reported, James Young Deer, a Native American, was the person in charge of Pathé's West Coast studio and directed many of the company's films.[21] The beginning was inauspicious, as the brothers were interested in Walsh mainly because he could ride a horse. When he showed up for work the first day, he was taken to the livery stable up the street from the "studio" where he saw ten horses or so that he immediately termed "jugheads" because of their heavy heads. Not thrilled—but determined to be an actor—Walsh picked one of the jugheads, climbed aboard, and galloped down the street, did a stop, got off, and did a flying mount back onto the horse again. The next thing he knew he had signed a six-month contract for three pictures with the brothers playing heavies and romantic leads with a few historical figures such as Paul Revere thrown into the pot.

Walsh always said that his first picture for Pathé was called *The Banker's Daughter,* a film in which he was featured with the ex-burlesque queen Dolly Larkin and whose plot involved bank robbery and mistaken identity. He actually played in that film after he left Pathé for Reliance and briefly became an actor under Griffith's Biograph banner. Still, he could tell a good yarn about his months working for the Frenchmen. "'You kees the girl—kees the girl, grab, kees, kees, kees,' they would yell. They'd be yelling at you all the time. 'Give another kees.' I'm running out of kisses, you bastard." The Frenchmen would talk over the director. "One time a girl was in love with me and I was dying and the camera was in close—she was kneeling down and this roughneck bastard director was yelling: 'Cry, cry, cry, you son of a bitch, cry, will ya?' And I was lying on the ground dying. It was a helluva place."[22]

Walsh said his second film for Pathé was a sentimental story called *A Mother's Love,* even though a record of the film does not exist. *Paul Revere's Ride,* which Walsh said was his third and last film for Pathé, put him on a horse again. But the French director, Emile Couteau, who had directed a couple of his Pathé pictures, called for trolley tracks to be included in the Paul Revere story, at which point Walsh reminded him that there were no such things in 1775. When Couteau confronted him, reminding him who the director was on the movie, Walsh thought seriously that maybe it was time he became a director himself.[23]

Walsh still lived at the big family home on Ninety-fifth Street and Riverside Drive, only now the household was shy one more female when Walsh's nineteen-year-old sister, Alice, secretly wed the billiard champ Willie Hoppe, who was two years her senior, on December 15, 1910. The couple had met three years earlier when Alice went for a swim in the beach at Atlantic City and nearly drowned. Hoppe was swimming nearby and fished her out of the water, saving her life. He courted Alice for three years, most of the time behind Thomas Walsh's back. When he could no longer wait to get married, he phoned her from Scranton, Pennsylvania, and told her to meet him at the corner of Forty-second Street and Broadway in Manhattan. Alice, whom the newspapers called one of the wealthiest and most beautiful girls in New York City, did what Hoppe asked, and the two were married at a nearby church that day. On learning of his daughter's elopement, Thomas admitted that he was dumbfounded and furious, but he put on a good show for reporters (starting a Walsh family tradition). He told them that he was certain the family could work things out, and he welcomed the couple into his home. Too busy working, Walsh never attended the ceremony.

Most of the films Walsh made for the Pathé brothers were westerns. "But there were others." Walsh played bank robbers, prizefighters, and ne'er-do-wells. But Walsh became disenchanted with this form of operation. It seemed unrealistic and redundant in the worst way. There was hardly an adventure here. Frustrated with Pathé and its operation, he knew there was a better way to meet the dream he had set out for himself. Little did he know that he was about to take a giant step toward it.

2

Griffith and Beyond
The Apprenticeship Years

> We've gone beyond Babel, beyond words. We've found a universal language—a power that can make men brothers and end war forever. Remember that. Remember that when you stand in front of the camera.
> —D. W. Griffith to Lillian Gish

"Notice," Sam Clemens warned at the start of Huck Finn's "stretcher" about his adventures with Tom Sawyer and the slave Jim in *Adventures of Huckleberry Finn*. "Persons attempting to find a motive in this narrative will be prosecuted; persons attempting to find a moral in it will be banished; persons attempting to find a plot in it will be shot."[1] The same may be said about Raoul Walsh's account of how he came to sail to Cuba with his uncle, how the two men got shipwrecked, and the route Walsh took to find his way to Mexico and the United States—and how he landed working in pictures. Anyone trying to find the truth in Walsh's narrative might be led astray. The only truth lies in the joy of telling, the art of being a storyteller. Walsh's life in the early 1910s escapes being documented; truth may be fiction, or the truth may be a story with more embellishment than fact.

Waiting for the Sun to Shine

Walsh recalled that he left Pathé for the Biograph Company in 1910, but more likely he left behind the *frères* with the bad English in the middle of 1913. Although he may have been just another name on the payroll in the early months of that year, the acting bug hit him hard. When he was not actually mugging for the camera, he could be found hanging around with the other actors waiting for a new assignment or just killing time until the weather cooperated on a current one. Oliver's Restaurant in Fort Lee, New Jersey, was a popular hangout for movie folk trying to make time stretch on a shoot. It had good food, good service, and cheap prices. Good thing, too, since movie folk, called *movies* because they moved around a lot, also spent a lot of time there waiting for a sunny day. Sunlight was the only illumination possible for a shoot—and nature was in charge of that. If there was no sun, there was no picture.

On one particular day, Walsh happened to be sitting atop a horse "working a rope," as he liked to say, showing off his array of rope tricks after an overcast sky had interrupted a shoot. A few people stood around watching, and one in particular began talking to him. Christy Cabanne was a former actor turned director who was making a name for himself with D. W. Griffith at Biograph (though Cabanne's directing career was undistinguished, it was one of the longest running in Hollywood). Cabanne yelled up to Walsh that his tricks were some of the best rope handling he had seen. He also complimented Walsh on how he handled a horse. Then came the clincher: he mentioned that Walsh looked pretty good sitting on one. Walsh later said that he knew he was good with a rope, and that he looked good on a horse, but that there was something in the way Cabanne said so that really pleased him. Cabanne said that he could use a man like Walsh and advised him not to sign a new contract with Pathé. He wanted him to come act for D. W. Griffith's company and to consider himself hired.

Walsh did just that. He considered the few Biograph pictures he had seen "not as God-awful as the stuff Pathé was making."[2] His instincts were good. In the past several years, between 1911 and 1913 especially, Griffith had been experimenting with new techniques for narrative storytelling in the movies that would push the art form forward in unexpected ways. Walsh would be right there beside him.

So, when Cabanne walked away, Walsh later recalled, "I took stock of myself, feeling a bit chesty and pleased with the way things were shaping up. Not many weeks earlier, I had been riding that treadmill and feeling more foolish each night. Now I was a full-fledged actor and had played the lead in three motion pictures, terrible as they were. When I got home that evening and Father asked me what I had done with my day, I mumbled something inane because my head was full of dreams."[3]

Walsh agreed to go over to the Biograph Studios on Fourteenth Street in New York the next day; he signed with Griffith a day or two later.

The time was right for Walsh to move to Biograph, even if the stay was a brief one. Griffith had had a short but already illustrious trial as a director in the fledging movie industry. In 1908, about the time he began working for Biograph, there were fewer than nine thousand motion-picture theaters in the United States. The seating capacity in most was small; many were storefronts converted to movie theaters that often seated fewer than one hundred patrons. A program of two films and an illustrated song, lasting less than an hour combined, was a typical evening's entertainment. With an audience that had more leisure time on its hands than ever before, and with a cheap admission price at a nickelodeon, for example, movies provided exciting stories for the working class, especially, that came to see the "flickers."[4]

The movie industry was growing quickly in the United States and had been for some time. By the 1920s, the United States would be unrivaled as the center of the filmmaking industry. It simply suited the American sensibility; it was in our mythos. On a practical, business side, an "unrivaled" number of immigrants arrived in this country during the last two decades of the nineteenth century, many with "the muscle and the imagination" to work in a fledgling industry, especially one with so many imaginative possibilities.[5] Also, the nickelodeons that turned up did so in the unrestricted economic conditions of turn-of-the-century America. When men such as Griffith moved to California to make their pictures, they found a paradise of inexpensive real estate and welcoming Mediterranean weather conditions. But, even more so, the movie industry, new as it was, fit right in with a culture bent on creating myths for itself. Myths of American self-making had already been set in place in the mid-nineteenth century by Toqueville, Emerson, and Whitman. America would always be seen (more importantly, see itself) as just being born, as always being in the process of being born anew. The movie industry offered one more opportunity for men to create new notions of selfhood, especially selfhoods that were visionary and that could soar to any size and, in a grandiose way, be seen by many at once. Images of men and women larger than life were projected onto a screen; the self was a new creation with proportions never before imagined. And the men and women behind it all had reinvented themselves into a new industry, a new culture. What better idea than an industry so rooted in the imagination?[6]

Cabanne put Walsh to work right away, directing him in several one- and two-reelers with various other Biograph feature players, including Blanche Sweet, Dorothy and Lillian Gish, Donald Crisp, Lionel Barrymore, and even Mary Pickford. But Walsh was just starting out, so his roles were far from enticing. Neither were they terribly noticeable to audiences. He even took to going to the theater itself after one of his movies opened just to make sure he was actually in a picture he recalled making.

Given his eagerness to get ahead, Walsh understandably suffered a nagging sense of disillusionment at Biograph. While he didn't expect his acting career to take a meteoric rise as soon as he arrived there, neither did he expect to be kept in such abeyance from getting actual screen time. *The Detective's Stratagem* from 1912—of which only fragments survive—is the one picture Walsh is certain to have appeared in, even though he long claimed to have appeared in *The Musketeers of Pig Alley* in 1912, which is unlikely. *Pig Alley* is one of Griffith's more important one-reelers—not the first, but certainly the earliest surviving gangster film, also said to be possibly the first to use follow-focus, where the camera blurs out the background as three gangsters walk toward an alley in the opening scene. (*Pig Alley* is also said to have influenced Martin Scorsese when he directed *Goodfellas* [1990] and *Gangs of New York* [2002].) Walsh may simply have confused the picture with the landmark gangster picture that he himself directed for William Fox in 1915, *Regeneration*. Walsh's earliest documented work was actually as a director for Griffith, a 1914 two-reeler, *Mexican War Pictures,* with actual Mexican War scenes. Most likely it was shot later, when Walsh went to Mexico to work on *Life of Villa.* It hardly marked an auspicious career move—the kind Walsh would soon make as a director in Griffith's company.

Walsh was now so frustrated and disillusioned that he was ready to leave pictures and maybe head back to Vera Cruz. But just when the thought hit, Christy Cabanne gave him the news that Griffith was about to leave Biograph and make a permanent move to California. He had been trekking back and forth for some time and now wanted to settle there permanently and to start his own company, Fine Arts Studios, for the Mutual Corporation.

Now, at the end of 1913, only twenty-six years old, Walsh found himself on Griffith's short list and then on the train that took him to California, a land he'd never heard of, to say the least. Standing on the cusp of his new life, he was leaning forward. He didn't venture to the new land alone, however. Also on that train was a handful of Griffith players, including Mary Pickford and her younger brother, Jack, Donald Crisp, Henry B. Walthall, and Cabanne—along with Griffith himself and Griffith's chief cameraman, Billy Bitzer. Had it not been for Walsh's great self-confidence, he could not have fathomed why Griffith picked him to join the troupe. But Griffith took special notice of the young actor and promised him, "Someday, I'll make you a director." "I don't know why he said that," Walsh later quipped. "Maybe because he thought I was a lousy actor."[7]

A Fatherless Girl

The train heading for Los Angeles carried another Biograph feature player, an attractive actress named Miriam Cooper—and, before Walsh truly had time to settle into what eventually became his luxurious Los Angeles lifestyle, Cooper would change her name to Mrs. Raoul Walsh.

Miriam Cooper considered herself a true Biograph ingénue, and certainly she found good-enough roles in Griffith's pictures to warrant her self-confidence. With her dark hair and large, luminous dark eyes, she made quite a contrast, along with Blanche Sweet, to some of Griffith's other working girls, such as the more fair-skinned Mary Pickford and the Gish sisters. This left a corner of the market open to Miriam, and Griffith eventually gave her history-making parts: she earned the part of "The friendless one" in *Intolerance* and, better still, a leading part as Margaret Cameron in *The Birth of a Nation*. While she garnered two history-making roles in Griffith films, the mark she left on Walsh's life was just as history making—and far more dramatic, leaving a greater emotional impact on him than any fiction could have managed.

Miriam grew up mostly poor in Baltimore. Her mother received financial assistance from her mother-in-law, but, after the mother-in-law died, the fatherless family lived in poverty, with Miriam's mother scraping by as best she could. This included a move from Washington Heights to Little Italy, and, even though Miriam was put in an orphanage for a short time, later her mother managed to educate her at St. Walburga's Academy, a convent school, and then at Cooper Union High School in New York City. During the time Miriam set out on an unplanned career in pictures, she also modeled for Charles Dana Gibson.

Miriam and a girlfriend named Rita set out looking for the Biograph studios, which at the time occupied a large brownstone at 11 East Fourteenth Street. The building itself had once been a mansion owned by a millionaire on a street where other such mansions were now turned into rooming houses, restaurants, shops—and one movie studio. The rooms were huge with high ceilings. Once inside, the two women noticed a man Miriam soon learned was D. W. Griffith; he was shooting a ballroom scene for one of his pictures. Griffith needed extras for a scene he was shooting, and, before she knew it, Miriam was in pictures and being paid for it. The five dollars she earned turned her head, and she wanted more.

Before landing a full-time job at Biograph, where she was cast in ingénue parts, Miriam worked for Kalem Features in various pictures in New York and on the road. But she ended up back at Biograph, working for Griffith and making numerous pictures with Walsh. When Griffith first met his new actress and took a personal interest in her, he took special care to learn about her background. She told him that she was from Baltimore and now lived with her mother, brothers, and sister. She also told him that her father was long gone. "Most of the girls in the Griffith Company had the same kind of background. None of us had fathers; they all had disappeared before we ever saw Mr. Griffith," she later wrote. "I learned later that this was the kind of girl Mr. Griffith liked—young, beautiful and supporting her mother. He didn't care particularly about talent since he felt he could mold anyone into the type of performer he wanted."[8]

It would be a while before Walsh and Miriam became an item since Walsh also had his sights set most on becoming an integral part of Griffith's new setup in California. But, on the train out west that October, Miriam spent her time with Walsh, Christy Cabanne (who brought along his wife, child, and mother-in-law), and a Native American actor called Eagle Eye, this despite a warning from Cabanne's mother-in-law that the three were not exactly good influences on Miriam. "She was right, but she was only half right," Miriam wrote in her autobiography.

"I was safe; my money wasn't." Walsh and Cabanne taught Miriam to play poker, even if the two men cheated her left and right. "I would sit next to the window with my cards held out in front of me. 'Hold your cards up, Miriam,' Raoul said. When I did, the cards were reflected in the train window and he and Christy could see everything I had."[9] The trip west marked the last time Walsh ever took money from Miriam. For years to come it would be the other way around.

The Gold Rush

When the train pulled in to the Los Angeles station, the Griffith players were in for a surprise. Very few hotels in the city allowed actors inside their doors. Eugene Pallette, one of Griffith's established actors, who was already in the city, arranged for them to stay at the Gates Hotel on the edge of the city proper, one of the few places that allowed actors in its doors. While people posted signs on their front lawns advertising apartments for rent, they usually read, "No dogs or picture people allowed." Most Californians at that time were either retired midwesterners with very middle-class ideas or second-generation Californians who were, in Miriam's words, "just far enough away from their Gold Rush ancestors to be bluenoses."[10]

Some of Griffith's people, such as Miriam Cooper, considered Los Angeles and its environs to be a hick town when they arrived in 1914—hardly an attractive place. The downtown area was quite built up at the time the company arrived, but the same could not consistently be said for the adjoining areas. A few miles to the west, Hollywood looked much better. The area was still residential, showing off large, comfortable houses set back from the streets with well-manicured lawns to buffer them from what little traffic noise there was. Sitting on a small knoll, well back from the street, was the Hollywood Hotel, which did allow actors inside. Many took up lodgings there and, apparently, were not evicted for the large parties that often took place.

With his stock company now in California, Griffith left Biograph behind—for one reason, because the company did not believe, as Griffith did, that lengthy feature films could be financially viable. Griffith joined the Mutual Film Corporation and also joined forces with the Majestic Studio manager, Harry Aitken. Now called Majestic-Reliance Studios, it would later be named Fine Arts Studio. Griffith's new production company became an autonomous partner in the Triangle Film Corporation, along with Thomas Ince and Keystone Studios' Mack Sennett. Griffith would produce *The Birth of a Nation* through Majestic-Reliance a year or so later.

For now, the Griffith players faced the challenge of adjusting to a new locale and customs, or so it seemed. They were not exactly reenacting the seventeenth-century myth of the City on the Hill facing the hostilities of Native American tribes, but they faced the natives of southern California nonetheless. It would have been difficult to believe then that the motion-picture business would come to represent glamour to the rest of the country. Glamour would have to be built from the ground up, just as the studios themselves would have to take shape in this new landscape.

Christy Cabanne put the actors to work almost immediately so that they could bring in some money—and keep busy. Griffith's advance men set up and built a studio and outdoor stage at the intersection of Sunset and Hollywood Boulevards. That first Fine Arts Studio was an open-air structure that made use of movable props and backdrops. Before Griffith and his company arrived there, it had been making color films, one of them *The Clansman,* which was never finished.[11] It mimicked a theater stage but had difficulty getting light. Reflectors had to be used to catch the natural light, even though they hurt the actors' eyes. As Walsh wryly noticed, the paraphernalia of early moviemaking must have looked out of place situated among the surrounding citrus groves and cow pastures. Griffith hired three or four directors who had been with other stock companies, and, with his supervising hand, they turned out maybe ten pictures a week. Electric lights being unreliable back then, the actors and directors still relied on the sun. When it was cloudy outside, Griffith would use that time to rehearse upcoming pictures; then they would all go outside when the sun came out again.

Walsh found a small bungalow in Hollywood near the studio and persuaded Mary Pickford's mother (who was also on that train to California) to let fifteen-year-old Jack Pickford room with him. Then he began scouting extras for Griffith. One day while traipsing into the Los Angeles stockyards he literally ran into a dime-store gospel show setting up in the back stables of the studio. He noticed a man called Bear Valley Charley sitting in a wheelchair "as drunk as the proverbial fiddler's bitch."[12] Charley's job was to supply the makeshift preachers with customers, but he was too drunk at that moment to do any good. Although Charley was three years Walsh's junior, his habit of taking "firewater" had already put years on his face. The mangy-looking character was a former cowboy; Walsh liked his spark and hired him on the spot as an extra. Their friendship lasted many years. This is what Walsh liked to do and would continue doing: surround himself with coworkers who became good friends. In this atmosphere, he now familiarized himself with cameras, lights, and action. For Walsh, the gold rush was on.

In Walsh's eyes, Griffith was a genius and the man who influenced him more than any other. He made it a point to stand behind Griffith whenever he could. He learned the importance of movement and particularly the dramatic crescendo that became Griffith's "race to the rescue" at a story's end. He learned the importance of the shots Griffith used: the high-angle shots; the close-up shots—in one actor's eye the spectator could find the movie's emotional core—so newly interspersed with long-range shots. He learned to limit the use of titles just as Griffith did, especially in action scenes that carried a lexicon all their own. Griffith told him always to shoot the most difficult scenes first, advice he followed religiously. He also followed from his first days as a director Griffith's habit of memorizing the script and doing away with it on the set whenever possible. Walsh could never really recall the older man looking at a script during shooting. For the rest of his career, Walsh surprised both cast and crew by referring to the picture's script infrequently and sometimes not at all. Like his mentor, once Walsh read the script, he had memorized it visually. There it stayed—no need to look further at the written word.

Walsh may have learned about the camera from Griffith, but he also learned how to conduct himself on and off the set. Griffith came onto the set but did very little to interfere with a setup. He might make a comment about regulating the tempo; he might tell his men and women, "Well done," if a shot pleased him. But Walsh noticed that he was all about business—silent and quick paced. Walsh picked up the habit; for years to come as a director he left cast and crew trying to puzzle out his frequent habit of looking or walking away when a scene was being shot. Like Griffith, he knew the scene in his head; he listened after that. If it sounded good, he knew it looked good. Walsh learned two great lessons from Griffith: get your picture finished on time, and take a businesslike, no-nonsense approach to work on the set. Both would serve him well in years to come.

Walsh appeared in the cast of a number of Reliance and Majestic/Mutual productions during 1914. Christy Cabanne directed Miriam and him in two-reelers such as *For His Master* and *The Dishonored Medal*—so Walsh said. He stood out as the smarmy villain-fop—the real Walsh not so hidden—who twirls his handlebar mustache with finesse before and after he attempts to swindle an innocent Blanche Sweet out of her honor in *The Little Country Mouse*. But he disappears into the scenery when he stars with Lillian Gish in two-reelers such as *The Rebellion of Kitty Belle*. At this early time, westerns were cheaper to produce, and Walsh often found himself as Griffith's right-hand man in scouting locations and rounding up local residents (whether they were old cowhands or just men and women he saw on the street). It did not take long for him to move up to being assistant director—until the day Griffith made good on his promise that one day he would let him direct.

Although Walsh considered the 1915 one-reeler *Home from the Sea* a picture with a humdrum plot, there he stood, nevertheless, on the threshold of his own career as a director when Griffith gave him the reins to Fine Arts' first sea picture. He did double duty in the picture, playing an errant son who finally repents, along with Francelia Billington, and getting only occasional supervision from the boss. Walsh chose to shoot in San Pedro, at the time a fishing village just south of Los Angeles with a large Portuguese population. The locale was ideal, and Walsh took control of the job as if he were standing at heaven's gate itself. There was no going back now; he knew it, and Griffith knew it. Walsh standing at the helm—leaning forward, of course—was so natural an event it could have made one of the greatest entries in the autobiography he would write at the end of his life. But, when he wrote that book, he shied away from blowing that horn. Still, he took to the job so easily that it was no surprise that Griffith gave him more films to direct, including *The Mystery of the Hindu Image*, *The Double Knot*, and *The Gunman* (codirecting with Christy Cabanne). There was nothing like the first morning Walsh took the reins. He choreographed the action as if it were second nature to him. Soon enough, he felt as though he was in his second skin.

On it went like this, with Walsh doing either single or double duty, in front of the camera or standing in back of it as well—until the day he met the big bandit.

Running with Pancho Villa

Walsh always thought Griffith an expert on inventing pieces of business, and one of the best ideas his boss had, if not also the craziest to some, was the idea to sign the notorious Mexican bandit Pancho Villa to a one-picture deal, as it were. Walsh got involved in the Villa project around March 1914 and drove down to Mexico to shoot footage of the famous Mexican renegade. The proposed picture was a can of worms that created opportunity and chaos from the start.

Villa had been flirting with the movies for a while before Mutual became involved. He would approach movie companies to film his escapades, this way financing them in the process. Now he was ready to negotiate again. The company executive Frank Thayer had gone down to Juarez, Mexico, twice in the early part of 1914 to get a commitment from Villa to let the company film him. The bandit had just captured the city and had approached the movie people covering the event to make a deal. He would allow cameramen to accompany him on his campaigns; he would even provide food and animals for their travel. In exchange, he wanted 50 percent of the profits. Mutual was the only film company to agree. In March, the project finally looked viable. Thayer returned with an agreement from Villa to let Mutual direct a feature film about him, to be entitled *The Life of General Francisco Villa.* Griffith would direct, Villa would play himself, and Walsh would play Villa at a young age as well as direct background footage. As it turned out, Griffith became much too involved with plans for his upcoming epic film, an adaptation of Dixon's *The Clansman,* and sent Christy Cabanne down to Juarez to direct. Walsh would act as assistant director—but it turned out that he had a much more prominent role in the Villa fiasco. He had to persuade Villa that Mutual had a worthy story for him.

One afternoon that March, Griffith called Walsh into his office; he asked him about his experiences in Mexico and wanted to know whether he could speak Spanish. Walsh told him he had learned the language from an Apache Indian—a typical Walsh tease—and did not think anyone would be able to understand him when he spoke. Nevertheless, Griffith asked him whether he would like to go down to Juarez and film some Villa battle scenes. Walsh said yes without question. He was to give Villa $500 in gold—and, since there still was no story for this picture, Walsh would have to think it up himself as he went along.

As Walsh recounted many years later, Villa met with him and, after fingering the gold Walsh had brought, asked him, through his translators, to tell him the story for the film. Walsh thought quickly:

Well, General . . . a young boy, a fine looking young boy . . . everybody in this little town loved him. He was a fugitive, not even allowed in the town. The farm that he had there . . . there was no rain. Then he had to leave, to go seek employment at a big ranch as a cowboy, to get money for his widowed mother and his little sister. While he was away working to get money for his dear old mother and his sister, the Federals came into the town [Walsh knew Villa was at war with the Federals, the heavies, as he called them]. They came into the town; they burned down the church. Then they came to burn down his house. His mother got out but they grabbed his sister. But he didn't know this. He got the money at the Ranch Terrazas, where he worked, and he was coming home and he bought presents for his mother and his sister.

Then he comes home. He sees the house half burned down. He sees an old man standing there. He asks where his mother is. They tell him that his mother is at this place over here and he runs over and he wants to know where his baby sister is. He finds out his baby sister died and they buried her back of the church or something.

Then this young boy, this handsome young boy, this terrible calamity that hit him just in the prime of life. He stood before his mother, he lifted up his hands and he vowed to kill Federal after Federal till the whole army was wiped out! From then on, he had nothing but hatred for the Federals, and he decided to collect an army and he went from town to town to town to tell them what these Federals did to his family, what they did to the poor. Finally, he got a great following of people and right now they're here in Juarez, and here is the great General that accomplished all this.[13]

Then, Walsh said, the general got up and shook hands with him. They had a deal.

Mutual paid Villa $500 in gold a month to photograph him, his battles, and his executions. Villa liked movies, and he liked gold—what could go wrong? "I had a terrible time," Walsh later said. "Day after day, I would try to take shots of him coming toward the camera. We'd set up at the head of the street, and he'd hit that horse with a whip and his spurs and go by at ninety miles an hour. I don't know how many times we said, 'Despacio, despacio—slow—Señor, please!'" He continued:

> I used to get him to put off his executions. He used to have them at four or five in the morning, when there was no light. I got him to put them off until seven or eight. I'd line the cameramen up, and they'd put these fellows against the wall and then they'd shoot them. Fellows on this side with rocks in their hands would run in, open the guys' mouths, and knock the gold teeth out. The fellows on the other side would run in and take the shoes and boots off them. Later on, they made the picture, but D. W. Griffith didn't direct it—he was busy on something else. Christy Cabanne directed it, and I played Villa as a young man.
>
> Of all the people I've seen executed—not one of them ever wanted to be blindfolded, not one of them gave a damn. Some of them stood up there and cursed, you know, but no cowards—no falling down or anything like that.[14]

Walsh was able to shoot some of Villa's battles, although he thought them none too spectacular. When the crew returned to California, they had to invent some of them.

The film the studio put together was released under a confusing range of titles, not only *The Life of General Villa*, but also *The Tragedy in the Career of General Villa* and *The Tragic Early Life of General Villa*. Moving Picture World described vivid action scenes, showing the rebels advancing under fire, in the "actuality" section of the film. The dramatic section concentrated on the story of Villa's sister, raped by a Federal officer. Villa (whose real name was Doroteo Arango) killed the officer and took to the hills as an outlaw. When the revolution broke out, he linked his bandit army with the rebels, and the film envisioned his final victory over the Federal army and his proclamation as president of the Republic of Mexico.

Griffith and then-writer Frank Woods congratulated Walsh on the "Mexican coverage," even though Walsh hardly felt as enthusiastic about it as they did. He wondered who had directed whom? Had he directed Villa, or had Villa directed him? Griffith commented that some of the shots were good and bloody. The censors might faint, but that was Mutual's headache, not his. There was one more point to make, however. Mutual was pushing him for the complete feature. So Walsh would play Villa, and Cabanne would direct, just to get the picture finished. Because, on the whole, money was hard to come by in the 1910s, movie crews did not travel to far-off locations. *Life of Villa* studio sequences were filmed at Fine Arts; most of the exteriors were shot in and around the San Fernando Valley, not far from the studio's Hollywood headquarters. Eventually, the studio had a five-reeler for its trouble. The project was eventually taken out of Walsh's hands when Mutual decided to beef up what it had. Weak linking and replacement footage was filmed, and *The Battle of Torreon* was released in 1914, in a double bill with *The Life of General Villa*, with Walsh playing the young Villa in the latter film, on which the direction was attributed to Christy Cabanne—although much of the footage shot by Walsh was inserted into Cabanne's work.[15]

Walsh was never entirely certain how much the film grossed but remembered that it ran for what seemed like a long time at an all-Mexican theater on Spring Street in downtown Los Angeles. It became a staple at the Cinco de Mayo festivals in the city, but, over the years, the film, and any footage from it, became lost.[16]

Walsh hoped that his negotiations with Villa demonstrated to Griffith his verve and imagination—and his sheer American know-how. Griffith was impressed but kept his words to a minimum. Still, Walsh always claimed, his antics with the Mexican revolutionary brought him some measure of fame outside the studio. One day, shortly after the Villa episode, not one but two American legends, Wyatt Earp and Jack

London, came by the lot to congratulate Walsh on riding with the man who thumbed his nose at President Wilson.

Facing the Nation

The Villa adventure only enhanced Walsh's appeal to the women in the Griffith company—especially Miriam Cooper. Walsh was a kind of local hero after completing the footage of the Mexican revolutionary. After the Biograph players arrived in California, Walsh was far more interested in the actress Mae Marsh than in Miriam, but that changed quickly one Sunday morning when he asked Marsh to go to church with him and Marsh talked Miriam into going along. Then Marsh reneged at the last minute so that she could accompany Griffith, whom Miriam thought she was probably seeing on the sly (although evidence of this has never surfaced), to look at some land he had purchased in the San Fernando Valley. Miriam and Walsh spent the day together, felt a mutual attraction, and saw each other regularly after that. They made a handsome couple—dark-haired Miriam with her petite stature and fine chiseled features and Walsh with his sleek figure and that abundance of wavy brown hair. Everyone at Fine Arts knew they were an item soon enough. Walsh always behaved as Griffith himself would behave—like a gentleman.

Walsh had already picked up some of Griffith's behavior off the lot. He drove around Los Angeles in a two-seater White Steamer; he and Griffith were the only two men in the company to have one. By now, Walsh also shared a larger two-bedroom apartment with his fellow actor Eugene Pallette. The rest of the company thought him to be rolling in money, although they could not understand how. It could not have hurt his ego when producer Jesse Lasky made him an offer to come and direct for him at the Jesse Lasky Feature Play Company, but Walsh decided to stay with Griffith until he had put a few director credits under his belt.

The work was not easy, much of it physical, what with the heavy lifting of equipment and constantly helping gather the troops around so as to position them before the camera, including himself—but it was steady. Griffith included a battle scene or chase scene in every movie, and, since there were no stand-ins at the time, Walsh the actor performed his own stunts. He broke both his arms at least once and his nose three times and counting. He had to write the scripts as well, a skill that served him well later on. Walsh was ready to tackle any role, any job that needed doing, any call from Griffith when he needed assistance.

All the time Walsh was in Mexico handling Villa, Griffith stayed in Los Angeles already shooting scenes for the film that truly drove him westward from New York and away from Biograph: his epic adaptation of *The Clansman*. It may have been Walsh's familiarity with Dixon's play that moved Griffith to ask Walsh to be one of his assistants and to help direct the battle scenes that eventually became *The Birth of a Nation;* more likely, Walsh impressed Griffith with directing *Home from the Sea,* also demonstrating finesse in handling the often unpredictable Pancho Villa. Griffith had numerous assistants on the picture, but Walsh took on much of the tough-going action involving Indians, cowboys, soldiers, and horses when the company shot in Newhall, California. By now, Walsh was at Griffith's side. He told Kevin Brownlow in 1967, "That was a real tough job. . . . I would have to stay up half the night, you know, one, two, three, four o'clock in the morning [because] these cowboys lived in wagons down at a place called Edendale [the east side of Los Angeles] with no phones or anything. I used to have to go and roust them out of bars and stuff and get them on horses two or three o'clock in the morning and send them off on location . . . and of course when they got up there in the morning, half of them were drunk . . . [a] couple of them would be in jail."[17]

Walsh helped direct the military charges, a task that quickly changed from being a great challenge to an enormous headache. The extras hired to play Confederate and Union soldiers had to be truck loaded to location. Walsh liked to embellish the story. Not only did they have no idea what end of a rifle the bullet came from, he said—they didn't even have a conception of how to behave in front of a camera (much less know what a camera was). He had to think and act quickly. He had the Confederate soldiers move from left to right and the Yankees move from right to left so that the audience would know the difference. When he asked the men to change sides, many revolted (he also liked saying that they had been soldiers in the Civil War) and left the scene. He then had to give each man a number; that man would have to fall into battle when Walsh called his number. The plan was such a success that, when Walsh finished the sequence, Griffith was known to have told him that, had he had been a Confederate general, the South would never have lost the war.

Griffith cast Miriam Cooper in the pivotal role of Margaret Cameron, who represented the symbol of southern womanhood. Griffith rehearsed his actors for hours before he shot important scenes—sometimes getting lines from them in his office or in a bare room with kitchen chairs for furniture. When Walsh later directed Cooper at Fox, she recalled that he would shoot and reshoot a scene endlessly—not at all the way Griffith worked: with endless rehearsals but with hardly a reshoot once the camera rolled. Little wonder that each could walk away in confidence when a scene was actually being shot.

Griffith was looking around for an actor to play the pivotal role of Abraham Lincoln's assassin, John Wilkes Booth, and coming up empty. One day he looked over at Walsh entertaining a group of starlets, noticed his handsome face and easy charm, and thought that he might be just the actor to play a character who aspired to be a matinee idol. He told Walsh to make up for John Wilkes Booth; Walsh was given dark curly hair and lots of dark eye makeup for dramatic effect. He would play Booth. When it came time to reenact the assassination itself, Walsh not only looked the part but also simulated the act in an uncanny way. Just as Booth did when he jumped onto the stage after firing the fatal bullet to Lincoln's head, Walsh jumped over the chairs to get to the stage and make his getaway and, just as Booth himself had done, injured his leg. Now he had more fodder for a story.

Walsh liked the drama—and the attention. He continued acting and made other daring leaps—some that won him the free publicity he began to enjoy. A May 22, 1915, issue of the popular movie magazine *Reel Life* caught him at a good moment and made the most of it in its pages:

In a recent Reliance production Raoul Walsh, fearless leading man of the Hollywood forces, made a forty-foot dive off a bridge into a river. The consternation of persons passing on the bridge at the time may easily be discerned in the accompanying snap-shot of the daring feat. "I sauntered along," said Walsh, "carelessly glancing now and then, through the railing at the water below. It is one of the highest bridges near Los Angeles. A man behind me was walking at a normal pace, and

another unsuspecting individual was approaching from the opposite direction. Suddenly, the director gave the signal. Before
the two laymen could grasp its meaning, I had sprung upon the
edge of the rail and flung myself headlong into the river. The
fellow behind me started to run and shout for help. The other
man, who at the time I leaped was scarcely five feet away, just
doubled up and hung onto the railing with both hands, precisely
as though he had received a blow in the pit of his stomach. It's
worth the risks one takes to be able to thrill your audience from
the screen." "But," added Mr. Walsh, with an expansive grin,
"after all, there's no sport like giving folks the scare of their lives
in person."[18]

Walsh liked being in the spotlight from the start; it appealed to his
sense of himself as a daredevil and adventurer. He craved publicity because the Griffith company kept him more or less in the background as
an actor, and he had not yet taken off as a director. The flavor of this
early piece of publicity forecast Walsh's future; he would come to be seen
as a young filmmaker whose offscreen and onscreen escapades collapsed
into each other and spelled out brashness and candor. A big picture
emerged that forever wed Walsh to his publicly constructed persona:
a young man living on the edge, looking for excitement, and willing to
take chances to get it. The edge was a comforting place.

Given all his success in California, Walsh summoned his brother,
George, to come west to act for Fine Arts. The company put him in a
few battle scenes in *The Birth of a Nation*. Griffith and Cabanne both
liked George's handsome face in front of the camera and cast him as
the bridegroom in Griffith's next epic picture, *Intolerance* (with Walsh
also working as an assistant director). George embarked on a brief but
noticeable career that would carry him for at least ten years.

But, just when Walsh had his brother with him, his own plans turned
dramatically. Soon after the February 1915 New York City premiere of
The Birth of a Nation, William Fox, rising quickly on the mogul ladder
and then still in New York, also took notice of Walsh. He wanted him to
direct for his then-fledgling studio and sent his representative, Winfield
Sheehan, to Los Angeles to woo Walsh by taking him out to dine at the

Alexandria Hotel and offering him a huge amount of money to leave Griffith. Walsh claimed Fox took note of his directorial work on *Home from the Sea* and was immensely impressed. Walsh began negotiations with Fox Film Corporation. Griffith paid Walsh $40 a week, and Walsh said that, since he thought Fox might be a fly-by-night company, he told Sheehan he would want $400 a week—that way he could get rid of him. He never thought Sheehan would go for it—but he did. So Walsh figured he had better sign. Griffith happened to be in the Chicago courts at the time, defending against the charges of racism that were leveled against *Birth*. Although Walsh heard that Griffith did not want to lose him, he signed on with Fox and made plans to head back to New York to Fox before long. Frank Woods told him to go ahead and do it; it was probably just a one-picture deal anyway.

Before leaving California, Walsh directed one more picture for the company that Griffith himself supervised. The full-length *Pillars of Society* was an adaptation of Henrik Ibsen's 1911 play of the same name and featuring Henry Walthall, who played the protagonist in *The Birth of a Nation*. In *Pillars*, Walthall plays Karsten Bernick, a basically decent man whose character flaws prove fatal. The story also indicts the social hypocrisy and corrupt politics characterizing the environment surrounding Bernick. Walsh was called in to direct after the original director "hit the laughing water," as Walsh liked to say (and as he often said). Griffith supervised the production yet made only a few minor adjustments to Walsh's conception of the story.

Now directing—and about to leave Griffith—Walsh did not want to mind that he was suddenly alone, after spending so much time with Miriam Cooper. More offers came in, including one from Jesse Lasky again. Miriam then left for the East Coast to visit her family and help promote *Birth*. Griffith himself suggested she make the trip; very likely Miriam and Walsh's romance was not quite as secret as the two supposed, and Griffith, not especially supportive of his players' emotional entanglements—despite his own entanglements, such as that possibly with Mae Marsh—might have been very happy to see the couple separate. *Birth* was playing in theaters when Miriam and Walsh began sending cables back and forth to each other, their wires often crossing, but their growing passion for each other coming across very clearly.

While in New York, Miriam kept tabs on Walsh. After she returned to New York from a trip to Chicago to promote *Birth,* Walsh wired her on April 24, 1915: "Glad you arrived safely. Acquaint me with your actions in Chicago. The Lasky Co. has made me another offer. Did you receive my letters? Wire me all the news as soon as possible. Miss you. Very much love. R." But Walsh never mentioned his negotiations with Winifred Sheehan. Miriam took offense at his questioning how she spent her time in Chicago. After she told him so in a wire, Walsh rebutted with an April 27 cable: "I trust you explicitly. My inference was why no wire from Chicago? Mr. G. complimented me on my pictures and started me on a four-reel feature with Walthall [i.e., *The Pillars of Society*]. Everything going fine. The auto is like new. Wire when you intend returning. Love, R."[19]

The Griffith player Mary Alden wired Miriam on May 2, 1915, telling her that Walsh, whom she called "the old fisherman," was doing fine: "The old fisherman is well and very good wearing hair on his upper lip. I am working for him. The French Lady is vamping again so do come back soon. I miss you. The Chief is going to remain here for a month. Wire me when you arrive."[20] Then Mary sent another cable saying Walsh was miserable without Miriam and suggesting that she return to California as soon as possible. Miriam was panicked enough as it was, having not heard from Walsh for at least three days at one stretch. She cabled him and received word back right after that. He wrote, "To forget you already is so absurd. I miss you more and more every day. I have worked day and night all week with about four hours sleep. Have not been away from the studio. I have the opportunity of my life on this picture and am going to fight all the way as much as I want you here. Do not leave until all is settled for when you return we never part again."[21] Clearly, Walsh was still thrilled to be directing for Griffith, but Fox awaited.

Miriam returned to California as soon as she could but arrived in Los Angeles on an ill-timed wind. Just as she reached Walsh, he was about to leave for New York to work at Fox. They declared their undying commitment to each other; still, he had little choice but to leave her behind in California, where she was about to start work on Griffith's next picture, *Intolerance.* For the time being at least, they would have to carry on their love affair long-distance.

In his later years, Walsh chose not to mention Miriam Cooper's name in his autobiography; he found another woman to replace her on the pages describing his departure for New York—a Russian beauty whom he said he was seeing at the time. "Olga[22] came to the train to see me off," he wrote. "She started talking softly to me in Russian, while I had my arm around her. When I asked her what she was saying, she told me, 'I have a feeling in my heart that one day we will meet again. And wherever you are, you will never be far away from me.' I kissed her pretty mouth and walked sadly to the train."[23] Both Miriam Cooper and, later, Walsh's second wife, Lorraine Walker, were ousted from his autobiography. The narrative of the Russian beauty Olga Grey serves him better in those pages, good for a romantic escapade. But, in reality, in the moment of spring and summer 1915, Walsh and Miriam Cooper were very much in love. Their love had grown, and they could hardly bear to be apart.

3

Leaning Forward at Fox

> You're Irish, but you have a Yiddisher head.
> —William Fox to Raoul Walsh

The one-picture deal at Fox turned out to be a three-picture contract at $400 a week—just the salary Walsh bargained for but never expected to see. Before Walsh left for New York, Sheehan called to tell him he had two scripts in mind for him but was giving first choice to an older director in the company, Oscar Apfel, who had recently come over from the Jesse Lasky Feature Play Company. Apfel made what Walsh thought was the poorer choice, and Walsh was handed a project called *Regeneration*. He was in New York by before mid-1915, ready to direct what would be the first feature-length gangster film in American cinema. At twenty-eight, Walsh was poised to seize the day, certainly to take hold of a new studio. This directing business was not exactly new to him as he had been watching Griffith vigilantly, but it was unknown territory to be on his own. The little he lacked in confidence he more than made up for in seriousness. His lean frame mirrored the energy racing inside him. He seemed almost to be leaning forward.

Like Walsh, Fox Pictures was just starting out in the business. William Fox began his career buying nickelodeons, where he offered vaudeville acts as well as pictures. Noticing that audiences were flocking less to the vaudeville portions of the shows and more to the flickers, he quickly omitted the vaudeville acts. Then he moved to change over from film distribution to production, but first he had to challenge Thomas Edison and the chokehold he and the Edison Company had on distributors, who were forced to buy film product only from him. Fox sued Edison and emerged the victor, and the studio head now used his winnings to open a full-fledged production company, the Fox Film Corporation. He was determined to get ahead fast, and, the way Walsh remembered it, he was more than willing, at least at this early stage of the game, to pay big salaries to get prestigious movies made.

Walsh moved back into the large family home on Riverside Drive and lived there with his father, his sister, Alice, and her husband, Willie Hoppe. Alice and Hoppe had been married for five years now, with Hoppe still making occasional money as a championship billiard player. His marriage to Alice would be short-lived, and eventually Alice would remarry, take the last name Berghoff, and, tragically, lose herself to alcohol as she grew older. Always close to his father, whose figure was a little pudgier than the last time he saw him, Walsh found him no less handsome in his eyes. He was happy to be with him again. If he noticed that his late mother's room had not changed one bit since her death, he made no mention of it to Thomas.

Ensconced in the environment that shaped him—the great city with its infinite variety of neighborhoods and characters—Walsh would come to know all of it in a new way as he began casting and directing his pictures for Fox. He would soon be back, figuratively, at least, at New York's Bowery and Lower East Side, picking up where he left off. While he would have enjoyed the company of his brother in all this, George was in California working for Griffith now, and it pleased Walsh that he'd had a hand in that.

Walsh could not have found better material for his first solo outing as a director than what he had in *Regeneration*: a story about rough-and-tumble lives in the Bowery that mirrored almost uncannily the adventures he and George dreamed up about it when they were kids. Being privileged as they were, they could not have really understood a life lived there, but now Walsh had the opportunity to flesh out the imagined narratives he had cooked up long ago. As a director, as a human being, he needed to demonstrate the extent of his sympathies for strangers so as to tell a compelling story about a world he only half knew.

Regeneration is based on Owen Kildare's popular and very touching book *My Mamie Rose*, which recounts the author's harrowed life in the Bowery, beginning with the death of his mother and father in his infancy (something Walsh could partially understand), and tracing his subsequent years as an orphan living in a virtual hell on earth. As he grows to manhood, the protagonist becomes "a beer slinger and a pugilist in a tough Bowery dive," by necessity a man "whose fighting capacity and brutishness made him a bouncer in one of the most infamous resorts New York has ever known." When he meets a young woman named Mamie Rose (who becomes Marie in the film), he steadily transforms himself. He and Mamie Rose are to be married, but, tragically, she dies of pneumonia shortly before the wedding. Nevertheless, she has changed his life forever; because of his "regeneration," he discovers that he has the gift of writing and sells his story to a newspaper. After its publication, he ends up a newspaper writer and novelist, telling his reader, "When a man at thirty cannot read or write the simplest sentence, and then eight years later is able to earn his living by his pen, his story may be worth telling."[1] Kildare wanted to show his readers how his characters' hearts hungered even more than their stomachs, how despair mapped out all the days of their lives. The book sold well, even garnering a theatrical adaptation that opened in New York City on September 1, 1908—even if Owen Kildare may have been a pseudonym for a Russian writer.

It is unclear what form the story was in when Walsh got hold of it. The claim in his autobiography that he wrote the script conflicts with other comments he later made that he and a man called Carl Harbaugh worked on it together. He also said once that he did the work while Harbaugh did very little. Harbaugh, who also was cast in the film as the district attorney (a character who never appears in the book), was a new friend Walsh had made at Fox; he would be a constant companion and coworker throughout Walsh's life, either writing with Walsh or appearing in his pictures. Both Walsh and Harbaugh were credited with adapting Kildare's novel;[2] little attention was paid to the book's New York theatrical production.

Regeneration is rife with the dramatic elements that pleased broad audiences of early cinema—violence and redemption, heavy sentiment, romance and tragedy. Walsh knew Kildare from the inside—at least in his storytelling intellect—his camera pointed always on the tenement culture, capturing and closing in on a man, and men, so hungry in body and soul, so long living in emotional and physical impoverishment, that to grab a necessity when it came along was everyday fare. The film follows the book almost faithfully, although Walsh omits the death of the protagonist's father and focuses only on that of his mother—a change he obviously made so that he might feel closer to Owen. When a neighboring couple that turns out to be abusive adopts the boy, Owen learns to live on his own and soon runs his own gang in the neighborhood.

Walsh found a leading man, Rockliffe Fellowes, who had great charisma, taking audiences on a roller-coaster ride of emotions—menacing one minute, heartbreaking the next. Fellowes's boyish good looks provide Walsh's camera with a love object that could carry a feature-length picture. No less affecting is Anna Q. Nilsson, a popular actress of the day, who plays Marie, the woman who abandons her upper-class roots to work in a settlement house and reach out to the needy. Nilsson has the earthiness and the gentleness to appear at once enticing and maternal, a woman Walsh and his camera blatantly adore. Her death is a shocking moment in the film, leaving audiences, and no doubt the director—who understood such a loss—feeling as if the world has suddenly darkened.

Regeneration was an auspicious moment in Walsh's early career. The film is more artful than Walsh would ever admit, especially with its harrowing close-ups, its painterly mise-en-scènes, and its concise, fast-moving storytelling. The threat of anyone noticing this kind of aesthetics taking hold in his work—or calling it such, as the critics did—was disturbing enough to him that, in response, he adopted an attitude of nonchalance about it. This kind of posturing continued throughout his filmmaking career—and here was the first example of it. If nothing else, the picture displays a great range of technical know-how and storytelling conceits, showing that Walsh had been paying close attention to Griffith. Yet much more than technical brilliance is on display in *Regeneration,* more than simply the display of a young filmmaker's innate awareness of the camera. The film shows Walsh getting inside his material, finding the interior terror in his characters' lives; his actors, especially Fellowes, have a look of desperation and yearning on their faces, rendering them three-dimensional souls who chip away at the spectator's complacency.

Yet, at such an early time in Walsh's career, this film initiates a conscious decision to invent the persona of an artist claiming he is not an artist at all. While movies were not yet viewed as an art form, as they would be later in the twentieth century—Walsh and many of his fellow directors often ignored gathering theoretical and aesthetic discussions of their work—Walsh no doubt had a self-consciousness about what he was doing, an awareness that there was an artfulness on some level to the way a scene or a shot—or an emotion—played out on film. Later in his career, as he chose material often far inferior to his talents, he could certainly disclaim any artfulness in some of his pictures. But, at the time of this picture, his material was stirring, and he merged his finely tuned sensibility to it. Still, he disclaimed. If he called himself a storyteller, that was fine. But he claimed nothing more. When he took a chance, four years later, with *Evangeline* and called it poetry, he was stunned at the film's public failure. But, for now, when *Regeneration* opened on September 13, 1915, to critical and box-office success, he never talked about *art*. He talked about the picture as a project that he needed to complete on schedule. If there was a humorous moment during the shoot, he might talk about that. This was to become an emotional place from which he would never really venture. In talking about *Regeneration*, Walsh always chose to focus on the excitement of the production itself.

Regeneration provided Walsh with another episode to add to his growing repertoire of crazy-making moments on the set. While he was still a rather serious fellow at this juncture in his life, as he got older he loved to dip into his abundant collection of stories recounting his true adventures and the bizarre mishaps that occurred on the sets of his pictures. This one was an adventure of the first order. For the second half of *Regeneration,* Walsh had to create a scene where a crowded riverboat catches fire while going down the Hudson River. He needed a large group of extras to jump off the boat into the river, so he recruited them from the Bowery—the women looked like hookers and the men like criminals awaiting execution, he said. But, during filming, one problem cropped up; he noticed that many of the women's undergarments were missing and that this could be seen in the printed shot. As it turned out, some of those women were actually male actors; when he could not find enough female performers for the scene—the first one he filmed, remembering Griffith's advice always to shoot the most difficult scenes first—he offered a dividend to any male actor willing to dress in women's clothing. To fool the audience, he went to the "negative doctor," a man he remembered from his days working at Pathé. After some coaxing, Walsh convinced him to doctor the footage so that it looked as if the women were wearing pants.

Another mishap occurred that Walsh always spoke of with great pride—as if he had nearly caused a riot during the film's production.

When the actors began jumping into the river, three New York City fireboats and a police launch showed up to put out the "fire" and calm the "crowds." Walsh was hauled off to the local station house, but he was more amused than miffed, and the studio relished all the free publicity the incident garnered. Word of mouth about Walsh and his picture was building. It was no surprise that the press made note of what was considered to be the film's unusual emotional complexion. "There is a grim sort of humor in many of the scenes," wrote Lynde Denig in *Motion Picture Weekly*. "There is an abundance of excitement in others, and through the picture carries a genuine heart interest."[3]

Regeneration was the first collaboration between Walsh and the brilliant French cinematographer Georges Benoît, newly arrived from Paris and also making his first Fox picture. The two men worked together over the next few years and between them produced stark yet lyrical images in such pictures as *Carmen, Blue Blood and Red,* and *The Honor System*. William Fox was so taken with the box-office success of *Regeneration* that he bought Walsh a Simplex automobile and raised his salary to $800 per week. Walsh now entered a period of his career where he produced a virtual feast of riches at Fox, but he was still hard-pressed to concede that he had the artist in him. He was making a noise at the studio. By August 1915, Fox put into effect a plan to produce at least one picture a week to be based on the work of a famous author and to feature one of his famous stars. The directors on the short list for this plan included Walsh, Herbert Brenon, Edgar Lewis, Oscar C. Apfel, Frank Powell, Frederick Thompson, Will S. Davis, Marshall Farnum, and J. Gordon Edwards.

Hot Property

One of those famous stars and Fox's hottest property at the moment, the Vamp, Theda Bara, took up some of Walsh's time—off and on the set. Now he was slated to direct her in several vehicles that showed off her already well-appreciated sex appeal as a screen siren who lured men to their end—pleasurably or not. Secretly, Walsh thought Bara had very little to offer as an actress, although he would never let the thought escape his lips until many years later. Ability or no, he certainly didn't mind the notoriety she brought to a picture since he was always looking for a little of that himself. The studio touted Bara as being descended from gypsies, but, in fact, she was Theodosia Burr Goodman, a Jewish girl from Cincinnati who took her career very seriously. She wanted meatier, more dramatic material than Fox had so far given her; now about to work with Walsh on *Carmen* and *The Serpent,* she continued to make headlines and to see box-office success, even if the films were not especially serious material.

Walsh always took credit for the idea to make *Carmen.* He claimed that he was reading *Variety* one day and noticed that Cecil B. DeMille was about to direct a movie adaptation of Bizet's opera *Carmen* with the opera sensation Geraldine Farrar playing the lead. He told William Fox that he wanted to beat DeMille to the punch and put his version into production first, with Bara playing the lead. Fox was so pleased that he told Walsh to go ahead with the production almost immediately. Even if Bara had larger goals in mind for her career, Fox still saw her as the woman who vamped American men and brought them to the box office in droves.

Walsh's *Carmen* would be an adaptation of Prosper Mérimée's popular novel of the same name, and it would be a six-reeler, one of the first pre-Hollywood epics. The Spanish city of Cordoba was erected on the Fox back lot in Fort Lee, and five thousand extras were brought in for the shoot. But Walsh needed a bull too. Sheehan had the executive Sol Wurtzel send to Tijuana for the animal, which also arrived with a matador in tow. Walsh was thrilled. To get the matador's cooperation, Walsh promised him that he would be a big movie star one day—just as he had promised Villa. Attempting to get a frontal shot of the bull's horns as he charged the bullfighter, Walsh used a French camera, the Debrie, which he strapped onto the bull's back. But the bull ran amuck when one of the "toreadors" yelled "Toro" one too many times; it chased the matador out of the arena and ran off the set and into the street, causing Walsh to yell out, "Que chingaos pasa?" A day later one of the grips found the bull grazing in a meadow near the studio; Walsh never got his frontal shot. Ultimately, the negative cost the company $200,000.

At the start of their relationship, Bara was less fond of her new director than he was of her. According to her biographer, Eve Golden, even before Bara began working with Walsh, she heard that the twenty-eight-year-old director was considered by some to be "a maniac" with a "Rabelaisian sense of humorous filth." According to John Goldfrap, a frequent visitor to the set, Walsh "was besieged by a non-stop fit of hyperactivity" and "suffered frequent temper tantrums and kept a supply of cheap pocket watches to 'dash into a hundred pieces against a convenient wall.'"[4] Even now, no one would have enjoyed this description of Walsh better than Walsh himself.

Bara was not pleased that Walsh's script for *Carmen* emphasized "action over character and plot development." As Walsh told one reporter visiting the set, "My main object was to put plenty of action in it. I saw to it that there is something doing every minute the picture is on the screen. . . . I write my own scenarios, and I cut all my own pictures." Walsh already considered himself a great success and ascribed this to the fact that he and his cameraman Georges Benoît "shaved their heads for good luck on the day they started each film."[5]

Fox released Walsh's *Carmen* on November 1, 1915, the same day as DeMille's version. DeMille's brought in better reviews, but Walsh's made more money, which was just fine with Fox. Still, Fox's version found good reviews across the country, even in smaller venues. One reviewer called Theda Bara "Hades' hand-maiden . . . literally a rage from coast to coast." Walsh was touted as a "vastly experienced master-hand" and "indissolubly associated with extraordinary notable photoplay achievement." His picture moved "past all precedent in pomp and lavish splendor" with "the true spirit of ancient, picturesque Spain."[6] Another reviewer, in a Montana newspaper, called Walsh "one of the greatest" and Bara "remarkable" and raved that Fox Film Corporation had scored "a triumph": "From the first to the last the Fox *Carmen* holds the interest with a tempo which never lags."[7] Fox was so pleased with the picture that he raised Walsh's salary to $1,000 a week and gave him an assignment about prison reform called *The Honor System*.

Reports of Walsh's alleged "hyperactivity" on the set of *Carmen* probably held some truth—at least the public might have thought so after Walsh and Bara made headlines around the time that Fox released *Carmen*. The Associated Press reported (or lathered up) an incident that occurred—supposedly on the set of Bara's next picture, *Sin* (although it may have botched the name of the picture—it was more likely *Carmen*).

A story appeared at the end of October that Bara looked to be "out of control" during a fight with another actress on the set and that Walsh himself stood on the sidelines cheering Bara on during the catfight:

> The sunlight was falling in full mid-afternoon flood upon the players in a slum scene at one of the four William Fox studios across the Hudson. In the background were two huge buildings of glass that looked like overgrown greenhouses. In the fore-ground stood a group of men and women who were watching a strange figure.
>
> Its head was shorn to the scalp. It was coatless. Its big blue-gray Irish eyes were wide and ablaze. It jumped up and down, 'round and 'round, from side to side with the quickness and angles of a jumping jack. And it was calling aloud to somebody in tones of command, then of entreaty. . . .
>
> "What's the matter with that man!" I asked. "Is he a maniac?"
>
> "No," my escort from the Fox film offices [said], "he's Raoul A. Walsh, a director."
>
> Presently, when the escort had spoken the words of introduc-tion, I discovered that Mr. Walsh is a boyish man with the large eyes of a dreamer and the quick, nervous movements of the doer. He is a graduate of the film city suburb of Los Angeles—Holly-wood—and the three pictures he has done for the Fox Company will be a revelation. Generally there is a man at the bottom of a woman's evil deeds. Mr. Walsh incited Theda Bara to fight.
>
> Walsh shouted at Bara to "Go at her . . . Get her down! Jump on her! Scratch her! Bite her! Good!" She became a "fury, and sank her teeth deep into the girl's shoulder." When Walsh stopped his jumping and said, "That's enough," Bara got up with an impassive face and walked away, leaving the other ac-tress shaken and in tears.[8]

A more flattering, or at least a more level-headed, picture of Walsh emerged several months later when a reporter wrote of him, "Aloof with newspaper interviewers almost to the point of shyness, Mr. Walsh does everything quietly and without fuss. He never raves at principals or 'extras' or tears his hair after the fashion of some directors. After the biggest scene he generally confines his comments to two words—'pretty feeble' or 'very good.'"[9] Likely both descriptions of Walsh were publicity pieces released by Fox to promote the reputation of its young superstar; it hardly mattered which direction that reputation took.

The name Raoul Walsh became more familiar to the general movie-going public thanks to Fox's fast-turning publicity wheels. But, despite the notoriety he received, Walsh felt less than satisfied about his career—good material was not coming in fast enough—and even less satisfied about his personal life. He and Miriam frequently corresponded. His letters to her were far less desperate cries of loneliness than hers to him were. Still, he missed her. As would be the case throughout their courtship and marriage, whatever Walsh felt, Miriam felt a much more dramatic version of it. By that same October, having been separated from Walsh for almost six months, she planned a brief escape from California by lying to Griffith and telling him that she had to visit her sick mother in New York. She was on the next train east and arrived just as Walsh was finishing production on *Carmen*.

Miriam had counted on Walsh being on the set, but she hadn't counted on Theda Bara. The two women disliked each other almost immediately. Miriam thought Bara a "horrible" person who seemed to have only one expression, to "duck her head and stare at the leading man or the camera with what appeared to be a searching look. . . . [She was] overweight, coarse and unattractive, entirely different from the slender young Griffith girls [meaning Miriam herself])."[10] Bara thought just as little of Miriam, which Miriam interpreted to mean that, since Walsh had a girlfriend, that was one more man off Theda's market.

Miriam's two-week visit to New York only fanned the fires of loneliness. She and Walsh would have to do something about it. Walsh didn't express the same emotional turmoil, no matter what he really felt. He was about to direct his next picture with Bara, and Miriam would just have to wait. Production on Fox's *The Siren of Seville* began that winter with the studio building new sets on its back lot. After the Spanish city was complete, Walsh was still looking for his male lead when it began to snow heavily in New Jersey. Instead of sunny Spain, he later remembered, they had Lapland. The picture was already sold (as was the

practice then of booking a film into theaters even before it was finished),
and there was no choice but to come up with a different kind of picture
and use the sets and the weather they already had.

Walsh suggested they make a Russian picture instead. The idea
took, Bara was notified of the change (she took it quite well), and Walsh
got together with a few other Fox writers and rushed out a story about
Czar Nicholas, his daughter Anastasia, and the underhanded Rasputin's
shady dealings with the family business. Walsh wired George to come to
New Jersey to play the part of Anastasia's beautiful boyar. Not only did
George star in the picture; he and Walsh concocted the script for what
was to become *The Serpent,* based on Philip Bartholomae's "The Wolf's
Claw." The story has Bara playing a Russian peasant girl who is seduced
by a grand duke (Charles Craig) only to seek revenge on his entire family. The municipal censorship boards were in place, and to get by them
Walsh and George decided to encapsulate the entire scenario into a bad
dream, as if to suggest that what happens in the picture never really
happens. Instead of luring her betrayer into a horrid death, Bara ends the
picture seeming only to wish for his death and instead goes off with her
good-mannered fiancé. The studio released the picture on January 23,
1916, to decent notices and a respectable box office. Just then, the snow
in Fort Lee melted, and the studio no longer had the streets of Moscow
and St. Petersburg on its hands but once again the Grand Plaza and the
avenues of Seville.

Miriam's time in New York only made her feel worse. She missed Walsh
and he her. They began corresponding in earnest, declaring their un-
bridled passion for each other in letters and cables that flew back and
forth for several months, sometimes at the rate of two or three a day.
Traveling with George on the way back to New York from Chicago after
the release of *The Serpent,* Walsh wrote to Miriam on January 25, 1916:

> My Darling Sweetheart,
>   We are somewhere in Missouri and it is snowing. The time
> is about seven o'clock. I have been awake for an hour and you
> my darling have been my only thought. . . . Even a single day
> [without you] is like a year. When we arrived in Chicago the
> Fox Company's manager met us and took us for an auto ride

and gave us a dinner. I also received a telegram from Mr. Fox congratulating me on the success of my picture, which he said was greatly received at the Academy and the [illegible] Theatres.

I wish you were here, Miriam. It is snowing quite hard and the country looks wonderful. Little groups of cattle are scattered here & there & they look so cold, but then they look strong and I guess they will [illegible] this year. There are mostly men on the train, with the exception of a young girl about eighteen traveling with her mother. They look quite refined, despite the fact they have more make up on than either my sister or Dorothy [Gish?]. They are scandalous. Darling, I will close so that I can mail this at [unreadable], which town I can now see in the distance. Bye Bye till tonight. All my love and a big hug & a kiss from your own,

Boo Boo[11]

Throughout Walsh and Miriam's courtship, and during the first years of their marriage, they used pet names in their correspondence. Walsh was "Boo Boo" or "Daddy," and Miriam was "Mommy."

Miriam wrote Walsh a letter the very same day, saying, "Oh, Boo Boo . . . I miss you so much that I hardly know what to do. The awful feeling of knowing you are going farther away from me every minute and that I cannot even talk to you over the phone. Oh, Boo Boo, I am so lonely and I love you so much that everything loses interest for me when you have gone and I count on the days when I leave to go with you."[12]

Miriam was more adamant about getting married than was Walsh. But there was no doubt that he loved her. They decided to marry, and Miriam was the one who made the arrangements—he more or less followed her lead. Since she knew that Griffith would disapprove and that she might jeopardize her career at Fine Arts if she married Walsh, the couple married secretly. Georges Benoît got the idea that they should say their vows on the Hopi Indian reservation near Albuquerque. Walsh traveled to Albuquerque from New York and Miriam from Los Angeles. They said their vows the second week of February 1916.

But the marriage ceremony didn't solve the problem of their continued separation, so Miriam took it on herself to fix that. On the train back to California she realized that, with Walsh on the East Coast and

she in California, they had nothing to look forward to but continu-
ous good-byes. That wasn't what she wanted. More than anything she
wanted to be on the same coast as her husband; she wanted to be a wife
and a mother. If she had to give up her movie career, so be it.

So it mattered little to Miriam that, a few weeks after she returned
to California, Griffith offered her a part in a new production he planned,
an adaptation of *The Rubaiyat of Omar Khayyam;* he presented her
with a leather-bound edition of the poems inscribed "David" on the
inside to solidify his offer. As an excuse to get out of the assignment,
she told Griffith that she could not understand any of the poems in the
volume and that she could never appear in a picture about which she understood so little. Soon after that, telling no one but Walsh, she slipped
out of Los Angeles and headed back to New York. When Griffith did
find out, he showed no anger but politely congratulated her. They never
saw each other again.

Walsh and Miriam decided to make their marriage more official and
had a second ceremony in a Catholic church where the shared their first
High Mass. Again, never a religious man, Walsh followed Miriam's lead.

Life with Father

Walsh had always been "polite around women," Miriam later said. But
living with him brought with it an altered vision of the man. Unlike
the subdued D. W. Griffith, the only other man this fatherless girl had
consistently been around, "Raoul swore all the time. It was the way he
started the day. He'd get up in the morning, go to the window, look
out, and say, 'Christ, what a hell of a fine day!'"[13] The nice Catholic
boy she imagined she married turned out to be a little rough around
the edges—and her fantasy that she would be a wife and a mother to a
husband who stayed home with her had to be rearranged as time went
on. Walsh displayed little interest in religion being part of their lives; in
fact, he barely showed an interest in Catholic characters and themes,
such as redemption and salvation, in his films. That would have been
difficult for Walsh, who, unlike a John Ford or a John Huston, was over
the years often hard-pressed to find a true emotional connection to those
themes and characters in his pictures. He would always be more inclined
to shout "God-damn" out the window or on the set than to sit down

quietly and contemplate others. A man seeking adventure, the pleasure of the hunt, as it was, was a different husband than the one Miriam romanticized.

With the success of *Carmen* and *The Serpent,* William Fox was more than pleased with his new hire and, after raising Walsh's salary, also increased his responsibilities at the studio. Walsh had wanted to return to California for some time and blamed Theda Bara and their box-office successes for his not being able to do that sooner. Bara just loved being on the East Coast, and Fox just loved Walsh's work with her. Fox had another, bigger idea: he had been making plans to open a studio on the West Coast, and now he offered Walsh the opportunity to return to Hollywood to work there. Walsh practically jumped at the opportunity. He and Miriam packed their bags, boarded a train at Grand Central, and were back in Los Angeles before April 1916.

Fox wanted Walsh to work hand in hand with his former secretary, Sol Wurtzel, who now ran the business end of the new studios on the corner of Western Avenue and Sunset Boulevard in Hollywood. Walsh would be in charge of sets and technical advice and, of course, of finding scripts. The Fox money bought his loyalty. His first business was to hire five new directors, and he promptly suggested men such as Jack Adolfi, Eddie Dillon, Billie Beaudine, and Jack Conway, the last three Griffith bred and raised. He also told Wurtzel to "sniff around" Mack Sennett's "bird cage" to find screenwriters. When Wurtzel mentioned the three-acre vacant lot across the street from the studio, Walsh decided to use it to build a western street, a "cow town" with a saloon, a sheriff's office, a bank, a post office, and a Wells Fargo express. He said to sprinkle in "a doctor's office, a barber shop, a bank, a brothel and a funeral parlor." When Wurtzel asked, why the saloon, Walsh said, "What do you think cowboys do when they come to town? Spend all their time drinking bad whiskey and trying to shoot the bartender? Whoring was legal then, not controlled by mobsters and pimps like today."[14] When Walsh walked across the street to the studio and saw five huge indoor stages, he thought that Hollywood was really coming of age!

Though Wurtzel wasn't keen on the idea, Walsh convinced him that westerns were the most popular movies around. *Blue Blood and Red* would be Walsh's first West Coast western. He again hired his brother, George, to star in the picture and to write the script with him. The story would forecast Walsh's western spoof to come over forty years later, *The Sheriff of Fractured Jaw*. Similarly, this picture is a semicomic western tale centering on a blue-blooded college dropout (George Walsh) whose angry father sends him out West to see whether he can ever amount to anything. He arrives a fish out of water, replete with a white racing car and a butler in tow. But, when he falls in love with a red-blooded minx (Doris Pawn, who soon wed the director Rex Ingram), he finds a way to tough it out, get comfortable in his western environs, and even win the girl.

The picture turned George into a full-fledged star and soon a matinee idol—even if his status as a heartthrob was short-lived, halted when MGM promised to cast him as the hero in its 1925 *Ben Hur* and then reneged. But now, and for the next decade, after Fox signed him to a contract, he enjoyed first-billing status.

Publicity was heavy for the April 2, 1916, release of *Blue Blood and Red*. Walsh became a news celebrity as stories turned out nationwide detailing every angle of the picture's production, especially his travels to New Mexico to obtain what critics later called "some of the most remarkable photographs ever taken of a cattle round-up." Newspapers were smitten with his bravura, particularly when he learned that cowboys were bringing in five thousand head of cattle from some ranges in Albuquerque and coordinated his large cattle scenes with the event so that he could "use" the roundup in the picture. Critics called the film the first great outdoor western photoplay.[15]

Walsh took as naturally to the press as he did to the western terrain, both becoming landscapes in which he maneuvered with ease and felt completely at home. He liked being the center of attention—when he held the reins—and peppered his interviews with as much color and animation as he could. If he had to stretch the truth a little so that the drama suited him, it was easily done with no second thoughts. Enthusiasm for the film was so strong that papers could not get enough gossip about it. One paper even printed an anecdote about a behind-the-scenes moment that occurred on location. Even though the crew was "far from civilization, director Walsh insisted that two or three scenes just taken be developed." In lieu of having a darkroom, Walsh's cameraman, Georges Benoît, "crawled beneath the covers of his camp bed, sealing all possible holes where light might enter and went to work."[16]

Walsh had seen Griffith stage huge outdoor scenes; he also found Pancho Villa to be the kind of ornery bandit he liked. Villa churned out one tall tale after another, and Walsh took a liking to that immediately. The West that Walsh either dreamed up or lived in before making his way to the movies just fed his imagination for the huge outdoor spaces he came on when he met Griffith and Villa. No matter what other terrain he scouted, he would return to the West, his truest homeland.

Walsh was gaining a reputation at a fortuitous time: since the early months of 1916, motion picture revenue soared in the United States. As early as January of that year, newspapers across the country announced that the movie industry was now the fifth largest business in the country, with only agriculture, transportation, oil, and steel, largest to smallest respectively, ranking above it. A "conservative" estimate of $5 million had by now been invested in the industry, and the amount of money spent annually in making movies far exceeded that figure. At least ten million people went to the movies annually, and there was scarcely a community in the country with a population of more than one thousand that did not have a movie house. To get to this happy state of affairs, articles touted, the bulldog had to yap at both ends of the elephant (the conglomerate), and the exhibitor bulldogs had to sign an agreement that they would buy only from the big conglomerate. The little bulldog that could was William Fox. "One day, William Fox, president of the Greater New York Rental Company, went to Washington and laid a few facts before George W. Wickersham, then Attorney General. Shortly thereafter, the Sherman anti-trust law was taken from its shelf, dusted off and applied to the elephant. Oct. 1, 1915."[17]

Also, since the appearance of the nickelodeon just after the turn of the century, it was only a matter of time until the debate took shape comparing the stage actor to the newer breed, the movie actor and, in that vein, the stage director to the new kind of artist now appearing on the American scene—the film director. "A new type of actor has been developed by the movies," the *Dallas Morning News* reported. "The motion-picture industry has also developed a new type of artist, separate and distinct from the movie stars. This artist is the director. Five years ago the motion-picture director who received a salary of $50 weekly considered himself fortunate. Today there are directors whose annual income is equal to that of the President of the United States." It was reported that D. W. Griffith's income rivaled that of the U.S. president. Down a notch or two, Walsh was listed as one of those directors whose salary shot upward of $25,000 annually. Others at that pay scale included Reginald Barker, Thomas Ince, Mack Sennett, Allan Dwan, J. Gordon Edwards, and Cecil B. DeMille.[18] (Both salaries and reputations were on the rise.)

Walsh and Miriam's move back to California triggered a period when they traveled extensively, sometimes together, but more often apart. During the first two years of their marriage, they considered themselves workhorses. Although Walsh was now making more money, they still worked hard and, to Miriam's way of thinking, "without glamour." At times they had both an apartment in New York and a house in Los Angeles, but very rarely were the two of them in the same place at the same time. Walsh would be on location in Los Angeles and Miriam somewhere on the East Coast. But, when they were together, Miriam saw to it that she and Walsh kept up with certain status symbols, including health fads of the day: wherever they went, they made it a point to get massages and high colonics. Walsh went along with his wife, never thinking to object: "They were all the rage with picture people then. . . . We had them in New York, Santa Monica and San Francisco."[19]

Miriam managed the Walshes' social image. Walsh went along with her on that also, giving little consideration to how much money she spent. He had little concern about spending it—a habit he had learned long ago when he was a child. His parents' household was luxurious, and he and his siblings grew up privileged, his sense of entitlement something he never entirely outgrew. Now with Miriam, the money spent seemed to make sense to a man trying to build up a reputation in a movie and often-moneyed community. But, no matter how much Walsh made, Miriam never thought they had enough.

Miriam hired a full-time cook and called it their one luxury, admitting that having one was really a matter of keeping up appearances. She fussed over the woman, making certain her uniform looked appropriate, but never gave thought to whether she could cook. "All I was interested in was the show," she said later. She was aware, even from the beginning, that her love for Walsh existed alongside her love of the "show." Walsh, on the other hand, cared about the cook's culinary skills. In her autobiography, Miriam recounts a stringent moment one night when

Walsh finally showed he cared. When the new cook brought to the dinner table two overcooked lamb chops, Walsh roared that they looked more like "dog turds." "Don't you know what I like?" he asked. "You ought to—you sat across the table from me for a whole year."[20] He fired the cook and found another, named Theresa, who stayed with them for years, to the end of her life.

Walsh had his career to attend to. Two visions loomed before him: he saw that his output as a director could be voluminous if he handled it right. He also realized that the medium itself embodied huge possibilities. He still loomed forward, looking for unusual material to put on the big screen. He stayed friends with the Griffith cameraman Billy Bitzer, amazed at Bitzer's childlike curiosity about the camera and what he might capture with it. He would be out and about in Los Angeles, catching big tufts of fogs rising over the hills along with frequents shots of the sun setting over the beach at Santa Monica. Walsh was out there with him, learning technique, and also staying close to someone he considered a master. If Walsh could be somewhere other than in the house with Miriam, he would be there. Seeing other women under innocent social circumstances meant hardly a disruption to his life.

As early as the first year of the Walshes' marriage, there were signs of trouble to come. For one thing, Walsh developed a penchant for betting on the horses, a habit that unnerved Miriam, especially the day he won $90,000, a good deal more than their combined salary, which often totaled $300 a week. More disruptive, Walsh's love of being around women other than his wife wore away at Miriam from the start. Before their first anniversary, believing her husband to have been with another woman (and, just as were Walsh's wives to come, Miriam was uncertain who), she claimed having tried to kill herself by swallowing a bottle of carbolic acid that Theresa had left on the sink. Walsh was very tender with her after the episode, but she never trusted him again. Miriam was histrionic at times, it was true; but she would always be left wondering about Walsh's whereabouts during his evenings out without her.

With Honor

There are conflicting stories about just how Walsh came to direct what would be his great film of this period, *The Honor System*. One story has it that the *Los Angeles Times* writer and drama critic Henry Christeen Warnack approached Walsh to help him develop a script from his book on prisons that he called *The Honor System*. Another version has Fox giving Walsh a finished script that Walsh rewrote. In his autobiography, however, Walsh says that he and the studio were about to cast the picture (he doesn't mention who scripted it) when he received a phone call from the *Los Angeles Times* sports editor Paul Lowry asking Walsh to talk to his friend, John Twist, the *Chicago Tribune* editor, who had just published a story in *Collier's* magazine about Arizona governor George Hunt and the new program—an honor system—he initiated for the state's penal system, letting prisoners take short, unsupervised leaves. Walsh says that it was Twist's idea to "have a prisoner, your star, released on his honor to testify in some case and see what happens."[21] Since the story had no central character at that stage, Walsh was only too happy to listen to Twist. The two worked on the picture together (eight years later, Twist returned to Los Angeles, where he and Walsh worked on scripts for the rest of their careers and remained the closest of friends).

Just as Walsh had written the scenarios for most of the one- and two-reelers he appeared in and directed for Fine Arts (or that he carried around in his head rather than on paper), he was doing the same with his early Fox projects. He was also completely responsible for casting them, finding locations, and overseeing production. He was, that is, producing before he ever officially called himself a producer or ran his own small production company. So it would not be unusual for a man such as Warnack to approach Walsh with a story idea.

Walsh wanted to research the program himself and traveled to Florence, Arizona, to see about Hunt's new program. Prisoners were let out of the facility on their honor, with a promise that they would return in an allotted amount of time. Walsh lived in the prison for three days while he studied the prisoners and then returned to Los Angeles to work on the script. He managed to get an actor he liked very much, Milton Sills, to play the lead. He convinced Miriam to play the daughter of the prison warden. Although she considered her career over since her marriage, she agreed to be in the picture—not so much to restart her career after leaving Griffith's company but because she feared a separation from her husband when he went on location to Arizona. To her chagrin, she stayed, not with Walsh, but with the warden's family during the shoot. But at least she felt more comfortable being in the same city as her husband.

Using the name Raoul A. Walsh, which he did frequently during his early acting and directing career, Walsh now set out to direct a ten-reel picture that thematically and technically far outdistanced its similarly titled predecessor released by Kalem Productions four years earlier and featuring Carlyle Blackwell in the lead. Unfortunately, both the Kalem film and Walsh's more sophisticated version were lost early on—Walsh's version considered by most historians to be an especially tragic loss—leaving only stills, newspaper stories, and Fox's original program to rely on in order to understand the enormous impact Walsh's picture had on the filmgoing public at the time.

Walsh took his crew and cast members to Yuma, Arizona, to shoot inside the Arizona State Prison. He and Miriam always worked well together on the set; he was gentle with her, and she, in turn, had no problem seeing him as a mentor. No matter the turn their marriage took, Miriam always believed Walsh to be one of the best directors working. The production then returned to Los Angeles and finished up in Inglewood, a suburb just a few miles south of Hollywood.

The story begins with a scenario Hitchcock would use repeatedly some thirty years later: the fabulous journey of a man accused of a crime he did not commit. Joseph Stanton (Sills) is a New England inventor who ventures west to get money for a new project. When he arrives in Howling Dog, Mexicans raid the border town, and, unintentionally getting involved in the action, Stanton is attacked and, fighting back, accidentally kills his attacker. An unscrupulous attorney swears that the man Stanton killed was unarmed. Stanton gets a life prison sentence and endures all kinds of physical atrocities, including being flogged and having to live in severely unsanitary conditions in the prison. During a staged prison break, Stanton and others escape, but Stanton pleads to the governor that he should see for himself the horrors of the prison. The governor does just that and subsequently allows the now blind and emaciated Stanton, who has just endured another flogging, to participate in the newly installed honor system. The governor also decides to support Stanton's new invention and allows him to leave prison to test out his idea—with the promise that he will return. Stanton intends to do just that but is sideswiped by thugs working for the unscrupulous attorney who make sure that Stanton misses his train back to the prison. Now having to walk back through the desert, he makes it to the prison just in time to meet his deadline but is so exhausted from his ordeal that he dies right at the prison door. In the meantime, the warden has been informed that Stanton actually did act in self-defense during his initial offense. In the film's tragic ending, the warden and his daughter, Edith (Miriam Cooper), wait in vain through the night to give him his pardon.

The studio removed this tragic ending and replaced it with a more cheerful one that has Edith nursing Stanton back to health. This incident is significant in Walsh's career, being the first of many times censors would frustrate him in the coming years. No matter the ending, *The Honor System,* released in New York on February 6, 1917, had an initial six-week run that brought in close to 100,000 customers.

Walsh was excited about directing *The Honor System* and poured his heart into every detail. Some of the film's images were difficult to take, even for those with a strong stomach: maggots crawling on pieces of bread the prisoners eat; rats and other vermin sharing cells with the prisoners. All of it was real, except the one touch of humor Walsh devised: a close-up of cockroaches walking around carrying messages on their backs written by prisoners as a way to communicate with one another.

The studio went all out and offered movie patrons a twenty-four-page program, elaborately designed with dialogue and photographs from the film and, more interestingly, extensive messages about prison reform, including words about the honor system from Governor George Hunt himself. Fox went overboard in promoting the film, including all the publicity schmaltz it could muster. The top of the program's front page read, "Am I My Brother's Keeper?" Beneath it, just before the film's title, is the announcement, "William Fox Presents The Gigantic Prison Problem Film."

Walsh went into the project with his heart on his sleeve, allowing himself to believe firmly in the romance that his picture might actually further the cause of prison reform. He had been swayed and now felt uplifted by the belief that Governor Hunt's experiment with Arizona prisoners might take hold across the nation and become routine. At this still early stage of his career, he could be called a director with a large hopeful vision—a vision of what a powerful medium movies might become and how influential he might be as a director.

The studio chipped away at his idealism in little time. He looked forward to editing *The Honor System* at a careful pace, but William Fox thought differently and assigned Walsh to another picture right away. Walsh found himself directing a series of smaller pictures, calling these his day job, and then rushing to the editing room at night to shape *The Honor System.* The smaller pictures added up to a clear sign that William Fox was not all that interested in pouring money into large productions. Walsh directed smaller-budget affairs, beginning with an eight-reel, still fairly substantial story about General Sam Houston called *The Conqueror* (also called *A Man's Revenge*), which he scripted with Henry Warnack, released later that year. The picture's initial six-page scenario announces that it is "suggested from the life of Sam Houston, that romantic character and early prisoner, which had so much to do with the freeing of Texas from Mexican rule, and who did so much for the Indian." The story, however, recounts that period in Houston's life before he emigrated to Mexican Texas, from his boyhood life among the Indians up to the time he became governor of Tennessee in 1827.[22] Romance outdistanced history in this story.

Walsh stayed with a spate of what, in his estimation, were trivial pictures such as *Betrayed* (also called *The Heartless Senorita*), featuring Miriam as a woman named Carmelita who lives with her "lazy, fat father in a small adobe shack." The story notes reveal that, even though her father had gotten slovenly, "in Carmelita there still remained some of the dignity and the grace of the peon." In spite of "her filthy father, the instincts of a senorita prevailed."[23] Other small pictures were *This Is the Life, The Pride of New York* (featuring George Walsh), *The Silent Lie,* and *The Innocent Sinner,* the latter two again featuring Miriam and released the same year as *The Honor System.*

The Honor System nevertheless established Walsh as a director of substance. John Ford claimed that it was his favorite picture of all time after *Birth of a Nation.*[24] The reviews were glowing. "*The Birth of a Nation* at last eclipsed," the reviewer for the *New York American* wrote. The *New York Times* critic called the film "the motion picture pretty nearly at its best." The critic for the *New York Dramatic Mirror* concurred, waxing on about the film's ability to influence social discourse, a view that greatly pleased Walsh. *"The Honor System,"* he wrote, "is undoubtedly the most powerful philippic against the prison system under which prisoners are held as wild beasts, rather than humans, that has ever been produced. If reform propaganda has a place on the screen, then assuredly this picture deserved first rank."[25] But Walsh was equally impressed by a mishap that followed the film's New York premiere. Governor Hunt asked William Fox if he could send a "life prisoner" to the premiere. Thinking it a good idea, Fox heartily agreed—not failing to consider the publicity such a stunt could garner for the picture. But the prisoner outsmarted everyone, escaping the night after the event. After he was on the train traveling from the New York premiere back to Arizona, he escaped, most believed in Chicago, and was never heard from again.

Fox decided that he wanted Walsh back at the Fort Lee studio, so Walsh and Miriam returned to New York and took up residence in a new apartment in the east seventies that Miriam enjoyed decorating. But, before leaving California, Walsh directed Tom Mix in a two-reeler called *The Lone Cowboy,* shooting it on Mix's own ranch just outside Los Angeles (credited with a 1915 release, the picture was probably released late in 1917 or early 1918). Back on the East Coast, Walsh continued to work on a string of what he considered entertaining and serviceable pictures that used up little film (Fox's and other studio heads' wish at the time) and that he edited the way he liked. (Walsh never made it clear over the years how much or how little he edited his films. Clearly, his involvement varied with each film—for one thing, Warners, where he would go later, had its own editors, but he said he outsmarted them and the censors by shooting enough scenes his way to override any cutting.) To Walsh, his pictures *remained* his pictures.

One film he enjoyed making was *This Is the Life,* featuring his brother, George. On its release, an advertisement in local newspapers across the country read, "Here is a typical George Walsh vehicle, a play that gives him ample opportunity for his smile and his acrobatics. He climbs up the side of houses, fights a whole army of revolutionists, carries people around at will, and gets the girl he wants." Walsh and George were still extremely close, especially since George had married the starlet Seena Owen and the two had a young daughter. George's career stayed on a steady track still, and he and Raoul continued to write scripts together, whether or not they were produced. In fact, as late as the 1940s, long after George's divorce from Seena, and during his much happier second marriage, he sent Raoul story ideas on a regular basis. Even after George quit the picture business and settled down near Walsh in California—to help raise horses for his brother and others in the film community—he never ran out of story ideas, which he continued to mail to his brother.

With World War I now raging in Europe, and with the United States soon entering the hostilities, Walsh was a good candidate to go off to Europe. He was now just past thirty years old and had had three hernia operations, yet he received a classification of 1A. He claimed later that he wanted to go overseas, but Miriam told a different story, that he had no intention of giving up his career. William Fox thought the same way, along with Miriam, who did not want to be separated from her husband. Walsh was drafted in May 1917 but ended up staying in New York. On the East Coast, he was a member of the Signal Corps and assembled footage for the War Department until the war ended. But he also directed what could be called a serious war film of the period, *The Pride of New York*, a story of men in battle that featured a Walsh favorite, Anna Q. Nilsson—earlier featured in *Regeneration*—and George Walsh. He also directed a film expressly made for the war effort, titled *18 to 45*, a short subject aimed at convincing young men about to register for the draft that the system was completely impartial. On another note, another picture he directed during this time, *The Woman and the Law*, gave Miriam a substantial role as a woman who murders the husband she finds has been faithless to her. Miriam could not have missed the irony of Walsh putting her in a film based on a real murder trial of the time since she herself was becoming increasingly agitated by what she believed to be her husband's growing attraction to other women.

At the end of November 1917, believing that his contract with Fox was about to expire, Walsh signed on with the Samuel Goldwyn Company, also set up at Fort Lee, New Jersey. Goldwyn had just formed the Goldwyn Pictures Corporation with the Broadway producers Edgar and Archibald Selwyn, who were leaving Famous Players Lasky (the company with the ever-changing name); he had made overtures to Walsh before this. Walsh now felt more confident of his position in the industry and billowed a few of his feathers as he gave an interview to *Motion Picture Weekly* on a matter he thought close to his heart, the exhibitor's role in a motion picture's success or failure: "Frankly, I have been very much disturbed over the way I have seen many of my own pictures run. The Twentieth Century Express is a horse car [*sic*] beside some of the speed I have seen careless operators or short-sighted house managers put into their films." On one side is the director, Walsh said, who has "timed his action as closely as possible to the right tempo." Then an exhibitor might speed up that tempo in order to get in an extra showing that day and make a few more dollars. "I take the bulk of my straight scenes at 13 or 14 exposures a second. When it is swift comedy or big melodramatic action—a chase or a fight or a raid, for instance—my cameraman slows it to 11 or 12." When the complete film is run through the projector "at a normal, constant speed of 14, all the tempo runs true." This should be the director's business, not the operator's. Unfortunately, he concluded, the director is at the "absolute mercy" of the "man who shows it."[26] Walsh liked to think that he had significant control of his pictures, and sometimes that was true.[27]

But he would have to continue making those pictures at Fox for a while. Walsh was unaware of the clause Fox had written into his contract stating that Fox had the option of retaining his services for another year—or at least he had failed to remember it or pay attention at the time he initially signed with the studio. Fox refused to release Walsh—he was too valuable at the moment—and Walsh had no choice but to stay.

His next picture for the studio, *The Prussian Cur,* released in 1918, drew impressive reviews, inspiring critics to suggest that he may have even stolen some of his mentor's thunder when it came to huge mob scenes. He surely had been looking and listening as he stood behind Griffith in the early years, one reviewer suggested. The picture's huge mob scenes were impressive enough to inspire another critic to say, "One should remember that Raoul Walsh was a Griffith assistant on *The Birth of a Nation*." Walsh did not agree with this kind of praise. "It was the worst picture I ever made," he said at the time.[28]

While Walsh focused on his career, sometimes with Miriam on his set—and sometimes not—Miriam herself grew more despondent at not being able to conceive a child with her husband, the one thing she believed might make them closer. She would have been just as happy playing wife and mother as leading lady in Walsh's pictures. Never one to give up on her plans, Miriam convinced Walsh that they should adopt a child. As always, he gave in without giving it much thought. Before he finished editing *The Prussian Cur,* Miriam found a child she loved immediately. She found him at the New York Foundling Hospital. He was a five-year-old named Jackie whose parents, Miriam and Walsh were told, were killed in the Halifax disaster of 1917. The Walshes adopted him in July 1919. But Walsh was not prepared for fatherhood, nor was he willing to invest too much time in this kind of responsibility. As he usually did in response to Miriam's plans, he went along but wasn't entirely emotionally present in the matter.

Walsh joined a growing list of sterling Fox directors, including Frank Borzage, John Ford, and Allan Dwan, each putting out pictures popular with audiences. In 1918, however, William Fox had to be as frugal as other studio heads since the United States had just entered the war in Europe. Many studios on the East Coast were only too cognizant of hard choices that had to be made. Some even closed down, even if temporarily, while others cut back on costs as much as they could. William Fox was one of the lucky ones since his pictures continued to bring in audiences and make money. Despite this, Fox warned his people not to get "too complacent." But Walsh grew increasingly restless with Fox's belt tightening, which amounted to smaller budgets and little publicity to speak of to exploit a picture on its release. All this led him to think seriously—and not for the first time—of going independent. But, before actually making that move, he took a smaller step in that direction. He wanted to write a script that was very different from the kind of stories he had been directing; he was feeling rebellious. His thoughts turned more and more to classic literature, to something with substance. He and Miriam had long discussions about this as they pored over volumes of fiction, poetry, and drama looking for a great work. One night, they talked about Henry Wadsworth Longfellow's poem *Evangeline,* and Walsh became more interested in the romantic story of love and loss. The poem told the story of a young French Canadian woman who follows her lover, now fighting in the army. But she is unable to find him for a long time. Every place she travels to, to locate him, she finds he has just left. At last she is reunited with him. But, as she holds him in her arms, he expires from the plague. This was a classic star-crossed-lovers scenario the likes of which might excite D. W. Griffith himself and most likely had in one form or another over the years. Walsh could not see the heavy sentiment as being problematic in any way.

He produced the film for Fox and had a personal stake in its success. He wrote a script and began casting the picture. But he had trouble finding his female lead and after much imploring convinced Miriam to star in the film. Never a fan of the Longfellow poem, she tried to find a way to keep feeling sad (and, therefore, in character) throughout the production; she had an organ brought onto the set everyday and hired an organist to play mournful music, angering many in the cast and crew. One day on the set, when Walsh directed her to hold a bouquet of flowers and look sad and angelic, he managed to make her angrier than anything else. Not thinking she could hear him, he said in a low voice to the cinematographer, "You'd never know she's such a devil, would you?"[29] Miriam threw the flowers at Walsh and walked off the set.

The Walshes had moved back to California for the film's production. Among his cast members, Walsh hired a young William Wellman, the future director, to play a British officer. Walsh later remembered firing Wellman because he was "a great bottle man" in those days and got drunk more often than not. Walsh recalled that Wellman was having marital troubles at the time and started drinking and "fooling around." He added, "It was much easier to throw an actor off a picture in those days." Wellman didn't mind leaving the production. The way he was costumed ("with a powdered wig"), he said, he "looked like a fairy."[30]

Perhaps influenced by Griffith's *Broken Blossoms*, released the same year, and even *The Bluebird*, Walsh was clearly enamored of his subject matter. He wanted something that was, as he later told Peter Bogdanovich, "a little more poetic," and he worked diligently on what he considered a work of art. A little over three weeks into production the picture became a labor of love. The critics indeed called it a beautiful work of art when it was released. Walsh said, "I like the flow of it, the poetry in it, and the softness and the sweetness. It took me away from violence."[31]

Or so he thought. When *Evangeline* failed to make money at the box office—despite its sterling reviews—Walsh was crestfallen, devastated, in fact. He later said that the failure of the film changed his life forever: "The picture didn't make a quarter. So I said, 'That's the end of art. Give me the dagger, the sword and the gun.'"[32] Walsh flirted with "art" so quickly, then abandoned it when he thought it had failed him in its inability to garner large audiences. He was, as always, halfway out the door before even stepping wholeheartedly into the room.

4

The Dagger, the Sword, and the Gun

The mishap with the Samuel Goldwyn contract, coupled with the failure of *Evangeline,* only helped feed a deepening sense of disillusionment with Fox. Walsh began to think seriously about going independent and forming his own production company. After writing and directing three more pictures for Fox—*The Strongest, Should a Husband Forgive?* and *From Now On,* none of them very distinguished in his eyes—he moved away from the studio for a short time and formed Walsh Productions, signing a three-year contract with the Mayflower Corporation (and, by extension, the Realart Company) on October 24, 1919, to distribute his films.

Miriam recorded this time in her autobiography, logging in on the chaos that ensued. "Raoul and I, and our entourage, always seemed to be in the wrong place," she wrote. "We'd be working in New York, then Fox sent us back to California, and now when Raoul decided to become an independent we had to go back to New York to see the big money men." Walsh and Miriam left Jackie with Theresa and the dogs in the big house in California and headed off to New York with their chauffeur, Pat, in tow ("in order to drive us around—as though you couldn't get a cab in New York").[1] They were an assorted group, large enough to fill more than one house. Even Miriam saw the humor in their lifestyle, although not enough to alter how they lived and behaved.

On the day they were to leave Los Angeles, while they were packing their bags, Miriam looked out the window to see a little fat man running up their front lawn. Louis B. Mayer knocked at the front door; he came to make another overture to Walsh to come work for him. Walsh turned him down on the spot, but all Miriam could remember about the visit was the way Mayer smelled. She kept backing away from him. "He was short and fat, with squinty eyes and a big nose and the worst case of halitosis I'd ever been this close to. There was green stuff on his teeth, like moss. The more I retreated, the more he came on. He backed me all the way from the front door to the backyard."[2] Her repulsion at the sight of Mayer would one day come back to haunt her.

As an independent, Walsh drew a salary of $2,500 a week. Back in New York now, he surrounded himself with a group who could be considered his regulars—a few of them family members. He gave them jobs at every chance, and, no matter who happened to be his family over the years, he continued the tradition—even in the 1960s. Miriam would star in the pictures, George would return soon from California to play male lead, and Miriam's brother, Gordon, along with another friend, Jim Marcus, were Walsh's assistants; Marcus would also serve as assistant director. Before he began as an independent, Walsh brought in a little extra money acting as production supervisor on a picture called *Headin' Home*, a biography of Babe Ruth featuring Ruth himself. Lawrence C. Windom directed the picture for a company named Kessel and Baumann, and the Yankee Photo Corporation produced. The picture's major investor was Abe Attell, known to have helped Arnold Rothstein fix the 1919 World Series. Walsh now had some connection to the mob world he'd concoct so well when he directed Cagney and Bogie later on at Warner Bros. But, for now, this was no fiction.

Walsh and Miriam moved to an apartment on West Sixty-fourth Street and sent for Jackie and Theresa. Then Walsh settled in to cast his first movie as an independent—an adaptation of a successful play, *The Deep Purple*, written by two close friends of his, Paul Armstrong and Wilson Mizner. Not deterred by the play's two previous film adaptations, in 1912 and again in 1916, he hired Earle Browne to write the script, even though he put his two cents in every chance he had. The story hinged on the travails of a beautiful young country girl (Cooper) who is lured to New York by a group of crooks, then miraculously rescued just in time by the story's hero, played by Vincent Serrano. The picture brought in fairly good box-office receipts, and Walsh went on to produce several more films with Miriam in the lead. Walsh loved directing her, no matter how chaotic their personal life off the set. Miriam's beautiful white skin and dark flowing hair gave her an especially expressive demeanor; at times, she could look harrowing if the character called for it. Her presence in a Walsh picture practically ensured a mood of high drama bordering on the histrionic, very popular at this time.

Walsh and Miriam's next picture together, *The Oath,* was a favorite of Miriam's because it was such a tearjerker and it allowed her to display what she especially liked: a wide range of emotions. The story centers on a wealthy Jewish girl who secretly marries a gentile; if the father discovers his daughter's marriage, he will cut off her inheritance. When her father is murdered, the girl becomes the chief suspect. Walsh hired Ralph Spence to write a script adapted from W. J. Locke's novel *Idols.* The story was as flimsy as Walsh's next production, the melodrama *Serenade,* made the same year, which centers on aristocratic Castilian rivals in New Mexico who fight over the same woman. George Walsh returned from California to play one of the male leads.

Walsh surrounded himself with talented people. Paul Bern, a screenwriter who later married the screen siren Jean Harlow, also wrote for Walsh during this period. This period also marked the art director William Cameron Menzies's first outings with Walsh. Soon they would work together on *The Thief of Bagdad,* and their association continued on and off during the decade. There was, however, at least one fly in the ointment. After working with George Walsh for what Miriam considered one too many times, she complained to Raoul and implored him not to pair the two again. She found George impossible to work with and considered him a lousy actor. She dreaded her scenes with her brother-in-law, calling him a stick instead of an actor of any worth. Walsh complied, not surprisingly since he was apt to give Miriam anything she wanted at this point in their relationship. He needed her to remain satisfied as a member of their troupe. She required no salary, and audiences loved her.

Walsh's brief foray into independent filmmaking came to an abrupt halt, however, when Mayflower fired him in February 1921, charging that he had violated part of his contract. The violation was never clear, even though Walsh accepted the termination. He moved quickly and signed then with Associated First National. The month after that he sued Mayflower, alleging that he was wrongfully discharged and that the company owed him back pay of $10,000 for four weeks' work in addition to another $235,000 in back salary. It is not known whether Walsh ever received any settlement from Mayflower. Either way, Walsh

Productions was short-lived; *Kindred of the Dust,* another picture to feature Miriam, would be his last independent production in this period—and, more significantly, Miriam's last film with Walsh.

Kindred of the Dust tells the story of a poor girl (Cooper), the daughter of a squatter, who falls in love with a wealthy young man (Ralph Graves). The two want to be together but are kept apart by their different stations in life. Walsh could not have had more fun with the imagery to signal their different socioeconomic status. He literally separates the two by placing physical objects between them, a rug in one shot, a huge leaf in another, as the lovers struggle to find unity but are kept apart. They play out their love affair against the backdrop of another schism: the clash between nature and society, one bringing them together, the other keeping them apart. The heroine, Nan (Cooper), leaves her father's house at one point only to find a doomed life. Walsh recalls Griffith's *Way Down East* as Nan, the innocent, carries her and her lover's baby in her arms. Nan is also an earlier embodiment of Ida Lupino's character, Marie, in Walsh's Warner Bros. picture *High Sierra.* She is vulnerable and almost emotionally frail, trying with great difficulty to navigate an indifferent society in which she lives. Released on February 27, 1922, *Kindred of the Dust* is the only film shot during this period to survive. At the very least, it survived longer than the Walsh marriage would. Byron Haskin, the assistant cameraman on *Kindred of the Dust,* noticed the director and his star fighting on the set more than once. Others on the picture couldn't help but see the discord between them.

While Walsh stayed in Los Angeles cutting *Kindred of the Dust,* Miriam returned to New York to be with Jackie, who by now lived with his nanny more than his mother or father. When Walsh did return to New York, he had some startling news for Miriam—he told her he thought he no longer loved her. After six years of marriage, he said, the separations were putting too much of a strain on their relationship. Miriam was shocked but still wanted to keep the marriage together. They decided to stay together and make another go at it. They began to live more extravagantly than before, Miriam calling them "the beautiful people." While they lived in Los Angeles they found a house near the exclusive Wilshire Country Club just south of Hollywood. But, since the club didn't allow movie people as members, the couple joined the more forgiving Rancho Golf Club and shored up their status in other ways.

Since owning a dog was a status symbol, Miriam and Walsh owned five. Their Airedales came fully loaded "with more papers than we had," Miriam noted.[3] While Miriam took lessons in golf, bridge, ballet, and water skiing, Walsh bought an $8,000 Locomobile for himself and a Packard for his wife. He also insisted that she have a chauffeur. Walsh's car remained in California when the family made the trek across the country to New York in Miriam's Packard. In California, where they settled more than New York, they made another move and rented a house in the fashionable West Adams district, just south of Hollywood. Their landlord was the actor Fatty Arbuckle, who had rented the house to various film people over the years—including Norma Talmadge. Walsh also began buying racehorses, boarding them at nearby racetracks.

The Walshes spent money almost recklessly, with Miriam dictating where they would spend and Walsh going along with her—an early sign of his lifelong inability to handle money with any frugality. As a family member later said of him, he simply wasn't good with money. During their marriage, Miriam paid the bills and kept (or did not keep) track of their expenditures. She was more concerned about money—more obsessed with it—than Walsh. For his end, he would often wire her from California asking her to deposit money in their account because he needed to pay a bill or, later, to buy a horse.

A fashionable address seemed a natural idea to a couple who, while they worked hard for their money, still thought it important to spend as much as they could to keep up appearances. Walsh's days with his father served him well. Thomas's career as a haberdasher left a lifelong impression on Walsh; nice clothes were always part of his expenditures, and he simply loved fashion. Photographs taken of him at every stage of his career show him wearing expensive suits, some bought in England (with boots to complete the outfit), others purchased in the finest New York men's shops. Pictures of Walsh throughout his life show him to be sporting a mustache and most often a curly, or at least wavy, head of hair. The first time Miriam walked into their bathroom to find her husband curling his hair with her curling iron she showed surprise. After that it became routine.

Walsh's dream of being independent seemed to vanish before him during a time when the Hollywood moguls began to take hold of the industry; he would be working for others most of his life. Leaving Miriam and Jackie in New York, he went back to Los Angeles, where work was more plentiful. When Samuel Goldwyn again approached him (after seeing *Kindred of the Dust*), Walsh signed with him, giving up on his own production company. He thought Goldwyn would mean a long-term contract, but their association produced only one picture, *Lost and Found on a South Sea Island*.

Goldwyn already had a script for the picture but thought it lacked panache; he asked Walsh to work on a new script for this South Seas adventure. Walsh and Miriam thought it a lucky break since they continued to spend money at a rate that outdistanced their combined salaries. Walsh tightened the script, adding more dramatic points than the original writer, Paul Bern, had included. Then he scouted locations, not going on salary at Goldwyn until he actually began shooting the picture. Since Miriam and Walsh agreed they needed even more money than this picture would bring in, Miriam sent Jackie and Theresa to live with Walsh in Los Angeles and went off to Detroit to shoot *Is Money Everything?* for the D.M. Film Corporation.

Fixated on the idea that Walsh no longer loved her (and with good reason), Miriam wrote him in early June 1922 from Detroit, "I am so tired. We have been on location thirty miles away every day since we started the picture. . . . Not even one letter have I received. I am quite sure you do not expect me to believe you care for me and I am fully convinced you have ceased to love me. I do not blame you. These are things which are not controlled by us." But Walsh convinced his wife (and may have believed) that he still loved her: "My heart is breaking for you. If you tell me you are not coming back I will not live without you. Let me but have you in my arms and one day of love shall widen into eternity. Who knows the earth may crack tonight—or the Sun go down forever in his grave—Who knows tomorrow god will begin to finish the judgement of the world—and when it is all over find you sleeping in my arms."[4] Sounding as romantic and melodramatic as the movie *Evangeline*, Walsh made an impassioned plea for their love to continue. Miriam would never know whether he truly felt the passion he claimed or simply got carried away with the romance of his words, even the romance of what he needed at the time. He was, after all, in the midst of writing a South Seas adventure.

Walsh was about to live his adventure when he convinced Goldwyn that he could save money by actually filming *Lost and Found* in the South Seas. Walsh asked Miriam to accompany him to Tahiti and suggested they bring Jack along. On June 17, 1922, he wired her at the Statler Hotel in Detroit and signed their son's name to it: "Dear Mother. Hurry and come to Los Angeles. We are going to the South Seas. Daddy mad because you say he don't love you. Patsy, Theresa and all send love. Wire me at once. Jack." Ignoring the "Daddy mad" jab, Miriam wired back that she still had three weeks of filming left but would try to follow afterward. On June 25, she wired that she would take a boat in early August and meet Walsh in Tahiti. He wrote back, again as Jackie, "Dear Mother. Are you coming back to your Jackie, Patsy, Daddy and Rexie? We all miss you very much and want you here on the seventh. I am a big boy now and want to see my mother before I forget what she looks like.[5] All my love. Jackie."[6]

Miriam worried about becoming sick in Tahiti as she had heard all nonnatives did. Put out by her concern, Walsh wired back, "The information you have received about Tahiti is absurd. July and August are the choice months. It is winter there now. Fever is unknown and it is declared by all who have been there to be a veritable paradise, a bower of flowers and enchantment. If you come on the August boat you will be able to spend ten days with me. If you think that worthwhile, come. Love, Raoul."[7] Walsh tried in earnest to convince Miriam he wanted her with him, but his defenses were up all the same.

Without yet hearing back from Miriam, in early July 1923, Walsh left Jackie and Theresa home and boarded a ship for San Francisco, then changed over to a ship for the two-week voyage to Tahiti. His coterie went along, including his associate Jim Marcus and Gordon Cooper, Miriam's brother, who went as Walsh's assistant. Also on board was Jim O'Donohue, who would work with Walsh to finish the script. The Walshes' chauffeur, Pat, went along as an all-around handyman, as did Walsh's lifelong friend Carl Harbaugh, who would act as a feature player, writer, even crew member—whatever Walsh needed.

Walsh told Peter Bogdanovich in a 1971 interview that he took "a lot of money" to Tahiti (Goldwyn paid a good salary, at least $20,000— one reason Walsh took the assignment). "I had just got rid of the squaw and I took along eighteen thousand dollars (that I had here) before she could lay her hands on it."[8] Although Walsh took a stab at Miriam with that comment ("before she could lay her hands on it" was a jab at the coming years when she would be hauling him into court for alimony), in fact, Miriam did follow Walsh to Tahiti as soon as she finished her picture and picked up Jackie in Los Angeles. She later said that another Los Angeles resident, the evangelist Aimee Semple McPherson, and her young son were on board the same ship bound for Tahiti but that McPherson would not allow her son to play with Jackie because his mother was an actress.

Tahiti loomed as the most exotic locale Walsh had seen so far—a romantic landscape that he used as fodder for stories for years to come, for example, that the French government gave him trouble and arrested him for bringing guns and blank cartridges with him. This may or may not have been true, but Walsh was gaining on reality with the stories he garnished time and again—all told in the name of adventure and romance. The Tahiti production actually lasted well over a month, and at its conclusion Walsh organized a feast for the natives who had been so hospitable to him. With that came another story never substantiated: after drinking too much liquor at that dinner, Walsh later said, he allowed himself to get a nose piercing: he also claimed he carried around the disfigurement, slight as it was, for the rest of his life.

The film had two original titles, *Captain Blackbird* and *Under the Skin*, both of which were written on the script Walsh received. Eventually, the picture was called, simply enough, *Lost and Found*, a somewhat serviceable title for what turned out to be a serviceable tale (it even included the obligatory chase scene) and little more. The story (of which one reel survives) centers on a seventeen-year-old Tahitian girl named Lorna and her boyfriend, Lloyd, who are terrorized by an evil white trader. Lorna is "a moral derelict on the shore of life as well as an actual derelict on the beach of Tutuila, an elfin, wistful, love-starved little waif"; Lloyd is a young man with too much kindness, sympathy, and idealism. He's devoted himself to "books, study and the ethical things of life." Together, they are no match for the "smiling devil of a modern pirate," Captain Blackbird, described in the initial script as "Wallace Beery at his worst."[9] The picture performed poorly at the box office after its release in February 1923 yet remained for Walsh a grand memory because he could make so much fiction out of the time he spent in Tahiti and the South Seas. He collected such fodder with great seriousness.

On their return to Los Angeles, although they had some money in their pocket, Walsh and Miriam rented hotel rooms instead of settling down. Not long after that, Walsh instituted his alternate career of doctoring scripts and pictures—and, as usual, without taking credit. When his friend Mary Pickford called to ask him to help salvage *Rosita,* a picture she was making with Ernst Lubitsch that also featured George Walsh, he jumped in to direct and recut parts of the film. But Pickford still later referred to it as the worst film, bar none, that she ever made.

A Magic Carpet Ride

Walsh thought of the early 1920s as the time when talent agents literally descended on Hollywood. Now back at Fox again, he looked around for an agent to represent him until he found someone he thought he could trust, finally signing with Harry Wurtzel, Sol's brother, in late 1923. He was keeping it close to home. Harry Wurtzel was good for Walsh from the start; he managed to get Walsh a loan-out from Fox and set up a meeting between Walsh and Douglas Fairbanks to talk about Fairbanks's latest project, an ingeniously conceived Arabian nights fantasy called *The Thief of Bagdad.* Walsh always claimed that Wurtzel must have talked magic to Fairbanks to convince him that Walsh was the man to direct the picture. But Walsh was unsure whether he wanted to undertake a project as large as the one Fairbanks had in mind. So Fairbanks took him on a tour to see what William Cameron Menzies had already designed and set up on Fairbanks's studio back lot. Walsh later said, "I caught my breath when I saw the sets. . . . [Menzies'] artistry was great enough to convince me that I was walking the streets of old Bagdad. . . . I changed my mind then and there. I would make *The Thief of Bagdad* and it would be the best picture I had ever directed. That is what one man's genius can do to another man's ego."[10] Walsh then went to work at United Artists, the company Fairbanks formed in partnership with his wife, Mary Pickford, along with Charlie Chaplin and D. W. Griffith. When Walsh arrived at United Artists to begin work, Fairbanks set down in front of him the completed and "enormous" script for *Thief.* Walsh was one of the last to join the production. Right off, Fairbanks needed his help finding extras for the mob scenes. Fairbanks said they needed "Oriental" types, and Walsh got to thinking about it. Then he came up with a plan to go to "Mexican town," in Los Angeles. As he later explained his rationale, "A dark-faced Mexican with a head-rag hiding everything except his eyes and nose and mouth will pass for an Arab any time." Walsh thought of himself as a lifelong liberal when it came to racial tolerance, and he never once considered himself a racist even when uttering a racial joke or slur if the moment occasioned a good joke.[11] That, too, was a lifelong habit.

If he brought anything to the film, it was his clear, no-nonsense approach to handling Fairbanks's convoluted story. As the audience learns in the film's prologue, the story's overriding theme is that "Happiness Must Be Earned." No one learns that better than the main character, Ahmed (Fairbanks), a crafty thief who bounds around the city of Bagdad, leaping from balcony to balcony, house to house, palace to palace, as he steals purses, food, even a magic rope—which, of course, comes in handy. His philosophy is simple: "What I want, I take. My reward is here. Paradise is a fool's dream and Allah is a myth."

But, when Ahmed sneaks into the palace of the caliph, he falls for the ruler's daughter, the beautiful princess, and decides to impersonate a prince in order to pursue her. He becomes one of four suitors for her hand until he is exposed as the thief of Bagdad, after which he is flogged and thrown out of the palace. But the princess saves his life, reinstates him as one of her suitors, and sends all four on a journey to find the world's greatest riches—she will marry the one who returns with the greatest treasure. Ahmed travels to many lands and fights many monsters (and even visits an underwater realm inhabited by beautiful mermaids whose temptation he is hard put to ignore) until he finally finds the Chest of Nazir, which confers on him the power to conjure anything he wishes.

When Ahmed returns to the princess, he conjures an army from his magic chest (in one of the grandest and most expansive battle scenes put on celluloid, literally with a cast of thousands of soldiers who multiply before our very eyes) and defeats the Mongol prince. What is more, he has earned his great find. Now, with the princess at his side, Ahmed sails through the skies of Bagdad on the magic carpet, heading to the Land of Love. The film ends with a reprise of the opening, with the stars twinkling the message, "Happiness Must Be Earned."

The forty-year-old Fairbanks was almost fanatical about keeping in shape for the part and worked out daily at the Hollywood Athletic Club, sometimes with Walsh, now thirty-seven, and their mutual friend Charlie Chaplin joining him. Fairbanks not only looks lean and muscular in the part of Ahmed; he exudes a sexuality, almost a pure eroticism, that made him irresistible to the female moviegoers who watched *The Thief of Bagdad*. He also surrounded himself with beautiful female leads, casting Anna May Wong as an unsavory female slave and the newcomer Julanne Johnston (who bore an uncanny resemblance to Miriam Cooper) as the princess. Both women are beautiful creatures, but neither, Fairbanks made certain, looks quite as appealing as he does.

Filming began on "The Lot," at 1041 North Formosa Avenue, in West Hollywood, soon after Walsh entered the picture, although Fairbanks had been in preproduction for at least a year. Critics and historians have since debated the extent and influence of Walsh's contribution as director on a film that from the start was so personal to Fairbanks. Some have argued that Walsh simply played yes-man to Fairbanks, who directed most of the picture himself. Some have also said that not enough credit was given to the film's art director, William Cameron Menzies, and that, if Fairbanks collaborated with anyone, it was with him. The argument has been, in part, that the film's style was set long before any cameras rolled and that, once they did, Fairbanks's choreography and narrative control hardly waned. Even by then, Walsh was seen as an action director with a no-nonsense approach. The question has always remained: How much influence could he have had on such a fairy-tale fantasy whose centerpiece is a magic carpet ride?

But Walsh brought a straightforward, problem-solving sensibility to the picture, something Fairbanks intuitively knew he would. Fairbanks's sense of myth and fantasy were so all-consuming, visually and thematically, that he needed the exact kind of no-nonsense movement, measured action, and pace that Walsh provided. Walsh's knack for economy and realism kept Fairbanks's extravagance in check. Walsh later said, "I purposefully heightened the action so that the build-up to the fantastic finale would not drag and become tedious. The rival princes got more than the script called for. Toward the end, I had them running his head on a platter. The idea of making The Thief invisible was my own. I trust my blatant ad-libbing did not cause the clever Scheherazade to turn over in her grave."[12]

When planning the magic carpet ride at the story's conclusion, Walsh "racked" his brain to think of some device that would make the carpet "fantastically plausible." Unless there was at least some sense of reality, he thought, the picture would be destroyed. He found the answer when he inadvertently passed by a construction site at the intersection of Highland Avenue and Hollywood Boulevard one day. He saw one of the construction workers riding a load of girders being hoisted up from the ground by a large crane. He thought that Ahmed and the princess could also ride a steel girder if it was covered with a large carpet and some way was found to hide the supporting cables. He got the characters off the ground by installing an overhead pulley and a hand winch (both were kept off camera) and then used a burly extra to wind the crank. "When the drum winch began to turn," he remembered later, "the whole thing, with Fairbanks and Miss Johnston sitting cross-legged on it, rose before the eyes of the suitably astonished spectators and thin wires pulled it toward the window." When the crane caught up with the open window, the cameras caught it again once it reached outside the building—and Walsh called "cut."[13]

Walsh kept the balance between the fantastic, which threatens to overtake the picture at various turns, and the believable. He also balanced Fairbanks's enthusiasm and grace as the actor alternates between the balletic and the acrobatic. Walsh was always aware of the audience's need for a satisfying story, and he made certain that the narrative did not fade into the fantastic. As director, he brought his matter-of-factness to bear on Fairbanks's sheer aestheticism. He packed movement into his long takes and brought Fairbanks back down to earth when he could.

The Thief of Bagdad, which carried a price tag of over $1 million to produce, held its first premiere at New York City's Liberty Theatre on March 18, 1924. Walsh planned other premieres and parties in Los Angeles even as Miriam returned to New York. She convinced herself again that her husband was cheating on her, even though her only proof, what little there was, stemmed from his flirtatious behavior with women on the *Bagdad* set, where she was a constant visitor. While in New York, she wired Walsh to tell him of her worry. Walsh wired back in defense and told her, in a June 18 cable, "If I believed all I heard about you I would be in China now. I am at least entitled to a hearing, so come on home as I am getting up a party for you for the opening of *Bagdad*. Wire when you leave." Instead, Miriam wired her friend Lillian, who answered by defending Walsh: "Raoul has been with us constantly. . . . I am positive there is and has been no other girl that he loves. Don't believe all the stories carried to you by meddling outsiders who would like to cause trouble between you and Raoul, as I am certain he cares only for you. He has convinced me of this. You know I am for you only and would not take his part unless I thought he loved you. Please listen to me as your friend and come home soon. Lillian."[14]

Miriam returned to Los Angeles. Worried that her marriage wouldn't last much longer, she did what she could to keep it going, convincing Walsh to buy a home at 629 South Plymouth Boulevard, south of Hollywood in what is now called the Wilshire district. She also began proceedings to adopt another child. She and Walsh chose a boy named Patrick who very quickly seemed too aggressive with Jackie. They returned Patrick to the New York orphanage where he had lived and adopted another boy in his place, naming him Robert. Miriam hoped they now might be the family she had always wanted. Walsh may have participated in Miriam's plan to shore up their marriage, but at the same time he invested little emotional energy into it. He was far more interested in shoring up his career.

After leaving Fairbanks's lot, Walsh's contract with Fox was about to end; Harry Wurtzel convinced his brother, Sol, to let Walsh out of it. Walsh waited awhile before making another picture and then signed with Jesse Lasky in July 1925 in conjunction with Famous Players and Paramount Studios. He directed five pictures with Lasky, three in 1925 and two the following year, none of them especially memorable, with the exception, in Walsh's view, of the memorable event of getting the chance to work with the Polish actress Pola Negri, whom he thought had great talent. Miriam also appreciated Negri—the actress didn't go after Walsh, even though she did come to the Walshes' home several times a week, her purpose being to confide in Miriam about her latest romantic trauma.

Or at least Miriam chose to believe that Negri and Walsh were never intimate. Walsh, however, implies otherwise in his autobiography, recounting the period when he worked with Negri—of course omitting

Miriam and the two boys from the narrative—and, as a "single" man, had a great flirtation with her. His narrative is curious, not only for its deliberate inaccuracy about his marital status, but also for the way it reveals his attitude toward Negri and other women he "knew." He devises a complete fantasy:

> Since burning my fingers at the matrimonial clambake after get-
> ting out of the army,[15] I had shied away from serious feminine
> contacts. I was not bitter, but some bad memories lingered.
> Becoming involved with female stars beyond what the script
> calls for is something every sensible director learns to avoid like
> poison ivy. If he indulges his amatory appetite, he is liable to
> discover that the star has become the boss and is busy directing
> him. After almost twenty years in close association with motion
> pictures, I had seen more than one promising executive fall on
> his face because he could not keep his hands in his pockets and
> his mouth shut. Not that I had become a monk. I did my share of
> shepherding Hollywood pretties in the direction of the casting
> couch but they were some other director's meat and potatoes,
> not mine. All of them were luscious and transient; that was what
> I wanted. . . . Beautiful girls came from everywhere under the
> sun to try their luck in a screen test. When most of them lost
> out, they had to sell something else besides nonexistent talent.
> This profusion of penniless pulchritude may have had some
> bearing on the current divorce rate. While it might be fun to get
> married; it was also fun to play the field. . . . The Roaring Twen-
> ties did not come to Hollywood, they were born there. Bosoms
> and bottoms and bathtub gin were common enough to become,
> at times, a bit of a bore.[16]

The troubles he and Miriam had at the time, coupled with the sub-sequent years she spent trying to get alimony from him, understandably prompted Walsh to eliminate her from his life as he recorded it in the autobiography. The fiction is far better to remember than the reality during that time. Miriam permeates the autobiography nevertheless. In it Walsh displays a jaded view of women and portrays himself as the lover of many and tired of the current "scene." He certainly became that man, even if this fantasy, written late in his life, reads more like a movie script than anything else.

Walsh's 1925 outing with Negri, *East of Suez,* was based on the 1922 play of the same name by W. Somerset Maugham and centers on a torrid love affair between an educated Chinese half caste—Negri's eyes were taped back to make her look Asian—and the young Englishman she loves. Negri plays Daisy Forbes, educated in England and now returning to China, where she suddenly finds herself a social outcast after word gets out that the Chinese nurse who raised her was really her mother. The Englishman is talked into renouncing her, and, in turn, she marries another man out of desperation. But eventually she and her Englishman reunite and travel back to England. Walsh had fond feelings for the picture and was incensed to find out later that the entire reel where she marries the Englishman was cut. He must not have known that the Hays Office had installed a do-and-don't code at that point; he always blamed Paramount for not knowing and letting the censors butcher his picture.

The film featured a young actor named Edmund Lowe whom the camera adored without hesitation. He could be serious, humorous, even flippant when necessary. Walsh admired his ease on film and would use him again a year later in *What Price Glory?* and its two sequels. He would return to Maugham also. In 1928, Walsh would adapt another Maugham play, *Rain (Sadie Thompson). East of Suez* was released on January 12, 1925; afterward Walsh went on to direct four other Lasky-Paramount productions released in 1925 and 1926, *The Spaniard, The Wanderer, The Lucky Lady,* and *The Lady of the Harem;* the latter two pictures Walsh considered a means to an end.

The Wanderer, an adaptation of the parable of the Prodigal Son (originally only a five-hundred-word passage in Luke 15), blew up into an all-out Hollywood biblical spectacle, complete with an all-star cast that included the Swedish actress Greta Nissen (who also appeared in *The Lucky Lady* and *The Lady of the Harem*), Wallace Beery, William Collier Jr., and Tyrone Power Sr. Somewhat shocking was a scene in which Nissen dances and appears to be wearing little other than a rose on her person. The picture also marked Myrna Loy's first appearance in a film; she plays a reveler in an orgy scene. At the time of its release, much was made of this "daring" Walsh in publicity pieces that turned up in newspapers around the country. One in particular marveled at Walsh's seeming lack of fear of the lions used in the film. "Well, if Walsh weren't a great director, he could be one of our very best wild animal trainers," the story read. "He is absolutely fearless where lions, tigers and other ferocious man-eating animals are concerned, and that's his secret—an absolute lack of fear. He is still a little eleven-year-old boy who either hasn't heard or doesn't believe that wild animals are man's enemy. He just hasn't grown up this way. They fascinate him . . . he just isn't afraid of them." The story concluded with a description of Gloria Swanson's visit to the set of *The Wanderer* with her husband. When a lion lunged at them, Walsh evidently "saved the day by taking a nearby rake and batting the lion over the head and into submission."[17] Walsh did what he could to keep himself myth friendly and ready to jump into a good story.

After this solid but unextraordinary string of productions, especially striking given his wildly creative turn with Fairbanks just the year before, Walsh made an auspicious return to Fox when he directed the first of a trilogy of masculine adventure stories that made a lot of noise at the box office and put him back on top in the public eye. With *What Price Glory?* he signed a new seven-year contract with the studio, proving to everyone, himself first, that he no longer wanted to be independent. Being so would mean having to be cagier about getting money instead of being able to rely on a large studio paycheck. He always would be more comfortable with the latter. There was more to his story of himself than looking into the camera's eye. If money was hard to find, he could not indulge in his growing passion—the horses.

Maxwell Anderson and Laurence Stallings's antiwar drama *What Price Glory?* opened on Broadway in 1924 to immediate controversy (two other plays with the same subject, *Nerves* and *Havoc,* opened that year but did not have the same strong impact on audiences). The play "amazed its first-night audience with its blunt honesty, its raucous language, and its unprecedented lack of respect."[18] Originally entitled *None but the Brave, What Price Glory?* centered on two carefree soldiers, Captain Flagg and Sergeant Quirt, whose fight against the Germans during World War I was not enough to get in the way of their sophomoric rivalry with each other concerning women, bravado, and honor. The two were quintessential boys who never grew up. They had immediate appeal for Walsh. Here was great aplomb and tenacity.

Stallings initially was signed by MGM to write a screen adaptation of his and Anderson's play. But Fox bought it soon after, "when it became obvious, from the acclaim given *The Big Parade,*" that war films would be commercial again as they had been right around the time of the first World War.[19] Walsh then came on board and cast Edmund Lowe as First Sergeant Quirt. Lowe was the affable actor who could ham it up onscreen at a moment's notice. Lowe played the character as a cocky, almost slithery ladies' man, as shallow as he sometimes appears, and his natural charm rendered Quirt more a sympathetic character than a louse. Lowe would also come on board for Walsh's 1929 project *In Old Arizona.*

Casting Captain Flagg proved thornier. The British-born actor Victor McLaglen was determined to have the part. Born in Tunbridge Wells, near London, McLaglen had the background and the right kind of swagger and size for the part. Half-Irish, half-Scots, he was a huge man who had run away from home at age fourteen to join the army, eventually becoming a boxer, and later taking part in the gold rush at Kalgoorlie, Australia. After getting into the movie business, he'd landed the lead in the British color production of *The Glorious Adventure.* After that, he arrived in the United States to star in J. Stuart Blackton's *The Beloved Brute.*

At first Walsh was dead set against McLaglen having the part of Flagg: he thought it would be impossible for him to understand the American marine mind-set. McLaglen worked diligently to wear Walsh down and change his mind. "I had seen the play on the stage and had realized immediately that if I was born for nothing else I was at least born to play Captain Flagg in that full-throated yarn of the American Marines," he later wrote in his autobiography. He was determined "to get the lead in this super-picture." After making inquiries, McLaglen discovered that his name was "already on the list of potential candidates for the coveted part" and "immediately went to see Raoul Walsh who was to seal his reputation with the direction of the picture." "You're English," Walsh told him, "as though that finished it," McLaglen said. The actor argued that his nationality did not matter. But Walsh would not agree. "He said," McLaglen remembered, "that I could not possibly portray the prototype of the American Marine. I knew nothing of the American service, or of the mentality of its troopers. Arguing very fiercely with him, for I was dead keen on that part, I told him that there were no soldiers in the world tougher than the men in my own old Middlesex Regiment. A soldier was a soldier all the world over, I said, and if a man could handle the tough Cockneys of the Middlesex he could act the part of handling equally tough men in the American Marines."[20]

Walsh agreed to test McLaglen even though he was still against hiring him. "Nothing but an outstandingly 'different' test would keep me in the running," the actor later said. "The thing was to get something original." Asking the British producer George Ridgwell, who was on the scene, to act as a bartender, McLaglen borrowed a set for a Buck Jones picture and, after writing a hasty scene with Ridgwell, "charged into the bar-room and tried hard to behave as I thought Captain Flagg would have done had he wanted a drink in a hurry and found himself confronted with an idiotic bartender."[21] McLaglen got the part and happily signed a contract for the picture. Dolores del Rio had the female lead.

Shooting *What Price Glory?* turned into Walsh's wildest ride to date, one he needed badly after the inertia he developed after his previous four outings. The battle scenes were shot on the studio's lot, called Movietone, just west of Beverly Hills, on 250 newly purchased acres that Tom Mix once used for his ranch and that he sold to William Fox in 1923, five years before the studio moved there permanently in 1928, then calling itself Fox Hills Studios. (Decades later, in 1961, owing to a financial fall, Fox Studios sold off much of the land to the Alcoa Corporation, at which point the area was renamed Century City and subsequently became heavily developed with high-rise offices, hotels, and apartment buildings.)

John Ford directed some second-unit scenes on the picture. Often the shoot was a fiasco—there were so many villages built. "Most of [the area] has been converted into foreign villages," the reporter Eugene V. Brewster wrote in *Motion Picture Classic*.

> The first I came to was a Spanish city and it was hard to believe that I was not actually in Spain, although it was devoid of people because nothing was being filmed there just then. The next place was a complete French village with hundreds of dwellings, ho-

tels, churches, saloons, etc., and thousands of French peasants, shop-keepers, children, and soldiers in uniform.

Walsh has the ability to do anything he sets out to do. . . . Just imagine a director standing near the cameras on a platform shouting orders to a thousand people who were scattered about in every nook and corner of a scene that extended nearly half a distant mile! There was the keeper of the geese, the men in charge of the horses and mules, the girls in the windows, the captains and corporals, the men who were letting water from the tanks into the stream, the women who were doing their laundry on the banks of the river, the principal players in the cast, and I don't know how many others who had to know just what to do and when to do it.

Yet, in a short while this vast human machine moved like clockwork, the cameras clicked, the regiment marched down the hill thru [sic] the village, the populace waved, the geese quacked and scampered to cover, Dolores del Rio ran along the street in search of her sweetheart soldier, and before I realized it the cameras stopped grinding and the scene was finished.[22]

Walsh told numerous stories over the years about his battles with neighborhood residents who lived near the studio. He shot the film's battle scenes at night. The explosions broke nearby windows and caused damage to bungalows in the area. Walsh loved to talk about the way he chose a different assistant each evening just so that, when the sheriff arrived and asked who was in charge, all fingers, including Walsh's, pointed to the lucky "assistant," who was then hauled off the premises—after which Walsh would simply pick up and resume filming. Walsh liked to add some salt and pepper to the tale, describing how one time a neighbor in the area ran onto the set yelling that his roof had caved in just in the middle of his taking a bath. Walsh quieted the man down by taking down his name and address and promising to send him a check to reimburse him for damages.

During production of the film, one of the actors died of injuries he sustained in one of the battle scenes (a tragedy that would repeat itself in *They Died with Their Boots On* in 1941). But Walsh had a tendency to recall the lighter moments front and center. He told Charles Higham in 1974 a story he repeated time and again about the consequences of making the film: "The only trouble came from lip-readers. It was a silent movie. Victor McLaglen would say to Edmund Lowe, silent, 'You great big, fat, son of a bitch,' but the title would say, 'How are you today?' Well, the lip-readers picked it up, and there was a hell of an explosion over it. But the result was everyone went back a second time to see if they could read the lips—and that helped to make the picture one of the biggest hits Fox ever had.'"[23]

William Fox decided to take advantage of the huge battle scenes of *What Price Glory?* and show off the studio's sound-on-film process, this in addition to adding a customized musical score. Also, Earl Sponable and Ted Case recorded the sound effects as well as the orchestral score for the film. Fox's first showing of its sound-on-film process (Movietone) took place on November 23, 1926, at the Sam H. Harris Theatre in New York City. Raquel Meller treated the audience to songs before the screening, and the studio gave the audience a thrill by including a stage show that included exploding bombs, machine guns going off, and red flares that illuminated the auditorium while scenery toppled all around. If this wasn't enough, the picture itself had viewers riveted to their seats. The film became an artistic and financial hit for Fox and ranked as number three on the *New York Times* ten best films list for that year. Walsh was less concerned about its artistic reputation than whether he had directed an audience pleaser—or so he told others. It had not been that many years since his guard went up after the box-office disappointment of *Evangeline*.

With a production cost of $800,000, the picture grossed $4 million. It is little wonder *What Price Glory?* became such a hit for Walsh and the studio. Audiences may not have seen its antiwar sentiment coming at them at first, but Walsh's characters suffer enough physical and emotional pain that an audience could easily put two and two together to understand the film's attitude.

The picture, with titles by Malcolm Stuart Boylan, is an economically wound melodrama that moves at a fast clip—another earmark of Walsh's films to come. Audiences went wild over the film's artful treatment of the big subjects: love, war (or antiwar), valor, loyalty, and friendship. Walsh uses a three-part structure that holds together pieces of time—each leading to the characters' realization of war's human toll.

In the first section, we meet the rivals Flagg and Quirt, marine officers during World War I who fight over everything, but especially wom-
en. When they travel to France to face combat, they meet the woman
they both come to love, Charmaine (Dolores del Rio). Neither man sees
her as a human being; rather, she is a conquest.

In the second section, the war comes into play, and the two men
actually go into battle. The lead image in this section is a stunning
full-body shot of a soldier (the symbolic soldier of all wars), a body
dressed in black outlined by the flames of hell that take up the entire
frame. While at war, Flagg and Quirt learn very little about friendship,
but they do learn about death—especially in a touching scene when a
dying soldier enters the underground shelter to find Flagg and, leaning
against the wall, says, "Capt . . . Captain Flagg. Stop the blood," then
dies in Flagg's arms. These words are the film's first suggestion of its
antiwar position.

In the third section, the two men return to Charmaine in her village
but still fight over her. Their rivalry is actually their own love story—the
undying ties that they have to each other but that they do not recognize
until the film's last scenes, when they are called off to battle again. In a
close-up, Charmaine sees them off; the audience sees that they are beautiful and too young to die. The last shot has Flagg and Quirt walking
with their arms around each other, committing at last—in romanticized
close-up—to their love for each other. With this kind of sentiment, it
is understandable that John Ford remade the film in 1952 with James
Cagney, although it was not nearly as successful as Walsh's film: the
male bonds of attachment, the two friends' transformation from callous-
ness (they never see Charmaine as a human being until the last scenes) to
humanity are themes Ford saw as clearly as did Walsh.

The film's greatest antiwar statement is a profoundly touching scene
in which Charmaine visits the killing fields–now–become–graveyard
(called the "Field of Glory"). "What price, glory?" another captain asks
Flagg. Walsh would have to confront his own words with this film—he
might have gone for the sword, the dagger, and the gun, but his artfulness led the way. The picture anticipates, sometimes even scene for
scene, Stanley Kubrick's *Paths of Glory* thirty years later: the same antiwar theme, similar tracking shots moving down the trenches catching
soldiers as they fall dead into this early grave, even similar battle scenes,

with the men looking like ants scowling across the deadly landscape as enemy bullets fall on them.

What Price Glory? was both a critical and a box-office success when Fox released it at the end of November 1926. It was for Walsh his strongest foray to date into the masculine experience of adventure and romance that he would embrace more and more. His career loomed large again. He became active in the newly formed Academy of Motion Picture Arts and Sciences, formed in mid-May 1927. Walsh was in good company; attending the first honorary dinner were its thirty-six founding members, including the actors Richard Barthelmess, Jack Holt, Conrad Nagel, Milton Sills, Douglas Fairbanks, and Harold Lloyd, the directors Cecil B. DeMille and Henry King, and the producers Sid Grauman, Jesse L. Lasky, Louis B. Mayer, Joseph M. Schenck, Irving Thalberg, Mary Pickford, and the Warner brothers.

What Price Glory? is a watershed moment in Walsh's evolving career and development as a storyteller. In it, we see the moment that his male characters become archetypal in his body of work. Quirt and Flagg, for all their bragging and rivalry, in the end come to rely on a more deeply rooted bond, a male camaraderie based on an acknowledgment of their need for each other. This is an innocence that Walsh could imbue in his male characters but that he could not allow anyone to see in him—that pervasive vulnerability that he throws into his stories as a child would. His heroes have been called *childlike* more than once, and for that very quality they've been seen as consistently appealing. Like Quirt and Flagg at the story's beginning, smaller obstacles (such as their everyday rivalry) are overcome easily. Yet, eventually, the obstacles become larger, as the two comrades discover, and require a vision of themselves in the world that is much larger than a child's. This is not always possible for Walsh's men, not at least until much later on, in the older male characters of the 1950s films. For now, and for the most part through Walsh's Warner Bros. years, no matter how far his characters see, these men always remain, at some level, childlike, often alienated from the adult world around them. They welcome the world and travel out into it, but they do so as romantic rather than realistic human beings.

This quality follows the films Walsh made with Errol Flynn, as Flynn's characters consistently embody chivalrous, heroic qualities at the expense of mature relations to the world—and to women. Walsh's characters' relations to women are often childish in these scenarios. A full-bodied relationship is not always possible with the women in their lives. They are too uncomfortable in the world. Walsh's men, like Walsh himself, stuck in the loss of a fundamental woman (his mother) early in his life, often can't move forward and create a satisfying bond with women. In this way, Walsh's stories fall into the larger archetypal American male story so beautifully articulated in the 1960s by Leslie Fiedler, who spoke of American male writers and characters wedded to the forest, or to each other, more than to a woman.[24] The irony in all this is striking. Walsh insisted time and again that his films centered on a love story always. If there was no man in love with a woman (whether or not he won her or ended up with her), there simply was no story.

The Rupture

Also important, Walsh now stood at a brink in his personal life, where the feminine constituted its own war zone. Miriam became even more convinced as time went on that her husband regularly cheated on her— and she was usually not far off. The older Ethel Barrymore and Beatrice Lillie were two of Walsh's dalliances that she knew of and whom she confronted. But, in 1926, she herself brought home the woman who helped end her marriage once and for all. Miriam met Lorraine Helen Walker, who was married, and her sister, Ruth, who was single (but who would soon marry Walter Pidgeon, a marriage that lasted until his death decades later), in the summer months of 1926 and often played bridge with them. On returning from one of her frequent visits to New York, to keep up with and purchase the latest fashions, she was told by her young son Jackie that "Aunt" Lorraine had been "sleeping over" in her absence and that "Daddy would not let me into the bedroom" as he usually did. Miriam discovered that Lorraine and Walsh had, indeed, been sleeping together. She immediately left for New York, filing for divorce at the end of May 1927. William Fox advised her that, if she chose to end Walsh's career with gossip and an accusation that he and Lorraine had been having relations, she would suffer as much as Walsh. Without a career, he could never give her the alimony and child support she needed. Rather than drag Walsh down with accusations of adultery, Miriam took the high (or smarter) road. She agreed with Fox and told the *Los Angeles*

Times that her husband had "declared himself to be temperamentally unfit for matrimony," telling her that "a man in his profession had no business marrying."[25]

As part of the divorce settlement, Walsh was to pay Miriam $500 a week. It was not until 1939, when he decided to stop paying her that sum, that their troubles started and she began hauling him into court at every turn. Part of her actions stemmed from her anger over his often-unsavory financial treatment of her. But deeper than that lay the real source of Miriam's dismay: she never truly recovered from losing Walsh.

Now, Walsh's masculine landscape—personally and cinematically—would became as troubled as it would be joyous. Walsh always thought of adventure first, especially of the fictions he could make of it. But it didn't always erase the deepest source of the adventure, the loss of the feminine in his world. He needed to find it again.

5

Pre-Code Walsh
The Big Camera

Walsh became increasingly disenchanted with Fox after he directed *What Price Glory?* When he first arrived at Fox in 1915, the studio seemed a much better oiled machine. Back then, William Fox spent good money for good directors and the best material he could get so as to build up his enterprise. As a result, good scripts were much more likely to come down the pike. Now, Walsh thought those days were waning. The year before, Sheehan had bought *What Price Glory?* for him; this year, he bought *Seventh Heaven* for Frank Borzage. "[These were] two good silent stories," Walsh told Kevin Brownlow in 1967. "And they were both terrific hits. I think [*What Price Glory*] grossed $169,000 in one week at the little Roxy when the top was sixty cents. So you can tell how they lined up for that. Then, for some unknown reason, Sheehan, who had been a newspaper man, . . . brought quite a few writers and reporters and stuff out and gave them the job of writing scenarios, and they never bought any more big properties."[1] Fox directors now had to make the best of it. It made no sense to Walsh that the studio would hire writers and reporters to pen original (and inferior) scripts when, in the "old days," they could just adapt a good novel or short story and "put it on" for less money.[2] In these years at Fox, Walsh still got fired up over good scripts; he'd had some good ones. They weren't as personal to him as they were just good stories. Later in his career, as he felt more comfortable at Warner Bros., his need for good material tapered off. He never wanted for good writers at Warners. He became, in a way, complacent—there was no need to be anything else, in his eyes. When he ended his contract years later at Warners, he cared less about the material than about simply being on the set making a picture.

For now, however, Walsh was looking at two pictures he knew he'd aim directly at "Main Street," the term he still used for pictures he sent out to the masses strictly for entertainment's sake, not for the sake of "art," as he put it: he still hadn't recovered from the box-office failure of *Evangeline* in 1919. Despite the haunting, even poetic imagery he'd found in himself for *What Price Glory?*—a soldier caught in the midst of flames of war surrounding the edges of the frame, another dying soldier pleading for the blood to stop—Walsh committed to directing for the adventure of it, the challenge of building a story, but not for art, and not ever for personal expression. This attitude strengthened over the years.

The Monkey Talks, released February 20, 1927—one of those pictures headed straight for Main Street—is an absurd tale about a physically undersized man in a circus who after impersonating a monkey is literally taken for one—with tragic results. The critics didn't buy it but warmed a little more to Walsh's next picture, *The Loves of Carmen,* released in September of that year. Walsh had liked working with Dolores del Rio in *What Price Glory?* so much that he cast her in this *Carmen*. A humorous remake of Walsh's 1915 Theda Bara vehicle, *Carmen* borders on making fun of its title character, a feature that earned it good box-office figures even if the critics were not so enthusiastic. Herbert Cruikshank later said of Walsh in *Motion Picture Classic,* "We'll forgive him his *Carmen,* if for no other reason than in translating the ancient story into cinematic terms, he disclosed an independence of spirit, a willingness to blaze new trails, a disregard for precedent, which are much needed and seldom found in the celluloid industry."[3] What Cruikshank might have meant in calling Walsh an independent spirit "willing to blaze new trails" was Walsh's fearlessness in flying in the face of censorship. As Kevin Brownlow has said of *The Loves of Carmen:* "The degree of sexual innuendo was surprising for a film of its time. Walsh established a reputation [in *What Price Glory?*] of being able to smuggle more exposure of a female thigh than any other director. He pulls this off (literally) once again in *The Loves of Carmen.*"[4]

Walsh had invested so much physical and emotional energy in directing *What Price Glory?* that, not surprisingly, he felt depleted, literally depressed, and for a long time after could not shake it. Miriam was gone, and so were the two boys; he had begun seeing Lorraine Walker on a regular basis. Lorraine was in the process of getting a divorce, and she and Walsh would marry the next year. Still, he felt out of sorts even if he couldn't put his finger on it. If the separation from Miriam had anything to do with it, he would be the last to admit it. If he missed his two sons, he would never say so. He had been an ambivalent husband and an absent father. He made no request to see the boys after the separation.

Breakfast with Gloria

But his spirits lifted and his energy surged in every sense of the word when Gloria Swanson came bidding in the early summer of 1927 and asked Walsh to direct her next picture. She had no idea what the picture might be—or so she told him. Swanson was doing a slow burn over the box-office failure of her first outing as an independent producer with Gloria Swanson Productions. Desperate for a hit, and looking to take a big gamble to get one, she thought Walsh might give it to her. She was so impressed by *What Price Glory?* and *The Thief of Bagdad* that she turned a deaf ear to entreaties from people around her warning her not to work with this action director. Walsh held a certain mystery for her—his masculine energy appealed to her in no uncertain terms, and she simply wanted contact with him. She said as much to Joseph Schenck, the production chief at United Artists, where she had been working, who told her to forget about Walsh; he was a crazy Irishman who wandered into the movies by accident. Anyway, he was a man's director, not for her. Even the fact that Fox had Walsh under contract did not deter Swanson, however. She phoned him one evening, they had a good conversation, and he was at her breakfast table the next morning, where he, Swanson, and her current husband, Henri de la Falaise, got along famously and talked about possible scripts they could do together.

Walsh and Swanson had been drawn to each other even before this meeting. They had met briefly at a party given by Pola Negri, and Walsh was immediately attracted to Swanson. Walsh later wrote, "I had not seen Gloria since Pola's party. After calling her number when I was really low, I had hung up before she answered. Now she was looking for me. I could have won the post position at Indianapolis by the way I drove [to her house]. . . . Lindbergh had just landed at Le Bourget, but he could not have been more happy at spotting Paris than I was to see Gloria. I had to throw a half hitch around my feelings to keep from hugging her, because she looked so beautiful."[5] For her part, Swanson wrote in her memoir of

Walsh's entrance into her house the morning of their first story meeting, "He was tall and robustly good-looking, with a huge boyish grin and a shock of curly fair hair, and so shy that he blushed when Henri and I started to praise *What Price Glory?*"[6]

Walsh was the one to bring up the play *Rain,* a recent Broadway sensation based on W. Somerset Maugham's short story "Miss Thompson." Walsh was feeling sexual and mischievous sitting at that table with Swanson. Her husband's presence didn't make any difference. He probably suggested "Miss Thompson" as a way to be playful because he knew its controversial story line—the conflict between a prostitute and a clergyman—but Swanson secretly hoped that he might bring it up; she had read the short story in Maugham's collection *The Trembling of a Leaf* and loved it. (The story had first run in the magazine *Smart Set* in April 1921.) She was equally impressed with Broadway's *Rain,* starring Jeanne Eagels in what she considered a riveting performance in the title role. She wanted the part badly and only hoped she could do as well as Eagels had. Walsh's mood suited her own, and getting hold of Sadie also meant getting hold of Walsh.

The film that became *Sadie Thompson* is the deceptively simple story of a prostitute who arrives in Pago-Pago (in American Samoa) by ship along with a group of passengers, including the "moralists" Mr. Davidson (Lionel Barrymore) and his wife (Blanche Friderici), who have come to Pago-Pago to Christianize the natives and rid them of their sinful (natural) ways. The passengers all stay at the same hotel (naturalistically designed for the film by William Cameron Menzies). When Davidson sees Sadie, a "sinful" woman who drinks beer and flirts with the soldiers around her, he becomes obsessed with her and makes it his goal to change her and make her repent her loose lifestyle. But Davidson really lusts after Sadie and hides his desire behind a facade of moral reform.

Also on the island is a group of marines whom Sadie likes to pal around with in the evenings. She falls in love with one in particular, Sergeant Timothy "Handsome" O'Hara (played by Walsh), and the feeling is mutual. O'Hara tells Sadie that he doesn't care about her past life. He wants her to go to his home in Australia and to wait for him there. The two make their plans, but soon Davidson gets to Sadie and threatens her. He will report her to the governor of the island and have her sent back to San Francisco. Before she can defend herself, Davidson has her believing that she really is sinful and must repent. After three days of heavy praying and nearly reaching insanity, Sadie tells Handsome that it's too late for them—they can't be together. She thinks she should return to prison in San Francisco and repent for her sinful life just as Davidson has instructed her to do.

But, before Sadie and Handsome separate, Davidson's lust for Sadie overtakes him; he goes to her bedroom at night and rapes her. Then he commits suicide; the next morning the natives find his body floating in the river. In a tagged-on happy ending, Sadie and Handsome make plans for their future together.

Walsh and Swanson chose Maugham's story as their picture together, both of them knowing full well that they would have to fight the censors over it. It would be a challenge to get the play, even the story, produced at a time when the Hays Office bore down hard and held a firm grip on Hollywood and the studio heads who complied with its dictum—*the formula,* as it was called. Walsh was no stranger to the censors, and the fight against the Hays Office's monitoring of the film industry would become the defining one of his career. Even near the end of his life, he considered censorship the greatest problem he faced over the years. He told James Child in 1973, "My greatest disappointment was censorship, which until recently was very strict. I could remake some of the pictures I made way back; it would be great. All the stuff that was cut out."[7] No matter how much Walsh shot around the censors, his battle with them waged on relentlessly.

Walsh had just won a battle of sorts with the Hays Office—from there on out claiming amazement that *What Price Glory?* had skinnied past them as much as it did, especially given the prostitutes, blatant sexual innuendo, and the female form and male bravado on display. He loved to talk about the way Victor McLaglen mouthed "Son of a bitch" during the film. The censors didn't catch it, but Swanson, among others, did: Walsh's bravado intrigued her. It didn't hurt either that, in October 1927, a list of "Do's and Don'ts and Be Carefuls" appeared on the industry horizon, written by a committee chaired by MGM's Irving Thalberg. One of the "don'ts" pointed to *What Price Glory?* The industry was asked to be mindful of limited "pointed profanity—by either title or lip." Also on the forbidden list were scenes involving illegal drug traffic, sexual perversion, white slavery, miscegenation, VD, childbirth, children's sex organs, ridicule of the clergy, and willful offense to any nation, race, or creed. The "be carefuls" included everything from the use of the flag to attempted rape.[8] Swanson and Walsh would have to be mindful of sexual perversion, attempted rape—and lip readers.

Both director and star knew they faced an uphill battle. Swanson's first smart move was to ask Will Hays to breakfast with the idea of selling him the Maugham idea as a literary work—more kosher than a stage play about a prostitute. He went along with her, and she paid Maugham for the rights to "Miss Thompson." Eventually, Hays insisted that the character of Reverend Davidson, a man of God who lusts after Sadie, be altered—the character became a self-appointed missionary and social reformer. But Swanson did not anticipate the Hollywood backlash: studio after studio, including Walsh's home studio, Fox, attacked her as being a traitor to the enforcement of a code they all "knew" was in everyone's best interest. As she and Walsh well knew, their actions amounted to a move to save their own skins in the face of any future trouble from the Hays Office. In essence, they won the battle they looked forward to and enjoyed.

Moving away from Fox briefly, Walsh wrote a script (portions of a written script actually do survive on paper) and urged Swanson to write to Maugham asking for another original story about Sadie Thompson. Swanson wrote Maugham: "Could you not write an original story for me, THE LIFE OF SADIE THOMPSON, tracing the woman from the moment she leaves Pago-Pago and goes on with whatever life your imagination has created." Swanson and Walsh hit on a good idea that, unfortunately for both of them, never materialized—this despite the fact that Maugham agreed to write a new story, for $100,000.[9] Walsh knew Sadie was going to be a hit; they should have a sequel ready to go. The way Walsh remembered it, two sequels to *What Price Glory?* were already in the can, *The Cock-Eyed World* (begun while *The Loves of Carmen* was still being cut) and *Women of All Nations* (in his estimation a turkey—and a good observation on his part since asking audiences to follow Quirt and Flagg a third time was asking too much). *The Cock-Eyed World* was released on October 20, 1929, in both a silent and a sound version, and *Women of All Nations* would not be released until May 31, 1931, as a talkie.

What Swanson *did* produce was that backlash among others in the community that could make it difficult for her to get a top-notch cast and crew. This picture was Swanson's project. She especially wanted to hire George Barnes, Goldwyn's cameraman, to photograph *Sadie Thompson*. Goldwyn agreed to the loan-out but stalled as long as he could. In the end, Barnes came on board and was credited along with two other cinematographers, Robert Kurrle and Oliver Marsh. Walsh still hired family when he could. He cast his father, Thomas, as the governor in Pago-Pago. Then he wired George in New York on June 22, "Sorry you are not here. Opportunity in this picture but cannot wait. When you come home bring Leo Burns with you. Can give him small part with me."[10] Lionel Barrymore was hired immediately to play Davidson. Swanson had no one in mind but Walsh to play Handsome, although she feigned looking at other actors. Handsome O'Hara did not exist in the Maugham short story but was written for the American stage version and kept for the two film remakes to come. Swanson told Walsh he should play Handsome. At first, Walsh blushed, but then he agreed, although he had not been in front of the camera since *Birth of a Nation*.

Cast and crew were on their way to Samoa to film, but the expense turned out to be too great, so Swanson and Walsh settled for shooting on Catalina Island, twenty-six miles out in the Pacific off the coast of Long Beach, just south of Los Angeles. The company departed for Catalina in the early summer of 1927. One end of the island was turned into a South Sea paradise, while the interiors were shot on United Artists' studio stages. After shooting began, Barnes was called back to Samuel Goldwyn Studios, and Walsh had to find a new cinematographer. Eventually, Robert Kurrle, who had worked with Walsh on *Regeneration* and who could match what Barnes had done, was a good fit to do the exterior shots and came on board. Swanson also turned to her friend Marcus Loew, who sent over Oliver Marsh to finish the interior shots. Swanson then told her husband that he would have to take full charge of their two children; she would be much too busy with the production.

Walsh looks uncomfortable in front of his own camera in many of the scenes, especially in long shots, where the most striking thing about him is his relentless habit of hitching up his trousers. But the chemistry between Walsh and Swanson is unmistakable, certainly strong enough to veil his discomfort in being fully exposed in those long and medium shots he hoists on himself. The sexual sparks between star and director-star onscreen are strong enough to suggest that they were intimate off-screen. Their working relationship was sometimes stormy—he walked off the set more than once because she refused to relinquish control of scenes she wanted directed a certain way. As the shoot continued, the two remained suspended somewhere between sex and agitation.

At least one critic was equally agitated about the film as production neared a close. Welford Beaton's *Film Spectator* piece must have had Swanson and Walsh either laughing or biting their nails:

> United Artists, with a false opinion of the box-office value of coarseness, secured Walsh to direct *Sadie Thompson,* a picture that required discriminating direction to make it passable. . . . Instead of the kind of director that the story needed, one of fine instincts, culture and good taste, Raoul Walsh, whose obsession is that the public is degenerate, directed the picture and turned out [a picture] that the United Artists people had the greatest difficulty in cleansing sufficiently to make it fit to be released. A picture that has to be put through such a delousing process as *Sadie Thompson* was subjected to cannot emerge as a good example of screen art. In removing the filth it is not possible to avoid scraping off some of the healthy substance. . . . Quite apart from a consideration of good taste, it is the greatest economic folly to peddle rottenness to shoppers for screen entertainment. The producers who chafe under the restraint of censorship have only themselves to blame for it.[11]

From the accusation Beaton throws out, readers would hardly have recognized the same Walsh who, Miriam Cooper once said, refused to let her enter the home that William Randolph Hearst built for Marion Davies because Davies was a kept woman.

Walsh's female characters could be tough—especially the women he put on the screen in the 1940s and 1950s, from Ida Lupino to Jane Russell—but he saw them through an affectionate lens, as if standing on the sidelines rooting for them. He had created bad girls before Sadie (Carmen, for one), but Maugham has the corner on feminine evil—such as the vindictive Leslie Crosbie in the story "The Letter," all the more evil because she covers up what Maugham sees as degenerate in her with pleasantness. Sadie Thompson is not so much a bad girl as she is an innocent lost at sea. She literally folds when Davidson convinces her to repent. Walsh's Sadie is treated sympathetically—no doubt a collaboration between director and star. She is quickly softened by Handsome's presence in the story. She can express love and be loved.[12]

Sadie Thompson was a box-office success and marked the third time—after *Thief of Bagdad* and *What Price Glory?*—that a Walsh picture appeared in *Film Daily*'s best ten list (eventually, *In Old Arizona* and *The Cock-Eyed World* also made the list). Swanson received the first of her three Oscar nominations for her performance. She threw a large party at her home when actual production ended. Arriving at the front door, Walsh realized as he was about to ring the front bell that he felt like a lovesick teenager chasing after a married woman. He later wrote in his autobiography that he never went in. He stood at her front door, waved good-bye to her in his own way, turned around, and drove off. But, almost fifty years later, while he was happily married to his third wife, Mary Simpson, Swanson easily floated back into his imagination. Contacting her after an appearance they made together at the Museum of Modern Art in New York in 1974, he wrote:

My Dear Gloria,

My trip for the festival was worth while, just to see you again.

My quip I made at the luncheon about you finding the fountain of youth is all too true.

Your lips, your eyes, your hair have been with me for these many years. To me, I can see my lovely Gloria. I will always remember her as a new phenomenon like some April evening, the downy breast of spring. She was like a rippling brook, singing among willows where kingfishers skim.

But now the sun is going to rest. I can hear the wild ducks flying over head, and the mountains were drawing themselves off to sleep, and at night fall would be the singing of the crickets.

Somewhere a Mexican is playing guitar, and somewhere else a dog barked into the stillness of the night. A queer eerie sound . . .

Good night my dear one[13]

Back at the Fox lot, Walsh directed *The Red Dance,* another picture featuring Dolores del Rio, and one in which Fox used all synchronized music, save for the picture's theme song. This time del Rio is a fiery Russian peasant girl at the time of the Russian Revolution whose talents as a dancer (the picture was also titled *The Red Dancer of Moscow* at one point) bring her much attention. Her true love, the grand duke (played by a rather laconic Charles Farrell), has married a princess, a woman he doesn't love, and del Rio later gets involved in a complicated assassination plot—all this before the two lovers find each other again. In this fast-moving yet melodramatic film, Walsh's camera (at one point mounted on a monorail during a scene involving the murder of the notorious Rasputin) creates a chaotic tempo when necessary, along with long takes that let the action build. The film's art director, Ben Carré, later said that the scene involving Rasputin's murder had been cut after the picture's release. Despite his well-staged action scenes, Walsh was never particularly proud of the picture, although it is an enjoyable mess of potboiler action and over-the-top histrionics. Filmed in Truckee, California, near Reno, Nevada, the picture saw its own drama when one of the actors was killed during the filming of a battle scene. *The Red Dance* suffers the same fate as many of Walsh's later pictures when he began freelancing in the early 1950s: his camerawork was far superior to the mostly mediocre story material he filmed.

Released eleven months after *Sadie Thompson,* at the end of 1928, *The Red Dance* didn't garner Walsh much favor at the box office or with the critics. But it does survive to this day—as does a publicity shot depicting Walsh holding del Rio tightly in his arms as he demonstrates a scene to Charles Farrell. As Walsh told Alma Whitaker, a reporter for the *Los Angeles Times,* he would be "directorially content" if he could alternate between Dolores del Rio and Gloria Swanson for the rest of his career. Then "he mused discontentedly," saying: "But directors are the doormats of the industry. Outside of Cecil B. DeMille, they never get proper recognition for the work. . . . You will find everyone [on a picture] given credit but the poor doormat of a director. We do all the work, suffer all the anguish, but all the rest get all the glory." But Whitaker found a flaw in his thinking. "I don't know," she wrote. "Directors don't seem to suffer from suppressed personalities as a rule. Even Raoul looked very dashing and triumphant—and felt important enough to be half an hour late for his interview. Which is a privilege I only concede to editors—and husbands. Until Raoul appreciates that even royalty should be punctual, I shall approve any suppressions that are put upon him."[14] Whitaker had little sympathy for *this* doormat.

If Pictures Could Talk

> The transition from silents to sound pictures didn't hit me in any way. I just kept the thing moving regardless of the sound. I took them out of the room and let them talk in the hall, if they didn't talk inside the room. I just kept going. . . . I handled it the same way. Of course, there was a great upheaval amongst the directors when talking pictures came in. They called me a renegade because I was one of the first ones to do an outdoor talking picture. They said that they'd created such a medium with pantomime, you know, and now this talking stuff was going to destroy it all. I said it was going to destroy us if we didn't get along and get in with it. So they finally all came in.
> —Raoul Walsh[15]

In 1928, Walsh's friend Wilson Mizner added to the publicity pot and published a story in the *New York Times* describing the way Swanson and other colleagues most likely experienced Walsh on a set. He walked around without a script in his hand (it was in his head by now), and the only sheets of paper anyone saw him read were pages of the *New York Racing Form*. According to Mizner, on the set of Walsh's 1928 *Me, Gangster* (which strikingly included red-tinted sequences and sound effects, just as the earlier *The Red Dance*, a.k.a. *The Red Dancer of Moscow*, had), Walsh asked one of the stars, June Collyer, to hold on to something for him, a crumpled-up piece of paper with smudges all over it. When Collyer asked what the paper was, Walsh whispered in her ear that it was the script for the picture. Not only did he skip looking at the script; he skipped viewing the dailies as well.[16] Walsh was already a subject the press liked to follow. The reporter Herbert Cruikshank noted that one scene for *Me, Gangster* required that an African American butler steal and eat a banana. Walsh shot the scene no fewer than eight times, and, when asked why, he told Cruikshank he knew that the actor was down on his luck and not eating regularly. "This way he could get the man a square meal without hurting his pride."[17]

The divorce from Miriam became final in 1927. Ever since Miriam left the house in Los Angeles and moved back to New York with the boys, Walsh had been seeing quite a lot of the would-be actress Lorraine Walker. A woman almost twenty years his junior, Lorraine was born in Missouri in September 1906. At the time she met Walsh, she was still married and had a two-year-old daughter, Marilynn. Now separated from her husband, who lived in northern California, Lorraine put plenty of effort into becoming the second Mrs. Raoul Walsh. Her sister, Ruth, nine years her senior, also made a stab at acting but became secretary to the actor Walter Pidgeon and married him in 1931. At the time, Pidgeon was a widower with a ten-year-old daughter; he and Ruth stayed married until his death in 1984.

On August 2, 1928, Walsh and Lorraine Walker drove down to a little town called Agua Caliente, Mexico, just outside Tijuana, and were married. The director Allan Dwan and his wife, Marie Shelton, were on hand as witnesses. (In his autobiography, wiping out any mention of Lorraine and Marilynn, whom he later adopted, Walsh writes instead that he went down to Agua Caliente for the derby and a tan.) It was a fact that, just to make certain he was able to do a little betting while he was in Caliente, Walsh left the ceremony quickly. *Life* magazine reported on August 20, "After the ceremony, Mr. Walsh played roulette, won $18,000." Walsh kept his intentions about the marriage secret. Only his very close friends the Dwans, Carl Harbaugh, and his immediate family knew. California newspapers later reported that Judge Francis Miranda read the ceremony in Spanish in the Governor's Suite at the Agua Caliente Hotel.

For over a year now, Fox had been experimenting with Movietone, its sound-on-film process, but Warner Bros., ironically on the verge of bankruptcy, released *The Jazz Singer* in 1927 and at least publicly made sound pictures its second name. These were exciting times, and no one felt more enthusiastic and inspired about sound pictures than Walsh. When he returned to Los Angeles from Caliente, Winfield Sheehan told him to go see the latest picture playing at the Beverly Theatre on Beverly Drive. He went to a matinee and could hardly believe the hackneyed picture he saw up on the screen—still, more important than anything, it had sound. "Here was revolution," he later wrote:

> The triteness of the sets and the obvious nervousness of the female lead made me want to jump up and start shouting. Then a thought struck me. If the tedious dialogue could be supplemented and broken up by more action, the result might be thrilling instead of soporific. . . . I got up to leave, but turned back at the top of the aisle, when a burst of sound from the newsreel caught my attention. There before my eyes, a Fox Movietone News truck was filming a dock strike. The shouting came from a man who was evidently a union leader. His exhortation did not interest me but the open-air news shot did. I broke the speed limit all the way back to the studio.[18]

Walsh liked the idea of taking a gamble and wanted to get moving at exaggerated speed on this. He told Sheehan he was going to be the very first to make an outdoor sound feature and asked for a good newsreel truck and a western script. He would make a picture that boasted sound and action, nothing like the stilted scenario he had just seen at the Beverly Theatre. In October, Sheehan announced to the press that, over the course of the next four months, Fox Pictures would produce eight new features with dialogue and seven all-talking two-reel comedies. Five of the full-length productions would be entirely in dialogue. Walsh would direct one of them, an adaptation of O. Henry's story "The Caballero's Way," a western about the Cisco Kid that Fox called *In Old Arizona*.

Walsh rode the crest of the coming of sound pictures with great enthusiasm—more than some others who believed that sound was going to be the industry's demise. But Sheehan was with Walsh, and he gave Walsh the go-ahead. Fox had Tom Barry write a script from the O. Henry story, and Barry turned in a fairly bare-bones screenplay that still had rough edges. But that was not the first thing on Walsh's mind now; he could easily improve the story. He was about to take a production crew into Bryce Canyon National Park and Zion National Park in Utah to see locations. He had just what he wanted; he would direct history itself: the first outdoor talkie, the first western to use the new technology.

At Sheehan's urging, Walsh kept the production a secret at first. After the two men decided on the O. Henry story, Walsh put together his cast and production crew. He added chase scenes to the script and looked at one actor after another to play the Cisco Kid. Unsatisfied with them all, he decided to play the part himself. "The Cisco Kid was a Mexican," he wrote years later, "and I was tanned sufficiently after Caliente to look the part." Fox casting had plenty of cowboys on call, and the story moved well. He and his assistant, Archie Buchanan, headed first for Bryce Canyon. He took only his star, Dorothy Burgess, three cowboys, including his pal Bear Valley Charley, two vehicles, the property van, and the Movietone truck. Production on *In Old Arizona* started on September 9, 1929. "The cowboys were gaunt enough to pass for Indians," Walsh wrote in his autobiography. He was certain that the audiences would never suspect that their long black hair "was chopped from horsetails and glued inside their headbands." He added, prophetically and, of course, unknowingly, "What the eye does not see, the mind does not worry about."[19]

But Walsh would have to take the golden ride into sound pictures armed with even more stamina than he ever could have anticipated or imagined. Sheehan was so happy with the rushes Walsh sent back to him that he told him to make the picture a feature-length film and to write the script as he went along. He didn't care how long they stayed out there. Walsh asked for a stagecoach, which was sent on a flatbed, and six horses. The chase scenes turned out fine; so did the shots of the stagecoach coming at the camera. The next plan was to move out of the flat desert and into the hills so that Walsh could get some good holdup scenes with the Cisco Kid. Then the truck broke down, and Walsh decided to leave Utah and finish the picture on Fox's back lot. Lorraine was with him on location, so they headed back to Los Angeles.

"I think it was about then that the gods started laughing at me," Walsh wrote in his autobiography. On the night of October 4, he was driving back from Zion National Park on his way to Cedar City, Utah, with Lorraine sitting in the passenger seat. All of a sudden, the headlights stunned a rabbit, which the Jeep then hit, hurling it up through the windshield. The rabbit hit Walsh's head, along with a gale of glass splinters, before landing in the back seat. Glass flew everywhere on Walsh's side of the Jeep, piercing his right eye. Blood flew everywhere as well, Walsh recalled afterward. He knew he was in trouble. Lorraine immediately had him taken by train to a hospital in Salt Lake City, where Dr. E. M. Neher began working to save his eye. "I caught a glimpse of the rising moon with my left eye, but when I shut it I was blind," he later wrote.[20] The damage was extensive, and Walsh was then transferred to a hospital in New York for further evaluation. Doctors realized that there was no hope of saving the eye.

Sheehan told Walsh not to give a thought to the picture; he would handle everything. Irving Cummings took over as director; all Walsh's long shots, where his face was not too distinguishable, were retained, along with chase scenes he directed in Bryce Canyon. The actor Buddy Roosevelt was cast as the Cisco Kid after Walsh was forced to drop out. But Roosevelt soon broke his leg and was replaced by Warner Baxter, who had recently played the title role in a film adaptation of F. Scott Fitzgerald's *The Great Gatsby*. Ironically, the studio continued to expand the picture's length from two reels to seven, and it turned into an almost $2.5 million project. The movie performed well at the box office, and Baxter won an Academy Award for his lively performance. But *In Old Arizona* is Walsh's film no less; he is credited for being the first director to use sound recording equipment on location—even though Lewis Milestone shot large portions of *All Quiet on the Western Front*, released in April 1930, as a silent and then postsynchronized the battle sequence sounds in the studio.

Three of Walsh's recent productions saw release at the close of 1928. *Me, Gangster* was released on October 20, *The Red Dance* on December 2, and *In Old Arizona* premiered in Los Angeles on December 25 but was not released to other venues until late in January 1929. For many Fox releases, sound still meant the virtual orchestra. Walsh's *The Red Dance* (1928) contained mostly synchronized music, save for its theme song, "Angela Mia," sung by Andre de Segurola. The release of *Red Dance* at this time—along with these other films—certainly gave the impression that Walsh had been working steadily at Fox. *Red Dance* played at the Globe in July, billed with *The Family Tree,* the first two-reel Movietone all-talking comedy.[21] George Bernard Shaw's famous Movietone News recording also debuted on this program.[22]

But *In Old Arizona* caused the most stir at that moment. Audiences took to the actor Edmund Lowe's melodious voice, and an upbeat theme song, "My Tonia," added even more verve. Donald Crafton summarizes the reaction in the press:

> "The microphone caught everything," bubbled [Maurice] Kann. "When the caballero sings as he rides out of the picture his voice grows fainter as it would in real life. Then the cows moo, you hear them and when the stage coach driver cracks his whip, your ears get that too." The lively Western broke the Roxy's weekend record with a gross of $54,000. The *Daily News* found Edmund Lowe's voice thrilling and Warner Baxter's Mexican accent "simply swell." "The most interesting talking picture yet to be heard in this town," the *New York Post* declared. Hall's portentous *Times* comment again emphasized "forgetting" sound as something positive: "Often the story is so well told by the dialogue of the characters that one forgets for the moment the novelty of the Movietone."[23]

Walsh was not on board for much of the ride, but the picture would still be called his. Maybe not at the moment, but soon enough, he felt inspired enough to think of an even bigger outdoor western.

A few weeks after doctors removed Walsh's eye, he and Lorraine boarded the Twentieth Century Limited out of New York and headed back to the West Coast. Transferring to the Santa Fe Chief in Chicago, which would take them to Los Angeles, Walsh had plenty of time to think. He experimented with new ways of seeing himself, trying on different emotional and psychological hats. How would he view himself as a man with one eye? "Comparing myself to Floyd Gibbons and Wylie Post smacked of reaching for a crutch," he said years later. "One-eyed Connelly, Manhattan's champion moocher, seemed a more apt comparison. If he could crash the Dempsey-Carpentier fight, I could still crash any studio I wanted. And I would not be lugging around an empty box either. It would contain fifteen years of motion-picture directing." Work—going back to work—was the answer. While he told himself that the loss of the eye would make little difference in his life, he didn't quite believe it yet. He needed to find out, and he assured Wurtzel and Sheehan that he was so ready to direct that he would even "direct Victor McLaglen as *Little Red Riding Hood*."[24] The humorous scenarios masked the deep emotional pain—even years later.

How had the accident affected Lorraine? Married only two months to Walsh before he ran into this tragedy, she hardly had time to get to know her husband before being asked to turn around and see him in another light. Walsh would not confide in Lorraine, or in any woman, willingly or easily. He pulled back even further than he might have had he not lost an eye. He knew about hiding pain. He became emotionally protective of himself—even as photographs show him wearing as little as a small bandage over his right eye socket when he was not sporting a black eye patch. He compensated for this loss for years to come by supplying the press with comic anecdotes about his eyeball. It was either loose in his pocket, dropped unwittingly into a glass of beer, wrapped in a cloth in his pocket—or, most truthfully, not in his possession at all. When the doctors first asked him if he wanted a glass eye, he quipped that, no, he'd only lose it or have to take it out if he got into a fight. The truth was just that: he never did have one.

Accident or no accident, Lorraine grew into her role as Walsh's wife, remaining in the background of her husband's directorial career. She enjoyed the social status and the money his career brought, but she made very certain to play a limited role in his everyday comings and goings from the studio to the set. Marilynn, her three-year-old daughter, became close to Walsh; she took his last name after he adopted her. Later, when she married and had children, she named her first son Raoul, after her stepfather.

Walsh stayed in the spotlight when he could, keeping his name in the public eye. He took to the media in February 1930 when he endorsed an ad for Lux Soap that showed up in national newspapers and magazines. Under the headline "You Can Keep Your Skin Lovely Just as 511 Hollywood Actresses Do," the copy read, "98% of the lovely complexions you see on the screen are cared for with Lux Toilet Soap. As Raoul

Walsh, famous Fox director puts it, 'Smooth, beautiful skin is the most
potent charm a girl can have . . . and an absolute essential for stardom on
the screen.'" Alongside the copy, the advertisement ran the photographs
of the most popular actresses of the day: Clara Bow, Evelyn Brent, Janet Gaynor, Anita Page, Mary Brian, Esther Ralston, Olga Baclanova,
May McAvoy, Bessie Love, and Fay Wray.[25] This free publicity touting
"Raoul Walsh, famous Fox director" also appealed to Walsh's flair for
the humorous, part of the public persona he was perfecting, even if it
was a defense against anyone knowing the man—the deep feelings of
sadness—behind the persona. He nurtured this public face even more so
since he lost his eye. An eye patch was only one cover.

Walsh liked being in the papers, but not as bad news. As if his recent
troubles were not enough, three months after *In Old Arizona* premiered
in Los Angeles, Walsh found himself in hot water with the IRS, although
perhaps indirectly. A federal grand jury had been inquiring into the income tax returns of various "high salaried stars of the Hollywood film
colony," as it was reported in the *New York Times*. On March 15, 1929,
the grand jury indicted Edward H. Hayden, an income tax counselor,
for various violations of the Revenue Act. Hayden was charged with
eighteen counts of feloniously aiding the preparation and submission of
"false income tax returns," said the *Times*. "The indictment names specific instances of alleged fraud in preparing the returns of Fred Niblo and
Raoul Walsh, directors, and George O'Brien and Ramon Navarro, actors." Hayden was indicted along with another "tax counselor" named
Marjorie Berger. The two, along with what the paper called "other
counselors," were alleged "to have made out the returns for their clients
on the understanding that they would receive as their 'fee' one-half of
the amount 'saved' in taxes." Walsh was thought to be among a group of
"victims" who believed the returns made "were actually legal."[26]

This involvement in the Hayden fiasco was an uncanny predictor
of things to come. Walsh would find himself involved in some sort of
litigation from now on and to the end of his life. The frequency with
which he sued another party or was *himself* sued (the suits having to do
mostly with business dealings, although divorces from Miriam and Lorraine fell into the pot as well) added up to a strange kind of excitement
for him. These episodes, unconsciously or not, became a way of stirring

up drama in his life. They were another means of loving an adventure. Lorraine would later say that Walsh was never as happy as he was when he was cooking up some way to go to court.

As a result of losing his right eye, Walsh was left suddenly with monocular vision and some loss of depth perception in his total field of vision. He had always been successful (and would continue to be) seeing the world through the myopic scope he created, paying less attention to the real social world around him (including landmark social and political events) and more to the fictional one he lived by (and in). But now he literally *did* see the world in a different way. Even so, the time was still right for him to get creative with sound equipment—something he had wanted to do since *In Old Arizona*. In June 1929, Paramount, Fox, and MGM announced that at least 169 full-length features were scheduled to be produced over the next year, almost all of them talkies. He needed as much ego boosting as he could get and received a good dose of it when his name showed up on *Film Daily*'s list of the ten best directors of 1928–29. Others included were Ernst Lubitsch, Frank Borzage, Clarence Brown, Cecil B. DeMille, F. W. Murnau, and William Wellman.

Walsh began to feel more secure on the set since the accident. Even so, he could not have missed the irony of the title of his next picture. He shot both a silent and a sound version of *The Cock-Eyed World*, a sequel to *What Price Glory?* that he altered slightly by changing the story's location to Central America and adding a number of musical numbers. The picture was certainly good practice for the upcoming epic journey *The Big Trail*, which Walsh would shoot in thirty-five millimeter as well as in Fox's new Grandeur process, or seventy millimeter. He would also reshoot *The Big Trail* to accommodate different language versions. He worked again with Victor McLaglen and Edmund Lowe, who reprised their roles as Flagg and Quirt, and added the voluptuous Lili Damita (who replaced Dolores del Rio as the love interest), who had been a star in French silents and would soon marry Walsh's close friend Errol Flynn.

Walsh added the comic touches to Stallings and Anderson's play himself. Flagg and Quirt are the same raucous duo beating their chests in Damita's presence and scowling over who is going to get the girl. Americans ate it up; *The Cock-Eyed World* proved to be the third biggest grossing picture of 1929 and the biggest grosser Fox had had up to that time. The picture used a two-director system, which had worked well with *In Old Arizona,* though under some different circumstances. For *Cock-Eyed World,* Walsh directed the action sequences, and William K. Wells wrote and directed the dialogue. Given the stir caused by the words Victor McLaglen uttered in *What Price Glory?* the censors were more astute than ever about this one, and the rough language of the barracks had to be toned down. Still, Walsh managed to get one by them—when "Yump Olson" (El Brendel), walking with a prostitute, shouts out to Flagg (McLaglen), "Captain, I'm bringing you the lay of the land," and at the same time reaches into his pocket and produces a map, saying, "Here's a map that will tell you where the enemy is sleeping." Also, hardly a viewer or reviewer failed to notice the sergeants' argument over which one had fathered a mutual girlfriend's child. According to one reviewer, the language was vulgar, salacious, and more ribald than rollicking.[27] An ongoing stream of corny songs, such as "You're the Cream in My Coffee," helped temper the raucousness, but the picture is little other than high-powered burlesque as the two rivals chase skirts and show each other their muscles and masculine prowess. More than one reviewer found it entertaining but at the same time vulgar and smutty.

Walsh kept working at a brisk pace; as always, going to the set was the surest way to ward off the unwanted feelings that threatened to invade. Depression over the loss of his eye now hovered over him. Completing a picture swiftly became a habit, defining his method from here on out: think about getting the job done quickly and savor the time spent on honing a technical prowess. Monocular vision or no, original story ideas invaded his imagination just as frequently. By June 1929, he had an original story in hand called "The Duke of Kakiak," which, after three revisions and counting, became the popular picture *Hot for Paris.* In its earliest phases, it was known at Fox simply as "The New Raoul Walsh Picture." A month later, Dudley Nichols wrote up a story outline, then ten days later wrote dialogue for the story. Then Walsh wrote an eight-page tentative outline, calling the story "Well Dressed Man," and noting on the cover, "There is no connected story here, only a number of gags"—a clear indication of the film's perpetual disconnectedness to come.[28]

Hot for Paris benefits greatly from the giggly personality of its star, the French-Canadian singer and dancer Fifi D'Orsay, whom Fox had just taken off the vaudeville circuit to star opposite its popular moneymak-

ing star Will Rogers in *They Had to See Paris*. Walsh saw her on the
set with Rogers and liked her enough that she became a staple—albeit
briefly—in Walsh pictures. She played opposite Victor McLaglen and
El Brendel in *Hot for Paris* and appeared in *Cock-Eyed World*. Brendel
would work with Walsh on *The Big Trail*. *Hot for Paris* tells the story of
the first mate (McLaglen) of a sailing vessel who wins the grand prize in
a sweepstakes and, in a funny turn of events, goes on the run trying to
ditch people who attempt to give him his prize money. McLaglen meets
D'Orsay, a singer-dancer in a café he frequents, and the two hit it off,
leading the way to a series of episodic gags and song-and-dance routines
that include a perky little number from D'Orsay called "Sweet Nothings
of Love" and a grand effort at singing from McLaglen called "I'm the
Duke of Kakiyak."

The picture opened in theaters five months after production began,
several days before Christmas, crediting two other men, Charles J. Mc-
Guirk and William K. Wells, as screenwriters. Audiences loved it, even
if the critics were sometimes hard-pressed to understand why. The critic
for the *New York Daily Mirror* called it "a rowdy, raw affair," expand-
ing to say, "The comedy is very frank. The dialogue is very staged. . . .
But it's still an hilarious comedy, particularly for men."[29] Walsh looked
more than ever a man's director.

Walsh was not in Los Angeles when *Hot for Paris* opened. In early
November, he, Lorraine, and four-year-old Marilynn flew to New York
and then to Europe. In New York, he gave an interview to the *New York
Times* telling a reporter that he thought up the story for *Hot for Paris*
while flying on an airplane from Malibu to Los Angeles (they believed
him) and then just created dialogue as they shot the picture (probably
true). "You can't very well give a written script to Victor McLaglen or El
Brendel . . . and expect them to do it any justice," Walsh said. "McLaglen is liable to get tripped up on a single word, and the whole sequence
goes wrong. So we mostly improvise."[30] On November 4, the Walshes
left for Southampton, England on the SS *Bremer*. Arriving on November
20, they stayed at the Grosvenor Hotel in London; then they traveled to
Cherbourg, France, and then Vienna, where Walsh met with Sheehan to
look over material for future Fox productions. They had a chance to see
some of Europe before they returned to New York on December 24 and
then headed home to Los Angeles.

Walsh keep his ties in Caliente, the city where he and Lorraine married. In fact, he enjoyed the town more and more as the years went by, and he especially liked playing the horses there. In the last week of December, he was proud to be named to the board of governors of the Agua Caliente Jockey Club, an organization set up to regulate horse racing. Having been a horseman since his childhood days riding around New York State, Walsh harbored a passion for buying and selling horses and entering them in competitions. Stories of his presence on movie sets over the years are littered with tales describing his habit of reading racing forms before reading a film script. Just before the new year, Walsh went to Caliente to attend the first meeting of the new club's board of governors. He was in good company; also on the board was filmdom's Joseph Schenck and the sugar tycoon Howard Spreckels.

Grandeur

The beginning months of 1930 were both opportune and perilous times for the motion-picture industry. Over time, the stock market crash of 1929 sent audiences to the movies in increasing numbers as a way to escape the stifling reality of economic depression, but it also caused the studios to tighten their belts on production costs. This would seem an odd moment for Fox Studios to begin production on a picture that would cost upwards of $2 million (this would translate to $100 million today) and was to be a western with sound, still a relatively unknown commodity. The studios were skeptical about using sound in westerns, especially since the genre still embraced simple storytelling that often translated to very little dialogue—the exact opposite of what using sound implied. Equally problematic were the large, clumsy cameras that had to be enclosed in boxes to keep their whirring sounds away from the likewise clumsy microphones. The heavy cameras could not be moved around easily on soundstages, let alone be maneuvered outside. The notion of going outdoors with sound equipment was still a stretch, but Walsh loved the idea that audiences might now be able to hear the authentic sounds of the West: horses hooves thundering, horses neighing, and especially gunfire. This would be *The Big Trail*.

Fox got busy putting *The Big Trail* into production. The story of those months of its production—from the beginning to the end of

1930—is fantastic enough even without taking into consideration the scope of the film ultimately produced. The feat of taking to the open trail to film this story was remarkable even in its conception, and there was a litany of remarkable circumstances surrounding the filming of *The Big Trail.*

The legend has been printed (and remains unproved) that a script for *The Oregon Trail,* later to become *The Big Trail,* was first offered to Walsh's Fox colleague John Ford, who was not pleased with it—and so it was passed to Walsh. It was not uncommon for projects to float from one director to another at Fox; oddly enough, at this very time Ford took over direction of *The Seas Beneath,* a project intended for Walsh. *The Big Trail* had some large acts to follow—for one, John Ford's silent *The Iron Horse* (1924), a railway saga that boasted the largest location shooting to that time. One year earlier, the director James Cruze's *The Covered Wagon* (1923) dramatized the westward push from Kansas City to Oregon. And, though each of these pictures turned out to be somewhat ponderous—even meandering—as stories they nevertheless impress with their great reach.

Hal Evarts, who initially penned the story "The Big Trail," wrote his version of how he and Walsh began throwing ideas around for the film, all of it recorded in his eighty-eight-page log of the film's production. The saga began on the hundredth anniversary of the Oregon Trail: "While sojourning in Paris [after completing a large production] [Walsh] overheard Americans commenting upon a pioneer serial of mine then running in the *Saturday Evening Post.* He read it and decided to ask me to write the story for his next picture. Upon his return to Hollywood we took up the matter." A few weeks later Walsh and Evarts had mapped out the general story and considered suitable locations. Walsh wanted complete accuracy in detailing the pioneers' march from the Mississippi to the Pacific Northwest.[31]

Walsh, Evarts, and a production secretary, Miss Postal, recorded the story as it developed. "The scenario, dialogue and continuity were," Evarts noted, "to be carried along at one and the same time."[32] The picture was Walsh's second chance at a sound western since having to give up partial directorial duties on *In Old Arizona* after the loss of his right eye, and that very fact had great meaning for him. He was willing to invest enormous energy in this project, both physical and psychological, to see it through to its completion, and there is little doubt that the massiveness of the production was directly related to Walsh's need to compensate for what he had lost out on, not only *In Old Arizona,* for which history would have recorded him as being the first to direct an outdoor western, but also his eye itself. The idea of having vision—more urgently, of having a vision—became huge for Walsh. It also threatened to require of him a personal, artistic vision, the notion he swore to shy away from but could no longer avoid with this picture.

The Big Trail is, at heart, a simple story of adventure and romance that grows into a large historical cinematic document. The story offers little complexity of plot and character as it tells the tale of a huge wagon train that departs the banks of the Mississippi River and travels to the northwest corner of America. In his first starring role, John Wayne plays the simple, honest, almost Cooperesque trail scout Breck Coleman—a man who embodies the innate goodness of American manhood, a type Wayne would go on to etch in stone in his long film career. As Coleman tries to keep the wagon train on track during the sometimes horrendous trek, he also fights a personal battle. He has taken the job of trail scout in part to seek revenge on the wagon master Red Flack (Tyrone Power Sr.), an evil sort whom Coleman knows killed Ben Grizzel, the father figure in Coleman's life. Coleman is out for revenge, along with the simple pleasure of getting a good job completed. Along the way he falls in love with a young single mother named Ruth Cameron (played by Marguerite Churchill), who is making her way west and often needs Coleman's protection. The wagon train encounters all kinds of setbacks and tragedies, including attacks from hostile Native Americans, not to mention threats from Mother Nature herself. The fearless pioneers do all they can to survive the elements in order to find the new life they seek.

From the time filming actually began, on April 20, 1930, through the next four months, and until filming finished, on August 20, 1930, Walsh found himself in the midst of a shoot complex enough in its technical requirements that it threatened to topple one of the best movie minds in the business—his. The picture required shooting at upwards of fifteen separate locations, including Buttercup Dunes, Imperial County, California; the Grand Canyon National Park in Arizona; Grand Teton Pass, Wyoming; Hurricane Bluffs, Zion National Park, Utah; Imperial County, California; Jackson Hole, Wyoming; Moise-National Buffalo

Range, Montana; Moise, Montana; Oregon; the Sacramento River in California; Sequoia National Park, California; St. George, Utah; Yellowstone National Park, Wyoming; and Yuma, Arizona.

The screenplay was credited to Jack Peabody, Marie Boyle, and Florence Postal, based on a story by Evarts. But Walsh already knew too much about himself to follow any script strictly. More than likely, he improvised as he went along. The picture was to be shot with the Grandeur process in addition to the old standard cameras. In the standard, a good amount can be blocked off and camouflaged. Not so with the Grandeur, where, as Evarts described it, "one may portray a couple making love in the foreground yet so universal is the focus that a cabin on a mountainside miles away shows up with microscopic distinctness."[33] The cinematographers Lucien N. Andriot, who shot the thirty-five-millimeter version for general release, and Arthur Edeson, who shot the Grandeur, seventy-millimeter version, easily captured Walsh's spectacular setups, each painstakingly composed. Since sound editors at the time did not have experience in dubbing, Walsh had to shoot four more thirty-five-millimeter versions—Spanish, French, Italian, and German—each using different casts and directors, each of which Walsh oversaw. El Brendel, who played Gus, a foolish but lovable pioneer, repeated his performance in German. All five versions were shot simultaneously, and the feat of actually finishing the film—or films—was as spectacular as the journey itself. Fox made a promise to help equip theaters in order to run the Grandeur version of the film, but the results of that promise remained to be seen.

Gary Cooper was originally slated to star in the picture, but the script took much longer than expected to complete, and he had to move on to another project. So Walsh looked around for another actor, the result of which became legend—his discovery of John Wayne. He found him almost as serendipitously as anyone could. After Cooper's departure, Walsh gave a great number of screen tests but still came up empty-handed. Then one day he walked by the property department and saw an extremely good-looking young man who was about six-foot-four. As Walsh told Richard Schickel in the late 1960s, "He picked up a big stuffed armchair. So I went over and waited till he came out." When Walsh asked Marion Morrison whether he had been in any pictures, Walsh recalled him saying no. (This is where Walsh's story is misleading since Ford had already used Wayne as an extra in several Fox features.) Walsh told Morrison to let his hair grow, which he did, and, when the young man showed up in Walsh's office about two weeks later, Walsh "got him into a good buckskin suit and took a good test of him—a silent test—and the company ran it. Winnie Sheehan [said,] 'That's a hell of a good-looking boy. Can he speak? And I said, 'Sure he can speak. He's a college boy.'[34] So he said, 'All right. We'll sign him up if you want to take a chance with him, a newcomer.' I said, 'All right, I will.'"[35] Wayne asked Walsh whether he could also find a small part in the film for a friend of his—named Ward Bond. A small repertory of two was born that later moved to John Ford.

But Wayne didn't please everyone. "They [the studio executives] didn't like his name—Morrison—and got changing it around," Walsh remembered, "and called him Joe Doakes and Sidney Carton and all those sort of names—and I remembered I had read a book that I liked one time about Mad Anthony Wayne. I thought this Wayne was a great character. So I said, 'Let's call him Anthony Wayne or Mad Wayne or whatever the hell you want to call him—call him Wayne.' Well, they called him John Wayne. That's how he got his name." (Wayne initially fought the change, along with the green shirt and yellow boots that Fox insisted he wear to promote the film. "Don't make me do this," he said. "You don't put a red dress on an elephant.")[36] As the story was told numerous times, Sheehan and Wurtzel thought Wayne needed help emoting for the camera and brought out five character actors from New York City who were considered the best in the business. But Walsh took one look at them and considered them nothing if not green themselves. He thought he'd have "a hell of a time with them on location."[37] Later, he embellished his story about them to include their fondness for "fire-water," one of his favorite quips.

Many found it astounding that, as *Film Daily* reported, "Fox had chosen for a principal role in Raoul Walsh's *The Oregon Trail* an actor whose only experience had been in bits, extra work, and assisting in the Fox prop shop." A writer for the *Hollywood Filmograph* noted: "Just how he [Walsh] can expect a youth to carry such a picture is beyond my conception. If he brings in a winner with Mr. Wayne he will be entitled to a Carnegie medal."[38] Still, *Film Daily* noted later, "Winfred Sheehan was enthusiastic about the neophyte actor with the honey voice and was 'laying out big plans for a smashing meller [i.e., melodrama] with all the trimmings called *No Favors Asked*.'" Wayne signed a long-term contract with the studio that August. But the press also noted numerous goings-on in the film. It was also reported,

> Recorded sound overlays are used extensively to create atmosphere. A distant figure sawing logs, for example, is accompanied by sounds of her work. Most of the camp scenes have the sound of dogs barking—though not coming from any visible canines. Orchestral music is used much like that in silent films. When Coleman [Wayne] is telling Indian stories to the children, ersatz Native American music plays. A homey tune plays as he says good-bye to his girlfriend, Ruth (Marguerite Churchill). Sometimes the balance between the planes of sound effects is not good. On the steamboat landing, for instance, the actors can scarcely be heard through the layers of din.[39]

Occasionally, it sounded as if some of the voices did not come from the mouths of the actors—which some thought to be caused by the image of the wide-screen Grandeur process.

Not surprisingly, the shoot itself was grueling, for many reasons. The number of actors used was staggering, not to mention the extras, even animals needed for the shoot: 20,000 extras, 1,800 head of cattle, 1,400 horses, and 500 head of buffalo traveled with the production. Walsh used 725 Indian extras from five separate tribes and almost enough props to warrant the movie documentary status, including 185 wagons. The production crew was equally impressive: a staff of 293 principal actors and 22 cameramen. Then there were the 12 Indian guides and the 123 baggage trains that trekked over 4,300 miles in the seven states used for locations. Also brought along were the picture's 700 barnyard animals, including dogs, pigs, and chickens.[40]

Location shooting became monotonous when not broken up by small disasters such as a piece of equipment going haywire or a problem with a local extra. More difficult, and less welcome, were the events that played out when Walsh bought a horse named Grayola, the first mare to win the Caliente Derby in fifteen years. He paid $12,000 for her, and the next day she won the $30,000 purse—the same day that he was offered $30,000 by another buyer. He had no intention of selling because he was crazy about the horse. But then disaster struck. As Evarts recorded, "One day on location Walsh was handed a telegram telling him that Grayola had contracted pneumonia and had to be put down." Walsh was bereft, and more than one crew member found him weeping "unrestrainedly." "He loved that little mare."[41]

There were painstaking scenes to master—for one, reenacting the slow, labored chore of lowering humans, livestock, and wagons down the side of a cliff, the only way to get the wagon train off the mountain and onto the next part of its destination. Walsh insisted that all shots, all sequences, be true reenactments of the original journey taken decades earlier. The technical challenges were staggering, as Evarts noted:

> Microphones were arranged to carry the sound to the sound trucks, cameras must glide smoothly with the scene. A great sled was constructed, on which the six cameras, from different angles and elevations were trained on the subjects. Twenty odd mules were hitched to it. Then the chain that pulled the sled was extended on through to the tongue of whatever wagon was to be the setting for that particular bit of dialogue. In that manner, naturally, sled and wagon must move together so that the cameras would not be thrown out of focus. Out on either side and back in the rear, by way of atmosphere traveled the other wagons, horsemen, etc.[42]

At least a dozen cables were extended from the sound trucks to the camera sled to mikes in the wagons. In order to make them move along with the cavalcade, fifty or more men walked along, invisible to the camera, carrying the cables with them.

Walsh needed a six-year-old girl to play Marguerite Churchill's sister, Honey Girl, and gave the part to his stepdaughter Marilynn (Lorraine also had a small part in the picture). Walsh was skeptical that Marilynn would be able to carry it off and so hired another young girl (the sister of the future director Robert Parrish, who happened to be on the set working alongside his mother as an extra). Marilynn quickly bowed out and was replaced by Helen, Parrish's sister.[43]

Walsh and company covered seven states during production, traveling from blistering heat to severe cold. There was a problem with massive drunkenness off and on the set. Sometimes the cast members downed so much liquor that Walsh (who didn't drink much) began to call the film *The Big Drunk*. There were also instances of actors and extras getting seriously hurt. Parrish went along when the cast headed for Jackson Hole, Wyoming, and spent three months there. "A luxurious tent city was constructed on the shores of Jackson Lake in the Grand Teton Mountains," he remembered. "The wagons, cameras, lights, and wind machines were brought from Hollywood by train. Most of the actors and livestock were also brought from Hollywood, but in such a big western there was work for a number of local cowboys, Indians, and extra horses and mules."[44] There was plenty to do for Walsh's head wrangler on the film, Jack Padjan, an ex-cowboy who had played Wild Bill Hickock in *The Iron Horse* (1924) and now supplied livestock and wagons to the studios from his San Fernando Valley ranch.

Parrish recalled numerous dramatic moments that occurred during the shoot. Cheyenne Flynn, one of the film's cowboys, got drunk one night and began accusing an actor named Charlie Stevens, who played a half-breed in the film, of cheating at cards (Stevens was among Douglas Fairbanks's closest friends and the alleged grandson of Geronimo). The end result of the fight was that Cheyenne bit off a mouthful of Charlie's ear, which Parrish discovered the next morning outside his own cabin. He put a piece of rawhide through the lobe and hung it on his family's cabin door until his mother made him remove it. Walsh's reaction to being "faced with a one-eared half breed" was to write a scene in which a squaw bit Charlie's ear off in an Indian-raid sequence.[45]

As a follow-up to the ear-biting episode, Walsh rode by Parrish on a horse and noticed that the boy had put the piece of ear (still hanging on a piece of rawhide) around the neck of a horse named Annabelle, one of Parrish's favorites. "He stopped his horse, rolled a cigarette with one hand, lit it, and watched me for quite a long time," Parrish recalled. "Finally he said, 'What's that hanging around Annabelle's neck?'" When Parrish told Walsh it was Charlie Stevens's ear, Walsh quipped that it looked "a hell of a lot" better on Annabelle than it did on Stevens.[46]

It was hardly a secret to anyone on the set that Lorraine Walsh—described as a gorgeous redhead who had nothing to do all day while Walsh was miles off on location—was having a bit of an affair with Ian

Keith, who played the heavy in the picture. When Keith was not on call, he might take Lorraine riding or fishing. One time, during an all-night shoot, she was seen stepping out into the darkness from Keith's cabin. Walsh seemed the only one unaware of this—or at least he was saying nothing.

When a good portion of the shoot was completed, Walsh sent most of the company home and kept a skeleton crew to accompany Keith, Wayne, and himself from one location in Utah to another so as to stage the final fight scene between Keith and Wayne. Walsh kept Parrish with him, telling him he was the best muleskinner around. And on the last day of shooting Walsh staged the fight scene and decided to show Wayne how to throw the punch at Keith. Walsh called for the cameras to roll as Keith braced himself. This is probably just what Walsh had been waiting for. He "feinted with his right, then threw his left."[47] Keith could not keep up with him, and Walsh's left hook crashed into Keith's jaw, fracturing it in three places.

Fox had big plans for *The Big Trail*. On July 15, 1930, Winfield Sheehan told a government official that the production cost to that date hovered around $2.5 million and that the studio expected to spend considerably more before its completion. He was, therefore, eager to regain some of that cost. A big blowout campaign might be one way. He stopped at nothing short of inviting the president of the United States, along with his cabinet, to see the picture before its official release. For the world premiere at Grauman's Chinese Theatre in Hollywood on Thursday, October 2, the theater program notes, written by George Brown, described the film as an epic the world waited to see: "Visualiz[e] a mighty surging wave of humanity coming from the East into the West, land hungry, liberty hungry, home hungry, turning their faces toward the wilderness and pushing into the setting sun." Brown found "candor" and "honesty" in Walsh's reenactment of the pioneering spirit and heroism.[48]

Walsh needed to cut loose and get rid of his bottled-up energy. When he put his signature in cement at Grauman's Chinese Theatre (one of only two theaters in the country equipped to show the Grandeur version), he punched his fist into the cement, signed his name, and wrote in the date: November 14, 1930. Above the imprint of his fist he wrote "His Mark."

Unfortunately, the box-office and critical reception of the film was far from grand, some of its failure owing to American theaters not being equipped to show the Grandeur process. Fox's promise to so equip its own theaters never came to pass. Financially, it failed to reap anywhere near its production cost. *Variety* called Walsh's direction elegant but found the story lacking in drama, saying, "But the recurrence of the same thing, interrupted now and then by a 'big scene,' such as the river or cliff crossing, or El Brendel's dragged-in comedy with his mother-in-law, or the simple romance, and the silly melodrama, commences to weary."[49] The film was little seen after its opening. But, in 1980, the Museum of Modern Art made a CinemaScope print of the film. Despite being a commercial disappointment, *The Big Trail* did draw its audiences and enjoyed notoriety at a White House screening in October 1930 when President Hoover showed it to Chief Justice and Mrs. Will D. Mitchell and most members of his cabinet and their wives.[50]

Walsh's vision for *The Big Trail* is layered with personal meaning for him. The connection between the loss of his eye and the way of compensating for it, or the way of creating a new cinema from his altered vision, shows the profound psychological investment he made in the film as a way to achieve that. Understanding his huge vision is essential to understanding the film's importance in Walsh's body of work. The way he strove for authenticity—the wagon train's precarious moments; the Indians circling around one wagon; the sheer drive to reenact the settlers' often excruciating physical and emotional course—represents his striving for a pure vision of his subject, the natural view that had to be as massive as its subject if it was to be authentic.

At times, the film's frame seems static, with an awkwardness that is strikingly unlike Walsh. With the loss of his eye, with the nonstop and clearly momentous decisions concerning the placement of cameras and the newfangled sound equipment, Walsh at times seems almost stopped dead in his tracks—as if halting to ponder what to do next so that he might reconsider his entire approach to moviemaking for a new age. Characters talk uncomfortably to each other, the action almost stopping so that Walsh can take in the breadth of the vista before him—these are milestone minutes in the career of a director who segued from the silents to talking pictures better than many others. But the new technology was, nevertheless, daunting.

In directing *The Big Trail,* Walsh installed himself squarely in a public and very mythic narrative. The picture in one sense is yet another embodiment of Raoul Walsh, storyteller—whose stories of himself and his culture, as told through a body of verbal and visual imagery, place him in the tradition of our country's greatest storytellers and mythmakers. His confidence in the still untested, still young John Wayne points directly to his fundamental understanding of the film camera. Wayne's presence in front of it, his physical beauty and natural grace, gives the film another layer of meaning. He is the first physical, visual embodiment American audiences ever had of the mythic Adamic male so important in our literary and cultural history. He is pure and unfettered; as Toqueville wrote in *Democracy in America,* he is the product of the soil from which he grows, natural, innocent, immediate. He is morally untarnished, bereft of any history that might weigh him down and spoil him for the immediacy of experience. Instead, he is Emerson's male figure: forward looking and at ease in his environment. Walsh instinctively understood this.

John Ford may have picked up Wayne in 1939, almost ten years after the failure of *The Big Trail* at the box office pushed his career back to the B-movie bin, yet Walsh understood Wayne better than anyone and put him in front of the camera—a man both beautiful and natural, camera ready for American cinema.

But Walsh did more with Wayne than merely embody a mythic man on the big screen. He placed him in the center of the more important story, the one that, for Walsh, not just permeates, but actually engineers every one of his pictures: the love story between a man and a woman. Walsh often told the public that at the center of all his films lay the true narrative: the man and the woman finding each other in one form or another. After all the struggles taking place during the trek from St. Louis to Oregon, after all the hardship and male competition between Breck Coleman and his adversaries, the story moves forward fueled by the impulse of men and women to come together and to make a home for future generations. The last shot of *The Big Trail* reenacts this paradigm: Breck and Ruth embrace and profess their love for each other just before Walsh's camera pans upward to display the glorious trees pointing heavenward in this new land. Not only does Walsh place Wayne in the midst of an epic gesture and story; he positions him in his first role (and one of the few) showing him to be a sexual, loving creature—something Ford would rarely do for Wayne in all the years they would work together.

Walsh's picture started what some industry analysts called a "Western trend" in filmmaking that year. After the picture finished production, a score of other sound westerns were announced as being in the works, including *Rose of the Rancho,* RKO's adaptation of Edna Ferber's novel *Cimarron* starring Gary Cooper, and the popular William Haines's latest vehicle *Way Out West.* The word was out that exhibitors ought to begin educating the public about westerns because, clearly, they were coming in full force.

The film's disappointing show at the box office halted Wayne's career for almost a decade, relegating him to B westerns, and robbing him of the celebrity even Walsh thought he would get. But no one was more disappointed than Walsh by the failure of *The Big Trail* to impress at the box office—although he hardly ever spoke of it publicly and, instead, looked to his next picture. After such a staggering accomplishment just to get the film shot, simply to orchestrate a production of such huge proportions, the picture's mediocre returns and critical word delivered Walsh an emotional blow. Although he remained with Fox until the mid-1930s, the studio was hard-pressed for production money: William Fox lost his shirt in bad investments just at the time *The Big Trail* was released. Walsh would move around during the next decade, even though he would still work at Fox. He could not find a sure stylistic footing for much of the next decade, and much of his work looked like a shadow of what he had already accomplished. But his ties to another love, horse racing, grew stronger. In mid-December, he became one of a number of stockholders from the Hollywood community who poured money into the racetrack at Agua Caliente. He joined Al Jolson, Eddie Cantor, Joseph Schenck, and Winnie Sheehan. He had enough affection for both directing pictures and racing horses that he remained true to them simultaneously for the rest of his life.

6

Salt of the Earth

Walsh's film titles, whether consciously or not, are humorous and ironic comments on his life. His next film, aptly called *The Man Who Came Back,* again carried an odd meaning for a director who needed to find a way back to box-office grace after the financial failure of *The Big Trail.* Walsh was the first one to want to forget about this new picture. In his autobiography, much like the two wives he ousts from his life, he omits any mention of *The Man Who Came Back;* and, with the exception of *Women of All Nations,* the second and woefully mishatched sequel to *What Price Glory?* he also glosses over his other pictures of this period: *The Yellow Ticket, Wild Girl, Me and My Gal,* and *Sailor's Luck.* With the exception of the brash and exuberant *Me and My Gal,* which survives along with *Wild Girl* and *Sailor's Luck,* these titles carried much potential but deflated at the box office. Yet each shows Walsh's buoyancy behind the camera—his exuberant characters moving at top speed and edging ever closer throughout the decade to the renewed wit and the sophisticated pace he would infuse into the Warner Bros. pictures to come in the 1940s.

Now in his early forties, Walsh had been directing for two decades; he knew that a box-office failure was no reason to derail. If the story was entertaining, whether it be dark or light, it was worth pursuing. *The Man Who Came Back,* a remake of the 1924 film directed by Emmett Flynn and released January 11, 1931, shows Walsh in an uncharacteristically grim mood. He takes Frank Borzage's favorite cinema couple, the popular Fox contract players Janet Gaynor and Charles Farrell, and darkens their souls. Gaynor plays a drug-addicted cabaret singer who meets up with Farrell, an aristocratic fellow with a heavy drinking problem. Although easily forgettable today, this proved one of 1931's highest-grossing pictures. It marked one of the young William Holden's earliest screen appearances, but it also inspired Gaynor to call it one of the worst pictures of her career.

Now in a new decade ushered in by the Depression, Walsh and his moviegoing public were in synch: style and consistency were less a concern than finding flickering moments of pure entertainment. Once in a while, Walsh might stumble on or himself shape a gem of a picture, but the experience of work itself topped his list of priorities. As with many of Walsh's colleagues, the move toward being guns for hire looked easy and rewarding. The work itself mattered more than mood or genre. The self-defining moments that engendered a *What Price Glory?* a *Sadie Thompson,* or an epic effort such as *The Big Trail* were behind him now—at least for a decade—replaced by a quick pace and a brash sentiment.

While Walsh spent days on the set, he spent weekends at Agua Caliente without Lorraine or Marilynn. In March, he entered a recent purchase into the race, a filly named Bissilla, who, to his disappointment, finished in second place behind a horse named Sharp Thought. The races at Caliente offered a definite getaway from home life, a locale Walsh was never too comfortable frequenting, at least not until he was much older. He was no more keen on fatherhood at this time in his life than he was on marriage. He never saw his boys, and Marilynn seemed to grow more fond of her stepfather than he of her. Caliente was a far easier place to frequent. Unfortunately, the races also provided financial losses, a personal habit that grew more troublesome for Walsh in the years to come.

It did not help Walsh's reputation that the moviegoing public was much less generous to his biggest mistake of that year, *Women of All Nations,* the second sequel to the Flagg-Quirt yarns, released on May 31. Walsh knew from the start that it was a bad idea, but he went ahead anyway, later lamenting (but in a not too serious tone) that the public didn't need a third trip around the world with this duo. More than the previous two outings, this picture strained unsuccessfully to be humorous. Quirt and Flagg look to be caricatures of their former selves, as if all the steam had been blown out of their competition and their friendship (the bit player Humphrey Bogart was hardly noticed). The writer Barry Conners's dialogue is trite and often meaningless, and the fact that Walsh himself does not seem to care, instead simply moving ahead with a story that is clearly inferior to its predecessors, points to a troublesome aspect of Walsh as a filmmaker. As the years went by, and certainly just before and after his great success at Warners, he very often seemed hardly to care about the stories and writers he directed, focusing instead on being out on location getting the job done. The thrill was personal, it seemed, only in the getting and doing—not in the quality of the story. This lack of personal connection to story lines did not hurt Walsh later in a film with as splendid material as the 1951 *Captain Horatio Hornblower,* but he seemed uncaring that the writing became watered down as the adventure sequences took up almost all his enthusiasm. He seemed almost uncaring of the weak scripts he directed in the 1930s—although there were a few exceptions—and in the last years of his career seemed almost unconscious of them. What he needed in the last years was to be on the set—any set.

As for *Women of All Nations,* where Walsh displays a full-blown case of poor story choice (and Fox was not pulling all the strings at the time), McLaglen and Lowe already look to be in dire straits for a good line by the time the two sparring buddies pull out of Brooklyn after the Great War and travel to Sweden, where, of course, they fall for a girl named Elsa (Greta Nissen) and duke it out to see who wins her. Audiences were numbed enough to the duo at this point that even the appearance of popular faces such as El Brendel and Fifi D'Orsay failed to help the picture with either critical esteem or box-office success.

But Walsh found a little excitement anyway off the set about this time when he became a witness to a catfight that secretly delighted him. An actress named Alona Marlowe accused Edmund Lowe's wife, the actress Lilyan Tashman, a favorite of Walsh's, of kicking her and attempting to beat her up in front of Lowe's dressing room on the Fox lot on the afternoon of May 9. Marlowe named Walsh and several other Fox players as witnesses to the beating. Although police were called to the scene, local newspapers never reported Walsh's statements or the outcome of the case. But the brief episode held more dramatic punch than Walsh had seen in any recent script.

Walsh fared no better with his next Fox picture, *The Yellow Ticket,* released on October 30. Despite a distinguished cast that includes Lionel Barrymore and Laurence Olivier, this previously filmed melodrama, originating from a stage play written by Michael Morton, concerns a young Jewish girl (Elissa Landi) in czarist Russia who manages to get a "yellow passport," given only to women of a certain class, so that she can track down her father, who is imprisoned on political charges. Tragically finding that he had died, she vows to expose the system that imprisoned him in the first place. Barrymore plays the head of the secret police, a rather terrifying Count Andreeff, who tries to seduce Landi. Olivier plays the honest English journalist who ultimately saves her. Even camera work by the illustrious James Wong Howe could not save this picture from falling into critical obscurity, despite a review calling Walsh "the best of all directors for causing old stories to look like new": "The general freshness of 'The Yellow Ticket' is his masterpiece of face-lifting. There is much pleasure to be derived from the palatial settings and regal costumes all on an Ernst Lubitsch scale." The same critic wrote, however, "We don't know whether you call what Mr. Barrymore does by the name of acting. It is a fascinating mélange of grimaces, tush-tush gestures and growls from the diaphragm." Still, he also notes, "These Barrymores do things in their own way but you like it."[1] This was hardly a big wave to stir moviegoers into the theater.

But now William Fox was in financial boiling water. After the MGM head Marcus Loew died in 1927, Fox conspired to buy out the family's holdings and, in 1929, finally did so. But it took little time for the MGM studio bosses Louis B. Mayer and Irving Thalberg to retaliate by persuading the Justice Department to sue Fox for violation of the federal antitrust law. In the same year, Fox was seriously hurt in an automobile accident, and, just as he recovered, the stock market crashed. All these forces worked to pull him down until his financial holdings were virtually wiped out. The Loews-Fox merger never came to pass, and Fox lost control of Fox Film Corporation in 1930 during a hostile takeover. From then on, the time Walsh spent at Fox saw William Fox fighting to stave off bankruptcy. Money belts were tightened, although no less than in other studios, given the economic crisis at hand since the crash.

At this auspicious moment, Walsh would sign, in 1933, with Darryl F. Zanuck, who had just come over from Warner Bros. to head up Twentieth Century Pictures, which absorbed Fox's company. Their first film would be 1933's *The Bowery*. Twentieth Century Pictures would partner with Fox Film Corporation in 1935 to form Twentieth Century–Fox Film Corporation. Walsh saw a new reshaping of the studio.

But, for now, Walsh worked again with Charles Farrell in 1932's *Wild Girl,* with a cast that also included Ralph Bellamy, Hollywood's perpetual second romantic lead, and Joan Bennett, whom Walsh would direct a few more times in the coming decade. The source material, Bret Harte's short story "Salomy Jane's Kiss," seemed just up Walsh's alley, telling the story of three fearless pioneers in a period setting. For this film Walsh worked with the cameraman Norbert Brodine; the picture is a charming western that has a boundless spirit (owing much to Bennett's bouncy performance). Given the times, however, the story is laced with strongly stereotyped images of African Americans, including the actress Louise Beavers as Bennett's metaphoric girl-in-waiting bowing to Bennett one too many times. Bellamy later said, "[Walsh] was an interesting one to work with. He knew what he wanted and he knew when he got it, as opposed to some people in those days who took many, many takes of a scene and sometimes you didn't know why you were doing it over again." At this early time, Walsh began to perfect a habit that eventually became legendary among the actors and crews he worked with: after he put in place a particular setup, he walked away instead of looking in the camera. In essence, he left his people floating. But he had good reason: he preferred to hear how a scene sounded; he already knew it by heart, and that was good enough for him. With this behavior, Walsh never wandered far from Griffith, who did the very same thing. Asked if he ever saw Walsh walk away from a scene after the setup, Bellamy said he never saw it personally but had already heard about it.[2]

If this first foray with Bennett was only a mediocre success, the next with the actress was golden. Walsh directed Bennett and Spencer Tracy in a robust romantic comedy that made the most of its story and cast and hit big commercially and critically. *Me and My Gal* was his only time working with the new Fox contract player Spencer Tracy—although, eighteen years later, Tracy and Bennett would team again in MGM's *Father of the Bride.* In *Me and My Gal,* Tracy plays a city beat cop who falls for a local waitress (Bennett). They're in love head over heels when the story is complicated by Bennett's sister's (Marion Burns) relationship with a bank robber (a wonderfully wise-cracking George Walsh) who holes up in her attic and threatens her along with her boarder (Henry B. Walthall) if she tells the cops. But, in the end, Tracy and Bennet figure it out and save the day, and Tracy gets a shot at being a hero. Predictably, the two lovebirds end up getting married. Arthur Kober received screen-play credit for adapting Philip Klein and Barry Conners's story "Pier 13." But Walsh's fingerprints stray all over the story, most noticeably in the spirited pace and catchy verbal bantering, reminiscent of the Flagg-Quirt jabbering in *What Price Glory?* and their subsequent outings.

Walsh also infuses some autobiographical humor in the picture. In one scene where Tracy and Bennett share a kiss over a lunch counter, Walsh's camera jumps to a close-up of Bennett's leg stretching up in the air and then Tracy's legs doing some fast shakes, both mimicking Walsh's energy level. When the couple tries to get information from Burns's boarder, Sarge (Walthall), who can't speak since being wounded in World War I, he uses his eyes to talk to them. He keeps moving his eyes upward and sideways, as if pointing to the attic, prompting Tracy to ask, "He was in the war, wasn't he?" "He was in the Signal Corps," Ben-nett says, referencing Walsh, and Tracy quips, "He's trying to telegraph it in. Maybe he's giving us the winner at tomorrow's handicap." Tracy is an early formation of Walsh's more sophisticated men to come: Cary Grant in 1936's *Big Brown Eyes* and especially the wisecracking Jimmy Cagney in Walsh's Warner Bros. gangster tales. But the robust romantic high jinks between Tracy and Bennett, which anchor the film, are pure Walsh, his energy dashing at top speed, his humor at its wisecracking best. The close-ups of Tracy's and Bennett's bodies, the mannerisms as these two fall in love with each other, seem to come directly from Walsh's unconscious. This man, who at this point in his life keeps his romantic yearnings at a distance (he hardly felt for Lorraine what he felt for Gloria Swanson), falls in love with Tracy and Bennett's falling for each other. He cannot have enough of it, and his love of the romantic ignites this film's high energy level.

Walsh's favor to his brother, George, was to cast him as Duke, the thug who gets mixed up with Burns. George's performance adds siz-ably to the picture. With his husky voice and sure demeanor, he easily made the transition from silents to talkies in an unfortunately truncated career. He had appeared only intermittently on the screen since losing *Ben Hur* in 1925. He would have been a natural presence in the films Walsh later directed at Warner Bros. beginning in 1939, but he retired to his ranch in California to manage his brother's growing interests in horse breeding and racing.

Walsh continued doctoring other directors' pictures even as he helmed his own; he would do that for the next thirty-odd years. James Wong Howe told an interviewer that, in late 1932, Walsh was called in to shoot the Coney Island sequence for *Hello, Sister,* Erich von Stroheim's last film for Fox. The studio took the film away from von Stroheim and sent him on "a permanent vacation." After Walsh finished his sequence, Fox brought in the director Alfred Werker to finish the film and to shoot new sequences. *Hello, Sister* nevertheless failed at the box office when the studio released it in April 1933. The popularity surrounding *Me and My Gal* did little to lift Walsh's career in the remaining years before he went to Warner Bros. in 1939.

During the decade Walsh looked for ways to stay afloat financially and not jeopardize his growing passion for the horses or Lorraine's growing passion for society life and the money it took to stay there. He found very few good stories, even though he invested his energy in all the scripts he directed and usually altered them to his liking. The story didn't necessarily have to be of particularly good quality, but it did have to be entertaining and have Main Street appeal. In March 1933, Fox released *Sailor's Luck,* a small, very spirited romance starring Sally Eilers and a very entertaining James Dunn. The picture garnered scant critical praise, one reviewer saying, "Any motion picture bearing the directorial stamp of Raoul Walsh may be expected to contain the very limit in ribald and racy humor and no little amount of good stiff drama. 'Sailor's Luck' is no exception to the Walsh rule. It follows the rowdy brand of screen comedy which the director fashioned in the first two of the Flagg-Quirt opuses, 'What Price Glory' and 'The Cock-Eyed World,' only this time we have a sailor, played humanly by James Dunn, and a helpless girl, acted with charm by Sally Eilers, in place of the two hardboiled marines."[3] *Sailor's Luck,* though not well received, contains many Walshian signal moments, especially the story's theme, contained in a musical number, that "love makes the world go 'round," the adage Walsh later confirmed to be the axis around which most of his movies turned. If a man loved a woman, there was a movie in it. There was no movie, no story to be told, if a man could not love a woman. Another signal moment is the way (or the mere fact) that the picture danced around the censors, especially since Sally Eilers and James Dunn rent a hotel room together, lie in bed together (the camera never reveals whether their feet are on the floor), and kiss in bed, and Eilers runs around the room in an extended sequence wrapped in nothing other than a bedspread.

A week after Walsh finished the production of *Sailor's Luck,* Miriam Cooper filed the first suit in what would be two decades of financial bickering between her and Walsh. As she would do innumerable times in the coming years, she claimed that he failed to pay her the $500 due her weekly as part of their 1927 divorce agreement. Though the figure would change in every suit she filed over the years, and although continually dragging him to court would cost him no undue anguish—far less than it would cost Lorraine—the fact was that Walsh was remiss more often than not in paying Miriam. Between the money he owed and often failed to pay Miriam and the monies spent on Lorraine's lavish lifestyle, not to mention his love of quarterhorses—the buying and the selling, not to mention the betting—Walsh embarked on an emotionally and financially costly roller coaster throughout most of his life. Miriam claimed in this first suit that, since the divorce settlement, Walsh had managed to make a payment of only $650 in monies that were supposed to go to helping her support herself and raise their two sons, Robert and Jack. This action was just the beginning.

Boys Being Boys

> Directing Raft and Beery . . . was like trying to keep the
> peace between a lion and a tiger.
> —Raoul Walsh

Then Walsh found a better gamble. Somewhere between the smart-alecky bravado of Quirt and Flagg, Spencer Tracy's self-assuredness in *Me and My Gal,* and the more sophisticated gangsters he would create at Warner Bros., Walsh fashioned two cocky, wisecracking Irish characters, Chuck Connors and Steve Brodie, in 1933's *The Bowery.* The picture that put Walsh back on top again was his first picture with the brash and very independent producer Darryl F. Zanuck. Walsh was looking to be fired up again with new and exciting scripts, especially if he would be in a position to seriously tinker with (and in some cases rewrite) them. He needed the kind of rush that only a new producer could give him. Walsh signed with Zanuck on June 12, 1933, to direct *The Bowery,* in what was the very first contract for Twentieth Century Pictures. Walsh had little to complain of in the deal: he would receive a salary of $25,000 to be paid in eight weekly installments.

The Bowery was partly based on a story about Brodie, a Brooklynite who skyrocketed to fame for five minutes after he took a dare and jumped off the Brooklyn Bridge. But it was much more: a rollicking tale of the rough-and-tumble times of New York's Bowery district in the early years of the century. The story is shot through with racial epithets. No one escapes unharmed—not the Chinese, not the Jews, not the women. All Walsh saw was the exuberance, the male bonding, and the thrill of good drinking and rivalry among men.

George Raft, whom Walsh had never met, was set to play Brodie. Zanuck wanted Wallace Beery for a supporting role, but Beery was under contract to MGM. So Zanuck called in his studio vice president, William Goetz, who arranged a meeting between Zanuck, Walsh, and Beery, after which, Walsh said, they all went into a huddle. Beery was "thorny" and had lots of objections.[4] Walsh said he bellowed when he was told the picture had a twenty-five-day schedule, complaining that at MGM no production ever ran under sixty days. He also told Zanuck and Walsh that under no circumstances would he work past five in the afternoon. Zanuck gave him what he wanted and hoped his promises would coincide with the picture's shooting schedule. The writer Howard Estabrook and the actor-writer James Gleason turned in a final script based on a novel by Michael L. Simmons and Bessie Roth Soloman along with a story, "When the Bowery Was in Bloom," by Roy L. McCardell, published in the December 19, 1925, issue of the *Saturday Evening Post.* Three days later, after MGM loaned out Beery, Walsh started shooting. A lament that appeared in the story also landed in the film's closing credits. It's a "sad little sad tune" about "the Broadway and Tenderloin of New York" where "saloons peppered the city" that was not only "rowdy, impudent and ribald" but "young, crude and virile."[5]

George Raft would not be a favorite of Walsh's, a fact that Walsh grew into during his five films with the actor—beginning with *The Bowery* and extending through the 1940s at Warner Bros. It was not Raft's mob connections (he was known to be friends with Bugsy Siegel) that

Walsh minded. In fact, in his autobiography, Walsh relates (or, perhaps, creates) a brief meeting he had with Siegel in the early 1940s: Siegel asked Walsh to his home to help him bribe Hearst to get out of the way of the gangster's plan to open a dog-racing track in Culver City, near MGM studios. The episode has Walsh refusing Siegel's request, then walking out of his living room, leaving him high and dry. The romance of this encounter notwithstanding, what bothered Walsh about Raft was the actor's utter lack of professionalism on the set, his insistence on controlling the script and interfering in the way a fellow actor might read a character. Raft set his own rules and stuck to them; he and Walsh would have words on more than one occasion.

But, when filming began, Walsh put his thumbprints all over a story that took only one month to complete. Here were the dueling buddies and the countless mugs who show up on the streets of the Bowery to give it the authentic flavor of New York street life ca. 1898, even as the racism stands out: the Chinese are Chinks, Jews are aggressive, money-loving tailors, *niggers* is frequent terminology, and the two principals kick their women in the behind every chance they get. Walsh was no racist at heart, but neither did he have a quarrel with a racist joke if it was humorous for the times.

Walsh's choreography is fast and spirited; there is no end to the teeming activity in this Bowery as the camera pans left and then right to nonstop dance numbers, minor brawls, and characters pawning each other and generally trying to make a buck or make a sucker out of the guy to their left. From the two main lugs to young Jackie Cooper's tragic little street urchin, to the homeless waif (Fay Wray) whom Berry takes under his wing, the picture teams with exaggerated street-smarts that render it nothing less than authentic. Beery commands attention in every frame he inhabits. The attention he and Walsh give to emotional (facial) nuance is the film's foreground; it is understandable that Walsh agreed to Beery's terms in order to have him in the picture.

The story centers on two dueling men, the historically true (but not necessarily accurate) Bowery boys Steve Brodie (Raft) and Chuck Connors (Beery), vying for everything they can lay their hands on, from the saloon they both want to own, to the girl, to the brawls they both claim to win. Unintentionally or not, Walsh by now had staked out the conceit that almost had him cornered: the unending parade of male characters who fight it out to see who is the strongest, the most attractive to women, the smartest, and, of course, the most adept at telling a tall tale. The film delivers the same turn-of-the-century sense of nostalgia Walsh later delivered in *The Strawberry Blonde,* even though the latter film has a more settled feeling to it, a kind of acceptance and maturity that replaces the pure exuberance and optimism here. Despite the numerous times Brodie and Connors get knocked down, either by the other or by Lady Luck herself, they get right back on their feet again to plot their next move.

Fay Wray later talked about working with Walsh. "He wore an eye patch for one thing," she said, "and that made him seem almost mysterious. He was a big, physically strong looking person. With women he didn't do much directing. It was kind of a feeling you got from him without too many words."[6] Walsh was not a tall man—under six feet with a medium frame, although he was in excellent physical shape. To the tiny Wray, he seemed almost larger than he actually was.

The studio planted a good piece of newspaper publicity for the picture. "George Raft Does a Brodie" appeared in syndicated columns and had potential moviegoers wondering about the real-life Steve Brodie and whether he actually made his historic leap off the Brooklyn Bridge. The story noted that, among the film's two hundred players and extras, there were also scores of old-timers who, as children, lived in the Bowery when Brodie's jump was a cause célèbre for many fistfights. Most of the Boweryites believed Brodie made the jump, it was said. But George Raft raised a skeptical eyebrow. Young Jackie Cooper wagered twenty-five cents of his allowance that the entire episode was a myth. There was never definite proof of the jump, although Brodie's claim to have made the leap rendered him the idol of the metropolis and brought many of New York's big shots to drink and spend at his saloon. The story wasn't bad for Fox publicity either.

In the early 1930s, Walsh needed the kind of optimism the picture's success brought with it. He especially needed firm ground, having shifted from high-powered stories to low-key set pieces and back again. His career was unsettled now, and Lorraine offered him little stability at home. But he found his outlet. Legalized pari-mutuel wagering had not yet returned to California, but Walsh moved ahead and decided to breed

Thoroughbreds. Now, he purchased a twenty-five-acre parcel on Petit Drive in Encino (in the San Fernando Valley, over the hill from Fox) and made it into a showplace. This small horse farm meant a great deal to him, and he imported twelve top-class broodmares from England and Ireland and put them behind beautiful white fences and let them eat lush green grass. He spent a good deal of time at Agua Caliente as horse racing and betting also had not yet returned to California. In 1939, he sold the Encino ranch to Clark Gable and Carole Lombard and bought a three-thousand-acre ranch in Willets, in northern California, where he tried to produce Thoroughbred stock. But his directing career ate up so much of his time that, eventually, in the 1940s, he parceled off and sold the Willets property too.

Lorraine's time was more taken up with social events than Walsh's, although he joined her on some occasions. When she was at home, Walsh probably was not. Walsh's nephew tells the story of a time when Walsh's father, Thomas, contemplating a move to California, came to visit his son and Lorraine. One day before Walsh arrived home, Thomas spent a good amount of time in the kitchen preparing a lobster dinner. After the lobster was cooked, Thomas sent one of the housekeepers up to Lorraine's room with the lobster to see whether she would like a taste. After a long while, he couldn't imagine what had happened to it. The housekeeper finally arrived back in the kitchen to inform him that Lorraine had thought the lobster was for her alone and had eaten the entire meal. The story circulated in the family for years.[7]

The greatest satisfaction for Walsh now came from raising horses and being on the set. He was even more satisfied when *The Bowery* saw good box-office numbers on its release that October. American moviegoers took it to their hearts; it was now three years and counting into the Great Depression, and nostalgia was number one in movie theaters. If Walsh thought he had played to the sentiment of the American public, that was fine with him—and he didn't mind veering left or right, up or down, to do it, as long as he could be on the set.

Walsh's pictures rode a brief crest of popularity, especially his next one, *Going Hollywood,* which easily garnered positive public sentiment. In the late summer of 1933, Walsh received a call from Ed Hatrick, a representative for William Randolph Hearst, who wanted Walsh to meet with him to discuss Walsh's directing Hearst's paramour, Marion

Davies, along with Bing Crosby, in what would turn out to be a spirited yet ultimately light musical called *Going Hollywood*. Hearst was looking for a way to pump energy into Davies's then sagging career and low box-office numbers—this despite her long-held popularity with American moviegoers. He believed a picture called *Going Hollywood* was a good shot.

From all angles, the movie looked promising—a frothy romantic musical focusing on a pretty teacher (Davies) who is just too bouncy and spirited for the staid atmosphere of the school that employs her. She meets a crooner and falls head over heels for him, then heads off to Hollywood to follow him, becoming a star herself. The scenarist Francis Marion, who had directed Davies several times, wrote a treatment called *Paid to Laugh,* and Hearst's production company, Cosmopolitan, created by Hearst especially for Davies, had turned the treatment into a screenplay by the up-and-coming playwright Donald Ogden Stewart, who would go on to pen scripts for *Holiday, The Philadelphia Story,* and Leo McCarey's Irene Dunne–Charles Boyer weepie *Love Story.* Although Crosby was set to star opposite Davies, Hearst was none too happy about it (although Walsh was a big fan of the singer). Word had it that the newspaper magnate was no fan of Crosby's singing style. Probably closer to the truth is that Hearst was jealous of Crosby and considered him a "womanizing hellraiser."[8] The MGM lyricist Arthur Freed had to convince Hearst to give Crosby the part, mostly because Freed, along with Nacio Herb Brown, had written six songs for the picture, including "Temptation," which he believed only Crosby could put over.

Walsh was one of the last on board, happy to work for MGM for the one picture (although he would not feel that way for too long). He arrived in time, as he often did these days, to have some say about casting. He was having a fling with Fifi D'Orsay, who by now had appeared in several of his movies, but he was typically quiet about that. But he hired D'Orsay to play Davies's naughty girlfriend who competes with Davies for Crosby's affections. Davies backed Walsh on the decision, but only after she and Hearst sparred over the choice. Although Hearst really wanted Lily Damita for the role, in the end Davies got her way, and Fifi was in. To fill in the rest of the company, Walsh cast some familiar faces: Stu Erwin would play a bumbling producer, and the ever-reliable "girlfriend" Patsy Kelly would play Davies's best pal.

Walsh got the idea to use his own backyard on Petit Drive for the picture's exterior shots. At the same time, he had the opportunity to spend time with Hearst, who was considered to be American royalty. Walsh and Lorraine were both enthusiastic about the friendship with Hearst. Davies liked to throw parties, and the Walshes were frequent guests: they especially enjoyed Davies's costume parties, where Walsh particularly got the opportunity to sport fake mustaches, hairpieces, and outlandish (if stylish) costumes. At one such soiree for hundreds, held at the Malibu beach house (with "110 bedrooms"), Walsh engaged in some high jinks and claimed that a fake Romanian prince was working the party, bothering every woman he could find, married or not. When the prince approached Davies, Walsh had had enough. "In any other ambience than the morally relaxed atmosphere of Tinsel Town, he would assuredly have had a bullet in him," he said. "I belted him on his Romanian nose and floored him with a right on the jaw. At which point Buster Keaton in a gorilla suit came over and counted the prince out."[9] Walsh said that he was just trying to save Marion Davies's honor. But it was more enjoyable than that.

Even after shooting on this picture ended, Walsh and Hearst remained friends and often saw each other socially. It seemed that Walsh was no longer as offended by the idea of his wife entering the home of a kept woman as he had been when he was married to Miriam. Lorraine and Walsh were in Marion's house often. Lorraine Walsh must have enjoyed being part of the social set Hearst and Davies offered.

In his autobiography, Walsh recalled his first response when asked to direct the picture. He had to learn about his producer. Hearst's representative first told Walsh "the Chief" wanted to see him; Walsh, being Walsh, with his love of Native American life, thought to himself, "The chief of what?"[10] Walsh soon found out, as Hearst took some of the cast and crew—Walsh, Crosby, and the songwriters—and flew them to his San Simeon castle, that 350,000-acre estate that commanded thirty miles of California shoreline. Hearst had the film's crew and cast up to the castle often, and it was not unusual for them to find other guests on their arrival—even Winston Churchill, who, it was said, would puff vigorously on a cigar and just as vigorously ignore them (although Walsh always claimed that he and Churchill called each other "Walshie" and "Winnie"). Rehearsing and socializing blended together day and night.

On one of those evenings, at dinnertime, Davies, who hailed from Brooklyn, asked Walsh whether as a boy he had ever visited Rockaway Beach. When he said yes, she called him Rockaway Raoul, after which Crosby "sang a tune of the same name."[11] From then on, Walsh was Rockaway Raoul to Davies.

The shoot took three months. Other than the exteriors in Walsh's backyard, the film was made on the MGM lot, where Davies had a bungalow described as "fit for the mistress of the world's wealthiest press lord: fourteen rooms." The powers-that-be at MGM soon began tiring of Hearst, especially his tirades about Norma Shearer, the executive Irving Thalberg's wife, and the roles he thought Marion and not Shearer should have been given.[12] To say the least, Marion and Hearst were operating in hostile territory, which was not helped by the couple's love of throwing or attending a good party. This put a dent in Walsh's habit of getting on the set and getting off as swiftly as possible. The film's producer, Walter Wanger, was no taskmaster in the face of Hearst, at least not to Walsh, and Walsh could not get the picture moving at a brisker pace. As time went on, it accrued a cost of over $900,000—a hit that could not recoup its own production costs. Wanger soon moved to Paramount, where Walsh later joined him to make a number of pictures.

The production could be called a *fiasco with fun*. Davies often didn't know her lines when she walked onto the set, which was just before noon. Crosby arrived earlier and waited. When Davies did make her entrance, a five-piece band that "serenaded her between shots" often accompanied her. As Gary Giddins described the atmosphere on the set: "[The cast and crew] would listen to pop tunes for half an hour, at which time Walsh would tear himself away from such pursuits as driving golf balls into a canvas net or playing cards . . . blackjack or gin rummy with a prop man and an assistant director." Then they repaired to lunch, a two-hour Lucullan production in Marion's bungalow: Rhine wines, foie gras, chicken in aspic, Bombay duck. Now they needed to make up again, after which they paused for another musical interlude, finally preparing to shoot around five. If Walsh wrapped as much as 150 feet of usable film in one day's shooting, it was a good day.[13]

At the San Simeon wrap party, Crosby told cast and crew that he and the film's musical director, Arthur Freed, had written a song for Walsh sung to the melody of "The Bowery" (to make it all the more personal), following the words Davies had used to describe her director. Crosby sang it for the others and later recorded it just for Walsh:

Rollicking Rockaway Raoul
When clad on the beach in a towel,
He's terrific, colossal, stupendous, and grand.
He's the lay of the land, of the land.
Oh, the Bowery, the Bowery,
He never goes there anymore.
A good pal and true,
That old Kerry blue,
Rollicking Rockaway Raoul.

[Spoken] Hello, Greenwood! Greenwood! Get me a bottle of that Royal George. What? No Royal George? Oh, Newman, is it too late to replace Greenwood? And where's my Bull Durham, goddamnit, where's my Bull Durham? No Bull Durham? Nuts! I tell you what we'll do, Bing, we'll go over to Davies' bungalow. Maybe she'll pop out with a drink. Okay, let's go. Wait a minute, wait a minute, wait a minute. There's Wange-er, Wanger. Turn 'em over quick! Wanger's here, Bing, otra vez.

Rollicking Rockaway Raoul,
He thinks highbrow operas are foul,
But bimbos and sailors and chippies and such,
He gives them that old Rao-oul Walsh touch.
"Otra vez," "Otra vez,"
We'll never hear that anymore.
And now that we're through,
MGM can go screw,
Says Rollicking Rockaway Raoul.[14]

When the front-office men at MGM heard the last line, they concurred that Walsh and company had been fooling around too much. Although Hearst was picking up the tab for the picture, Louis B. Mayer still became incensed. Walsh later claimed that neither he nor Crosby were ever again invited back to make a picture there—which is not the case.

Walsh, for example, returned to direct several times in the next few years and again in the 1950s. When *Going Hollywood* opened just in time for Christmas 1933, the critics loved it. One said, "Mr. Walsh has evolved a joyful, tuneful, often satirical essay on the types he cleverly directed."[15] Walsh was not especially fond of directing musicals, but he would helm a few more before the decade was out. They helped pay the bills and made him all the more grateful to land at Warner Bros. by decade's end.

After *Going Hollywood,* Walsh's career stumbled again, then hit one more high note, then faltered afterward until the decade closed. In early 1934, Hearst fired both Walsh and Walter Wanger off a picture that was to be called *Operation 13.* He could no longer tolerate their gingerly approach to picturemaking demonstrated on the set of *Going Hollywood.* Walsh found it difficult to regain a sure footing throughout the rest of the decade. In the next three years, he directed five pictures that he considered just programmers; their real function was to fill "the demand for double features."[16] He directed the undistinguished *Under Pressure* for Fox, a story based on Borden Chase and Edward Doherty's novel *Sand Hog,* the title of which offers some idea of the picture's story line: another tale of two workers and rivals (Victor McLaglen and Edmund Lowe once again) who work in an underground tunnel and vie not only to win the same woman (Florence Rice) but also to see who will complete his half of the tunnel first. The most remarkable thing about the picture, initially called *Sand Hog,* was its screenwriting team, which included, along with Chase and Noel Pierce, Lester Cole (who would later collaborate with Walsh on 1945's *Objective, Burma!*), and a young writer from Vienna, Billy Wilder, whose contributions unfortunately are meshed in with those of the team enough so as not to distinguish themselves at this early point. Unfortunately, more than one reviewer noted the obvious formula that viewers had come to expect from a McLaglen-Lowe vehicle. Although some saw intermittent flashes of excitement, the episodes now just seemed to repeat the antics of the wisecracking "bellicose" team.

Walsh then returned to MGM, despite vowing after *Going Hollywood* never to do so again, to direct a mediocre picture called *Baby Face Harrington* that follows the misadventures of a meek small-town bookkeeper (Charles Butterworth) who inadvertently gets involved with the town's most notorious gangsters and can barely get himself unhooked from their claws even as his wife (Una Merkel) threatens to divorce him. The picture came and went as quickly as *Every Night at Eight,* another in a series of collaborations with Walter Wanger that Walsh directed for Paramount after a long absence from the studio. George Raft starred along with Alice Faye, Patsy Kelly, and Frances Langford as three young working women who try to get a singing act going in the midst of a hub-bub of romantic complications. When Paramount released the musical in August 1935, the film's poster promised, "It's the Busiest, the Snappiest Musical Picture of the Year," although box-office receipts proved otherwise. But the picture received more fame in the 1960s when the American critic Andrew Sarris, fronting for French New Wave critics of the late 1950s and early 1960s, called *Every Night at Eight* almost "maddeningly routine" but nevertheless argued that a dream sequence in the film anticipates a dream Bogart's character, Mad Dog Earle, has in *High Sierra* almost six years later.

In January 1935, MGM announced plans to make *Public Enemy 2* with Walsh directing, but nothing came of the project. Walsh was becoming disillusioned with the business. In the spring of that year, he ventured further into his love of horse racing, joining a group of local citizens to help organize what would become the Hollywood Park Jockey Club, which opened three years later with the help of Hollywood's elite. Santa Anita Racetrack, also in the city, would not allow Jews into its arms. So the studio head Jack Warner and other Jewish industry notables in the Los Angeles area decided to open their own park, one far more tolerant of racial difference and religion. Walsh applied for a race permit from the California Horse Racing Board in March 1935. He would be president and general manager. William Randolph Hearst wielded so much power in the state, however, that, when he opposed a second racetrack in the Los Angeles area, the idea looked doomed. But Walsh went to his friend and convinced him to step aside and look the other way. When Hollywood Park finally opened, Walsh actually became president and general manager of the club behind it. Also on the board were some Warner Bros. heavyweights, the singer-actor Al Jolson and Jack Warner. The board planned eventually to open four sites between Beverly Hills and the Pacific Ocean, but only one ever developed. The formation of Hollywood Park, nonetheless, not only strengthened Walsh's friendship with Hearst but also forged a new one with Warner that would flourish to an even greater extent in the 1940s.

In the beginning of that decade, Walsh would buy and sell horses in quick succession. He bought Grand Manitou in Ireland and Sunset Trail II in France, and he had them both imported to the United States, where they ran successfully—Sunset Trail II won the three-year-old championship at Tanforan, and Grand Manitou once defeated the great mare Marica in a handicap in Chicago—even giving Seabiscuit a run for the money at one point. When George Walsh left the movie business to raise and train his brothers' horses, their luck even improved. The two brothers had a winner called Lady Peenzie brought over from England, and two others, Frexo and Mount Vernon, were also high-caliber runners. Later on, another horse Walsh bought, Bounty Bay, was a stakes winner, first in California, then in the Midwest.

Walsh and Hearst remained on good terms, and the two couples continued seeing each other socially. When Hearst and Davies were not entertaining, they traveled with the Walshes intermittently and even more often sent wires to each other for birthdays, anniversaries, or just to keep in touch. "We are mad at you, Pintsy [Marion's nickname for Lorraine]," Hearst and Marion wired when Lorraine failed to remind them of the Walshes' anniversary in the mid-1930s. "Hail to the chief on his brand new birthday and best wishes for health, appetite, peace and pleasure in the years ahead," Walsh wired Hearst around the same time.[17] Hearst even went through the trouble of trying to find Pancho Villa's original saddle for his friend—a reminder of things past. The magnate combed the terrains of Mexico in order to find it and thought he had managed to do that. When he presented it to his friend, Walsh knew that the saddle was too expensive looking to be Villa's. He knew that the Mexican bandit would never have ridden something that nice—but he never let on and accepted the gift with much to-do and a great show of appreciation. When legalized racing came back to California in 1934, Walsh made sure that he and Hearst were in on racing deals together.

Walsh and Hearst shared increasingly close political views of the world situation as World War II approached. Walsh may have been liberal in his view of the way minorities were treated in the movie business—and he tried to hire as many as he could, especially during his tenure at Warner Bros.—but his political views remained for the most part conservative. At the polls, he and Lorraine voted a Republican ticket in the years leading up to the war, although Lorraine strayed once or twice toward a Democratic vote. But neither strayed as far left as some actors Walsh directed over the years.

Around this time, Walsh signed with the Hollywood agent Sam Jaffe, staying with him until Jaffe closed his agency twenty-five years later, in 1959. Jaffe, who worked briefly for Harry Cohn at Columbia Pictures in the early 1930s, represented A-listers such as Bogart and Bacall, David Niven, and, later, Richard Burton. Jaffe is also credited with creating the production method of shooting "night for day," a brainstorm that allowed Paramount Pictures to continue making pictures on the fateful day of January 16, 1929 (just subsequent to Jaffe's association with Famous Players Lasky), when an electrical fire destroyed one of the studio's soundstages being soundproofed for talking pictures.

West of the Klondike

But Walsh grew increasingly frustrated with directing fillers. By 1935, he seriously considered leaving the movie business to raise horses instead. At that very juncture, however, Mae West showed up on his landscape and offered him a directing job he agreed to almost immediately. Sassy and irreverent (much more so than Walsh at that time), West may not have been exactly his female alter ego—but certainly she was the female equivalent of the next best thing, the Walshian smart aleck whom McLaglen, Tracy, and Raft had so vividly fleshed out in recent pictures. Wisecracking, fast on the verbal draw, and sly as a fox, West gave Walsh a run for his dollar on the screen as well as behind the camera. Not only did she prove to be a tough character on celluloid; she pulled most of the production strings on the one picture they made together, *Klondike Annie*.

The picture went through various revisions and smacks in the face from the censors—even being held back from final release until February 1936—as Walsh, West, and every studio in town now had to contend with Hollywood's latest censoring arm, Joseph Breen, the enforcer of the Hollywood Production Code Administration. Mae West took up much of Breen's attention, as Gloria Swanson had earlier done with Will Hays. If Swanson and Walsh had their share of maneuvering to do with

Sadie Thompson, Mae West's tsuris with the censors was an ongoing life adventure.

Just as Gloria Swanson had earlier, Mae West liked Walsh's chutzpah and insisted that he be her director on *Klondike Annie.* When Walsh arrived to work with her for what would be the first of four consecutive pictures he would make at Paramount, she presented him with a finished script, a compilation of a play she had written, *Frisco Kate,* itself a reworked version of another of her writings—this was pure West. Although the story really belonged to her, when it came to screen credit, she insisted that the writers who worked with her also put their names on it as well: she added Frank Dazey's name alongside hers for the actual script and gave story credit to Marion Morgan and George B. Dowell.

The story line follows the adventures of a woman called Frisco Doll who lives in 1890s San Francisco Chinatown at a gambling club called the House of Chan Lo. In truth, she is Rose Carlton, a woman "kept" by the house's proprietor (and her assumed master-lover), Chan Lo himself. Rose is miserable since Chan Lo has imprisoned her to the point that she is not allowed to see anyone of her own race. Soon she makes plans to escape Chan Lo and heads off on a frigate bound for Nome, Alaska. It is suggested, although never seen onscreen, that Rose murders Chan Lo in order to make her escape.

Rose boards a tramp steamer manned by the gruff Bull Brackett, played by Victor McLaglen, who still doesn't seem to have much to do other than walk in and out of rooms following Rose. Brackett of course falls madly in love with the very sexual Rose, and, when he learns that she's wanted for murder, vows to protect her. When a kind missionary woman boards the steamer at Vancouver, she and Rose attempt to understand each other. After the missionary, named Annie, tells Rose that she must repent for her wanton ways, she falls ill and dies. Rose assumes her identity and escapes the law after she arrives in Alaska. Rose then flirts with the idea of actually doing Annie's missionary work, but, by picture's end, she is back in the arms of McLaglen dousing him with her sexual charms, and all is well in the land of Mae and the rest of the world.

Although eight minutes were cut by the censors, the picture still invited all kinds of wrath, and not just for its aspect of miscegenation, the sexual relations between a Caucasian woman and an Asian man.

Also troubling to many critics was the strong suggestion that a loose
character like Rose could ever be redeemed by donning the clothes and
the demeanor, not to mention the good works, of a missionary woman.
But West was fine-tuned in her dealings with censorship. Not only her
swagger and sexual innuendo stayed intact. So did the story she initially
wanted. Walsh was only too happy to put one over on the censors, especially in using enough setups so blatantly sexual that, no matter how
many had to be cut, there were still plenty left to go around. He never
had to expose her thigh; her swing let each spectator know it lay inside
her tight skirt.

Walsh and West also fought battles of wits with each other—for
one, her slow working style angered him to no end as it collided with
his penchant for speed, or at least moving through the job at a good
clip. Eventually, however, they worked out their differences. The picture
turned into a great success for both star and director. Walsh serves West
well in *Klondike Annie,* giving her long takes to highlight the facial
expressions that so epitomize her style. If there was any compromise
for Walsh, it was the picture's pace, almost so slow going at times that
it takes its toll on McLaglen's character even as Walsh gives West's lot
of kick. Too often he appears to stand around looking for a physical
footing, seeming as if he is ready to be off and running while Mae is still
slowly approaching his side of the room to share the frame. But Walsh
does West a great service; setups for the musical numbers give her ample
space, and he never lets her often halfhearted delivery bog down the
story. The censors may have irked West, but she hardly shows it.

The hatchet that threatened to come down on West also included a
bout with William Randolph Hearst, formerly a friend of hers (and still
one to Walsh), who, on viewing the picture, issued a statement that ran
throughout his newspaper empire (but evidently did not threaten Walsh's
relationship with Hearst): "The Mae West picture, *Klondike Annie,* is a
filthy picture. I think we should have editorials roasting the picture and
Mae West, and the Paramount Company for producing such a picture—
the producer—the director and everyone concerned. We should say it is
an affront to the decency of the public and to the interests of the motion
picture profession. Will Hays must be asleep to allow such a thing to
come out but it is to be hoped that the churches of the community are
awake to the necessity of boycotting such a picture and demanding its

withdrawal. . . . After you have had a couple of good editorials regarding the indecency of the picture then DO NOT MENTION MAE WEST IN OUR PAPERS AGAIN WHILE SHE IS ON SCREEN AND DO NOT ACCEPT ANY ADVERTISING OF THIS PICTURE."[18]

Another voice piped in. The *New York Times* film critic wrote, "Mae West's *Klondike Annie* does not merit the agitation it has caused. Neither as healthily rowdy nor as vulgarly suggestive as many of her earlier pictures, it emerges a combination of lavender and old japes. . . . If she attempts to please the censors the more she displeases them. . . . It is unfortunate that there can be no truce between Mae West and the censors. . . . We found *Klondike Annie* quite unconvincing, quite witless, quite archaic and quite a bore."[19] Other critics spoke of the "new" Mae West, suggesting that she had diluted her acerbic wit to please her censors, or at least to get past them in a way she could tolerate and still believe she had not been toppled by the censors. It mattered less to Walsh than to West, obviously, and, even though the picture took in more money at the box office than anything he would direct throughout the rest of the decade, he thought of it more as another bow to Main Street than anything else. He always believed that the picture belonged to West. He didn't need it as much as she did; he enjoyed the challenge more than anything else.

Given *Klondike Annie*'s popularity, Walsh decided not to quit the movie business after all—at least not for the moment. In late January 1936, he and Lorraine threw a rare party at their Beverly Hills home; they were in a celebratory mood. West was just one of the many guests invited to the party. It was reported that Douglas Fairbanks and Mary Pickford were seen huddling, giving way to rumors that the couple may have had thoughts of getting back together after their recent separation. It was also reported that the singer Matt Moore was seen leaning up against the Walshes' English bar, pretending to be tired and muttering to passersby that he only wished he could get some rest.

On an even keel professionally, Walsh helmed a lively and under-rated comedy as his next Paramount–Walter Wanger project, directing Cary Grant, Joan Bennett, and his brother-in-law Walter Pidgeon in the spirited yarn *Big Brown Eyes*. Cary Grant plays a slick gumshoe wannabe who is more interested in chasing after Bennett than in catching a local thief who habitually absconds with the jewels of wealthy women unable to defend themselves. Walsh took a story by James Edward Grant and wrote the script with Bert Hanlon (the two also worked on *Sailor's Luck* and *Every Night at Eight* as well during this time, with Hanlon writing additional dialogue for these pictures), having a great time infusing the story with the shenanigans Grant pulls with the other characters. Walsh's pace matches Grant's at every turn as if they were in complete synch and in a hurry to get the plot moving. The *Variety* critic said, "Smartly played and directed, strong in story interest and plot novelty angles. . . . Offers excellent entertainment and will take ample care of itself as a program money-maker. . . . A fast-stepping, exciting melodrama, well paced with wise-cracking and sardonic comedy."[20] The tale is slight but witty and consistently exuberant.

Teaming up with Wanger and Paramount again, Walsh next directed a flimsy yet entirely entertaining reverse-Cinderella story featuring Henry Fonda and written by Bert Hanlon and Walsh (from a story by Eric Hatch). Frank S. Nugent, reviewing the picture in the *New York Times*, nicely summed up its failure to understand the reality still biting the country:

> There is some heartening news at the Paramount these days for dashing young playboys whose incomes have shifted from the upper brackets to the starboard side of the decimal point. "Spendthrift," which Walter Wanger has produced in celebration, apparently, of prosperity's arrival from around the corner, bids the indigent wastrel pluck up his courage when the last of his $23,000,000 has sped away and creditors harass him and his charming bride turns out to be merely a fortune-hunter. Make the supreme sacrifice, it counsels; confound your friends by announcing you are going to get a job; become a radio sports commentator at $1,000 a week and marry your stableman's lovely daughter.[21]

As the polo-playing Cinderella (who goes from riches to rags), Fonda displays his considerable romantic-comedic charms, yet none of the principals lifted the lightly drawn fable to the status of memorable fare. Walsh was in a light, spritely mood, and the work he produced mirrored that fact. Fonda later claimed to have forgotten ever making *Spendthrift*. Then Walsh left for England to make two pictures.

Walsh took Lorraine and Marilynn to England. He also took advantage of being in Britain for a period, walking around Saville Row in London, and frequenting men's clothing stores in other parts of the British Isles. Gieves and Hawkes was a favorite men's clothier. The silk ties and formal shirts were one thing, but Walsh's passion was houndstooth jackets along with riding pants and riding boots. Even though he never used one, a whip was a good accessory to complete the outfit. He thought about purchases he might make and traveled throughout England, Ireland, and Scotland in search of racehorses he might bring back to America (this became a lifelong passion). He was not fond of the weather in Britain, but the traditional and often staid British lifestyle in no way conflicted with his increasingly playful sense of humor. He could call on both simultaneously.

The writer-director Bryan Forbes, who became a close friend of Walsh's in the 1950s, later said, "Raoul was a passionate Anglophile (bought his shoes at Lobbs and his shirts in Jermyn Street). I remember I once went with him shopping there and he bought a dozen Eton ties. The shop owner asked him why, and he replied, 'My boy here (meaning me) went to Eton.' [Then] I asked him what on earth they were for and he told me, 'When I make a Western upon the Reservation the Indians will do anything for an Eton tie. There's a whole tribe that wear nothing else.'"[22]

Walsh's two British pictures were spirited romps. Released by United Artists, *Jump for Glory/When Thief Meets Thief* began shooting in November 1936, immediately after Walsh directed the Gaumont-British (Fox's British subsidiary) production *O.H.M.S./You're in the Army Now*. *When Thief Meets Thief* is a sophisticated romantic thriller featuring Douglas Fairbanks Jr. (who also produced the picture). Walsh displays an urbane wit, with Fairbanks giving a bouncy, tongue-in-cheek performance in a light comedy that, despite its lack of depth, has great charm and infectiously endearing characterizations. Fairbanks is a slithery burglar whose plans go delightfully awry after he meets his female match (Valerie Hobson) and the two fall in love and join forces. About the same time, Walsh was to direct a third film in Britain, an adaptation of Kipling's "Soldiers Three," featuring Victor McLaglen, but nothing came of it. Interestingly enough, just a few years later, RKO built a script around Kipling's poem "Gunga Din," which centered on the adventures of three British soldiers in India. Directed by George Stevens (who took over after Howard Hawks left the production), the picture did feature McLaglen and paired him with Kipling after all.

More disappointing was *O.H.M.S.*, which, despite a solid, dependable cast, including Wallace Ford, John Mills, and Anna Lee, made little splash when it was released in 1937. Ford plays an American racketeer who travels to Britain and, in a case of mistaken identity, ends up joining the British army. The film was far-fetched but still lively. Even though Walsh quickly forgot the experience of making it, he liked working in Britain enough to venture back there on frequent visits to buy clothes from London's well-known haberdashers. Later on, Walsh had little, if anything, to say about directing either film, but he always remembered the weather—a factor that seriously complicated his schedule, enough so that it got in the way of his scheduled return to Paramount to begin shooting *Artists and Models* just before summer 1937. Walsh hated to be late.

Artists and Models is one of a string of middle-of-the-road musicals for which Walsh was given the title "director of mediocre musicals" for a short while—a hat he could not take off soon enough. By now he could do lively in his sleep, whether or not it was personal. What was *truly* personal were his friendships on the set. *Artists and Models* tells the story of an advertising executive (played for laughs by Jack Benny) who must find a young woman to be the winning contestant in a beauty contest. The only notoriety to emerge from the picture was its ability to anger a newspaper editor from Louisiana who was appalled to find black and white dancers on the same stage during a musical number. In a letter sent to Paramount, the man ranted about "the practice of mixing races in pictures," to which, he believed, "the Southern reaction will be very hurtful to the movie industry."[23] This kind of anxiety never occurred to Walsh.

Walsh held on to his "musical" moniker for just a little longer. He directed the musical *Hitting a New High* at RKO and later said of the picture, "I didn't know what the hell it was all about—this girl singing her head off. Andre Kostelanetz using footage and stuff. 'What the hell,'

I said, 'let 'em do what they want. I don't know what's going on.'"[24] That statement may well have summed up those several years Walsh floated around the musicals he never truly liked (although he never let it look that way). It also sums up his sense of the absurd, the dissonance he could be so comfortable with when events called for it. He felt that same way when he returned to Paramount to direct another group of pleasant but mostly forgettable musicals such as *College Swing* in 1938 and *St. Louis Blues* in 1939. They were all-star affairs that afforded him the opportunity to work with actors such as Bob Hope, Dorothy Lamour, Martha Raye, George Burns, and Gracie Allen, but they were choreography driven, grinding work and hardly stimulating. Walsh was certainly not challenged when he directed *St. Louis Blues* (released in 1939), a mildly entertaining picture with Dorothy Lamour playing a New York actress who tires (ironically) of having to wear her sarong and South Seas getup onstage and heads out for a more serious career, ending up on a showboat run by Lloyd Nolan (who is serviceable but hardly charismatic in the picture). The film is perky and, if nothing else, benefits from Walsh's energetic pace. Walsh moved around quickly himself. Just before this, in late 1937, he helped out Samuel Goldwyn and took over director duties for John Blystone on the picture *Woman Chases Man,* which introduced Broderick Crawford and featured Miriam Hopkins and Joel McCrea, whom Walsh would direct over ten years later in the western *Colorado Territory.*[25]

Walsh kept up friendships, many for a lifetime; they were that important to him. Cast members and crew he had known in the 1920s and 1930s he still knew at the end of his life. He especially wanted to keep William Randolph Hearst's friendship during this time—the magnate could always be a friend worth knowing. In the fall of 1938, Walsh showed his allegiance to Hearst's political conservatism in an incident involving Hearst's reaction to Britain's stand over Hitler's takeover of parts of Europe. Hearst vehemently opposed any American involvement or intervention. On October 16, 1938, Winston Churchill "replied" to Hitler's expansion and broadcast a speech that went out over the NBC airwaves across the United States. He made an impassioned appeal to the American government, calling for its involvement in Europe's growing struggle against Hitler. "We must arm," he said. "Britain must arm. . . . America must arm. . . . But arms . . . are not sufficient by themselves. We must add to them the power of ideas. People say we ought not to allow ourselves to be drawn into a theoretical antagonism between Nazidom and democracy; but the antagonism is here now. It is the very conflict of spiritual and moral ideas which gives the free countries a great part of their strength."[26]

The fact of both Churchill and Hitler writing for Hearst newspapers in the 1920s and 1930s aside, Hearst responded to Churchill's broadcast with a lecture of sorts on the front pages of his newspapers after Hitler's troops marched into Austria and annexed it to the Third Reich. He demanded a "right of reply" and went on the airwaves on October 23 condemning what he called this British propaganda. He believed that, no matter the threatening events unfolding in Europe, there could still be peace. Most importantly, Hearst believed, England had no right or reason to ask Americans to support what he believed to be British propaganda in a scheme to dominate Europe, absorb Africa, and control the Orient. Despite his characteristic lack of political involvement, although he could be thought to swing to the right on occasion, Walsh defended Hearst's stance and sent him a telegram on October 24 from Van Nuys, stating:

LISTENED WITH GREAT INTEREST TO LAST EVENINGS BROADCAST AND SALUTE YOU AS A TRUE AMERICAN FIRST IN THE PUBLISHING BUSINESS FIRST IN BUILDING UP YOUR COUNTRY AND ALWAYS THE FIRST TO DEFEND YOUR COUNTRY AND ITS PEOPLE STOP MAY I SUGGEST THAT YOU INQUIRE OF MR CHURCHILL WHO SEEMS SO WILLING TO HAVE OTHERS TAKE UP ARMS AND GO KILLING EACH OTHER JUST WHAT ACTUAL MILITARY OR NAVAL EXPERIENCE HE MAY HAVE TO HIS CREDIT STOP JUDGING FROM HIS OPEN HANDED LIBERALITY WITH THE LIVES OF OTHERS ESPECIALLY AMERICANS ONE WOULD IMAGINE THE HONORABLE MR CHURCHILL HAD BEEN DECORATED FOR VALOR UNDER FIRE BY EVERY NATION IN THE WORLD STOP KINDEST REGARDS RAOUL WALSH.[27]

Despite this bidding for Hearst's continued friendship, the only political divisiveness or combat Walsh would know would be the cinema's fictive soldiers trampling through brush and sidestepping ground bombs as they made their way to enemy lines. They would be heroic and as far removed from the real world as Walsh was from political convictions.

Those fictions of combat, enemy lines, westerns, and gangster wars awaited him now at Warner Bros. At Jack Warner's bidding, Walsh made the move to the studio's Burbank lot, about to enter his golden period. But, whether he liked it or not, when the now forty-two-year-old Walsh departed Paramount for Warner Bros. in the fall of 1939, he stepped into the role of artist, and, for the better part of two decades, he would create a world of soldiers, cowboys, gangsters, and gun molls that saved his career no less than his soul. He never anticipated that the world he made for himself and for his audiences might be considered artful. But his best years were about to begin, even though, during his tenure at Warner Bros., he would vehemently shrug off any notion of the artist in himself—as much as the public, and film history, vehemently disagreed.

7

Beshert
The Early Warner Bros. Years

> We were sitting at this fancy dinner party one time—Jack Ford and me and a bunch of people—and he's complaining about his bad eye, the one with the patch over it. . . . Oh, he was complaining about the pain and all, don't you know, so I picked up my fork and I says, "Well, come on, Jack, let me pop it out for you and then you'll be OK." He gives me the dirtiest look, you know, but at least he stopped complaining.
> —Raoul Walsh to Peter Bogdanovich

> Working for Jack Warner and working for Pancho Villa? They're about the same. Both of them bandits.
> —Raoul Walsh

Walsh's quip describing how he put an end to John Ford's bellyaching about his bad eye says everything about Walsh's approach to making pictures at Warner Bros. When he finished one, which he usually did on time and on budget, it was like putting an end to the bellyaching around him: last-minute complaints from producers and actors, script changes that had to be made on the spot, or last-minute maneuvering because there *was* no script. For Walsh, the idea was to get the picture done. Always waiting on the other end was Jack Warner, bandit, businessman, and friend. For thirty years, the two men kept it going. Jack and Walsh. In Jack's native Yiddish, they were *beshert,* two people who were "intended," who found their "meant to be."

Walsh liked to say that he was one of the few men who got along with Warner, a claim not many writers, directors, or actors at Warner Bros. would even want to make—certainly not top workhorses such as Bette

Davis, Olivia de Havilland, Humphrey Bogart, or James Cagney, all of whom found themselves at one time or another in a career-defining moment involving either a contract or a script dispute with "the Colonel," as he liked to call himself once World War II came along. In actuality, Warner would not begin to refer to himself as "Colonel" until the United States entered World War II a few years later. According to Otto Friedrich, Warner responded to the government's call of service by saying that he wanted to start out with the rank of general, adding that he'd be happy to phone the White House to get President Roosevelt's approval. Willing afterward to settle for the rank of lieutenant colonel, and assigned to a public relations post in Los Angeles, he outfitted himself for his role, aided by the studio's tailoring shop. He let everyone know he wished to be addressed as "Colonel." He ended his "Colonel" days when an authentic colonel arrived at the studio to advise on a film project. When Warner shook his hand, his guest said, "You should have saluted me."[1] But Walsh and Warner enjoyed a long friendship and mutual respect—at the very least they stayed shy of the kind of public disputes that Warner and his other talent frequently displayed in newspaper headlines. Just as Walsh could have taken care of John Ford's troublesome eye with one fell swoop of a fork to make Ford stop complaining, so could he swoop down on a picture—it didn't even have to be his own—and bring it in on time and on budget just to get the job done efficiently. No wonder the Colonel liked him.

Signing with Warner Bros. provided an immediate end to the slump into which Walsh's career had fallen during the past five years; before Warner's offer, he had even contemplated giving up directing to raise horses full-time at Willowbrook, the ranch he had bought in northern California. He needed the backing of a studio with a uniform style to bolster him and keep him developing his film sensibilities—just as he benefited from his early tenure at Fox Pictures during the 1920s. Now, after the two box-office flops he had directed in Europe and the mediocre reviews for the Paramount features he had made in Hollywood, Warner Bros. gave him the chance to work with a studio that had a consistent style all its own. The deal could not have been more serendipitous—not only did Walsh salvage what would have been an abbreviated, albeit stellar, career, but at the age of fifty-two he was about to enter into what would be, hands down, his golden period.

As much as their shared interest in horse racing brought Walsh and Warner closer together since the formation of Hollywood Park, it also tested the Colonel's friendship for Walsh, now at the studio, since Walsh would so often borrow money or get an advance on his salary to help pay for his horse buying, his frequent losses at the track, and, when Miriam Cooper hauled him into court, alimony. Miraculously, however, nothing truly got in the way of Warner's support of Walsh—at least not for the next decade—and Walsh felt close enough to Warner to kid around with him by peppering his studio memos with well-intentioned but botched Yiddish phrases. "They're after my tuchus again, Jack," he wrote, referring to Miriam Cooper's attorneys when they came after him—just as she had been doing since the early 1930s. "I have a chance to pick up a M'tseha on a piece of property," he wrote in 1947, asking for a loan. "I will either make a fortune out of this or go machoula [meshuga, crazy] again," he wrote a few days later. "Dear Colonel," he wrote in August 1945, "The Irish and the Jews are always in trouble—that is what makes the world go 'round.'"[2]

Walsh boasted that Warner had been wooing him for years to come work for him. The Colonel and Walsh—or "Irish," as Warner called him—got along, not only because of their personal interests, but also because Walsh's pictures always made money for the studio. In turn, Warner gave him crackling, fast-moving stories that he knew were "Walsh" material. "I've been trying to get you away from Fox ever since you went to work for them," Warner said in 1939 when Walsh made his move to the studio. "I had no idea then that . . . when I signed the seven-year contract with Jack Warner," Walsh wrote in his autobiography, "the seven years would turn out to be thirty."[3] In an interview late in his life, he reiterated, "I got along with Jack for pret' near thirty years." "When they'd buy a story," he also noted, "they'd generally know it was my type of story. Adventure or gangster or suspense or whatever. Jack would call me in and say, 'Here.' I turned down a couple of them and made him cry, but he finally found out later on that I was right."[4] "[Warner] didn't like a scene to drag on," Walsh said elsewhere. "If, for example, you saw a man walking down the street and the shot appeared too long to him, one could hear [Jack] looking at dailies and muttering, 'Kill the son of a bitch and get it over with.' Jack looked for rhythm and he knew that

I had a sense of tempo."[5] Warner could also count on Walsh to come in and take over a picture on a pinch, get it right, and, then, like him, go to the races at the end of the day.

Known in Hollywood as the San Quentin of the movie studios (some of its talent certainly felt locked up), Warner Bros. earned the moniker, not only because the company's signature product—dark social realism and gangster pictures—made great profits during the 1930s and 1940s, but also because Warner's obsession with running a tight ship was almost legendary. For the Colonel and the front office men he had around him, making pictures was hardly that different from running a factory with a smoothly run assembly line. Warners operated a "superior" organization. "It was conceived in order to make a product and to produce without stopping."[6] Formulas that worked, even (or especially) if they contained similar "plots, incidents and characters," were recycled from one picture to another, usually with great success. It was business as usual that a good story (one that audiences flocked to) could be packaged, then repackaged, in a different genre with different players. The studio played musical chairs, always to its advantage:

> When *Captain Blood* is a hit, do it again, more or less, as *The Adventures of Robin Hood* and then *The Sea Hawk*. When the gangster film is condemned by the Production Code Administration as well as by outside censorship organizations, revive it as the G-man film and then bring it back again in the guise of a sociological study of environmentally bred criminal behavior (*Angels with Dirty Faces,* inspired by the success of the play and film versions of *Dead End*). . . . When *Dodge City* works, follow it with *Virginia City, San Antonio* and others. If Bette Davis dying from an incurable disease in *Dark Victory* is big box office, repeat it in *'Til We Meet Again* (a remake of *One Way Passage,* except that Davis refused to do the picture and Merle Oberon had to be hastily substituted).[7]

The family-run Warners had its share of domineering men. President Harry Warner and his brother Sam, the studio's chief executive, ruled from New York, and Jack, the vice president in charge of production, made his actors miserable in person in Burbank. Jack Warner was smart enough to put Hal Wallis, with his brilliant story sense, in place as executive producer in charge of production after Darryl Zanuck vacated the spot in 1933 to form Twentieth Century Pictures with Joe Schenck. Wallis ran the day-to-day business of overseeing most of the studio's films in production, and his rein was tight enough that it often looked as if he were directing and writing the pictures himself. If he was unsatisfied with the dailies he ran after a day's shooting, he would fire off a memo instructing changes in every aspect of the work, from camera angles to dialogue to the actors' costumes. Walter MacEwen was Wallis's executive assistant, and between him, Wallis, and the studio's general counsel, Steve Obringer, a myriad of memos flew daily. Most of these memos have survived since Warner Bros. had a strict rule to commit everything to paper instead of communicating verbally: at the bottom of the interoffice memo letterhead was written, "Verbal messages cause misunderstanding and delays (please put them in writing)."

Walsh thought that he had found studio nirvana, especially after his freelance days following his parting from William Fox nine years earlier. To him, Warner Bros. was "a plum for any director."[8] Not only did Warner's no-nonsense style in turning out pictures suit him, but the studio's essentially somber, naturalistic view of the world—which produced stories about men and women trying to change their often unalterable fate or rallying against it—also suited Walsh's own worldview. His heroes, usually fleeing from one world to find a better one and not usually succeeding, made him a good choice for the top material Warner Bros. contract writers produced. Walsh was not out to make personal statements in his pictures at Warners; again, he simply wanted to entertain, and, if good material came his way, especially a script with action and sweep, with a feisty character on the emotional run, he was happy. In truth, he would most likely retool the script his way in the end, just as he had always done. He told Hedda Hopper in 1965, "They used to have ten or twelve pictures going all the time. You'd finish one on schedule and they'd deliver another script. When you'd ask who was to be in it, they'd say, 'We haven't decided yet—you'll know when you start working tomorrow.'"[9] Walsh said that he never bought any Warner Bros. stock because he used to hear them fighting among themselves and got worried.

The World Moves On

"We are engaging Raoul Walsh to direct a picture," Hal Wallis informed Warner's general counsel, Steve Obringer, in a May 13, 1939, memo, "his starting to be June 5. He will work ten weeks at $2,000 [per week]. Thirty days after the preview of the picture we are to have the following yearly options 40 out of 52 weeks: 1st year at 1,750 [per week]; 2nd year 2,000 [per week]." There was also to be an increase of $250 per week every year after the second for the next five years. "We now have him assigned to the picture *20,000 Years in Sing-Sing,* but should there be any change in plans and should we wish to put him on another picture in place of this, we are to have that right."[10]

Warners exercised that right, and the first contract Walsh signed with the studio gave him a one-picture deal (not the initial seven-year contract he recalled years later in his autobiography). He never saw the set of *20,000 Years in Sing-Sing;* instead, the studio assigned him *The World Moves On,* whose title later became *The Roaring Twenties.*

The World Moves On, penned a year earlier by the newspaper columnist Mark Hellinger, was an epic production looking to happen. Unfortunately, it began life looking like the little engine of a picture that could—and almost didn't. Hellinger, who would later be associate producer on Walsh's third film at Warner Bros., *High Sierra,* and after that pen *The Naked City* with Malvin Wald, the brother of Jerry Wald, was a character so colorful he could have jumped out of one of his own stories. In New York City during the 1920s, he had been a crime beat reporter who also liked hobnobbing with Broadway royalty and celebrities. The idea for *The World Moves On* grew from his own experiences as a nationally known syndicated columnist; he wanted to take a nostalgic look back at the 1920s. Dapper and well connected to Hollywood insiders (and claiming to have connections to the mob), Hellinger was hired as an associate producer—although, in truth, no one was sure what he actually did at the studio. *The World Moves On* also happened to be the name of a Broadway play running at the time, and the studio had to take care of any potential copyright problems by buying up the rights to the play. Later on, some also thought that the name was changed to avoid any confusion between the picture and a 1934 picture John Ford had directed at Fox that had the same title.

"This is a big picture," Hellinger wrote at the beginning of his story. "It is either big—or it is nothing at all. For, while it deals with a specific set of humans, the background is far more important than the characters. And the background is the history of an era." But, from the start, the studio had problems shaping Hellinger's story into a workable audience pleaser. First called *Night at Tony Pastor's* before the studio went back to calling it *The World Moves On,* the property elicited little enthusiasm from studio principals. In an attempt to save the studio some money, the producer Bob Lord sat down and wrote a treatment himself from Hellinger's original story and sent it for review to the screenwriter Niven Busch, who wrote to him on July 25, 1938: "Dear Bob: If you will walk up to a mirror and take one of those long, horrifying looks into your soul that a writer has to take occasionally, you will realize that you don't like the treatment you wrote on *The World Moves On.* Much as I love you, I don't like it either."[11] This story was not the first to elicit witticisms between Warner Bros. writers.

By March 1939, the plot still had not thickened. In a March 7 memo to Wallis, the screenwriter Warren Duff had some thoughts about his own work on the script, which he thought not nearly strong enough yet as a story about the Prohibition era:

> I'm of the opinion we'd wind up with a couple of dissolves (and the majority of the incidents would be old stuff), and then be left with a threadbare story on our hands all about a gangster (emasculated by the Hays office) whose main purpose in life is to make a lot of money and make love to a little girl, and the girl, whose main purpose in life is to demonstrate that the love of blue-blood is better than the love of a mugg. And the terrific wallop at the end proves that while the mugg may have been a dirty heel and murdered dozens of the boys, he still has a heart of gold . . . where that little girl is concerned. If that isn't maudlin—I'm a green-eyed grasshopper, and if it is an exciting premise, I've been playing marbles for the last fifteen years. . . . On the other hand, there may be an angle to it. Somebody may see something in it that completely escapes me. I don't know. I only know that for me to attempt to make a good script out of it

would hurry my inevitable entrance into the booby-hatch. And you could spare me that.[12]

By May, the picture at least had a director, Anatole Litvak, although not for long. Production files indicate that, since the script was so long in the shaping, Litvak had to move on to another picture. When Walsh was given the assignment in June, no explanation was given—but he was not asking for one either, a habit he kept over the next couple of decades. He was now on board directing his first picture for Warner Bros.

Yet what would soon be retitled *The Roaring Twenties* still lacked a cohesive script. As was the studio's habit, a long list of contract writers found themselves assigned to the picture and subsequently taken off of it. By the time Hal Wallis invited Jerry Wald and his writing partner, Richard Macauley, along with Robert Rossen and Walter McEwen, to his house on the evening of July 13 to discuss the picture, a more permanent script was in the making. Many fingers were in the pot before a workable script emerged, however, including those of the writers John Huston, Bob Lord, John Wexley, Frank Donoghue, Earl Baldwin, and Niven Busch. Final writing credit went to Hellinger for the story and to Wald, Macauley, and Rossen for the screenplay.

Wald, who was gaining clout at Warner Bros., had a background similar to Hellinger's. He had been a fast-talking, fast-writing newspaper reporter himself. Wald has been (inaccurately) identified as the model for Budd Schulberg's scenery-eating character Sammy Glick in the 1941 novel *What Makes Sammy Run?* Wald and Macauley would go on to pen several hard-boiled scripts at Warners, including Walsh's *They Drive by Night* and *Manpower*. Later, as a producer at the studio, Wald would restructure the studio's adaptation of James M. Cain's novella *Mildred Pierce*, writing a screenplay for it that put the story in flashback form and added the murder of Mildred's husband, Monty Barragan, neither of which was in James M. Cain's novel.

Hellinger's story of three men who survive World War I and return to a less than welcoming world at home had kick to it by the time Wald, Macauley, and Rossen finished with it, but no one could have foreseen the romantic rush that Walsh would give it, how much sweep his camera would infuse into the story, and how seamlessly that large sweep would be bound up with the intimate story of its main characters' lives, as if each character, each life, represented a much larger story. Walsh transformed *The Roaring Twenties* into a romantic saga of an exhilarating American decade—a formidable performance by a director, considering it was Walsh's first Warner Bros. venture.

James Cagney and Humphrey Bogart were cast as two doughboys who survive the trenches of World War I and return to American soil. George Hally (Bogart) is a confirmed criminal mind, and Eddie Bartlett (Cagney) is thrown into a life of crime when he cannot get his old job as a taxi driver back and has to make a living somehow. A third character, Lloyd Hart (Jeffrey Lynn), who was in the trenches with Eddie and George, is able to resume his law career even though he ultimately uses it to serve his two criminal buddies.

When Eddie returns home and cannot get his job back, he starts his own taxi business but soon slides all too easily into bootlegging as a way to stay on top of the money game. He also falls in love with a young woman he met before the war, Jean (Pricilla Lane), and gets her a job in a nightclub owned by a big-hearted dame (who is really soft for Eddie), Panama Smith (Gladys George, in a role supposedly based on the real-life Texas Guinan and slated to go to Glenda Farrell, then Ann Sheridan, even Lee Patrick, before George nabbed it). In a paradigm that Orson Welles later used in *Citizen Kane,* Eddie tries to push a singing career on Jean, even though it is obvious that she has little talent to sustain it. But she has more charm than Kane's Susan Alexander and, it seems, more smarts; she gets out of her mediocre career pretty quickly and falls in love with and marries Lloyd Hart. For Eddie this is betrayal—and he begins a downward spiral that ends only in the stunning closing sequence, when he takes a bullet and dies on the steps of a church in Panama's arms.

Walsh had actually worked with Bogart before, directing him in a very small part in *Women of All Nations,* the Victor McLaglen–Edmund Lowe starrer for Fox eight years earlier, even though Bogart's part was so small that, when the picture was released, his scenes ended up on the cutting-room floor. But *The Roaring Twenties* marked Walsh's first picture with Cagney in what would become four memorable outings for the two at Warner Bros. *The Roaring Twenties* would be Cagney's last gangster picture for ten years after playing a thug for nearly a decade and until Walsh directed him ten years later in *White Heat*. The two men formed an immediate and lifelong bond.

In fact, much bonding in general went on between Walsh and the actors during the shoot. When Walsh first saw the script, he went to William Cagney, James Cagney's brother, and pleaded with him to talk Jimmy out of doing the picture. The script was that bad, Walsh told him—a real potboiler. But William Cagney assured him that he would get Jimmy to rewrite it as much as possible. Both Walsh and Cagney found a kinship in doing that, and working on this script brought them closer together. Others also gave the script some help: studio files reveal that Bogart, Cagney, and Frank McHugh, Cagney's great offscreen buddy, who plays Danny, Eddie's close pal in the picture, also worked after hours on revisions. Cagney later said, "Raoul Walsh asked me how I liked the opening scene as written, and I said I thought it was pretty bad, as indeed it was. 'I think so, too,' Raoul said. 'I've got a new one. Want to hear it?' I told him to fire away, and after he finished telling it, I told him the one I had in mind. Then Frank McHugh said he had one, so Raoul and I listened to Frank's, and by the end of his description, Raoul and I said, 'There it is!' So we shot Frank's, and one hell of a good opening it was."[13] Walsh and Cagney developed a style of working: no matter what the script said, they thought to go one better and set about revising and molding Cagney's characters as they saw fit. They scored few points with Hal Wallis on this. Cagney told interviewers more than once that he especially liked working with Walsh because, if Cagney was unsure about "what the hell to do," Walsh would just get up and show him how to do it.

As soon as shooting began on *The Roaring Twenties* on July 10, 1939, Walsh and Cagney of course got to work softening Eddie Bartlett's character, which angered Wallis to no end since he saw it as a transgression; memos began to fly when, while watching the dailies, he also noticed new dialogue. He ordered the associate producer Sam Bischoff to "check on this immediately and if the script is being rewritten on the set I want it stopped." Finding that Walsh was the culprit (Cagney escaped notice), Wallis implored Bischoff,

Have a talk with [him] about this immediately and tell him that when the script comes down to him as final, it is to be shot that way. Of course, I don't mind, and as a matter of fact will welcome, any comedy lines or business that he can add to the present script, but I do not want him to rewrite complete scenes on the set, as, for example, the scene where the boys get their mail. Also, you might talk with Walsh about the shooting of those huge close-ups. I don't like to cut those big heads in from medium and long shots and I don't think he ought to move up quite so close on people unless it is for an important reaction, a love scene, or something of the kind.[14]

Wallis was just beginning his campaign to have Walsh shoot fewer close-ups and far more expansive shots. He wanted those sets the studio spent so much money to build to be caught onscreen as well. The campaign raged on for several years.

Wallis wrote Walsh even on July 26,

I notice that you are still changing lines occasionally, and particularly when Cagney is involved in a scene. For example, the other night in the scene in the garage where he hires the three mugs out of jail, you cut out the speech at the end of the scene where Cagney told the three men never to try to pull anything on him or he'd take care of them—or something to that effect. I assume it was cut because Cagney didn't want to be the tough guy again, but you must insist on keeping these things in because they are necessary for his characterization. He is a very nice guy all through the story and if he occasionally has a scene where he has to be tough, you must insist on having it done that way in order to keep the characterization correct. After all, he is a tough guy and in a tough racket, hijacking liquor, raiding warehouses and all of that, so that occasionally if he does have lines of this kind he must deliver them. I can see no reason for cutting them.[15]

Wallis lost little love for Walsh, even if he had to admit that this director cost him little money by almost always coming in on budget and on schedule. Walsh's early responses to Wallis have been lost.

Memos especially also flew regarding the picture's famous last scene, when the cops shoot Eddie in front of a church and he staggers down the steps and dies in the arms of Panama Smith. Wallis, Walsh, Cagney, and even Warner had a hand in it. Walsh later said, "We always walked through a scene like that, of that length—from the house all the way down the street to the church. We walked through that with the cameraman, for the lights to follow Jimmy. It was Jimmy's idea to fall into that ashcan and knock it over, and then I told him, 'Stagger up the steps.' What I figured for him to do was die in the gutter. So he got halfway up the church steps, he staggered, fell, and rolled down and died in the gutter."[16]

The picture's production files tell a more convoluted story of the picture's last scene, with both Wallis and Warner trying to orchestrate the way Walsh shot it. Warner wrote to Wallis on August 29, 1939:

> I ran *The Roaring Twenties* dailies last night, and unless Walsh has more stuff of Cagney dying on the church steps, we will have to take all the long shots over. . . . In the first place, you do not know it is a church. Secondly, he has four drunks come by and somehow or other unless he uses at least 20 people with a little more excitement than the one cut of the policeman taking it, one shot of him running, a real long shot of the small figure and Gladys George on the bottom of the church steps, so that the audience has the feeling it is in front of a church, it doesn't mean a thing. . . . The way it is now, outside of the close-ups it is almost worthless and will have to be carefully cut because you will notice in all the takes where Gladys George is bending over talking to Cagney, and light coming on his gray shirt, shows his breathing and that he is very much alive.

In addition to instructing verbatim the dialogue that has the cop asking, "Who is this fellow?" and George answering, "He used to be a big shot," Wallis wanted the last scene shot a certain way: "At the end of the scene from her close-up, after she reads the line . . . pull back and up into a long shot, so that we leave the three small figures on the church steps, the girl holding Cagney in her lap, the cop standing alongside, and we can use that for our fadeout shot."[17] The final shot of the released version includes no people in the background. Later, Walsh took credit for devising the last shot as audiences finally saw it.

The Roaring Twenties encapsulated and commented on a stellar decade of Warner Bros. gangster films, but Walsh kept in character and never took credit for his overall achievement. When students or interviewers asked him why it took Cagney so long to die in that scene, he threw out a joke instead: "Well, it's damn hard to kill an actor."

Cagney's Eddie Bartlett is a character true to Walsh's screen lineage of the conflicted man with a soft core wrapped in a harder-than-nails demeanor. Walsh had been honing this character since his silent-movie days and came up with Eddie's truest prototype when he created the character of the hoodlum in *Regeneration* in 1915. He knows goodness in himself even though he is attracted to the evil in all men's souls. When he embarks on an adventure, the huge social forces that work against him outmatch him. Warner Bros. was adept at fine-tuning pictures where these social forces are darker and more powerful than the individual men and women swept up in them. With his first Warner Bros. feature, then, Walsh was at home. He never compromises Eddie's integrity as a man who does the wrong thing but remains aware of what the right thing is and what he has given up. Walsh transforms his seemingly small, intimate conflict into a grand, representative conflict of a generation and a nation. His camera foregrounds the intimate drama, setting it up against sweeping crowds and huge social forces.

When Warners released *The Roaring Twenties* on October 23, 1939, Walsh found himself on the inside track at the studio; he had a critical and financial hit on his hands. *Boxoffice* magazine wrote, "It will roar its way across the showmen's ledger leaving a trail of black figures and satisfied customers, this lightning-paced action melodrama of the prohibition era, its evils and its laughs."[18] The *Variety* critic wrote, "Warner Brothers comes through with a semi-historical film about the hysterical prohibition era that should exact a nice toll at the box office."[19] *The Roaring Twenties* took its place among a crowd of pictures in 1939 that made that year into one of the most talked-about years in Hollywood production. The picture was popular enough at the time of its release that Warner Bros. planned a sequel, taken from a Milton Krims scenario, that Walsh would direct: *The Fabulous Thirties,* also set to feature Cagney and Bogart. Nothing came of it, but Walsh had already met with the kind of good script he had needed for years.

Penance for John Wayne

As soon as he finished shooting *The Roaring Twenties,* Walsh took advantage of his option to work outside Warner Bros. From November 1, 1939, through the beginning of February 1940, he went to Republic Pictures to direct John Wayne in the western *Dark Command.* He no doubt appreciated the $25,000 the studio paid him. If nothing else, this way he could put some distance between himself and the confining, often claustrophobic soundstages that made up the Warner lot's "New York Street." Walsh always sought location shooting. Now he took the opportunity to enjoy a vacation, of sorts, outdoors on location, first at the Placenta Ranch in Newhall, California, then at Sherwood Forest, north of Los Angeles. He also wanted the chance to work with Wayne again and maybe do penance for the havoc *The Big Trail* wreaked on the actor's career ten years earlier when it performed so poorly at the box office. Wayne's career then landed in the B-western bin for almost the entire 1930s, until, as legend has it, John Ford rescued him and made a star out of him in *Stagecoach* (1939).[20]

Walsh took a great liking to W. R. Burnett's novel *Dark Command* (Burnett also penned what would become Walsh's 1941 *High Sierra*) and convinced Republic's Herb Yates to put it into production. Republic poured more money into the picture than it usually did at the time—as a way to enhance its new hot property, Wayne. Coming off Warners' hit *The Roaring Twenties,* Walsh only enhanced the production. The story was a somewhat fictional rendering of Quantrill's Raiders, with Wayne as a young Texas marshal who opposes the murderous and guerrilla tactics of the politician Will Cantrell (Walter Pidgeon). Claire Trevor plays the woman they both love, and Roy Rogers has an early role as Trevor's younger brother. Some of the film's highlights are an engrossing scene where the town of Lawrence, Kansas, burns to the ground and a spectacular cliff jump by the ace stuntman Yakima Canutt (who also handled second unit for Walsh on the picture) and three other stuntmen.

"But the story's banal," Walsh later said. "There was a bad man,

Quantrell's Raiders, the hero's love for the girl and finally the death of the bad guy. Truly a classic story! But because many of the scenes were cut, the film seems a bit odd; probably due to the fact that the action doesn't run on, the whole thing seems confused and badly directed."[21] Walsh had no final cut on this picture.

Walsh's producer was Sol C. Siegel, and their working relationship was brief enough that no conflicts arose. In 1987, Claire Trevor said, "Raoul Walsh was very impersonal. Very often he'd say, 'Now we're going to do this scene,' very cold. He'd sit down, 'You know what to do,' and sometimes when the camera was rolling, he'd turn his back and walk away. But that was his style, and he cared, I know, but he looked like he didn't care. I don't know why he did that."[22] Walsh had a habit of leaving his actors and crew confused about his motives. He seemed nonchalant about his job, but especially at this early point in his Warner Bros. career, even if out on loan to Republic, he felt anything but nonchalant. He had eased up from his noted manic behavior in the 1910s, but he still meant business when it came to getting the picture completed on time.

Now, in 1940, though Wayne and his career hardly needed boosting, *Dark Command* garnered large critical and box-office approval and became the only Republic Picture to be nominated for two Academy Awards: for John Victor Mackay's art direction and Victor Young's original musical score. The word around Hollywood was that, since John Ford had come to Wayne's rescue in 1939 by casting him as Ringo in *Stagecoach,* he should have been the one keeping Wayne at the top of the list for good roles. Instead, Walsh hoisted Wayne up there again by giving him star billing in *Dark Command.*

Although it had always seemed a good-natured competition between the two directors as to who really discovered Wayne, Ford apparently resented Walsh in no small measure—or at least more than Walsh or Wayne realized. Henry Fonda once told the Wayne biographer Michael Munn, "Duke Wayne loved Ford, and I'm sure that from time to time, Ford loved Duke. But Ford was just so jealous when Raoul Walsh beefed up Duke's career after *Stagecoach* [with *Dark Command*]. It was just unforgivable, and I know that Ford made him pay for it by letting him stew in films that really kept Duke out of the so-called A-list of stars for a long time. Duke was still part of the Ford clan and we all went on fishing trips together."[23] The Ford biographer Joseph McBride confirms another version of Ford's "mysterious" snubbing of Wayne, indicating how far back it went. Ford did not speak to Wayne for three years after Wayne appeared in Walsh's *The Big Trail,* and, since Wayne could not figure out the reason, he soon gave up trying to understand.[24] What seemed a good-natured rivalry to Walsh was far more threatening to Ford.

Sandwiched between Walsh's two more celebrated Warner Bros. movies *The Roaring Twenties* and his upcoming *They Drive by Night, Dark Command* tends to be overlooked. Yet it is a marker of Walsh's ever-evolving body of work with historical figures—insofar as he could romanticize them. He painted Steve Brodie as a daredevil, devil-may-care young upstart whom the audience identifies with like mad because he is so likeable. Walsh's George Custer and Jim Corbett would be far more polished, sophisticated versions of this type. In between them is Pidgeon's Will Cantrell, a heavy, but still of the gentlest ilk. Pidgeon and Wayne go at it as if just emerging from the pages of a chivalric novel. Walsh admired Burnett enormously and found his characters to have a depth he could play on. Burnett's characters here mark Walsh's deepening expression of men who meant something to him: heroic, almost cavalier, yet dangerous around the edges.

On April 20, 1940, William Lewin at the National Education Association sent Walsh a letter accompanying a study guide to *Dark Command,* published by Educational and Recreations Guides, Inc. Lewin told Walsh that the guide would be used in more than ten thousand schools and colleges across the country and in Canada "where photoplay appreciation" was now being taught. Although he may have been flattered by this, it was far more important for Walsh that he go for the quip. He later said of *Dark Command,* "It was one of the biggest moneymakers Republic ever had. I put everybody in it. Walter Pidgeon—he gave one hell of a performance—Marjorie Main, Roy Rogers, Gabby Hayes. I put everybody in it but my mother-in-law."[25]

Walsh offered these throwaway lines to shield himself from others peering in too closely, using this kind of humor to create a facade of self-mockery and self-deprecation. He was no stranger to making himself the object of verbal jabs, a trait that also seeped into his characters onscreen. They are often shaken by the real world, often making them defensive in front of others: Ann Sheridan's cocky waitress in *They Drive by Night,* even Bogart's Roy Earle in *High Sierra*. Their painful self-deprecation makes them sadly but fully three-dimensional. Their wisecracks reveal a jaded soul and a sad view of themselves in a dark world. Walsh's easy sympathies for these kinds of characters easily spilled over into his off-screen life, often taking shape as his habit of taking care of actors who had fallen on rough times, his penchant for making sure he could spread the wealth around to friends. If he could hire them, he would—just as he had when he hired family and friends on the set in the 1920s. His empathy for people around him deepened his art as well—coloring his fictional men and women as being real and natural in their surroundings.

With *The Roaring Twenties*, Walsh entered into an even more complex artistic and psychological nexus that, little wonder, would make him a darling of the French New Wave critics some thirty years down the road. He could have been the poster boy for the director as auteur that Truffaut, Godard, and their group defined, the director who works within the studio system committed to genre yet struggles against the system and the markers of its generic product. The American film critic Manny Farber, writing in the early 1970s, saw Walsh's films as quirky, unconscious oddities and saw the man as a director who, though he believed strongly in the genres he worked with, couldn't help but break out of them at the same time. He especially liked Walsh's "little big shot" in *The Roaring Twenties*, a character type who could reincarnate into many Warner Bros. "types" in other pictures.[26] Farber thought it a mistake for Walsh to be seen as the director of the grand sweep of the outdoor adventure story. Farber is correct—as a Warner Bros. workhorse, Walsh got in touch with his own poetry. He became the poet of the down and out, the sorrowful soul. This much he shared with the Warner Bros. paradigm of the down and out, even as he busted out of it now and again by changing dialogue, contouring characters to fit his own perspective. He inched closer to his own deeply felt yet secreted sorrows.

Farber's observations of Walsh again point to him as being an unwilling, perhaps unconscious artist of the American social scene. Whether his scene was an outdoor landscape or the anxiety of the urban street, Walsh always became lost in the telling of a story. As it often is, the love of telling stories emerges from a psyche that is chipped in some fundamental way, having experienced a deep sadness, a great loss, that finds expression in fiction—in the alternate world that fiction provides. Now at Warner Bros., Walsh found material that suited him. His gangsters lighted out on great adventures even as they were doomed. They never escaped the wish to light out, just as they never escaped the doom. Walsh saw this as generic packaging, never as artfulness or psychology that emerged from his own soul. "I just did my job," he always said. Yet his three-dimensional characters emerged effortlessly from what his colleagues often noted as his deep sense of humanity—onscreen and off. His friends the French producer Pierre Rissient and the filmmaker Bertrand Tavernier, both of whom he met in later life, talked about what they always considered his easy embrace of various moods within one story, something Rissient would call "Shakespearean," Walsh's ability to flow effortlessly from one emotional pitch to another, one kind of action to another.[27]

Walsh was accomplishing much more than just "doing the job," as he would call it. At Warner Bros., he found the consistency he needed and the independence he craved. At this early point at the studio, he felt supported by Jack Warner (if not always by Hal Wallis) without having to feel emotionally connected to anyone, save for Errol Flynn later on and his Irish cronies Cagney, Alan Hale, and Frank McHugh now. In this kind of environment, he could make pictures he considered entertaining but not necessarily great works of art; movies as art, personal expression, or social statement had no conscious meaning for Walsh. He meant to entertain—to *be* entertained—and to create a character and a situation he believed plausible. Then he went home at the end of the day.

In turn, to some who worked there, Warner Bros. was not a studio that necessarily cultivated close relationships or emotional bonds between directors, actors, writers, and producers (the other studios did no better at it either). "At Warner Bros. there was not a feeling of rapport, or of caring," said Joan Leslie, whom Walsh would direct the next year in *High Sierra*.[28] Now in his early sixties, Walsh was financially secure and studio supported. He needed little more than that, he believed, just the time to have an enjoyable day on the set and afterward just as much time to attend to his love of horse buying and betting. Every time he could he would go on location to some exotic part of the world or, at the very least, somewhere away from his own backyard.

A Woman Scorned

But, no matter how much success Walsh enjoyed in directing Cagney and Bogie, his relationship with the front office was dictated by personal finances. Miriam Cooper was the main reason Walsh borrowed money from Warner and the studio throughout his years there—although the debt he occasionally incurred from his betting on the horses ran a close second. Although divorced since 1927 and married to Lorraine since 1928—even if Lorraine never figured as prominently in his psychology as did making movies and playing the horses—Walsh could never be rid of Miriam. By 1939, he and Lorraine were living in grand style, up above the city at 624 North Doheny Road in Beverly Hills, in an estate just across the road from the fabled Doheny mansion. Walsh had less than half an hour's drive to the studio in Burbank and, in general, thought himself very lucky.

Back in 1939, Walsh had sold the Encino ranch to his friends Clark Gable and Carole Lombard, just prior to their marriage. He had bought the ranch on Petit Street in 1931, and he and Lorraine had been using it as a weekend getaway cottage. Gable and Lombard thought of Petit as their dream house, with its creamy white wood interiors and, of course, its stables at the back of the property. Walsh said that Gable had been trying to buy the property from him for years ("I waited a few more years after his last plea to me before I sold it to him").[29] Though frequently savvy with real estate, Walsh was also frequently in financial trouble. "He was not a man who was taking care of his money—a fact that many friends understood. Everyone said that of Walsh," Pierre Rissient later said.[30] Also, he was becoming fed up with his social life with Lorraine, and that would finally take its toll and lead to their divorce in 1946. But, for now, he continued to face financial problems, much of this owing to the fact that he could never fully free himself from Miriam's financial hold. She continued accusing him of reneging on alimony and hounded him with a court battle every few years. She first took him to court in 1933 for unpaid alimony of $2,350, accrued because, according to Miriam, he "refused" to pay most monies and what he did give her amounted to a total of $650.[31] Just as Walsh began warming up to Warner Bros., in 1939, his financial battles with Miriam also began to heat up and often made headlines in the *Los Angeles Times* and the *New York Times*. In one instance, Miriam tried to "recover" $46,000 from Walsh and attempted to attach his Doheny Road home.[32]

Miriam still lived in New York, and the boys were now grown. In 1940, wanting to get away from his mother, eighteen-year-old Robert petitioned and won the right to live in California with Walsh, placing himself under his guardianship. In March of the same year, during what was otherwise a good financial time for Walsh, now earning more recognition and better projects at the studio, he was forced to open a new kind of relationship with Warner and the higher-ups. Miriam still received money from Walsh, whose reliability in prompt monthly payments to her could often be wanting. In the time that he directed his first five films at the studio, he began to use those pictures as collateral for monies he had to pay to a woman who still drained him of his emotional energy. He often depended on the studio to loan him money, make advances on his salary—all in the name, so he said, of getting the very emotionally sticky Miriam off his back. He was not able to do that for years.

8

Out of the Night
At Home at Warner Bros.

Walsh now prepared to direct his next venture at Warner Bros., the Jerry Wald–Richard Macauley scripted *They Drive by Night,* another hard-knocks drama produced by Mark Hellinger and executive produced by the ever-vigilant Hal Wallis. With its dark and gritty palate, its broken-down characters who try to but cannot outdistance or overcome their milieu of psychological and economic hard times, *They Drive by Night* is quintessential Warner Bros. of the 1940s, a picture in the tradition of what the critic Manny Farber later called the "broken field journey," his descriptive way of talking about films in which characters break down emotionally on a road fraught with peril. Drawn partly from a novel by A. I. Bezzerides, and partly recycled from an earlier Warner Bros. picture, *Bordertown,* starring Bette Davis, this picture, like Walsh's *Manpower* to come, offers moviegoers the cinematic equivalent of literary naturalism—a story characterized by the inability of men and women to control or to get out from under the unforgiving social forces that loom large and significant around them. Walsh gave his hard-knocks characters both a lyricism and a biting wit in this story of two brothers who try to make a go of it as truckers in Los Angeles but find only heartache and hard times for their efforts. Halfway through, the story gets sideswiped by another completely different plotline when one of the brothers becomes romantically involved with a woman who turns psychotic, murders her husband, and implicates the brother in her crime. More intimate than *The Roaring Twenties, They Drive by Night* offers one of the best demonstrations in Walsh's body of work of how effortlessly and naturally he segues between hope and hopelessness, humor and pathos. It is ample proof of just how easily Walsh and Warner Bros. entered into a marriage of shared artistic and storytelling sensibilities.

Working with Wallis, the brilliant taskmaster, directing from scripts by some of Hollywood's greatest writers—Wald and Macauley, John Huston, and, of course, W. R. Burnett—Walsh saw his output take on a new edginess, a forceful creative drive. There was never as much poetry or tightly wound tough-guy aesthetics in a Walsh picture as there was in his work during these Warner Bros. years.

Field of Broken Dreams

They Drive by Night became one of the most noneventful shoots Walsh had encountered in a long time, the easiness of his work at the studio standing in direct contrast to the chaos swimming around him in his personal life. Walsh's checks to Miriam Cooper were very often late—even no-shows; he resented giving her his money. When it was time either to send her some or to spend it on a horse instead, Miriam ran a distant second. In turn, she continued to drag him into court. During production on this picture, Walsh was in a Los Angeles courtroom twice and even missed a court date because his adopted daughter, Marilynn, opened the door to their Doheny Road home, took a subpoena in his absence, and neglected to give it to him. To further complicate Walsh's life, his son Robert now filed to have Walsh appointed his guardian. Robert won the case, and Walsh found himself with a son whom, to be truthful, he neither wanted nor wanted to be close to. Everything associated with Miriam seemed to be sucking the life out of him.

Now, still trying to extricate himself financially and psychologically from Miriam, Walsh no doubt approached *They Drive by Night* with a vivid understanding of the human abyss into which a woman could send a man—just the kind of awareness he needed to get this film made. As if his life were designed by some kind of perverted serendipity, he now found himself directing a picture whose emotional centerpiece was a deranged woman who attempts to bring down her lover since she cannot have him to herself. Walsh could have had little doubt that the psychological havoc unleashed in this film by a woman bore an uncanny resemblance to that brought on by the first Mrs. Walsh. He could hardly have missed the irony.

The woman on the screen was Lana, played by Ida Lupino, in a recycled version of Bette Davis's psychotic wife in Warners' 1935 *Bor-*

dertown. She makes life miserable for the man she loves and for the husband she eventually kills. She was just part of a pattern that Walsh's life fell into in these months during production. Days were spent watching Lana destroy her husband, destroy the brother, and subsequently fall apart in a psychotic break in the courtroom where she stands trial for her husband's murder. Then evenings were spent walking in the front door of his home only to find a letter or receive a phone call from his or Miriam's attorney relaying the latest litigation and torture. Truth was worse than fiction: just as Lana kills her husband, clearly Walsh thought Miriam was killing him, or at the very least taking a good emotional chunk out of him.

Warner Bros. bought the rights to A. I. Bezzerides's novel *Long Haul* in March 1940 for $2,000 with plans to turn it into a screenplay; Hal Wallis changed its title to *They Drive by Night* a month later. Jack Warner was so pleased with Walsh's rendering of *The Roaring Twenties* that he gave him first crack at directing the project, another scripted by the crackerjack writing team Jerry Wald and Richard Macauley. From the beginning, Wallis saw the picture as a vehicle for George Raft, who had inched his way up in the studio's estimation and now had clout. Raft plays Joe Fabrini, the story's main character, and Humphrey Bogart—in his last time as second fiddle—plays Joe's brother, Paul Fabrini. Warners' "Oomph Girl" Ann Sheridan was cast as Cassie Hartley, Joe's girlfriend, and Alan Hale plays Lana's unfortunate husband, Ed Carlson. As the Fabrini brothers' trucking chums, the zany character actor Roscoe Karns and the ever-reliable funny man George Tobias add plenty of flavor.

Wallis was excited early on about the story and in the middle of March told Walsh in a memo, "I am glad that you are hopped up on the trucking story. I too feel that it will work out as an excellent vehicle for George Raft. I am entirely in accord with your idea to go out within the next few weeks whenever we get good weather and clouds and make some of the road shots. Will you please begin to line up a truck immediately and after you have made a selection let me see it?"[1] Actual production on the picture had not yet begun, and Wallis still spoke in a friendly tongue to Walsh.

Mark Hellinger again produced and brought Walsh in with him on the process of fine-tuning Wald and Macauley's script. He wrote Wallis a few days later, "Wald, Walsh and I never stopped talking about it all evening—and when guys are that enthused, something good must come of it." Hellinger wanted the young British actress Ida Lupino for the part of Lana, but Walsh had several other actresses in mind, including Frances Farmer and another, as yet untested, starlet, Catherine Emery. He wrote Wallis, "I saw the test of Catherine Emery and she is a splendid actress and I am sure she could give a fine and intelligent performance of the part of Lana. I think she can be photographed a little more attractively. She has a refined quality, that if she plays the part, I would like to modify." "I would prefer to withhold my decision," he added, "until I make a test of Frances Farmer."[2] But Hellinger moved faster than or played harder than Walsh, and Lupino was signed soon after Walsh's memo to Wallis.

Warners lathered up short biographies for each of the principal characters. Joe Fabrini, the protagonist, is "a quiet, forceful man in his thirties, stubbornly convinced through all adversity that his destiny lies with the trucking business." His brother, Paul, dreamed of a better life than that; he saw nothing but grief in spending his life in a truck cab. Cassie, Joe's girlfriend, is a product of the urban soil that produced her, "a good-looking girl who would do better in better times. She has no particular breeding or background but she is a pretty solid person, who knows her own limitation, and doesn't try to exceed it." In essence, Cassie is a generic Warner Bros. girl of the 1940s. Ed Carlsen, the man who hires Fabrini, is a hearty, beefy lug who rose to wealth through "the happy accident of a shrewdly invested and managed inheritance." Ed's wife, Lana, finds him loud and vulgar. She is a complete Warner Bros. fabrication—a psychotic about to blow.[3]

Production began on April 22, 1940, and finished five weeks later. Walsh shot the film in sequence, using studio soundstages for interiors and the highways on the outskirts of Los Angeles for exterior scenes. Lupino considered this her first important picture and later said, "When I was on the [witness] stand . . . I wasn't maniacal. I was quiet. I was simple. I was a child who was not a child. That's madness."[4] Walsh got on well with Lupino; they would work together again soon. Bogart was easy to be around—when he was in a good mood, which, of course, depended on the kind of night he'd had with his then wife, Mayo Methot. He would complain more than the others, maybe about the food, maybe about the hotels they stayed in on location. Walsh learned quickly enough that Bogart enjoyed complaining.

But Walsh had not forgotten working with the irritable, argumentative Raft and didn't look forward to what could be another bout with the actor. Typical behavior for Walsh, he kept his concerns to himself and never complained to Wallis. Instead, he showed only enthusiasm for the picture. As it turned out, production on *They Drive by Night* remained uneventful. (It was not until Walsh's next time directing Raft, one year later on *Manpower,* that Raft became troublesome and directed his wrath at Edward G. Robinson, not at Walsh.) For right now, Walsh remembered, "Raft was speaking to me again. . . . He seemed to have forgotten *The Bowery.* His acting had improved since the day I told him to jump off the Brooklyn Bridge. He was better at memorizing dialogue and he was careful about the way he dressed. He was also a star in his own right."[5]

But the conflicts between Wallis and Walsh began again. As was becoming habitual, Wallis accused Walsh of closing in on the actors' faces too often. He wrote him on May 6:

I remember okaying a budget of 10,000 or 15,000 to fix up the street down there and get a little bit of atmosphere into it, but so far, I have seen nothing but close shots of the cab, the boys getting out of it and panning them into close action with other people as in the scene where they sold the lemons to George Tobias. . . . Everything is done in short pan shots without any of the atmosphere of the street being shown, and for the amount of background that has been shown in this stuff so far, we could have used the New York street without spending any money on it. It isn't so much that I'm trying to get our money's worth out of the set, as it is that I'm trying to get the atmosphere into the picture, and I wish that when you go back there you would watch this and get some interesting setups, some long shots of the street, and then when the truck comes into it you can pan with it, but at least let's get back a ways and see what the boys are coming into and establish the fact that it is a market.[6]

Walsh capitulated somewhat to Wallis because he had his mind on other aspects of the film. The lightning pace belongs to Walsh, as it did throughout his years at Warners. *They Drive by Night* moves forward with a relentless, driving, masculine energy, making it a rhythmic precursor to Walsh's highly energized *White Heat,* which would come almost a decade later. The view of the world in *They Drive by Night*—that the downtrodden have to tough it out, even though that does not ensure success or happiness—is a theme that Walsh and the studio crafted well. Walsh moved the camera back, but just enough to give the characters some leg room. Raft and the not-yet-above-the-title Bogart play two brothers who try to start a trucking business in California just before World War II. But they are held back repeatedly from getting things off the ground. It is almost impossible for the small guy to get successful when the bigger guys, the corporations, the tough and the mean, stand in the way.

Trying to get ahead in a universe that dares them not to, Bogart's and Raft's characters go from hard knocks to tragedy. Transporting fruit from grower to seller, they are able to make a few dollars and buy their own truck. But, one night, Bogart falls asleep at the wheel, the truck turns over, and Bogie loses an arm in an accident that demolishes the truck. Raft, always the steadier and more ambitious of the two, is forced to work for a friend, Ed Carlsen (Alan Hale), who owns a larger, more successful trucking company. Although Raft has already met Sheridan and plans to marry the street-smart waitress with a heart of gold, Ed's flirtatious and up-to-no-good wife, Lana, falls hard for him and makes countless plays for his affections. So unstable is she that she eventually murders Ed to clear the path to having Raft for herself. But Raft still will have nothing to do with her. When he learns that she murdered Hale, he turns her in. But she convinces the DA that Raft forced her to murder her husband, and Raft finds himself on trial. While on the witness stand, however, Lana suffers a breakdown (driven mad by her guilt over killing Hale), spilling the truth, and Joe is cleared of any charges. This is storytelling so dark that Walsh's dark humor seeps through every scene—also driving the story on.

The picture cost almost $500,000 to make; the studio paid Walsh $17,500. After he finished shooting, however, the studio called in the director Vincent Sherman to shoot another scene. Sherman was asked to keep the shoot under his hat and to complete it "as soon as possible." It concerned a group of newsmen at the trial just as they learn that Lana has broken down and confessed the murder: "City desk! . . . [Each man reaches for a phone.] The doctors say she's daffy. Yeah, she's gone nuts. . . . They had to take her away in a straightjacket. The case has been thrown out. Fabrini goes free." Ironically, however, the scene blended in seamlessly.

Warner Bros. released *They Drive by Night* on August 3, 1940, premiering it at the Stanley Warner Theatre in Beverly Hills—this despite a legal threat by the American Trucking Association that had both Harry and Jack Warner worried. The ATA claimed that depicting Bogie's character as asleep at the wheel was "detrimental to the trucking industry" and "a direct slap at the effective safety regulations of the Interstate Commerce Commission (a driver can't go more than ten hours and must rest every eight hours before returning to work)."[7] However, the studio headed off any legal action, and the film's story stayed intact.

The studio tapped its brilliant publicist Martin Weiser to invent a creative exploitation tactic to promote the picture. He made plans for a fifteen-ton big rig to motor across the country collecting a host of "good wishes" from the 500,000 members of the International Brotherhood of Teamsters that, on reaching its West Coast destination, would be delivered to Ann Sheridan. Making numerous stops between Chicago and Los Angeles, the truck accumulated the painted autographs of truckers, mayors, and members of fan clubs. The big rig became big news and was called "'the Sheridan truck.'"[8] Sheridan was not actually present.

The grittiness of *They Drive by Night* negotiates the world on uneasy terms, a sense of loneliness and doom that never seems to lift. Sadness and gloom exude from the characters' faces, from their bodies, in fact. Walsh managed characters such as these with great ease even though he would never want to be praised for creating complex characters. He would be far more interested in talking about the mechanics of a setup, the aesthetic of creating a bit of action (curious for a director who Wallis believed closed in on characters' faces far too much). He also preferred to talk about this film's production itself—about its unevenness and its sudden change of focus about two-thirds of the way through, moving it from Raft and Bogart to Lupino's increasing nuttiness. "I guess they ran out of the trucking idea and tacked on that ending with Lupino going nuts on the stand. . . . That got her a seven-year contract at Warner Bros., you know," he said, as if standing far back from being the major creative force driving the picture. As it turned out, a decision was made to rehash Bette Davis's murder of Paul Muni and subsequent nervous breakdown on the witness stand in *Bordertown*. But Walsh never made it clear who called for the change. He had nothing to do with it.

Walsh maintained a curious relationship to the studio's front office during his early years at Warner Bros. He had little say in final decisions about a film's editing but made it clear, publicly at least, that it never bothered him. He had not been in the business for all these years for nothing. He repeated his old adage: the director was not supposed to have the right to the last cut, so he found a way to work around it. He shot scenes in such a way as to make it impossible to cut the picture any other way than the way he planned it to look. Before he arrived at Warners, Walsh was one of the few directors to have fights with Darryl Zanuck over cutting. He recalled Zanuck being a ruthless editor. But he couldn't cut Walsh's films simply because there was, according to Walsh, nothing to cut.

For Walsh, the highlight of making any picture was the personal contact he had with actors and crew, but not during actual shooting because he never fooled around or talked much on the set. He spoke to others only if he had to ask a question or make certain they understood him. His behavior baffled many, and it never altered: year after year, actor after actor described Walsh as looking enthusiastic about directing large-scale scenes of armies, horses, and chases yet looking away from the camera, even walking away from it and heading into the dark crevices of the soundstage, when the camera focused on an intimate scene between two actors. Still, Walsh could talk incessantly about the friendships he made and kept. He called Bogart "Bogey the Beefer," his affectionate term for a man he thought complained about anything having to do with picturemaking. He and Bogie got along, but sometimes it was touch and go, depending on whether Walsh was up for hearing Bogie's latest complaint—and there were many while he was still married to Methot. He complained that moviemaking was little more than long hours on the set. He hated every aspect of it. Walsh enjoyed reminding him that he liked the paycheck at the end of the week.

The Height of Gloom

> Chase scenes are very easy to shoot. Just keep going, keep
> going, keep going. Get on top of the mountain, turn around,
> bring them down again, and just hope there's nobody on the
> road.
> —Raoul Walsh

At the time Walsh was shooting *They Drive by Night,* Warner Bros.
was negotiating a deal to buy the writer W. R. Burnett's latest novel,
High Sierra, which had been a *Redbook* Magazine Book of the Month
in March 1940, before Doubleday published it a short time later. From
the start, Jack Warner knew exactly what he had with *High Sierra:* a
first-rate gangster yarn from one of Hollywood's most prolific novelists and screenwriters. Burnett had already penned *Scarface* and *Little
Caesar* for Warner Bros.; both pictures made the studio a good amount
of money. In a few years he would go on to write the screenplay for
This Gun for Hire (1943) and would pen the novel, *The Asphalt Jungle*
(1950). Burnett also wrote Walsh's recent picture for Republic, *Dark
Command.* Walsh never had better material.

Loosely based on the life of John Dillinger, *High Sierra* follows the
story of a hard-edged gangster named Mad Dog Earle who, now just
released from prison in a deal finagled by his cronies outside, reboots
his life of crime by setting out with a group of thugs to rob a casino in a
California mountain resort. When the job is botched, Earle goes on the
lam with a woman he meets in the group, a dance hall girl named Marie.
Although he really loves a young girl named Velma who rejects him, the
desperate Earle begins to soften and falls for Marie. But, with the police
hunting him down, he attempts to escape by climbing atop a mountain
in the California Sierras, where eventually he is shot and killed.

Warner Bros. paid Burnett $12,500 for *High Sierra* and had a lucra-
tive property on its hands. It changed the story's name several times—
from *Back Canyon,* to *Gunman,* to *A Handful of Clouds,* to *I Died
a Thousand Times,* to *The Jagged Edge*—before mercifully reinstating
Burnett's original title.

The studio first offered the part of Mad Dog Earle to Warner top
dog Paul Muni, who reluctantly agreed to take the role if the studio

would also agree to back a favorite idea of his for a picture, a biography of Beethoven. At first Warners agreed to the deal then reneged, angering Muni, who decided to get out of the *High Sierra* project—not directly, but by rejecting each draft of the screenplay brought to him. Essentially on his way out of the studio anyway, Muni got out of the role of Mad Dog Earle in the end. Now all front office eyes fell on George Raft, not the most well-liked actor at the studio, but one who brought in decent enough box-office returns. He was raking in a good salary, and Jack Warner wanted to take advantage of it and make him work harder for it.

Two other men in particular had their eye on Burnett's Mad Dog Earle. One was the up-and-coming writer-director John Huston; the other was Bogart. The two would go on to collaborate on some of the biggest box-office and critical successes Warners would see, including *The Maltese Falcon, The Treasure of the Sierra Madre, To Have and Have Not, The Big Sleep,* and *Key Largo.* When Bogart got wind of the negotiations with Burnett and then heard that Paul Muni might not do the picture (although the word around town already had him signed for the part), he wired Hal Wallis but received no response. He wired him again in a few weeks: "Dear Hal . . . You told me once to let you know when I found a part I wanted. A few weeks ago I left a note for you concerning High Sierra. I never received an answer so I'm bringing it up again as I understand there is some doubt about Muni doing it."[9] Wallis let it go for the moment.

A big fan of Burnett, the Warner writer John Huston became very interested in *High Sierra.* Huston was up and coming on the Warner lot after penning scripts with Lillian Hellman for Samuel Goldwyn Studios and working on the screenplay for Goldwyn's William Wyler–Bette Davis project *Jezebel* in 1938. But, before Huston got a word in to Jack Warner and Hal Wallis about *High Sierra,* the project fell into the hands of the screenwriter Warren Duff, who informed Wallis that he thought the story was "somewhat preposterous." "The best part of the book," Duff said, "is the chase which covers the last third. Here again, the relationship between the man and the girl, the dodges he uses to escape the law, etc., would all give Mr. Breen [the top-dog censor] a severe case of hiccoughs." "The book would," Duff thought, "film as it is and come out as a hard-boiled, sexy gangster-ennobling picture. But that, I understand, is very naughty."[10] None of Duff's wit made the book-to-script process move any faster.

Huston admitted being "a pushover" for W. R. Burnett's "stuff."[11] His enthusiasm matched Mark Hellinger's, who was on board as associate producer, with Hal Wallis as executive producer on this picture. Huston sent a memo lamenting the way Warners had so far misunderstood Burnett:

> It would be very easy for this to be made into the conventional gangster picture, which is exactly what it should not be. With the exception of LITTLE CAESAR, all of Burnett has suffered sadly in screen translation. IRON MEN and DARK HAZARD are both little masterpieces, I think—between covers—and on the screen they were nothing, for the reason, I suppose, that only the outward forms of the novels were followed and the spirit within ignored. . . . Take the spirit out of Burnett, the strange sense of inevitability that comes with our deepening understanding of his characters and the forces that motivate them, and only the conventional husk of a story remains.[12]

Huston's good story sense was helping ensure his rise at the studio. He was no fan of George Raft and was less crazy about the idea of Raft playing Mad Dog Earle. "Everything was intended for George Raft at that time, and I was not among George Raft's greatest admirers," Huston said later. "I thought he was a clown, walking around in his white suit with the padded shoulders and form-fitting hips, and bodyguards. He was very much a Mafia type and liked to display it. And it turned out, poor devil, he came to nothing. He refused everything that was thrown at him. And he refused *High Sierra*. You know, he was really an ignorant man. Poor devil. And I was delighted he didn't do it because Bogie would then play it. And I knew Bogie was a fine actor."[13] Huston could analyze Raft in a way that Walsh would not attempt.

At this juncture, the studio still saw Raft in the role of Earle. By now, *They Drive by Night* was a box-office and critical success, and Jack Warner wanted to repeat that success and keep the winning team of Walsh, Lupino, and Raft for *High Sierra*. He assigned Walsh to direct and signed Lupino to play the part of Marie, Earle's girlfriend. Since she made such an impression in *They Drive by Night,* Lupino received top billing. Walsh later told people that Warner asked him to go to Raft's house to try to convince him to take the part. Nothing could convince Raft, however, since he was adamant that he didn't want his fans to see him die in a movie. With Raft out of the picture, Walsh always claimed that he came up with the idea to use Bogart. Now was Bogart's moment, and Jack Warner should take advantage of that, he told his boss. Warner—of course having faith in Walsh's film sense—went along and gave Bogart the role that, as history now knows, turned him into a major film star.

Despite Walsh's claim, in fact Bogart lobbied heavily on his own behalf to get the part.[14] He also, according to the actor himself, talked Raft out of doing *High Sierra* by playing into his wish not to die at the end of a film, repeatedly pointing out to him how bad it would be for his career if he did. The truth was that Raft gave up the role of Mad Dog Earle because he preferred to make more money on a junket of personal appearances promoting *They Drive by Night.* Everyone was taking credit for all things *High Sierra.*

As often happened, Walsh was one of the last to join the production. He'd be put on the payroll for the picture after Warner had a good enough sense of the script and could call it Walsh material. After getting the assignment, however, Walsh still made it his business to work actively to fill out the cast, something Bogart also did. The fifteen-year-old Joan Brodel, whom the studio had just put under contract and renamed Joan Leslie, won the part of Velma, a teenage girl Earle falls for early in the picture, after his release from prison. The part was a small but significant one. Velma jilts Roy after he pays for a surgical procedure to cure her clubfoot. Roy then turns to Marie for comfort.

Leslie recalled that she was given a screen test without anyone letting on that it was for *High Sierra.* The producers brought her in, asked her to play the scene where Velma lies in bed recuperating from surgery and tells Roy she does not love him. Bogart fed her lines from off camera, and Walsh sat next to her in a chair, holding her hand off and on. Leslie had heard that Walsh was tough on actors, but she didn't experience him that way. Still, she also remembered his not giving her "a lot of direction." Also, he was beautifully dressed, she said—no doubt referring to his characteristically colorful wardrobe, from which he would often choose an ascot tied around his neck whether or not it clashed with the plaid jackets he liked to wear.[15] Walsh insisted a deal be struck on the set. No one was allowed to swear when the "young lady" was anywhere in sight. She was still a teenager, after all. Walsh seemed serious about his plan, even though he may have smiled when he turned around and walked off the set. He had a teenage daughter at home also; Marilynn was only a year or two older than Leslie.

Before shooting started, the Production Code boys jumped all over Huston and Burnett's final script. On May 29, 1940, Joseph L. Breen, who ran the office and dictated to the studios, told Jack Warner to eliminate any suggestion of an "illicit sex relationship between Marie and Roy." "Also," he continued, "the words 'sub-machine gun' were not to be uttered by any criminal. There could be no unnecessary display of firearms in the hands of the criminals." Neither could the film reveal "definite details of crime, as suggested by the dramatization of the hold-up in the hotel and later in the drug store." All swear words were to be eliminated, and no mention of "God words" or "swear words" could be heard. Also eliminated were lines from the script, such as Roy's speech: "We're getting ready to knock over a bank . . . a bunch of coppers are laying for us down at the bank . . . the fink fell out of his chair dead."[16]

With a shooting script now in place, filming began just outside Lone Pine, California, on August 5, 1940, even though numerous other locations in the area were also used. Walsh shot the climactic chase scene fifteen miles west of Lone Pine on a slope at the side of Mt. Whitney, about eighty miles from the "sink" of Death Valley. A group of twenty men from the studio worked for four days to clear a path so that mountain-trained mules, packing cameras and other equipment, could get up to the shooting area. But the event most everyone remembered was Walsh's colorful wardrobe. Since the cast and crew did a good amount of hunting and fishing, Walsh wore a seven-colored jacket at Arrowhead and Palm Spring locations—to make certain that hunters there would not mistake him for a deer.

Bogart had to run three miles up a mountainside for two days for the ending sequence, and everyone was surprised that the only injury he received was a skinned knee. Walsh ordered all the big boulders removed from the path of his final fall, but the little ones remained, and Bogart complained about that plenty. As a matter of fact, Walsh found him

full of complaints in general—at least more than Walsh thought necessary. Bogie especially did not want to trek up that mountain. This was
the shoot on which Walsh gave him the nickname "Bogey the Beefer."
One day, after the lunch wagon showed up on the "set," Walsh took a
sandwich up to him. "When I reached Bogey," he remembered, later,
"he was sitting on the largest rock, sweating like a run horse because
there was no shade and beefing even more than usual. I asked him how
he liked the great outdoors and he answered that the great outdoors
could go and screw itself. 'I'll take the parlor, bedroom, and bath any
time. When you think what an actor has to do to earn his salary in
this goddamn business.'" Needless to say, Bogart was not very happy
about the food sent up to him on the mountain either: "'This goddamn
sandwich must have been made last year! . . . I wonder how they can
afford it? Christ, they feed the cons in San Quentin better than this.'"[17]
The moment gave Walsh another opportunity to remind Bogart of the
salary he was drawing.

Shooting lasted until late September. Locations stretched to different
areas around Los Angeles, including Bartlett's Cedar Lake, Arrowhead
Springs (for the cabin sequences), Glendora, just northeast of Los Angeles, and "Hoppie's Place," an isolated gas station in the middle of the
Mojave Desert—where Earle first meets Velma and Pa (Henry Travers).
The shoot was not without its mishaps: At one point, when some of the
actors had to climb the mountain in pursuit of Roy, they were almost
pulled from the high cliffs by a forty-five-mile-an-hour downdraft. Walsh
used everything from a four- to a twelve-inch lens to film the scene of
Earle's flight and the ensuing gun battle. The tempo followed the quick
action sequences, just the way Walsh first envisioned the story's pace.
He was very satisfied by the time filming ended on September 26, 1940.

Word circulated for years after *High Sierra* finished production that
Ida Lupino refused to work with Bogart again because of the verbal
abuse he leveled at her during filming, although she often denied it.
When Warner Bros. released the film on January 25, 1941, it became an
immediate box-office hit. Pressbook advertising emphasized the melodramatic aspects of the story: "No man ever reached greater heights . . .
to wait for death. He knew he'd be killed . . . but what about his dreams?
A fireside, a farm, a woman's arms?"[18]

High Sierra is Walsh's riskiest film of the early Warner Bros. period because of the emotional depth he gives the characters. Unlike *They Drive by Night,* which is moved by the same kind of raw swagger that would characterize the sensibility of the upcoming *Manpower, High Sierra* swiftly dives inside the hearts of its characters and finds in them a deep sense of sadness and loss. The pervasive sorrow that defines Earle and Marie originates, of course, in Burnett's novel. But Walsh taps into it so readily, clicks into place with it so firmly, that at some level his own psyche merges with those of his characters. Unconsciously or not, he allows himself close proximity to their vulnerabilities. His camera catches them in medium shots and close-ups—close enough to their faces, earmarking their sad posturing. Their anxiety and worry pervade the entire film frame. Earle and Marie are not the hard-as-nails firecrackers from *They Drive by Night.*

The first page of Burnett's novel makes it explicit that Earle is a conflicted soul, easily joining Walsh's repertoire of characters longing for an unattainable sense of peace who emerge in his 1940s Warner Bros. films. Burnett first paints him clearly: "Roy came blinking out into the sunlight. He had on a neat blue serge suit Big Mac had sent him. He didn't look so bad except for his prison-bleached complexion. But his coarse dark hair had silvery streaks in it and his dark eyes were weary and sad."[19] Earle is "weary and sad" from the start, and Walsh could understand a man like him without much trouble. Earle the gangster is still a human being with a soft side. He remembers a childhood that he lost long ago and now idealizes. Walsh could claim the same thing. Roy Earle is on the run from his past, not only his criminal past, but also an innocent past that left him long ago. Walsh always was fascinated with characters on the run, running somewhere better than where they had been before and where they are now. The past was traumatic, just as Walsh's had been. Walsh and Earle idealize the past nevertheless. For Walsh, it is the life he had as a child with his mother before her death, the privileged life his parents created for him—the charming dinner guests, the lavish stories at the dinner table, the doting, loving parents—up until he lost it all.

For Earle, it was "the swimming hole," "Aunt Millie's kitchen where Aunt Millie was always cooking or baking something with fine sweet odors." Also it was "the Sunday afternoon baseball game" before he began to turn inward, to get in trouble with the law, to bring his childhood to a slow burning close.[20] Like Walsh, Earle idealizes the past. In both Burnett's novel and Huston's screenplay, he walks out of prison and into a park where children play, almost as if he has walked back into his own childhood. Walsh knew people like Earle, people who are hard on the outside but soft and hurting on the inside. Marie is very much the same the way Ida Lupino plays her. She loves Earle and clings to him because she has nothing else, no one else, in her life. She shares her loneliness with him, and, in the end, this sends her to her emotional doom. These are characters lost at sea. It is the kind of loss that is not temporary but defining of a character's entire movement and view of the world. The child in these characters prevails.

The last scenes in the film sew up Roy and Marie's fate: the long car chase, the couple's separation, after which police continue to chase him until he abandons his car and runs up the mountain that he mistakenly, or desperately, hopes will be his escape to freedom. He does manage to get to the highest point on the mountain, but that turns out, ironically, to be where the police shoot and kill him. The exciting chase is laced with poignancy and action simultaneously.

Walsh paints Earle and Marie as lost and confused, even desperate—enough to stay alive, but even more so to be able to belong to another human being. He moves them slowly, and they are often tentative in their actions and words. He closes in on their vulnerable faces and their almost innocent plans (plans that are fruitless) to escape the world that victimizes them. Responding to Pard, their dog, does Earle in. Another Warner Bros. writer, John Wexley, looking at Burnett's story early on, prophetically saw the characters that Walsh ultimately gave the audience. Wexley wondered how Earle could ever be presented accurately, yet Walsh delivered Earle on target:

> What lends the story any real value is its pervading mood, its primitive, simple, earthy quality—attained chiefly in the intimate relations between Roy and Marie, and secondarily in the uninhibited dialogue.
>
> There is a vital question. . . . The author's penetrating study analyzes our gunman hero as a maladjusted farmboy who never really escaped adolescence. It is this factor which continually motivates every major act he undertakes. And how to success-

fully capture this factor, which is largely responsible for the effectiveness of the story, but which is never dramatized outside the mind of Roy Earle—I am afraid [it] will be a terribly difficult problem, it's so insurmountable.[21]

Yet Walsh's Earle is consistently part grown man, part vulnerable adolescent, part experience, part innocence. He is a hint of what is to come in Walsh's protagonists of the 1940s and 1950s—characters who traipse on to a desperate adventure (consider, e.g., *Desperate Journey, Objective, Burma!* and, later, *Distant Drums* and *Gun Fury*): they are up for the adventure even as they display their vulnerabilities in the face of having to be tough. Bogart as Roy Earle and Ida Lupino as Marie are the personification of Walsh's own vulnerability. Projecting onto his most heartfelt fictive characters to date at Warner Bros., Walsh can express his own sense of vulnerability without anyone catching him at it. But he also put Earle and Marie at the center of the most crucial Walshian narrative: the love between a man and a woman. This was, he insisted again and again, the fundamental motivation for his pictures, the hope that a man and a woman would come together—or at least die trying.

Walsh always claimed that he had to kill off Earle at the picture's end because of the censors. These outlaws had to pay. But he always wished that Earle and Marie could have escaped. "Yes," he said, "him and the girl and the little dog. I would have liked to see them ride away into the desert somewhere with the sun setting, but the damn censors were pretty strict in those days."[22] That's the essential Walsh, the sentimental undercurrent lying somewhere just beneath the surface just threatening to jump up and scream at his characters to "get the hell out of there." Both that sentiment and that danger show in Marie's face every second she's in the frame.

Michael Curtiz was a candidate to direct *High Sierra* before Jack Warner gave it to Walsh. W. R. Burnett later said, "Technically, Mike may have been as good, but Walsh was much smarter, much cleverer. Walsh didn't need anybody. If he'd have wanted to, which he didn't, he could have produced and directed. It's true Walsh is not much interested in complexities. He's interested in making a certain kind of picture, mostly action. Which is the motion picture."[23] Burnett shows the simpler view of Walsh, one that was (and still is) commonly held—that Walsh wouldn't want to venture near psychological complexities. But, truth is, his characters are caught in (maybe trapped in) these complexities every minute. They made him uncomfortable enough to walk away from the camera when he shot these types of scenes, saw these characters suffering these emotional dilemmas. He'd get close to them, then need to leave. Complexities were too emotionally exhausting, too dependent on *his* emotional commitment to them. He'd rather position himself halfway out the door, halfway off the set or the stage, when he had to confront personal, intimate scenes requiring him to puzzle out the *details* of a painful psychological dilemma. He had an easier time maneuvering complex emotions in his action films, where they feel more distant, more removed, more entangled in physical acts that must be completed. Yet, even in those films, the human entanglements and the psychological warfare show on his characters' faces. When the studio released *High Sierra* on January 25, 1941, box office was more than solid, even in the face of such reviews as that of the *Variety* critic, who wrote that the script brought in "too many side issues" despite Walsh's tight direction.[24]

Burnett also had misgivings about the script:

John and I had to fight Hellinger. Hellinger was a swell guy, don't misunderstand me. I like him. But he was a sentimentalist. We got into an awful struggle about the character of the lame girl with him. He just couldn't take it, after Roy had her foot fixed, that she turned against Roy . . . that was too much for Hellinger. So we had to give a little on a couple of scenes like that. The main point wasn't as strong as it should have been. I corrected that in the remake, *I Died a Thousand Times* [Stuart Heisler, 1955].[25] The remake is a better picture. Except we had two repulsive people in it—Jack Palance and Shelley Winters. . . . I think the script is much better. I cleaned up the script. . . . I cut it down, shortened it. A lot of that dialogue [in the first picture] was in as a result of Hellinger. He'd say, "Bill, I don't understand that, I don't understand that . . . line." Huston would look up at the ceiling and say [Sing-song] "Got to have another line in here so he'll understand that line." In the remake I took all that bullshit out. [It] is a much better picture, script-wise, although not pictorially, because Raoul Walsh did a hell of a job.[26]

He nails a Walsh essential in this comment—the "pictorial" sense, the ratio of human emotion to physical landscape. Where does each stand in the frame? and who moves *whom?* Walsh's *High Sierra* advances *pictorially,* be it the chase, the face of a character, the language in his or her demeanor. The dialogue is surpassed by the film's physical, visual language.

A Revised Childhood

> I'll give you *The Letter* for *One Sunday Afternoon* and ten points and a new bicycle.
> —Hal Wallis to the producer Bob Lord

In one interview after another, Walsh said that *The Strawberry Blonde*—based on the 1933 Broadway play *One Sunday Afternoon*—was his favorite of all the movies he directed during the sound era. He liked the time travel, as it were: what he considered the old-fashioned music, the simpler characters, and the period dress. In other words, it brought him back to his childhood, as he often said, probably unaware of that loaded confession. After all, he also said, he grew up in that era. He deliberately tried to sweeten the memory of his past, not so much because it was that sweet when he was a youth as because that was the way he wanted to remember that time in his life. He would sweeten his youth and extract the bitterness from it for himself.

Walsh began working on *The Strawberry Blonde* almost immediately after *High Sierra*. Working consistently, even with time off for travel to purchase quarter horses, was the best defense against watching his financial fortunes fall, rise, and fall again as quickly and as frequently as Miriam Cooper could get him back in court. Segueing from the tragic *High Sierra* to the light and sentimental *Strawberry Blonde* proved no problem. He continued to practice what he preached—if it had good dramatic potential, take hold of it. He was open to any genre because he always felt confident that he could supply the emotional and physical action to keep the story moving and make it entertaining. Little had changed since his early years, and less would change in the future. At this particular time, Walsh was as fired up as Jack Warner was about keeping the ball rolling on projects in development and production. During the first half of the decade at Warner Bros., he was less in charge of his material than he recalled in hindsight. Nevertheless, he was stuck with the best.

Now, with *The Strawberry Blonde,* Walsh could reimagine the past. *The Strawberry Blonde* centers on two pals at the turn of the twentieth century, Biff Grimes (Cagney) and Hugo Barnstead (Jack Carson), both of whom fall in love with the same girl, the strawberry blonde Virginia Brush (Rita Hayworth). Biff is crestfallen when Virginia runs off and marries Hugo. On the rebound, he marries another girl who is part of their circle, a nurse named Amy (Olivia de Havilland). Later, when Hugo lets Biff take the fall for some of his shady business dealings, Biff ends up spending a few years in prison. On his release, he realizes that Hugo and Virginia are miserable and that he married the right girl, Amy, the one he truly loves.

Based on a Broadway play of the same name, *One Sunday Afternoon* had been adapted in 1933 by Paramount as a vehicle for Gary Cooper. But Stephen Roberts's picture turned out to be the only real flop of Cooper's stellar and very carefully orchestrated career. Jack Warner knew that the script needed a complete retooling, but he believed in it—one reason being that it was a Cagney production from the start, beginning as a pet project of James Cagney's brother William, mostly in service to the production company the Cagney brothers had set up so as to get good parts for Jimmy. This nostalgic look back to the turn of the century was their gift to their mother, Carrie Cagney, who would live only a few more years.

Problems with scripting *The Strawberry Blonde* started almost immediately after Warner saw the previous Paramount picture and sent a memo to Hal Wallis: "Dear Hal . . . I ran *One Sunday Afternoon* last night at my house. Of course the picture is very bad, but anyone who has seen the show or read the script claims there is a great picture in it. It will be hard to stay through the entire running of the picture, but do this so you will know what not to do."[27]

One of Wallis's first moves was get the brothers Julius and Philip Epstein on the job transforming a bad script into a good one (they later penned several classic Warner hits, including *Casablanca*). The trick was to transform James Hagan's play into a vehicle for Cagney, who had yet to commit to William and to the project—even as Hal Wallis also considered giving the part to a young John Garfield. William Cagney was brought in first to confer with Wallis before approaching Jimmy Cagney, who wanted a nostalgic part—any part—to take him away from the gangsters he was loathe to play now. Wallis told Walter MacEwen on April 20, 1940, "The Epsteins have gone into *One Sunday Afternoon* very carefully, and conferred with [Bill] Cagney on it, and it is their opinion that it requires a very complete new job. They feel that to get a good picture out of it today would call for as much work as was represented in getting *Daughter's Courageous* out of *Fly Way Home*."[28] One thing was certain—Bill Cagney and the Epsteins wanted the story's midwestern locale changed to New York City because they all knew it so much better. They were taking no chances.

Harry Warner wrote Jack from New York on July 26, 1940, "The other day I discussed with Bill Cagney the subject of him discussing with Jimmie Cagney the idea of him making an extra picture a year for us without pay to help us along while the war is on. He advised me he would take it up with Jimmie." He was even prepared, he admitted, to "give [Cagney] 10% of the gross."[29] But, by August, Jimmy Cagney still had not signed on. Before he would, he needed some changes made. He wasn't crazy about the idea of a "remake," but he knew he wanted Walsh to direct. More importantly, he didn't like the idea of playing scenes with the very tall Jack Carson. Cagney objected—in his polite way. He preferred Brian Donleavy instead; better still, he suggested the even shorter Lloyd Nolan. But Nolan would cost the studio $2,000 per week, and Carson could be had for $750. Despite Cagney's misgivings, Carson was cast in the part.

Though the part of Virginia Brush, the strawberry blonde, had initially been intended for Warners' Oomph Girl, Ann Sheridan, she was deep in another of her contract disputes with the studio and refused to work in the film. Jack Warner asked Walsh to go talk Sheridan into doing it. When she refused, the actress Brenda Marshall was tested. But Walsh also recalled a girl named Rita Hayworth whom he had seen in a few Columbia Pictures productions. He thought she was perfect for the part and, after she was cast, without a hitch, from then on always referred to Hayworth as his "find" (despite 1939's *Only Angels Have Wings*).

Rita Hayworth received $450 per week to play Virginia Brush and began work immediately with the makeup man Perc Westmore to find the right look for the main character in what would shortly be retitled *The Strawberry Blonde*. Hayworth required certain considerations. "When you are making your decision of hair coloring for Rita Hayworth," Westmore told Wallis on Oct 21, "will you please keep the thought in mind that her head is so large and she has so much hair that it will practically be impossible to put a wig on her. Whatever color you decide on, she will be happy to have it made that color. Then, at the end of the picture, we will dye it back to its natural color."[30] The picture marked the first time Hayworth was seen as a redhead and the first and only time in her career that audiences heard her real singing voice.

Always pleased to get free publicity, especially when it allowed him to display his sense of whimsy, Walsh did a brief stint as a judge in a local competition called "Baby Stars of 1940," where new female talent was on tap. Thirteen young women were chosen and considered to be the best bets for future stardom. "I am very interested to hear that Raoul Walsh is back of a plan to revive the old Hollywood tradition of selecting the 13 baby stars who have the most promise of succeeding," Louella Parsons wrote in her column. "A director from each major lot will act as judge. Each studio will be privileged to submit two or three girls under 21 years of age who have played not more than two speaking parts."[31] Former winners of the contest included Janet Gaynor, Clara Bow, Joan Blondell, Fay Wray, and Lupe Valez. The starlets chosen for 1940's contest included the teenager Joan Leslie.

Shooting got under way on *The Strawberry Blonde* on October 21, 1940, with Wallis again complaining that Walsh shot too close to the actors' faces. In turn, Walsh kept his vow of silence whenever he could. "I have spoken to you so many times about establishing shots and not choking up on the people and I just don't understand why you keep doing it," Wallis wrote to Walsh on October 29. "You have so much opportunity in this picture for atmosphere and composition that will bring a nostalgia to the audience and I hate like hell to see one set after another go by without full advantage being taken of what we have."[32] There was Walsh, moving in closely on the characters' faces again and changing dialogue on the set. Wallis seemed to be the only one disgruntled by the close-ups.

Wallis's troubles and frustration varied according to which director he supervised. With Michael Curtiz, on the set of *Yankee Doodle*

Dandy, for example, he would send memos saying, "Mike, can you just get the story on film, get it from the actors' faces, instead of going all over the place?" With Walsh it was, "Can't you just use more of the surrounding set, even getting an over-the-shoulder shot, instead of focusing so intensely on the actors' faces?"[33]

Walsh was not answering Wallis—nor was he always taking his suggestions, causing an angry Wallis to fire off another memo: "I don't understand how you miss these things. Put the camera on a dolly and move it a little bit—move up on people instead of those short cuts from one to another all of the time. . . . I wish you would think out ahead of time every sequence you go into from now on, and figure the best way in which to shoot it to get the most out of it in the way of business, camera angles, and everything else. Let's try to get some composition, and some moving shots, and some interesting stuff in the picture."[34] Wallis wrote to Walsh unaware that Walsh had already not only absorbed and memorized the script but also created in his head a visual map of how he would shoot. If anyone understood "the way of business," and "camera angles," and especially moving shots, it was Walsh. If any director's sensibilities merged with Warners' sense of realism, Walsh's did. Eventually, the memos stopped—and the finished film has barely a frame in it that doesn't hug the actors. Wallis's insistence that Walsh open the frame to include the sets also faded into the background.

Olivia de Havilland had no recollection of Wallis's frustration with Walsh, nor did she have problems with Walsh's decision to move in closely on the actors. In the tender reunion scene between her character, Amy, and her husband, Cagney's Biff, near the close of the film, she had a good opportunity to debunk Walsh's tough-guy reputation. "I loved working with Raoul," she said. "He seemed to understand perfectly the characters we were playing and to understand, too, the 'actor' approach to them. It was a happy, harmonious set, a happy picture to make. I felt Raoul was absolutely real with me. He inspired trust. He understood humor and humorous situations."[35] Julius Epstein, in an interview late in his life, said that Walsh "was great," that he was "very businesslike," and that he "never changed a word" in the script (a point Epstein got wrong as Walsh changed lines religiously). "Some writers complained about Walsh," he also said. "My experience with him was very good." Although Michael Curtiz "was a good director with the camera," Epstein noted, he thought Walsh the "better director."[36] When Warner Bros. released *The Strawberry Blonde* on February 21, 1941, the studio knew it had a hit on its hands. Walsh received accolades, with most critics scratching their heads wondering how a fast action director could take a sentimental tale and keep it so poignantly on target.

Critics at the *New York Times, Variety,* and the *Hollywood Reporter* also said that, despite Hayworth's eye-popping beauty (very heavily exploited in studio advertising), de Havilland literally stole the picture, not only with her softer beauty, but also with her flair for comedy. Closing in on de Havilland's face, emphasizing her soft beauty and her playfulness, Walsh comes the closest he ever would to embodying his mother onscreen. In this nostalgia piece, he reimagines Elizabeth Walsh as a beauty with a verbal flair, a steady demeanor, and a self-certainty that renders her psychologically rock solid. She is the emotional centerpiece of *The Strawberry Blonde,* holding together the shenanigans of all the male characters around her. Her Amy is striking enough, sufficiently idealized, that Frances Fuller's Amy in the 1933 film and even Dorothy Malone's Amy in Walsh's own 1948 remake, *One Sunday Afternoon,* pale by comparison.

Walsh considered *The Strawberry Blonde* his most successful picture to date, all wish fulfillment notwithstanding, and from then on he called it his favorite film—not only because it gave him the chance to revisit the time of his childhood, but also because it was for him one of his purest expressions of what he called "entertainment." Walsh looked for a good, entertaining plot in a script, and he went public with the idea when he wrote a piece called "Leave Me Out of the Literati" for the *Hollywood Reporter* at the close of 1940 in response to a comment the director William Dieterle had recently made complaining that Hollywood movies were "losing their intelligence" as of late:

> Mr. Dieterle seems to take the attitude that a film lacks "intelligence" and "artistry" unless it conveys a "message" with the heavy tread of a multi-ton truck. . . . Is that, after all, the big thing? Is that the prime service of the screen to its audience—to continually "needle" its intellect?
>
> Frankly, I don't think so. I think there is altogether too much serious thinking pressed now upon the man in the street for him

to be able to shoulder any more. He has his job to worry about, his son is being called for the defense program, he tries to figure out what is going on in Washington, he has the war. . . . The most important thing the screen may be able to do is to furnish a laugh, or a day dream, or an adventure in a make-believe world to the man in the street—make him forget for the moment how earnest and real is the life he finds on the front page of the newspaper. . . . Hollywood's job is simply and directly to furnish entertainment. The man in the street pays his four bits at the box office and he wants a good show. To hell with sermonizing.[37]

From a man who read the front page of the race track forms as much as anything else and whose pictures for the most part lived separately from the political and social world around them—rather, in the realm of fantasy and adventure—this piece is predictable, a ploy to sell a movie to the public during the holiday season. Walsh was not the type to rally support for the man in the street trying to puzzle out Washington, and he would be hard pressed to direct a movie with a personal or political agenda.

Walsh's problems dealing with Wallis during *The Strawberry Blonde* were not serious enough to curb his enthusiasm—which quickly doubled when he learned that he would work with Bogie again on another Warners tale from the dark side of life, *Manpower.* But his old nemesis, George Raft, whom he tolerated well enough on the set of *They Drive by Night,* was up to his old tricks again. The first thing he did was try to get Bogie taken off the picture and replace him. According to Bogart's biographers, Eric Lax and A. M. Sperber, Raft contacted Bogart's agent, Sam Jaffe, to tell him he thought Bogie was wrong for the part. Raft also went around the studio telling executives that he refused to play opposite Bogie. Raft's anger at Bogart apparently stemmed from Bogie's one-time complaint that reading lines with Raft was impossible because Raft would read every line the same way. Eventually, Raft refused to appear in *Manpower* unless Bogie was ousted. Since Raft still had more clout on the lot, Edward G. Robinson was cast in Bogie's part, even though the new pairing of Raft and Robinson turned out to be trouble anyway.

Manpower centers on two friends, Hank McHenry (Robinson) and Johnny Marshall (Raft), who work as linemen for a power company. One night they meet a woman named Fay Duval (Marlene Dietrich, loaned out from Paramount for the picture), a hostess in a clip joint, and competition for her affections begins—territory Walsh knew well from his McLaglen and Lowe days. She soon marries Frank, although it is a mismatch from the start. The rivalry between the two men, stemming from their love for Fay, reaches its breaking point during a terrible storm that puts the lives of both men in jeopardy. The picture is pure male-rivalry hokum and has been called a remake of Howard Hawks's 1932 *Tiger Shark*, which also stars Robinson. In that Warner Bros. picture, he plays a tuna fisherman whose woman (Zita Johann) falls in love with the friend (Richard Arlen) he lost his hand helping to save. Warners recycled this plot just as it had many others.

Walsh would again direct a Jerry Wald–Richard Macauley script—glad to do so since the three were a natural and easy match. Whatever the two men wrote seemed to flow directly from their pens and effortlessly out through Walsh's camera—*The Roaring Twenties* and *They Drive by Night* had already demonstrated that. Shooting on *Manpower* began on March 24, 1941, although Wald and Macauley had been tinkering with rewrites on the script for over a year before Walsh came on the scene. First called *Handle with Care*, then *Danger Zone*, *Manpower* was most memorable for Walsh because he finally had a chance to direct Marlene Dietrich, whom he recalled even in his late life as being one of his favorite actresses. And at least he met some interesting people with Raft on the set. Stories later circulated that, when the mobster Bugsy Siegel came on to Walsh's set to see his pal George Raft, he met his future mistress, Virginia Hill, who, though not in the picture, was nearby during the shoot.

The studio had other reasons to call the film memorable—the shoot made headlines from the start. An item in Hedda Hopper's gossip column gave the studio executives pause: "'Man-Power' must have made Marlene Dietrich too heady. I hear she's been giving Warners so much trouble already that they wanted to put Ann Sheridan in her part. But Marlene reminded them of her contract. Let's hope it goes through from now on without any more bickering."[38] That same day, having read Hopper's column, Walsh replied to her in a telegram, possibly in response to the studio's request that he handle damage control, but it would not have been uncharacteristic for him to act on his own. He was polite and quite emotionally removed in his words to her: "Dear Hedda . . . Somebody's been pulling your leg—which may be o.k. on a Dietrich story, but I do rise to defend the lady. Because she's been a pleasure to work with on *Manpower.* There's been no trouble of any kind. I thought you'd like to know the facts. Sincerely, Raoul Walsh."[39] Walsh thought to forgo the humor he could have gotten out of this; he went for chivalry instead.

Trouble came, not from Dietrich, but from Raft, who took an immediate dislike to Robinson. No one knew why. He repeated the behavior Walsh knew only too well from the time they shot *The Bowery* in 1933. On April 30, 1941, the Screen Actors Guild executive secretary wrote to Warner and Wallis about an incident already widely known. On the previous Saturday, as the cast was rehearsing a scene, Raft began pushing and roughhousing Robinson because he didn't like the way Robinson delivered a particular line. Robinson asked, "What the hell is all this about?" At this point, Raft began to "direct toward [Robinson] a volley of personal abuse and profanity and threatened Mr. Robinson with bodily harm and voiced numerous filthy obscene and profane expressions." Robinson left for his dressing room, returning to the set a few minutes later, went up to Raft, and said, "George, what a fool you are for carrying on in such an unprofessional manner. What's the use of going on? I have come here to do my work and not to indulge in anything of this nature. It seems impossible for me to continue." This triggered another round of profanity from Raft, "whereupon director Raoul Walsh, assistant director Russell Saunders and others, fearing further personal violence on the set between the two men, jumped in and separated them, and Mr. Robinson left for his dressing room off the set and the entire production was stopped." Two days later, Walsh sent a memo to Wallis saying, "Robinson and Raft shook hands this morning and we are off to a good start. I will try to make up the time we lost." Walsh loved a good fight, but he loved finishing on time even more. Warner Bros. filed charges against Raft with the Screen Actors Guild so that the guild would take disciplinary action against him. It took the help of Ken Thompson, the head of the Screen Actors Guild, Raft's attorney, and Wallis and Obringer to straighten out the mess. Wallis asked Raft to work nights to make up the time. But, when Walsh asked Raft to "cooperate" and work two nights on the time they lost, Raft refused. Walsh then threatened him, saying they might cut out the tag if he did not stay and do the work. But Raft just said "that was ok with him" and walked off the set without completing one more shot needed. Warner Bros. suspended him, and Walsh sent a memo to Wallis, "This is one picture I will long remember."[40] Shooting ended on May 20, 1941, but not before Raft and Dietrich had time to engage in a secret affair. At least someone got on with Raft, if only temporarily.

Manpower earned critical praise when the studio released it in August 1941. Walsh's frame is charged with energy, beefing up the rivalry between the two protagonists and infusing the visual storytelling with high-voltage effects: storms rage, power lines are downed, and lives are constantly threatened. His camera is energetic and continually moving. But, however great the rivalry between the two men in the script, they fail to ignite onscreen to the degree they did offscreen. Dietrich, who was fulfilling a final picture obligation with Warners, seems a fish out of water in Walsh's (and Warner Bros.') gritty black-and-white landscape. Her cavorting with Raft and Robinson seems forced, as if she would rather jump out of the picture and into a lighter Paramount espionage tale. *Life* magazine didn't see a problem, however, and wrote, "As the clip-joint babe, Marlene Dietrich sings a husky song, crosses a pair of nifty legs, bakes a batch of biscuits and, as has become customary in recent successes, gets slapped around."[41] Dietrich did look out of place in the kitchen, as if her persona was too overbearing for the character, a housewife married to Robinson, even if she did project the right kind of world-weariness for a Warner Bros. picture.

And God Created Bette Davis

In December 1941, Miriam was far from letting up, Lorraine was no comfort at home, the Japanese bombed Pearl Harbor, and Jack Warner sent Walsh his most brilliant and difficult star, Bette Davis, who had been finishing up *In This Our Life* with her good friend Olivia de Havilland. John Huston directed the two women, along with Charles Coburn, Dennis Morgan, and George Brent. A good sister, bad sister melodrama, with Davis as a woman who steals her sister's husband, then quickly rids herself of him, this was the kind of "parlor" picture Walsh knew to avoid. But, when Huston, who was having great trouble keeping Davis in line, suddenly became unavailable for a while, Jack Warner called Walsh in to finish it, something Walsh was used to doing. Walsh was not the first man to fight with Bette Davis on this film, but he was the last.

Olivia de Havilland later said that she was unaware that Walsh shot final scenes with Davis.[42] Walsh, of course, had his own tall-tale version of the episode, positioning himself as Davy Crockett taming the wild bear of Warner Bros.:

> John Huston was directing her in a picture, and they had a fight about how the picture was going to end just before the end of the shoot. She wanted it to end one way and he wanted it to end another way, so he took a walk. Warner called me up and said, "Raoul, this is one tough dame and I think you can handle her." That was the way he approached it. He said, "Will you go over to Pasadena and make this ending so we can get this thing done and get this dame out of the studio." Nice girl, but really tough. She'd demand this, that and the other thing. So I got into a car with Bette. On the way to Pasadena we stopped for dinner [to discuss the script with a new ending]. I said, "Bette, this will probably interest you," and passed it over. She read it and you never heard such a volley of oaths in your life. The ceiling went off from her screaming and yelling. People started to get up, but I finally talked her into it after a couple of shots of laughing water.[43]

Walsh's version played down the real antagonism between the two of them that evening. If not as Crockett, he serves himself up as a cowboy in a western tale who rids the town of the potential villain through sheer wit and guile. Davis had completely exasperated Wallis, and Walsh sent him more than one memo saying, in effect, "What am I supposed to do with this woman who won't budge?" On January 2, 1942, the assistant director Jack Sullivan sent a memo to studio production manager T. C. Wright: "In answer to your request for an explanation why Mr. Walsh did not get the scenes with Bette Davis on the location that Mr. Wallis wanted, all I can say is that Mr. Walsh tried to the best of his ability to get Miss Davis to do these shots but she absolutely refused to play it that way, to be tied up with the cops, and I had a tough time talking her into doing it any way. It took me about twenty minutes to talk her into staying there on the location and doing the scenes that we did get." As Wallis became more frustrated, Lou Baum, also on the set with Walsh, said, "Please be advised that Walsh most conscientiously tried to cover this sequence in the manner and in accordance with the instruction given him by Mr. Wallis in my presence. Inasmuch as Bette Davis was adamant about not doing them in accordance with these instructions, he definitely went into great detail . . . to make sure that the sequence was covered as best as he could under the circumstances."[44]

Walsh threatened to walk off the picture just when Davis finally submitted to a compromise—playing the scene a little Walsh's way, a little her own. Soon after that, word went out that there was to be a change in the script: Davis was to be slapped around and thrown on the sofa by her screen husband, Dennis Morgan. With this bold fantasy, Walsh found a way to get his revenge on Davis and that Huston found a Walsh-altered script when he returned. Walsh always did like his version of any story best, and he did enjoy tinkering with a script. After all, with its rocky start, 1941 had not been one of his most successful years as far as the women in his life were concerned. And the road would be rocky for some years to come, including a divorce from Lorraine and Miriam Cooper's continued attempts to take him to court, which mirrored this battle of wits with Davis. Yet one light would beam down soon. The next year, still married to Lorraine, Walsh would meet his third wife, Mary Simpson, the love of his life.

9

One Thousand and One Nights with Errol Flynn

> Hero: A person in a book who does things which he can't and the girl marries him for it.
> —Mark Twain

Now happily ensconced at Warner Bros., Walsh kept on speaking broken Yiddish to Jack Warner and getting away with it. That way he stayed on Warner's good side. He could borrow money from the Colonel when he had to pay off his horse-betting debts, and he could try to stay on top of the barrage of lawsuits Miriam Cooper still hurled at him. In turn, Jack Warner was indebted to Walsh; he could get him onto a picture in no time when another director walked off or was fired. Walsh was gold to him—and it was all working, as long as Walsh kept the pictures coming in on time and on budget. Now he was about to take on the story of General George Custer and expend a great amount of energy in the doing—something he was used to by now. But the pleasure it gave Walsh was even greater than usual. Directing the Custer picture opened and then deepened his friendship with the picture's star, Errol Flynn, who became a lifelong friend—*mishpocha,* in fact.

They Died with Their Boots On materialized in the same way as many other male-driven Warners projects of the late 1930s and early 1940s—as a possible vehicle for James Cagney, still the studio's biggest box-office draw. It was par for the course, then, that, at the close of 1939, Cagney's producer-brother William was again looking for a new project for Jimmy and enlisted the help of many Warners writers and producers to find possible material to develop. "At Mr. Cagney's suggestion," the contract writer A. E. MacKenzie wrote to the Warner executive assistant Walter MacEwen on December 29 in a studio memo,

"I shall spend tomorrow in search of material at the public library. This to account for my absence on the doorman's daily report."[1] MacKenzie was on another hunt for good Cagney material.

As it turned out, it hardly mattered that MacKenzie found little at the library that day because he would soon be half of the writing team on *They Died with Their Boots On,* a story that came to the studio by another route—although Cagney would not be its star. A few weeks earlier, Jack Warner's good friend William Randolph Hearst wrote him about a western book called *They Died with Their Boots On* written by a Thomas Ripley, one of Hearst's *Atlanta Georgian-American* editors. Doubleday, Doran and Company had just published it, and Hearst, wanting to further Ripley's reputation, thought Jack Warner ought to know about a book based on the life of the infamous outlaw John Wesley Hardin. To make the project seem even more attractive, Hearst told Warner that it "included a number of famous old Western characters."[2] It was loaded with legend.

Hal Wallis immediately put a reader on *They Died with Their Boots On,* only to receive a negative report. The book "offered very little in the way of picture possibility." "The story itself concerns a very bad man who goes around very indiscriminately killing people for no other good reason than he is a very bad man," the report said. "I doubt if we could make him sympathetic enough to have him kill a Negro slave, three Union soldiers, a company of Union soldiers, a Texas Ranger, and eight or nine other people."[3] Box-office potential appeared dismal.

With that report—and a story that looked "so ordinary"—Bill Cagney told Wallis he doubted that "Jimmy would want anything to do with it." But Jack Warner liked the title at least and wanted to make something of it. He paid Ripley $750 for the title alone and went looking for a writer to develop an original script around it. Four months later, the studio was still looking, and, on April 18, 1940, Wallis received a memo saying, "Bob Sherwood [the playwright who would soon pen *The Best Years of Our Lives*] too busy with other work to undertake 'They Died with Their Boots On.' Would you consider either Maxwell Anderson or Stephen Vincent Benet?"[4] The studio was aiming high and literary, although neither writer would ever be attached to the script.

After Jerry Wald and Richard Macauley agreed with Warner that he should develop a western story around the title, Wallis hired MacKenzie and his fellow contract writer Wally Kline to do just that. They came up with a fictional biography (emphasis on *fictional*) of General George Armstrong Custer. Hardin got lost in the shuffle to find a larger-than-life American icon. By December 1940, Hal Wallis okayed their treatment and told them to develop an actual script. The two writers finished their first draft in early May 1941.

Warner Bros. was not alone in thinking that Custer had box-office potential. Sam Goldwyn was also developing a film about him—and this may have been why Jack wanted a story so quickly, to beat Goldwyn to the box office. Goldwyn got wind of Warners' Custer story and fired off a letter indicating his dismay. In response, Warner fired back his own missive a few days later, on February 3, 1941, saying, "All the producing companies in the industry cannot sit back and be stopped from making a picture about the Royal Air Force just because one studio proposes to do so."[5] Both Warner and Goldwyn had gone through this before. Although speaking metaphorically, Warner let Goldwyn know in no uncertain terms that he wasn't running the show in this town.

By now, James Cagney was out of the picture, and after a brief flirtation with Fred McMurray to play Custer (McMurray was ultimately not available), the bad boy Errol Flynn was in—with Flynn's most frequent director, Michael Curtiz, set to direct. Flynn was finishing *Dive Bomber* and would soon be available—and, to Jack Warner's way of thinking, he was taking home such a large paycheck he should be at the studio's beck and call.

After the actress Joan Fontaine turned down the role of Custer's wife, Elizabeth (Libby), the part went to her sister, Olivia de Havilland, who had already made seven pictures with Flynn. This would be their eighth and final film together. Even years later, de Havilland looked back fondly on this picture—the two actors were barely secreting a mutual passion that now spilled over into what they knew would be their last picture together. For Flynn, the prospect of working with de Havilland again was enticing, but, when he failed to show up on time (as was his habit) to begin work on *They Died with Their Boots On,* he found himself facing the firing squad in the person of his nemesis, Curtiz, who had just directed him in *Dive Bomber,* where they continued their rocky relationship. Now, as was his habit with Flynn, Curtiz began flinging a barrage of criticisms at the actor. Flynn, as well as many others, saw it as nothing short of abusive and complained to Warner, saying that he was through working with Curtiz. Warner, no fool, decided to keep his star happy and replaced Curtiz with Walsh—probably at Flynn's request. Flynn knew Walsh but not terribly well. This would be their first picture together.

They Died with Their Boots On follows the life of George Custer from the time he enters West Point to his death at the Battle of the Little Bighorn. Walsh paints him as a dashing upstart unwilling to play by the rules, a romantic who is self-reliant and will no doubt find his own path. When Custer meets Libby Bacon (de Havilland), the story quickly turns sentimental: first they spar, but only because they are destined to fall in love. Although Custer the bad boy doesn't graduate with the rest of his class, he still obtains an officer position with the Union army after the Civil War breaks out. His irreverence now opens doors for him. He works his way to Washington, DC, where he befriends General Winfield Scott (Sydney Greenstreet), a man who furthers his career. On his return home to Michigan, he marries Libby, and the two go to the Dakota Territory, where he whips his regiment into shape. This ultimately leads to his taking his men into battle at the Little Bighorn. He knows that they won't have a chance against the thousands of Native Americans who stand ready to fight them. He says a tearful good-bye to Libby and goes into battle to meet his end. The film ends with a grand heroic gesture. Custer and his men have fulfilled his promise to them: they have died with their boots on, going out as heroes; their legacy of great dignity lives on.

The months prior to starting work on *They Died with Their Boots On,* Walsh had been negotiating again with the studio to get more money. He owed a good amount to creditors from betting on the horses and again turned to Jack Warner for help. On January 4, 1941, the studio's general counsel Jerry Obringer told Warner he had received a letter from Walsh's agent, Sam Jaffe—who now had replaced Wurtzel—saying that he, Jaffe, had been "trying to keep Walsh cool for the past few months: that Walsh has threatened to come in and talk to you or Mr. Wallis on a number of occasions about giving him a new deal; that he figures he has directed four outstanding hits in succession and that he knows Bacon, Curtiz, Howard Hawks and possibly others outrate him in salary." "I discussed this with Jaffe," Obringer told Warner, "reminding him that

Walsh was not doing so badly because his next option term, which starts February 23, calls for $2,000 per week, and also that Walsh should not forget the fact that he was given the chance of a comeback here when we put him under contract with Howard Hawks' deal, because Hawks had a free-lance, one-picture deal only. I also reminded Jaffe that you had been very nice to Walsh in advancing him funds in his financial difficulties during the past year, etc."[6]

Jaffe told Obringer that Walsh was perpetually on his neck, saying that MGM, Paramount, and RKO "are after him for a picture and he could get $60,000 or better on the outside." "I told Jaffe," said Obringer, "that the same was true with Bette Davis and any other artist—they could get more on a one-proposition than under a term contract, and that Walsh should not forget that he has the security here of forty weeks guaranteed pay."[7]

On February 8, 1941, Obringer again told Warner, "Raoul Walsh is badly in need [of] five thousand cash . . . [but] Walsh still owes sixty five hundred on ten thousand recently given him." "Walsh wants additional money," he said, "and we get back at two fifty a week. As you know, all his funds [are] tied up in account litigation. Please advise." By March, Warner agreed to give Walsh another $5,000, agreeing to postpone the deductions on that amount until after Walsh finished repayment of the $6,500 "heretofore" advanced him. Walsh was hurting badly, and looking for ways to get funds was not an unusual situation for him during these years. Warner refused to discuss this directly, even after Walsh went to see him. Instead, he offered to loan Walsh more money, which only frustrated Walsh, who responded: "Jack, as I told you, I have a very grave problem and it cannot be solved with the bonus of $9,000, although I greatly appreciate the gesture. Nevertheless my predicament involves a great deal more money and the only way I can work myself out of what has been a harassing and depressing condition is for me to do an outside picture. This will give me enough money to pay off all my creditors and enable me to have peace of mind once and for all." Still, Warner refused to let Walsh do an outside picture. By May, he decided to loan Walsh $20,000 instead, and Walsh accepted. "It was indeed a nice gesture," Walsh wrote him, "and I will never forget you for it. If at any time I can do anything for you, please feel free to call on me."[8] The fallout from betting on the horses had reached a crisis at this juncture and would wax and wane for the rest of his career.

Walsh could rest a little easier now. He had what he wanted and a promising picture to direct to boot. All bargaining aside, he was his usual congenial Warner self throughout the production of *They Died with Their Boots On*—business-like and even-tempered. He seemed untouched by money problems and especially got on well with the film's cinematographer, Bert Glennon, a veteran who had worked with Cecil B. DeMille on *The Ten Commandments* and was a favorite of John Ford's, having just been nominated for an Academy Award for shooting that director's *Stagecoach*. Walsh would take Glennon out and ask how it would be if they shot a particular scene here or there, this way or that. If Glennon wanted Walsh to move a certain number of feet from where he already was, and if it didn't affect the background, Walsh would do it. Walsh might ask for a change in lens, say, from a two inch to a thirty-five millimeter. Also, Glennon was very cognizant of Walsh's penchant for using low-angle shots—Walsh called them side angles and extremely low angles. The two worked easily together; their sensibilities simply blended. Walsh was enormously pleased.

Walsh scouted locations and turned up a variety of areas to the east and west of the studio. He spent a good part of July shooting scenes set in West Point, Washington, DC, and Monroe, Michigan. The main gate of West Point was really the Busch Gardens in Pasadena, California, with the Warners back lot or its huge Calabasas ranch providing the film's other important sets. He was gathering Sioux Indians if he could find them; if not, he hired members of the local Filipino community to be background extras. Anna Q. Nilsson, a young Gig Young, and the athlete Jim Thorpe also joined the cast uncredited.

The script that came to Walsh for *They Died with Their Boots On* is less historical documentation than escape into romance and hagiography—a romantic rendering of Custer that heroicizes his life. Walsh's setups only heroicize Custer more, framing him in the center of the action, catching him as robust yet quixotic. Olivia de Havilland recalled that she was happy when the ace screenwriter Lenore Coffee was called in to write additional dialogue.[9] She would add a sense of realism, especially to the last scene between Flynn and de Havilland depicting the Custers' final parting. Coffee received no screen credit for her work (a condition to which she had agreed beforehand). She had been in the business for years, adapting popular women's fiction for the screen. She wrote Bette Davis's tearjerker that year, *The Great Lie,* and would soon pen the Bette Davis–Miriam Hopkins melodrama *Old Acquaintance.* Coffee was also the writing equivalent of Walsh, a "fixer" who could come in and tighten up a baggy script. The emotional tenor of the love scenes between Custer and Elizabeth mirrored the real-life love affair and the warmth they felt for each other during their happy married life.

A copy of Elizabeth Custer's autobiography, *Boots and Saddles,* was on the set during the production, but Coffee was probably the one to take it most to heart, especially in writing the Custers' last moments together. As husband and wife, de Havilland and Flynn play it as if knowing they'll never see each other again. The dread Elizabeth/de Havilland suppresses in those moments comes directly from *Boots and Saddles.* Saying good-bye to her husband as he leaves for the Battle of the Little Big Horn, Elizabeth Custer actually writes, "In the morning the farewell was said, and the paymaster took sister and me back to the post. . . . With my husband's departure my last happy days in garrison were ended as a premonition of disaster that I had never known before weighted me down. I could not shake off the baleful influence of depressing thoughts. This presentment and suspense, such as I had never known, made me selfish, and I shut into my heart the most uncontrollable anxiety, and could lighten no one else's burden."[10] Elizabeth Custer's words inform the dread in this parting scene. Each knows it is their last moment together. Walsh pulls back, allowing a subtle tenderness to hover over them.

At the end of July, Walsh began shooting the Civil War sequences to simulate Bull Run and Hanover. Always shooting the more difficult scenes first, he'd already filmed the spectacular sequence of Custer's Last Stand, in which the stuntman Yakima Canutt doubled for Flynn and helped supervise the battle scenes. Walsh used approximately one hundred mounted extras, many of whom he considered too inexperienced for the work. Neither did this escape Wallis, who sent a memo to Walsh on September 8, 1941, saying, "Please watch your choice of bit men carefully . . . make sure that [each] is a capable actor, so that the scenes do not let down." This was not the first time Walsh had problems with extras, but now they would worsen before production finished, during which time three men were tragically killed. One man, George Murphy, was drunk during shooting and ignored instructions to get off his horse, then fell off the animal and broke his neck. A second man had a heart attack while on top of his mount, and a third, an extra named Jack Budlong (also known as William Meade), was actually impaled on his own sword after his horse threw him. Worried, the studio wrote up a full report, saying,

> The scene was rehearsed twice after full instructions had been given by loud speaker to the troop. In the scene which then followed and which was shot by four cameras, the deceased appeared to get as far as the division in the road, at which time he appeared to swing a little to the left toward the bridge, his horse balked in some way, and then reared. The deceased was thrown or fell from the horse to his own left and apparently was impaled on his saber when he landed on his back. . . . Mr. Budlong, after his fall, apparently arose and walked toward the side of the road to a fence or barricade of some kind. There he was given help by the men who first arrived, and almost immediately Mr. Roy Baker, the first aid man in attendance arrived . . . the entire episode not taking more than three or four minutes from the time of the fall until he was taken away.[11]

Budlong died three or four days later in the hospital from apparent peritonitis.

Later, Walsh said that he was the one who put Budlong into the limousine that arrived. Although he took the incident seriously and wrote a moving letter to Budlong's family about it, as the years passed the episode and the entire production became filtered through his love of a good, colorful story. In 1972 he remembered:

> There was a young actor playing the part of a lieutenant. When doing a long shot where they have swords, we would supply them with wooden swords with a silver tint to them so it looks like a real blade. When the property man went to take this chap's real sword away from him and give him the phony sword, he

said, "No, I'm going to use this one." The property boy argued with him a while and couldn't get anywhere, so he let him keep the real sword. So we shot the scene and there were a couple of explosions on either side, and he was thrown off the horse. The sword was thrown up into the air, came down like that into the ground, and him on top of it. I saw the whole thing and ran down and pulled the sword out of him, called a limousine and sent him to a hospital. Unfortunately, his mother wouldn't sign to let them operate and in three days the boy died. Another cowboy who was pretty drunk fell off a horse and broke his neck. Another fellow was watching the scene and evidently it didn't look too good because he had a heart attack and died.[12]

With a smattering of Twain-like logic, Walsh tied up the loose ends of his tale, being sure to take a poke at his film as well.

In with Flynn

Boots lives in the "reality" of romance, what Nathaniel Hawthorne called the landscape way above our heads rather than the real ground we tread. By living in the imaginary, the film forfeits much historical fact. Walsh's interest lies with heroes waging battles, men larger than life, the province of imagination—the embellishment of true events. Nowhere is this more evident than at the conclusion, when George Custer delivers a touching and heroic speech to his regiment just before they ride off to their fatal encounter at the Little Big Horn. Not only does he recall the birth of the Seventh U.S. Cavalry; he does so in a way that encapsulates the romance at the heart of the film: "Men die, but a regiment lives on because a regiment has an immortal soul of its own. Well, the way to begin is to find it, to find something that belongs to us alone, something to give us that pride in ourselves that will make men endure, and, if necessary, die—with their boots on. As for the rest, it's easy, since it's no more than hard work, hard riding and hard fighting." Beyond the script's romanticism, this speech identifies Walsh's romantic view of Custer just as it binds director and actor. Walsh and Flynn found a common thread in creating characters seeking to look heroic, men who above all else wish to leave a legacy of uncommon valor (suggestive of Flynn-Walsh films to come) and dignity. This began with *Boots* and continued on with *Gentleman Jim* and their cycle of war films. Flynn was the perfect embodiment of Walsh's wish to escape the real social world on film and leap into a romantic one. Heroism and dignity are imaginary concepts that both director and star found far more often on film than they did in their personal lives during the years they remained close.

Boots views history as the province of fiction, and no one could look and behave in a more fictional manner than Flynn. As the story subverts, then changes and reinvents, real historical fact, Flynn plays Custer the way Walsh imagines him—as part and parcel of a storytelling impulse. For Walsh, a true story could be authentic only once it became the property of fiction—then he would go to great lengths to ensure that historical detail, such as uniforms, West Point protocol, even cavalry life, looks accurate. His is, however, a love of detail only once it has been retooled into the borders of storytelling. Flynn is the ultimate boy-man, the romantic who takes a fictional world to be a real one. The hero must be sympathetic even if he embodies villainy. He must be sympathetic even to his enemies. If there is no hero moving toward his romantic end, there is no story, no storytelling.

Among cavalry films released during the 1940s and shortly thereafter, *Boots* finds a good companion in John Ford's *Fort Apache,* both stories being rooted in the personality of an errant, erratic hero and offering a romanticized view of its historical time. Of course, the two films diverge and converge in their treatment of a central hero. Ford places his hero (perhaps, even at this early date, antihero), Lieutenant Colonel Owen Thursday (Henry Fonda) in the center of a characteristically idealized community, where men truly love others as brothers and sisters, and where family is the vision of the ideal (although, in this case, it may not always hold fast, given the hostile environment of nearby Native Americans). But Thursday is a slightly more realistically drawn renegade—stubborn and dangerous in his cynicism—than is Walsh's Custer, who is dangerous only in his idealism. Ford's idealized community of men doesn't exist in Walsh's world; Custer is singularly alone (even with the love of a woman), more apt to trot off because of some romantic notion of heroism than because of the kind of arrogance that inspires Thursday to go against the social grain and act defiantly. Much like Walsh and Ford, the two films seem friendly rivals in their views of history and romance.

As successful as *Boots* turned out to be at its release in December 1941 and January 1942, the true success for Walsh was, as always, played out off camera—the close personal relationship he developed with Errol Flynn. It could be said, in fact, that Walsh's relationship—both personal and professional—with the swashbuckling Flynn was one of the most satisfying of his life. Without question, Flynn became several people symbolically collapsed into one in Walsh's life: the son who could substitute for the two real ones, Robert and Jack, Walsh neglected and then lost, as well as a drinking buddy who was more of a brother than a mere colleague.

Flynn was the "Baron," and Walsh was "Uncle," an affectionate name Flynn used especially when he needed something from Walsh. And, more often than not, what he needed was help getting out of a jam with a woman or with Jack Warner. During the time they made seven pictures together, Walsh often held Flynn together. At one point, at Jack Warner's request, Walsh literally had to get Flynn up every morning, drive to get him, and deliver him at the studio on time. Had Walsh not promised Warner that service, Flynn could easily have been ousted from the picture. Also, as Flynn began one of his many episodes of flirting with a young starlet and promising her a part in a picture, Walsh was in on it too. They had the scenario down pat. Flynn would see a girl he liked. He'd call out to Walsh, "Uncle, Uncle, quick! . . . You see what I see?" Walsh would snap his fingers and say, "Of course, you're dead right. You mean for the part of the sister?" There was no part, of course, but they could whip one up if necessary. And, if Walsh saw a girl first, he'd say, "Hey, Baron, quick! What do you think?" And Flynn would answer, "'But of course—the part of the sister. What else?'" Flynn called it "great teamwork; it worked like a charm."[13]

The teamwork worked in life and on film. On the screen, Flynn embodied Walsh's dreams—walked around in them, made them move. Together, they were a tough-guy version of Fred and Ginger—two artists in synch. Walsh supplied the fantasy; Flynn supplied the charm. When Warners released *They Died with Their Boots On*, the reviewer for the *New York Times* saw the finished product and put it generally, calling

Walsh and Flynn's pairing "an adventure tale of frontier days which in sheer scope, if not dramatic impact, it would be hard to equal."[14]

On the Edge of Danger

> The shot of the boys . . . they need to have trouble and hard-
> ship. So far they are having a pleasant journey rather than a
> desperate one.
> —Raoul Walsh to Hal Wallis

By December 1941, the studio had in the works what would become its first wartime drama to show in theaters. Hal Wallis asked both Walsh and Michael Curtiz to read the treatment of a story called *Forced Landing* that the studio had just purchased for $1,000 from the writer Arthur Horman. A month later, he asked Walsh to screen Carol Reed's film *Night Train to Munich,* with Rex Harrison and Paul Henried—a war melodrama about a couple who work to fight Nazis. *Forced Landing* became *Desperate Journey,* and Walsh was paid $41,000 and change to direct. He was soon out scouting locations.

Warner's first choice for the lead, Errol Flynn, received $80,000 to star, and the entire production, with a shooting schedule of forty-eight days, cost the studio $1 million. Wallis wanted Flynn to look as appealing as possible and told Horman, who adapted the script from his book, "Please bear in mind that Flynn is the star of our picture, and that we must give him plenty of situations and business. He must also have some of the comedy routines as we cannot have him playing straight for all the other characters at all times."[15] Horman didn't disappoint; neither did Walsh. The picture turned out to be a drama with a comedic edge.

The story of *Desperate Journey* follows the adventures of the British flight lieutenant Terrence "Terry" Forbes and his crew (which also includes Ronald Reagan and Arthur Kennedy), who are forced to land their aircraft in Silesia after hitting their bomb target against the Germans. Once on the ground, they are captured by the enemy and must escape disguised as Germans. As they make their way across enemy lines, they discover the location of a Messerschmitt factory, steal a German bomber, and scramble back to England to report their findings to the Air Ministry. Despite some implausible moments—British antiaircraft establishments never try to shoot down their bomber, for one—Walsh loads up on some breathless action in this fast-paced drama, one of the more thrilling in the Walsh-Flynn cycle. Ronald Reagan, Raymond Massey, and especially the Warner regulars Alan Hale and Arthur Kennedy (Wallis's personal choice for the part) give good support in a picture that delivers the prototype for Walsh's tough-guy action with "guys" who are vulnerable but courageous in the face of the enemy, supportive of one another because it's really the masculine way to behave.

Before Horman finished the first-draft script, Universal Studios informed Jack Warner that Walter Wanger was producing a film similar to *Desperate Journey* called *Eagle Squadron* that, similar to Walsh's film, included a scene where a British or Allied bombing crew, shot down or otherwise grounded in Germany, attempts to make its escape back to England by mosquito boat. Warners altered its story and used an escape device of capturing a German airplane for the American soldiers' return. The device allowed the surviving principals, Flynn, Reagan, and Kennedy, to bomb German targets on their way back to England, thereby amping up the heroics. After Horman finished, at the beginning of February 1942, Robert Rossen was hired to oversee his work. No stranger to tough actioners, Rossen had cowritten *The Roaring Twenties* and would go on to script *All the King's Men* in 1949 and write and direct *The Hustler* in 1961. More titles were considered, including *Stars on Their Wings* and *Objective Berlin*, before the studio went back to calling the picture *Desperate Journey*.

Shooting got under way on February 2, 1942, and lasted through the middle of April. Walsh was on the set from 7:30 A.M. until 5:30 P.M., hardly altering his schedule once he began. Again, he had to keep Flynn in line. Flynn began acting up right away, refusing to start work the day the studio first needed him (he told them he might be in New York or he might be on the set), causing Wallis to worry throughout production that, without Walsh on hand, Flynn would never make his 10 A.M. call in the morning to brush up on his German with Walsh and to get his wardrobe fitted.

Warners rented a European street set from Universal Studios and a plane from the British air ministry—a Lockheed-Hudson—and used it on location at Sherwood Forest above Los Angeles. This is the bomber that Flynn, Reagan, and Kennedy use to escape the Germans at the film's conclusion; they tag it the Lockheed-Hudson GK. Walsh also shot chase scenes at Point Magu, a spot of beach north of Malibu. Then Warners went all out and got hold of some MGM newsreel footage of the bombing of Singapore. Walsh wanted as much realism as he could get in this yarn. Wallis was just as much a stickler for it and sent Walsh a memo telling him he wanted the cars used to be "of foreign type," not "the usual Buicks being used by the Gestapo, German Captains, etc."[16]

Even on the first day of shooting, Walsh knew that he was unhappy with the script. It was not realistic enough, therefore not good storytelling. "I have just been reading the new pages of DJ [*Desperate Journey*]," he wrote to Wallis, "and I may be entirely wrong but to me the story lacks suspense. Each time a dramatic situation is created, it is spoiled by a lot of gab that takes away from the urgency of the chase. We have reached page 81 and have only just arrived at the first big climax of the chase."[17]

He told Wallis,

I have always felt that the story should be told in briefer, more varied scenes. For instance, [a] shot of the boys drifting down stream, carrying bush over their heads so that the guards would not see them, would be most effective. They need to have trouble and hardship. So far they are having a pleasant journey rather than a desperate one. Following the present construction, I would like to suggest that, after the "Peat Bog" scene, instead of cutting to the men by the brook, we should have a short scene with Baumeister. He could be ordering soldiers to cover all bridges, roads, etc., since he knows that these men will try to work their way toward the coast. This will give us some menace.

Walsh was full of ideas for change, all this to head off what he believed was looking like a programmer. His approach to talking to Wallis was level-headed and calm, the best weapon he could find. "Another thing that occurs to me," he said, "instead of picking up Lloyd on the empty bridge we might have the men from a distance see the bridge crowded with soldiers, as an officer dispatches them to search in many directions; then let our fliers catch up with Lloyd as he is almost discovered. Finally, though the train scene begins with great suspense, it becomes much too talky. And to me, having the men kicked off the train has always seemed an easy way of getting them out of their predicament."[18] Although the scene on the train remained somewhat talky and glib, at least the men were put in more jeopardy than before.

The script changes displeased Walsh, even after he sent that extensive memo. He told Wallis a week later the story was still "very flat and dull." "I don't believe anybody is going to take it seriously that one plane is going to do any damage to England or the water-works that can't be repaired over night," he said. "The scene with the police is ridiculous. Blood hounds are the only dogs that can run down a scent. The only suggestion that I can make is to hold Baumeister off until they are just about ready to take off; as though he picked up their trail further back. It is probably unjust of me to criticize this ending for at the moment I can't suggest anything other than this; [the] plane might be on its way to intercept Churchill on his way back from America." He ended with, "I wish I could feel your enthusiasm about this whole script, Hal."[19]

Wallis disagreed, as usual, and sent Walsh a memo to that effect. Then he mounted an attack on Walsh, the same day he complained to T. C. Wright that Walsh was not using his extras as best he could:

> The attached letter to Walsh is self-explanatory. We have had this trouble with Walsh on practically every picture, and if you will recall, I objected on several occasions to Russ Saunders[20] as the assistant because he did not have his extra talent properly rehearsed when the camera started cranking. If you wish, you have a talk with Russ immediately—along the lines of the attached letter so that between Saunders and Walsh they will have these extra people knowing what they are going to do before the camera starts, and not after. All we get in the latter case is a lot of confusion with men milling around not knowing what the hell they are doing.[21]

Wallis never thought that Walsh rehearsed his actors enough, even though Walsh was well known around Warners to rehearse at great length before setups. Wallis also resented Russ Saunders on some level.

Saunders, much like Carl Harbaugh and the writer John Twist, were bosom pals of Walsh's; where Walsh worked, they found jobs. Saunders was Walsh's perennial assistant director throughout both their lives.

Still not entirely happy with the film's script, Walsh wanted additional dialogue written. The studio hired Julius and Philip Epstein, who were also working on the script for *Casablanca,* to add some dialogue. Walsh sent a memo to Wallis on February 13 telling him, "The Epstein boys have added a little zip to the script, why not let them continue with it, and keep a little ahead of me. In going over the script last night, I think for the story and laughs, we should try to carry Hale a little longer in the script, where he uses his brute strength, chokes a guard or something, or holds a closed door, and lets the others escape, and he could be shot through the door."[22] Walsh thought he was almost there. Hale was gone early enough to miss out on the Three Musketeers antics during the picture's ending heroics. He voiced this to Wallis.

"As there is quite a lot of joking in the script now," Walsh said a little later on, "I like it. I think it might be a good twist to have a sort of a 'Musketeers' feeling of great comradeship between our men, frankly they don't think they have a chinaman's chance of ever escaping, so they are going to have a 'Roman' holiday, and do all the damage they can, blow up all the military equipment they can lay their hands on."[23]

But, throughout the film's entire production, Wallis was still never happy with Walsh—or with Flynn. Soon after, he thought Walsh was fooling around on the set when he should have been more serious. Warner himself got into the picture after Wallis complained to him. He sent Wallis a memo, "I had a talk with RW last night and told him emphatically that he must concentrate on his work and just not shoot and talk while the scene is on, the usual routine we have both been talking about. I also told him about adding some importance to the papers that Flynn will pull, not just depend on the Messer-Schmitt victories. I told him the next time he talked to you he should get your idea as from what I gathered he did not know much about it. He answered with words to the affect that Flynn's mind seems to be somewhere else, etc."[24] This was not an unusual turn of events.

Walsh and Wallis still sparred. Wallis wrote to Walsh a week later, on February 19,

Dear Raoul.

In your scenes today, please try to get a little more bite and little more forcefulness into the performances. The last stuff of Reagan in the bomb bay was so casual that he appeared to be sitting there playing a piano—and I would like to get something into the scene so that we get a tenseness and an excitement into the scene—particularly where he is releasing the bombs. Don't just have him sitting there pressing buttons. When you get on stage 16, please spend a half hour or an hour rehearsing your action before you make a take, so that when your cameras finally do start grinding, everyone will know exactly what they are to do, and the performances will look finished instead of ad lib.[25]

Then the picture—and the complaints—stopped abruptly for a day on February 27. A large oil truck and trailer jackknifed and overturned a short distance from the bridge near Piru where the company was shooting. Both truck and trailer caught fire instantly, and the frantic efforts of Flynn, Reagan, and others to save the twenty-five-year-old driver were futile. The incident so unnerved the actors and crew that shooting halted. When it resumed, it was Flynn's turn to complain. He wrote to Wallis that it seemed unconscionable for the film's characters to leave Arthur Kennedy's character "dead in the bomber while I talk cheerfully to Reagan and jokingly to the C.O. in England over the short wave." "It is, to say the least," he continued, "callous, and I don't think the audience will forget for one moment the corpse flying with us in the back seat while we ignore him. Can he be wounded—or killed outside of plane? Please let me know. . . . Errol."[26] Even a scoundrel (as he was in Wallis's eyes) could have a heart. The script's ending was rewritten: Flynn and Reagan fly off in the bomber, taking the wounded Kennedy with them. Suddenly, his wounds were serious enough, says Reagan, to land him in the hospital for a brief stay. All three men are on hand for the picture's patriotic ending.

Hardly a detail escaped Wallis or Walsh, and soon a minor battle ensued concerning the kind of dogs to be used in the picture. Wallis told Walsh that his research indicated that contrary to what Walsh said earlier—that only bloodhounds could trace scents—German Shepherds were trained to do the same. Walsh responded, "Dear Hal, I still think we are wrong to use German Shepherd dogs trailing our men. This is to verify the report from our research department."[27] (A long memo followed on the differences between the two types of dogs.) The conflict was never resolved, and Doberman pinschers were used instead. Walsh decided, however, and Wallis agreed, that he would use a good number of miniature machines—and, when he had to leave the set for two days, during which time Eric Stacey and William Keighly filled in for him, the miniatures stayed.

On March 23, Walsh told Wallis that he wanted to shoot the rest of the daytime shots immediately and leave all the night work until the end of the picture: "I am afraid that Flynn or somebody else might get sick, and then if anybody catches a cold . . . we would at least have most of the work done." Walsh thought constantly about staying on schedule, unaware that Warner was having his own difficulty with Flynn's unpredictability. Three days later, Warner told Wallis:

At lunch today I want to have a long talk with you about Errol Flynn as this has become a very serious matter which I will tell you about in person. You, Walsh and the others should run the picture and see what we can cut Flynn out of in order to finish it. If there are any retakes Flynn is in, maybe we can use a double, and if they can dig up enough work along these lines, by all means it should be done. Also you could give the script a fast once over and cut it down to a minimum, for I am sure Flynn is going to delay this picture as long as he humanly can and we are going to be tied up with a cast and a tremendous expense. However, I have another plan after this picture for Flynn and he will probably wake up when it is too late.[28]

One more glitch arose before the end of March, when Wallis notified Don Siegel (then directing footage at Warners, as he had done for *The Roaring Twenties*), who was doing montage scenes on the picture, "Ronald Reagan has been ordered to report to the army next week and it is impossible to get any postponement of time on him. It is essential, therefore, that you have all your shots for montages which involve Reagan laid out for shooting at such odd moments when you can use Reagan—or in any event to start on the day following the completion of his work in the picture." This hurried production along even faster.

Shooting officially ended on April 14, just in time for Walsh to head to court again in a personal litigation case. Warner Bros. waited until September 26 to release the picture; this was actually a very short shelf life considering that, during these war years, there was such a glut of product at the studios waiting to get released. Pictures were being held up because those already in theaters were staying longer owing to increased audience demand. *Desperate Journey* opened to lukewarm reviews. To many it looked unruly, a series of chases peppered by too much talk and horseplay. Also, the British response to the picture was generally poor, especially since the British press resented Errol Flynn "winning" the war. That was the same as the Americans winning for the RAF by proxy.

In another problem with Flynn, Jack Warner was forced to cut one particular line from the picture: "They know but one command—attack!" The reason for this was that, by that November, Errol Flynn was in court defending himself against a statutory rape charge (and Walsh was right there defending him, as he always did). One of the women accusing him, Peggy La Rue Satterlee, had been an extra in *They Died with Their Boots On*. She accused Flynn of nothing less than attacking her. Because of this incident, reminding American movie audiences of his ease in yelling out "attack" was decidedly bad publicity.

Despite Walsh's repeated efforts to boost the script's action quotient (and, perhaps in one or two instances, *because* of them), *Desperate Journey* is comedy first and adventure afterward. Among the Walsh-Flynn cycle, it has the least heart and soul, being instead an adventure yarn that pokes fun at itself repeatedly and wears down its believability factor. Implausible and unfocused, it is, nonetheless, a Three (and sometimes Four) Musketeers romp around Hitler's Germany that succeeds as a diversion from the real world at hand.

Desperate Journey marked the last time Hal Wallis directly oversaw a picture Walsh directed. Two years later, Wallis left the studio in a dispute with Jack Warner over the Academy Award speech Warner made when *Casablanca* won Best Picture. With Wallis's departure, Steve Trilling, the studio's former casting director, would take over as Jack Warner's executive secretary. Walsh spent the rest of his time at Warners working closely with Trilling, who, as most of those familiar with Warner Bros. operations knew, was a genius at getting Jack Warner out of awkward situations and potential lawsuits. He had the gift of diplomacy, a gift the gods never bestowed on his boss. Trilling knew how to run Warner and, if necessary, Warner Bros.

Walsh took the poor notices for *Desperate Journey* in stride as he had family matters to contend with for the moment. Miriam was on hiatus from pulling him back into court, but, on March 27, 1942, to his and Lorraine's embarrassment, Walsh's adopted seventeen-year-old daughter Marilynn secretly wed her beau, Don Phillips, a struggling actor who had been put briefly under contract to Warner Bros. Walsh had given him a small part in *Desperate Journey*. But the studio canceled Phillips's contract when it became clear that he was about to be drafted into the army air corps. The marriage was later announced in the *Los Angeles Herald Examiner*. To save face, Walsh and Lorraine told the press they were pleased about the union and said that Marilynn and Don had met a year earlier at the home of Walsh's brother-in-law, Walter Pidgeon. The couple then publicly wed at Santa Barbara Mission, with Walsh and Lorraine in attendance. Although the marriage lasted only a few years—Marilynn later married the pilot Jean Charlebois and moved to England—she named her first child with Phillips after Walsh. Her son, born in 1944, was named Raoul Donald Phillips. A second child, Melinda, followed two years later, before the couple divorced. As for Walsh, at this point in his now fourteen-year marriage to Lorraine, the two lived at the same address but essentially led separate lives—other than the few occasions their name as a couple emerged in the social section of the Los Angeles papers. Walsh managed to stay at the studio for most of the day, until he could break away for the racetrack. He would imply that, while movies were his livelihood, horses were his passion. Before long, his emotional distance would drive Lorraine to divorce court.

Just to add some chaos to his schedule, ten days after he finished shooting *Desperate Journey* Walsh was slapped with a slander suit in the amount of $100,000. A man named Summers Stickney claimed that Walsh had called him a convict during a court appearance with Miriam a year earlier. At that time, Walsh apparently backed up his statement about Stickney with the comment, "Here is his criminal number from San Quentin Penitentiary." The case was thrown out, but Walsh failed to learn the lesson that some of his quips could come back to bite him.

Walsh was not behaving badly; he was behaving recklessly. After four successful years, he was feeling his oats at Warner Bros.; he was more comfortable letting loose. His friendship with Flynn didn't hurt. Walsh still had that wild side to him; as the years progressed, he let the tiger out of the cage. The fact that he had owned a pet lion when he and Lorraine lived on Petit in the San Fernando Valley—and kept it on the property—might have meant something.

Adventure yarns were the easiest kind of escapism for Walsh, and he directed them adeptly, coming away with the moniker *action director*. But with his next outing, *Gentleman Jim*, he had the chance again to live out a fantasy of childhood, just as he had when he directed *The Strawberry Blonde*. These escapes into the past, where one easily reimagines a lost childhood, brought as much pleasure as the actioners did. This new picture, a biography of sorts of the boxer Gentleman Jim Corbett, centers on family ties and close-knit friendships. The look back at the past brought with it for Walsh more possibility of seeing what his own life was when he was young. Much like *The Strawberry Blonde, Gentleman Jim* is a conscious (perhaps even unconscious) yearning for a more perfect world, certainly a simpler one. In this kind of film, Walsh creates a stream of consciousness between genres: drama, comedy, romance, and nostalgia, all fluidly changing from one into the other. One scene, one form, flows easily into another and back out again, inspiring the French producer Pierre Rissient, Walsh's close friend, to say later that, with *Gentleman Jim*, Walsh showed that he could have directed any Shakespearean play with ease, moving swiftly and naturally between tragedy and comedy with hardly a disruption.[29]

Jim Corbett first published his memoirs, *The Roar of the Crowd*, in the *Saturday Evening Post* in five weekly installments beginning on October 11, 1924. The Curtis Publishing Company later published the memoirs as a book in April 1925, then sold the rights to Putnam that same year. Warner Bros. bought the rights to Corbett's story from his widow, Vera Corbett, in August 1941. She also furnished the studio with Corbett's personal letters, photographs, and various other papers. The story department later sent a report on *The Roar of the Crowd*, noting that it contained "excellent possibilities, but not as a Cagney vehicle, since he is scarcely the *Gentleman Jim* type of fighter."[30] With Cagney

always first in mind but now out of consideration, the studio went down
the list to look for the next possible candidate—and for a director.

In March 1943, the studio assigned Lewis Milestone to direct the
Corbett biography in what would have been his first assignment at Warner Bros. had he not so vehemently disliked the script shown him. On
April 3, 1942, he told the picture's producer, Robert Buckner, "*Gentleman Jim* is dull, slow, and in my opinion, without any entertainment
value whatsoever, both as a character and as a story." He then added,
"The script so lacks all elements that go to make up any kind of picture
that this script comes off as a dull documentary on the prize ring."[31]
Warners had the wrong director, even though he seemed right at first.

Warners also showed the script to the director Vincent Sherman,
who actually liked it, before handing it over to its rightful owner, Walsh,
who told Jack Warner right away that it looked like "a swell set up." "I
think," he said, "I will be able to get a picture that will top 'Strawberry
Blonde' and that I will have no trouble in selling it to Errol Flynn as this
is the best part he has ever had." Walsh then wanted to use Barry Fitzgerald and Sarah Algood as Corbett's parents. "You probably remember
them from the picture, 'How Green Was My Valley,'" he told Jack. He
saw Ann Sheridan for the romantic lead. "I believe the combination of
Flynn and Sheridan on the marquee would make a great box office attraction. If Sheridan is not available I would settle for Rita Hayworth."
Just for good measure, Walsh reminded Warner, "My old man used to
tell me I was an Irishman with a yiddisher kopf. What do you think?"[32]
Actually, William Fox said that to Walsh years earlier—but why not
make his father look good?

Warner wrote to Walsh on May 19th, "Dear Raoul: I want to wish
you every success on the starting of *Gentleman Jim*. As I told you before,
I am sure it is going to one of the biggest productions you have ever been
in charge of."[33] Walsh appreciated Warner's enthusiasm but was hardly
ruffled by the picture's size. He was comfortable in having gotten Flynn
to play Jim Corbett, and he now thought Alexis Smith was just the right
match as Corbett's romantic interest, Victoria Ware. Walsh surrounded
himself with the usual suspects in his extended Warner Bros. family. The
studio cast Ward Bond, often part of the Jack Ford stock company, to
play John L. Sullivan; also on board were Jack Carson, Alan Hale, William Frawley, and Carl Harbaugh. Even if he didn't know it consciously,

Walsh was thinking family when he planned this picture. He also cast his seventeen-year-old stepdaughter Marilynn (although uncredited) to play Corbett's sister, Mary. Marilynn had just gotten married, and she and her husband, Donald Phillips, still lived with Walsh and Lorraine in the house on Doheny Drive.

Walsh began shooting *Gentleman Jim* on May 21, 1942, and finished two months later on July 23, even though the studio held its release to November 25 of that year, just in time to exploit the picture's nostalgic hue and, no doubt, collect some Thanksgiving turkey. The shoot was unremarkable despite Warner's words to Walsh about the film's huge parameters. The sportswriter Ed Cochrane and Mushy Callahan, the onetime junior welterweight champ, coached Flynn until he got the boxing moves down to a fine art. Flynn's schedule was simple and kept him showing up on a regular basis: he would work out for two hours every morning and be on the set by 10:00 A.M. It was not until the third week in July, when the production was coming to a close, that he became ill and had to be hospitalized, which put the schedule three days behind. But Walsh caught up quickly; he refused to turn the picture in late—he cut out three pages of the script just to save time.

Errol Flynn always considered *Gentleman Jim* to be his favorite film of his career—and, whether or not he was aware of it, this thought was a reflection of his feelings for Walsh. Of all the films the two made together, in no other did Errol Flynn better inhabit Raoul Walsh's persona—the brash sentimentalist, the reckless bad boy, the charmer of women, the man who never stops longing for a chivalric world in which to be a knight. From his first frame to his last, as he walks out of the picture sparring with Virginia Ware, Flynn is playing Raoul Walsh. When the film opens and the camera almost haphazardly finds Flynn as Jim Corbett strutting up to a boxing ring with his pal Walter (Jack Carson), he struts as Walsh would want to: leaning forward, he almost dances as he moves. The first opportunity he gets, he shows his all-American ingenuity: he takes an opportunity when he finds it, and he does it with aplomb, almost bombastically. Flynn is always playing Walsh—the Walsh of Walsh's dreams—brash, forward looking, light on his feet, smile flashing, opportunistic, and, handsomely, ready to win the jackpot, even to go look for it if there is a chance it is anywhere nearby.

Flynn is playing Walsh because *Gentleman Jim* is Walsh's great autobiographical tract, another version of the book he would write in the
1970s, but still a young man's look back at his own fantasies—the way
he would have liked his early life to play out, with his family grounding
him and his life overflowing with corny one-liners that spell out love
from people around him. From the first overlay on the screen, "1887,"
the year of Walsh's birth, the picture is a fantasy of Walsh's own life
and times. The family is loving, the best friend is lie-on-the-railroad-
tracks loyal, and, above all, the woman in his life is intelligent, spirited,
independent, and beautiful. To make this picture complete, there is the
goal: not too far away so that he cannot reach to touch it, but far enough
away to make the getting of it a sporting event in which he is challenged
to show his American gusto. He is boyish, good-looking, honorable, and
sensitive but, above all, a champion. This is not the Flynn of Custer's life,
where sadness seeps through into tragic proportions; this is Flynn and
Walsh still buoyant, still looking at a future of possibilities, still seduced
by the American dream (and the Irish) that one's life lies in the future
and the process of one's life is to reach to get it.

Walsh's setups and camerawork flesh out this fantasy of robust
young manhood. Movements are swift, stages are large public arenas for
success. In one particularly energetic scene, Corbett fights Joe Choyn-
sky on a San Francisco Bay barge. Walsh's first work with a favorite
cinematographer, Sid Hickox, is large in scope and captures the crowd's
enormous enthusiasm; in one instance, Corbett lands in the bay with the
camera moving back to catch the disbelief, then the roar of the crowd as
Corbett gleefully climbs out of the water onto the platform and swoops
down on his opponent to win the fight. This fantasy avoids gloom.

The picture's movement ebbs and flows from high moments to low
moments, just like a life, just like a man's life. During scenes in which
Flynn moves deftly from one part of a huge hotel lobby to another,
Walsh positions the camera far back and moves easily as Flynn walks
down a huge staircase, glides to the left of the screen, then to the right,
as he practically floats out of the hotel entrance. The camera moves
carefully with him; this moment in Corbett's life, part of his calculated
move to the top of his game, flows naturally and without disruption.
Walsh's camera, along with the pace of the film, moves quickly, then

slows down, and then picks up again, before the cycle repeats itself. But there is never a break in any of the action, any of the character's growth.

Warners released the picture to equally robust box-office returns and critical praise. Flynn's genial performance, supported by Walsh's exuberant yet graceful depiction of his main character and the times in which he lived, generated an infectious enthusiasm for the picture that has grown by the decade. The *New York Times* said that the picture had a "warm, earthy spirit" and enough good qualities "to make it a satisfying show for anybody's money."[34] Walsh could take pleasure in the work he accomplished with *Gentleman Jim,* and it was a personal triumph to boot—one that consisted of drifting back into his own past and finding the best parts of what made him *him.* He liked himself best in moments such as these, and he would almost have to concede that filmmaking could be personal.

Gentleman Jim was a good defense against the financial and emotional chaos Miriam threw into his life. Lorraine was not much of a buffer in their marriage, but at this time Walsh met someone who could be: Mary Edna Simpson, a nineteen-year-old beauty whom Walsh fell madly in love with the moment he met her and who became his third and final wife. In his autobiography, Walsh writes about the time he first met this striking blue-eyed blond, thirty-six years his junior. He had gone to look for horses in Lexington, Kentucky, and when he went to a breeder's home, Mary opened the front door. For a man uncomfortable with love scenes, Walsh found himself smack in the middle of one. The story of how the two met may be truth, and it may be fiction, but nevertheless, by the early 1940s Walsh was in love again.

Mary Edna Simpson, born in Lexington in 1923, had had a childhood not unlike that of Miriam Cooper. When she was a young child, her mother, Inez, died, leaving Mary, two sisters, and one brother to be cared for by their father. Unable to meet that responsibility, the father put his children in an orphanage. Six years later, their paternal grandfather took them out and raised them himself.

After meeting Mary, Walsh stayed away from the Doheny house more often, telling Lorraine he was going out with friends—or even going away fishing for a few days. It didn't take Lorraine too long to figure out what was going on. By the mid-1940s, Walsh and Mary moved into a house together in the San Fernando Valley and lived there, "illegally," as Lorraine later claimed, until they married in Mexico in 1948, two years after Walsh and Lorraine would divorce. Walsh loved Mary deeply, but whether he could be faithful was another matter entirely. For now, at least, he saw no farther than the beautiful Mary.

10

In Love and War

By now Walsh was living fully the scenario he'd concocted long ago: he'd hardly finish one picture, and the next morning the studio would throw a new script on his front lawn. He used to say this about working for Griffith, but now he could just as easily say it about Warner Bros., where the fictions he'd already directed came barreling out of the pen at a quick pace. It seemed as though there was no space of time between them. And, when he wasn't on the set, he was at the races, not much with Lorraine, but instead with Mary, the new love in his life. Mary was born and raised in Kentucky, where he often went to buy horses. If he imagined that he had met Mary there, so be it.

In early September 1942, just before the studio released *Desperate Journey,* and before Walsh began work on *Background to Danger,* Jack Warner and the producer Jerry Wald asked him to help get them out of a jam. Wald was producing *Action in the North Atlantic* with Humphrey Bogart, who had just come off the set of *Casablanca.* But, in the middle of the production, the director Lloyd Bacon's contract with the studio ran out. Refusing to finish the picture without talk of a new one, Bacon walked off the set, and Warner fired him. Warner and Wald asked Walsh to step in and direct some of the action sequences until the new director, Byron Haskins, took over. Those sequences are the only mark Walsh left on the picture, even though its second unit director, Ridgeway (Reggie) Callow (who would also work with Walsh on the upcoming *The Man I Love* and *Cheyenne*), learned a thing or two from them: "Walsh . . . taught me more about action set-ups than anyone in the business. . . . For instance, if you're shooting a sequence of horses riding down a mountain, and they couldn't come down very fast, he had a way, an absolute knack of placing his camera in the right position to get the greatest effect

236

out of the stunt. In other words, many directors would do the same stunt as Raoul Walsh would do, but they'd have the camera in the wrong position. It was a question of enhancing the stunt."[1] Walsh would quip that it was just part of the job, tossing it off nonchalantly the way Flynn would toss off the danger involved in saving the life of one of his men in his last espionage picture. He kept silent about the great pleasure he took in manipulating a complicated shot.

But Flynn was nowhere around when Walsh shot the first of what he called the "three quickies" he "knocked off" the next year—*Background to Danger, Northern Pursuit,* and *Uncertain Glory.*[2] He went into production on *Background to Danger* almost immediately after his work on *Action in the North Atlantic.* He knew that it would be a business-as-usual adventure yarn. Still, he probably wasn't smiling when he learned it meant working with George Raft again. Like him or not, Walsh produced a more than credible adventure film with this project.

Initially intended for Flynn, the part went to Raft instead. In this entertaining thriller, Raft plays a very crafty American in neutral Turkey during World War II who gets mixed up with some smarmy characters: Peter Lorre as a Russian agent and Sydney Greenstreet as a Nazi. But Walsh's nonchalant attitude toward the material did not get in the way of his capable direction and hardly lessens the story's excitement, which is characteristically nonstop in this picture as well as *Northern Pursuit* and *Uncertain Glory.*

Not surprisingly, Walsh playfully subscribed to the script's view that good old American ingenuity and know-how can seize the day in any situation, especially during wartime. The scenario is simple: Americans are smart; Europeans (especially Nazi-affiliated ones) are not. One of the earliest scenes in the film has Raft outsmarting one of the locals when his character, Joe Barton, skinnies out of paying for a pack of gum, pulling one over on the local merchant who sold it to him and who is dumbfounded by Raft's quick getaway. Sly fox that he is, Raft leaves the man looking beguiled.

This sets the playful tenor—until the game playing becomes more dangerous. Barton unwittingly gets involved in a series of dangerous plots. He is asked to protect some photographs that prove Turkey is about to invade Russia and then is even asked to become a Nazi agent.

But no one can outwit Raft in this movie and get away with it. In the end, he helps get the evildoers put away and lights out for his next European assignment.

Despite all the action, Raft was no Flynn, and although *Background to Danger* traipses across dangerous European terrain with the rhythm of a high-speed train, as a story it lacks a certain charm and depth with Raft doing the running. Warner Bros. took the novelist Eric Ambler's fairly complex hero and the wartime spy situation and essentially made milquetoast of them. Raft insisted that the screenwriters give his character a great deal of swagger, insisting also that they change him from the ordinary guy, Joe, Ambler wrote to a supersmart secret agent. Joe Barton's depth of soul became lost in the doing.

The story was in trouble long before its production start date, September 1942. The producer Robert Lord told Wallis that the script looked as if "it might have been written at Monogram or one of the small, independent studios": "It is quick, slovenly, cheap and sloppy. The characters are conventional types, mechanically forced into preposterous situations."[3] The melodrama looked to be on a level with *Flash Gordon* and similar comic strips. Wallis wanted the picture taken off the schedule—that is, before the studio did a turnabout and put not only W. R. Burnett on it but also an uncredited William Faulkner, this just before Faulkner asked to be released from his contract with the studio because he disliked screenwriting so much. John Huston briefly showed an interest in working on the script but at the time was distracted by attempts to film an adaptation of Herman Melville's *Moby Dick* with his father, Walter Huston, playing Ahab. After sitting in on story meetings for a brief time, Huston walked away from *Background to Danger*. Eventually, Warners had Burnett write the script, one of the few he produced at the studio that barely rises above the superficial.

Jo Graham, a Warners dialogue director, had just been promoted to feature director and was scheduled to direct this picture before the studio decided to go with Walsh instead. Once Walsh got working, the picture started moving—this despite the behind-the-scenes scuffle between Raft and Peter Lorre in what seemed to Walsh a repeat of the Raft-Robinson fight on the set of *Manpower*. Walsh liked a good boxing match as much as the next man but not if it interfered with him getting a picture finished. Raft's personal assistant, Mack Grey, recalled that, in one particular scene, Walsh had Raft sitting tied up in a chair when Lorre walked around him blowing smoke in his face. Raft asked Lorre to "knock it off," which only encouraged Lorre to blow more smoke and laugh at Raft. Later on, Raft retaliated by clobbering Lorre over the head while he sat in his dressing room. A different version, offered by Lorre's stuntman, Harvey Parry, had Lorre doing his own stunt work with a cigarette in a scene that also included Raft and the actress Brenda Marshall. When asked by Raft what he was doing, Lorre replied, "I'm stealing the scene." Raft asked him whom he was stealing it from, and Lorre replied, "From you and Brenda." Raft asked how, and Lorre said, "They're like you, they all watch me." This remark irritated Raft, who then called Lorre "a son of a bitch"—and after the scene finished, he asked Lorre not to do it again. Lorre responded with, "Georgie, I do what I want, you do what you want. I wish you good luck." So Raft later went to Lorre's dressing room and belted him, knocking him from the sofa where he sat. Walsh then grabbed Raft and told him, "Now come on, George. He's just a little guy." Walsh tried to make peace between the two but no doubt had to turn his face the other way to hide a smile.[4]

The otherwise uneventful shoot, which lasted from September 28, 1942, to the middle of November 1942, was shorter than the shelf time the picture put in. Warners didn't release *Background to Danger* until July 3, 1943. Word was not great. The ever-astute film critic James Agee wrote:

> Eric Ambler's stories are not yet getting very good breaks on the screen. Orson Welles's *Journey into Fear* had sophistication without much journeying, in the kinesthetic sense of the word, still less fear. *Background to Danger* has plenty of danger, in lively motion at that, without a background keenly drawn enough to make it really dangerous. Short of the really "creative" men, Raoul Walsh is one of my favorite directors; but—besides thoroughly enjoying it—you could use this film for one kind of measurement of the unconquerable difference between a good job by Hitchcock and a good job of the Hitchcock type.[5]

Around Christmas 1942, turning away from *Background,* Walsh was set to direct *I Was Born Yesterday,* a film featuring Bogart and adapted from a W. R. Burnett novel. But the assignment turned out to be a fluke; no such picture made the production logs at Warner Bros. Walsh moved on to *Northern Pursuit,* the second of his self-proclaimed unholy three, which began as a two-part series by Leslie T. White called "Five Thousand Trojan Horses," published in the June and July 1942 issues of *Adventure* magazine. Warner Bros. bought the rights to the story in August 1942 and put together a script called *The Last Man* before learning that Paramount Studios had that name on its permanently protected list. After a brief change to *Night Shift, Northern Pursuit* became the title that stuck. Even though Walsh would direct Flynn again, and even though a fine team of writers worked on the script, including Frank Gruber, Alvah Bessie, and an uncredited William Faulkner (who actually worked on films into the 1950s), the picture impressed few critics or filmgoers when Warner Bros. released it in November 1943. Filmed between mid-April 1943 and the first week in July, it was kept on the shelf a good seven months. Interestingly, Walsh sent a memo to Warner a month before starting the picture, saying, "I saw the German picture entitled 'Leave on Your Honor,' this morning. This can be made into a great picture. I have two ideas and if you are interested I would like to tell them to you."[6] It is unknown whether Walsh was referring to the upcoming *Northern Pursuit* or another picture. At this juncture, he very often suggested ideas to Warner; it was only in the 1950s that he more characteristically took on assignments to bring in the money.

Northern Pursuit was the first picture produced for Warner Bros. by Jack Chertok, who had just left MGM and would go on to produce the Bette Davis vehicle *The Corn Is Green* (1945). The company traveled up to Sun Valley, Idaho, where forty-two sets were eventually built: all but two were snow covered. Two weeks after filming began, Walsh asked Steve Trilling to arrange a screening of Fox's new film *Desert Victory* as he wanted to watch the battle sequences. He briefly took the company to Ketchum, but Sun Valley was the main location. Filming was as smooth as any Walsh and Flynn worked on since Flynn seemed generally to behave and show up to the set every day. On this production, he found a way to spend his off-camera time; he sat offstage and finished his second novel, *One Man in His Time.* He also found time to pose for the portrait painter John Decker. He was too busy not to show up.

Although the picture's story line resembles Michael Powell's *49th Parallel*, Walsh's version of the material didn't impress audiences in the same way as the British Powell's more successful film, released in 1941. Also a World War II espionage tale, *Northern Pursuit* has Flynn portraying a Canadian Mountie of German descent who feigns guiding a band of Nazi saboteurs to their mystery base in the area of the Hudson Bay. But of course he is really working for the Allies and is able to prevent the Nazis' plan to bomb the Panama Canal. In between, Walsh mounts the action in nonstop fashion, and Flynn charms his way through every episode, inspiring a *Variety* critic to call the picture one of the best "of the traditions of outdoor melodrama."[7]

Walsh and Flynn decided to treat themselves to a vacation after they finished shooting *Northern Pursuit,* and during the last week of July, they went to Mexico City to watch the bullfights and then flew to Acapulco to get in some fishing. In fact, they spent a good amount of time in each other's company—Walsh always without Lorraine or even Mary, in fact. Then Walsh and Flynn followed *Northern Pursuit* with *Uncertain Glory,* this time joined by the feature players Paul Lukas and Faye Emerson, the elegant Lucile Watson, and the newcomer Jean Sullivan as Flynn's love interest. Although the picture has gained a reputation for being implausible if anything, Flynn's performance is still a winning one; he brings an edge to his character that foreshadows the conflicted protagonist he would portray in Walsh's 1948 western *Silver River.* As he aged, Flynn displayed gruffness more than swagger; Walsh was on hand to put it to use.

Initially called *The Last Vacation, Uncertain Glory* is another World War II thriller that has Flynn playing a condemned French criminal named Jean Picard who, when we first see him, is heading to the guillotine. But, when a bomb hits the prison, Jean escapes and soon poses as a resistance worker, albeit a cynical one after his narrow escape from death. Lukas is the French police inspector who initially arrested Jean. After a series of both heroic and criminal acts, Jean eventually gives himself over to the Nazis in order to save the lives of one hundred other people. In the course of the story, he learns to be honorable, an irony so winning for Flynn's character that it almost carries the picture over the line to melodrama. More and more, Flynn had wanted to play characters with a dramatic edge to them—heroes still, of course, but heroes who were more complex than those his swashbuckling roles called for. Walsh gives him the opportunity here. Jean Picard is a double-edged hero, as dishonorable as he is honorable, as prone to being opportunistic as he is to being valorous. He retains his doubleness right to the end. Again and again, Walsh frames him dead center in the midst of chaos (battles that are as physical as they are psychological) until he is forced to find a way out of it.

The film's leading lady, Jean Sullivan, recalled the gingerly way Walsh treated Errol Flynn on the set. "Errol decided he wanted to rewrite a scene. Raoul said, 'No problem.' We did Errol's version, but I think what ended up on the screen was the original." Sullivan also recalled Walsh's sudden jaunts to the telephone in between shots. "I found out later he loved the racetrack. He was just trying to find what horse had come in first at Hialeah!"[8] Sullivan's recall has a familiar ring to it as Walsh had for years often chosen to read racetrack papers over scripts during these daytime hours.

Actual shooting began on August 26, 1943, and finished November 3. As the production moved along, Walsh began to speed up noticeably, constantly changing and shortening the script and getting Flynn to go along with him on that. The film was shot partially at the Warner ranch in Simi Valley, and the unit manager Frank Mattison wrote in the production log that Walsh just continued to "hammer this stuff out right on schedule."[9] When Walsh did go back, it was to pick up an added shot, but this still didn't slow his pace, and he stayed on schedule to the end. He was in a hurry to get it finished. It was probably coincidence that the picture's title was taken from two lines of Shakespeare's *Two Gentlemen of Verona*—"Oh how this spring of love resembleth / The uncertain glory of an April Day"—and that Warners waited until April 1944 to release it.

School for Scoundrels

As quickly as Walsh could salvage another director's weak action sequence, so could he turn around and abruptly create his own bad action sequence off the set. Just when *Uncertain Glory* opened in theaters,

Raoul Walsh's mother, Elizabeth Brough Walsh, the year before her death in 1902, when Walsh was fifteen years old. Courtesy Mary Walsh Collection.

Thomas Walsh, Raoul Walsh's father, taken in California sometime in the early 1930s. Courtesy Mary Walsh Collection.

Albert, on the far right, as a young student in New York City, in school but not for long. Courtesy Mary Walsh Collection.

Albert, already handsomely dressed, already the horseman—taken about the time he gave his parents a scare and rode off solo to Virginia on a horse. Courtesy Mary Walsh Collection.

"Raoul" Walsh, after touring with the road show of Thomas Dixon's *The Clansman,* now making the rounds of New York agents looking for work as an actor. Walsh inscribed the photograph to the cinematographer Philip du Bois and signed his real name, Al. Courtesy the Academy of Motion Picture Arts and Sciences.

Raoul Walsh as a young actor. Courtesy Mary Walsh Collection.

Walsh soon after arriving in Los Angeles with the D. W. Griffith players. Walsh took his cues from Griffith, both on the set and off. Walsh had his initials, RW, engraved on the door of his roadster. Courtesy Mary Walsh Collection.

Raoul and George Walsh in dramatic dress, probably about 1915. Courtesy Mary Walsh Collection.

Raoul Walsh as the young Pancho Villa, who probably never looked this good. Courtesy Wesleyan University Cinema Archives.

Marie (Anna Q. Nilsson) is threatened by the Bowery hood "Skinny" (William Sheer) in Walsh's first picture for Fox, *Regeneration* (1915), the first feature-length gangster film in American cinema. Courtesy Kino Video.

The young lovers Raoul Walsh and Miriam Cooper at the time of their marriage in 1916. Courtesy the Academy of Motion Picture Arts and Sciences.

Promotional material for Walsh's early opus *The Honor System* (1917). John Ford considered this lost classic one of his favorite American films of all time. Courtesy the Academy of Motion Picture Arts and Sciences.

REDEEMED FROM THE DUNGEON

THE WOMAN
(Gladys Brockwell)

THE VICTIM
(Milton Sills)

"HARD LABOR"

EACH MAN TO HIS CELL

THE BOSS
(Charles Clary)

THE YOUNG WIRELESS INVENTOR

FOOD UNFIT FOR DO

THE BRUTAL KEEPER

THE GRAFTER
(Bay Rice)

THE ATTEMPTED ESCAPE

The newly formed Independent Screen Artists Guild holding its first national assembly at the Ambassador Hotel in Los Angeles, CA, on December 15, 1921. *Seated from left to right:* William Selig, Buster Keaton, Thomas Ince holding young Jackie Coogan, Charlie Chaplin, Allan Holubar, Sol Lesser, Maurice Tourneur. *Standing from left to right:* Lou Anger, J. Packer Read Jr., James Young, Jack Coogan Sr., J. Walton Tully, King Vidor, Carter De Haven, H. O. Davis, J. D. Williams (a producer at First National), J. L. Frothingham, Rudolph Cameron, Joseph M. Schenck, Louis B. Mayer, Marshall Neilan, Benjamin Percival (B. P.) Schulberg, Raoul Walsh, Hubert Henley.

Walsh directed his wife, Miriam, along with Ralph Graves, in the 1922 drama *Kindred of the Dust.* The more melodramatic the part, the more Miriam liked it; there were plenty such parts to go around as Walsh and Miriam worked together frequently during their marriage. He remained her favorite director. Courtesy the Academy of Motion Picture Arts and Sciences.

Walsh thoroughly enjoyed mingling with the natives in Tahiti when he shot *Lost and Found on a South Sea Island* (later shortened to *Lost and Found*) in 1923 for the Samuel Goldwyn Co. Miriam and their son Jackie accompanied Walsh on the trip, but Walsh deleted their presence on the island when he published his autobiography in 1974. Courtesy Kevin Brownlow.

Walsh and Douglas Fairbanks fooling around on the set of *The Thief of Bagdad* in West Hollywood, late 1923, early 1924. Courtesy Mary Walsh Collection.

A handsomely arranged promotional photograph of Walsh directing Pola Negri on the set of *East of Suez*, released in January 1925. Courtesy Kevin Brownlow.

Walsh among the Fox elite during a company luncheon in the mid-1920s. Courtesy the Academy of Motion Picture Arts and Sciences.

Captain Flagg (Victor McLaglen) holds a dying young soldier (Barry Norton) and learns the humility he sorely needs in Walsh's eloquent and haunting antiwar film *What Price Glory?* Courtesy the Academy of Motion Picture Arts and Sciences.

Walsh and Gloria Swanson burned up more than the screen and the censors during production on 1928's *Sadie Thompson*. Photograph in author's collection.

(*Above*) Walsh was to play the Cisco Kid and direct 1929's *In Old Arizona* before a freak Jeep accident cost him his eye and forced him to bow out as the picture's director and lead actor. Irving Cummings finished directing, and Warner Baxter won an Oscar for playing the Kid. Courtesy Mary Walsh Collection. (*Below*) Walsh was at the center of the action when he directed the spirited 1929 release *Hot for Paris*. The actor El Brendel hams it up on Walsh's right, and two of the director's favorites, the French actress Fifi D'Orsay and Victor McLaglen, sit at Walsh's left. Courtesy Eddie Brandt's Saturday Matinee.

Overdressed for the Oregon Trail, Walsh and the writer Hal Evarts (*left*) are dashing as they meet on the Fox lot just before Walsh directed and collaborated with Evarts on his story for the epic 1930 epic *The Big Trail*. Courtesy Kevin Brownlow.

Walsh directs a difficult sequence involving lowering wagons, animals, and pioneers down a cliff during filming on *The Big Trail*. Somewhere down the cliff, the Walsh discovery John Wayne sits awaiting the rest of the party. Courtesy Mary Walsh Collection.

Spencer Tracy and Joan Bennett tie the knot in the innocently sexy *Me and My Gal*. Photograph in author's collection.

(*Right*) Two good friends: Walsh and Marion Davies on the set of *Going Hollywood*, filmed partially on Walsh's Encino ranch on Petit Dr. Courtesy Mary Walsh Collection.

(*Below*) When not on the set or at the races in the mid-1930s, Walsh could be seen with Lorraine at Marion Davies's frequent costume parties held at the Hearst Castle (or one of the homes Hearst built for Davies). Walsh is on the right sporting a fake handlebar moustache. Courtesy the Academy of Motion Picture Arts and Sciences.

Marlene Dietrich visits Walsh and Mae West on the set of the naughty *Klondike Annie,* released in 1936. Courtesy Photofest.

The Walshes (*on the right*) joining in for a weekend with William Randolph Hearst (*center*), this time without Hearst's mistress, Marion Davies. Courtesy Eddie Brandt's Saturday Matinee.

Walsh and his wife, Lorraine, in the mid-1930s, visiting his horses at a California stable. Courtesy the Academy of Motion Picture Arts and Sciences.

Walsh, Lorraine, and Lorraine's daughter, Marilynn, returning to Los Angeles from a European trip in the mid-1930s. Walsh adopted Marilynn when she was very young, and the two stayed connected even after Marilynn's marriage in the mid-1940s. She named her first child Raoul Donald Phillips, partly after Walsh, and partly after her husband, Don Phillips. Courtesy the Academy of Motion Picture Arts and Sciences.

The interior of Raoul and Lorraine Walsh's home on N. Doheny Dr. in Beverly Hills in the early 1940s, styled by the Hollywood interior designer Harold Grieve. Drawings and photographs of Walsh's beloved horses decorated the walls of all Walsh's homes. Courtesy the Academy of Motion Picture Arts and Sciences.

Cagney and Bogie in Walsh's first film at Warner Bros., *The Roaring Twenties*. The 1939 picture marked the beginning of Walsh's golden period—and his thirty-year relationship with "Colonel" Jack Warner. Photograph in author's collection.

Bogart, Ann Sheridan, and George Raft steer the hard-knocks drama *They Drive by Night*, Walsh's blend of darkness, gloom, and poetic lyricism. Photograph in author's collection.

Walsh and his adopted son, Robert, stand outside a Los Angeles County courthouse on April 3, 1940. Although eighteen years of age, Robert sought to have Walsh named his legal guardian, stating in his petition that the alcohol abuse of his adoptive mother, Miriam Cooper, made his home life in New York intolerable. Robert won his bid and lived intermittently with Walsh. Later on, the two became estranged. Courtesy Photofest.

Walsh and Bogie enjoy a good laugh on the set of *High Sierra*. Everything turned out right on the picture: Bogie got his first shot at being a leading man, and Walsh solidified his standing as a Warner's gem. Courtesy Photofest.

(*Above*) Errol Flynn, Walsh, and
Olivia de Havilland share a light
moment on the set of *They Died
with Their Boots On,* a serendipitous film for all three: Walsh and
Flynn began their close working
relationship, while de Havilland
and Flynn saw the end of their
eight-picture run together—and
the romantic fire between them.
Photograph in author's collection.

(*Right*) Mary Edna Simpson,
Walsh's third wife, in the early
1940s. Mary was nineteen when
Walsh met her; not yet separated
from Lorraine, Walsh was smitten
with Mary, and there was no
going back. She was the love of
his life, and their marriage lasted
more than three decades. Courtesy
Mary Walsh Collection.

Walsh and Rita Hayworth ham it up during the production of *The Strawberry Blonde*, the movie Walsh called his favorite of all his pictures. He always believed that he gave Hayworth her big start with this film. Courtesy Mary Walsh Collection.

Ida Lupino and Walsh at the Macambo nightclub in Hollywood, 1945. The two made four pictures together: Lupino had the right combination of toughness and vulnerability that made her the perfect Walshian dame. Courtesy Photofest.

Walsh and Errol Flynn on the set of *Objective, Burma!* the classic war picture that gave Flynn one of his most successful roles. Courtesy Photofest.

Walsh and Mary with Dennis Morgan on the set of *Cheyenne* in 1945.
Walsh sometimes removed his signature eye patch and sported only a
bandage over his missing right eye. Courtesy Eddie Brandt's Saturday
Matinee.

Teresa Wright, Walsh, and Judith Anderson on the set of the psychological western *Pursued*. This film and the upcoming *White Heat* and *Along the Great Divide* mark Walsh hitting his stride with a spate of Oedipal-driven stories of male anxiety. Courtesy Mary Walsh Collection.

Trouble ahead: the psychotic icon Cody Jarrett holes up in the car with the two reasons he goes up in a great ball of fire in *White Heat*, Ma Jarrett (Margaret Wycherly) and the always unfaithful Verna (Virginia Mayo). Photograph in author's collection.

Mary and Raoul Walsh greeting the 1950s on a European vacation.
Courtesy Mary Walsh Collection.

Gregory Peck, Virginia Mayo, and Walsh go over the script on the set of 1951's *Captain Horatio Hornblower* at Denham Studios in England. Walsh considered this sea adventure the most difficult film of his career. Courtesy Sir Ken Adam.

Rock Hudson dries off after dipping in the water during production on 1953's slippery tale *Sea Devils*. The picture also took a dip with audiences and critics. Walsh personally groomed Hudson when he had the actor under personal contract before placing him at Universal Studios in 1949. Courtesy Peter Newbrook.

Walsh and his "bad boy" friend, the writer John Twist, in the early 1950s. Twist and Walsh were close for years, although some attributed Walsh's box-office fall in the 1950s to the screenplays Twist wrote for him. Courtesy Mary Walsh Collection.

Walsh in Spain in 1958 during production on the spritely western spoof *The Sheriff of Fractured Jaw*. This image is telling: Walsh lost in the landscape of his own adventures. Courtesy Kevin Brownlow.

Walsh entertaining visitors at his Simi Valley ranch in the early 1970s. *From the left,* Walsh; the director Peter Bogdanovich; Walsh's old friend, the director Allan Dwan; the actress Cybill Shepherd; and the actress Dolores Moran, who worked with Walsh in the 1940s. After Walsh retired, visitors frequently came to the ranch. Mary characteristically stayed in the background, serving freshly squeezed orange juice from the many orange trees on the property. Dwan last saw Walsh shortly before Walsh's death in December 1980. Dwan died a year later. Courtesy Mary Walsh Collection.

The quintessential Raoul Walsh, adventurous, forward leaning, and posing with one of the many Native American actors and extras who appeared in his films over his long career. Courtesy Mary Walsh Collection.

Walsh was back in legal hot water again, settling out of court charges of misrepresenting a horse he sold for $700. The Berman Stock Farm accused Walsh of representing that thirteen of fifteen mares he sold were in foal and that three colts, also included in the sale, were registered Thoroughbreds. Berman contended that only one colt was born, that four of the mares were blind, and that one horse was so starved that it could not be moved. Additionally, he charged that Walsh provided no registration papers to the stock company. The story made the local papers even though Walsh was able to settle without too much more notoriety. His financial worries never truly abated, and if he saw a way to find extra funds, he might take advantage of it.[10] Bad behavior sometimes lurked in the background.

Colleagues who worked on pictures with Walsh would never think of him as a dishonest man; instead, they might assume he made a mistake or overlooked the small print on a legal document. Most of his colleagues viewed him with an affectionate eye. He could be impishly irreverent on the set, and, certainly, he brought a bundle of idiosyncrasies to the plate. For one, he dressed impeccably, whether he wore a sports coat or a western jacket. He might have a scarf or an ascot tucked into his shirt, and he was sure to finish off the ensemble with a pair of English riding pants. All this presentation offset—or seemed oxymoronic to—the loose tobacco he continually spilled on his pants, a hazard that came with his incessant habit of rolling his own cigarettes and creating a circle of tobacco all around the chair he sat in or the area in front of the camera should he happen to be looking through it. If he ventured away from the camera, as he did more often than not, his crew and actors could easily trace his whereabouts by following the tobacco trail he left in his wake.

By the mid-1940s, Walsh had established his reputation at Warners as a tough action director who occasionally dipped into nostalgic set pieces or light comedy. But, when he now stepped onto the set of the implausible comedy *The Horn Blows at Midnight,* he took what many considered a wrong turn. The lightweight plot had the comedian Jack Benny playing a trumpeter in a radio orchestra who falls asleep during commercial readings and dreams he is an angel in heaven commissioned to destroy the earth by blowing his trumpet at midnight. The character pulling the strings is the Big Chief (the character actor extraordinaire Guy Kibbee), who is disgusted with the way people treat each other on our planet. Benny does his bidding for him.

Mark Hellinger seemed an odd choice to produce this out-of-sorts comedy, adapted by Sam Hellman and James V. Kern from a story written by Aubrey Wisberg. Even a lilting score by Franz Waxman could not alter the awkwardness of the action; in fact, it seems to enhance its dissonance. The actor Richard Erdman, who would appear in Walsh's *Objective, Burma!* recalled years later that *The Horn Blows at Midnight* was the talk of the Warner Bros. lot when the shoot began but that it was considered ruined because Walsh was the wrong director for the light-footed comedy.[11]

Initially called *Come Blow Your Horn,* the picture had a golden cast that included Benny, Alexis Smith, Dolores Moran, Reginald Gardiner, Guy Kibbee, and Margaret Dumont. The picture was actually a reunion for Walsh, Alexis Smith, and the cinematographer Sid Hickox, who had all worked on *Gentleman Jim,* although Walsh and Hickox would pair fairly often at the studio. The script was still unfinished when Walsh began shooting on November 27, 1943, but that never bothered him; he was just as happy to write it himself as he went along. Walsh shot the picture on the Warner Bros. lot and, for the exteriors, took his actors down the road to Griffith Park, just southwest of the studio. When shooting concluded on February 3, 1944—although Warners did not release the picture until a year later, on April 28, 1945—Walsh had mixed feelings about what he had in the can. Those feelings were matched by the *Variety* critic, who called the picture "a lightweight comedy that never seems able to make up its mind whether to be fantasy or broad slapstick. There are some good laughs, but generally *The Horn Blows at Midnight* is not solid. . . . Generally the chuckles are dragged in and overworked. Heaven as depicted, is certainly not a very soul-satisfying spot."[12] Benny quipped for years afterward that blowing this horn spelled taps for his movie career, albeit brief as it already was.

But Walsh never measured real success by a picture's performance at the box office—he saw it in the personal friendships he came away with afterward. Good box office or not, this picture left him with a touching momento he kept for the rest of his life on his living-room table—a silver cigarette case his good friend Jack Benny gave him. The top of the case had "RW" engraved on it; inside, Benny had a personal message engraved: "Dear Raoul, This case is for cigarettes so that you don't have to roll your own. Jack Benny."[13]

Before Warners released *The Horn Blows at Midnight,* Walsh was back in court again, this time pursuing an embezzlement suit against his former secretary, Frances Morehead, who had worked for him since November 1938. As Walsh learned to trust Morehead over the six years she was in his employ, he gave her increasingly more responsibilities, including, she claimed, allowing her to endorse checks made out to him and deposit them in his banking account, saving him the trouble of doing it himself. But now Walsh was claiming that she deposited checks made out to him in her own accounts, not his.

When Morehead was cross-examined on the witness stand on November 16, 1943, she claimed that, the longer she worked for Walsh, the more responsibilities he gave her and the more access to his personal finances. She said that her duties for Walsh expanded from secretarial/banking to include such personal responsibilities as scheduling with Walsh's wife, Lorraine, and with his mistress (Mary, although she went unnamed in the trial) and helping him look for a ranch. Morehead said that Lorraine often called her while very drunk, looking for Walsh. This was private information, although Walsh would have cared little had it leaked to the press. Lorraine drunk? Mary known to Lorraine? He no doubt loved the possibility for a titillating news story—if only secretly. These years with Lorraine had been dragging on, it seemed.

In turn, Walsh often called Morehead at night to make or break appointments. She claimed that his financial situation was good when she started but that then he withdrew all the money from his private savings account and his other account was attached by Miriam Cooper. She said also that, per Walsh's request, an account was opened in her name and that she was responsible for depositing and withdrawing money for, for example, paying the servants. Although Morehead insisted that she never put Walsh's funds to her personal use (if anything, the accounting between her and Walsh was haphazard), by the time she was called into the office of Walsh's attorney, she had destroyed canceled checks and vouchers. Walsh denied ever authorizing her to deposit his paychecks into her personal account. Eventually, Morehead was found guilty of all charges. As part of the money she owed Walsh, the constable of Beverly Hills was instructed to seize her 1941 Cadillac Sedan from her address on South Reeves Drive. Apparently, working for Walsh was profitable on many accounts.

This case marked another episode in the ongoing financial instabilities of Raoul Walsh—and his constant concern over having enough money. He was up one day, down the next—and, despite the good money the studio paid (and loaned) him, it was never quite enough. Nor was he ever really on top of his financial affairs. His money often just slipped through his fingers—or through someone else's. It seemed that Morehead had gotten away with more than Walsh had bargained for, although she received her comeuppance in the end. The episode had the making of a good thriller if someone had just added a good clip to the events.[14] It might have been no coincidence that Walsh's litigation episodes throughout the years bore more than a passing dramatic resemblance to the adventure stories he directed.

Dueling Memoirs

> Dear Jack: The trailer I saw yesterday on "Objective, Burma!" had a good sock wallop to it. Why not put my name on it and make it a knockout?
> —Raoul Walsh to Jack Warner

By the middle of April 1944 Walsh was out of the courtroom and back at the studio immersed in directing what would be a full-fledged critical and financial knockout for both Flynn and him—the producer Jerry Wald's pet project *Objective, Burma!* Alvah Bessie wrote the original story, although, after that, many hands dipped into the till. Finally, Walsh also put in hours on the ever-evolving script, collaborated with Wald and the screenwriters Ranald MacDougall and Lester Cole, and carved out a taut, hair-raising story. Final screenplay credit went to MacDougall and Cole. This was MacDougall's first big project for the studio.

That month Walsh began scouting locations that would simulate the heat-drenched terrain of Burma and decided to shoot the film on the outskirts of Los Angeles: in Whittier, at the Providencia Ranch in Glendale (later the site of Forest Lawn), at Busch Gardens in Los Angeles, and at the Warner ranch in Calabasas. Filming began on May 1, 1944, and finished August 26, 1944. The cast member Richard Erdman, who played Private Nebraska Hooper, recalled years later that, since it was a summer shoot, the locations were pretty miserable places to inhabit. The summer months made for hot, humid, sometimes torturous weather, even for southern California. The weather turned out to be Walsh's great nemesis during this production.

The story centers on a group of men who parachute into Japanese-occupied Burma during World War II on a mission to locate and then blow up a Japanese radio station. But it isn't until after they accomplish their mission that the real danger begins: they find Japanese soldiers waiting for them at the location they are to rendezvous, and they are forced to do an about-face and traipse back into the Japanese-occupied jungle to escape. It was later said that the story was a composite of the adventures of Merrill's Marauders and Wingate's Raiders. Wingate's Raiders was a brigade of British, Gurkha, and Burmese guerrillas that harassed Japanese forces in the jungles of northern Burma. Merrill's Marauders was an American long-range-penetration special operations unit that fought in the Burma campaign. The producer Jerry Wald also said that some of the script relied heavily on the 1941 Spencer Tracey–Robert Young picture *Northwest Passage (Book 1: Rogers' Rangers),* a story set during the French and Indian War but a good yarn about traipsing across outdoor terrain.

The film marks a high point in Walsh's Warner Bros. career: the action is nonstop, with the troops confronting one frightening, sometimes tragic moment after another. Walsh's great collaboration with the cinematographer James Wong Howe, the composer Franz Waxman, and the ace Warner Bros. editor George Amy—along with the use of World War II stock footage (when the crew members were not being transported in the ever-reliable C47s)—gave the picture a sterling look of authenticity. But the production had its own perils too as conflicts arose among cast and crew. The journals and reports that emerged from the shoot show an equally exciting sideshow, from the humorous to the ludicrous, from anger to amusement. For one thing, Flynn may have looked more complacent than usual—something Walsh often noticed—but he found his own pockets of misery now and then when it was absolutely necessary that he show up on time.

Flynn seemed to be on a creative bent during the production, later writing in his autobiography, "Jack Warner wasn't around the studio at the time, so Raoul Walsh and I made the picture, but it was Jerry Wald's baby. I was not the producer, but I had my way with many of the creative aspects." In this he stood side-by-side with Walsh when he said, "Sometimes make-believe is not so far from reality as you might suppose. Sometimes make-believe is reality and presents reality better than life itself. Often pictures seem more real than the things they're supposed to portray."[15] Flynn could wax poetic about the real world versus the fictional one, and Walsh would be right there beside him, similarly rhapsodizing, albeit with more grit.

Walsh simulated the conditions of the Burma campaign with the help of a technical adviser who had literally been though the whole of the British retreat. Jerry Wald found the man, who had been wounded in Burma, and brought him to the studio. The locale and the weather conditions that Walsh rendered were realistic enough that audiences later had trouble believing that what they were seeing was, in fact, the Santa Anita Ranch in California. Flynn put his two cents into the production also, taking credit for making sure that there was silence and not a musical score at strategic points in the action.

The newcomer William Prince, who played Lieutenant Sid Jacobs, had only one film under his belt when he worked on *Objective, Burma!* He remembered being picked up in a limo every morning along with Henry Hull and being driven up Mulholland Drive to pick up Flynn, whom Prince also remembered as stealing his lines whenever he could. As for Walsh, Prince recalled, he would say, "All right, boys. No Hamlets in the jungle."[16]

The picture's unit director, Frank Mattison, reported on May 5 that "Mr. [Steve] Trilling called me yesterday and was worried about Mr. Walsh speaking during the takes. . . . As you know, we cannot rehearse these takes as once the shot is made the grass has been trampled down and the JUNGLE broken through so that there is no chance for a retake on that same setup."[17] Walsh, who was used to this kind of directing from his silent days and would verbally position each actor without a thought to being heard, was following an old habit. Trilling suggested that Walsh direct the men from behind the camera, telling them to go to the right or to the left. Close-ups would be cut into those shots, and the track could be removed in those particular spots. Walsh, who never liked calling for numerous takes, wanted the story as lean as possible—a fact that again got him into some hot water with the studio. Warner execs thought he wasn't getting enough backdrop into his shots, a complaint that he fought off yet again so that he took the shots he wanted of the actors. There were scenes in the picture where two, maybe three cameras were used—not necessarily the six flaunted by the publicity department when it came time to write up production notes for exploitation.

Mattison also reported, on May 11, that Flynn was being Flynn. He had tried to get Flynn on the phone twice in the afternoon the day before and four times that night but couldn't reach him. A woman answered the phone, promising that Flynn would be back after dinner. But another call found the phone to be off the hook. Then Mattison reported on May 22 that he talked to Walsh about the problem and was told that they had better prepare and have a couple of days ready for work without Mr. Flynn. Walsh knew Flynn well by this point, and he knew exactly when to anticipate an episode of "Flynn missing-in-action." He also knew how to work around him. Said Mattison, "You know that Mr. Flynn has worked for five days straight and about one day in nine he usually stays home. However, we are protected and can work at least three days without Flynn if we have to."[18]

Jerry Wald was writing scenes as the shooting progressed, and Flynn was unhappy with what he was getting. Mattison reported on June 19, "As you know, Mr. Errol Flynn has refused to come out to work today. I had Mr. Jerry Wald on the phone last night and again this morning and it is up to him to straighten it out." Flynn was waiting for some promised script changes, but what he received looked unchanged. He felt that he was walking through the picture and that "not a damn thing has happened since the picture started where anything other than routine dialogue and walking has been photographed." The fact was that the picture's story line called for Flynn and his men to be walking endlessly through the terrain. If Flynn had complaints, he never made them well known to Walsh. "This is in Jerry Wald's lap and I just hung up the phone, telling him that we could take about nine setups without Mr. Errol Flynn," Mattison said. Flynn returned the next day and accomplished a great deal of work.[19]

But Flynn was perturbed by the studio's treatment of him, meaning the insistence that he fly right. He was also upset by what he considered the substandard living conditions he had to endure during the production. He never told Walsh a thing. He took his flair for words and later compiled a clever but biting letter to the production manager, T. C. Wright:

Dear Mr. Wright,

For the last four months our company has been on a number of different locations and I wish to acquaint you with a few facts concerning the dressing rooms. As you know, locations are never comfortable, particularly the sort we have had on "Objective Burma."

My dressing room, as we laughingly call it, had certain novel features. I counted as many as ten holes in the canvas sides through which I found some children examining me in the act of robing and disrobing. One other quite noticeable feature was the floor. At Whittier, for instance, it consisted of a thin strip of moth-eaten matting, much torn and ratted. It only covered a minute portion of the dressing room, the rest was solid cow-dung. This undoubtedly explains the fascination [it] held for ten million assorted insects. There was no privacy of any kind, and perhaps you are not aware that not one of these dressing rooms had a latch unless you can call one of my shoelaces jammed in the opening [a latch].

I cannot adequately explain the general filth. But the topper came when I discovered one day that my dressing room had been changed overnight and that I was now dressing in one that I had myself used the previous day as a toilet (in company with two or three hundred gentlemen). The only marked change between the toilet and the dressing room was that it now had a broken down chair instead of the usual receptacle. I am enclosing a picture by way of illustration.

Conditions such as these are pretty bad but I might never have gotten around to complaining had it not been for the day before yesterday. When I came down from the top of the mountain, where I am currently working, my dressing room had completely disappeared! At present, I am not familiar of its whereabouts (unless Eddie Blatt is using it for a set). A hue and cry was raised to find my clothes. Several gentlemen at last located them by the side of the road beneath one of the curious dilapidated matted things we refer to as the mattresses. I dressed by the open roadside—fortunately no Tanner Busses passed—but upon plugging my hand into my pocket I discovered that I had been rattled for all the money that was in my pockets. No, pardon me, the sum of 78 cents was left. But the $62.00 green was on its way to Glendale or elsewhere. Your unit manager is to blame for the loss for ordering my room struck while my clothes were in it.

Frankly, Mr. W, everyone is familiar with your rooted objection to actors being comfortable on locations. So, actually you might just as well dispense with dressing rooms all together. . . . By contrast, I would refer you to the trailer dressing rooms both Fox and MGM use on locations.

Yours, sincerely,
Errol Flynn

P.S. Without wishing to draw envious comparisons between my own plight and that of others, consider Miss Bette Davis. When Miss Davis goes on location, even for a day, her dressing room is loaded on a truck and sent along with her. Miss Davis is thus accorded a double-edged advantage, for Nature is on her side too. If, reluctant to enter the nauseating precincts of the canvas structure marked WOMAN, she seeks fragrant solace of the California shrubbery, there is little chance of her acquiring a dose of poison oak upon those hanging appendages with which nature has endowed the male of the species.[20]

Flynn had copies of this letter made and sent to Warner and Trilling.

If Walsh knew of the letter, he no doubt found it amusing despite his own occasional irritation with Flynn. But he was most perturbed about the weather, which was too hot and steamy more times than not and put a huge dent in his schedule. To make matters worse, for the first time in their association, he and James Wong Howe sharply disagreed about some of the shots and almost came to blows. On June 16, Mattison reported, "The difficulty between our cameraman and the director continues, and I heard yesterday that we are going to come to a complete stop. Mr. Raoul Walsh told me that he is going to talk to Jimmy and if Jimmy doesn't like it he is going to walk off the show." While they eventually worked out their disagreement, Walsh was still perturbed at his losing time because of the weather. At one point, Mattison wrote that he and Flynn were "foaming" about the loss of time.[21] Almost twenty-nine days behind by the week before shooting stopped, Walsh tried to eliminate some shots, but Wald made certain they went back in. Walsh also decided to transpose some of the scenes in the jungle as originally written in order to save time—and cut ten people off the payroll. If it worked, maybe no one would know the difference. The last day of the film's production report was noted as November 13, 1944, nearly forty days behind schedule, a first for Walsh. Actor Richard Erdman later recalled the hot, humid weather during the shoot but noted that Walsh's unique style of directing often took his mind away from the discomfort. He remembered Walsh's idiosyncratic verbiage. It may have been the cryptic directions "Roll 'em boys; easy does it" and "Give it some action," but the voice had a humorous tint to it.[22]

But the film that Walsh produced is a taut, lean adventure yarn likewise tinted with an emotional depth of character throughout the action. In one scene where Flynn and his men come on an American soldier severely wounded who asks Flynn to kill him as an act of mercy, Flynn's face is a map of deep emotional chaos. Mercifully, the soldier dies before Flynn has to make a decision, but the agony of the decision is already on his face. Walsh keeps the soldier's body half hidden, knowing that American audiences were not ready at that time to see the ravages of war portrayed realistically. The fact that the audience must use its imagination makes the suspense greater and the possible pain more effective. These intimate moments blend effortlessly with the excitement of the action sequences and the suspense of the soldiers' trek through the terrain, not knowing where the enemy might be and when he might next jump out at them. In the film's final battle sequence, with guns and explosives going full blast, Walsh's camera catches individual soldiers almost in close-up as their bodies fling into the air and they seem almost to pop out from a fiery backdrop—a throwback to his *What Price Glory?* almost twenty years earlier and still the prototype of his war films. *Objective, Burma!* looks back in that way—but it also looks forward to Walsh's westerns of the 1950s as his camera opens up to give the audience a good view of the surrounding landscape. The men in battle are but small creatures wandering in this landscape, just as his cowboys wander among the mountains in *Colorado Territory* and *Pursued*. The imposing landscape towers over them and places them in the arms of a huge heroic adventure both perilous and exciting.

Alvah Bessie found few heroics in one particular portion of the *Objective, Burma!* script. He had misgivings about some of the film's dialogue. Concerned about the picture's inherent racism, he sent Jerry Wald a letter voicing his objection to a scene in the film in which the newspaper correspondent says, "The Japanese should be wiped off the face of the earth." He thought, as, he noted, did Lester Cole, that the statement was dangerous and should be taken out of a picture that "so sedulously avoids political statement of any kind." While he thought Japanese "atrocities should be dramatized," it should be made clear that "such atrocities are not the private property of one nation or one race or people." If the studio left the line in, it would be "falling into the enemy's trap." Bessie reminded Wald that the studio had deftly handled the same problem in *Destination Tokyo* when Cary Grant "made it plain that people can be trained from childhood to be brutes—or they can be trained to be decent human beings." He suggested that, if it were technically possible, the correspondent who makes the statement should be rebutted by one of the soldiers; otherwise, the speech should be cut.[23] But the statement (uttered by the Walsh regular Henry Hull) was left untouched and remained in the picture. Walsh liked to think of himself as the epitome of racial tolerance, but he often failed to see a racial slur even when it was under his own nose.

Warner Bros. gave *Objective Burma!* a big promotional blitz, beginning with a press screening in New York. Against his better judgment, Jack Warner wanted Flynn to be there. So he made certain his star had an escort who could get him to the theater on time and keep him out of girl trouble to the best of his ability. Who better than Walsh, who could coax a screen performance out of Flynn even when Flynn didn't have it in him and could make sure that he showed up on the set in the mornings? Jack Warner refused to speak directly to Flynn anymore—especially since Flynn had marched into his office and offered him a bucket with the word *tears* printed on it, to be used, said Flynn, the next time the studio screamed poverty—so he called Walsh into his office to ask for his help.

Objective, Burma! received sterling reviews, and Warner Bros. decided to make the most of any publicity it could get. Walsh talked for years about the time Warner sent him to accompany Flynn in New York in conjunction with publicizing *Objective, Burma!* He had to keep Flynn from drinking too much whiskey (the studio would have to foot the bill)—and from buying too many dozens of roses for all the women Flynn met and fell in love with during their brief stay. But even Walsh could not keep Flynn from falling in love while in the throes of a romantic and whiskey stupor. When Flynn threatened to jump out the window of their room at the Waldorf-Astoria, Walsh looked on with affectionate chagrin. He even managed to get some photographers into the room to talk about the picture they were there to promote.

Objective Burma! didn't cause the racial stir Bessie feared it might; instead, it caused a different kind of stir in Great Britain, first among veterans groups, then among the military, and later among the press itself. Since the Burma campaign was primarily a British and Australian one, the picture seemed an insult to these men in the way that it Americanized the Burma campaign, just one more example of the way Americans portrayed themselves as winning the war single-handedly. Flynn's heroics were so believable that the film was pulled from release in Britain just one week after it opened. While it opened in New York on February 17, 1945, the British held the film up one year. The lord chancellor pulled the picture after the British press became enraged. But that didn't stop filmgoers in England from trying to get into a screening, especially when one turned up at Leicester Square before the picture went on hiatus.

When Warners reissued *Objective, Burma!* in Britain in 1952, the film appeared with a statement claiming that it contained no anti-British sentiment. Anti-British or not, Walsh was inspired enough to reuse the story of *Objective, Burma!* when he directed Gary Cooper in *Distant Drums,* his 1951 film set in the Florida Everglades.

After finishing *Objective, Burma!* Walsh convinced Jack Warner to loan him out to Paramount, and, on August 28, 1944, he began production on *Salty O'Rourke,* a horse-racing drama starring Alan Ladd and Gail Russell—the first feature he directed about the subject so close to his heart. On hand in supporting roles were William Demarest, Bruce Cabot, and Spring Byington in a production that lasted two months, until October 21. Walsh's agreement with Paramount stated that he would begin work at that studio "within forty-eight hours after completion of director's services for Warner Bros. in connection with their production, *Objective, Burma!*" He would be at Paramount for a period of not more than fourteen weeks without Warners' written consent. Walsh received $6,000 per week, with a guarantee of $85,000 to aggregate. He needed these loan-outs and the extra money to offset his mounting debts from horse betting. They ebbed and flowed for years to come.

Paramount had purchased an unpublished story, "Salty O'Rourke," in January 1943, although it would be a year before the picture went into production. The story went through six title changes—including *Lady Luck, There They Go, Salt of the Earth, Mr. Racket, Big Stakes,* and *Pride of Kentucky*—before the studio settled on *Salty O'Rourke.* The story centers on a definitely salty gambler (Ladd) who finds himself in hot water when the picture opens. He has one week to pay off an important debt, or his life will take a serious turn for the worse. To pay off the debt, he hires a banned jockey (Stanley Clements) who has to fake a different identity in order to win the race that will mean money for Salty. Along comes a schoolteacher named Barbara (Gail Russell), whose positive effect on Salty changes the story's outcome. The story moves effortlessly to its predictable conclusion.

There were few surprises on the set, and Milton Holmes's script was delivered piecemeal to Joseph Breen's office as Walsh was directing. Breen made a few red pencil marks: there should be no reference to illicit sex, and, in addition, the audience should never see horse racing in a bad light. Neither of these "requests" caused Walsh any sleepless nights. They were par-for-the-course intrusions. Paramount released the picture at the end of April 1945. On May 3, a review of *Salty O'Rourke* appeared in the *Dallas Morning News* praising Walsh in the subtlest way possible: "This is a stalwart product from the directorial hands of one-eyed Raoul Walsh, who knew the movies as far back as 1912. Since turning director he has mastered a technique as profitable as it is artistically unimportant. His characters consist of a few, recognizable cartoon strokes. His plots heave rather than thrust. His dialogue is sparse, little more than spoken subtitles for pictorial effects. He wins no Academy prizes and makes no dull movies."[24] Other reviewers called it a picture of bold deceptions, a story Damon Runyon might have penned about the double-crossing that goes on in the backrooms near the tracks. The picture opened without audiences understanding how much Walsh put of himself in the setups—the mischief, the playfulness, and the flirtation with being a bad boy as much as a good one.

As long as he was making a film about horses, Walsh got it in his head that he wanted to return to the western frontier. As early as January 1945, he mentioned to Jack Warner that he was interested in a western story called "Cheyenne." "I told Bogart the *Cheyenne* story the other night and he wants to do it," Walsh wrote in a memo. "The girl's part is a natural for Sheridan and we might get Flynn to play the bandit. This script can be written in five or six weeks. By that time the weather will be turning good, and with all the exteriors, I know I can make this picture under a million."[25] Nothing was yet jelled.

Although John Huston agreed to write the script for *Cheyenne,* as the studio pursued the idea, Walsh's interest waned—although he would return to it later. He feigned interest in a story called "Wallflower" but, in truth, just wanted some time off. He told Steve Trilling he was exhausted. "When I returned to Warner Bros. after my Paramount commitment [i.e., *Salty*]," he wrote to Trilling on January 29, 1945, "I started preparing 'Manhattan Fury,' then 'Melancholy,' then 'When Old New York Was Young': and now 'Wallflower.'[26] I have discussed the outline with Lou Edelman and Miss Pierson[27] for the 'Wallflower' and we have reached an agreement. It will take Miss Pierson at least four or five weeks to finish the script. . . . How about that trip to New York now, while I am marking time, that you promised Sam when we signed the new contract? It has been nine years since I last saw the Big city as I have averaged three pictures a year. I know the trip would stimulate me. How about it!"[28] He wanted to visit New York, but he didn't want Lorraine to go with him. He could spend the time with Mary.

The studio gave Walsh what he wanted and then some. He didn't start another picture for Warner Bros. until July 1945. In the meantime, by March, Warners' front office, concerned about rising production costs, sent out a memo dictating that scripts had to be shorter. Ever the agreeable workhorse, Walsh wrote to Trilling on March 30, "I received your good sound letter on over-length pictures and I for one will go on record by stating that I will not start any picture with a script over 140 pages."[29] Walsh was well versed in bartering with studio boys.

The Women He Loved

Nothing worked out the way Walsh planned, but that was fine with him. He was, as usual, committed to no particular story. All came down the pike equally. Starting in mid-July 1945, Walsh spent two months directing one of his favorite actresses, Ida Lupino, for the fourth and last time. He and Ida had become more than friends during the years they worked together; they had a flirtation, even if briefly. He might have been in love with Mary, but there was room for Ida. The two of them spoke the same language, rough-and-tumble, and understood each other's bent toward irreverence on and off the set. By now, Walsh and Lupino were close enough that they formed, with Errol Flynn, an "elite triumvirate dedicated to fun."[30] Joining "the Baron" (Flynn) and "Uncle" (Walsh), Lupino became "Little Scout."

The Man I Love is a curious picture in Walsh's career—more a woman's film and admittedly from him the kind of parlor picture he would ordinarily avoid or else poke fun at after the fact. Although, with Walsh's no-nonsense direction, the film adds bite and cynicism to the woman's-film genre, it retains that genre's signature plot: the story of a self-sacrificing woman who essentially goes about the picture putting out domestic fires that erupt in her family's emotional lives. Lupino's talents were well showcased with a script in which she could seethe as much as she wanted and carry around a cynical chip on her shoulder. Unlike Bette Davis, to whom Lupino was often compared—the well-worn adage being that she took the parts Davis turned down—Lupino could show anger and not feel remorse about it, something Davis could never do. Like Davis, however, she could fall apart at her psychological seams and not feel the need to explain herself. Hers was the perfect psyche to showcase Walsh's hard-boiled woman, and the director and star made good sense together.

Warner initially wanted Ann Sheridan to play the film's heroine,

Petey (Sheridan was often first choice for many starring roles, even though many of them ultimately went to other actresses), and he then saw Lupino—or even Olivia de Havilland—playing Sally, Petey's sister. But continuing problems with finishing the script made it necessary for Sheridan to move on to another picture. Warner also considered Bogart or Gable to play Petey's love interest, San, a piano player with a melancholy past, and John Garfield to play her troubled neighbor, Johnny. None of these choices worked out any better than the Sheridan idea. Tunes written by George Gershwin give *The Man I Love* a serious edge, even though the mood often swings over to a kind of cynicism that clashes with Gershwin's more classic mood. Uncharacteristic of Walsh, the story's tone is moody and melodramatic, but he and Lupino's cynical view of the world tone it down just enough.

The story follows a very independent single woman and New York nightclub singer, Petey Brown, who, when the story opens, we find singing with a band after hours in a club, moving around the musicians, a cigarette in her hand and the blues in her heart. Petey has a world-weary heart when it comes to men and the resigned attitude to prove it. After singing a soft, lulling little number with the guys, Petey tells her girlfriend that she is leaving New York and moving to Long Beach, California, to be near her brother and two sisters. She misses them, and, anyway, there's no man to keep her in New York. He got away long ago, and, as Petey tells it, a good man is hard to find. She doesn't expect one to be stopping by anytime soon.

Once in California, Petey snuggles into the family's emotional discords, trying her best to take care of everyone while coping with a preying mantis of a new boss (Robert Alda) at the nightclub where she now sings and a lover (Bruce Bennett)—that guy did show up, it seems—a talented has-been of a piano player who cannot forget his first wife and sulks about the life he once had and cannot seem to reclaim. He takes Petey's ready heart with him wherever he goes. Petey goes on being the solid base for her family and the understanding woman to her man, who ultimately leaves, just as the audience thought he might stick around for Petey.

Even though she plays the good girl here, Lupino does at least get a chance to be Lupino and to throw some verbal zingers at the audience. In one scene, walking up the stairs in the nightclub, she sees her troublesome next-door neighbor and says, "Well, well . . . the people you run into when you're not carrying a gun." The line seems straight out of a gangster yarn, which this film is certainly not, and its tenor comes straight from Walsh, who tinkered around with the script all through production. Taut and tangy, Lupino still puts out those fires and slaps a louse good and hard in one of the film's better moments. Petey still embraces a longing and long-suffering look in the picture's last shot—as her lover leaves town for a stint with the merchant marines (he wants to straighten himself out). She turns from him at the dock and walks away from the station and into a close-up that tells the audience that she sees a future where happiness might find her someday soon. As she tells her sister in the previous scene, she is leaving Long Beach and heading out for who knows where; she believes something she cannot exactly name. But the audience knows that the something has a man's name on it.

Irving Rapper (whom Bette Davis always claimed took direction from her exceedingly well on the set of *Now, Voyager*) was Jack Warner's first choice to direct *The Man I Love*. But Rapper had other commitments, and Warner then considered both Vincent Sherman and Walsh and for a short time could not decide between them. The Warners screenwriter Barney (Benjamin) Glazer sent Warner a memo suggesting that Vincent Sherman would be better suited because "he knows these young people better and is more sensitive to their language and their problems."[31] Not easily swayed by this missive, Warner chose Walsh in the end. He could depend on Walsh to take Petey and get her cynicism on the screen quick and dirty.

The unit manager Frank Mattison called Walsh "very pliable" on the set and hoped that this meant they would get through the picture on time.[32] Lupino didn't have much of a singing voice, so Walsh had all her numbers dubbed—as close to her speaking voice as possible. Also, Bruce Bennett continually found it difficult to learn how to play piano—the instrument his character, San, is an old hand at—so Walsh kept him practicing throughout the shoot. Lupino, who was exhausted from the "grind" of her oncoming divorce from Louis Hayward, was often late to the set, claiming either that her alarm clock was not working or that she didn't have one. Mattison, who was usually pleased with the steady pace that Walsh kept on a picture, complained to Trilling about him almost daily. He was rewriting so much of the script that the production fell behind schedule and went over budget—very unusual for Walsh. What was worse, Walsh was rewriting off the cuff and jotting none of it down on script pages. Walsh kept saying to let it go and forget it; he was satisfied with the progress the company was making, and he had given the screenwriter Catherine Turney (and himself) a free hand to do as he pleased. He was comfortable with this, but the script girl found it impossible to keep track of what had and had not been shot. As late as three weeks before production was to end, Walsh was still rewriting material, even if he was being patient with all the chaos on the set these changes caused.

Still, the assistant director on the picture, Ridgeway Callow, remembered Walsh going at a "very fast" pace:

> I don't think Raoul was much help to the cast at any time, but he was great as far as set-ups were concerned. I remember . . . Ida Lupino . . . came up to Walsh and asked a routine question about a scene, but her language was earthy, to say the least. Raoul's answer was equally rough in the language department. And I was looking at them back and forth like a tennis match. It was the same on any of Raoul's films. And you know, as far as coming in the morning and knowing what he had to do for the day—he used to say to me, "What the hell happens in this sequence?" You'd have to go into detail and tell him. But by God it didn't take him any time at all to pick a set-up. I'll say that. Raoul probably picked set-ups faster than anybody I've ever worked with. He'd say, "All right, put the camera there, boys."[33]

Walsh's script changes held as much weight as his frequent nonchalance to what went on around him.

Lupino's social life also angered Mattison. He wrote in the logs on September 7, "I wish we could do something about the incoming calls to Miss Lupino on the set when she is working and busy with a lot of dialogue. One certain party, an actor in this studio, yesterday made four or five calls that I know of and Mr. Walsh wants to see if we cannot curb this somewhat or eliminate it entirely—at least until we get through with this picture."[34] Boyfriend or no, Lupino caused further disruption when at the end of shooting she developed ringworm on her face and Walsh could not shoot the angles he wanted. The shoot finished on September 22, nine days behind schedule—unusual for Walsh. Midway through production, another event sent shivers and worry throughout cast and crew: the United States dropped the atomic bomb on Hiroshima. In this state of unrest, the production went on.

On first reading the script, Breen's office found it unacceptable because of its "low moral tone" as well as the "implications of adultery and illicit sex on the part of the principals."[35] When Warner Bros. released the picture two years later, critics were unkind, but moviegoers loved it. Newspaper ads showed Lupino sitting on a piano with a cigarette in her hand, wearing a tight, sexy gown. "There ought to be a law against knowing the things I know about men." Another ad had her saying, "The more you know about love, the more you'll love this picture." Petey was a woman who "had a song on her lips and a man on her mind." The picture left an impression on the director Martin Scorsese years later: he claimed that it was the main inspiration for *New York, New York* (1977). This was the woman's melodrama rearing its head again; Walsh had directed a woman's film with a bite to it.

Completing the picture also marked a time of striking changes in Walsh's personal life. In mid-September 1945, Walsh moved out of the house on Doheny he shared with Lorraine and in with Mary Simpson. Though they were not married, they shared a rented, furnished six-bedroom estate at 13141 Addison Street, in the San Fernando Valley, for six months—until they purchased a house in Toluca Lake.

The Hollywood art director David Garber, who owned the house on Addison, ended up suing Walsh for damages to the property (including cigarette burns to the tables and cushions, liquor stains on wood, and the storage of too many weighty pieces of furniture, causing the floor to break); Walsh turned around and sued Garber for violation of section 2c of the rent regulations of the Office of Price Administration. It seemed that Garber charged Walsh $1,000 per month when he should have charged not more than $600. Both men dropped their suits eventually, and Walsh tried to buy the house on a lease option. Nothing came of it—but at least he had another day in court.

In the meantime, two weeks before production ended on *The Man I Love*, Lorraine Walsh had had enough of what she considered the lonely life and officially separated from her husband. She told Louella Parsons in a phone call that she was "definitely through" with Walsh and that he had not been home "for the past three weeks." The only thing to do, she thought, was to separate from him. The news appeared in Parsons's syndicated column the next day.[36] (Walsh later said that he had gone on a fishing trip without telling her.) When Lorraine eventually filed for divorce, her chief complaint against her husband was that he would never talk to her anymore.

11

Oedipus Wrecked
The Late 1940s at Warner Bros.

> JAMES CHILD: One critic, Andrew Sarris, said, "The Walshi-
> an hero is less interested in the why or the how than in the
> what. He is always plunging into the unknown, and he is
> never too sure what he will find there." Do you feel that's
> too precious a criticism, or that it's on the nail?
> RAOUL WALSH: I guess it's so. Everybody has his own impres-
> sion of things. Maybe the guy was drunk.
> —*Sight and Sound* (1973)

Walsh was in good spirits. In January 1946, three months after he and
Lorraine separated, she began divorce proceedings, seeking a property
settlement involving the house on North Doheny. Claiming mental cruelty, Lorraine said that she wanted to end her eighteen-year marriage to
Walsh because he no longer would talk to her. She knew who her rival
was, even if she never said so directly. Walsh was glad to give up the
Doheny house; he was already living with Mary in the Valley—for the
rest of his life he would remain on the outskirts of Los Angeles, where
he could have the horses close to him and not have to pay good money
to board them at a racetrack or purchase a separate piece of property in
order to house them.

While he was still shooting *The Man I Love* in the fall of 1945, Walsh
rekindled his interest in *Cheyenne,* a rather routine western adventure
yarn he had thought about, then dropped, in the beginning of the year.
The writer Alan Le May, whose novel *The Searchers* later became the
basis for John Ford's classic 1956 film starring John Wayne, originally
brought the story to Warners' attention. The author was Paul Wellman,
who would later pen two popular novels of the day, *Apache* and *The*

Comancheros, both later filmed as vehicles for Burt Lancaster and John Wayne, respectively. Both Le May and Wellman had occasional ties to Warner Bros. and, more importantly for Walsh, also had deep interests in action stories set on the western landscape. That wide-open space with its huge mountain ranges in the backdrop would always be Walsh's favorite place to film, and, from the late 1940s on, he'd be there more than anywhere else, directing westerns.

Cheyenne tells the tale of a gambler named Jim Wylie, a good-looking, velvety-voiced smooth talker who arrives in the city of Cheyenne having escaped from a nearby town after killing a man in a gambling dispute. The local sheriff in Cheyenne catches up with him, and in order to save his skin and not get sent back to be hanged, Wylie makes a deal to help track down a mysterious local bandit known as the Poet, who is responsible for a series of Wells Fargo stagecoach robberies. Setting out to catch his thief, Wylie also gets tangled up with two women—one, Ann Kincaid, thought to be the Poet's wife, and another, Emily Carson, who may or may not be his girlfriend. One more notch in the script has Wylie forced to do battle with another small-time outlaw named Sundance who adds some color to the story but is killed off early in the picture. *Cheyenne* was a run-of-the-mill western that nevertheless grabbed Walsh's attention: he wanted to get back to the West.

Walsh thought Humphrey Bogart would be perfect to play Wylie, along with Ann Sheridan, of course, as Anne Kincaid and Errol Flynn as the Poet. In August 1945, Walsh asked Steve Trilling for the script. Worried that it wasn't fine-tuned enough to show to Bogart, and with Le May and another writer, Emmett Lavery, working on it, Trilling took over three months to deliver it to Walsh. At this point, Robert Buckner was on board as producer.

Walsh and Steve Trilling were unhappy with the script they saw. It was full of plot holes and inconsistencies, and they said so in a memo to Jack Warner while including their own idea for a new plot outline. This so outraged Buckner, who wanted control, that he began sending a barrage of long memos to Warner and Trilling stating his disapproval. He thought that Walsh sabotaged him and demanded that, if Walsh was to have that much control over the story line, then he, Buckner, should be taken off the picture. "Walsh's attitude toward the entire script has been obstructive from the beginning," Buckner said. "Last week when

I gave him the last half of the script to read, he had no criticisms or suggestions for changes. I asked him to come to my office before I sent through the last half for mimeographing so that we could discuss any point of objection, which he might have. He told me on the phone that he had nothing in mind and that I should send it through as it was. . . . Now he turns around and wants to tear the whole thing apart again." "I think in all fairness," Buckner added, "it should be remembered that I have done a great many more Westerns than Walsh and that I should certainly be consulted before Walsh's changes are forced into the script." He also said, "I never had a script on which there has been this much friction with the director, and under the circumstances I do not look forward to going into production on it with him. If he does not like the script, you know as well as I do that he will not shoot it with conviction or communicate any enthusiasm to the actors."[1] Walsh wasn't intentionally playing with Buckner or trying to anger him; neither was he always forthcoming with the producer about his reworking of the script. He was sometimes less than communicative.

Eventually, Buckner cooled down, even though he obviously knew Walsh better than some—he could easily lose his "conviction" and "enthusiasm." In all this, Walsh never blew up; he just kept quiet and kept moving, never again mentioning his disapproval of the script. The finished screenplay was credited to Le May and Thames Williamson, but Jack Warner's fingerprints were there also. "The Colonel feels very definitely that the character of Ann Kincaid should not be a Goodes saleslady," Trilling told Buckner in January 1946. "If it is possible to get the girl to sing a good hit song similar to SOME SUNDAY MORNING or ALONG THE SANTA FE TRAIL, so much the better as this type of song never misses. Although a dancehall girl is always used in every Western picture, we will take the chance that it is a cliché setup—SAN ANTONIO is the answer to it and while we do not want to repeat everything we have done before, we do want a good colorful success as a picture in CHEYENNE."[2]

Of course, the higher authority, Breen's office, had approval rights over the script and ordered some changes. There could be no use of the word *outhouse* if it meant "outdoor toilet." Nor could dialogue contain the phrase *she excites me* or *she contents me*. Care had to be taken with animals, the sheriff was not to die at the hands of bandits, and there was to be no suggestion of prostitutes. Walsh at least appeared to cooperate with these suggestions, even though the picture was never shy about sexually charged moments between the characters.

Bogart was never cast in the film, though he was first on Walsh's list. Errol Flynn, Ronald Reagan, Dennis Morgan, and Bruce Bennett were also considered. Morgan was finally cast as Wylie. In the running to play Wylie's love interest, Ann Kincaid, were Barbara Stanwyck, Ida Lupino, Eleanor Parker, Alexis Smith, and Jane Wyman. Wyman took the part in the end. She had usually been cast as second fiddle up to this point at the studio yet in 1948 would play the lead in *Johnny Belinda* and win an Academy Award. Walsh wanted Zachary Scott to play the Poet, the story's villain. Also considered were Robert Alda, Craig Stevens, and Bruce Bennett, who was cast in the part. Janis Paige was cast as Emily Carson, the other woman in Wylie's life, even though Eve Arden was also considered. Arthur Kennedy had the part of Sundance, the bandit who makes trouble for Wylie, and the ever-entertaining Alan Hale took on the small part of Sheriff Fred Durbin. Walsh's old friend "Bear Valley" Charley Miller was also cast in a small part. Cast and crew were ready to shoot, partly on the Warner Bros. soundstage, at the Warner ranch in Calabasas, and also in Flagstaff, Arizona, for exterior scenes.

Eventually, Buckner and Walsh found something to agree on—problems with Jane Wyman's choice of hairstyle. "Both Raoul and I are not at all pleased with Jane Wyman's hairdress [*sic*]," Buckner wrote in a memo to Trilling. He continued:

> It is too plain and is completely unbecoming to her. We anticipate some trouble with Miss Wyman who has extremely set opinions about herself, but this will have to be thrashed out very definitely before we start. Neither Walsh nor I agree with you about the color of Wyman's hair. We believe she is much more effective as a blonde and it gives us a much better dramatic contrast with Janis Paige's black hair. Wyman's hair looks absolutely mousy in its present color and both Walsh and I feel there is a very strong possibility of Janis Paige taking this picture from under Miss Wyman's nose, on looks alone. Had I known that Wyman was going to dye her hair I would have protested loud and long at the time.[3]

With Wyman's hair bleached a lighter color, the cast began shooting March 11, 1946.

Walsh's behavior on the set was consistent with that of someone who had lost his enthusiasm, except for those times when Mary came by to visit. He was on the set by nine in the morning if need be, and he shot the film without getting behind schedule—retaining his reputation as the ever-reliable workhorse. Shooting concluded on May 27, 1946. But, when *Cheyenne* opened in New York City on June 14, 1947 (some accounts say June 6), audiences saw a story fueled by Walsh's characteristic energetic pacing but also seriously muddled scriptwise, a judgment that Buckner would, no doubt, see as a reflection of the ambushes he thought Walsh earlier carried out against him. Looking more than a little schizophrenic around the edges, if not straight up the middle, the picture shows signs of having had too many hands involved. If, as Buckner claimed, Walsh tried to take over the script and make it clearer, or at least alter it to his liking, the move did not altogether work. Mood swings characterize the story's quick transitions from comedy, to romance, to adventure story. If Walsh tried to outmaneuver the Breen Office, as he often said he did, the picture is good proof of that. The characters throw blatant sexual verbiage at each other throughout. The sexual tension between Wylie and his two female cohorts is the picture's most consistent conceit. Wylie and Ann enjoy sexually charged chitchat, and they pose as husband and wife in the story, a masquerade the censors let go. Also, there are some sexual moments involving Paige and Wyman and a bathtub, an unusual circumstance for the time. Ultimately, and by no means consciously on Walsh's part, *Cheyenne* is far more interesting as a sexual farce than it is as a western action story. Walsh's way of handling Breen's office was, as often happened, to get around it.

Out of the Past

Lorraine received her divorce from Walsh in early March 1946. She repeated her story to newspaper reporters: Walsh refused to talk to her anymore and objected to having her friends over to the house, although he was essentially occupying another house, with Mary, as well. In the settlement, Walsh would pay Lorraine $300 a week alimony for six months, then $200 a week for the rest of her life or until she married.

Although Walsh denied the charges of mental cruelty, he didn't contest the divorce. Despite her closeness to her stepfather, Marilynn Phillips corroborated her mother's charges. A short time later, Lorraine married the retired tennis pro Fred Perry (although the union was a relatively brief one) and found an entirely new social circle in which to travel.

Walsh took a two-month hiatus, and he and Mary did some traveling in Europe, with him frequenting fine men's clothing stores, before he started on his next picture, *Pursued*. The film turned out to be one of the most complex and controversial in his body of work, not only because of its haunting visual imagery, but also because it embraces so many psychological conceits thought by many to be uncharacteristic of Walsh. Again, as a Warner Bros. house director, he came onto the project late in the game, well after the film's author, Niven Busch, got the kinks worked out with the studio on a script he treated with kid gloves. Busch and Milton Sperling (who was married to Harry Warner's daughter, Betty) had recently formed a partnership to get the film made. This way, Busch figured, he could get the control he wanted over how the studio treated his script. Sperling had formed United States Pictures, a banner under which he would produce films distributed by Warner Bros. *Pursued* was produced under this USA Pictures banner.

Originally a newspaper journalist, Busch had already coscripted such classics as William Wyler's *The Westerner* (produced by Samuel Goldwyn in 1940) and *The Postman Always Rings Twice* (MGM, 1946), the Lana Turner–John Garfield sensation crafted from the James Cain noir novel, and the producer David O. Selznick had just that year produced a film adaptation of his novel *Duel in the Sun,* for which he also wrote the screenplay. The inspiration for *Pursued* (as well as for *Duel in the Sun*) came to Busch a few years earlier when he roamed the Southwest looking for local legends to put into his stories. Visiting El Paso, Texas, he read an old newspaper story about a bloody feud between two families that left the little boy of one of the families orphaned. The family that murdered the boy's parents now was raising the boy as their own. Busch wondered what kind of life the boy would have. The material was fodder for all kinds of psychological traumas and drama.

Pursued centers on a boy named Jeb Rand who, when the film opens, witnesses the slaughter of his family as he hides underneath the floorboards in their home. Afterward, he represses what he sees: images of a large man killing his father and mother. From then on, all Jeb can recall is an image of a pair of boots with spurs on them—maybe belonging to the killer. At the scene of the slaughter, however, Jeb is whisked away by a mysterious woman (Medora Callum, played by Judith Anderson) who takes him to her own home and raises him as her son along with her natural children, a boy, Adam, and a girl, Thorley. When they become adults, Jeb and Thorley fall in love and marry, and Jeb must contend with Adam's growing resentment of this outsider in the house. Jeb never shakes the sensation that some menacing force is after him, which is true since Medora's sinister brother-in-law, Judge Grant Callum, wants Jeb dead and will not rest until he is. But, in all his innocence, Jeb knows only that he must solve the mystery of those memories that haunt him.

Busch thought of the story as a Greek tragedy set in a western terrain. Given its grounding in a family tragedy, coupled with Busch's interest in dark, secretive motifs, *Pursued* was Greek tragedy rife with Freudian themes: notions of forbidden sexuality, repressed memories, the longing for the idealized family, childhood trauma, and more than a hint of incest. It also embraces elements of noir (given the story's dark themes and visual images), and some have called it a gothic western and/or a psychological mystery with biblical motifs, especially given the tragedy that emerges from Jeb and Adam's Cain-Abel rivalry.

For the important role of Jeb, Busch wanted an actor new to the screen whom audiences wouldn't especially know. Montgomery Clift was tested but looked too slender for the part and "too silly" in a cowboy hat. Busch liked the idea of casting Joel McCrea but, in the end, thought him too old for the part. Jack Warner didn't like the cleft in Kirk Douglas's chin, an ironic turn of events because, when Robert Mitchum, whom everyone liked right away, was cast, no one seemed to notice that he too had a cleft in his chin. Busch's then wife, Teresa Wright, got the part of Thorley, and Judith Anderson offered a lusty sexuality as Medora Callum, whose affair with Jeb's father (unknown to Jeb as well as the audience) sets off the subsequent murders. Walsh again worked with his longtime coworker the cinematographer James Wong Howe. The two had worked together on *The Yellow Ticket* (1931), *The Spider* (1931), and *Hello, Sister!* (1933) for Fox and on *The Strawberry*

Blonde (1941) and *Objective, Burma!* (1945) for Warners. (On *The Spider,* Walsh worked uncredited—credit went to the set designer William Cameron Menzies—and Howe was listed as James Howe, an effort to offset the racism he encountered in Hollywood for a long period in his early career.) Now, with *Pursued,* Howe and Walsh worked as they had previously—integrating their like-minded love of a realistic frame, this time so amplified that the shots take on almost a kind of surrealism, extremely appropriate for the often-fractured psychology that drives the film.

Many people who knew Walsh thought that Warner was crazy to give him the picture with its incest-bound family, a group of serious neurotics if ever there was one. Walsh, with his eye for natural landscapes and his deep enjoyment of lusty male bravado, seemed "one of the least neurotic men in Hollywood" and an odd choice to handle neurosis and deeply hidden anxieties. It was reported later that "Walsh asked Busch to stay nearby during shooting and be ready to tell him what the hell was going on."[4]

Walsh and Howe's collaboration went even further. Not only did they broaden the story and the characters by placing them in a huge and shadowy black-and-white physical and psychological setting, but Walsh also opened up Jeb's character by getting Mitchum's facial expressions to mirror a perpetual, natural innocence—thereby making him vulnerable to anything good or evil coming his way. Walsh's connection with the material, however, goes even deeper. The film's overriding concern is loss and grief, natural territory for Walsh, who in one way or another was drawn to these subjects and found his way back to them time and again. That Jeb loses his home is not lost on Walsh, who in the deepest sense lost his home when he was young. The homeless soul, like Roy Earle or Marie of *High Sierra,* fit Walsh naturally. As Jeb wanders about seeking a home while at the same time losing that place, he embarks on an unconscious, unplanned journey to recover a part of himself that he has lost. This is the only fact he knows about himself until the story's end. He takes a detour, if a slight one, from many of Walsh's heroes: like many, he seeks to recover something lost. But he is more innocent than the rest.

Walsh shot the picture from the first week in August 1946 to October 12 at Red Rock Mesa near Gallup, New Mexico, and Dark Lake Canyon, north of Gallup. Cast and crew traveled to shooting locations by means of a specially chartered train of fifteen cars that transported one hundred players, cameramen, and technicians, along with tons of equipment, props, and twenty-one trained saddle horses, from Hollywood to location spots.

Midway through shooting, Anderson spoke of her commitment to the picture in a publicity piece aimed at the broadest readership possible:

> Only a few weeks ago, Judith Anderson was in New York planning some plays, getting married and selling her home in Hollywood. Now you find her hard at work at Warners on what should be her finest picture role to date, the head of a feuding New Mexican family in 1890. The title remains unmentioned. But "It is a good part," she says. "The woman is chic and the story is dramatic." "You should have been on the ranch yesterday," she says. "We had a whole town built there. Certainly I shot it up and drove home wild horses around the place. This is quite a picture."[5]

And this was quite a public relations maneuver, typical of the press at the time—the oddest and the most ordinary scenarios roped together and delivered to readers hungry to know the details of movie production and actors' lives.

When Walsh first scouted the area of Gallup, there were no animals to be seen. Neither were there any after shooting began. But, soon, loads of sheep, cattle, and dogs showed up and had to be cleared away. Navajo braves in the area volunteered for the job at the rate of ten cents a head.

A week after shooting began, Walsh took a morning off to venture into a Los Angeles courtroom to defend his old friend "Bear Valley" Charley Miller of drunk-driving charges. Not only had Walsh just cast Charley in a small part in *Cheyenne;* the two friends went back to silent days. Walsh described him as one of the great "bottle men," his other major talent being his ability to drive a stagecoach and four horses "with terrifying skill." Walsh used him in most of his pictures, whether he was drunk or sober—"he drove better when he was drunk"—but, inevitably, the intake of what Walsh called "Napa juice" made Charley more a menace than a friend—a fact that Walsh could never see in all the years they remained close friends. Walsh kept his old friend on his personal payroll, and Charley was usually to be found on a Raoul Walsh set, working—or drinking—or not. The day Walsh went to court for Charley, October 23, 1946, a photograph showed the two men standing close together with Charley lighting a cigarette. He offered an outrageous story to defend himself but failed to get off without a fine.

Filming *Pursued* offered Walsh plenty of opportunity with this terrain to capture what became his signature long shot—lone men riding a horse and seen against the backdrop of huge mountains that dwarf them. This shot could open a film or show up in the midst of one, such as in the upcoming *Colorado Territory* and, using two riders, later in *The Tall Men*. Now Walsh again incurred Howe's anger (as he had done when they worked together on *Objective, Burma!*) over shooting these long and longingly held shots. Walsh in turn became irritated with his friend, who, to him, seemed more obsessed than usual with lighting setups. He tried to make the best of it—even with Busch, who was around for most of the shoot. He just referred to Busch as a man enamored of his own scripts. But Walsh and Mitchum became instant friends and stayed friendly for the duration of Walsh's life. Years later, Mitchum famously described Walsh's style of working on *Pursued:*

> Well, Raoul was good at getting things worked out. So we walked it out and talked it over so each one would know where he is and where we crossed and so forth. And Raoul said, "OK, you got it? Now you think you got it?" Then he said, "Roll it," and he turned around and walked away and he rolled a Bull Durham cigarette on the blind side and all the tobacco'd fall out. He'd light it and whoosh! And he'd roll another one . . . same thing. He rolled five or six of those. Finally there was a silence, and he turned and he said, "Over? Cut it!" And he said, "How did it look?" "Oh," I said, "a lamp fell off the table." He said, "Did it look natural? Did you put it back?" "Yes," I said. "OK," he said and ripped the page out. . . . "One for Macros . . . four Academy Awards! Number one's the scene." So much for your modern auteur.[6]

"It's just a day's work," Mitchum once told Richard Schickel later. In that vein, he said:

> I remember one time riding a horse out of a little box canyon—and they had set up another camera around the corner. I didn't know about it, and the horse jumped, fell down, and rolled right over me. Of course, I was up over his withers—and I was riding bareback, so I didn't get hung up in the saddle or anything. But the horse rolled over me so quickly that it just knocked the wind out of me. And Raoul came over, and he didn't say, "Are your ribs broken?" Or, "Are you all right?" He said, "Listen, bring him out a little faster next time, will you?" Nothing to it.[7]

But Walsh was the all-around nice guy, said Harry (Dobe) Carey Jr., who played Wright's doomed suitor in the picture. He found him to be "a tremendously nice man—too nice . . . maybe I needed more guidance. He left you pretty much alone." He remembered: "After I did a screen test for the part, Walsh said to me, 'Let your hair grow,' instead of 'You've got the part.'[8] Walsh was easy to please. Judith Anderson had attitude. And Teresa Wright, who was a total sweetheart, was terrified of Mitchum, and was afraid he would deck her and wreck her. As a joke, Walsh had Mitchum carry Teresa over the threshold and over to the bed and drop her there, looking down at her as if we were going to rape her."[9] Wright never trusted them after that. Walsh continued his habit of setting up a scene, then turning his back and walking away when the scene actually was being shot. It was the same. He knew exactly when to turn around again and yell, "Cut!"

When the studio released *Pursued* in the first week of March 1947, the reviewer in *Film Daily* wrote, "Introducing the neurotic to the Western scene, 'Pursued' . . . is a sound dramatic offering holding attention from the outset and delivering a story that mounts to a fair peak of suspense. Raoul Walsh handled the plot with skill and his chief players manage constant conviction. . . . This is an adult tale of twisted personalities, ulterior motives and lurking threat of death arising from dishonored families compounded of such basics as profound hatred, murder, brawling and love that degenerates into homicidal intent."[10] It may have been too early for viewers and critics to embrace this portrayal of deeply rooted human anxieties. The film was banned in cities such as Memphis for just that reason.

Steve Trilling saw a script for a picture called *Silver River* early in February 1947, just prior to the release of *Pursued*. Two weeks later, he suggested to Walsh that he read it. Trilling had Flynn in mind for the lead in this new western and sent him a copy also. Walsh was willing to do it. But, after reading the script, Flynn wrote Trilling, "I have read most of the script. As a Western, I think it's damned good. I wish it would have been given me for one of the five other Westerns they had me do. . . . I have nothing against it. [But] I'm not going to be the Gene Autry of the future. Yes, tell the front office. By all means, they might as well know what the score is."[11] Flynn was not looking to be a cowboy again. He'd had enough of sitting on a horse. But the forces were against him—and, anyway, Walsh was directing. Flynn was in.

Silver River has hardly been viewed as one of Walsh's or Flynn's greatest efforts—looking at times like a stock western that falls flat after the early action sequences. But the picture contains some of Walsh's and Flynn's most complexly drawn characters of the period. Walsh mustered a fair amount of enthusiasm while directing it; after all, it was a western, and Warners had roped Flynn into doing it. *Silver River* was based on a story written by Stephen Longstreet, who also penned *Stallion Road* in 1945. Warners hired Longstreet to cowrite the script with Harriet Frank Jr., a new writer at the studio who later went on to carve out a long and sizable career, also writing the screenplays for adaptations of Faulkner's *The Long, Hot Summer* and *The Sound and the Fury* and, after that, for films such as *Hud, The Reivers,* and *The Cowboys*. Flynn plays a Union officer, Mike McComb, who has been disgraced by his superiors and now looks at the world through vengeful eyes. He wants to become the wealthiest man in the territory and has no qualms about stepping on anyone who gets in his way. He heads out for Nevada, becomes a mining baron, and later butts up against a fellow officer, Stanley Moore (Bruce Bennett), the husband of a woman Mike truly loves (Ann Sheridan). To get rid of his rival, Mike sends him into a hostile Indian situation that causes his death. Now free to marry Georgia, Mike does so and gains even greater wealth. But, eventually, his sins turn people, and fate, against him, and he must ultimately decide whether he wants to face up to them and find redemption.

Flynn's character is a complex man straddled by ambiguity and conflict. While Walsh shot large battle scenes for the story's beginning sequence, the bulk of the picture stays focused on Flynn, Sheridan (he would finally direct her again), and Bennett—and on the interiority of their personal conflicts. Like many of Walsh's characters, especially in the upcoming decade of the 1950s, Mike contends with a trauma in his past (his treatment by the military) and then strikes out on his own adventure to avenge himself and stumbles as he tries to reinstate himself back into the human fold.

Walsh began shooting *Silver River* on April 21, 1947, alternating between three locations: Bronson Park at the southern tip of Griffith Park in Hollywood, Sherwin Summit at Inyo National Forest, and the always-reliable Warner Bros. ranch in Calabasas in the western part of the San Fernando Valley. Walsh faced a relatively long production schedule, not finishing until August 2. Flynn was one good reason why—not showing up when he should and, as in the past, not available when the studio tried to reach him. Six or seven weeks into the shoot, as much as he loved his friend, Walsh became frustrated with his drinking and too-frequent no-show status. Then Jack Warner read Flynn the riot act in a memo to Flynn's agent at MCA, Lew Wasserman:

> So there will be no further misunderstanding, our company is reserving the right to keep track of the things that transpire during each day [*Silver River*] is in production.
>
> If Flynn is late, if liquor is being used so that from the middle of the afternoon on it is impossible for the director to make any more scenes with Flynn,
>
> If liquor is brought on the set or into the Studio—we must hold Flynn legally and financially responsible for any delay in the making of this picture.
>
> We may go so far as to abrogate the entire contract and sue him for damages. . . .
>
> We will never again make pictures where Flynn or any other artist becomes incoherent due to liquor or whatever it may

be. When a director informs Production that it is impossible to shoot further because the actor or actress cannot properly handle their assignment we may as well quit. This has happened repeatedly during the last pictures we have made in which Flynn has appeared and we cannot permit it any longer.[12]

The memo did little to halt the problem.

But this picture belonged to Walsh and Flynn and in the most personal way, and in light of their work over the past years, it was fortuitous that the two men came together to work on this picture. Of all the actors in Walsh's life, no one hit Walsh harder—or softer—than Flynn. The two men now working on their eighth and final film together, Flynn's complex performance as Mike McComb is a testament to his entire body of work with Walsh. In the saloon scene when Plato (Thomas Mitchell) begs Mike not to send Moore to the mines—and surely to his death by Indian attack—Flynn at first turns a blind eye, then reconsiders, looking pained, almost as if tortured by his own conscience. Plato tells Mike the story of David and Bathsheba, how David sent one of his soldiers into battle, to the fore of the battle, and when the soldier was killed, married the soldier's wife, with whom he was in love. Plato shows Mike his own selfishness—and for the first time in the story Mike shows his deep conflict. Flynn goes quiet while still talking; he's talking about one thing but thinking about another. He allows himself to bear his pain and alienation for all to see—but, more than that, for Walsh to see, as if he is telling Walsh and the camera about himself as a message of love to a director he adores. The words roll out of his mouth and come from his heart, almost reenacting the emotional pitch of his last scene with Olivia de Havilland in *They Died with Their Boots On*. Although Mike Mc-Comb is talking to Mitchell, Flynn seems more to be talking to Walsh, uttering in his own way, "It's been an honor to walk through life with you." He is speaking to his director and his friend, making his love clear to the man in this final performance for him.

Silver River failed to bring in a substantial box office. While moviegoers at the time found little action in what looked to be a mediocre story line, over the years they have shown increasing appreciation for Flynn's complex performance. But the immediate reaction was hardly positive. The *New York Times* reviewer wrote, "The opening sequences are full of sound and fury, sweep and dash . . . but [Walsh] handicapped himself unmercifully in filming 'Silver River' by cramming all the excitement into the first ten minutes or so. As a consequence . . . the picture . . . runs downhill for most of its remaining length."[13] But Walsh now stood inside the film, ruminating about his friendship with Flynn, who caused so much trouble on his sets yet had his heart. Box-office receipts ran only a distant second.

Walsh and Mary Simpson were fully committed to each other by this time. Walsh later said that he secretly married Mary in Mexico in 1947 and then again officially in a July 1949 New Mexico ceremony. Married or not, they now settled into a home on Kling Street in Toluca Lake, northeast of Hollywood. Mary loved the house as much as Walsh did, even though he had no room for his horses; he boarded them at Hollywood Park and kept the ranch in Willets in northern California. The Kling Street house was a short drive from Warner Bros. and gave Mary easy access to the modest social life she had set up for herself—lunching with girlfriends, traveling now and then with her husband either on vacation or on location, and keeping house for him. She was a stickler for housework, preferring to go around their home barefoot and in pigtails (the way Walsh liked her hair) as she did her work. They made a striking couple, Mary with her youthful beauty, and Walsh looking still extremely virile while nearing sixty.

In the midst of settling into his home with Mary, Walsh went on to direct his next few pictures for the studio, two of which were remakes of earlier pictures. He learned, at least with one, that you can't go home again. His remake of *The Strawberry Blonde*, now called *One Sunday Afternoon*, could never have repeated the good experience, and the good box office, of the earlier picture. Although he had the producer Jerry Wald on his back, instead of his older taskmaster, Hal Wallis, this shoot had no Jimmy Cagney, no Olivia de Havilland, and no Rita Hayworth. It was a perilous time to do remakes, especially with postwar audience attendance dwindling and the potential embarrassment that they might not ignite audiences at all. As early as 1943, Harry Warner in New York sent a memo to Jack in Hollywood. "You can't do this and succeed," he said, referring to Jack's proposed remake of a 1936 Bette Davis picture, *The Petrified Forest*. "That is all right when you are making 50 or 60 pictures and shooting them out like cheese, but when you have built up a reputation such as you have, you cannot continue it if you keep on making remakes."[14] But that didn't stop the spate of remakes that emerged from the studio at this juncture, some belonging to Walsh. *The Petrified Forest* was, in fact, the basis of a remake, *Escape to the Desert* (1945). Also, the film *The Unfaithful* (1947) was a partial remake of the Bette Davis vehicle *The Letter* (1940).

Wald was the more forceful personality on this picture, and it could very well have been his idea to remake *The Strawberry Blonde*. Walsh was never one to turn down an assignment. It was as simple as that: work equaled money; work also equaled being on the set all day; being on the set meant getting a picture made and spending time with people you usually liked. There was nothing in sight to lose, except maybe down the road at the box office. Also working on him, although he may not have been entirely cognizant of it, was the fact that Walsh had so enjoyed the earlier picture he would not pass up the chance to go home again to the time of his youth.

The picture still followed the James Hagan play, and now Robert L. Richards was brought in to write the screenplay. Walsh knew the material by heart and just followed his own instincts. Jack Warner was unsupportive, thinking more about cutting budgets, convinced that the picture would not recoup its cost—still, he didn't stop the production. But, even before the cameras rolled, Walsh had creative disagreements with Jerry Wald, who was clearly in charge. Preproduction on the film had already seemed convoluted—requiring more energy than Walsh thought necessary. His relationship with Wald never reached out-and-out contentiousness, but it easily could have were Walsh not so mild-mannered and easygoing with studio executives and producers. Still, memos show his discontent. Before he left for a brief vacation on November 11, 1947, he telephoned Steve Trilling and mentioned that he was very concerned about *One Sunday Afternoon* because Wald seemed so preoccupied with other matters that he was unable to give "proper attention to this property." Trilling sent a memo to Warner:

Evidently, Jerry is still talking about the OKLAHOMA flavor and/ or the possibilities of keeping to the stage play which Walsh is opposed to, as he feels it is and was a flop once before when

Paramount made it with that formula. Walsh wants to go back more to the *Strawberry Blonde* story, moving into a St. Louis or small town atmosphere and doing the beer garden sequence aboard an excursion boat, etc. He feels they could resolve these differences if Jerry only spent two or three solid hours in a story conference and worked out all problems, rather than giving him a few minutes here and there and no concentrated organization. I called Jerry to arrange a story conference with Walsh and settle these differences.[15]

It took several story conferences for Walsh and Wald to work out their differences and get a story they liked. Walsh had his remake.

Like its predecessor, the picture ended up on Warners' New York street, circa the turn of the twentieth century. Walsh cast the film quickly but not necessarily happily. He'd had a good experience working with Dennis Morgan on *Cheyenne,* and since Morgan was showing off his singing talents at this time, Walsh thought he would be a natural to play the Cagney character, Biff Grimes. Wald disagreed and saw the young actor Dane Clark as Biff and Eleanor Parker as Virginia—and without too many musical numbers at that. But Morgan eventually was cast. Then Wald had the idea of casting Donna Reed in the part of Amy. "This girl has the correct warmth and looks for the role," he wrote Warner, "and she will add a tremendous amount to the overall picture. Don't forget that Miss Reed played opposite Jimmy Stewart in *It's a Wonderful Life* . . . and I feel we can get a couple of extra pictures with her."[16] Even though using Reed would have held up the picture's production (she and Alan Ladd were making *Chicago Deadline*), Walsh agreed that she should be cast. But, after much shifting, and after Walsh tested the newcomer Doris Day for the part, the role of Amy went to someone else entirely—Dorothy Malone, who, among other roles, had had a small part in the studio's *The Big Sleep.* Janis Paige, who actually was a singer and a dancer, won the part of Virginia Brush. This casting move, made against his wishes (he had wanted Virginia Mayo cast as Virginia), made Walsh angry enough to fire off a letter indicating his general dissatisfaction. "When I made The Strawberry Blonde," he told Warner on January 7, 1948, "it had a great cast, all 'kosher.' I think you are making a mistake in not casting Virginia Mayo for the part of

Virginia. I'm sure this girl has great possibilities. . . . The title One Sunday Afternoon is 'traffe' [he meant *trafe,* 'not kosher']." "The pictures I direct have 'gutsy' titles," he added. "Please find one. . . . Remember, 'men Ken nisht fen zaetz macken succar' [his broken Yiddish for 'Don't try to make salt into sugar']."[17]

Walsh shot the picture from January 27 until April 5, 1948, without any further turmoil on the set. When he was finished, five days behind schedule, the studio had a picture that came and went without much notice, remembered only as the remake of one of the studio's most successful and loved pictures of the last decade. The box-office take was fair, and the critical response on the picture's release was mediocre but upbeat. Walsh, who was never an avid attendee at previews, again missed the two for *One Sunday Afternoon* in May and June. He had already left Los Angeles for Oscoda, Michigan, to begin shooting his next picture, *Fighter Squadron.* Again, he was eager to depart the studio's New York street for an outdoor location.

The actors Walsh knew best at Warner Bros.—Cagney, Bogie, and Raft—were getting older, and Flynn was fast losing his stamina, not to mention his looks, to alcohol and bad health. Walsh looked for new faces, as did the studio; they were always to be found. For his next picture, *Fighter Squadron,* Walsh found what he thought he was looking for, a fresh face with the kind of masculinity he liked in his characters—virile and camera friendly. *Fighter Squadron* is a solid air cadet action film not terribly well remembered but significant for its introduction of two young actors, Jack Larsen, who later went on to play Jimmy Olsen in the 1950s television series *Superman,* and another unknown, Roy Fitzgerald, who soon changed his name to Rock Hudson and went on to make four films with Walsh. Hudson would not only have a bona fide love affair with the camera; he was a bona fide Walsh discovery, something akin to the young John Wayne he discovered almost twenty years earlier. At least he seemed to be at the start.

There are conflicting versions of the way Walsh met Rock Hudson. The casting agent Billy Grady claimed he was dining at Chasen's Restaurant in Beverly Hills one evening in the late 1940s when Walsh, also dining there with Mary and with the then Roy Fitzgerald, came over to

Grady's table and asked whether he could bring Fitzgerald, whom he had taken a great interest in and now represented, over to meet him. After the meeting took place, Grady was so taken with Fitzgerald that he promised him a $300 a week contract with MGM starting that very evening. On his way out of the restaurant, Walsh grabbed Grady's arm and said, "I hope this isn't a dream."[18] Another version has Hudson's agent, Henry Willson, bringing him to Walsh's office at Warner Bros. for an interview. Knowing Walsh made a lot of westerns (and thinking him a tough guy), Willson insisted that Rock dress in jeans. Even though Hudson appeared nervous as he read, Walsh was still impressed with him and, after walking a circle around him, pronounced him "green but ripe." "At the very least," Walsh later said, "he'll be good scenery."[19] Walsh asked Hudson whether he could ride a horse. Hudson answered in the affirmative. It hardly seemed to matter, however, since, in *Fighter Squadron,* there was no horse anywhere near the set.

The story of "hot rocks" air force pilots who fly fighter planes to battle the Luftwaffe in 1943–1944 over France and England, the picture featured Edmond O'Brien, Robert Stack, and Tom D'Andrea. While Walsh drove the action to a feverish pitch, and a Technicolor one at that, the showstopper was the mesmerizing aerial photography inserted in the story. He thought this might be Hudson's good shot also.

Walsh spent considerable time and money on Rock Hudson and put him under personal contract. He told Hedda Hopper in a 1965 interview:

> I couldn't use him while I was at Warners—they wanted me to turn him over to them. I took him on location to New Mexico where he had to get up at 5 A.M., ride horses and everything. It helped to toughen him—but he got away from that. At the time I saw him he was going on the soft side; I suggested he watch Cary Grant—"you don't like this rough side of the work." I took him to see Hal Wallis, sent him to see Walter Wanger—but they weren't interested. I called Jack Ford and he agreed to see him. When he went in Jack said, "What's your name?" He said it was Rock Hudson. "No, I mean your real name." When Rock said it was Fitzgerald, Jack said, "Why did you change it! Now, get out!"[20] Everybody turned Rock down—even MGM. Finally I

sent him back to Yates and Republic. They wanted me to direct
him but I couldn't because I was under contract at Warners.
Then I sold him to Universal.[21]

Hudson was so green at the time that he even had trouble with the one
line Walsh gave him to say in *Fighter Squadron:* "You've got to buy
[get] a bigger blackboard." Walsh in turn was not kind to Hudson. As
Hudson's biographer noted, "Walsh was not too good at putting the
[actor] at ease [and] at one point, seeing Hudson standing in the scene
without anything to do, said to him, 'Jesus Christ—you're standing there
like a goddamned Christmas tree—get out of the middle of the shot, for
Chrissake, or stand sideways so you don't block everybody!'"[22] Others
on the set were taken aback.

The one defining word to describe Walsh's feelings about Hudson was *ambivalence.* He both mentored him and scratched his head
about him, for years to come hardly ever moving past that splintered
attitude. Hudson was a disturbance to Walsh, something he himself
could probably not even articulate. Hudson represented some kind of
"lack," physically and psychologically. Walsh wanted him to be tough
and masculine, something he just couldn't be at that time. All he could
do was look handsome, with a body that the camera couldn't help but
follow. Perhaps Hudson's homosexuality was clear, although, if he truly
understood that, Walsh would never utter a word; he'd much rather talk
about "bottle men" than a too-pliable actor, which Hudson was to him.
But the two went on to make numerous pictures together. The friendship
was there, even if it later waned. For now, Walsh kept it quiet that he was
sponsoring Hudson, and his treatment of the young actor was nothing
out of the ordinary for the time, when studios nurtured young actors
with a combination of all-out support and a tough-love attitude.

Hudson worked uncredited on *Fighter Squadron* for two months at
$120 per week. Walsh signed him to a personal contract that guaranteed
him forty more weeks at the same pay whether or not he worked. To fill
the time that Hudson was not working, Walsh gave him little jobs to
do—even chauffeuring Walsh around the city. Despite his poor showing in *Fighter Squadron,* Walsh told Hudson he had a good future, and
Hudson believed him. Walsh paid for acting lessons for Hudson and
kept bolstering his ego.

Walsh also made sure that Hudson kept his hair long, instructing him that he never could tell when a western part might come along. Walsh and Willson had seven of Hudson's teeth capped and continued flaunting their find in front of studio executives all over town. Universal Studios eventually put him under contract for $9,700, a sum equal to what Walsh and Willson had invested in him. Although *Fighter Squadron* never helped Hudson's career, Walsh continued his association with the young actor through three more uneven and quirky collaborations spanning the early years of the 1950s—*The Lawless Breed, Sea Devils,* and *Gun Fury.* He never could get a good performance from him.

An item in *Boxoffice* magazine on August 28, 1948, noted that Walsh was set to direct Errol Flynn and Alexis Smith in another Warner Bros. western called *Montana,* but the assignment never came through for Walsh, even though he directed some of the action scenes without taking credit for them. Instead, he became involved in a story he convinced Jack Warner to make, *Colorado Territory,* a remake of Walsh's *High Sierra,* made seven years before. "I remade *High Sierra* as *Colorado Territory,*" he later remembered, "because Warners was stuck for a release. Everybody had turned down scripts and nothing came up. I had a talk with Warner and said to him, 'Make a Western.' He said, 'All right. Start tomorrow.'" Now that the war was over, turnaround on a picture was fast. "The director could turn down a script, if it didn't fit him or something. But then they'd generally plead with you. . . . Most of these pictures were already sold and had to be released on January 15 and here you were in December. 'How are you coming? Do you think you'll finish tomorrow?'"[23] Not having learned from his experience working with Hudson on *Fighter Squadron,* Walsh considered giving him another chance—the lead, in fact—playing the doomed hero Wes McQueen. He put Hudson to work feeding lines to the first-time Walsh inductee Virginia Mayo, who was testing for the female lead, the half-breed named Colorado. She got the part even though Hudson did not fare as well. According to Mayo,

> [Hudson] had a rather bad attitude about commitment. Raoul had him under contract, hoping he'd become a big star. . . . But Rock just didn't get it. He would wander onto the set around

noon, after the rest of us had been working since 6 A.M., and Raoul would say, "Rock, you have to get on the set and work with the cowboys at dawn. You do not just decide to show up at noon or one o'clock." [Rock] would show up finally on the set, and then just goof around. He liked to play! He was just a huge kid. Raoul would scold him, but Rock would just pour on that gigantic, charming grin outline and all would be forgiven—until the next time.[24]

Walsh couldn't figure out what he thought of Hudson, but he knew enough not to hire him as the lead in the picture.

With *Colorado Territory,* Walsh took *High Sierra* and situated it on the western frontier. As Wes McQueen he cast Joel McCrea, an actor who had the right kind of good looks and cynicism for the part of an outlaw who has pretty much given up on life. McCrea brought the same kind of sympathies to the part that Bogie had earlier, playing a likeable bandit who can't escape the grip of the bad luck that pulls him down. Like the most characteristic of Walsh's heroes, McQueen has good intentions but can't change his life; he's too deeply rooted in his past. Walsh's western landscape gave the picture a vast scope, rooting it in a tradition as sure-fired as the gangster genre—the scenario of good versus evil that lends the characters mythic status.

At the beginning of the film, McQueen is sprung from jail by his new gang so that he can help them pull a train holdup. The dance-hall girl Colorado is the woman who tries to shield him from his fate: his gang eventually turns against him, and he falls for a woman (Dorothy Malone) who abandons him as well. With a $10,000 reward on his head, he attempts to outdistance the law. Instead of retracing Bogie's path into the Sierras, however, McQueen flees to the Colorado Mountains, where he is cornered by the local sheriff and his posse. Colorado stays with her man and also dies trying to protect him.

Like its predecessor, *Colorado Territory* was taken from W. R. Burnett's novel *High Sierra.* The studio wavered over giving Burnett screen credit, and eventually that went only to Edmund H. North and Walsh's good friend John Twist. The picture suffered through a long list of titles, including *Colorado Bound, Dark Canyon,* and *North of the Rio Grande,* until it became *Colorado Territory.* On September 2,

1948, the day shooting began in Gallup, New Mexico, Jack Warner (egged on by Steve Trilling) sent Mayo a bouquet of flowers, no doubt tilting her mood in the right direction. For Mayo, the biggest payoff was the chance to be directed by Walsh, and it would always be so. Years later, she recalled how he inspired McCrea and her during a particularly difficult scene, telling them to imagine some "reward" at the end of it. He would "invent some idea for us to think about," Mayo said. "For example, if we were supposed to run away fast, he'd say, 'You're very, very hot and thirsty, and you've just heard that free beer is being served just around the corner.'"[25] The cast and crew saw little other location shooting. After spending time in New Mexico, Walsh shot the plaza, church, and courthouse scenes at the Warner Bros. ranch. Filming ended on November 2, 1948.

On its release in June 1949, the picture received a much better response than Walsh's previous remake, *One Sunday Afternoon*. Though the film was banned in West Germany for what that government considered its antisocial elements and the fact that it still looked like a gangster film—attitudes Walsh enjoyed hearing about—postwar American audiences found an easy empathy for Walsh's characters McQueen and Colorado. In a decade when film noir bleakness crept onto American movie screens, Walsh's picture caught on (as it continues to do today) with audiences who innately understood the psychological darkness of these characters who are, by contrast, playing out their lives (and the end of their lives) in the almost breathtaking beauty of their physical surroundings. McQueen and Colorado are, in their ironic innocence, almost more heart wrenching than Earle and Marie in *High Sierra*. They have been called noir characters in a decidedly noir western.

About this time, Walsh began making inquiries about his ex-wife Lorraine's alleged marriage to the tennis pro Frank Perry, even hiring investigators to find out whether what he suspected was true (which it was). With Lorraine again married, he no longer had to pay her alimony; he could spend it on his horses instead. Two weeks after shooting began on *Colorado Territory*, Lorraine wrote Walsh's attorney, Julian Hazard, from Stockholm, Sweden, crying foul about Walsh sticking his nose into her business and her marriage to Perry. Walsh's actions rekindled Lorraine's not-so-deep-seated anger and frustration:

Would really dislike to be waiting for my next meal depending on Raoul to answer a letter. . . . Am afraid whatever you advise him he will never be satisfied. He not only wants a copy of my marriage record but a written letter to the effect that it was the only marriage? And then what will he want? He loves intrigue and thrives on it. He was never happier than he was during the Morehead case.[26] He is so used to having his secretaries tell him what hour to go to the bathroom that when one makes a mistake he fires her and hires another. Miss Steffen not only told him when to go to the bathroom but went with him. He was so helpless that he couldn't sign his own checks but had Morehead do it for him. It's too bad he didn't marry Constance Bennett, as they ran each other a close race for several years being sued or suing someone themselves. It's the only time Raoul gets a sparkle in his eye if he thinks there is going to be a bit of dirt flying. Will be home very soon and as I have waited this long you can see my attorney when I arrive. Don't forget he married Mary Simpson and lived with her illegally and of course he judges me the same. I have always been a friend of Raoul's and never intended to treat him as Miriam Cooper did.[27]

After eighteen years of marriage, Lorraine knew Walsh well enough. He enjoyed a little litigation now and again; it served up some drama in his life. He also didn't want to give money away if he didn't have to—especially to an ex-wife. Money was always at a premium: the horses always beckoned, as did betting on them.

The Monster from the Id

> Gentlemen: Do you HAVE to make money this way? . . . There is no knowing the untold harm "WHITE HEAT" will have done before it is off the screens of the world.
> —Anonymous

When anyone asked James Cagney what he had thought of *White Heat* before he started work on it, he said that it was just more of the same—a predictable mobster yarn that he hoped audiences would enjoy. That was before he and Walsh became coconspirators on the set, retooling a first-rate script by Ivan Goff and Ben Roberts, and twisting the story's main character, Cody Jarrett, until he gave new meaning to the word *psychopath*. The controversy stirred up by the film's deranged urban outlaw—and there was plenty—was just what Walsh loved.

Beyond all those western landscapes, here was the best reward: fiction that made waves. This was the reason he made movies—controversy was good drama, therefore, to Walsh, good storytelling.

Even though *White Heat* was a box-office hit when it reached theaters in September 1949, Jarrett was a disturbance of the first order that no one could see coming. So too was the movie itself, a vortex for postwar American angst that proved anything but comforting. With a script that could have been ripped from the pages of Freud's *The Interpretation of Dreams,* the film unleashed the image of a terrifying, unruly force of psychological chaos. Its main character, the psychotic Cody Jarrett (James Cagney), was (and remains) troubled enough to embrace all the collective cultural angst that Americans felt after World War II. He has a mother fixation that is the mother of all mother fixations. In between cold-blooded killings, he climbs onto his mother's lap to cool down from his latest emotional fit. He reminded audiences (as if they had forgotten) the lesson of war and its aftermath: war was such a disturbance and rupture of culture that, in its aftermath, all kinds of monsters from the id could bubble up to the surface.

As the conduit of Cody's psychosis, James Cagney was all but ensured that he could regain his crown as the top Warner Bros. tough guy even after a hiatus of eight years and a much-needed break from Jack Warner (the feeling was mutual, Warner was sure) playing softer souls in his own independent productions. If, as Cagney claimed, he also left the studio because he wanted to get away from the gangster roles that he began to find repetitious, then Cody would cure that. *White Heat* was a repetition of nothing that Cagney had done before.

Walsh, of course, would be the last one to take credit for the film's cultural impact. He might admit to the powerful effect it had on audiences, but he would also deny its obvious broad social underpinnings and influence. That would be too much to ask of a man who still intended to get onto the set, jump into a fiction, get the job done, and "get the hell out." Walsh remembered his sense of disappointment in the box-office failure of what he considered his true work of art, *Evangeline,* and even now still would not admit that his pictures possessed any artfulness. Instead, he remained committed to "playing to Main Street." If this picture made money, well and good; if not, well, it was an adventure while it lasted. Walsh, that is, would be the first to say that he had no idea why a picture worked. Still, he was in top form when he worked with the firecracker material that became *White Heat.*

With its dark and gritty take on the life of a small-time mobster, *White Heat* sits on the edge of two genres, the gangster film and a film noir tale. Walsh gets the feel of the urban jungle down pat: the war going on inside his protagonist's head is but a metaphor for the ugliness of the people and the landscape outside. Cody Jarrett (Cagney), the leader of a gang of robbers, is tough and menacing on the outside but psychologically frail and ready to crumble on the inside. His one true love—and one true downfall—is his mother, Ma Jarrett (Margaret Wycherly), more ruthless than her son and the true leader of Cody's gang. To say that he is pathologically attached to her is to say a mouthful, especially after he gets one of his debilitating headaches and gets nutty and Ma comforts him back to reality. The other woman in his life, his wife, Verna (Virgina Mayo), is a beautiful dame who is crazier about money than she is about Cody and who is ready to betray him at the drop of a fur coat.

After pulling off a train robbery with his unlucky band of thugs, Cody avoids a federal rap by pleading to a lesser state robbery and goes to the pen, where he can run his gang with no trouble. But the Feds are still on to him, and the undercover cop Hank Fallon (Edmond O'Brien) poses as another prisoner to get close to him. Once Fallon gets Cody's confidence, he is in. The great prison scene occurs when Cody learns of Ma's death; he goes berserk and jumps all over the mess hall tables as if he were an animal in the throes of death. But he survives, and when he gets his release from prison, Fallon is right there beside him. The two return to the gang as Cody makes plans to pull off his biggest heist yet—he and his gang will stow away inside a gas truck to get inside a chemical plant and rob it. Instead, Fallon turns on him, and Cody runs amok in the plant trying to escape (or does he really *intend* to escape?). He gets nuttier by the minute, puffed up by some fantasy that he will get to the top of the world just as Ma promised he would. In the film's shot-blast ending, he is on top of a gas storage tank as it explodes and takes him with it. He goes up in a great ball of fire.

The origins of the testosterone-driven *White Heat* lay, not with a male, but with a female writer. Virginia Kellogg was a one-time correspondent for the *Los Angeles Times* who began writing for the studios in the early 1930s. She penned original story ideas for films such as *Mary Stevens, M.D.* (1933), *Stolen Holiday* (1936), and *Meet the People* (1944). She originally approached Milton Sperling and his United States Pictures (which two years earlier had produced Walsh's *Pursued*) with her new story. When nothing came of it, she negotiated directly with Warner Bros. and sold the story for $2,000 in November 1948. Then she was out of the picture, although the studio gave her five weeks of employment after the sale.[28]

The two thirty-page drafts that Kellogg sold to Warners were similar in plotline but different in locale. Neither, however, looked very much like the picture Walsh directed. The story Kellogg wrote first has a Washington, DC, opening where a post office has just been robbed of new currency from the Bureau of Engraving and Printing. What follows is a complex field investigation focusing on two Feds—Hank Fallon and the younger Vic Parker—whose father-son relationship can hardly be missed. They sniff out clues in St. Louis for the notorious Black Flynn gang, believed to be responsible for the heist.

Kellogg's second draft moves the action to a western town and focuses on the two Feds and a hood, Blackie Flynn, who has a strong woman in his life, but a wife, not a mother. As in the movie, Blackie voluntarily surrenders to the authorities and goes to prison, and Parker the Fed has to go undercover and befriend him. While in prison, Blackie goes nuts when he learns his brother has died in a holdup (Kellogg writes that he has "orange eyes and cunning, criminal features"). At the story's end, replete with a shootout with the Feds, Blackie throws himself through an attic window and lands on the pavement below screaming, "They'll never get me on the Insane Express alive!"[29]

Although Kellogg titled her story "White Heat," it bore little resemblance to the final screenplay put together by Ivan Goff and Ben Roberts, the two Warners writers who turned the title into a story of Cody Jarrett's demented psyche. The Australia-born Goff and the Bronx-born

Roberts first crossed paths at Republic Studios in the late 1930s, just
a short time before Walsh went there on loan from Warner Bros. to direct *Dark Command*. A little while later, during World War II, the two
worked together at what used to be the Astoria Studios on Long Island
producing military propaganda shorts for the U.S. Army. After the war,
they teamed up to write a play, *Portrait in Black* (one version of which
later became a 1960 Lana Turner vehicle). Soon after, they ventured out
to Hollywood and wrote a feature film that never saw the light of day,
The Shadow, adapted from a play by Ben Hecht. Warner Bros. asked
them to redo a troubled script called *Backfire* (released in 1950) and
subsequently put them under a five-year contract. Then, Steve Trilling
handed them Kellogg's story and asked them to turn it into a screenplay.
As they remembered it:

> We said, "We don't want to do this. It's simply a bank robbery.
> It's ordinary, conventional, banal." They said, "What would
> you like to do?" We said, "We don't know. Give us some time
> to think about it." So we thought about it and we synthesized
> Ma Barker down to having the one son instead of four, and we
> put the evil of all four into one man. Then we went back and
> said, "We'd like to do Ma Barker and have the gangster with a
> mother complex and play it against Freudian implications that
> she's driving him to do these things, and he's driving himself to
> self-destruction. Play it like a Greek tragedy." They said, "Fellas
> . . . ?" We said, "Believe us, it will work. And there's only one
> man who can play this and make the rafters rock."[30]

The last thing Jack Warner wanted in mid-1949 was to see James
Cagney ("that little bastard," as he referred to him) back on his studio
lot. For Cagney, the feeling was mutual—even with an Oscar coming for
1942's *Yankee Doodle Dandy*. Not only did Cagney not want to return
to gangster parts; he never forgot the contract hell Warner had put him
through since the early 1930s. He could speak some Yiddish from his
childhood years, but it never sang in Jack Warner's ears as Walsh's did.
Yet Goff and Roberts were adamant about Cagney playing the part of
Cody Jarrett, and in the end, the prospect of big box-office returns, and

Cagney's return as the ultimate tough guy, was too much for everyone to ignore. Fighting ceased, and Cagney returned to the lot.

No doubt the prospect of working again with Walsh was one reason. The two had collaborated on *The Roaring Twenties,* together tweaking Cagney's character and Walsh framing his ever-changing emotional map of a face. They were lightning quick and understood each other's pace. Walsh understood Cagney enough to draw out of him not only his character's depravity but also his humanity—his frailties. As Roberts later said, it didn't hurt that Walsh's cinematographer on *White Heat,* Sid Hickox, was one of the director's favorites. He had given *Gentleman Jim* a nostalgic sheen and would photograph this picture to look rough, almost emotionally and visually grainy. Now Walsh's story would look even darker and more foreboding—as if the characters' psychological innards were not already dark enough.

Walsh began shooting on May 6, 1949, finishing six weeks later, on June 20. He made use of various southern California locations, first going to the Santa Susana Mountains, near his home, for chase scenes, then on to an old Southern Pacific railroad tunnel and train to stage the opening robbery scenes. The hideaway lodge sequences were shot on the Warner Bros. ranch, the interior scenes in the studio itself, and the climax at a plant near Torrance, south of Los Angeles.

Cagney was not in as great a physical shape as he would ironically be in a few years when Walsh directed him in *A Lion Is in the Streets.* So, for now, to compensate for Cagney's being away from the grind and having put on some weight, Walsh decided to shoot him from the waist up whenever possible, using close-up and medium shots as much as he could. What might have been a hindrance turned into a benefit: with so much emphasis on Cagney's face, on Cody Jarrett's physical twitches, rapid eye movements, and a more than occasional cock of the head to one side, his character embodies even more psychotic shadings than he might otherwise have had.

There were some interruptions from Jack Warner during filming, one of them relayed by Roberts. Warner was getting angrier by the minute over the picture's rising costs. He wanted to change the location of the scene where Cody goes berserk hearing of his mother's death—which, as it now stood, was to be shot in a mess hall, requiring six hundred extras for one line of dialogue. He called Walsh, Roberts, and the producer Louis Edelman into his office and asked if they could change the scene to a chapel—which would require fewer extras. All three men said, "Cody in a chapel?" Not likely, since the point of it all was Cody's being in a loud mess hall that suddenly goes silent when he begins to yelp at learning Ma is dead. So Walsh finally said to Warner, "Give me three hundred extras and the [Warner Bros. actual] machine shop, which we'll convert into a mess hall, and we'll be out by noon so the men can go back to work." Warner said, "You've got it." Walsh did the scene "in three hours," said Roberts, "and was out for lunch. One take."[31]

The Rhythm of Bullets

Cagney always claimed it was his idea to have Cody climb onto Ma Jarrett's lap and sit there being soothed after one of his psychotic migraines—even if legend always put it that Raoul Walsh was the only director who could ever get Cagney to do something like that. In *Each Man in His Time*, Walsh says that he found the script on his own—probably not true—that he came across *White Heat* by accident while reading scripts. "After only a couple of pages I knew it was for Cagney. Only he could play the snarling paranoid with a mother fixation. It was a natural for his brand of talent," Walsh writes. "The story called for some of the most vicious action I had ever directed." "No standard mold would fit [Jarrett]," he continued, "because he was unstable, raving against society one moment and whimpering at his mother's knee the next. With such a script, I had to take a few chances. In one scene I wanted to put Cagney in his mother's lap. Even the cameraman looked doubtful when I posed the shot. We got away with it because Cagney and [Margaret Wycherly] were absolutely convincing."[32]

In his autobiography, Cagney mentions stopping by Roberts's office one day after shooting and telling him that he had just done something "startling." He was not sure it would work, but Walsh thought it would. When Roberts asked what he had done, Cagney said, "I sat on Mama's lap." He and Roberts thought it would work because, truthfully, that was what the movie was about—Cody's Oedipal complex, being the child who needs his "mama."[33]

Cody Jarrett's cheating wife, Verna, played by Virginia Mayo, is one of Walsh's sadder women, beaten up by Cody and unable to get even except by betraying him with his cohort, Big Ed (played by Steve Cochran), who abuses her as much as Cody does. In one scene, Verna is a preview of things to come in Walsh's films—a tough broad maneuvering in a man's world. But, as the 1950s rolled in, Walsh's male characters would be less vicious and easier to love. Relations between men and women would become more even keeled. Verna's character borders on being played for laughs, the script making fun of her more often than not.

In Walsh's hands, *White Heat* moves to the rhythm of bullets, each one shooting out from the frame as if the entire scenario, with its psychotic, mother-loving killer and its trigger-happy anger, wants to rouse postwar American society in even newer ways than Warner Bros. had already managed to do with nearly two decades of the gangster genre. Walsh gave the film its frenetic rhythm, its robust energy, as if he had dipped back into his days on the set of *The Bowery* and found a crazier version of bravado to match the psychotic edge Cagney offered up so well. Cody may be psychotic, but the film is lusty and good-humored, smart-alecky and typically Walshian in its hero's relentless search for a way to escape the stray bullet that will end his life.

Walsh's personal touches go beyond the script. When the gang hides out in their cabin just after their early train heist, as Cody's debilitating headache comes on, he falls from his chair, and the .45 he's cleaning drops and goes off, causing everyone in the room to panic and scatter. The gunshot was Walsh's idea—it is not in the script. Also Walsh's is Verna's leg swing as she gets up out of the bed just minutes earlier. She bares enough of her upper thighs in the movement to make anyone wonder how Walsh got that one past the censors. Sometimes the story plays with and teases Verna. When Verna tells Cody that Ma went to buy strawberries for her "boy," the script simply has him giving her a seething look. But Walsh has him actually knock her off the chair she is standing on, causing her to fall onto the bed.

Walsh blows Cody to bits in as big an explosion as he can imagine. He found that plant one day driving around Los Angeles County. He wanted to go crazy because with Cagney he could. He could tweak and wreak havoc because Cagney was the physical actor Walsh needed in a story where popping bullets set the rhythm. Cagney's face and body move in perpetual motion. His angst can run amok in the midst of Walsh's fast-paced action—until Cody is so dangerous, so on the loose, that he's a force only psychoanalysis (or an explosion) knows how to fix. Like the A-bomb that might have made him, he's a wrath of chemicals on his way to destruction. The bullet rhythm emanates, not from the script, but from Walsh's pure enthusiasm for this story. It's his last great action story at Warners, and the film's car chases, crackling exchanges between fast-talking characters, and sleek, economical setups that move quickly are extensions of his almost organic responses to his fiery material.

After getting in that one good explosion in *White Heat,* Walsh tamed himself and returned to the set, appearing in, of all things, a movie—playing himself. On August 1, 1949, he made a cameo appearance in *It's a Great Feeling* (originally called *Two Guys and a Gal*); since he was on the Warner Bros. lot anyway, he took advantage of the chance to ham it up on the screen for a fellow director. David Butler directed this stock-in-trade Warners musical comedy starring Dennis Morgan, Doris Day, Jack Carson, and a handful of Warner contract actors playing themselves. Carson is a producer who cannot get anyone to direct his next picture. In the opening sequence, he approaches three of the studio's big guns, Michael Curtiz, King Vidor, and, first up, Walsh, who, sitting in his director's chair on a set, tells Carson, "Arthur, you're my favorite producer in the world. I'd do anything for you, but not *this!*" Walsh then turns back to his own crew and says, "Now, let's get on with this clambake. . . ."

12

By Land and by Sea

If *The Big Trail* proved to be the great adventure of Walsh's early career, then the biggest challenge later on came in spearheading the massive production of *Captain Horatio Hornblower R.N.*, a picture that took four months to complete and severely tested the mettle of the now sixty-three-year-old Walsh. Confronting unpredictable weather conditions, soaring production costs that had to be held in check, and the staging of naval equipment both huge and small, he would call it the most difficult film he had ever directed. The production that began January 24, 1950, practically turned Walsh and Mary, who accompanied him, into British subjects as they spent six months settling in England, then traveling to France and back to England again, before returning home to California.

Warner Bros.' intentions to put the picture on the screen were long in the making. In fact, the studio's connection to *Captain Horatio Horn-blower* even predated its relationship with Walsh himself. Jack Warner handed over the sum of $10,000 back in 1939 as a first payment to the British writer C. S. Forester for the picture and allied rights to his *Captain Horatio Hornblower*, actually a trilogy, consisting of the novels *Beat to Quarters*, *Ship of the Line*, and *Flying Colors*, centering on an officer of the British navy during the time of the Napoleonic Wars. From the start, Warner had Errol Flynn in mind to play Hornblower, but the film took more than a decade to come to the screen, long enough for time and Flynn's health problems to erode his youthfulness and vigor; eventually, he was out of the picture. Various directors and writers had also been attached to the project, including the director William Dieterle and the then writer John Huston. At one point, the studio even had plans for a production featuring the husband and wife team of Laurence Olivier and Vivien Leigh. There was never anything small scale about this story. When Warner gave the picture to Walsh, it had been on the block for over a decade and was considered to be a massive undertaking.

The writer C. S. Forester was born in Cairo, Egypt, in 1899 and produced a long list of adventure stories. During World War II, he took up residence in the United States and, among his other activities, produced propaganda to encourage America to join the Allied forces. He published *The African Queen* in 1935, which was adapted as the 1951 film starring Humphrey Bogart and Katharine Hepburn. He also wrote *Hunting the Bismarck!* which became the basis for the 1960 film *Sink the Bismarck!* But his most popular work was the *Horatio Hornblower* series that traced the Hornblower character's career from midshipman to admiral, three of which formed the basis of this film.

Walsh's screen version of *Horatio Hornblower* falls into two parts, the first half delineating Hornblower's character as a solitary, taciturn human being who mediates his relationships with others by adhering to a strict code of honor, certainly of rules. Early on, when his second mate wants a crew member flogged, Hornblower carries through with the punishment, not because he believes the man to be guilty of a crime, but because he wants to show the second mate that, if he vowed to flog the man in front of the others, he must do so, right or wrong—even if he also believes that flogging makes for unhappy, broken crew members, not at all what the ship or the queen's navy needs. Hornblower is the polar opposite of Walsh's own nature; the officer is a rigid superego whose stiffness and unwavering self-assurance carry him through the film's first battle sequence—a huge confrontation between the *Lydia,* his ship, and a ship stewarded by a demented Central American autocrat. One can almost feel the glee Walsh experienced in concocting these dueling ships and canons—like a kid playing with the best toys in the chest and putting every fiber of his being into making it seem real, replete with sound effects shooting out of the side of his mouth.

For this reason, the second half of the story clashes in tone with the first. Hornblower soon falls in love with Lady Wellesley, and, even though another enormous battle sequence ensues, the story, and Hornblower, goes soft; he jumps out of an adventure script and into a love story created for readers of the *Ladies' Home Journal* as the lovers at last embrace amid a set of (literally) thousands of flowers. The picture is uneven at best, its standout features being the huge battle sequences staged at several intervals in the story. The man and woman are tender lovers, but the script shortchanges them by omitting a logical transition from star-crossed to full-blown lovers. One wonders whether Walsh noticed the leap—or perhaps became lost in battleship mania, failing to keep tabs on a script that falls victim to a love affair, always too tough for him to look closely at anyway.

Hornblower was produced at the time of the Eady levy, named after the British treasury official Sir Wilfred Eady, but also called the British Film Production Fund—a tax of a quarter of a penny per ticket. It began in June 1950 as a way to give the producers of British films an increased share of the box office and to spur homegrown film production in the face of an invasion by the U.S. studios, which began setting up British subsidiaries after World War II to skirt restrictions in the earnings that they could take from that country. But, of course, the fund also helped Hollywood since it made no distinction between British production companies and the British arms of American companies. Called *British runaways,* the American films made on British soil came to dominate British cinemas from the mid-1950s through the mid-1960s; one of the most popular was *Captain Horatio Hornblower.* Warners took advantage of the situation, using its British facilities to produce *Horatio Hornblower* (and, certainly, live ships were easier to obtain in Britain than on the Pacific Coast). Despite the fact that the film would be made at Warners' British studio, the cast would also consist of Americans, each of whom had to apply for a permit to work in the United Kingdom. Walsh was on board as producer (a moniker he had left behind in the 1920s), not only for the extra money, but also to gain more control over this huge production. He was so eager to tackle this picture that it seemed as if he were pacing the ground to get closer to this adventure, a fantasy that appealed to the boy still in him.

Walsh arrived in England on December 1, 1949, to begin his six-month commitment to direct *Hornblower.* He had with him a final script by Ivan Goff and Ben Roberts, who had penned *White Heat,* along with Aeneas MacKenzie, who had coscripted *They Died with Their Boots On* (and who later wrote DeMille's 1956 *The Ten Commandments*). He scouted locations and familiarized himself with his British outfit, as he might put it. Three days after Jack Warner sent him a gift basket of food for Christmas 1949, Walsh wrote him a detailed letter: "Dear Colonel . . . Many thanks for the nice basket you sent to the boat—they came in very handy for Christmas. As a matter of fact we are cooking the basket tonight. The food situation is a little rough here, also the weather, but I have been hard at it getting my staff together since we arrived, and we are making good headway. I do not get a cameraman [who turned out to be the talented Guy Green] until the 5th of January, but I've been lining men and women up for tests, which I will ship to you immediately."[1] A combination of jest and seriousness, this was typical Walsh behavior on the set.

Warner's decision to use American actors for the principals was, to say the least, unpopular with the British press. Gregory Peck won the part of Hornblower, and even though Walsh tested other actresses, such as Constance Smith, and almost settled on Patricia Neal even as the name of Alida Valli came up (she and Peck had gotten along well making Selznick's *The Paradine Case* previous to this),[2] the Walsh favorite Virginia Mayo, already under contract to Warners, won the part of Lady Barbara Wellesley. Peck rooted for Margaret Leighton to win the part, but the voluptuous Mayo also had Warner in her corner.

Peck had been interested in the part of Hornblower for several years. "I can tell Jack Warner a little secret," Louella Parsons had written earlier that year. "If he decides to make C. S. Forester's popular 'Captain Horatio Hornblower,' Gregory Peck would like to be his boy."[3] Peck had a three-picture deal with David O. Selznick at that time, but Selznick loaned him to Warner Bros. for $150,000 when *Hornblower* went into production. That amount easily exceeded the $60,000 Selznick had to pay Peck. Known for his painstaking research of the characters he played, Peck prepared for the part by studying accounts of nineteenth-century naval warfare, along with sailing and navigation. Peck took to his director immediately—although Walsh later said that he liked his star but found him a little too stiff for his taste, a little too serious.

Walsh was developing more of a crusty edge to his personality. His humor had become more ribald, and he was given to playing around with a young actor (if Peck could qualify as that), almost like a cat playing with a mouse and teasing it to distraction. He often coupled that with acting the part of the benevolent father, with a gruff yet affectionate tenor to his words and behavior. Like scores of other actors before and after him, Peck noticed right away that Walsh was not all that interested in dialogue. According to his biographer Gary Fishgall, "Peck recalled that sometimes during the shooting of a particularly talky scene, the director would sit in his chair, reading a newspaper." When he finished, Walsh just said, "Print." If Peck told Walsh that he might have forgotten a line or "garbled a word," Raoul simply replied, "Did you, kid, what was that?" If Peck asked for a retake, sometimes Walsh obliged him. But, if Walsh thought it wasn't that important—or that the audience wouldn't notice—he'd say, "Kid, it's fine, let's go, let's keep moving."[4] With his measured pace and great attention to detail, Peck could easily rub Walsh the wrong way. Walsh would never voice his anger to the gentle Peck; he would just look to the side with an odd expression on his face.

The British press was particularly hard on Virginia Mayo, whose introduction to England was not a pleasant one. From what the Brits had seen of her so far, she was nothing if not a brassy American screen dame. The press thought a British actress should have had the part of the British Lady Wellesley. But Mayo was good box office, and the studio insisted that she be in the film so that it could recoup its investment in dollars and pounds.

It was rumored at the time that Mayo was chosen only after several British actresses turned down the part; however, studio production files contradict that. Jack Warner cabled British Warners executive Gerry Blattner, "If the English do not agree, we will seriously consider revising out future production plans for England." Warner was not about to lose any clout that Mayo brought. Instead, the studio went to work to try to improve her box-office potential in Britain. Blattner wrote to Warner on February 7, 1950, after Mayo arrived in Britain,

> As you will no doubt have heard, Virginia Mayo arrived twenty-five hours late after one of the stormiest passages in the Queen Mary's history. However, I understand that Virginia is looking fine. . . . She gave a very good broadcast on Saturday in the peak hour programme, "In Town To-Night," which is heard by approximately 20 million listeners. I heard this broadcast, which she did extremely well and am convinced that it did a great deal of good. The main trend of the broadcast can be summed up by quoting the interviewer's last few words: "We are very

proud to have had you here to-night, Virginia Mayo. I hope you have as warm a welcome in Britain as Richard Todd has had in America." The whole press situation has now quieted down.[5]

If a small public relations fire flared up after this, it was not much of one, and Jack Warner and his men put it out quickly.

At one point during the production, Walsh relayed some tsuris he and Peck had had over the actor's insistence on making script changes. Peck thought, not only that the script should conform more to the book, but also that Lady Barbara's character ought to be less sexualized. To this end, Goff and Roberts later told Warner, "Principally we have changed Lady Barbara's attitude from hot-pants archness to one of interest, growing admiration, and eventual love. This modulated approach we feel preserves the dignity of the book and makes the love much less Captain Blood and much more Captain Horatio Hornblower." In short, they reported, "We have de-tarted Lady Barbara. She's NOT on the make."[6] The change didn't please Walsh, but then he also knew that a detarted Lady Barbara didn't necessarily a devoluptualized Mayo make.

Walsh, who produced along with Gerry Mitchell, arrived on the set the first day of shooting wearing an outfit that practically frightened his British crew: it consisted of "pink trousers, a tweed jacket over a white sweater, a plaid muffler covering the absence of either shirt or necktie and a blue beret, at an extremely unrealistic angle." "English directors did not dress that way," Albert Margolies reported for the *New York Times*. "But Raoul Walsh did, and as he rolled his thin toothpicks of cigarettes, his manner was as distinctly so-what as anyone's could possibly be." The crew expected Walsh to start the day with something like, "Action!" or "Camera!" Instead, they got, "Okay, let's go, hombres," which took some adjusting. Still, they found Walsh to be extremely even-tempered and full of patience. "Do that slower," he would say to an actor. "I want your family to recognize you when they go to see this picture." Or he would tell an actor, "That was fine for *Macbeth*. Now let's do it for us." "When one of the arc lights sputtered through a take, Walsh said, 'We'll have to go through all that again. There was a spotted dog getting cooked that time.'" But it was no less impressive that Mary Walsh brought her husband's lunch to the set everyday.[7]

Just after Walsh began shooting, he received a break-a-leg cable from Warners' front office: "Dear Raoul . . . Always knew with you at the helm that good ship Hornblower could set sail in January and you've made it. You have the very best wishes of everyone here for the successful making of a great picture . . . Jack, Steve, Walter." Jack Warner followed with his own cable on January 23, 1950: "Dear Pappy . . . Happy you're off. Be positive. Everyone understood in dialogue. Don't let them speak fast or too broad. We want no photo finishes on what they are talking about. Must make great picture as Hollypark [Hollywood Park] being rebuilt. Need mucho gelt [i.e., money] when this opens next summer. Don't want [to] disappoint stockholders. My best to Mary . . . Jack." Walsh also cabled Trilling and Warner on January 28, "All the cast winners. No Mayfair accents. One exception: Quist [a ship's mate]. Can dub in American as he is great type. Met Mr. Tsouris Munzer and trafe [Walsh's Yiddish, meaning 'bastard' and 'unkosher']. They had me down for the count of nine but am on my feet battling it out and trying for a knockout. Regards, Raoul."[8]

Then Walsh encountered weather problems that hardly let up for the whole of the production. Uncharacteristically, by February 3, 1950, he was two days behind schedule after only seven days shooting. "Severe storm prevented me from phon[ing] you last night," Walsh cabled Steve Trilling on February 3. "Shipped coloured dailies to you today. Some closer shots and over shoulders missing. Also some long shots. Wire me your opinion when you receive stills. . . . Sending you long cable regarding love scenes from Peck's reaction. Going is pretty tough but I'm still on my feet. Uncle."[9]

England was still feeling the effects of wartime food rationing, and Walsh had to have food sent over from the States. As early as January 7, he cabled his agent, Sam Jaffe, "Please arrange Trilling two shipments weekly meat, eggs, butter." Jaffe wrote to Trilling the same day, "Here is the cable that I got from Raoul Walsh, and also enclosed is my reply. Raoul is a small eater and if he doesn't get proper nutrition it is bound to affect his work and speed. I would like to see you within the next couple of days and I will set up an appointment."[10]

Walsh used a total of five ships for the production. Hornblower's ship, the *Lydia,* was actually a three-masted schooner named the *France* that had seen action as early as 1914. To help set decorators transform the *France* into a royal warship, a 1785 frigate called the *Ariel* was used as a model. Walsh also had a full-size, fifty-ton reconstruction built right on the London set that he could use for most of the filming. It was equipped with hydraulic machinery so that it could simulate the movements of a ship at sea. Even though, at 140 feet in length, the reconstruction was enormous, it was still a tight squeeze when cranes hoisted all the sound equipment, the camera, and the lighting fixtures onto it. Walsh, along with his longtime assistant Russ Saunders and the cameraman Guy Green, made the best of it. Sometimes the set was so crowded that there was room for the actors but not Walsh himself, forcing him to direct from the rigging. He made scrupulous notes on some points: adding detail to the flogging scene and Horatio's relationship to his crew and, on one occasion, noting that he doubted Peck would relish the shower scene he was expected to do, "on account of his physique." (The scene was later removed.)[11] Even in his sixties, and later than that, Walsh walked around movie sets shirtless; he was not a man who, at least outwardly, harbored any doubts about his own physique or his virility—a fact that made it easier for him to write such a note about Peck.

Warners sent miniature ships to Walsh from Hollywood. Steve Trilling cabled the production in England on May 2, 1950: "Ship and gun miniatures sent you for use Hornblower on temp loan basis and must be returned to us. The miniature ships are old models used innumerable times at Burbank Studio. Were built originally for Captain Blood and Divine Lady over twenty years ago. Have small intrinsic value. Would evaluate max $3000 for 2-inch models, $2000 for 1-inch models. $5000 total."[12] Walsh choreographed these disparate elements into a seamless whole.

Yet there is less discrepancy between the film's life-size ships and its miniatures than there is between the film's battle sequences and the heavily sentimentalized love story that Peck and Mayo fall into—enough to know that Walsh could not have had much personal investment in the more flowery aspects of this picture. It is not surprising, then, that the film's crew often reported seeing Walsh's behavior change radically from time to time. He seemed almost like a young boy, showing personal excitement and unlimited enthusiasm whenever he shot the battle scenes. But he would go completely silent and look around for something to read instead of looking straight into the camera when Mayo and Peck shot their love scenes. Walsh had exhibited this kind of fragmented behavior before, but it became more prevalent as he directed more character-driven stories into the 1950s and early 1960s. He avoided looking into the camera more than he ever had.

A highlight for Walsh and the entire company was the day Princesses Elizabeth and Margaret came to the set at Denham Studios and Walsh gave them the full tour. Elizabeth was especially interested in the organization of the battle sequences. But Walsh became fully energized when the company moved to Villefranche on the French Riviera to film the sea sequences. He had a new problem to solve. "I was at a loss to know where we could find period ships to represent the French squadron that Hornblower, fresh from harrying the Spanish-American ports along the Pacific littoral, was to take on single handed until the rest of the British fleet arrives," he later wrote.[13] He eventually found four old schooners for sale and rounded up "seagoing" carpenters to outfit them to replicate Hornblower's enemy squadron. While on the Riviera he also authorized a bloodstock agency to make an offer for a horse, an Irish-owned Grand National Steeplechase entry. He thought about going over to ride the horse himself (or so he told the press), but he never did.

But an adventure that Walsh never counted on once the company settled in at Villefranche occurred when Edmond Greville, a director of the French team (which, for trade union reasons, doubled for the English team there), took a great liking to Mary Walsh and it appeared that the feeling was mutual. Greville and Mary would occasionally go off together, causing Walsh enough agitation to walk around asking, "Where is Mary?" and even venture off himself to look for her. The three-decades-plus difference in their ages gave him pause, however briefly.

Walsh kept in shape, physically and psychologically. He took a swim every morning, often with his sidekick Bear Valley Charley, who still went with him almost everywhere as a good-luck charm. Word got out that now he would be raising Kerry blues in the future because he no longer had time for race horses. That, however, was just hearsay. Walsh had not let his duties on the *Hornblower* set squelch any opportunities he might get to see or purchase a horse while in England. He had the ranch in Simi Valley to house any animal he purchased. Soon, in January 1951, back home from England, he would write to John Huston, "If you are going ahead with the African Queen and if you need a good assistant, the chap I had helping me on Captain Horatio Hornblower is great. His name is Jack Martin and when you get to England you can locate him. Incidentally, knowing that you are a horse man, I know that you will pick up a horse over there, and the finest and most honest man I can recommend is Bert Kerr. . . . You can pick up yearlings very cheap over there and when this fellow has a horse running, you can win your-self a bet." Huston responded, from his home at 650 North Bronson, in Hollywood, "Dear Raoul . . . When I go to England I shall certainly avail myself of your tips. I am especially glad to know about the honest horse man in Ireland, as I definitely intend to buy some horses there."[14]

Captain Horatio Hornblower premiered in London in April 1951 and then in New York on September 13 at the Radio City Music Hall, ultimately earning $3 million and becoming Warner's top-grossing pic-ture in the United States that year. But Walsh was peeved when the stu-dio began mounting its publicity campaign as early as January. He wrote Steve Trilling, "I see by the enclosed clipping that they are starting to advertise HORNBLOWER. If I can remember correctly, there were 1,200 still shots on this production and out of these, two of the worst were selected by the publicity department. When I came back from England I rode on the plane from New York with Mort Blumenstock [Warners' head of publicity]. I suggested a blow-up of the two miniatures blazing [the] hell out of each other and suggested it for a twenty-four sheet."[15] No matter what stills the studio chose to exploit the picture, *Horatio Hornblower* was an immediate success with audiences and with the critics. *Variety* praised, not just Peck's performance, but also Walsh's direction of the story's action sequences, calling the film "a spectacular success," one "lensed with great skill"—albeit noting that the picture seemed to be divided into two parts.[16] Some years later, Peck attempted to make a sequel, but that never materialized.

Horatio Hornblower provided Walsh with one of his greatest plea-sures—to give in to his wanderlust. He subscribed fully to the belief that the grass might be greener on the other side of the fence, on the other side of the world, in this case, England and the French Riviera. But he also subscribed to the belief that you help your friends out when they come calling. And come calling his pal Humphrey Bogart did in late

July 1950 when he asked Walsh to step in and direct a picture he was making at Warners—*The Enforcer* (a.k.a. *Murder, Inc.*), a story that Bogie disliked (proof to him of the poor material the studio was giving him) and that turned out to be his last outing there.

Scripted by the ace writer Martin Rackin, and produced for the studio by Milton Sperling's United States Pictures, *The Enforcer* was Walsh material anyway—there was enough police action to keep him interested—and he was happy to step in. Slated for the European director Bretaigne Windust, who directed very few pictures at Warner Bros. in his short tenure there, the production hit a snag when Windust was said to have become seriously ill after a few days on the set and couldn't go on. But that was far from the truth—or so the film's writer, Martin Rackin, told Walsh's friend Pierre Rissient years later. The French-born Windust was originally a New York stage director specializing in dramas. He had already directed pictures for Warners, including two Bette Davis films, *Winter Meeting* and *June Bride,* both in the late 1940s. Neither was very successful. Windust, who happened to be homosexual, was assigned to direct *The Enforcer.* But, after a few days on the set, someone [possibly Milton Sperling, the film's producer] went to Jack Warner and told him he'd better look at the rushes because all the actors playing gangsters "looked like sissies." Warner took one look and yelled, "Bring in Raoul Walsh! He'll cure *that!*" Rissient said that Walsh was very much a gentleman, more than many others around. He directed the picture but refused to take credit, telling people—in error—that this was Windust's first feature at Warners and that he needed the credit more than he, Walsh, did.[17] Bogie needed Walsh to get the picture finished as fast as possible.

Right after *The Enforcer,* and before *Hornblower* premiered in this country, Walsh was at work directing another western for Warner Bros.—a curious, middle-of-the-road psychological drama in western dress originally called *The Travelers* but released as *Along the Great Divide.* This picture marked the last of Walsh's ongoing contract deals with Warners that had begun in 1939. From there on out, he would return to the studio on individual picture deals or two-to-three deals only. He was ready to test his mettle in more than just his own backyard.

Along the Great Divide took Walsh only as far as Lone Pine, California, just north of Los Angeles—an area long a favorite with studios for outdoor location shooting. Unlike the location for *Hornblower,* this landscape wasn't exotic, but at least it was outdoors and on dry land. The area had subbed for the Himalayas in George Stevens's *Gunga Din* in 1939, and Walsh used Lone Pine's Whitney Portal Road for the ending chase scene in *High Sierra.* Now he would use it to simulate the Mojave Desert.

Walter Doniger, who had cowritten Universal's *Danger in the Pacific* in 1948 and adapted *Tokyo Joe* for Bogie in 1949, sold his original story, "Along the Great Divide," to Warners in October 1948 and went on to cowrite the screenplay with Lewis Meltzer, who had coscripted the 1939 *Golden Boy.* As the two fine-tuned the script, Doniger kept Warners' research department jumping, loading up on details about the old West, the history of the state of Wyoming (where he placed his characters), and U.S. marshals in general. He asked for material on water rights, on court procedure in U.S. territories, how long a man and a horse could live in the desert without water, what cowboys ate, how to poison a well, where the gallows were located in western towns, and whether a fast horse with a rider could beat fast horses pulling a stagecoach. He had done his homework by the time Walsh came on board in October 1950. The script was complete, and Walsh was ready to go to work again with one of his favorite cameramen, Sid Hickox.

Virginia Mayo was hardly out of Walsh's sight for a minute after *Horatio Hornblower* (she and Mary Walsh would become very close friends) when he cast her in *Along the Great Divide* as the female lead. She would play opposite Kirk Douglas, who headed the cast as Len Merrick, a U.S. marshal trekking across the Mojave to civilization to make certain the prisoner in his keep gets a fair trial. This was Douglas's first western; he later claimed that he took the part only because it would get him out of his then current one-picture-per-year commitment at Warner Bros. Walter Brennan, whom Doniger later described as an actor who was "always polite,"[18] was cast as Douglas's nemesis and John Agar, whom Walsh had never directed before, as a deputy. Shooting began on October 16, 1950, and ended on November 25. The picture opened in the United States four months before the American premiere of *Horatio Hornblower.*

Outdoor shoots gave Walsh the natural lighting he liked best. He never again liked to be cooped up in a studio (in some kind of bedroom, he would say) for weeks on end. The light was too artificial, and there was no "weather," no wind, no dust to kick up if need be. Doniger thought that Walsh was in his element with action films, that "he had an eye for the image and moment of action to keep the image moving."[19]

On the other hand, Douglas was never shy about his dislike for Walsh, calling him, at the very least, "a brutal man." Feeling more as if he were doing time than having a good time, he looked back on his days on Walsh's set as nothing short of being in hell. "Walsh loved violence," Douglas wrote in his first autobiography. "I was disgusted one day to see him get excited almost to the point of orgasm while watching a dangerous stunt in which a stunt man almost got killed. I could see his sexual glee, watching the stunt man almost get kicked in the head as he ran through a stable full of kicking horses."[20] The statement says more about Douglas than it does about Walsh, however, as if the venom Walsh inspired in him was intense and long lasting.

For Douglas, none of this was helped by Walsh's habit of cutting corners on the script if he could get away with it. The crustier he became, the more impatient he seemed, sometimes looking as if he needed to be somewhere else—perhaps a race track. Douglas remembered objecting vehemently to Walsh omitting several pages of a particular scene. Walsh's response—after hearing the scene rather than looking at it during the shoot—was simply to say that it "sounded" fine the way it was. Angered though he was, Douglas nevertheless looked at the bigger picture later on—if nothing else, more able to appreciate the genre he liked so much. At the very least, westerns taught him "good horsemanship." "Westerns [perhaps even Walsh's] are an important part of movie history, of our country's history," he added.[21]

Although it traverses a psychological subject, the relationship between fathers and sons, *Along the Great Divide* lacks the power and the sheer neurotic fun of Walsh's earlier psychological western, *Pursued:* Doniger's script is far less complex than Niven Busch's twisted family saga of incest and seduction. But *Along the Great Divide* serves Walsh well, with its emphasis on the physical landscape that he so loved to photograph and that he favored time and again as a natural canvas on which to dramatize human behavior.

Douglas plays U.S. Marshal Len Merrick, who comes on a group of angry cattlemen determined to lynch a man named Pop Keith (Brennan), a homesteader with a penchant for rustling who is accused of murder-

ing the son of the local cattle baron. Merrick stops the lynching, takes
Keith into his custody, and intends to deliver the alleged murderer to the
local authorities to see that he gets a fair trial. Along for the adventure
is Keith's sultry daughter (Mayo), who begins to look more and more
attractive to Merrick, just as Keith himself begins to look less and less
guilty. Not only do the elements work against Merrick and his two depu-
ties (Agar and Ray Teal)—the gusty wind that Walsh loved so much for
atmosphere—but he must also outsmart the unforgiving desert terrain
and outrun an angry mob on his tail. Since the western genre so easily
lends itself to the play of good against evil, the conflict between conscious and unconscious feelings and behavior, Doniger makes it obvious that Merrick is also prey to a rehashing of unfinished psychological
conflicts with his own father that being near Pop Keith triggers. While
Walsh gives power to the psychological battles at hand—including the
complex issue of justice and living up to the law—the battles of man
against nature are the ones Walsh favors in almost every frame. The
characters find themselves trying to stay alive, not just as human beings
battling their own consciences, but more so as human beings battling
elements of nature—including intensely charged sandstorms and even
a poisoned water hole—much larger than themselves. Walsh had been
throwing men and women against unforgiving social elements since his
first days at Warner Bros. His view of an unforgiving natural world is
every bit as threatening.

When Warners released *Along the Great Divide* on June 2, 1951,
critics were quick to notice that Douglas was in virgin territory in western garb. One wrote that it made sense he'd turn up on the prairie sooner
or later since every actor, it seemed, had to go through the initiation of
appearing in the genre. As have many viewers since, others appreciated
the film's visual composition more than the story line, which was decent,
if not original. But Walsh was pleased with the results, especially the
look of the film and the natural effects he produced, saying, "We had
wind all right and plenty of dust. And when the horses gallop off into the
distance they are enveloped in clouds of dust. And that helps the actors,
shooting in natural surroundings."[22] He had insisted on that sand storm
and built it up in spades. He had also insisted that Mayo not wear pants
anytime onscreen, but that would have made things difficult for her
with all that wind. The trousers only made her look sexier, embodying

Walsh's signature view of his women in this decade—tough and feminine at the same time. This woman, after all, had to put up with more
than one tough guy in front of the camera and another one in back of it.

Friends, accusers, businessmen—that was how Walsh and Jack Warner
galloped along throughout their thirty-year association. Sometimes the
relationship was good, sometimes not so good. Good was better, for
better or worse. After *Along the Great Divide,* the two friends had to
talk turkey. On December 7, 1950, Warner Bros. made Walsh an offer
too good to pass up (or was it?), a two-picture deal at $60,000 a picture
for the first fifteen weeks, then two weeks with no salary if he went
over, and then $4,000 per week. Misunderstandings hit all sides of the
table, from Warner to Walsh to Obringer. The figure discussed became
$50,000 instead. Walsh wrote to Warner on December 8:

> Dear Colonel,
>   When I went home last night and told the Schikse I had
> passed up a two-picture deal for $75,000 per picture and was
> willing to accept $50,000 per picture, she sent for Dr. Hyatt
> and two psychiatrists. They worked on me until midnight, and
> I finally came to.
>   Then at the psychiatrist's suggestion, she phoned Sam Jaffe
> at his home. When he heard the news he passed out, and he is
> now at the Cedars [Cedars of Lebanon Hospital in Hollywood].
> I phoned him this morning to see if he was feeling better, and
> they had him in an oxygen tent. The doctors think that with a
> little good news he may pull through.
>   Well, Jack, all the kidding aside, as you said yesterday, I've
> been with the company fourteen years [Walsh's figure was off],
> and I'd like to stay another fourteen—and I'm willing to make
> a big concession to stay. Meet me halfway; give me $60,000 per
> picture, 37 weeks for other pictures, and I solemnly promise and
> guarantee that I will save you ten times the amount involved in
> shooting time. Mazel Brocha, Raoul[23]

Jack offered him $50,000 and stuck to it. Walsh at first agreed and
then left for a hunting trip in Mexico, telling Jack to deal with Sam

Jaffe instead. The deal never went through—with more complicated misunderstandings tossed around until no one understood what had happened. Walsh thought he would have some free time if he finished either picture under the allotted time, but Warners wanted him tied up for the full thirty-seven weeks. The studio said what it wanted to say; Walsh heard what he wanted to hear. He later signed a one-picture deal to direct *Distant Drums*. The future was up in the air.

The *Pursued* screenwriter, Niven Busch, wrote an original story, "Distant Drums," an adaptation of Frank G. Slaughter's popular 1951 novel *Fort Everglades,* published in January 1951, which Warners purchased the next month. A complaint mailed to the studio by the author R. J. Minney claimed that the studio had stolen the title of his book, *Distant Drums,* rendering it no longer saleable. But, since there were at least twelve other novels, plays, and short stories recently published with the same title, Jack Warner was not worried one bit. Busch then coscripted the picture with Martin Rackin, who earlier scripted *Fighter Squadron* and Jules Dassin's jewel heist film *Riffraff* as well as *The Enforcer* and would go on to pen *The Big Land* in 1957 and coscript, with John Lee Mahin, John Ford's 1959 *The Horse Soldiers*. As with *Pursued,* Busch took a deal with Milton Sperling's United States Pictures, which would produce, with Warner Bros. releasing the picture. Walsh shot *Distant Drums,* as the screen's closing credits say, "in the heart of the Florida Everglades at Silver Springs, and at Castillo de San Marcos in the Southeastern National Monuments."

Busch could easily have looked to *Along the Great Divide* in writing the plot for *Distant Drums* since the stories are so similar in depicting a lone hero who leads a party through dangerous territory and on to safety. Then again, this scenario could describe numerous films Walsh directed in the 1950s. But Busch always thought that his story closely resembled Walsh's *Objective, Burma!*—a fact he once said seemed to have escaped every critic who saw the film, although other people saw it easily. It's familiar Walshian territory: hostile forces surround a heroic protagonist who, even though he flinches internally, nonetheless (and even with casualties along the way) makes it to the metaphoric other side.

Distant Drums gave Walsh the opportunity to work with Gary Cooper, an actor he already called a good friend. The two had been hunting and fishing buddies for some time. His feelings for Coop, expressed in the autobiography, aspire almost to poetry: "I never met a finer man than Gary Cooper or, for that matter, a better friend. Together we had fished the lakes of the sierra for trout. In the shivery winter mornings, we had huddled in blinds on the Sacramento, waiting for the fly-out of geese and ducks coming south from Canada. Now we were to be together again, making a picture called *Distant Drums*."[24] Walsh signed another one-picture contract with Warners, a practice he would continue throughout the 1950s and early 1960s, and began production.

In *Distant Drums*, Cooper plays the kind of hero critics could call *Walshian* by now—a loner with a tragedy in his past who leads others into dangerous territory because there is a great need for an emotional reward and some kind of safety or solace at the other end. Here he is Captain Quincy Wyatt, a soldier who leads a small group of men (and the requisite female love interest, played by the relative newcomer Mari Aldon) into the Everglades to stave off war with the area's Native Americans. The story plays with the second Seminole War of 1835–1842 in Florida, a historical subject not many films had approached. Much like the wives in many western heroic quests, Wyatt's has been murdered, although, unlike in other such scenarios, revenge is not his motive. Wyatt envisions larger ideas, one being the wish to keep the landscape free of Indian attacks.

Production on *Distant Drums* began in mid-April 1951 and finished on June 7. Walsh and Mary traveled to Naples, Florida, where Walsh shot some footage before returning to the studio on May 20 to finish the film. Walsh once again worked with Sid Hickox, who enhanced the film's already beautiful Technicolor palate with some stunning underwater photography. Walsh either did not notice (which is difficult to believe) or did not comment on Gary Cooper's obvious attraction to Mary Walsh. The actor looked shy but smitten in photographs taken on the shoot. The attraction eventually played itself out, although Cooper carried it all the way back to California after the film wrapped.

Distant Drums was the first picture to tap what became known as "the Wilhelm Scream," a sound effect of a man screaming that would be used frequently from this time to indicate men in peril, attacked by either hostile forces or wild animals. It actually combines one long scream accompanied by five shorter screams—although variations have been employed since its introduction. The effect is especially useful as an alligator drags one of the characters underwater in the swamps. Walsh surrounded himself with wildlife. Snakes were flown in from Los Angeles for the sake of authenticity. But he was most proud of the fact that he shot the film in a swampland where no camera crew had gone before, in the territory of the Seminole Indians. He added a little color to the story, later saying, "The Seminoles are the only Indians who have not yet signed a peace treaty with the United States. They aren't the easiest people to 'domesticate.' Just try having a chat with them—they threatened to kill me."[25] This statement lives in the shoot-'em-up world of movie cowboys and Indians, a young boy's fantasy in which the Indians are the bad guys and the cowboys the heroes. Walsh often turned to this world without realizing that it was different from the social world around him.

Though the film is visually beautiful, with its lush Everglades backdrop (and with Russ Saunders heading a second unit that provided the animal footage), the *Variety* critic wrote of it after its release on December 29, 1951, "Had the screenplay . . . been as realistic as the locales used, Distant Drums could have counted as a better-than-average entry in the outdoor pioneer field. Plot situations are conventional and the dialog banal. However, Raoul Walsh's action-wise direction makes excellent use of the standard framework most of the time to keep the film moving along in an acceptable clip."[26] By now, Walsh was heading into often hostile critical territory: a good number of the pictures he directed in the decade to come—almost to the end of his professional life—were based on scripts that didn't always measure up to the visual beauty and the still-hearty action scenes he choreographed.

Soon after he finished shooting *Distant Drums,* Walsh received a letter from his adopted daughter, Marilynn, telling him of her recent marriage to the Canadian airline pilot Jean Charlebois, which took place without her mother's knowledge. Walsh wrote back with the latest news, mentioning filming *Hornblower* in England and France, and saying that he found the climate dismal there. He added that he had just returned from Florida, where Gary Cooper "went right along" with the swampy conditions. He told Marilynn that he was working very hard and never got a chance to see any of their old friends. Errol Flynn was now housebound with dislocated vertebrae. "I hear Bruce Cabot is getting married," Walsh added, "(to a girl who is half Portuguese and East Indian)." Walsh had also heard that "she throws knives at him."[27]

By 1952, Walsh was telling the press that he was glad to be freelancing. That way he could choose his own projects and travel more extensively, not owing any particular studio favors. But he partly hoped that he might form a group with others and brainstorm on a future movie or television deal. Television had begun to creep into his psyche, but it would never hold much meaning for him, and he stayed away from it as much as he could, fielding offers when they came his way.

Soon after, Walter Wanger sent him a copy of a Canadian romance called *Yellowknife,* asking him to look it over for possible film adaptation. That was the last word on the subject (a few months later, Wanger sent him a screenplay, "I Met You Too Late," which Walsh turned down). But the *Variety* review of *Distant Drums* noticed what would become a trend in Walsh's subsequent career. When he ended his long-term association with Warner Bros. in 1951 and moved from studio to studio, he never found the quality scripts he directed at Warners. No longer tied to the studio whose style matched his own, his choice of material suffered. The scripts did get poorer in quality for Walsh, but whether, as Jean-Pierre Coursodon and Bertrand Tavernier suggest, much of it had to do with his work with John Twist—and their close alliance during these years, fueled by a mutual love of womanizing—is debatable.[28] Walsh never lost his natural feeling for directing action and adventure films but worked with scripts much inferior to his talents. The good material became spotty, while his feel for pacing and action did not.

Walsh moved to his not-so-favorite studio, MGM, once again in the spring of 1952 to direct the popular newcomer Leslie Caron and Ralph Meeker in an atmospheric but critically unsuccessful melodrama called *Glory Alley.* He hardly had to make a request that his leading lady wear dresses and not slacks since Caron (in her only appearance dancing in a black-and-white picture) performs numbers that mystify in their getting past the censors. Caron looked all the better for Walsh's work with the cinematographer William Daniels, well known for getting tantalizing shots of Garbo in her home studio. Despite the story's often-implausible plotline, Walsh seems at home rendering another aspect of the story—the sleazy back alleys and underground dives, which come across as flavorful and nuanced.

Meeker plays boxer Socks Barbarrosa (a name changed from Kayo Janek), a local fighter of some fame in New Orleans. Socks has a dark secret he refuses to tell his girlfriend, Angela (Caron), who sticks by him despite his often neglectful treatment of her. Angela's father, Gus "The Judge" Evans (Kurt Kasznar), thinks Socks is a coward and refuses to let his daughter marry him. The story runs around itself in this manner, meandering through sometimes banal dialogue, but gets a little jolt now and then from the appearance of Louis Armstrong and his band. Then Socks leaves town to fight in the Korean War, comes back a war hero, reunites with Angela, and reveals his traumatic past, that, when he was still a child, his father murdered his mother and beat him up, leaving him for dead. Now Socks can get back in the ring.

Art Cohn, who wrote both the story and the script for *Glory Alley,* had earlier penned the script for Roberto Rossellini's 1950 *Stromboli* and later wrote *The Joker Is Wild,* the Joe E. Lewis biography adapted for the 1957 film starring Frank Sinatra. Cohn had a tragically short life, perishing in the same 1958 plane crash that killed the producer Mike Todd, whose biography Cohn was writing at the time. Walsh began reading Cohn's virtually untouched script in October 1951, then began shooting on November 15, finishing twenty-eight days later, on December 15. In her autobiography, Leslie Caron recalls Walsh on the set as if he were not so much benign as almost absent: "Raoul Walsh . . . the director every French film buff worships like a god . . . ever mindful of his one eye . . . was seldom near the camera. From way back at the coffee corner, his voice would call to the camera operator, 'Were they all in the frame, buddy?' 'Yep, they were.' 'Okay, print!' I would ask, 'How can you tell?' The answer came, laconic, 'Pace sounded good. Next!'"[29] In addition to his idiosyncratic work style, Walsh may have had problems working with Caron; she was not his favorite actress, especially since her refined MGM sensibilities were the antithesis of his earthier sense of realism.

Just as effective as the colored alleyways Walsh created, Ralph Meeker's tough demeanor fit effortlessly into Walsh's vernacular. Meeker represented a new crop of tough-guy heroes Walsh directed in the 1950s, a group that also included Aldo Ray and Richard Jaeckel. These young masculine actors drift in and out of his pictures—in between his work with the softer actors he began working with, such as Tab Hunter, Sal

Mineo, Troy Donahue, and, of course, Rock Hudson. They also shared space with the older icons Walsh still loved to work with: James Cagney, Van Heflin, Alan Ladd, and Gregory Peck. Bogie would soon be gone, dying of lung cancer in 1957; Raft was fortunately out of pictures for the most part. Although Flynn passed away in 1959, he had been essentially lost to Walsh and to the rest of Hollywood since the early 1950s as he drank himself to death slowly but with great determination.

Meeker was Walsh's kind of actor, terse, tough speaking, visually tormented. It was unfortunate that the two never worked together again and that by the close of the 1960s Meeker's career had come to a halt. But Walsh was out of that alleyway as quickly as he walked in. *Glory Alley* received generally poor notices. The critic for *Variety* called the script "both unbelievable and confusing almost from the very start," adding, "[It is] a tedious and pretentious film. . . . [It] seems to make an attempt at the psychological melodrama but veers out in all directions without ever striking a central theme."[30] The reviews helped no one's career, although Caron walked away generally unscathed, as did Walsh. If the picture seemed to veer out in all directions at once, it earmarks the various directions Walsh's career took during this decade and the next. The road was untamed, and Walsh never found a consistent style, even as his gift for setting up powerful action shots or a compelling composition never waned. The French critics later liked to call attention to, among other things, his use of diagonals, splitting the screen by having a lone figure or line move across it in a dissonant path for the eye to see. But American audiences were slow to find redeeming qualities in his 1950s films.

Walsh left MGM after *Glory Alley* and immediately signed a one-picture deal with Universal Studios to direct *The World in His Arms*. Later, on May 7, he signed another contract with Universal for *The Lawless Breed*, which he was to direct further down the road. Walsh later said, "These two films have points in common. With both of them we tried to arrive at the same colour scheme—pastel! As I don't like colours that are too brilliant, I asked the photographer on each occasion to try to find me a softer colour design, something a little different from the kind of thing you usually see."[31] The two pictures could not have had more different landscapes, the high seas and the western frontier.

Walsh teamed again with Gregory Peck and those high seas for

The World in His Arms. His first choice was John Wayne, who was not available at the time, so, having limited say in the casting, he again minced few words with the reserved but likable Peck. The actor's leading lady was Ann Blyth—in her only time working with Walsh—who played Peck's love interest and the metaphoric subject of the film's title. Universal paid the estate of the late writer Rex Beach $100,000 for the story. At least fourteen of Beach's novels had already been adapted into successful pictures—including *The Spoilers* (with five versions) and *The Avengers*—and Universal had high hopes for this one. Peck plays Captain Jonathan Clark, who, when the story opens, sails into San Francisco in 1850 with a fortune in seal pelts poached in the Pribilof Islands in defiance of the Russian authorities. When he attends a huge party given in honor of his crew, Clark meets the countess Marina Selanova (Blyth) and falls in love with her. But he is unaware that the countess is racing to her uncle (Sig Ruman), the Russian governor-general of Alaska, to avoid a forced marriage to the arrogant Prince Semyon (Carl Esmond). Her escort is none other than Clark's archnemesis, a man named Portugee (Anthony Quinn), a rival seal poacher. But Marina's fiancé, Prince Semyon, reaches her first and whisks her away. Thinking he has been duped, Clark begins drinking heavily and bets Portugee that he can race to the Pribilofs before him. He wins the race but is then captured by Russians. To save his life, Marina agrees to marry the prince if Clark is released. But, on Marina's wedding eve, Clark and Portugee forget their rivalry and steal Marina away so that she is free to marry Clark, the man she really loves.

Thinking that he would recapture the adventure of *Horatio Hornblower,* or at the very least get in some traveling, Walsh pumped lots of enthusiasm into this project and left for thirty-six days of shooting in Lunenberg, Nova Scotia, just sixty-five miles south of Halifax. He felt on top of the world as another adventure loomed in his immediate future. Universal estimated the cost of the production would be $1.5 million, which would give him some good leeway.

Walsh began shooting the picture on September 15, 1951, and finished on October 26, most of the time in Canada, and then back at the lot for interior scenes. He had little trouble with Breen's office, being told to cut down on excessive brutality in the fight sequences and to cut the scenes with prostitutes to a minimum so that there was no indication of them in the picture. One particular line he had to cut: when the seamen return to land, one yells out, "Who cares what her name is? A woman. Any woman. We've been two years at sea!"[32] But the best human (or nonhuman) interest story during the shoot occurred when a fourteen-year-old trained Alaskan seal named Tommy Tucker, who was supposed to be a background extra at best, began hamming it up to the point where he stole the scene focusing on dialogue between Peck and Quinn. Walsh had little choice but to get rid of Tommy. Any film that captured the seal was discarded.

Also cast in a small part was the future writer-director Bryan Forbes. Forbes later recalled: "I had no name in Hollywood. I was sent to see Raoul and much to my amazement he gave me a small role in *The World in His Arms*—a Universal potboiler of little distinction. I believe . . . he shot the entire film in eleven days [an exaggeration], but of course in those days we worked incredible hours which would not be tolerated today. [Walsh's] philosophy for action films was, 'When in doubt start a fight.'" Forbes also recalled that Walsh had a swear box on the set: "Anyone who swore in . . . the demure . . . Ann Blyth's presence . . . had to put money in it."[33]

The World in His Arms, much like *Horatio Hornblower,* collapses into a love story—and with far fewer exciting moments than *Hornblower* provides. Equipped with the requisite sea chases and the predictable arm-wrestling scene between Peck and Quinn, the good-natured film is significant for being one of a trend to come in which Walsh's pictures focus more on character interiority than on action to drive the story forward. The love scenes in *Horatio Hornblower* feel tacked on—certainly the rose-colored ending does. But, in Borden Chase's script for *The World in His Arms* (Chase had also penned Hawk's *Red River*), there is hardly a moment that doesn't service a love story. Russell Metty's beautiful photography heightens the action scenes Walsh pumps into the story. But, throughout the picture, romance comes first; the action supports it. On its release in June 1952 in an Alaskan premiere, and throughout the United States a few months after, *The World in His Arms* received generally favorable reviews and did respectable box office after that. Reviewers could find no real fault with the picture, except its somewhat slow pace and predictability. The sets were lavish, and the action was hearty, even salty.

Despite the enthusiasm Walsh tried to pump into the picture, he was plagued by back problems throughout the production. Anthony Quinn recalled how he "complained constantly of an aching back, and turned his ailments into a metaphor on aging." "I went over to him one afternoon, during a break in shooting," Quinn remembered, "and asked how he was faring. 'I'm sixty-five years old, kid,' he said, 'and at my age it's downhill and shady all the way.'" Age, and the stress being put on his one eye, were just beginning to take their toll on him.[34]

Walsh moved all over the Hollywood map as well as Europe and Asia during the 1950s and 1960s. Before finishing production on *The World in His Arms,* he signed an exclusive employment contract with the British firm Coronado Productions on March 14, 1952, to direct and produce *Toilers of the Sea,* which became *Sea Devils.* RKO would distribute the film. Then, in May 1952, he signed directly with RKO for a one-picture deal to direct *Blackbeard the Pirate,* for which the studio guaranteed him six weeks work with a salary of $45,000. If Walsh began to lose interest in this upcoming spate of adventure stories—and the scripts could be less than thrilling—he nevertheless enjoyed the travel and the camaraderie on the set.

Before heading to England to direct Coronado's *Sea Devils,* Walsh went to work on *Blackbeard the Pirate;* he began shooting on June 3, 1952, and finished on July 9 of that year. He hoped the picture would be pure action adventure. Alan Le May, who penned *Cheyenne* for Walsh and whose western story became Ford's *The Searchers* in 1956, wrote a script from an original story penned by DeVallon Scott about the infamous storybook pirate Blackbeard. The fast production went off with just one hitch: Robert Newton's Blackbeard was so much a comic-book pirate that William Bendix turned in the only performance audiences could take seriously. The cast of heavy hitters, including Linda Darnell, Richard Egan, Alan Mowbray, and Keith Andes, seems lost at sea in the unconvincing seventeenth-century shenanigans in Jamaica.

For the movie's fight sequences, Walsh had a handful of sports figures on the set, including Stubby Kruger, the onetime Olympic swim champ, the famous track star William Johnson, and the popular wrestler Chester Hayes—just in case the cast needed help handling the swirl of swords, guns, pins, and cutlasses that Walsh used.

The critics were kinder to the picture than they might have been, taking in its melodramatic high jinks good-naturedly and generally giving it good reviews. More interestingly, Walsh and Newton emerged from the project with intentions of being business partners. At the end of 1952, the two had plans to team up and form a new television outfit called Caribbean Pictures Corporation, with the idea of making fifty-two vidpix in the West Indies. Newton would play Long John Silver in thirty of them and Captain Blackbeard in the other twenty-two, all directed by Walsh (who obviously didn't mind Newton's histrionic acting style). But, unfortunately or fortunately, the project lost steam and never got off the ground. Newton, always an actor with a spotty career owing to excessive drinking, died four years later, at the age of fifty, of alcohol-related causes.

Walsh went to Universal for his second promised picture, *The Lawless Breed,* directing Rock Hudson as the infamous outlaw John Wesley Hardin, whose autobiography forms the picture's base. (Walsh's *They Died with Their Boots On* initially stemmed from a book about Hardin.) Now under contract to Universal, Hudson was still a fixture in Walsh's films, however sporadically. William Alland penned the story, and Bernard Gordon then wrote the script for this simply told, heartfelt tale. *Lawless* reveals Walsh's dominant aesthetic in the 1950s—looking more closely at his characters, the camera focused on how their motives move the story. Hardin's autobiographical work portrays the speaker as a man who might be larger than the life experiences he narrates. He heroicizes himself, no doubt, and, in so doing, sells out real fact for fiction, something Walsh knew about himself. Walsh set up camp at Newhall, Thousand Oaks, and at Agua Dulce, all north of Los Angeles, and he shot all exteriors on schedule and without interference from the weather.

Walsh, as the film's uncredited producer, cast the young Universal contract player Hugh O'Brian to play Ike Hanley, a Hardin foe who turns up early in the picture. O'Brian and Hudson had been high school classmates in Winnetka, Illinois, but now found themselves in front of Walsh's camera in the early 1950s. O'Brian remembered, "I was very impressed that [most of the directors at that time] knew exactly what they wanted from a character. [Most] would fight for that, and sometimes they would become tough to deal with because the performer didn't want to do it. Walsh was very specific. . . . He was one of the roughest directors I ever worked with. He was absolutely a no bullshit guy. I never had that feeling of lack of interest from him. I never felt that he was just directing it to get the money." He continued, "[Walsh] didn't have to spend as much time with me as he did with other actors, especially with Rock, because whatever I brought to it . . . I had a very definite approach to a role and [Walsh] felt that. So there was a huge difference between how he worked with me as opposed to Rock, because Rock did the lead . . . and Rock was not an actor. . . . He was a good lookin' kid but he was not an actor's actor. . . . It would have been interesting to see him on Broadway." O'Brian had some respect for Hudson's talent as an actor, "but not a great deal."[35] Still, Walsh liked the way Hudson looked in front of the camera; he and that "public eye" shared a deep affinity.

Although history books offer up Hardin as a brutal murderer whose number of victims may have exceeded fifty, Walsh and his writers portray him as heroic and honorable, sticking to the guns of his autobiography, fiction or not. Walsh was never at a loss to revise history in the name of romance, as *They Died with Their Boots On* had proved. Directors such as Anthony Mann and Budd Boetticher painted the western landscape as a grittier moral landscape where good and evil are hard to distinguish as they chew away at the story's borders. Walsh's western landscape dispensed with complex issues of right and wrong; it is easy to know on which side of the law, and the woman, his men stand. His love of historical truth extended no further than whether it made for a good story, whether it might entertain audiences. Nothing would interfere with a good story, even as fiction overtook truth. Conflicts between good and evil, innocence and experience, are fodder for the good story and for the travel it takes to go to location and shoot it. Ultimately, in Walsh's landscape, there is no greater story than the one about the guy getting the girl and having to go through his paces to get her. She might be his in the end, or he might meet his end before he can hold her. But she is the goal. Something larger than both of them pushes them together.

The Lawless Breed departed just slightly from Walsh's more simplified view of western male-female relations and from that of the western hero himself. Hardin is an ambiguous man, hoping his autobiography—which frames the story told in flashback—might help restore his reputation as a human being, might soften society's view of him. The woman he eventually marries (played by Julie Adams) also jumps out of the predictable mold, becoming—while her husband is in prison—a highly self-sufficient businesswoman. In a review published before the film's release in January 1953, the *Variety* critic saw the picture as slightly episodic, although he still praised Walsh's "robust action." He liked Hudson's performance also, no doubt owing to the slightly ambiguous moral character Walsh gave him.[36]

But soon after this Walsh was happy to leave California and take off for England again to shoot *Sea Devils* for the producer David Rose at Coronado Productions. He flew to London for a week of preproduction and probably started shooting the picture no later than July 31. He was paid $50,000 in weekly increments. Rose agreed to confer with Walsh about the picture's lead actor, but Rose had final say. He agreed to cast Rock Hudson (as Walsh seemed to be on a roll with the actor) on a loan-out from Universal. Yvonne de Carlo, Maxwell Reed, Denis O'Dea, and the future writer-director Bryan Forbes, now a Walsh pal, filled out the cast. RKO's publicity department described the picture as the story of a beautiful heroine named Droucette (De Carlo) who, while on a secret mission, falls in love with a handsome young fisherman-turned-smuggler (Hudson): "Through his assistance and daring [she] is smuggled from the British Channel Islands into France. Their romance is shattered when subsequent events cause the young seaman to believe Droucette to be a spy for an enemy country. But when her true identity is revealed . . . they are reunited in a dangerous game of hide-and-seek with death."[37] Walsh shot the picture in beautiful color, but, storywise, the adventure never truly got off the ground.

Borden Chase again wrote the screenplay, this time adapted from Victor Hugo's *Les travailleurs de la mer,* the title soon changed to *Sea Devils.* Walsh filmed in the Channel Islands and Finestère, France, before returning to Nettlefold Studios in Surrey for interior shots.

Bryan Forbes, who had recently worked for Walsh in *The World in His Arms,* later told an interesting story about landing his role in *Sea Devils:*

Raoul came to London to direct *Sea Devils* and we had kept in touch. I got a message from the casting director for me to come to The Dorchester and meet Raoul. He told me Raoul said

"Don't shave, talk with an American accent and you never saw him before in your life." I duly presented myself along with dozens of other actors and was eventually shown into Raoul's suite together with his producer. Bob Leonard the casting director said, "This is Mr. Bryan Forbes." And Raoul immediately said, "The kid looks virile to me. I'm tired of seeing all these British faggots; let's give him the part of Willy." I believe that role of Willy had originally been thought of for Barry Fitzgerald! The producer went into shock, but Raoul stuck to his guns and insisted they give me the role. He also managed to get me an extra fee for rewriting most of the dialogue, telling them I was a brilliant writer. And so it was I went to Concarno in Brittany with Yvonne de Carlo, Joan Collins' first husband, Maxwell Reed, and the young Rock Hudson, whom Raoul had under contract. I shared rooms with Rock in the hotel and was somewhat amazed one night when over dinner he confessed he was in love with me. I told him it was very flattering but I did not swing that way, so I suppose I was one of the first to know of his homosexuality.

There is one incident I remember: we were all having lunch in a French restaurant when Raoul was called to the phone and [then] came to ask Rock and me how much money we had. We asked why. He told us he'd just had a call from an Irish jockey in Dublin [who] told him to bet the limit on the 2.30. How the jockey ever found out where Raoul was is beyond belief. Anyway, Rock and I and both parties [gave] what cash we had—I think about £40 each—and Raoul duly made the bets. The horse came in at 20 to 1 and we made what was in those days a small fortune.[38]

The picture proved a minor moment in the careers of all its principals, including its director. A love story set in the midst of a mediocre swashbuckler hardly went over with any of the press or the audiences who came to see the picture. Hudson had yet to find his bearings as a romantic lead in a sea adventure, and De Carlo and he as lovers were simply unconvincing. When Walsh called some of his films "turkeys," he no doubt had *Sea Devils* foremost in his mind. But, happy to travel again to England and shoot on location, Walsh was in a good mood

throughout the production. The camera operator Peter Newbrook recalled the colorful, and off-color, moments Walsh provided before and
after production:

> We did a few artiste and make up tests at the Nettlefold Studios
> in Walton-on-Thames and then left for the Channel Islands in
> a hired plane which took off from a private airfield in Surrey.
> Raoul insisted on a few belts before we took off which was just
> as well because the plane leaked like a sieve with water coming
> through on to our laps! This caused Raoul to make some very
> pointed jibes at David Rose, who was not present. When we got
> to our first location, which was supposed to be a fishing village,
> all the ships had radar masts and were quite useless. Raoul went
> straight to the nearest bistro and ordered drinks for the senior
> members of the crew. After several other abortive attempts we
> finally got started, but because of the changed locations, some
> script changes were called for. Most of these were handled by
> Raoul and Bryan Forbes, and this pattern was repeated every
> time changes became necessary.

Newbrook also recalled:

> We were away quite a few weeks but by the time that we re-
> turned to the studio, all had settled down. I got on very well
> with Raoul. For some reason he always called me Pedro. He
> was quite relaxed on the set. He never looked through the view-
> finder or the camera—he would frame a composition by using
> his two thumbs and forefingers to illustrate what size picture he
> wanted. His rehearsals were quite minimal; he would listen to
> the dialogue and if he liked what he heard, he would say, "This
> is a very intelligent reading. Let's go."[39]

The assistant director Phil Shipway would get Walsh a copy of the
Racing Times each day. Walsh would study the form and get Shipway to
put some bets on for him. Sometimes during the stage changes he would
haul several of the crew around to the nearest hostelry, bang on the bar,
and say to the barmaid, "Give my friends here some good drink and none

of your goddamn cooking sherry!" He was a nonstop (and "fantastic") raconteur and would regale the crew with stories from his earliest days as an actor. "[Walsh] got on well with all the actors," Newbrook recalled, "especially Hudson and de Carlo, and there were never any disputes." There could have been, however, given the rather run-of-the-mill script Walsh was handed and had to change. "The script was pretty mundane," Newbrook said, "and every now and then [Raoul] would get Bryan to goose up the dialogue a bit." "We always ran the rushes first thing in the morning," Newbrook said. But Walsh never came in to see them:

> He stood outside reading the morning paper and when we came out he would say, "Well, Pedro, how was the projection? Could you see 'em, were they moving?" One day we came out of the room, his eye patch was up and tears were rolling down his face [and he was] holding a letter in his hand. He said, "Pedro, want a good laugh? Read this." It was a letter from the president of Universal offering him a job as director in a new 3-D picture. He said, "Of all the action directors in the business, they ask a guy with one eye to direct a picture in 3-D." He laughed at that all day.

Walsh himself could be a source of humor without trying:

> Some days were just unforgettable. One day almost the entire male cast was on the set and, given that it was a period piece, all the men wore tight trousers. And it was pretty obvious that one actor, Jacques Brunius, was very well endowed. Walsh noticed this and told Phil Shipway to get wardrobe master Charlie Guerin on [the] set. When Guerin arrived, Walsh told him to get Jacques a jock strap. Guerin told him that they had run out, and Walsh turned to Wilkie Cooper, the director of photography, and said, "Hey, Wilk, throw a gobo [shadow] over the guy's nuts and let's go."[40]

Sea Devils was the very last picture made using Technicolor three-strip color photography. The demise of Technicolor three-strip film was no doubt due to business reasons. Every time Walsh saw a plane overhead near the flight path to Heathrow Airport , he quipped, "There goes David Rose to pick up another load of short ends." "After the war, the U.S. government decided to start breaking up some of the big conglomerates by bringing anti-trust suits against them," Newbrook said, recalling:

> In the late 1940s they turned their attention to the movie majors and made them divide up their operations by separating the theaters from the production and distributing arms. As Eastman Kodak made all the film stock used by Technicolor, the government instituted a class action suit against both of them, alleging that between them they had conspired to prevent any further development of color motion picture photography. Kodak would have been happy for the status quo to remain, as every Technicolor picture made used three times as much raw stock as a monochrome picture. Anyway, the government prevailed, and so Eastmancolor single strip film became the norm.[41]

Walsh found himself on the edge of history once again, using a process that would soon be extinct.

Walsh was well aware of history moving quickly. As he grew older, he became more remorseful that he was not a father in the truest sense. His relationship with his two adopted sons had long ago dissipated, and Marilynn was not around. In the fall of 1953, Walsh took another chance at being a father, even though he and Mary never had children of their own (nor had he had children with his previous wives). One day he saw a story in the *Los Angeles Herald Examiner* about an orphaned fourteen-year-old boy from Mexico named José Toscano who sneaked across the California border "to pursue an education" and was turned over to immigration. Toscano appeared on the singer Bob Crosby's *A Friend in Need* program before ending up at a Franciscan mission in Los Angeles. The nuns gave him a "diploma" before he was deported, then helped him back into the United States again, where he obtained a permanent resident visa.[42]

Representatives from Paramount Studios heard about José and considered using his story as part of a series relating to the "Wetback problem" in the state. Their meeting with Toscano resulted in his wanting to be an actor, and, by coincidence, Mother Gertrude at the Franciscan Missionary of the Immaculate Conception wrote to Walsh asking whether he could arrange a screen test for the boy. Walsh's response was an offer to adopt Toscano. But, in the end, Mother Gertrude wrote to Walsh that such an adoption "would not work out satisfactorily," as they planned to send the boy back to Mexico.[43] In years to come, Toscano found his way back to Los Angeles again and took a job as a cashier at the city's famed Farmer's Market before attending Catholic high school.

Walsh never heard about him again, and the matter was dropped. Walsh was never forthcoming about his feelings for the children he did adopt in his life. Relatives later believed that he always did want to have children. While he clearly mismanaged the relationship he had with his first two adopted sons, Robert and Jack, he seemed to do better with Marilynn as the two stayed in touch for the remainder of Walsh's life. Marilynn returned to Los Angeles later on, where she died in 1987, seven years after Walsh. He was the only father she knew.

13

Reverie

Rouben Mamoulian once said, "No matter how you put it, a film for a director is always autobiographical. You see his outlook on life. You see how he looks at love, at honor, at life."[1] That is, the director and his characters share the same psychological space. Even before an actor comes along, the director wills to this character some part of himself, just as he authors and designs the world on the screen that they inhabit. He initiates their movements and contemplates their reactions to the world as if, in some fundamental way, they speak for him. As Walsh, now in his seventies, grew into old age and moved further into the decade of the 1950s, he and his characters grew closer together than before. Just as he put much of the young Walsh into Danny Dolan's (Spencer Tracy's) ribald sense of practical joking, along with the spunk in the Helen Riley (Joan Bennett) character in 1932's *Me and My Gal,* and just as much as Victor McLaglen and Edmund Lowe inherit Walsh's love of male camaraderie in *What Price, Glory?* Walsh's 1950s films reveal his psychology also, although now filtered through a somewhat different lens—contemplative, more tuned in to his characters' inner lives. They may not reveal themselves verbally at such an intense speed; now they move more slowly, act more deliberately, are far more meditative before acting than their predecessors were—as if Walsh replicates in them the way he now measures and contemplates his own life, his own actions in advancing age. There is more taking stock of things in a character's life; there is more reverie in the looking. It's far more satisfying now, this looking around and contemplating where one stands in the world. Clark Gable's and Jane Russell's characters in, say, *The Tall Men* to come, or Gary Cooper's Quincy Wyatt in *Distant Drums,* speak of Walsh's more serious consideration of the relationship between men and women, the way one man treats another, and the way characters live honorably in the social and physical world. While Walsh's physical landscape remains just as large, the characters in it are often more mindful of their place in that world on the screen. They can still be young, impulsive, and ready for action in war in the Pacific or on the American plain. But they also take more seriously the actions they perform, the adventures they seek. For Walsh, the cinema is still the great adventure, but it seems less an escape from the real world than before. Even as he directed Gregory Peck in a series of high-seas adventures, even as he directed a best seller such as *Battle Cry* because it gave him the chance to re-create another large actioner—and, thus, to place a man in the center of a conflict— Walsh begins now to peer more deeply into the interior lives of his men and women, no matter what the battle, as if he were peering more into himself than before.

Before Walsh finished *Sea Devils* and returned to Los Angeles, his old pal James Cagney contacted him about directing a picture he'd had on his mind for some time: a story about a corrupt southern politician based on Adria Locke Langley's 1945 novel *A Lion Is in the Streets*. Walsh could have cared less about the politics; he envisioned the drama. Naturally, he said yes and was ready to begin as soon as he saw the green light. It would be good to be back at Warners with Cagney, the man whose screen psyche he had messed with so seriously and successfully.

Cagney and his brother, William, who produced the picture, emphatically denied all along that their protagonist, Hank Martin, was a Huey Long prototype, thinking the fictional Martin's rise in politics did not parallel any living politician. Instead, Cagney said, the object of their film was "to stress as much as possible the fact that any deviations from the democratic processes are dangerous": "The sum and substance of our attraction to the novel and our purpose in making the picture, aside from its dramatic qualities as an entertainment, is showing the simplicity with which a demagogue can pervert the democratic system."[2]

The fifty-three-year-old Cagney thought that he needed to get in shape for the part so he could convincingly strut around the southern back roads and implore the crowds to vote for him in what was, no matter how you cut it, a loosely based knockoff of Long's career. He dropped twenty-five pounds by plowing the fields of his Northridge, California, farm himself, later saying that his foreman couldn't understand why he wouldn't use a tractor. By the time Walsh arrived back in

Los Angeles, Cagney was still working out. Production wheels began turning on November 10, 1952. After Claire Trevor and Nina Foch unsuccessfully tested for the part of Hank's wife, Verity, the less-known Barbara Hale was cast, and a young Anne Francis was cast as Flamingo, the young woman who comes between them. With Frank McHugh also set to appear, it seemed almost as if Walsh were back on an early 1940s Warners set with Walsh, Cagney, and McHugh back to their old "Irish Mafia" high jinks.

A Lion Is in the Streets, scripted by Luther Davis, tells the story of Hank Martin (Cagney), a charismatic peddler living on the bayou. When the film opens, he meets a pretty (and naive) schoolteacher, Verity Wade (Barbara Hale). Soon they marry, and Hank begins his rise in politics. It takes Verity a while to realize that Hank is an expert manipulator, which is how he manages to gain a foothold in local politics. He organizes the cotton farmers in the area and then in his first election proves his opponent to be corrupt. Along the way, Verity also discovers that a local beauty, named Flamingo (Anne Francis), has been in love with Hank since she was a child. Verity then understands that Flamingo is not her only rival. Hank is driven by enormous greed in his desire to control the people and politics around him—enough to cause his own eventual demise.

As much as Cagney denied Martin's resemblance to Huey Long, Warners did its own math and came up with different results. In the studio's estimation, both Hank and Huey Long were "poor white" men who "specialized" in selling similar goods—Hank sold a shortening called Sizzle; Long sold a shortening called Cottolene. Both received support from backcountry people. Both had the same campaign points: highways, education for the underprivileged, and the notion of "spreading the wealth" from the rich to the poor. Both had "close ties to gamblers." Both met their wives while peddling. And, most important of all, both had women on the side: Hank had Flamingo, and Long had "a cuddly brunette who was his secretary before he became governor."[3]

Walsh shot the picture's interior scenes at the Goldwyn Studios in Hollywood—before and after venturing back out to the Florida Everglades on November 25, 1952, to film all the exterior shots. The entire production lasted a little over a month. Anne Francis found Walsh to be a shy man who blushed when she planted a kiss on his cheek. Her recollection of him was similar to those of many others who worked with him in the 1950s: "I remember him setting up a scene and then before the cameras rolled him heading out for the dark ends of the sound stage, where he would stay until the scene was over."[4] Then he came wandering back into the light.

Despite all the energy the Cagneys invested in *Lion* (which Walsh neglected to mention in his autobiography later on), the film had a hard time when Warners released it. Much had happened between the time the Cagneys first bought the novel and the time they brought it to Walsh. Columbia Pictures, which had released the director Robert Rossen's *All the King's Men* (based on Robert Penn Warren's novel of the same name) in 1949, hit Warner Bros. with a plagiarism suit during production, and the picture was pulled right after its release, not to be seen for some years. Other than in the lead character, there is more difference than similarity between the films. Rossen's film is a darkly serious treatment of a corrupt political player, whereas Walsh's is a hard-boiled, hard-hitting melodrama whose beautiful Technicolor palette only makes the slightly unbelievable Hank Martin seem all the more implausible. While Walsh infuses weight into the story by giving Cagney a large physical arena in which to strut, and while Cagney is still the virile embodiment of anger and rage, the script renders Hank an unrealistic creation—more a slogan than full bodied. Walsh either didn't notice or didn't care since it's hard to believe that he no longer knew the difference between a character whose actions are plausible and one whose are not. Hank is hardly believable as a more-than-middle-aged man who still sells pots and pans on the back roads of a small country town and then all of a sudden meets a much younger woman and without reason heads out for a political career. Critics could not overlook the fact that Walsh and Cagney still made a dynamic team, even winning out over the script's awkward moments. The scenes in which Cagney confronts his naysayers, the conflicts between the farmers and the guards early on—all these dramatic moments deliver Cagney and Walsh lions still, vital and forceful. Cagney never loses his confidence, his gift of the gab, and Walsh keeps his pace quick and lively. If conflicts arise, they have to do with the director's and the actor's apparent brassy and pungent moves running head on into a story that doesn't keep up with their gusto. Critics noticed as much as audiences did that Walsh's pictures began to look more splintered, hanging an often-implausible or predictable story line on the side of an immensely dignified mountain range or on a beautifully lighted frontier.

The astute cultural critic Manny Farber understood the straight-shooting Walsh's world. He wrote: "The melancholic fact about this natural, unsophisticated humanist is that he is often alone playing straight rather than cynical (Hawks), surrealistic (Farrow), or patronizing (Huston) with genre material. Walsh, who wrote some scripts as bald copies of hit films he directed, and probably entered each new project with 'Christ, it's not bad. It reminds me of my last movie,' never fights his material, playing directly into the staleness."[5] Farber understands Walsh's startlingly natural approach to his material and to what he saw when he looked through the camera lens. If he put the diagonal line in the frame—which the French love so well—it was because that's what was there. Attempting to make fiction realistic—and often he missed that there was a difference—he forgot to be cunning. His story sense ebbed and flowed, but his simple, humanist instincts remained.

Then Walsh signed a one-picture deal with Columbia Studios, the same studio that censored *A Lion Is in the Streets,* and from late May to mid-June 1953 went off to Sedona, Arizona, to direct *Gun Fury,* another serviceable western whose only real distinction was its 3-D format, Walsh's bow to staying current. Just prior to that, on April 10, Walsh signed an agreement with Columbia to direct a picture called *Ten against Caesar,* a ten-week assignment for which he would be paid $60,000. But the picture never went past the planning stages; Walsh was off to location with another western.

The story of *Gun Fury* has a repetitive ring to it—not only the story line that hinges on an ex-soldier forced to rescue the woman he loves, but also what was by now pretty apparent, Walsh's ambivalence about Rock Hudson, who plays the hero. Walsh knew all too well Hudson's weaknesses as an actor but still saw him as a growing box-office draw. In this tale, Hudson is Ben Warren, an ex-Confederate soldier whose fiancée, Jennifer (Donna Reed), is traveling from Georgia by stagecoach to meet him. When she passes through Arizona, Ben surprises her by joining her for the rest of the journey. When the stagecoach is set on by a gang of outlaws, Ben is shot and left for dead, and Jennifer is kidnapped. After Ben recovers, he sets out to rescue her, trekking a perilous road to do so.

Gun Fury, based on the 1952 novel *Ten against Caesar,* written by Kathleen B. George and Robert A. Granger, was scripted by Irving Wallace and Roy Huggins. Unfortunately, this was Walsh's only opportunity to direct the actor Lee Marvin since Marvin could be a craggy-tempered Walshian villain if ever there was one and played one of the heavies, Blinky, in this picture. Marvin appreciated Walsh from the start. "We called Raoul 'Cotton-Eyed Joe' because he had lost an eye in a car accident," he said.

> I don't think he was much interested in dialogue. He was an action director. He loved horses, stagecoaches and explosions. He was an old timer and rolled his own cigarettes. If you had a scene to do with dialogue, he'd say, "You're over here, you're over there, roll it." Then he'd look down and roll a cigarette and when all this talking had stopped he'd turn to the script girl and say, "Did they get it all?" She'd say, "Yeah," and he'd say, "Print it." But for the action stuff he'd get all excited. . . . "OK, we're over here with a 35mm lens. Now the stagecoach comes rolling down the pass and the gunmen gallop out from behind this rock." Raoul would come to life![6]

Walsh had become more set in his ways. He was in a hurry to get out the back door—although for what reason he didn't always know.

But he could also be subject to bouts of nostalgia, or even some seriously misguided notions of what made good material in this decade. During the second week of October 1953, during production on *Gun Fury,* Walsh contacted H. E. Aitken, who still owned the rights to *The Birth of a Nation,* inquiring about a possible remake of the film. Aitkin wired back on October 15, "ANSWERING WIRE THERE IS NO COMMITMENTS OUT FOR REMAKING THE BIRTH OF A NATION. I HAVE CONTROLLED THE RIGHTS FROM ITS CREATION AND CAN ARRANGE FOR A REMAKE IF PROPER DEAL IS WORKED OUT. PREFER TO HAVE ROY [Obringer, Warner's attorney] COME HERE FOR MEETING OR IF SPEED IS NECESSARY CAN MEET YOU BOTH IN CHICAGO ANSWER BY PHONE OR WIRE AT FRANCIS HOTEL."[7] Nothing came of the deal, yet it's interesting that Walsh thought of returning to more glorious times, certainly to a period in his life when he saw the threshold rather than the steady boat that took him slowing on his course. He either didn't pay attention to the story's inherent racism or didn't think to consider how much it mattered.

If thinking about *The Birth of a Nation* pushed him backward, Walsh showed better judgment, in current cinematic trends, when he knew to embrace 3-D technology at this juncture in time—a repeat, although on a smaller stage, of his great enthusiasm for sound pictures when they loomed on the horizon back in the late 1920s. While shooting *Gun Fury*, Walsh gave an interview to the *Los Angeles Times* explaining his enthusiasm for the 3-D process. He disliked wide-screen cinema because it was, to him, unnecessary to see that much scope. He believed that a spectator could see everything in the action with a "normal" screen size. But 3-D excited him. He could cut a 3-D picture, he said, exactly as he would a "2-D one, close-ups and all." He thought that 3-D had great possibilities because it didn't depart from the principles of shooting a picture that he had followed from the earliest days. To Walsh, 3-D was part of the future. His excitement may have been for naught. Columbia released *Gun Fury* on November 11, 1953, but audiences could see it only for a short time. Columbia, like most of the other studios, quickly left 3-D somewhere in the dust.

Columbia Studios boss Harry Cohn, known to wander onto the sets of his directors and annoy them, sent one of the picture's writers, a very young Roy Huggins, onto Walsh's set, purportedly so he could learn a thing or two about the movies. Huggins later remembered his brief time with Walsh. It sounded familiar. Recalling one scene in particular where two actors were asked to yell and scream at each other, he said, "Walsh called 'Action,' and sat down with his back to the actors. The scene ended and Walsh said, 'Cut. Print.' Later, when the scene had to be re-shot, Walsh again called 'Action,' and sat down with his back to the actors. The scene ended and Walsh said, 'Cut. Print,' and stood up and said, 'Okay, that's a wrap.'"[8] Not reading anything in particular, Walsh had just decided to turn around.

A week after the release of *Gun Fury*, Walsh was already thinking about another picture that he had signed on for at Warner Bros.—*Battle Cry*. Although the film was not scheduled to begin until 1954, Walsh was back at the studio on November 19, 1953, and sent a memo to Jack Warner showing some concern for the picture, already in the planning stages. "When BATTLE CRY is released," he wrote, "we will be up against

CAINE MUTINY, with the following cast: Humphrey Bogart, Jose Ferrer, Van Johnson, Fred MacMurray. Where do we go from here?"⁹ No response was recorded.

The first place Walsh went from there was Canada, to shoot *Saskatchewan* for Universal Studios, a period picture set in nineteenth-century Canada. The studio handed him Gil Doud's finished script late in July, and then he took cast and crew to Vancouver and into Banff National Park for five weeks of shooting, beginning on August 4, 1953. While Walsh drew a salary of $60,000, the film's star, Alan Ladd, had him topped on that one, receiving $100,000. But Walsh also received a percentage of the picture.

Saskatchewan (a.k.a. *O'Rourke of the Royal Mounted*) concerns a Mountie named O'Rourke (Ladd) who is forced to do battle with the Cree and Sioux Indians as they try to wipe out the U.S. Seventh Cavalry in Saskatchewan. O'Rourke has several conflicts to cope with: a beautiful woman (Shelley Winters) who has survived a Cree attack, a Cree half brother, and, like many of Walsh's western heroes, a sympathy for the supposed enemy. O'Rourke sees the Sioux side of things as well as he sees anything else.

Alan Ladd's short physical stature had challenged the fleet of directors who worked with him over the years to get creative in finding ways to keep him looking as tall as, if not taller than, the women he romanced and the thugs who came after him. Walsh had faced this challenge a few years earlier when he directed Ladd in *Salty O'Rourke*. Also working with Walsh again, Hugh O'Brian, now cast as Ladd's adversary, later remembered:

> [Ladd] was . . . not too much bigger than Mickey Rooney. And we did a dolly shot on that. Whenever I did a scene with him, we would rehearse it and then the camera would set up and all that. And they would dig a hole for me to stand in. And the guy with the shovel, well, he's not too stupid, so he digs a half a hole. He takes my dirt from the first half and uses it as a mound for Ladd to stand on so that he only has to dig it six inches. And a couple of things happened. I mean, what bothered me most, I guess, was . . . well, the difference between Alan and Mickey Rooney. . . . Mickey [would say] "Hey guys, I'm short, that's why you're

all f——n' here—let's do it, OK? I'm short, I'm short—that's it. But you're getting paid, so let's do your friggin' film."

[But] Alan would kind of never admit that somebody else was standing in a hole. They began to work and there were a couple of things that happened. . . . I went to Raoul and I said, "Raoul, I've had it. Next time we do a scene together and they dig a hole for me . . . I don't mind that, and I understand it. But, goddamn it, don't use my dirt for his mound!"[10]

Walsh got such a kick out of O'Brian's joke that he roared with laughter and continued to chuckle to himself the rest of the day.

Ladd was not the only cast member Walsh found challenging. Shelley Winters, who played Ladd's love interest, gave him pause more than once. "Shelley Winters at the time was going with Vittorio Gassman," O'Brian remembered, "and Walsh was not too thrilled with Shelley, kind of from the front. And then Vittorio came up to location and it was very difficult to get her to concentrate. [Raoul] was not happy. And there was a sequence where I come face to face with Alan Ladd at the end in the final gunfight between the two of us. I've got hold of Shelley as a shield. And, when it comes time to actually have the gunfight, my character throws Shelley away. So the gunfight happens, and Alan Ladd shoots me. And, just before we went through the take, [Raoul] came over to me and said, 'Hugh, throw her as far as you can.' I really threw her across the view."[11] Walsh had gotten someone else to do his bidding.

Walsh didn't want any stand-ins for his actors during the production, so Shelley Winters let it be known to reporters who visited the set that she was covered in bruises from head to foot—she also commiserated with her friend Marilyn Monroe, who was nearby shooting Henry Hathaway's *Niagara*. But Walsh had a soft spot somewhere for Winters, or at least for lovers. She told him that she was lonely for Gassman even though he telephoned her every other night from Rome. So Walsh rearranged their shooting schedule so that she had the day off for her birthday, when Gassman flew to their location site bringing a birthday cake with him. He also had a soft spot for another actor, Richard Long, building up his part to larger proportions to help boost his career.

Again, the chance for Walsh to surround himself with new natural scenery and meet the locals was a top priority, almost as if he could never get enough of the new. After the production wrapped, he released a statement that September for a studio publicity piece. He didn't see the racism in his words; he saw only the humor:

> It was refreshing to join up with some enthusiastic redskins. The average American Indian, used to appearing in dozens of western thrillers a year has become lethargic about the whole thing. These Canadian newcomers to the trade wanted to do everything from love scenes to pratfalls. A lot of American Indians have learned to goof off on the job, hiding out in their teepees during big battle scenes and making themselves scarce in general when there's arduous work to be done. The Canadian bucks are new enough to the game that they out do themselves to be useful. We had so many of them falling off their horses in trick riding scenes that we had to shoot 'em over again. Nobody, not even Alan Ladd, could have killed that many pesky redskins with a six shooter.[12]

His jibes at working with Native Americans hadn't changed in decades.

Warners knew how to dress its director for the public and released a publicity piece for the picture that reinforced Walsh's already-established reputation as a ham:

> Walsh is a virtual one-man vaudeville act as he paces back and forth behind the camera lines while a scene is in progress. As leading men implant passionate kisses on cheeks of leading ladies, so does director Walsh implant equally passionate kisses on the cheeks of incorporeal actresses floating conveniently near him in the water washed sound stage air. When the hero swings a Sunday punch at the heavy, Walsh is likely to come up with a roundhouse from the floor which connects at just the appropriate moment with the jawbone of the octoplasmic alter ego of the villain. And when someone dies, Walsh dies a thousand deaths with him.

This story almost reached back to his antics with the actress Theda Bara years earlier. The release continued:

"We can tell when a scene is going to be good and okayed for printing," one of the crew said. "When Raoul is hitting on all six behind the camera, sipping tea with the gals and doing pratfalls with the stunt men we know everything's going right in front." "[He] detects when a scene is lapsing into lethargy when he exploits with facial contortions not unlike those of a man getting his initial shif of well-ripened Gorgonzola cheese." "Walsh wanted a fast moving tempo from the start. Ladd calls Walsh a one-man stock company (with his impromptu vaudeville act and all). Once when Ladd blew his lines, he excused himself by saying he was only waiting for Walsh to catch up with him." "Walsh said, 'Well, there's a little ham in everybody. I just got a second helping of it when it was passed around.'"[13]

By now, Walsh was a seasoned raconteur; the gift was native to him. He spent even more time talking to the media. He piled on the schmaltz and perfected his stories until he could recite them by heart.

With *Saskatchewan* completed, Walsh was ready to focus on a larger project with far more notoriety attached and, with that, a far greater chance to succeed or fail in a large public way. Leon Uris's best seller *Battle Cry* put Walsh to the test in just the way he liked: on foreign ground and with Jack Warner back home in Hollywood talking to him through cablegrams.

War Diaries

The name *Battle Cry* had been floating around the Warners lot since 1943, when Howard Hawks spent two weeks at June Lake, near Yosemite, California, with William Faulkner and the writer Steve Fisher (who scripted *Dead Reckoning* and *Lady in the Lake*) trying to etch out a script of a movie carrying the same name (though it had little relation to Walsh's film). Soon after that, Warners had the idea to base the film on a book by Ambassador Joseph E. Davies and to design it as a series of episodes, each scripted by a different author. A memo circulated around the studio noting, "A number of the leading novelists of America, England and France already have communicated to Warner Bros. their interest in the project and requested that they be allowed to submit material for inclusion in *Battle Cry*." Each of eighteen projected reels would tell the story of a different soldier. The idea behind the film was "to show the real brotherhood of man in this common struggle against Fascism": "We are all fighting the same thing."[14]

Ten years passed, and nothing happened with the title. Then, in July 1953, Warner Bros. purchased Leon Uris's popular novel *Battle Cry* for $25,000. The studio tagged it "a story about a group of Marines in the Pacific war"—which was not saying much about anything, not yet.[15] But Jack Warner had big plans for the book. The studio agreed to pay Uris and his publisher, Putnam's, an additional $12,500 should any sequels to the film be made.

Uris wrote the script himself, finishing just at the end of 1953. The studio considered numerous titles, such as *The American Sequence* and *The Lonesome Train,* before deciding to stay with *Battle Cry*. The story, which focuses on a group of marines as they go from boot camp to the battlefields of World War II, contains the requisite conceits of the genre: one marine has a girl in every port; his buddies run the gamut from overly zealous to running scared. Walsh signed a contract with Warner Bros. on October 6, 1953, three months before he began shooting *Battle Cry*. The contract stipulated that he would work for a period of fifty-two weeks for the production of at least two "but not more than three pictures" and would receive $3,000 per week during that time. When he signed with Warners, however, Walsh was still obligated to direct the western *Jubal Troop* for Columbia, although he could renege on the picture at his own discretion, which he did (Columbia released the director Delmer Daves's *Jubal,* starring Glenn Ford and Ernest Borgnine, in 1956—without Walsh attached to it at all). But, as part of the Warners' contract Sam Jaffe now negotiated and Walsh signed, in addition to directing *Battle Cry,* he was also set to direct, without screen credit, the battle scenes for the studio's *Helen of Troy,* to be filmed in Rome. That would come later.

Walsh claimed he worked on the script of *Battle Cry* with Uris, although it is unclear when that took place. The script was still not finished by the time shooting began, and sections of it were shipped now and then to the company after they began filming in Puerto Rico. But one thing was clear: Walsh saw *Battle Cry* as a chance to replicate his success with *What Price Glory?* These large-scale war pictures excited him the most, as if, the more mettle he could pump into a story, the more chance to live on the edge of danger, the more opportunity to choreograph action sequences—the bigger, the better. He had been doing some straight shooting recently with pictures such as *Gun Fury* and *Distant Drums*. But *Battle Cry* would mean firing the big guns. "It's one of my favorite films," Walsh told the British press later in a piece of puffery, "and one of the most ambitious":

> If you can bring a group of characters together . . . who can sustain your story, then you have a good film. That's one of the reasons why you sometimes shoot films with an enormous number of characters. But, as you're viewing the "rushes," you see three or four of them who are not going too well, and you're obliged to eliminate them or cut the parts down. With *Battle Cry* I had no chance—because the public liked *all* my characters. That's perhaps because I succeeded in making each of them entirely different. . . . I worked in collaboration with [Uris]. That was very pleasant, but it so happened that he didn't want to adapt certain scenes in the book for the purposes of the film, even though I wanted to keep them. Finally, I got everything I wanted. I included in my film all the scenes about which *he* was reticent.[16]

It's conceivable that Walsh worked on the script with Uris but more likely that he tinkered with it during production.

Battle Cry is a smorgasbord of personalities and dramatic events that intersect in 1942 as a group of young marines joins up to go into battle. They spend as much time playing out personal dramas as actually seeing battle, if not more. Aldo Ray is the girl-crazy Gyrene who somehow falls in love with the right girl; Van Heflin is the colonel who is a soft touch beneath his steely exterior; Perry Lopez is the Hispanic soldier (just one of many cultural types represented in the picture); and there is Tab Hunter as the guy who has a fling with a married woman played by Dorothy Malone. Also on board is Justice McQueen as the brash southern soldier L. Q. Jones (the name McQueen took after the film). Following Uris's script, Walsh portrayed his group of marines as a cross section of America; they spend more screen time defining them-

selves as types than they do fighting the war, a fact that many critics and
moviegoers noticed.

The picture's long list of characters triggered a casting call heard
around the world. Hollywood's and Broadway's best showed up to read
for parts. James Dean was considered first for the part of Ski and then
for the part of Marion, both supporting roles, but received no callback
for either. At the time, he was being groomed for Elia Kazan's *East of
Eden,* and Kazan, protective of the young actor, wanted it kept under
wraps that Dean had even come in to read for Walsh's picture. The up-
and-coming Warners producer William Orr wrote to Jack Warner's executive assistant Steve Trilling saying, "James Dean is a young man who
is gaining a reputation as a fine young actor whom we tested yesterday
for the part of Ski, even though we didn't think him quite right for the
part."[17] Neither did a young Walter Matthau impress when he read for
the part of Mac, another of the marines.

Paul Newman and Joanne Woodward came in together—Newman
first reading for two parts, with Woodward reading for one. Bill Orr sent
Steve Trilling a memo:

> We did the test of Newman and Woodward Wednesday, De-
> cember 16. Mr. Newman came in with a preconceived idea of
> what they wanted to do in this scene, which consisted of: rolling
> around the mattress and the floor, leaping to their feet, staging
> a mock boxing match, rolling her up in the blanket, and a few
> other sundry peccadilloes. In as much as they both had to get
> back to the theater, I tried to simplify their ideas sufficiently to
> shoot it within about a half hour and not keep the curtain from
> going up on "Picnic." So don't think we've all flipped our lids
> when you see it.

Walsh, who must have had word that the auditions were trying, wired
Trilling from San Juan after the Newman-Woodward episode, "I am
getting better stuff each day hereafter staging all my own battles. Give
my best to all. Uncle." He wired again on February 27, 1954: "Good to
talk to you. Don't let these actors annoy you. To me they are strictly dog
meat. I am here to put on a battle with the Marines, which I am going

to do. Uncle."[18] Walsh may have been joking, but battle scenes were for more serious enjoyment.

More successful was Justice McQueen/L. Q. Jones, who was working as a page at CBS but was trying to break into pictures when he went in to read for the film. Walsh was there, and, after the reading, all he said was, "Thanks, kid, we'll be in touch." Several days later, Jones got the call to head over to wardrobe at Warner Bros. Jack Warner argued against Walsh hiring Jones. "He's only a kid; he's got no experience," Warner said. "You're going hundreds of miles away on location; what if the kid freezes [up]? Just call him when the picture is over, offer him a small part in another picture, and everybody's happy." But Walsh told Warner, "If the kid doesn't work in this picture, get yourself another director." That was the end of it, and L. Q. was in. Walsh saw a quality in Jones that he liked and even offered to put him under personal contract; he had done that with Rock Hudson, after all. When Jones told him that the studio had already gotten him an agent, Walsh said, "Don't worry, kid, I'll take care of everything."[19] This was quintessential Walsh—open armed and in a hurry.

Jones had a singular view of Walsh. "At that period of time there were only three or four directors who did whatever they wanted to do, and Raoul was one of them. Ford was another; Wild Bill Wellman was another," he recalled. "Raoul ran his set the way Raoul wanted to run it, and you did what he wanted to do. Russ Saunders [Walsh's assistant director] had been with him for so long he knew exactly how to run the studio and keep them off [Walsh's] back. If you worked with Raoul you worked with Russ, and Russ did not like actors. He'd seen too many have too much crap. Russ ran a tight ship—there was no waste."[20]

Walsh took his cast and crew to the U.S. Marine Corps depot in San Diego on February 15, 1954, to begin shooting. He cabled Trilling: "Get Gloria Grahame for Pat [Nancy Olson was cast]. Think her name has some value with Marines. The best actors we have are James Whitmore, Spanish, L. Q. Jones, Pedro [Perry Lopez], Danny [Tab Hunter] and Andy [Aldo Ray]. The rest are dog meat. Everybody working hard here under tough conditions, but we are going to bring home the bacon and I hope it's kosher. . . . Uncle." They were in San Juan by the end of that month. Afterward, Walsh wrote Trilling on March 4: "Shipping artists back to their

agents this week. Don't give out any scripts until I get there. I am staying
here to photograph D Day landing's ship maneuvers and naval cannon
fire. If you have not yet selected a cutter, suggest Alan Crosland as a good
man. I have lost twelve pounds owing *traffe* [*trafe*, 'bad, not kosher'; he
probably meant food] and no sleep because of Kinnen [unknown]. But if
we can win the war that's all that counts. Give my best to JL and all the
misphoka [*mishpocha,* 'family']. Love, Uncle." He later added, "Everyone
down here beating their brains out trying to get a good picture."[21]

The Marines invaded three to four times a year on Vieques, an island municipality of Puerto Rico in the northeastern Caribbean; that
was their practice. Walsh was very aware of this, and he coordinated
his shoot with one of the invasions so that he could use their ships and
their men. That way he had twenty to twenty-five thousand men at his
disposal and knew exactly how to run them.

On March 8, Jack cabled Walsh: "Dear Uncle . . . Can you put
cameraman front of tank or shooting through gun turret or some other
intriguing way having tank bearing down on whatever is in front and
have camera vibrate when tank goes off? Steve and I have seen all film.
Looks really great. Everybody doing wonderful job. Be happy [to] see
your smiling *batesmer ponem* ['beautiful face'] again. Jack."[22]

According to Jones, Walsh didn't like to work on Saturdays since
he thought he already worked hard enough Monday through Friday. If
there happened to be a Saturday call, he would show up at 9:30 A.M.,
step out of the "limo"—a Jeep—and, if it was too hot, look up at the sun
and say, "My God, it's raining. That's it for the day."[23] He'd go home,
and the production would disband. That was only one of Walsh's quirks.
Another actor, Tommy Cook, who played one of the marines, later remembered him sitting in his chair as the cameras rolled, just reading the
Hollywood Reporter.[24]

Walsh returned to California in the middle of March. He was back
hardly one day when the Warner Bros. story editor Finlay McDermid
wrote him:

Welcome home! While you have been fighting the battle of Vieques, the home front has been staging a close-quarter battle
with the Breen Office. This has been a nip and tuck affair but I

believe we have successfully defended what the Breen Office describes as the most gutsy [he might have meant *gutty*] script (and
they include *From Here to Eternity*) to pass their inspection.
However, if the picture is to skate successfully over some very
thin ice, there are several spots, which you'll have to watch very
carefully. We could still fail to get a Seal unless the following
points are handled with extreme caution. Please, Uncle, protect
yourself, and the studio: Danny and Kathy way too intimate
on page 47; intimacy still a problem throughout script; wanted
dominant emotion to be tenderness instead of passion; scenes
with Dragon's Den [a nightclub] too much sexual innuendo; had
to take out mention of "cheap room."[25]

Walsh obliged but would always be sorry.

Staying at the El Cortez Hotel in San Diego, Walsh wrote Trilling
on March 22:

Dear Stevie,

We arrived in San Diego this morning and ran into very unusual weather for California. Plenty of rain and lots of fog. This
evening we had an earthquake and the two Indians went tearing
through the lobby in the nude. Guthrie was still chasing them
at 9:00 [P.M.]. We found one of them in a bar down the street,
and the other one was singing with a band. He said, "I wanta go
back to the reservation." . . .

The present script is lacking in humor. I thought we were
going to put in the scene where L. Q. [Jones] goes to the ranch
and has the disastrous affair with a country girl. This to me was
a very funny episode and I think the audience is more interested
in seeing the escapades and situations that our platoon gets into
rather than have two officers yakking all the time. . . .

The manager just phoned and said the Indians have gone to
bed with their clothes on, waiting for another earthquake. I have
had one good break here. The fleet is in Honolulu so Guthrie
can't call up any admirals and have them over for dinner.

Best wishes for a Happy New Year. Uncle.[26]

On April 17, Walsh began filming the Saipan battle scenes at Camp Pendleton, near San Diego. The cast and crew then left for San Juan again to complete most of the picture. Shooting ended July 2, 1954, five months after Walsh started out in this war.

Walsh could segue from seriousness—seeming almost distant—to humorous, throwing a curve and waiting for the reaction. Tab Hunter worked with Walsh on only this one film and came away with a bad impression. "Walsh remained aloof," he remembered. "If he got what he wanted, he simply moved on to the next shot. You could never tell if anything affected him." Nevertheless, even he admitted Walsh's playful side: "When Walsh had Jack Warner view rushes [of a love scene between Hunter and Dorothy Malone], he played one of his customary practical jokes: as Dorothy and I run outside for our swim, he spliced in Hedy Lamarr's skinny-dipping scene from *Ecstasy;* Everybody roared."[27]

Then, on December 10, 1954, in a serious mood, Walsh wrote to the commandant of the U.S. Marine Corps, General Lemuel C. Shepherd Jr., in Washington:

Dear General,

We press previewed the picture "Battle Cry" last night before a regular paid admission audience of approximately 2,500 men, woman and children at The Pantages Theatre in Hollywood. It was stirring to hear the enthusiastic response and it was the consensus of opinion, "A wonderful tribute to the Corps and unquestionably the best Marine picture ever made." I am happy to report this because of my promise to you at Vieques Island that I would endeavor to make "Battle Cry" a better picture than "What Price Glory?" and from last night's reception I feel we have accomplished that. My compliments to you, and the Marines have landed again.

Warmest Regards,
Raoul Walsh[28]

On the set, Walsh would often tell his actors where to be, what to do. Then again he might just trust them. They had to learn what to expect from him because he wouldn't always communicate. He liked rehearsing; he'd go through the dialogue and what each actor would do, and that way he'd be happy and talk to the camera and say what he wanted. And, when everyone was ready and the bell sounded, he turned his back and just sat and listened to the scene. L. Q. Jones recalled that, "He maybe could not see that well, but he could *hear* and see that well. And if you missed your mark by a quarter of an inch, he was up, out of that chair, screaming. He'd done it so many times, he knew where you were supposed to be, and you'd better know—although he wouldn't get on your case; and he'd do it with humor. But he'd undress you, right in front of God and everybody, if it was your fault. If it was somebody else's fault, then he got on their case." Jones (who would work many times with Sam Peckinpah before going on to his career as a director) recalled the difference between Walsh and Peckinpah: "[Walsh] still did it [got on your case]—unlike Peckinpah, who was snide and bitter when he corrected. Raoul enjoyed people, enjoyed directing, enjoyed pictures, and it came off when he directed."[29]

American moviegoers generally liked *Battle Cry*, especially responding to its young cast. One critic said that the picture was made "in peprally fashion and extended for two hours and twenty-seven minutes on the CinemaScope screen." He added, "No one can say that Mr. Uris and Director Raoul Walsh have missed many tricks in splashing a long, episodic, Rover Boyish service story on the screen. . . . From the opening accounts of the razzing and hazing of 'boot camp' Marines by the usual hard-pants drill sergeant to the big lump-in-throat episode, when the fellows fix bayonets in silence to go forth and avenge their colonel, killed by the Japanese, they have got this film loaded with characters, sentimentality and clichés. An old hand at watching these pictures can almost call the shots and repartee."[30] It was hard to miss the predictable moments that are peppered throughout the film. Still, Walsh could choreograph a large cast of actors as effortlessly as he could stage a battle sequence.

In early 1955, Walsh went off to Rome to fulfill the second half of his Warners contract and conducted the battle scenes for the director Robert Wise's *Helen of Troy*, released in early 1956. His good friend John Twist coscripted the picture, which featured the newcomer Rossana Podesta, along with Stanley Baker and a young actress named Brigitte Bardot. If nothing else, he received a trip to Rome and later made a good story out of it. He told Hedda Hopper in 1965:

> When I was in Rome polishing some battle scenes for *Helen of Troy,* I was in the lunchroom at [Cinecitta Studios] and saw a tall girl walk by. I asked the casting woman who she was, and she said it was Sophia Loren. I said I'd like to give her a test and send it back to America. She agreed to arrange it. Two days later she told me that Sophia was just going into Mr. [Carlo] Ponti's picture, and he thinks it might not be a good idea to test her and send it to Hollywood. It might give her inflated ideas. He asked me to wait until she had finished his picture. But I couldn't wait, or I might be able to say that I discovered Sophia Loren.[31]

Walsh's contract with Warners to direct *Battle Cry* was the last one brokered by his longtime agent Sam Jaffe, who would close shop in 1959 to become a producer. Although there was no animosity between the two, Walsh left Jaffe before the mid-1950s. When he signed with Fox, in February 1954, to direct his next picture, the western story *The Tall Men,* he signed with his new agent, Herb Brenner at MCA, whose other clients at the time included Shelley Winters, Robert Taylor, and Mervyn LeRoy. Walsh worked with Brenner for the rest of his career.

Tall Men and Long Shadows

The trip to Rome was short-lived, and by the beginning of February 1955, Walsh had returned to Los Angeles to begin work on *The Tall Men* for Fox. By mid-April, he took cast and crew to Durango, Mexico, to begin filming, but first it took a while to rewhittle the script. *The Tall Men* is another rugged, outdoor adventure, aided in good part by beautiful De Luxe Color and CinemaScope, both of which Walsh now used often (along with Technicolor)—although the former was not his favorite process. The two processes together give a feel of grandeur to what is, again, an otherwise ordinary story with a cast that could draw an audience. Clark Gable and Cameron Mitchell are two Texas brothers, Ben and Clint Allison, who, when the picture opens in the year

1866, are seen riding their horses into the Montana Territory. The two have emerged from the Civil War physically intact but psychologically wounded. The opening words on the screen tell as much: "They came from the South headed for the goldfields . . . Ben and Clint Allison, lonely, desperate men. Riding away from a heartbreak memory of Gettysburg. Looking for a new life. A story of tall men—and long shadows."

The country inside Walsh's frame is strikingly beautiful—blue sky and spectacular snow-covered mountains. This kind of grandeur filled Walsh with a soaring energy. The men who ride within its folds are minuscule and, as the story unfolds, made to look smaller still—physically *and* psychologically. Ben and Clint (Gable and Mitchell) arrive in a small town with the purpose of getting money any way they can. They spot Nathan Stark (Robert Ryan) in the back room of a saloon unloading a hefty amount of money onto a table. Within minutes, they ambush him outside, rob him of his money belt, and take him along until they reach an isolated spot where he can't call for help. Stark then turns the tables on them and offers them a job that he promises will make them rich. He needs men to accompany him to Texas with the objective of bringing as many head of cattle as they can back up to Montana, where the animals will bring in a huge profit.

The three become business partners and head out for Texas. But the blizzards are tough going, and when they take shelter, they run into a young woman, Nella Turner (Jane Russell), whom Ben rescues from an Indian attack a little while later. The two fall in love, but Nella has big dreams that do not match Ben's smaller ones. She goes along with him anyway, and she meets Stark, who has departed for a while, when they all gather in Texas. Hotheaded Clint is killed by Indians. From then on Nella fights with herself: she loves Ben but wants the life Stark's kind of money can fetch. All three make it back to Montana, where Ben and Stark wrangle the square up and Nella comes to terms with her love for Ben.

The picture's screenplay took some doing before the Fox production chief Darryl F. Zanuck thought it in good enough shape: if Walsh thought Jack Warner was a controlling overseer, Zanuck, a goy like Walsh, was a hands-on producer who liked a good story meeting but could just as easily walk a script through to production on his own.

The producers William Hawks and William A. Bacher bought Clay Fisher's novel *The Tall Men* early in 1954 and showed it to Zanuck with the highest of hopes. When Zanuck read the story, he sent a memo through the ranks on April 19, 1954: "I have read this story, which I understand has been purchased by Hawks and Bacher. While it contains a great deal of material seen in other spectacular outdoor films, nevertheless it does have the 'look' of a great, big, mammoth outdoor film. Too bad it comes from a third rate book. It is a colossal undertaking from a financial standpoint. It cannot be touched for less than three million, five hundred and be done in a way it should be done—particularly with an all-star cast." "Make a deal with the author and publisher," Zanuck said, "to have the book rewritten in such a way that you could sell copies and make it a best seller. It would of course be published under another title as this title is too close to 'Ten Tall Men,' which was a picture released last year." Then he had another idea—to combine the story of *The Tall Men* with a remake of *The Iron Horse*: "The picture would tell the story of 'The Tall Men' but would have the characters bringing cattle to railroad builders in Montana."[32] Zanuck eventually scrapped the *Iron Horse* idea, and Frank Nugent came in to write a revised script, which he gave to Zanuck on February 12, 1954.

Walsh had his own ideas about script changes and met with the producers to offer rewrite ideas amounting almost to an entire overhaul. The opening credits seemed uninteresting, and he asked to change them to include "some good shots of the wild country under the titles": "Then we come to a shot of a barren hill, hold for a moment, then the two men ride into it. Their horses should have long hair, and the men should look pretty rugged, indicating they have been on this trip for a long time." Walsh got what he wanted for most of the opening shots, but not those depicting Ben and Clint coming on "the hanging spot," where they find two men hanged by Indians (there is only one in the final film) and Ben says to his brother, "At least they died with their boots on."[33]

Walsh wanted the intimate scenes between Ben and Nella to be cooled down, especially the first time they are alone in the cabin: "While we want to have a sexy scene here, we also want it to be in the picture after the Breen boys see it." Walsh proposed: "Ben and Nella arrive at the prospector's cabin; we play it as it is, up through the kiss. Now it looks as though the next step will be in the direction of a bed, but before this can happen, the cavalry patrol arrives. Ben looks out, sees them, then looks back at Nella and remarks, 'This is the first time I've not been glad to see the Texas troopers.'" Then Walsh has the scene proceeding to "the next morning."[34] He received his "next morning," but the cavalry never arrive, and Ben and Nella have to go it awkwardly alone, falling in love, Nella even getting a foot rub without it looking sexual. Breen's office surprisingly left the scene intact.

Walsh didn't get all the changes he asked for, but he did get an important one: "The more scenes we can have between Nella and Ben, and the more arguments we can have between these two, the better it will be for the story," he said, wanting some sexual fireworks. He also said: "We should always have the big herd moving in the background, stirring up clouds of dust." (Walsh loved dust.) Fox's special-effects department contributed obvious matte shots of dust, cloudy skies, even towns and stampeding herds of cattle. In addition, Gable had a few ideas about script changes that he passed along through Walsh to the producers. He thought that "Ben should take complete control of the trek" and that "the scenes between Ben and Nella should be built up, and there should be more of them."[35] That way, Gable would be front and center, which he was.

Walsh later said that the shoot was a rough one: four hundred people from the production came down with dysentery, and, on top of that, Ryan contracted hepatitis. But the cast and crew still grew close. Walsh and Gable, both notorious practical jokers, went at each other constantly, at one point Walsh putting a descented skunk in Gable's hotel room, scaring the actor out of his wits. Russell recalled that, before she went on location with Walsh, she was told "not to go anywhere near a Walsh set" since he was "horrible to actors." She found him to be just the opposite. He was "a pussycat," she later said, who began calling her "Daughter" while she called him "Father." For the remainder of Walsh's life, Russell sent him a Father's Day card every year and later became close friends with Mary Walsh after the Walshes moved to Simi Valley.[36]

Although the film grossed $6 million after it opened domestically in September 1955 and put Gable—in his first real cowboy picture—back at the top of Hollywood's top ten list of actors, the critics were not kind, especially citing the picture's wealth of weather-weary clichés. However, the film's reputation has improved over the years, in good part owing to its physical beauty—the expansive picture Walsh paints. His signature wide panning shots are so free-flowing they seem almost haphazardly to catch one or two lonely figures traveling within them, dwarfed by the huge size of this physical space.

Walsh's characters interact with each other and their physical environment in a contemplative way, as if very cognizant of their behavior toward one another, especially the two men who see the woman they love. They are heroic travelers, the kind of traveler Walsh might want to be at this stage in his life—not the childlike Errol Flynn but a full-fledged, grown-up man. He might want to be, like Ben, a man other men want to emulate, one who still conducts himself with dignity around others. Ben Allison, as Clark Gable plays him, is the masculine yet soft-spoken man Walsh wishes to be. In fact, Walsh confuses Ben with Gable, unable to see a difference between the actor and the character he plays. In his autobiography, Walsh mentions directing Gable in this picture and talks of how he and Gable went hunting together, masculinizing and romanticizing the bond between them. Ben embodies a self-sacrificing nature, embracing not so much a fictional persona as a real one for Walsh. A sense of reverie seems to have settled on Gable, and Walsh sees it. It's triggered by a recognition of so much time, and life, having gone by. *The Tall Men* speaks to this: its characters are hearty, earthy, and organically rooted in the soil they travel. There is a realism to them that cancels out any holes in the script. Walsh gives them a physical presence that is almost staggering.

14

His Kind of Women

Although Walsh's brother, George, left the movies in the early 1950s to take up horse training and ranching, he kept his heart in the film business. When he began working with horses, he did so for Walsh until he branched out working for other members of the Hollywood community. But the two brothers had collaborated on scripts several decades earlier, and George never stopped suggesting project ideas to Walsh. He sent them along in a letter no matter where his brother happened to be. From 1955 to 1963, Walsh received countless letters from George, each with a new movie project, none of them realized, however. An early idea was Alexandra Orme's novel *Comes the Comrade,* a story about the Russian occupation of Hungary seen through "the eyes of an attractive woman" that describes a mysterious "Red" character taking over the land. This indictment of communism was not to Walsh's taste. The same year, 1956, George sent Walsh various other ideas, including a story of modern Mexico replete with bullfight action and "color and romance." He also tried to sell his brother on "The Life of Mary Jemison" (telling the tale of a white colonist captured by the Seneca Indians when she was thirteen). Along similar lines, he told Walsh about "Birch Coulie," a romantic story about an Indian uprising in 1862 Minnesota. George knew his brother well; the story was very sympathetic to Native Americans. Other ideas over the years had to do with horse racing, the Irish sweepstakes, and Senator Joe McCarthy, who was, in George's words, "the victim of a most undeserved censure by the Senate for the monumental crime of patriotism above personal popularity." Walsh did not go for any of those either, even though all the stories George sent his brother had one common element, a love story. Each wrapped around the love of a man for a woman or a man fighting the odds to fight the good fight while still knowing a woman stood waiting for him.[1]

Walsh hadn't changed. If the scenario didn't include a good love story somewhere in the plot, Walsh was not interested. He still insisted that his films turned on one central action: the coming together of a man and a woman. In spite of his being called an *action director*—which he has been tagged time and time again—Walsh believed more strongly in the love between man and woman than any other story in his life, and that belief found its way into all his pictures. Even though he said that women were more difficult to direct (both his female characters *and* the actresses who filled their shoes), his world is fundamentally a sentimental one where a woman plays a central role; if she does not unite with her man, he dreams of her just the same. Just as Mad Dog Earle topples from the High Sierras for love of Marie, even as Cody Jarrett sits on his mother's lap, Walsh's essential story, before anything, is that of doing the right thing for the woman you love.

"I wouldn't give you two cents for a dame without a temper," Mad Dog Earle quips in *High Sierra.* That statement said as much about Walsh as anything else, especially in his later films. Many of Walsh's 1950s films turn on a new kind of woman. *The Tall Men* unleashed, not only Walsh's heroic, more mature male traveler, but also a strong woman who could travel by his side. This woman is capable of setting up her own house on her own terms in any godforsaken wilderness. She has gotten stronger in Walsh's cinema over the past decade, but she would still rather be with her man than not. Jane Russell's Nella Turner may be along for the ride, but she carries a strength within her that could create a household if and when her man returns. The spitfire Amantha Starr, soon to emerge from *Band of Angels,* is equally strong yet equally ambivalent about leaving her man. A slave owned by the film's hero, Hamish Bone, Amantha can pass for white and can have her freedom anytime she wants. But she chooses Hamish's house nonetheless. A male-dominated universe binds the women in Walsh's cinema, and this often conflicts with their fierce desire for independence, their natural emotional and physical strength.

In *The Tall Men,* however, Jane Russell, or Nella Turner, as the two are truly the same woman, ups the ante for finding the Walshian woman who causes the earth to shake. She problematizes her man's journey as he treks across the frontier and, therefore, across the story's terrain in order to complete himself and show that he is a man. Russell is the toughedup version of (and with a better sense of humor than) Walsh's earlier women, Ida Lupino or Virginia Mayo. She sweetens Walsh's landscape at the same time as she rides horseback with the hero and boots him in the rear if he needs it. She is the perfect Walshian woman, tough, loving, entirely female. She completes her man's universe. "Woman are for loving. Walsh's never cry. They like watching their guy being beat up, knocked down, given comeuppance—and coming up off the canvas to win. For their world is full of outrageous injustice, mutilated bodies, innocent lives destroyed," says the critic Tag Gallagher. "Where your fights will take you and what you will find on the trail and who you will be when you get somewhere are unknowable. The only sure thing is that you will meet a damsel in distress, beautiful, erotic and alluring, and fall madly in love with her, to your ruin or regeneration."[2] Walsh met his other half, Mary Simpson, and set out to live a quiet life with her, all the while dramatizing how his fictional heroes would meet their women and how they might treat them. As Walsh once told Peter Bogdanovich, as he had told so many others, "In all my films, the whole story revolves around the love scene."[3] As much as critical looks at Walsh have minimized this feature of his work, the man's attraction to the woman (whether she is alive or a memory) stands out as central in his pictures—from the art films made at Fox Pictures, to the Paramount musicals, through the Warner Bros. tough-guy journeys, and into the 1950s and 1960s. Walsh's universe, Walsh's psychology, sees a man and a woman traveling together, rocky road or no. There is no other universe to which his loner might aspire.

An alternate Walshian woman would be the woman traveling alone, meeting a man to love, but finding in the end that she must light out for the rest of her life without him. When Walsh directed Jane Russell in his next Fox picture, *The Revolt of Mamie Stover,* he saw a woman unable to keep her man in the end. In Walsh's universe, this means going against nature—this is tragedy in a world where men and woman are meant to be together. When Walsh worked on Mamie's character at Fox, he went as far as he could to shape her as a valuable human being in a chaotic, male universe.

In William Bradford Huie's novel *The Revolt of Mamie Stover,* Mamie is a prostitute who sets up shop in Hawaii just prior to World War II. Neither Walsh nor Fox wanted that profession for her (it was too risky), so, in the film, Mamie is a good girl with naughty edges. When the film opens, she is escorted by the San Francisco police to a pier and then to the ship that will take her to Hawaii. In essence, she's told to get out of town. In Walsh's frame, this makes her the female equivalent of the sad, lone traveler out to escape a bad history and looking to redeem himself in a new one.

On the ship to Hawaii, Mamie meets the writer Jim Blair, who immediately takes an interest in her sadness and befriends her when they get to Hawaii. Mamie finds work in a gentleman's nightclub called the Bungalow run by a woman named Bertha; she entertains men in her room but strictly at the level of music and friendly conversation. Soon, Mamie and Jim realize that they are in love, and he sheds his more aristocratic girlfriend, Annalee Johnson. But Mamie is viewed as a whore all around town, and when Jim tries to take her to the local officers' club, they are shunned. A soldier himself, Jim is soon shipped overseas. He and Mamie pledge their love. But the Japanese bomb Pearl Harbor, and Mamie realizes that she has enough money to buy property in the hard-hit area of town. In order to make more money and to grab as much power as she can (as a man would), she keeps working at the gentleman's nightclub even though she promised Jim she would quit. When Jim gets wind of this, he asks her to stop, which she refuses to do. Jim leaves her, and at the story's conclusion, Mamie leaves Hawaii, passing through San Francisco on her way back home to Mississippi. She had made a fortune in real estate but gave her money away. Now alone, Mamie wonders whether the independence was worth it all.

Jane Russell's home studio, RKO, loaned her to Fox for *The Revolt of Mamie Stover,* and Walsh had his girl with him again. Richard Egan was cast as Jim Blair, and Agnes Moorehead played Bertha Parchman. Joan Leslie, who began her career in Walsh's *High Sierra,* made her final screen appearance as Annalee Johnson.

The *Mamie Stover* script went through almost six months of changes at Fox before Walsh began shooting the picture in late November 1955 in Los Angeles. A first treatment, dated June 1955 and written by Huie, has Mamie no longer an out-and-out prostitute but certainly something close to it: a woman living on the edges of proper society. She is "beaten up" and "wearing large, dark glasses to hide a black eye": "She is twenty-two. She is a lush woman; golden hair, tall, and proportioned

accordingly. She is not a tramp. She is a fresh and fairly sensitive girl who
has been treated harshly." In several subsequent treatments, Mamie is
already on the ship when the story opens, omitting the scene in the finished film that has her booted out of San Francisco, escorted to the ship
that will take her to Hawaii to make sure she is on it. A final shooting
script, dated October 31, 1956, does little to change that opening.[4] On
November 4, 1955, Zanuck met with Walsh to discuss the script. Also in
that meeting was the soon-to-be Fox production chief Buddy Adler, who
would take Zanuck's job in a short while after Zanuck left the studio in
what some say was a midlife crisis exemplified by an urge to chase the
young actress Bella Darvi around Europe (he returned to filmmaking
five years later as an independent producer).

Zanuck, Walsh, and Adler considered revisions to the script. Zanuck
liked the script "immensely," saying that it would make "an interesting,
off beat picture." But he worried that it didn't dig deeply enough into the
characters. "Are we too much on the surface?" Zanuck asked (prophetically). "As an example," he said, "take the character of Jim Blair. I like
him but I found it hard to believe that he was an author. I do not feel
wisdom in him. He is so obvious, it seems to me. Now take the newspa-
perman, William Holden's character, Mark Elliott [in *Love Is a Many
Splendored Thing*]. His observations on life, and what makes us tick,
and his observations on things in general were pretty adult." Zanuck obviously had a high opinion of writers. He added, "Jim Blair in this script
sounds to me like a lousy writer because, among other things, he doesn't
seem to be on a higher intellectual plane than does Mamie [Zanuck had
little respect for Mamie's intellect]. I do not feel any wisdom in him; he
seems a little naive. I think he should be more intrigued by Mamie, by
the kind of girl she is, and by her philosophy. At first we should see him
watching Mamie, and sizing her up. Then he gets hooked by her."[5]

Sydney Boehm's final shooting script, dated November 9, 1955, includes the opening scene with the San Francisco police escorting Mamie
to the ship. Mamie is a bad girl who, by story's end, learns a good lesson
and loses her man. She owns a good amount of property but is punished
for her transgression, not only because she is unable to quit her profession as a hostess, but also because she wants money as much as any man
does. In the 1950s, Mamie is still too aberrant in her desire for power.
A feminist reading (in which even Walsh's strong women are pieces of,

rather than owners of, property) would see Mamie's end as a punishment for her wish to be independent of a man, for no longer wanting to be a commodity but instead wanting to control a commodity—and herself. Mamie isn't punished for being a prostitute—not outwardly—but she is punished nonetheless.

Walsh shot the picture in Hawaii and on Pier 13 in Wilmington, California, just south of Los Angeles, before returning to the Fox lot for interior scenes. He and Russell often worked from 8:45 P.M. until 1:45 A.M., forming a close friendship once again, this time Egan joining them in playing practical jokes on each other, privately and in public. When they were in Hawaii, Walsh showed his affection for Russell by readjusting their shooting schedule so that she could get home to California for Christmas to be with her husband, the Los Angeles Rams quarterback Bob Waterfield, and their children. He made certain that she, Egan, he, and Mary changed to a hotel closer to the airport in Hawaii so as to catch an early flight to Los Angeles. The three remained close friends for years.

The riches of *Mamie* are many. Walsh and Jane Russell are natural-born allies, coming together serendipitously for *The Tall Men* and now for this tale of a woman who is the destination for all Walsh's celluloid women over the years. She is, of course, down on her luck, struggling to stay afloat, and using a cynical sense of humor to help her get by. Russell's earthy sexuality is the female equivalent of Walsh's male bravado and virility. *Mamie Stover* is Walsh's most important film of this decade, revealing an emotional landscape in which he lets his guard down and creates pure vulnerability on the screen. Mamie exists in a script with potholes, and she is pulled down by the weight of the world around her. Yet she is a real woman, full bodied enough to capture the spectator with the full force of her honesty.

But there was no love lost between Jane Russell and Buddy Adler. Getting Russell's hair color just right for the character was harder than expected. Her natural color, black, was wrong for Mamie, who in the book is a platinum blonde. Adler decided that her hair should be red, even though Russell preferred to go platinum. She called him on the phone one morning to make that suggestion, adding that Moorehead should keep her natural, "beautiful" red hair. "He sounded annoyed that I'd gotten him so early in the morning," Russell said, "and he told me to forget it. 'Just do as you're told,' he said." According to Russell, Adler also believed that the writer was "the living end, and all decisions were slanted his way." "Raoul was very unhappy," she added.[6]

Russell was likely unhappier than Walsh. The experience of working with Adler helped convince her to become a producer herself. Her reviews for *Mamie Stover* were not sterling. Critics found her performance more amusing than serious and saw the picture as awkwardly structured, even crude. But audiences disagreed; *Mamie Stover* enjoyed good box office and afterward built a large international following.

Russell and Waterfield were just forming their own company, Russ-Field Productions, and made a distribution deal with United Artists for their first feature, a western titled *The King and Four Queens*. Russell gathered her film family around her: Walsh agreed to direct, and Clark Gable came on board as the film's protagonist, Dan Kehoe, a confidence man who gets involved with a widow and her group of daughters-in-law. Gable also joined as a production partner in the picture, and the company became Russ-Field Gabco.

When Walsh signed with Russ-Field Gabco Productions on March 26, 1956, his contract stipulated that he would be paid $5,000 per week for the duration of the production. Just to make certain he would stay alive and healthy, he was forbidden to travel in any noncommercial aircraft for the duration of the picture. At this juncture, Walsh secured his immediate future. One month after this, he signed a five-picture deal with Fox and would be staying on. He committed to directing five pictures within seven years with a guaranteed compensation of $500,000 total, or roughly $100,000 per film, with regularly scheduled payments of $50,000. He was to work twenty weeks on each picture at $5,000 per week. The contract would take effect at the close of his commitment to Russ-Field Gabco. In June 1956, Walsh looked into being part of a syndicate that included Gable and several Detroit businessmen, all of them looking to purchase the Detroit Tigers. The Hollywood producer Bob Golshein represented the group. The deal never went through.

Originally called *The Last Man in Wagon Mound*, then *The King and Four Queens*, the picture was to shoot until July 31, 1956, but the schedule was later extended to August 15. Walsh directed the actresses Eleanor Parker (as Gable's love interest) and Barbara Nichols and Jean Wiles (as rivals for Gable's attention). But he was most impressed with

Jo Van Fleet, who played the story's matriarch. To him, Van Fleet was a powerhouse and a true professional.

Gable plays a middle-aged, still handsome cowboy who learns that a widow and her four daughters-in-law live on a ranch where $100,000 lies buried, money stolen by the sons in a robbery. Three of the sons are known to have been killed in the robbery, but one is said to be alive. Gable's character, Dan, wants the money and moves in on the women, telling them that he knew that son. The film, shot in St. George, Utah, shines little in Walsh's body of work but nonetheless earmarks once again the maturity of the characters he defined in his 1950s films. At the story's conclusion, Dan ends up with one of the daughters-in-law, Sabina (Eleanor Parker), who confesses to him that she and her supposed husband were never married. This leaves her free to ride off with Dan. The two decide to stay together not so much because of a passionate love for each other as because they realize they make a good team—and the best kind of life is one where you are not alone in the end. This was Walsh acknowledging that getting older affords, or necessitates, seeing the world in wider, more inclusive terms. The landscape grows broader and becomes more tolerant of human flaws. These flaws no longer necessarily kill his men (and sometimes his women) but instead paint them as more sensitive to their own vulnerabilities and their need for one another. The critics unanimously disliked the film, considering it melodramatic and implausible at best. Gable was none too happy and, after the stress of producing a film, decided he would do better working for someone other than himself. Walsh never much liked the script; when he was filming, he found out that his friend the director Sam Fuller was nearby filming *Run of the Arrow*. Walsh told Fuller that he loved his actors but hated his script and jokingly suggested that the two of them swap pictures.[7]

Walsh's maturing characters stem not only from his approaching old age—he was now nearing seventy—but also from his steady marriage to Mary, who more and more became his emotional foundation, even though he never gave up the habit of straying should the occasion ever present itself. Still, this was his idea of a happy marriage. When he left their home in Toluca Lake to go on location, he had a habit of leaving Mary little notes—addressed to "Gip Gip," his pet name for her. "Dearest Gip Gip," he wrote in one undated note, "Wherever I go, wherever I am, you are never far away from me because I love you. I told Gussy and

Shep and Gin Gin [the Walshes' pet dogs] to watch over you and protect you. All my love, Papa." In another note, also undated, Walsh wrote to her, "Dearest Gip Gip, I love you and I am going to miss you. But you are never far away from me. All my love, Papa. P.S. The little fellows will keep you company till I return." When Walsh left for Puerto Rico to shoot *Battle Cry,* he wrote her, "Now Baby, take good care of yourself while I am away and always remember you and you alone are the only one in this world I love with all my heart. If I can get good transportation to San Juan I will send for you. Love, Papa."[8]

In the first years of their marriage, Mary traveled with Walsh when she could but tired of it as time went on. A homebody at heart, her favorite pastime was to walk around the house barefoot doing housework and taking care of her husband and their menagerie of animals. Yet, when Walsh signed on with Warner Bros. to make his third and final picture with Gable, *Band of Angels,* Mary was still in traveling mode and accompanied him to Baton Rouge, Louisiana, for a ten-week shoot beginning January 18, 1957.

Glad as usual to be back at Warners, Walsh was also pleased to be working again with the cinematographer Lucien Ballard, although this picture would be their last collaboration. *Band of Angels*—the title refers to the short life expectancy of freed blacks who fought in the Civil War with the Union troops—is based on the celebrated novelist-critic Robert Penn Warren's *The Destiny of Hamish Bond,* a story of miscegenation in antebellum Kentucky and Louisiana, which Warners had purchased a year earlier. Gable plays the reformed slave trader Hamish Bond (although many saw Rhett Butler lurking inside the character), who buys a beautiful slave girl, Amantha Starr (Yvonne De Carlo), who has been raised as the daughter of a wealthy white plantation owner but now has found out that her deceased mother was black: Amantha has just been sold down the river, her father's plantation sold to pay off his debts. Hamish's guilt about his slave trader past forbids him from treating his slaves as slaves, and Amantha is given star treatment and soon enough becomes Hamish's lover—and eventual mistress. Also in the picture is a young Sidney Poitier, who plays Hamish's "son," a slave rescued, raised, and educated by Hamish who might also be his biological son. After a few life-threatening skirmishes, Poitier helps Hamish and Amantha escape, just as the Civil War begins and the slaves look toward a new freedom.

When the team of John Twist, Ivan Goff, and Ben Roberts completed the film's script, Breen's office had more than a few problems
with it. The office issued a memo to the effect that the script "in its
present form" was an "unacceptable treatment of illicit sex," though it
was agreed that anything "illicit" in it would be "removed": "In its place
would be substituted a desire on the part of the leads for each other, but
because of the fact that they are master and slave . . . they would refrain
from indulging in sexual intercourse until they are married."[9] What is
curious about the Breen Office statement was the explicit anxiety about
only sexual relations outside of marriage, not about what was undoubtedly the more disturbing subject in the picture and in Penn Warren's
novel: the sexual/power relationship between a white male slaveowner
and his half-black female slave. The issue of sexual relations and power
struggles between blacks and whites was only just becoming a subject
in American films, especially in pictures such as Robert Rossen's *Island
in the Sun* (1957), Delmer Dave's *Kings Go Forth* (1958), and, the most
well-known example, John Ford's *The Searchers* (1956), whose implied
subject of illicit sex between Debbie and Scar veils the film's true, hidden subject: black-white relations. Breen's office was unconcerned with
anything other than explicit sexuality between the races if the man and
woman were unmarried, even though there is more than a suggestion
of sexual attraction between Poitier's and De Carlo's characters as well.

Walsh initially wanted the young Natalie Wood to play Amantha
but couldn't get her. His attraction to the story lay in its possibility for
action, sweep, and romance. After the critics, and Gable himself, panned
Band of Angels, Walsh still defended it, thinking of it as a story with
mysterious undertones and layers of narrative that slowly reveal themselves. Walsh thought that the picture had an unusual beauty, especially
its opulent sets and sensual atmosphere—enlivened in great part by
Max Steiner's often-sweeping score (unfortunately burdened down in
the beginning credits with lyrics, as was a 1950s trend). But Gable never
forgave Walsh's having him take De Carlo in his arms in their big love
scene, as all the while a hurricane was raging outside the windows of the
room—curtains flowing madly, lightning piercing the sky with boister-
ously loud sound effects. Walsh loved the scene; he found it exciting. The
only part of the shoot he regretted was having to start the picture in the

month of January, when Baton Rouge looked brown instead of the lush green he wanted. But Gable had a limited amount of time to shoot, and Walsh was left with little choice.

The controversial subject of slavery and black-white relations was not the attraction for Walsh. He had always been fascinated by the South, and he knew that controversy—he saw it strictly as a story element, not a political matter—brought with it the possibility for great action, great drama. He was not a political animal in any sense, nor had he ever been during any time of his life—despite his propensity for wooing William Randolph Hearst and enjoying the celebrity Hearst could provide him on the world stage. Walter Doniger noted that Walsh was never active in the Director's Guild, a clear sign in Doniger's eyes that he had little interest in politics and might even be politically conservative.[10] Walsh consistently voted the Republican ticket and coupled that with true tolerance of anyone around him without regard to race or social status.

The *Variety* critic was somewhat kind to the picture on its release on August 3, 1957. But most critics found it to be a superficial, melodramatic treatment of a serious subject. The *New Yorker* said, "Mr. Warren was after . . . a description of Southern society when slavery was the order of the day. What we are offered [in the film] is a spate of romantic hokum."[11] As much as Gable respected Walsh, he decided not to work with him again.

Later in his life, when he looked back at this period, Walsh still seemed unaware of the political potential of Warren's book. He blew hot and cold about this period in his career, considering which films stood up and which did not. He dismissed *The King and Four Queens* as one of his "turkeys," as he liked to say. *Band of Angels* still stood high in his estimation, especially his good memories of working with Gable and De Carlo, despite the trouble he had with the Breen Office. But *Mamie Stover* was the great disappointment: "The biggest mistake we made—I didn't make it, the studio made it—was they bought that damn book, *The Revolt of Mamie Stover*. Well, that book is all about prostitution in Hawaii. They knew they couldn't show prostitution and yet they bought it. We wrote a script and we put it on. And it was nothing."[12] But eventually the picture gained a broad audience who appreciated the mediated rhythms in Walsh's films of the 1950s.

Back to the Battle Hymn

But Walsh worked up great enthusiasm for his next film, *The Naked and the Dead*, adapted from Norman Mailer's best-selling antiwar novel about World War II. He approached the picture with high hopes—it was, after all, another large-scale war effort—but later became disillusioned with the Breen Office cuts. The censors took out all the naked and left the dead, Walsh liked to quip. His one-liners, thrown out seemingly casually, were difficult to read at this point. They were ambiguous responses to disappointment—or maybe indifference. It was hard to know which. Mailer's lengthy, seven-hundred-plus-page novel follows an army unit stationed in the South Pacific and struggling for survival against the Japanese even as its own platoon leader, the sadistic Sergeant Croft, terrorizes the men in his charge. The higher-ups are split on whether Croft should be stopped, some believing that, the more the men are goaded and abused, the better fighters they will be. Individual soldiers' stories intertwine with the action sequences as the men gear up and go into battle. Mailer's novel was hailed as one of the greatest wartime novels ever written—as it follows a fourteen-man infantry platoon struggling to keep its dignity while experiencing the horrors of war.

After a lengthy journey to see the book adapted for the screen, Mailer sold the movie rights to *The Naked and the Dead*—for $250,000—to the independent film producer Paul Gregory, who had just produced his first film, Charles Laughton's *The Night of the Hunter*. Gregory tried to interest Laughton in directing Mailer's novel, and Laughton actually wrote a script for it. But, feeling exhausted after *The Night of the Hunter,* and in ill health, Laughton left the project. Then Gregory went to Warner Bros. The studio agreed to finance the picture but insisted on almost complete control. RKO would produce, and Warners would release it. Warners wanted Walsh and got him. Jack wanted "tits" in the picture, and he knew Walsh would put them in and damn the censors.

Before he began shooting *The Naked and the Dead,* Walsh followed through with some unfinished business with Rock Hudson, who had not worked for Walsh since 1953. He sued Hudson in September of 1957 for $1 million in damages and asked for a court order preventing him from working for anyone else. Walsh alleged that, in July 1952, Hudson agreed to appear in four pictures to be produced by Walsh and then reneged. Walsh filed the suit when he learned that Hudson had plans to appear in a film produced by Henry Ginsberg. (The picture was, presumably, George Stevens's 1956 *Giant*, which Stevens and Ginsberg produced for Warner Bros. However, Hudson worked on *Giant* in 1955 and made no other picture for Ginsberg.) The suit was eventually dropped, and Walsh and Hudson worked together again in 1961 when Walsh produced (uncredited) *Come September*, in which Hudson appeared with Gina Lollobrigida, Sandra Dee, and Bobby Darin. The urge to go to court hadn't yet abated.

Walsh left for location shooting in Panama in mid-November, and his cast and crew arrived on December 12, 1957, working until February 10, 1958, with no days open for rehearsal. Walsh rewrote the script—often and all during production, working with Terry Sanders and Denis Sanders, who had helped Laughton reshape James Agee's script for *The Night of the Hunter*.

Walsh had with him a large cast to flesh out Mailer's episodic tale of the gruesomeness of battle in World War II. Raymond Massey played the sadistic superior officer, General Cummings, and Cliff Robertson was cast as the liberal-minded lieutenant who clashes with Cummings and is really the story's heart and soul—and conscience. Aldo Ray was cast as Sam Croft, a sadistic sergeant who treats his men with great disrespect. Walsh had great hope that audiences would find some sympathy for Croft, not only as the story's central character, but also as the engine moving the action forward. To Walsh, Croft was an ambivalent man, an excellent soldier who instinctively understands what he has to do in wartime, even if this renders him as unsympathetic as sympathetic. Walsh himself felt an affinity for a man (a director) who needed to get the job done and sometimes angered those who didn't understand that.

The cast showed up for *The Naked and the Dead* before there was a script. Charles Laughton had written 620 pages, and Walsh refused to work with his material. He asked the cast member L. Q. Jones to come to location ahead of time and do all the tests, playing every character—that went on for three or four days. Then Walsh began rewrites—with Jack Warner's blessing. Jones later said, "It was Mr. Warner who decided who was going to write it and direct it." But Steve Trilling, a very astute man, was right behind Warner and the best thing that could have happened to him, even now. He made sure the Colonel did not self-destruct. "It was Trilling's job to make sure Warner didn't have a hissy fit or a heart attack," Jones also recalled. One episode to that effect stayed in Jones's mind for years:

> As I stood in Steve's office one day you could hear Warner [in his next-door office] screaming and absolutely having a fit. The door burst open and Warner burst in, screaming, "That bitch!" He'd go off on some woman, how he's going to sue her, how he's gonna have her killed. "I'm going to get rid of her!" he said. Then Steve would say, "You're right. Let me call and I'll get the thing going." And he'd get him out of the room, and he'd dial up and he'd say, "Look, Betty, we've got a problem here. And we've got to get the picture done. Do you want to get paid? I can maneuver *this* if you'll do *this*." When he was through, he'd go to Jack and say, "Now, she called, and she apologized, so why don't we just accept that and we'll go on." So, he, Steve, ran the business of Warner Bros. Jack Warner gave bad speeches and insulted people; Steve Trilling saw that A, B and C got done.[13]

Warner told Walsh to go ahead and write a script with Denis and Terry Sanders behind him. Sometimes, however, the writing went minute by minute and it had strictly to do with Walsh. He would show up every morning during filming and get Jones, Cliff Robertson, and Joey Bishop to do some improvisations. Then he'd shoot—without a formal script.

But the producer Paul Gregory was never happy with the picture, especially with Jack Warner's habit of cutting financial corners whenever he could. Nor did Gregory enjoy working with Walsh, who was surrounded by his own group of actors and crew and moved swiftly along to the finish. He especially disliked Walsh tacking on an alluring fan dancer, played by Lily St. Cyr, who appears in the film's opening nightclub sequence. But Walsh had his own adventures with Gregory. He would go up to Gregory's room every night because there was no script. One night he knocked on the door, and Gregory opened it. Gregory didn't have a stitch of clothing on, but Walsh said nothing. He walked in, and they sat down and talked for about two or three hours about the script. Then they got up, and Gregory opened the door for Walsh, who started down the hall. Then he turned around and saw that Gregory was about to close the door. Walsh turned back and said, "By the way, your fly is open."[14]

The episode went even further. "Now, Raoul dressed for himself," Jones said. "He wore the puttees, the riders, the cowboy shirt, the ten or fifteen gallon hat, and he carried the swagger stick. That's the way he always dressed. Well, about the fourth or fifth day we're out on the set and the limo pulls up, and it's Gregory. He gets out of the car and he's got on puttees, and the rider's pants and a ten gallon hat and a swagger stick."[15] Gregory was trying to look like Walsh, but the attempt failed, succeeding only in giving the crew laughing fits for hours.

Neither Gregory nor Mailer was happy with Walsh's finished film—nor was Walsh himself. Mailer could never have been satisfied with a picture that had to be sentimentalized and sanitized to please a wide 1950s audience. The one redeeming feature was Walsh's suspenseful war scenes and battle sequences—which even today drive home the tragedy of the waste of human lives so fundamental to Mailer's antiwar theme. In this regard, *The Naked and the Dead* could have had much more in common with *What Price Glory?* than Walsh believed *Battle Cry* might have had. Walsh saw no further than the censor's cuts.

Unfortunately, the studio thought it necessary to water down Mailer's violence and replace it with Hollywood conceits—a barroom brawl and some equally unconvincing flashbacks when soldiers recall the girls they left at home. Walsh's direction shows him to be interested in the battle scenes and deeply detached from the love scenes—not because they might be intimidating in their intimacy, but because they feel so detached from the film's central action. Back in 1950, Burt Lancaster thought about producing Mailer's novel but believed that the country was not yet ready for its antiwar story.[16] Eight years later, the country wasn't any closer to being ready. No one was more disappointed than Walsh to see so much of Mailer's gutsy story also expelled by the censors, and his battle with them was reminiscent of his troubles with *Sadie Thompson* and *Klondike Annie* years earlier. He worked furiously while on location to please Warners and Breen, but he could not restore all that had been lost. To say the least, the conventional treatment of Mailer's subject, the way it is dispersed to make it acceptable to the broadest popular audience, obliterates any thought about war's insanity. Walsh was more immersed in Hollywood conceits than he would ever understand at this point.

But, again, adventure and travel were Walsh's escape from disappointment. After seeing the censors slice up *The Naked and the Dead,* he looked at traveling again. In March 1958, he returned to Fox and began work on the western spoof—or, as it might have been called, the Jayne Mansfield vehicle—*The Sheriff of Fractured Jaw.* His Fox contract called for a twenty-week production schedule that sent him to Spain for exteriors and then to Fox England for interior shots. Jacob Hay's short story "The Sheriff of Fractured Jaw" was first published in *McLean's* magazine in April 1954. Four years later, Arthur Dales completed a script for the story, and the studio set about preparing to produce the picture. Walsh actually shot the picture in seven weeks—a fact that impressed many (although he never understood why). After its release in the United States on March 14, 1959, a short item appeared in newspaper syndication across the country on June 25, 1959, entitled "How to Make Movie Money": "Raoul Walsh shot [*Fractured Jaw*] with Jane Mansfield and Kenneth More in seven weeks for $700,000 in Spain and England. As of June 25th, the picture [has taken in] $2,300,000." Walsh had not slowed down, even now at the age of seventy-one.

Walsh began shooting at Pinewood Studios in England for the film's interiors and for the prologue, which is set in London. Then the production traveled to a remote location in the Spanish province of Aragon, the first time a western was shot in Spain. Walsh recruited men from a nearby gypsy encampment to play ranchers and Native Americans. He also recruited the actor Henry Hull, one of his oldest friends; the two had known each other since their Biograph days. Although Hull appeared in countless Walsh films at Warners, he was now in near retirement but came to work for Walsh.

Fox studios in Los Angeles put together a prefabricated western town and shipped it to the plains of Spain. The production was under way practically without a hitch, save for the moment Walsh and his crew were surprised by a number of high-powered explosives on the day they were to begin filming. Walsh found out that the Fifth Spanish Army Corps was holding its annual maneuvers, ignoring his request that they postpone.

Once maneuvers were over, cameras began rolling. Walsh found both Mansfield and Kenneth More amicable, although he often had difficulty with Mansfield's exaggerated baby-doll mannerisms, a pretense that he thought hampered her innate comedic talents. In what turned out to be a beautifully realized western spoof shot in Technicolor and CinemaScope (Walsh's fourth time using the latter), More plays a staid Englishman who ventures to the town of Fractured Jaw in the American West to represent his family's gun-manufacturing business. Since he inadvertently stopped a holdup on the stage he took into town, he is immediately appointed its sheriff. But he seems a fish out of water in his Saville Row attire, even though he has a secret weapon that his family back in England rigged up: a kind of James Bondian device that ejects a pistol down his sleeve so that he can protect himself. When he meets Mansfield, the owner of a local hotel, she takes a liking to him, tired as she is of all the "virile" thugs she has to put up with in town. Ironically enough, More finds a way to make peace with all the town's diverse citizens, including all manner of upright men and women, thugs, and the Native Americans. With its happy spoof of an ending, the unlikely couple, More and Mansfield, end up at the altar. *The Sheriff of Fractured Jaw* was an impressive hit with moviegoers on its release in October 1958, first in the United Kingdom and then the United States, and gave Walsh his last true box-office success.

Walsh stayed in the comedic mode, taking what Fox offered him in the way of inferior scripts, and closed out the decade with a trifle of a comedy called *A Private's Affair,* a story that Fox purchased in 1953 from the writer Ray Livingston Murphy. Initially called *The Love Maniac,* then *The Form Divine,* then, once again, *A Private's Affair* (although *The Love Maniac* was still used as an alternate title when it was released), the story circulated around the studio for a long time. When I. A. L. Diamond, one of several writers who worked on the script, put it on Darryl Zanuck's desk that same year, Zanuck wrote a note on the front page, saying he didn't need to read it at that point. He instructed Diamond and the others to keep it in their files; he'd read it later. Although many hands worked on the script, Winston Miller produced a final draft screenplay by January 21, 1959, long after Zanuck's departure.

When Walsh began shooting the picture in mid-March of that year, the studio still referred to it as *The Love Maniac. A Private's Affair* (its official moniker) seems more a television comedy than a big-screen theatrical release. Fox obviously wanted to make use of its young contract actors and saw the romp as a good vehicle for many of them. Sal Mineo, Barry Coe, and Gary Crosby (Bing's son, who enjoyed a short-lived movie career at the time) play three privates in the U.S. Army who, shortly after they are inducted, get involved in mildly funny run-around schemes that involve (not surprisingly) putting on a musical show, a case of mistaken identity, and marriage plans that go awry in several different directions simultaneously. Coe and the newcomer Christine Carère (a French ingénue whom Fox had just featured in its romantic weepie *A Certain Smile* but whose career ultimately plummeted) were paired as the comedy's lead couple. Also on hand are Jessie Royce Landis, Barbara Eden, Terry Moore, and Jim Backus. When the *New York Times* critic shook his finger at the picture, he noted, "The antics get even wilder as [the picture] bounces along." But the most charitable point he could make was that the powers at Fox "did a good deed in giving employment to a clutch of eager, young, decorative performers who cavort about in this light-weight imbroglio."[17]

These light comedies that Walsh directed late in the decade are throwbacks to the Paramount comedies of the late 1930s, although, at this late point in his career, Walsh no longer sported his *director of musicals* moniker. As those earlier Paramount comedies also showed, these 1950s romps indicate a director in large part disengaged from a studio that nurtures his finest storytelling instincts. They also point to the deep changes taking place in the studio system. Television had already chipped away at the big screen's audience, despite the introduction of CinemaScope and huge spectacles (which, ironically, may even have hastened the chipping—e.g., money-chewing disasters such as Fox's Taylor-Burton vehicle *Cleopatra* to come). Twenty years previously to *A Private's Affair,* Walsh's comedies could not have been compared to television products, but now they might very well be. These were thin comedies, not the weighty dramatic products of early television.

To make matters worse, Walsh lost good friends in the 1950s. Bogie passed away in 1957 from lung cancer, and Errol Flynn abandoned his good friend and "Uncle" in 1959. Mary never shared Walsh's affection for Flynn. In fact, she hated him, ever since the night in the 1950s he became a father and, instead of going to the hospital for the birth, stayed at the Walshes' Toluca Lake house with them drinking all night. Walsh's attendance as one of the pallbearers at Flynn's October 1959 funeral was too large an event not to contribute to his reverie about the changing face of Hollywood. But his adventures were nowhere near finished; he had a store of sadness he needed to escape.

15

The Adventure Is Larger
Than the Man

In this early poem to his wife, Walsh enjoys catching Mary's youthful,
voluptuous body, her ripeness and joy; not only are they a pleasure to
him, but they also reflect on him and the kind of virility a woman such
as Mary would love:

> I called to the house "Hello":
>   And at the door there did appear
> A lass who set my world aglow,
>   What e'er she said I did not hear;
> For suddenly the lightning flashed
>   As my heart thundered in my chest;
> Her lips, her cheeks, her eyes, her hair
>   Were rainbow colors at their best,
> Her body was a sculptor's dream,
>   With ripeness round and so alive
> With youth and joy that it did seem
>   Without her near I could not survive.
> I, who knew the world's beauties,
>   The glamour girls of the silver screen,
> Part of a director's duties . . .
>   But such a woman I'd never seen.
> This heart of mine so long free,
>   So long pursued but never lost,
> I surrendered to her instantly,
>   Willingly and gladly, what e'er the cost;
> It was thus I met Mary.[1]

Walsh sees himself as vigorous, masculine, sexual. He has known great beauties and appreciates them still. He would never want to lose that sense of himself. Now, approaching his midseventies, he saw himself as someone who still had adventures to seek, films to be made—those things being, of course, one and the same. In this poem, he holds on to, not only his wife's beauty, but also the man she has loved. Paths still lie open.

By the 1960s, Walsh had to travel many of those paths without Mary by his side as she was by now weary of traveling. She wanted to stay at home, tending to her animals and to their gardens and numerous orange trees. Those trees were becoming famous as the subject of many stories written by many visiting writers—Peter Bogdanovich, Richard Schickel, and others—who, on arriving at the Walsh residence in Simi Valley to visit and write about the older Walsh, were offered a glass of Mary's freshly squeezed orange juice before they even sat down, before Walsh proceeded to lament the encroachment of the freeway on his once-beautiful, once-expansive Simi Valley property nestled in the Santa Susana Mountains. Mary wanted to stay in California, but Walsh wanted to continue his adventures in the movies and was off to Rome, Japan, and other countries. He was alone, and he missed Mary for many reasons, even though one reason took precedent over them all—his failing eyesight

Unlike Walsh's hero Ben Allison in *The Tall Men,* whose heartbreak lay in his past, Walsh's heartbreak lay waiting for him in his future. Ben is a man revered by no one more than Walsh himself, and to behave as bravely as Ben in the face of grief had to be, for Walsh, the only path. As Walsh's one remaining eye deserted him, leaving him in almost total blindness the last years of his life, he had little choice but to call on those fictional men he created to know how to live—young George Custer, Horatio Hornblower, Gentleman Jim Corbett, and Ben Allison. After all, they came from his camera, his psychology, and were in his imagination still. They were *his* stories of himself.

Mid-June 1960 found Walsh in Rome—an opportune location to film given the strikes going on in Hollywood; the clash between the unions and the producers lasted at least through the first half of 1960. Walsh was now producing *Esther and the King* for Fox—which paid him $100,000—and his good pal John Twist acted as his associate producer.

Deviating from biblical history, Walsh saw the story of Esther as a love triangle between the beautiful Hebrew woman Esther (Joan Collins), her young lover, Simon (Rik Battaglia), and King Ahasuerus of Persia (Richard Egan). Although engaged to marry Simon when the story begins, Esther is abducted by the king's men and taken to the palace, where, eventually, she falls in love with the king. She agrees to marry him, and her actions ultimately save her people. Along the way, the king must also confront Haman, a confidant who betrays him until Ahasuerus has him assassinated at the story's conclusion. In his notes on the film's characters, Walsh saw Esther as "a girl of great beauty with a 'light in her' and an element of spirituality." He thought that there should be in Ahasuerus "a simplicity about this big, muscular warrior." There should be "no pompousness in him": "He is always more soldier than king. . . . A man of quick, dangerous violence, but capable of love and justice."[2] Ahasuerus was another expression of Walsh's hero, this time in the sands of Persia instead of riding on the American frontier.

A little-known writer, Michael Elkins, who hailed from Lichtenstein, produced an early screenplay for *Esther and the King* in February 1960. Two months later, Walsh wrote a story outline and added some comments on the front page of the script about the story's weaknesses. "It is especially important to emphasize a dangerous risk and a great sacrifice—and the memorial day of Purim," he wrote. "So let us establish something for Esther to sacrifice. I do not believe it is any distortion of the Testament to try to create what happened backstage—and what probably *did* happen. It would seem incredible that a girl of Esther's beauty did not have some young man in love with her. Hence, the building up of the script's character of Simon which provides the missing element of triangle-conflict which this story has always needed for theatrical dramatization." Walsh added, "I can find nothing in the Book of Esther indicating that Esther's joining of the beauty contestants was voluntary. To the contrary the Scripture states, 'Esther was also TAKEN into the palace and put IN CUSTODY of Hegai who had a charge of the women."

In early June, Walsh revised the script the way he liked it, and by the end of the month, he and Elkins produced a final-draft shooting script. Walsh shot the picture at Titanus Appia Studios in Rome. He assured the Fox front office that he could make the picture in six or seven weeks because, he emphasized, in Italy they shot on Saturdays. The studio was banking on Walsh's words. As it turned out, production lasted until September 1960.[3]

A letter from the producer Sid Rogell to the Fox casting director Lew Schreiber on July 8, 1960, noted that Walsh was unhappy with the actress Daniela Rocca, who played Queen Vashti. He thought that she was neither an accomplished performer nor a dancer, and he wanted to use a double in a scene where she actually had to dance. This caused quite a rift, but Walsh had his way. More trouble occurred when he took a line of dialogue away from Rocca and gave it to another actress. According to the production files, the girl objected strongly, especially when Walsh decided that he would have to "play her in bed" (meaning not let her move around too much in front of the camera), just as he had to do with Theda Bara years before (whom he apparently thought had less talent than he led Bara to believe).[4]

Mary accompanied Walsh to Rome but stayed only a brief time before returning to Los Angeles. Lonely, Walsh would phone her when he could and also wrote her frequently. In one letter he said:

Dearest Gip,

I was so lonesome last night I had to talk to you; am feeling better today—start the picture the 20th and hope to finish Sept. First. Then home—to you and the little fellows—However, will phone you from time to time and let you know about coming back & me. The script is finished and I have selected a good cast. Have interviewed about one hundred Italians and believe I have the best—the weather here is getting warmer and have had some rain. I see a lot of Dick [Richard Egan] and his wife [Patricia Hardy] and the baby is real cute. He likes the script very much. Eve gets here Sunday and John [Twist] is very happy. He has taken a violent dislike to all black poodles. We took Reggi some steak last night. Well, Gip, I love you more each day and miss you all the time. Write me and take good care of yourself.

All my love, Papa[5]

On July 18, 1960, Warners sent Walsh's agent, Herb Brenner, a note letting him know that Walsh had agreed in 1956 to direct a picture for them called *Bury Them Together,* which he was to begin on August 29, 1960, and complete by January 15, 1961. Ten days earlier, Warner had written Walsh personally asking him to cancel that picture; he did, and it never came to pass. Since Walsh was still in Rome shooting *Esther and the King,* Mary acted as signatory in his absence, sealing a deal with Universal to have the studio distribute Walsh's upcoming production *Come September,* scheduled to begin shooting in Rome in 1961, which was to star Rock Hudson and Gina Lollabrigida. Walsh would go uncredited as the film's producer.

Walsh always spoke casually about *Esther and the King:*

> I shot the film in six weeks. There was a writers' strike in Hollywood, and Fox had to get a film out very quickly. Mr. Skouras [Spyros Skouras, president of Fox at the time] and Buddy Adler asked me to do them a favor and make a film very quickly for them, because they had nothing at all, the studios were practically shut. That's why we made *Esther* in Italy. Working conditions were very different from Hollywood. Those guys, the Italians, work hard enough though. And I had the chance of using a very good cameraman, Mario Bava, who works very quickly. He is a master of everything that concerns lighting. He could do marvelous things with only the smallest amount of light.[6]

Mario Bava was Walsh's right-hand man, the two working seamlessly as an integrated team.

Fox released *Esther and the King* in December 1960. In an era saturated with wide-screen, big-budgeted biblical epics—and with Joseph Mankiewicz's *Cleopatra* about to eat up the budget of numerous Fox productions—*Esther and the King* performed poorly at the box office. But there was more to it. Some of the most scathing critical remarks noted that the story of Esther had been transformed into a crude costume parade that at times came close to looking like a lineup of Las Vegas showgirls waiting to wind the Persian king. Each review, one even suggesting that Walsh's direction looked almost funny, put one more nail in the coffin. The film has never been able to gain a good enough reputation to rise above the criticism. It did well in France, however, and helped Walsh gain a reputation there.

But Walsh kept leaning forward—at the same time as he gave more thought to his inevitable retirement. He and Mary bought their Simi Valley ranch in 1960 but let it sit before they built on it in 1963. In the meantime, by spring 1961, Walsh had an idea for a picture Fox would release as *Marines, Let's Go!*—a rehashed but also updated scenario Walsh liked, first essayed with *What Price Glory?* over thirty years earlier. He thought he might recover the magic that had recently deserted him with another marine tale. He wrote an original story for *Marines,* coscripting it with John Twist. Fox gave the go-ahead, and by May 1961 Walsh had flown to Kyoto for location shooting. He would also produce the picture—with an estimated budget of $2 million. Over the years, both Walsh and his films enjoyed great popularity in Japan; *High Sierra* and *White Heat,* for example, had never waned in popularity there.

On location in Kyoto, Walsh described the picture to the *New York Herald Tribune* reporter Walter Briggs as a story about U.S. Marines "fighting the Reds in Korea and loving the local belles while on 'rest and recuperation' leave in Japan." The action would be robust and fast-paced. Walsh also said that he liked using a cast of relatively unknown actors—including Tom Tryon, Tom Reese, and David Hedison. "I'm trying to break in some new faces to get youth and virility into the picture," he told Briggs. "In Hollywood movies we've got old men making love to twenty-year-old girls," Walsh said. These guys were old men in the 1930s. Walsh expected the newcomers to be as popular as McLaglen and Lowe's marines in *What Price Glory?* He said, "The audiences will really go for what these character do, no matter how outlandish. These are sympathetic characters because they're on borrowed time. They're going right back into the war."[7] At this early point, he believed that the picture would find an audience. He saw it as a buoyant, infectiously likable tale of three marines' misadventures in Japan. He had convinced himself that this was, again, another *What Price Glory?* He still lived so fully in his earlier prototype of male adventure and camaraderie that he no longer could see where it had ceased.

Walsh took along with him his new secretary, Hisayo Kawahara (later Hisayo Graham, after she married), a UCLA student who was bilingual and would help him with translation in Japan. Graham's first challenge was to teach all the Chinese actors Fox had hired how to speak with a Japanese accent—it seemed that the studio didn't know the difference between a Chinese and a Japanese actor. According to Graham, Fox paid these actors less money than the records indicated; she noticed that the studio cooked the books on the picture, charging out its production as being costlier than it really was.[8]

When Walsh arrived in Japan, he was treated like royalty. "Directors were even more respected in Japan than actors," Graham later said. When Walsh first arrived, she remembered, "it was the rainy season, and when he showed up at the hotel you could see all these umbrellas rushing toward him to get him into the building quickly." When Mary later visited Walsh on location, Graham recalled that she wore a fur coat, and when all the umbrellas rushed toward Walsh and left Mary standing in the rain, she decided right then and there that she hated the country. "You have to be a man to go there," she told Graham.[9]

The U.S. government gave Walsh permission to shoot on the marine base just at the foot of Mount Fuji in Okinawa for a huge battle scene he had lined up. He was also offered the use of U.S. soldiers as extras, but at the last minute the marines had to pull out for Laos, leaving Walsh with no troops. Although offered a few men and some tanks that hadn't been deployed, he didn't have enough to get the results he wanted. His enthusiasm didn't last long, couldn't sustain him. Not only were logistics working against him; he had to acknowledge that his and Twist's characters and misadventures were paper thin. "It just wasn't any good," he later said. He put up a good front, publicly at least, Graham said, "but he knew the film wasn't very good."[10] The reviewers concurred after Fox released *Marines, Let's Go!* on August 15, 1961. The critic for the *Dallas Morning News* considered the picture "dated, corny, juvenile and thoroughly predictable."[11] Another of Walsh's late films darted out into moviegoers' laps as a disappointment. His timing was on track; his material lagged far behind.

To outsiders, Walsh seemed to take the negative reviews in stride, but he had to understand that he was changing, however slowly. He was going back to Warner Bros. to fulfill his three-picture contract. At first, the studio assigned him a picture called *The Deathmakers,* the story of an American tank force during World War II scripted by Halstad Welles and based on Glen Sire's novel. Burt Lancaster was to be featured. Walsh looked forward to shooting the picture in Germany, but then Jack Warner replaced it with what he considered a more prestigious picture—he wanted Walsh to direct *PT 109*, a wartime adventure based on a best seller recounting President John F. Kennedy's harrowing but heroic (the hue chosen by the Kennedy family) experiences during World War II. The story by now had become legend, beginning years earlier with the adventure's lavish treatment in magazines, in books, and on television. John Kennedy was so pleased with Robert J. Donovan's *PT 109: John Kennedy in World War Two* that he pressed his father, Joseph Kennedy, who still had his Hollywood ties, to call up his old pal Jack Warner to get the wheels spinning on a film adaptation.

Warner started the wheels going right away, putting the veteran producer Bryan W. Foy (one of the original seven little Foys) on the case. Foy had earned the moniker *keeper of the Bs* since he ran Warners' famed B-picture unit. He had produced the fame-making 1943 *Guadalcanal Diary* and, more recently, the 1951 *I Was a Communist for the FBI*. First, Warner and Foy went to John Ford to direct *PT 109* since he had directed the only other picture about PT boats, 1945's *They Were Expendable*. But Ford passed on the project. Warner decided that Walsh would direct. Who better for a war film contingent on huge battle scenes and lots of action? Now the world would see Kennedy's story—again. Walsh and the studio went into preproduction mode.

By January 15, 1962, Walsh and Bryan Foy had been in Florida for about two weeks to scout locations for the pictures and had come back pretty satisfied. Warren Beatty was approached to play Kennedy, but he declined; then Peter Fonda (he had the clout of the Fonda name) was tested for the part of Kennedy, but he also declined. By now, Walsh knew Florida as well as he knew the business—but he was about to step into much more than a swamp: he was in for the surprise of his life. The alligators in this picture's swamp stalked territory far above the water.

White House press secretary Pierre Salinger established an ad hoc committee to oversee information going to support the film. Its other member was George Stevens Jr. (the son of the famed director George Stevens), who had just been appointed associate director of the U.S. Information Agency for Motion Pictures. Stevens arrived in Washington, DC, in January 1962 and became intricately involved in the process of deciding who would direct *PT 109*. Even though Walsh was already slated, Stevens aimed to change that. He was not a fan of *Marines, Let's Go!* Nor did he think Walsh the right man for the job. To him, Walsh was past his prime and not up to producing the tough, prestigious kind of picture this story needed. (George Stevens Sr. was sent a synopsis of *PT 109,* yet it is unknown to what extent this meant he might have been a candidate to direct—a misguided choice for sure since he was not a war-picture director. This may or may not have influenced his son to screen *Marines, Let's Go!* at the White House.) *Marines, Let's Go!* was an odd choice to show Kennedy since it is a comedy, not a war picture, and would have given little indication of the kind of war story Walsh would direct—something Stevens surely knew.

On seeing *Marines, Let's Go!* Stevens "was relieved" when Kennedy halted the screening "with a sailor-ly exclamation of 'Tell Jack Warner to go fuck himself.'"[12] Stevens disliked Kennedy's suggestions for a replacement for Walsh—either Fred Zinnemann or John Huston—a response that angered Foy. Nevertheless, Warner sent Walsh a check for $100,000 with an explanation saying nothing more than "circumstances beyond the control of each of us."[13] Jack Warner later tried to get Zinnemann for the job, but the director passed on the project. After a brief time on the picture, Lewis Milestone left it (he complained about never having worked at a studio that trusted him less than Warners did), and a young Leslie H. Martinson, who later directed for television, took Milestone's place. Martinson, along with the actor Cliff Robertson, who played Kennedy, failed to please moviegoers with the finished film. It has gone down as a misfired and mediocre moment in Warner Bros. history.

Months later, the studio had to decide how to write off the $100,000 sent to Walsh. On July 13, 1962, Steve Trilling decided to charge the figure "to the *PT 109* production." "At the present time there is no indication we will want to apply it to another picture, nor do we want to charge [it] off to overhead."[14] For his part, Walsh never commented publicly about the fiasco. It takes little to imagine Jack Warner's position: firing his close friend but bowing to pressure from Washington and a possibly robust box-office return. Walsh told friends soon after that he didn't want to direct the picture with the president still alive.

By now, Walsh and Mary were living on their Simi Valley ranch. After the *PT 109* incident, Walsh understood on some deep level that his position in the industry had shifted. It could have been that foreknowledge, coupled with that loner instinct that had always defined him more deeply than any other, that prompted him to leave Toluca Lake for Simi, a much further distance from the Hollywood lifestyle he barely allowed himself to have in the first place. "Walsh wanted to go to Simi," Graham later recalled, "but Mary didn't." When the Walshes finally built on their Simi property and moved into their new house in 1963, Mary became a different person—and she never recovered from the change. "She became bitter and almost seemed to withdraw into herself," Graham said. "She used to like to dress up and have lunch with the girls when she and Walsh lived in Toluca Lake; now she lost interest in all that."[15] It helped that Rock Hudson would come to visit; he would rather go shopping with Mary than stay and visit with Walsh.

The Simi house pleased Walsh: it was smaller than the one in Toluca Lake. He wanted it that way; he didn't especially want visitors staying over. The wood-paneled ranch-style home had a swimming pool in back, a myriad of orange trees and magnolia bushes on the grounds, and acres of property so that Walsh could bring his horses back from the stables he rented and have them close to him. The cook they had had in Toluca Lake retired now, and Mary did all the cooking herself. To compensate for her losses, Mary surrounded herself with even more dogs and cats—and other assorted small creatures—than she had had in the Toluca Lake house. The stream of pets coming and going in Simi was endless. She also spent more time managing Walsh's affairs. Although he understood how to budget a motion picture, he didn't really understand budgeting when it came to his private life—decades of horse-betting debts were proof enough of that. She was trying to prevent them from going bankrupt because of Walsh's continuing investments in horses.

Walsh didn't like parties, and he and Mary never attended them. He was more isolated now, but no matter who saw him or who didn't, he never lost his love of wearing custom-made clothes, a habit ingrained in him by his haberdasher father. It was as if he half expected someone to drop by—little had changed over the years. If he didn't travel to England, Europe, or some other foreign destination to buy suits, he had them custom made in Los Angeles. Never mind that they might seem at odds with the cowboy bent in him (he never left the bedroom without his cowboy boots).

Hank Kilgore, Mary's nephew, spent much of his childhood with his aunt and uncle. Kilgore remembered Walsh wearing cowboy boots no matter where he was. Once, when he was no more than five years old, Kilgore took his uncle's boots, put them on, and walked straight down the steps of the swimming pool in the Walsh's backyard. "I could see that he was angry, but he never yelled at me. He held in the anger and tried to explain how important those boots were to him. He asked that I please not do that again."[16]

A Distant Memory

Around this time, Warner Bros. sent Walsh Charles Schnee's estimating script for *The Marauders;* the studio wanted him to direct it as a replacement for *PT 109,* closing out the three-picture contract hanging over him for so long. But that picture never went into production. Instead, the studio replaced it with what would be the final picture of Walsh's career, a western called *A Distant Trumpet.* Fittingly, he would make it for Jack Warner. Rumors spread that Walsh was considered too old to be insured for the picture and that Warner posted the bond himself, but nothing in the film's production files supports this claim, although it would not be out of character for Warner to make this gesture for his old friend, especially to assuage the guilt he had over firing Walsh from *PT 109.*

When there was a finished script ready to go, *A Distant Trumpet* would evolve the same way as the first picture Walsh ever directed—and all the pictures since. Every action, every sequence, was committed to memory before he walked onto the set. Long before Walsh came on the scene, Laurence Harvey had plans to produce and star in a screen adaptation of Paul Horgan's popular book of the same name published in 1960. Steve Trilling sent word to Jack Warner on August 1, 1960, that Alan LeMay was interested and available; Harry Brown, the coscriptor of George Stevens's *A Place in the Sun,* among other films, was also interested. But, eventually, Harvey dropped out, and Richard Fielder and Albert Beich adapted Horgan's novel. Later, John Twist was brought in to write the final script. The studio had Leslie H. Martinson set to direct, but in an ironic twist, he was soon out of the picture.

Steve Trilling wanted to hire Walsh. He wrote to William H. Wright, the producer of *A Distant Trumpet,* on January 15, 1963, "Following are suggestions for a director for *A Distant Trumpet,* listed roughly in order of preference but without regard for price or availability: Gordon Douglas, Raoul Walsh, John Sturges, Jacques Tourneur, Phil Carlson, George Sherman, David Miller, Michael Anderson, Guy Green, Delbert Mann, Robert Parrish, Roy Rowland. Note that Raoul Walsh appears high on the list, despite the fact that you said that the picture was 'not his cup of tea.' Perhaps it would be if there were more sugar in it.'"[17]

The sugar was poured, and Walsh came on board in January 1963. The studio paid him $35,000 for twenty-three weeks' work. Walsh took the cast and crew to shoot in Flagstaff, Arizona, and then to Gallup, New Mexico, for location shooting, which began on August 16, 1963, finishing two months later on September 11, 1963.

When Walsh first read the script, he immediately thought of John Wayne. But, instead, he was slated to work with young actors the studio believed would bring in young audiences. The western featured Troy Donahue and his next wife, Suzanne Pleshette, both enormously popular with young viewers at the time, especially coming off their megahit *Rome Adventure* two years earlier. But the two have difficulty carrying the Walsh banner, partly because of their monotone performances, but also because John Twist's script runs on a slow and superficial register. Although Twist had written and tinkered with scripts alongside Walsh for decades, in this case for sure the two men were unable to see when a story looked implausible or just plain hollow. They were such good friends that they couldn't see beyond that.

Donahue plays the U.S. Cavalry lieutenant Matt Hazard, who is sent to Fort Delivery in Arizona just at the Mexican border. Attacks by Indians are an everyday occurrence outside the fort's boundaries, and Hazard is given the job of making peace with them. Once at the fort, he and Pleshette fall in love almost immediately, even though she is married and he is engaged to another woman. The story kicks up some dust when the new, older commander, General Quait (played by James Gregory), arrives and, after launching an all-out attack on the Indians, gives Hazard the assignment of gaining their trust and convincing them to relocate to an Arizona reservation. Although conflict with insubordinate officers almost does him in—not to mention additional Indian attacks, offering Walsh the opportunity to stage some exciting sequences—Hazard accomplishes his goal and gets the girl in the end

(Hazard breaks his engagement, and Pleshette's husband is conveniently killed off before story's end).

The shoot was more or less unmemorable, although a memo did pass from a crew member to the producer William Wright at one point indicating, "At a party [one night] Troy Donohue did a dirty pantomime of an astronaut." "Don't know how he does it," the writer went on, "but [Troy] pursues his hobby [partying] all night, gets two or three hours' sleep and makes his 6 A.M. calls. True, he does sleep a good bit of the time in the dressing room truck. His lines show it."[18] While Donahue may have been bastardizing his lines, Walsh was perfecting his. He made it a point to speak Navajo to the Navajo actors hired to play Apaches in the film. When it came time to shoot a cavalry battle against the Indians, the 300 Navajo warriors and 125 soldiers (who were actually local Gallup horsemen and students from the University of New Mexico at Albuquerque) received their acting cues from Walsh as he sat a half mile away sending messages via tiny earplug radios. His orders came down the pike both in English and in Navajo.

Walsh's cinematographer was William Clothier, who worked often for John Ford (he had most recently shot *The Man Who Shot Liberty Valence* and *Donovan's Reef* for him). He took to Walsh as if he had known him his entire life. "He was a great guy, just a great guy," Clothier later said. "That was his last film. He was a great storyteller. He used to keep me in stitches. We used to get along terrifically. Anything I wanted to do was OK with him. He'd pick out a long shot, he'd say, 'You want to get this shot?' I'd set up, say, 'Look in the camera,' [and] he'd say, 'Shoot it, looks good.'" Clothier told the story of the caricature he had of Walsh in which Walsh is sitting in his chair, waving his cigarette: Clothier says, "Say, Raoul, I don't have the actors in the picture but the clouds look terrific." "Great shot, Bill," Walsh says. "Looks much better that way."[19] Clothier said, "I was in love with the old man. It's a shame I didn't know him earlier, because he was such a nice guy to get along with. . . . He told me about the time he married an Indian gal and everything was great until they got up one morning and her parents had pitched a teepee in the back yard, and he decided to get rid of her. Raoul was a wonderful man to work with; he was like Wellman, or like Ford. He knew exactly what he wanted and that's what he wanted, and it's that simple with people like that."[20] Clothier also wondered whether in some ways—especially in setting up the strategy of large battle scenes (the sequences were that beautiful)—Walsh might not be superior to Ford and Hawks.

Even before completing *A Distant Trumpet*, Walsh, now seventy-six, felt invigorated and eager to direct another western. He knew Donahue meant box office. William Wright wrote to Steve Trilling on September 1963,

> Raoul Walsh told me today that he would like to make another outdoor picture with Troy Donahue. I told him about a new book called *Monte Walsh* by Jack Schaefer, which I read some months ago in galleys. Raoul asked why the book had not already been bought. I surmised that its long chronology, which takes its hero from the age of 16 to his death in his 50s, made it difficult to dramatize, but I told him I thought I knew how to do it by shortening the time lapses. He said that he would like to read the book. Should I get him a copy? You may hesitate about buying another western for Troy Donahue until the box-office returns on *A Distant Trumpet* give us a verdict on how the public likes him in such a vehicle—a verdict which may be a year away.[21]

When Warners released *A Distant Trumpet* at the end of May 1964, the mediocre box-office and critical reception may have cheated Troy Donahue out of his next Walsh western, but it is doubtful. Walsh never directed *Monte Walsh*. The picture was made—it starred Lee Marvin and was directed by William A. Fraker—but it came to the screen six years later, in 1970. By then, Walsh's directing days were long over, and Donahue's popularity had severely plummeted.

A Distant Trumpet marked the culmination of changes a long time coming in Walsh's career and in the film industry itself. The studio system had virtually disappeared by the early 1960s, leaving actors, directors, and producers roaming about in freelance situations (an image, if set on the frontier, Walsh would condone). For one thing, in an effort to keep up with the changing face of American public taste, Warner Bros. no longer bore its distinctive style, showering audiences with celluloid images of social misfits and hard-knocks loners. CinemaScope, Technicolor, WarnerColor, and Panavision—all these new technologies

changed the look of storytelling on the big screen. And many of the
iconic actors Walsh had worked with had died or retired. Walsh successfully kept up with the times, yet doing so often meant using a less
convincing actor such as a Troy Donahue instead of a Gary Cooper or
an Errol Flynn, which presented serious challenges to a picture's believability factor. The picture Walsh made his last also marked, ironically,
the changing map of movie faces, even in the background. Many veteran
cowboys worked on *A Distant Trumpet* "for the last time as a group,
playing cavalrymen who attempt to fight off an Indian attack."[22]

Walsh begins *A Distant Trumpet* with his signature shot, panning
across a huge natural vista of mountain ranges, snow-covered hills,
deep valleys—a natural backdrop in which a lone human figure rides,
so small that he is dwarfed by the nature surrounding him. Walsh fans
have commented that, much as in Michelangelo Antonioni's expansive
landscapes, in Walsh's the natural environment substitutes, or perhaps
speaks, for the emotions of that lone human being. More to the point,
however, in Walsh's body of work that human is dwarfed by the natural
vista because the vista always holds out the possibility of adventure—and
the adventure is always larger than the man. Its largeness holds unseen
promises, unseen places to reach, and unseen roads to travel. To the very
end, Walsh's cinema attempts to take men and women—and him—away
from misery, sadness, and adversity. It is the peaks of *High Sierra,* the
mountain ranges of *Pursued, Colorado Territory,* and *The Tall Men,*
even the steaming terrain of *Objective, Burma!* and the doomed but still
open range of *They Died with Their Boots On.* The open vista provides
the only landscape a Walshian character will inhabit if he or she wants
to feel truly free—not unlike Walsh himself.

Walsh saw the end of his filmmaking career staring him in the face. After
the mid-1960s, he had very few projects to consider. As he told Hisayo
Graham, he could no longer get good scripts. After *A Distant Trumpet*
was released, he was scheduled to make a picture in Japan for Fox, his
friend Pierre Rissient, the French film producer, recalled. "At a certain
point [maybe even before *Trumpet*] he was thinking of casting Stephen
Boyd in [a picture]. . . . [But] he was pretty off by that time."[23] Then there
was the notice that Walsh wanted to direct a picture called *Jack of All
Trades* to feature Dennis Hopper.[24] There was also a comedy with Jackie

Gleason and the Mexican superstar Cantinflas. This was to be shot in Japan, but Gleason refused to fly on a plane to get there. Neither of these projects came to anything. Nor did anything come of Walsh's brief attachment to the western *Rio Lobo,* which eventually became the 1970 John Wayne vehicle, the final film directed by Howard Hawks.

But, after Walsh visited Japan to shoot *Marines, Let's Go!* he developed a great affection for the country and its people—he liked the springs there and in Taiwan. In addition to his long-standing passion for horses, he had now developed a great interest in Akita dogs, difficult to get in the United States in the early 1960s. He returned to Japan to purchase an Akita and spent a month there to complete the necessary paperwork before bringing home a four-month-old puppy that he named Aki. But there was a price he hadn't counted on. While he was in Japan, Mary was convinced that he was having an affair there. After he returned and the dog went through the necessary quarantine, Mary refused to keep it in the house. Distraught, Walsh called Graham, who had gotten married the year before (Walsh gave her away at her wedding) and was living in Palos Verdes, south of Los Angeles. He told her that Mary had kicked him and the dog out of the house and that he had thrown some of his things into the car and left. Graham met him (he told her he did not want anyone to recognize him, so they met at a hotel). He asked her whether she and her husband would buy the dog and keep it at their house. When she agreed, Walsh said that he would visit the dog whenever he could. But, after his first visit, he cried miserably; he missed Aki so much, according to Graham, that he never visited the pup again. This was a repeat of Walsh's experience with a lion he had owned when he lived on Petit Drive in Encino during his marriage to Lorraine. He kept the lion on the property for as long as he could, but as it grew bigger, he had to give it up—he donated it to the San Diego Zoo. He was terribly broken up about it, and though he tried to visit it at the zoo, he was too overwhelmed by sadness and stopped himself. This was why he could never visit Graham and her husband again. The couple had to go to Walsh's house if they wanted to get together. They had his beloved Aki (who eventually became a blue-ribbon winner). "I'll never go back," he told Graham.[25]

His emotional attachments to animals—which, despite the Aki episode, he and Mary deeply shared and which, little known, he also shared earlier with William Randolph Hearst—spoke of a part of Walsh he tried to keep hidden. He often felt broken—an emotional response to the trauma of losing a loved one early on—but just as successfully deferred the sad feeling by jumping into the adventure of making a picture. His long-standing passion for horses was one avenue of emotional softness that he allowed himself to show publicly. Often hiding his feelings, he was a loner, Graham said, "but he put on a good show."[26]

In late 1964, the producer Nat Holt offered Walsh a western television series situated in nineteenth-century San Francisco, something Rissient recalled Walsh telling him. But Walsh was not interested in directing for the small screen and turned him down. Slowly but surely, the picture business dried up for Walsh. Mary told Rissient that it was very difficult for Walsh when he realized he would never direct another picture again; it hit him hard.[27]

"I'm a lone wolf in this business," Walsh told Hedda Hopper in an interview in January 1965. He made an issue of his more isolated lifestyle at his Simi ranch:

> Like all the Irish [he would call himself "the other Irishman" to John Ford], I like to have horses around. Our ranch is in Simi Valley. It was blowing a gale up there this morning—but nice and clear—a warm desert window, like the Santa Anas we used to have here. . . . I spend a lot of time traveling now. I have friends in Japan who want me to make pictures there. I have a good story but need Cantinflas and Jackie Gleason—but Gleason won't fly. And it takes fourteen days by boat to Japan. His manager agreed that this story is the kind that would put him on top in pictures. . . . I just turned down a picture because I didn't want to make it in Rome. I fly all over then go back to the ranch and the horses. . . . I expect to stay here for a while. The mares will foal in February and March. I love the ranch and love living there.[28]

He was not out of the business just yet; he and John Twist wrote a script that Walsh initially thought he might direct, but they sold it to Frank Sinatra shortly after that. Sinatra decided to direct *None but the Brave* himself, and Twist received coscreenwriting credit.

Walsh had always been extremely health conscious; the stories about his hard drinking (the "laughing water" he said he drank with so many buddies) was one more good story but hardly the truth. And though he was always close to John Ford even if he wasn't part of the Ford clan fishing trips, he preferred to stay home in the evenings and read instead of spending his time out drinking with an entourage. By the mid-1960s, however, Walsh had become nostalgic for the old days of Hollywood. He showed his deep disillusionment with the current film industry trends when he told Hopper, "Cooper, Gable, Flynn—all gone at once—it left a big hole. The Academy Awards are now a joke—a songwriter's holiday. It's, 'What song can we get him or her to sing?' This used to be a place out of the Arabian Nights in earlier times—now the so-called stars go around dressed like bums—in old jeans. It's unbelievable." When Hopper asked him where Hollywood was going to find new stars, he said, "Not from TV—all they have is a mop of hair—and many look a bit on the feminine side—no virility. We used to have a barn where we would box, we used to run—to ride—to keep fit. Now when they film a fight there are doubles all over the place—we never used to do that."[29]

Although Rissient had been corresponding with Walsh since the time of *Band of Angels,* they became closer in 1964, and Rissient came out to California to visit. He recalled that Walsh took him to the Santa Anita Race Track. The two men went over to where the horses were held, and Walsh was enjoying touching them. He asked Rissient whether he wanted to bet on them. Rissient told him he had no money. Walsh said that was all right; he would give him the money. Rissient still said no, so Walsh bet alone. "Four times out of five he won," Rissient later said, incredulous. Also on that visit, the two men went to the Gaslight Club on La Cienega in Beverly Hills and "smoked cigars and cigarettes." They had quite a time then. Rissient also recalled an incident that showed him Walsh's sense of humor. The two men were at a gathering, and a woman "about the age of sixty-four and wearing a mini skirt" approached them. She was talking heavily about film theory, which the United States had just discovered. She asked Walsh why his movies had so many crowd scenes in them, and she urged Walsh to give her "the semiotic answer." "You must teach us, Mr. Walsh," she implored him. Walsh answered, "I don't know . . . maybe because I come from a big family . . . the more the merrier!"[30] To get along with Raoul Walsh, Rissient said, and to get him to say more, it was better not to ask him to reflect on what he was thinking. Anything even remotely intellectual would bore him. At least that was what he offered the public.

Rissient recalled watching *The Enforcer* with Bertrand Tavernier one day and Tavernier mentioning that the picture looked as if Walsh (who was not the credited director) had directed it. It turned out that Tavernier was remarkably observant; Walsh had, in fact, directed the film. "The fact that Walsh did that without credit," Rissient noted, "was very important to French film buffs [at the time]—they had not heard of such a thing before."[31]

Walsh used to talk over his career with Rissient. He told Rissient that, while he and Lorraine had had a very busy social life and that he allowed himself to get caught up in it now and then, it was something he regretted later. Rissient thought that that explained why Walsh's Paramount films weren't so good. By the time Walsh went to Warner Bros., he had already removed himself psychologically from the marriage. His years at Warners meant a great deal to him, and now it was all winding down. The industry seemed to be changing before his eyes, and he didn't like everything he saw.[32]

"The screen has become a window on depravity," Walsh also told Hopper. "Why would they give a seal to a picture like KISS ME STUPID? They should never have let the salacious Italian and Scandinavian pictures be shown in this country in the first place. This started the trend. And it's unbelievable what's happening to the young in this country. We send missionaries to the Congo; they could do with some of them in some of the so-called dance places. And these are the people who are going to vote soon! When I made the Marine pictures with McLaglen and Lowe there was a little rough stuff, but it wasn't salacious. The studios used to protect their stars."[33] Walsh's worries for the studios ran all over the map.

After Hopper published her syndicated interview with Walsh, he wrote her, using his Raoul Walsh Enterprises, Inc. (under which no films were produced) letterhead, "Dear Hedda . . . I have just returned from Mexico. A fishing trip. Or I would have written you sooner to thank you for the nice write up. It was so kind and thoughtful of you to remember the Wild Irishman. Thanks again. And may God bless you always. Raoul."[34]

Strangely enough, one film Walsh did want to direct right after *A Distant Trumpet* was *Belle du jour*. He even went so far as to get in touch with the book's publishers in France and had begun preparing for the production. He would shoot it in Japan. But he was told that the rights had been sold to the Hakim Brothers, who became the film's producers when the Spanish director Luis Buñuel put his name to it.

By the mid- to late 1960s, French filmgoers had rediscovered American auteur directors and reinstated them in film history. The wave was a large one. Walsh himself became the subject of innumerable articles in French and English film journals. This wave of reverence unleashed a phenomenon Americans might not have thought of themselves—taking a second look at the directors they had taken for granted for decades. Beginning in the late 1960s, directors of Walsh's generation such as John Ford, Howard Hawks, Alfred Hitchcock, and Walsh himself became the subjects of retrospectives—countless exhibitions displayed at museums and universities throughout the country. The old directors, no longer really working, were available and more than willing to show up for these retrospectives when they could. Telling their stories became their new profession. Walsh soon began making appearances before adoring audiences.

Walsh had also been thinking about writing a novel for some time. Back in 1963, he'd found a brief story in the *Los Angeles Times* praising the novels of the western writer Louis L'Amour; Walsh had held on to it all this time. He underlined various passages, one in particular: "And lately, it seems, modern readers are finding Old West novels more appealing than ever. Western paperbacks—which now sell about 6 million copies a year—have enjoyed an increase in sales of nearly 20% over the last 18 months." He paid specific attention to the line saying, "Readers want to be entertained and they are curious about how other people solved their problems. . . . A good western does both."[35] Walsh had no problems to solve in public, but he still wanted to entertain others—and himself.

About 1969 or 1970, Walsh began to write his first novel, *The Wrath of the Just Ones* (initially titled *Days of Wrath*), which he dedicated to "Duke Wayne—a man as big as all outdoors, and the last living legend."[36] The book never found an American publisher but, in 1972, saw great success when it was published in France as *La colère des justes*

(The wrath of the just ones). The novel is an adventure yarn set at the close of the Civil War. Three men, each of whom has fought for the Confederacy, now head west in order to find adventure and make their fortunes. Johnny McGraw hails originally from California and, had he stayed in San Francisco, would have become the heavyweight champion boxer of the world. Jebnah, from Kentucky, studied the law before fighting in the war, and he puts his education to work for himself in his travels. Lord Wesley Connaught St. George hails from England but came to the Confederacy to fight, soon shedding his name in favor of the title "Pretty Boy." As expected, given Walsh's psychological aesthetic, the three men also come on some strong women along the way.

The characters in Walsh's novel, not unlike the characters in his films, are simply and straightforwardly etched. They embody an innate goodness of heart and of intention in the way they treat others. These fictional men are a compilation of Walsh's three uncles, who themselves set out to make their fortune after arriving in America from Ireland (whether or not they were real or imagined by Walsh), along with the characters he created on the screen: Gentleman Jim, Horatio Hornblower, and the actors Victor McLaglen, Errol Flynn, Gary Cooper, even Clark Gable. They are a chivalric group of souls, and Walsh can't help but like them as he moves them along. Somewhere in this group is Walsh himself, in as many guises as he can muster.

Rissient helped get the book to publication and later said of his work, "[It is] very impressive in terms of what happens in event and character . . . very Raoul Walsh. It's written with force as a great Raoul Walsh film. Of course Walsh would have liked it to become a script and a film. I don't think he was really thinking of directing at that time, because of his age and also because he probably realized at that time that no one would finance a picture of that magnitude directed by him. It was a big film. [The book] was very revealing of his feelings at the time. Walsh was very happy to write it."[37] The novel prepared him for another large project—his own life story.

Walsh wrote two other manuscripts. One, *Come Hell or High Water,* is another version of his Civil War manuscript. The other, *Only One Love Have I,* is a story that mirrors his life with Mary. He dedicated *Only One Love Have I* to Mary, saying, "I dedicate this story to my lovely wife who is the springtime in the autumn of my life."[38]

After that, Walsh began writing his autobiography, which Farrar Straus Giroux published in 1974. He initially titled the book *Here Lies the Truth* before changing the title to *Each Man in His Time,* using a line from Shakespeare's *Hamlet* that his friend John Barrymore inscribed on a photograph of himself after playing the part. (The inscribed photograph is reproduced in the book.) In the autobiography, Walsh approached his life as one more film script—as a huge adventure whose focus was color and fire, and run-ins with the famous and the infamous, and anecdotal humor above all. He looms larger than simply a player on the American scene and in the film industry. He emerges as a one-man adventure show, presenting himself in one rollicking adventure, one tight spot, after another.

As he might have done with James Cagney when the two rewrote and recontoured Cagney's characters in *The Roaring Twenties* and *White Heat,* Walsh shaped his life on the page to look more like a tall tale than a true account of the facts of his life. Of his three wives, Miriam Cooper, Lorraine Walker, and Mary Simpson, only Mary appears in the text—and even in his marriage to her he shape-shifts the true events, fudging them, if not outright changing them. Of his two adopted sons, Robert and Jackie, and his adopted daughter, Marilynn, there is silence all around. Written when his career as a director had ended, the autobiography was Walsh's last opportunity to imagine one more adventure taken—the greatest, the longest adventure of them all. For that, it is no less entertaining than one of his fast-moving action films. For example, in the book he recounted a story that had been circulating for years: that the day Barrymore died their mutual friend Errol Flynn was distraught. Walsh went to Malloy's Mortuary that night where Barrymore's body lay, convinced the mortician to let him borrow the body, and then propped it up at Flynn's dining room table. According to Walsh, Flynn nearly died himself after seeing Barrymore sitting in his dining room. The story has been passed around as merely legend, although Walsh's family always believed it to be true. Yet no evidence exists to support the story; it matters little whether the facts of *Each Man in His Time* are fact. They are true to Walsh; they carry great import—the signature of the freest part of himself, his greatest moment of telling a great yarn. The book packs the energy that is the essence of Raoul Walsh. In that sense, it is a true picture of Walsh, in his own words.

After he saw the autobiography published, Walsh wrote a second, far less successful novel. He wanted to see it published but never did. During this time, he was still very lively, especially when Rissient first got to know him, in the early 1960s and through the early 1970s. "He was still full of humor, great anecdotes—and pride," Rissient remembered. "Above all, he was very funny."[39]

Walsh had built a wall around himself since the mid-1960s. Rissient believed that he came out of his shell in 1972 when the retrospectives began to materialize. Until then, he had been very bitter about not working. He didn't say it, and he didn't show it, but he would much rather have worked. So, when he realized that work would not be coming his way anymore, he closed himself off and retreated to Simi Valley—just as he would toward in the last two or three years of his life.

Retrospectives of his work took him out of Simi Valley, as did invitations to appear at conferences organized to celebrate his films. Accolades carried him for the next ten years, the last decade of his life, and also triggered visits from younger scholars and filmmakers. In 1972, Walsh met Robert Bookman, a Yale law student who grew up in southern California, Walsh's home turf. Bookman later said, "I met Raoul through Dick [Richard] Schickel. We taught a class together at Yale called 'Art, Craft and Power in the American Film,' and Dick had just done a documentary called 'The Movie Crazy Years' for PBS and Raoul is interviewed in that. Out of that came the documentary for Eastman Kodak [*The Men Who Made the Movies*]. He is the one who turned me on to Raoul more than anybody else. I wouldn't know Raoul without Dick Schickel."[40] Schickel's influence went far and wide.

Bookman invited Walsh to Yale for a retrospective of his films to be held in April 1972. Walsh would also visit Richard Schickel's class at Yale and attend another at Wesleyan. After Bookman's invitation, Walsh responded by letter on March 2:

Roberto, My Lad,
    Good to hear your cheery voice on the phone the other night. As I told you, I am off to Japan for a few weeks to see the melancholy Geshisas [*sic*], also to catch up with a Japanese Producer who wants me to direct a picture in Mongolia [*sic*].

He tells me he can arrange for 1 thousand camels, 2 thousand horsemen, and many more thousands of soldiers. He also told me that the story is not yet written. I have made many trips to the Orient and enjoy their food, namely: stewed prunes, steamed lice, ladishes, lubarb, boiled mushrooms, labbit pie, lye whiskey, and then take a boat trip down liver, then go home and take rest. Write letter to Lobert at Yale University—say coming to New Haven April 13 & 14.

All the best,
Raoul[41]

After his appearance at Yale, during which students saw a screening of *They Drive by Night* and he held a question-and-answer session, Walsh was driven to Wesleyan University. The cinema professor Jeanine Basinger remembered Walsh visiting her class there. For his entrance, he stood behind a curtain, and when it parted, he walked out wearing full western garb, a holster, and a gun, which he proceeded to take out and hold up in the air. The students went wild.[42]

The Man Who Loved Women

The most satisfying part of his meeting Bob Bookman was the close friendship Walsh developed with him: he eventually called him his "number one son." Their friendship lasted until Walsh's death. Walsh often took Bookman to the races, but Mary hardly ever went with them. Said Bookman, "She never went anywhere. I never saw her leave the ranch, except one time . . . [for] Raoul's burial." Bookman recalled Mary Walsh's relationship to her husband in the early 1970s: "On one level it was caretaker. On another level, she really cared deeply about him. I was going out there at least once a month. I saw him right before he died. I was taking my dates and girlfriends out there because he fawned on them; he just loved being with young women. He was a man who loved women."[43]

Walsh's preference for kidding around with young women never waned, no matter his advancing years. When he traveled, it was often alone, so the opportunity to flirt was there. Bookman remembered, "We'd be in the hotel, and Mary had pinned different denominations of bills in different pockets and places of his coat so he knew what to do. He gave me a fifty-dollar bill, and this is a lot of money in 1972 to go out and have dinner. So Mary sends Raoul to New Haven, and he can't see [his eyesight was going]! He flew!"[44] Walsh had enough vision and enough chutzpah left in him during a Museum of Modern Art event to ask a nurse attending him briefly if she might like to join him when he took his nightly bath at the hotel.[45]

The festivals and retrospectives were a way of life now; Walsh appreciated each one of them. If nothing else, they gave him something to do, some sense of purpose. Southern Methodist University and the USA Festival in Dallas also honored Walsh, and President Nixon gave him a citation for a "lifetime of creative contributions to the motion picture industry." In October 1972, the San Francisco Film Festival paid tribute to Howard Hawks and to Walsh, both of whom attended the event. In his biography of Hawks, Todd McCarthy saw the event as a launching pad to discuss some similarities and differences between the two men whose careers paralleled each other but who never became close friends the way Walsh had become with Allan Dwan and even his legendary rival John Ford:

> While Hawks seemed quite formidable, intimidating and austere to visitors, even if he was, as always, utterly approachable, Walsh was considerably warmer and more affable. Both Pierre Rissient and his sometime publicity partner in Paris during the 1960s, Bertrand Tavernier, spent a good deal of time with both men. Tavernier placed the comparison on the intellectual and artistic plane: "I can say Walsh is a *wider* director; his interests were wide, but he . . . was never able to do anything as controlled as *To Have and Have Not* and some of Hawks's comedies. Hawks is a great director, but narrow; he always did the same three or four films. There are people who have a narrow vision of the world, and Hawks is one. You don't *feel* the world as you do in a Walsh film."[46]

Tavernier responded to a fundamental difference in the work of the two men. Hawks made the same few films repeatedly because the stories emerged—even if unknowingly—from a personal belief system around which he wrapped a story. Walsh made his stories from a conviction that movies were more about entertainment than a personal view of the world—a decision that ironically said more about him than he ever suspected.

Among the many film historians and young directors who made the trek out to Walsh's Simi Valley ranch house, Peter Bogdanovich was a frequent visitor. He interviewed Walsh twice, the first time in 1970. He remembered:

> [Walsh] was very friendly, and his wife [Mary] was very hospitable. She made us some great orange juice from oranges they had growing there. I remember the house. It was a sprawling ranch style, but not that big. The colors were a little garish . . . a little yellowy and orange. He was not that tall by then, maybe five foot ten or so. Oh, he was attractive, though, still attractive. He was very vital and funny. He was a guy. Men aren't like that anymore. He was macho but he was gentle, and he liked women. He wasn't the type of macho guy who doesn't like women that [we] mostly [have] now. He was kind of courtly.

Walsh was calling Bogdanovich Pedro by that time. Bogdanovich would call and ask how it was going since Walsh was going blind by then. Walsh would tell him, "It's tough, Pedro." "But he never complained."[47]

"[As a director] he worked on spontaneity," Bogdanovich said. "He wasn't so concerned about getting the dialogue perfect. Like many of those directors who really began in the silent era, the dialogue wasn't as important to them and they had much more ease in cutting it out than the talkie directors. The best films made in the 1930s, 1940s and 1950s were made by people who started in silent pictures. Raoul had fluidity. You never see him working."[48]

Walsh wouldn't talk about personal travails. "We didn't talk much about his personal life," Bogdanovich said. "He didn't want to talk about it [i.e., about Miriam or the two boys]. 'It's a nice day. Let's not ruin it,' [Walsh would say to practically anyone who ever mentioned Miriam's name]." Still, Bogdanovich thought that Walsh was very fond of women and heartily applauded their vitality in his movies: "I just feel that he liked women generally. He liked them vulgar and even a little crass. He liked tough women and he celebrated them in his movies, like in *Mamie Stover*. I see a movie that runs three hours and I say, Raoul could have done this in ninety minutes. There's no bullshit in his movies. He [just] told it. And the way he shot it—it was so tight and there was so much energy. *High Sierra, White Heat, The Roaring Twenties—High Sierra* has such a sense of doom." He then recalled: "At the end, he and Allan Dwan kind of shared some time together. [Then] I would call him and say, 'How's it going?' 'Pretty tough,' or 'Pretty good, Pedro,' Walsh would say. 'Old Allan came over.'"[49]

The accolades came from abroad as much as from the United States. Walsh traveled to the Cinémathèque in Paris in June 1972 to attend a retrospective of his work and, in a sense, to thank the French for the renewed interest in his pictures and his reputation. A week or so later, he was still in Paris to help promote *La colère des justes*. A journalist, Mary Blume, caught up with him in the lobby of the Paris Hilton, just around the corner from the Eiffel Tower, and wrote about him in the *International Herald Tribune*. Walsh gave her an interview and pretty much rehashed all he had been saying in other interviews for the past ten years. Blume also noted his appearance: "a windowpane plaid jacket, a neckerchief, a five-gallon hat, tiny cowboy boots and a dapper little white mustache." "Mr. Walsh looks the proper dude," she wrote, "but he isn't. He is a survivor from the old Western days when men were men and toughness was something to be proud of." The floor waiter attending Walsh at the Hilton told him he went to see *Gentleman Jim*. "One minute I laugh, one minute I cry. I never do that before."[50]

In early 1974, Charles Higham recalled going to Simi Valley to visit Walsh. He later gave an interview to the *New York Times* that was published to coincide with a retrospective held at the Museum of Modern Art. At the ranch, he found Walsh still very virile, still possessing a razor-sharp memory. One particular instance stood out: "As I arrive, Walsh's wife announces a dramatic little problem: a giant hawk has gotten caught in a bush and broken its wing. Walsh—a tall, grizzled, white-moustached man with a black patch over his right eye and wearing a green windbreaker, cream-colored Chino pants sprinkled with cigarette ash, and cowboy boots—tells her how to tend the bird's wing and what fodder to give it ('bread 'n scratch')." With this spirit, Higham went on to describe Walsh as a man's man of a director, someone who confessed to enjoy working outdoors on action pictures more than on anything indoors.[51]

The spirit was still vibrant. When Walsh still had hopes that his novel *Days of Wrath* would be published in the United States and then adapted into a film, he wrote to Bookman, now a book agent and living in Los Angeles:

> Number One Son,
>
> Honorable father was greatly pleased to receive postal card of your trip through the valley of the Gonniffs. Most of the hotels and restaurants you have enjoyed are run by descendants of the Jesse James gang of highway men. So, I look upon number one son to come home busted, disgusted, and not trusted.
>
> Welcome home, Bobby. I talked to Bob Giroux last week, after I sent him two great recommendations [blurbs] for the book, from Jimmy Cagney and John Wayne. . . .
>
> I have great faith in this book, Bobby. I know it will make a super western, and I would like to see you become the producer of it.
>
> So, when you get home have your clothes dry cleaned and pressed, and we both might take a trip to Japan.
>
> All the best to my number one son,
Papa San[52]

As his vision grew dim, Walsh stayed home even more, reading books. When he could not read the words himself, he hired girls to read to him—adventuring even in old age into the pages of his imagination—just as he had learned from his mother. He had always enjoyed reading popular novels of the day, and he loved reading Shakespeare. He also continued painting, a hobby he had taken up decades earlier. When he had difficulty seeing the canvas, he used a magnifying glass until that no longer worked. But he produced a great number of paintings: nudes of Mary and copies of works by other well-known traditional artists. Until very late in his life, he kept a separate studio in the San Fernando Valley, once inspiring Mary's rage when she walked in on him there painting a nude female model. Mary had no qualms about her wrath: she slashed the painting right then and there in front of Walsh. He took it out to the garbage himself.

Mary continued to care for Walsh, even as it became harder and harder to do so. She complained little but nevertheless felt the frustration of it all. Sometimes she was cold to him and stayed away from him, no doubt a result of his growing dependence on her as he became blind and more housebound. Still, she prepared his meals every day. One morning, Walsh sat in the dining room, barely able to see, but able to see enough to notice that Mary had not set the table with a tray of food the way she always had done: orange juice to the left, coffee to the right, eggs in the middle, napkin next to the plate, utensils in their place so that Walsh could reach for them instinctively. Something was missing, he noticed. He complained and asked Mary why one plate was not in its place. This was enough for her. She calmly walked over to her husband, took the tray of food, and dumped it upside down onto his lap. "How do you like it there?" she said, and walked away.[53]

Toward the end, when Walsh could no longer see at all and had difficulty moving about, Mary served him his meals in bed. He was more sedentary; Father James McCuen came out to the house every Sunday to visit him. Then Walsh dictated a letter to Hisayo Graham for Bob Bookman and relayed the thoughts he had about no longer being able to see the world around him:

Dear #1 Son,
    There is little I miss now that I am completely blind. Sure I must be telling you . . . there are scents, and sounds that I know the seeing people never have, the scent of grass and the scent of new-mowed hay.
    The trees speak to me in the wind. I know the soft dignified music of the pine tree, and the oak tree with the chatter of the little gray squirrels, and I know the sad music of the tall Eucalyptus tree.
    It is not a terrible thing at all to be old. I have seen the young folk start out in life, and before them there's the shower and lightning. But I am in warm, brown October.

You know, dear Bobby, the Irish are a wild lot . . . nomads,
who wander on the face of the earth.[54]

Living in darkness the last years of his life, Walsh did what he had
always done: created an adventure from the material he did have and
used his imagination, the landscape that never failed him. Mary could
do the same, sweeping away her little grievances and seeing the bigger
picture: the man she had loved for almost four decades now. At Walsh's
request, she signed an agreement never to contradict anything he had
said, or written in his autobiography, especially about the details of how
they met. Those were secrets locked away.

On December 29, 1980, Walsh complained to Mary of having chest
pains. She called an ambulance, and he was transported to Simi Valley
Hospital. He remained there two days and then was released. The next
day, December 31, 1980, his heart gave out, and Raoul Walsh passed
away at the age of ninety-three. At Walsh's funeral, Mary told Bob
Bookman that, upon being admitted to the hospital the day before he
died, Walsh was flirting with the admitting nurse. The spark had not
gone out yet. His time on earth had run out; there was no telling where
he could go from here. Several months later, on February 8, 1981, the
city council of Simi Valley passed an honorary resolution commemorat-
ing Walsh. His good friend Allan Dwan spoke lovingly of Walsh, calling
him "a student, a hard-working . . . sensitive man who made great motion pictures, some of the very greatest."[55] But Walsh would never have
tolerated such praise; it was a good thing he was out wandering again,
striking out to see where his imagination might now take him.

Epilogue
Walsh's American Scene

Raoul Walsh was known as Hollywood's adventurous, often impishly irreverent "one-eyed bandit." He carved out a career that spanned over half a century and upward of two hundred movies—and helped transform the Hollywood studio yarn into a breathless art form. He belonged to that generation of filmmakers who learned to make movies on a dime in a fledgling industry at the start of the twentieth century and invented a Hollywood that made movies bigger than life itself. In a generation that stretched from the likes of D. W. Griffith, F. W. Murnau, and Cecil B. DeMille to John Ford, William Wellman, and Howard Hawks, Walsh walked in the land of his imagination, his great adventures. It never failed him. Film historians, film buffs, and lovers of Walsh have debated for decades about where to place him in the company of directors of his generation and after—directors whose films generate heated discussion and will go on doing so. More than any others, the names of Walsh, Howard Hawks, and John Ford come up time and again as if they were a Holy Three who wander incessantly through the collective consciousness of American (and European) film culture and film narratives. By now, the word has become pretty distilled—set in place and unlikely to shift. As the word has it, John Ford is the great poet of American community captured in a diegetic frame—the arbiter of the communal experience, the tribe whose members together generate love and great affection. Hawks poeticizes the smaller group, the limited band of brothers, perhaps outcasts, such as we find in *Red River* and *To Have and Have Not,* where the loner can't be alone for too long since he is drawn into the fray and is forced to battle it out with his own kind.

But, in Walsh's American scene, so iconic in its depiction, understanding, and inventions of American types, no such community, large or small, exists. While the lines Walsh paints are vertical and strong, they point upward to the sky more than to a community of other men and women. When his men were young and full of themselves, their immaturity was held in check by others close by, such as in *What Price Glory?* and even *The Bowery*—by male comrades and a temporary band of brothers. But it was not a lasting formation, not a permanent experience. Walsh's characters are too compelled to light out for the territory on a small raft of sorts where there is room for no one else by their side save a woman. When they reach maturity and take stock of themselves in the world, they realize that they are meant to seek an adventure of necessity and to suffer the consequences of any of their actions. Although Walsh touched down now and then on a nostalgic collection of souls—such as in *The Strawberry Blonde* and *Gentleman Jim*—the truest Walshian character is the lone wolf. He is Mad Dog Earle, and he is the hero of *Distant Drums*. He is even George Custer and the Errol Flynn of the Walsh-Flynn World War II cycle. Should a character travel with a pack, he ultimately must fend for himself. In war—in battle—if he must do without his woman, he will seek her out when he can, even in his imagination if need be. Walsh's characters, like Walsh himself, are happiest living in their imaginations, pondering what might be. Like Walsh, they are loners more apt to be leaving the room than walking into it to stay.

Hawks's frame may capture a small band traveling together, but, if they are in outdoor country, they nevertheless crowd together (just as his characters tend to do in *Only Angels Have Wings* and *Red River*). Ford's visual language suggests that cropped hills and rocks are extensions of the community, the family of men and women who live within their borders; the physical plain is familiar and integrated into the action as if it were family. But Walsh's physical environment, his visual composition, whether one notices the vertical, the horizontal, or the circular patterns, is a beckoning place, a place the isolated character is driven to find: the Sierra Madres for Mad Dog Earle, the billowing combustion that consumes Cody Jarrett, the huge backdrop of the mountainside in which Walsh's western characters move along in *The Tall Men, Pursued,* and *Colorado Territory*. That environment beckons its lone wanderers with its false or true promise of an adventure yet to be had, an adventure that can be realized only by the sheer force of the imagination. The adventure must always be tinged with danger; the adventurer will always be standing on the psychological edge of a cliff.

Walsh's imaginary world is large and contains multitudes. One place he traveled after his death was into the imagination of those who loved and admired him. Stories about Walsh never cease to abound, just as he would have wished. "He was a very private man," L. Q. Jones said. "After we worked together, I was always afraid of intruding, saying 'He's too big; he's got too many things going on.' I didn't want to interfere. Raoul was a movement unto himself. I called him up at the end. I asked Mary, 'How's he doing?' 'Why don't you ask him yourself?' she said, and gave the phone to Walsh. He gets on the phone, 'Goddamn it, how you doin' kid? Listen, I'll get rid of Mary. I'll pick up some hookers. . . . No, you pick up some hookers; I'll get the booze. Come on out, let's have a party!' He was dead two days later."[1]

Walsh never won an Academy Award and, some say, never received the recognition he should have gotten in his lifetime. But, toward the end, his enduring and, indeed, revolutionary place in the history of American cinema became the subject of critics, historians, and friends. It would be no surprise, then, that when Miriam Cooper died in April 1976, a silver tea set she owned triggered an auction bidding war because so many famous lips had touched it, including those of Carole Lombard, Rudolph Valentino, Douglas Fairbanks, Mary Pickford, Pola Negri, and, of course, Raoul Walsh.

Two years earlier, in October 1974, Walsh wrote to his friend Richard Schickel that he was losing his eyesight—he was entering a dark world. Schickel wrote back the next week from New York:

Dear Raoul,

    I know you are in darkness. But what you can't see is the light you shed on the lives you have touched. You and some of the other men I did on the series [*The Men Who Made the Movies*] have given me so much. You gave to me before I even knew you with your movies . . . taught me a lot of what a young man needs to know about being a GROWN UP MAN, about strength and tenderness and honor and the need for love between man and woman, man and man. Now in your twilight you continue to teach me with your gallantry and sweetness of spirit.

One year ago I was guiding you around the St. Regis here. Someone asked me if you were my father. I said, "No, but I wish he was," and I do. Mine was not like you at all and so your example has meant so very much and always will.

In fact, you have many sons—many you haven't even met, I suspect. You, the essence of you, has been in your films and now it is in us.[2]

Walsh knew finally that he had "sons." He took to heart Schickel's words and counted dearly on his closeness with Bookman and with his nephew, Hank Kilgore. Yet his life soared above this. Walsh lived a life—in its truest sense—wandering within the boundaries of the fictions he made, from the earliest stories his mother told him, to the adventures he lived when as a boy he drove his horse out of New York State, to the fictions he and his brother, George, lived in lighting out for California when they were young men, and, finally, and in the grandest sense yet, to his fictions on the big screen. He was the New York boy who came out West and fell in love with California and the movies. He learned about his own life that way and what he could respect. He would always love the fiction of Gable's character, Ben Allison, in *The Tall Men*. As Ben rides away from town, Robert Ryan speaks of him as if speaking for Walsh himself: "There goes the only man I ever respected. He's what every boy thinks he's going to be when he grows up—and wishes he had been when he's an old man."

For Walsh loved the movies most. He was considered an action director who could dive into the heart of his sad, doomed characters trying to outrun the cruel social world for a world of adventure and escape. The truest characters he ever knew were Mad Dog Earle and Marie in *High Sierra*. "This is Raoul in absolute perfection," said L. Q. Jones. "He saw that everything *can* be better, that everything is going to a purpose. Bogie is going down. But look what he did for Velma; look what Henry Travers did for everybody. The progression of the characters is marvelous. How does he do the thing at the very end? What causes it? The dog! The damned dog! Now, who's going to hinge their whole picture on what a dog can do! But he did it for humanity. It's looking forward. It's just going there."[3]

That is why Raoul Walsh loved that day on the set of *The Naked and the Dead* when the budding young actor Jones did his first death scene. He was emoting; he was writhing; he was doing all he could to please Walsh and the camera, both just a foot away from him. Raoul Walsh laughed and said, "OK, kid, die, goddamn it, and let me get on with my picture."

Filmography

A Mother's Love (Pathé, 1913)

Director: Emile Couteau. *Running time:* 1 reel.
Cast: Dolly Larkin, Raoul Walsh.
Note: Filmed in Brooklyn, NY.

Paul Revere's Ride (Pathé, 1913)

Director: Emile Couteau. *Running time:* 1 reel.
Cast: Raoul Walsh, Dolly Larkin.
Note: Filmed in Fort Lee, NJ.

The Pseudo Prodigal (Reliance, 1913)

Director: Raoul Walsh. *Released:* December 20, 1913.
Cast: Sue Balfour, Miriam Cooper, Robert Harron, Ralph Lewis, Raoul Walsh.

For His Master (Reliance, 1914)

Director: W. Christy Cabanne. *Screenplay:* George Pattullo. *Running time:* 2
reels. *Released:* February 7, 1914.
Cast: Fred Burns, Miriam Cooper, Frank Bennett, Raoul Walsh (Father Walsh).

When Fate Frowned (Reliance, 1914)

Director: William Christy Cabanne. *Released:* March 17, 1914.
Cast: Miriam Cooper, Joseph Karl, Raoul Walsh.

The Great Leap: Until Death Do Us Part (Reliance, 1914)

Supervising producer: D. W. Griffith. *Director:* W. Christy Cabanne. *Screenplay:* Anthony Paul Kelly. *Cinematographer:* G. W. Bitzer. *Running time:* 4
reels. *Released:* April 1914.
Cast: Mae Marsh (Mary Gibbs), Robert Harron (Bobby Dawson), Irene Hunt,
Ralph Lewis, Raoul Walsh, Donald Crisp, Eagle Eye.

The Banker's Daughter (Pathé, 1914)

Directors: William F. Haddock, Edward M. Roskam. *Screenplay:* Bronson Howard. *Cinematographer:* Fred Dobson. *Running time:* 1 reel. *Released:* April 15, 1914.

Cast: Katherine La Salle (Lillian Westbrook), William H. Tooker (Lawrence Westbrook), David Wall (John Strebelow), Harry Spingler (Count de Carojac), William Bailey (Harold Routledge), Joseph Bailey (George Washington Phipps), Ethel Phillips (Florence St. Vincent), Kitty Baldwin (Aunt Fanny Holbrook), Mab Rae (Natalie Strebelow), Philip Robson (Mr. Brown), Raoul Walsh.

The Dishonored Medal (Reliance, 1914)

Supervising producer: D. W. Griffith. *Director:* W. Christy Cabanne. *Running time:* 4 reels. *Released:* May 3, 1914.

Cast: Miriam Cooper (Zora), George Gebhardt (Lt. Dubois), Raoul Walsh (Adopted son), Frank Bennett (Bel Kahn, son of Achmed), Mabel Van Buren (Anitra), Dark Cloud (Sheik Achmed).

The Life of General Villa (Mutual, 1914)

Producers: H. E. Aitken, Frank N. Thayer. *Supervising producer:* D. W. Griffith. *Directors:* W. Christy Cabanne, Raoul Walsh. *Writer:* Frank E. Woods. *Cinematographers:* L. M. Burrud, Raoul Walsh (Battle of Torreon sequence). *Running time:* 7 reels. *Released:* May 9, 1914.

Cast: Irene Hunt (Villa's sister), W. H. Lawrence (Federal officer), Walter Long (Federal officer), Teddy Sampson (Villa's sister), Pancho Villa (himself), Raoul Walsh (Villa as a young man), Eagle Eye, Mae Marsh, Robert Harron.

Notes: Filmed in Mexico. On April 17, 1915, a version cut down to four reels was reissued as *The Outlaw's Revenge*, a Mutual Masterpiece.

The Double Knot (Majestic, 1914)

Director: Raoul Walsh. *Running time:* 2 reels. *Released:* May 24, 1914.
Cast: Mary Alden, Jack O'Brien, Raoul Walsh.

The Rebellion of Kitty Belle (Mutual/Majestic, 1914)

Director: Christy Cabanne. *Story:* George Pattullo. *Running time:* 2 reels. *Released:* June 14, 1914.

Cast: Lillian Gish (Kitty Belle), Robert Harron (Joe Belle), Raoul Walsh (Bud Parker), Kate Bruce, Joseph Carle, Dorothy Gish, Alfred Paget.

The Angel of Contention (Majestic, 1914)

Director: John B. O'Brien. *Screenplay:* George Pattullo (from a story by Will Levington Comfort). *Running time:* 2 reels. *Released:* July 5, 1914.

Cast: Lillian Gish, Spottiswoode Aitken, George Siegmann, Raoul Walsh.

The Only Clue (Majestic, 1914)

Running time: 1 reel. *Released:* July 7, 1914.
Cast: Eugene Pallette, Irene Hunt, Raoul Walsh.

Lest We Forget (Majestic, 1914)

Director: John B. O'Brien. *Running time:* 1 reel. *Released:* July 24, 1914.
Cast: Elmer Clifton, Miriam Cooper, Josephine Cromwell, Ralph Lewis, Raoul Walsh.

The Mystery of the Hindu Image (Majestic, 1914)

Director: Raoul Walsh. *Running time:* 2 reels. *Released:* July 26, 1914.
Cast: Nick Cage, Dark Cloud, Richard Cummings, Eagle Eye, Raoul Walsh.

The Sheriff's Prisoner (Reliance, 1914)

Directors: Arthur Mackley, Raoul Walsh. *Released:* July 29, 1914.
Cast: Eugene Pallette, Vester Pegg, Arthur Mackley, F. A. Turner, Florence Crawford, Richard Cummings, Raoul Walsh.

The Gunman (Reliance, 1914)

Directors: Christy Cabanne, Raoul Walsh. *Story:* George Pattullo. *Released:* August 1, 1914.
Cast: Eugene Pallette, Miriam Cooper, Sam De Grasse, Ralph Lewis, F. A. Turner.

The Second Mrs. Roebuck (Mutual/Majestic, 1914)

Directors: John B. O'Brien, W. Christy Cabanne. *Screenplay:* George Pattullo (from a story by W. Carey Wonderly). *Running time:* 2 reels. *Released:* August 23, 1914.
Cast: Mary Alden, John B. O'Brien, Wallace Reid (Samuel Roebuck), Blanche Sweet, Raoul Walsh.

Sierra Jim's Reformation (Majestic, 1914)

Director: John O'Brien. *Running time:* 1 reel. *Released:* September 7, 1914.
Cast: Raoul Walsh (Sierra Jim), Wallace Reid (Tim), Gertrude McLynn, Fred Burns, Dark Cloud, Eagle Eye.

The Final Verdict (Majestic, 1914)

Director: John B. O'Brien. *Running time:* 2 reels. *Released:* September 13, 1914.
Cast: Francelia Billington (Mary), Raoul Walsh (King), Eagle Eye, Joseph Singleton.

The Unpainted Portrait (Majestic, 1914)

Running time: 1 reel. *Released:* October 6, 1914.
Cast: Mary Alden, Cora Drew, Raoul Walsh, Billie West.

Sands of Fate (Mutual/Majestic, 1914)

Director: Donald Crisp. *Running time:* 1 reel. *Released:* October 11, 1914.
Cast: Dorothy Gish (Helen), Robert Harron (Lee), Raoul Walsh (Holden), Cora
  Drew (Mrs. Robinson), Charles Eberts.

The Availing Prayer (Mutual/Majestic, 1914)

Director: Donald Crisp. *Screenplay:* Richard Barker Shelton. *Running time:* 1
  reel. *Released:* October 30, 1914.
Cast: Dorothy Gish (May Rock), Raoul Walsh (The doctor), Spottiswoode Aitken (William Rock), Bobby Burns, John P. McCarthy.

Paid with Interest (Majestic, 1914)

Director: Raoul Walsh. *Screenplay:* Anthony Paul Kelly. *Running time:* 1 reel.
  Released: November 1, 1914.
Cast: Robert Harron (Tom Taylor), Mae Marsh (Mame), Raoul Walsh (George
  Watson), Irene Hunt, Ralph Lewis.

The Little Country Mouse (Mutual/Majestic, 1914)

Supervising producer: D. W. Griffith. *Director:* Donald Crisp. *Running time:* 2
  reels. *Released:* November 16, 1914.
Cast: Blanche Sweet (Dorothy), Wallace Reid (Lt. Hawkhurst), Mary Alden,
  Raoul Walsh.

They Never Knew (Reliance, 1914)

Director: Arthur Mackley. *Running time:* 1 reel. *Released:* November 25, 1914.
Cast: Florence Crawford (Rose), Vester Pegg (Ben), Raoul Walsh (Carroll), Arthur Mackley, George Siegmann.

Who Shot Bud Walton? (Reliance, 1914)

Director: Jack Adolfi. *Running time:* 2 reels. *Released:* December 5, 1914.
Cast: Sam De Grasse (Lafe Johnson), Raoul Walsh (Bud Walton), Eugene
  Pallette (Jeff Hardin), Francelia Billington (Tillie), Beulah Burns, Thelma
  Burns, Fred Hamer, Bob Burns, Fred Burns, Dark Cloud, Eagle Eye, John P.
  McCarthy.

The Exposure (Reliance, 1914)

Director: Fred Kelsey. *Running time:* 2 reels. *Released:* December 26, 1914.

Cast: Wallace Reid (Reporter), Irene Hunt (Helen), Raoul Walsh (Joe Reed), Ralph Lewis (Phelan), Howard Gage, William Lowery.

The Old Fisherman's Story (Majestic, 1914)

Director: John B. O'Brien. *Running time:* 2 reels. *Released:* December 27, 1914.
Cast: Spottiswoode Aitken (The old fisherman), Raoul Walsh (Ben), Jack Conway (Ned), Mary Alden (The gypsy), Lucille Browne, Arthur Maude, Seena Owen.

Home from the Sea (Fine Arts, 1915)

Supervising producer: D. W. Griffith. *Director:* Raoul Walsh. *Running time:* 1 reel.
Cast: Raoul Walsh, Ralph Lewis, Francelia Billington.

The Love Pirate (Reliance, 1915)

Director: Edward Dillon. *Story:* Theodosia Harris. *Running time:* 2 reels.
Cast: Fay Tincher (Viola), Raoul Walsh (The magnate), Elmer Clifton (The Young Clubman), Beulah Burns, Bobby Ray, Frankie Newman.

The Double Deception (Majestic, 1915)

Running time: 1 reel. *Released:* February 5, 1915.
Cast: Elmer Clifton (Henry), Miriam Cooper (Laura), Raoul Walsh, Mazie Radford, Charles Courtwright, Jennie Lee.

The Death Dice (Reliance, 1915)

Director: Raoul Walsh. *Story:* George Pattullo. *Running time:* 2 reels. *Released:* February 13, 1915.
Cast: Eugene Pallette, Irene Hunt, Fred Burns, Vester Pegg, Joseph P. McCarthy.

The Fatal Black Bean (Majestic, 1915)

Director: Raoul Walsh. *Screenplay:* Russell Smith. *Running time:* 1 reel. *Released:* February 23, 1915.
Cast: Miriam Cooper, Elmer Clifton, Eagle Eye, Jennie Lee, Raoul Walsh.

The Birth of a Nation (Epoch/Majestic, 1915)

Producer: D. W. Griffith. *Executive producer:* H. E. Aitken (uncredited). *Director:* D. W. Griffith. *Screenplay:* D. W. Griffith, Frank E. Woods (based on the novel *The Clansman* by Thomas F. Dixon Jr.). *Cinematographer:* G. W. Bitzer. *Editors:* D. W. Griffith, Joseph Henabery, James Smith, Rose Smith, Raoul Walsh. *Music:* Joseph Carl Breil, D. W. Griffith. *Costume designers:* Robert Goldstein, Clare West (both uncredited). *Special effects:* Walter Hoffman, "Fireworks" Wilson (both uncredited). *Running time:* 12 reels. *World premiere:* February 8, 1915, at Clune's, Los Angeles. *Released:* March 3, 1915, New York.

Cast: Lillian Gish (Elsie Stoneman), Mae Marsh (Flora Cameron), Henry B. Walthall (Col. Ben Cameron), Miriam Cooper (Margaret Cameron), Mary Alden (Lydia Brown), Ralph Lewis (Austin Stoneman), George Siegmann (Silas Lynch), Walter Long (Gus), Robert Harron (Tod Stoneman), Wallace Reid (Jeff), Joseph Henabery (Abraham Lincoln), Elmer Clifton (Phil Stoneman), Josephine Crowell (Mrs. Cameron), Spottiswoode Aitken (Dr. Cameron), George Beranger (Wade Cameron), Maxfield Stanley (Duke Cameron), Jennie Lee (Mammy), Donald Crisp (Gen. Ulysses S. Grant), Howard Gaye (Gen. Robert E. Lee), Raoul Walsh (John Wilkes Booth [uncredited]).

Note: Filmed in Los Angeles and Calexico, CA, from July 1914 to October 30, 1914.

His Return (Reliance, 1915)

Director: Raoul Walsh. *Story:* Russell E. Smith. *Running time:* 2 reels. *Released:* March 5, 1915.

Cast: Miriam Cooper, Elmer Clifton, Howard Gaye.

The Greaser (Majestic, 1915)

Director: Raoul Walsh. *Running time:* 2 reels. *Released:* March 23, 1915.
Cast: Fred Church, Elmer Clifton, Miriam Cooper, Vester Pegg, Raoul Walsh.

The Tramp (Reliance, 1915)

Director: Raoul Walsh. *Screenplay:* Russell Smith. *Running time:* 1 reel.
Cast: Thomas Jefferson.

The Artist's Wife (Majestic, 1915)

Director: Raoul Walsh. *Running time:* 1 reel. *Released:* April 2, 1915.
Cast: Miriam Cooper, Elmer Clifton, Vester Pegg.

The Fencing Master (Majestic, 1915)

Director: Raoul Walsh. *Screenplay:* Raoul Walsh. *Running time:* 2 reels. *Released:* April 11, 1915.

Cast: Thomas Jefferson (Monsieur La Rogue), Frank Bennett (Claude, La Rogue's nephew), Teddy Sampson (Yvette, La Rogue's ward), George Walsh (Morode, a duelist).

The Outlaw's Revenge (Mutual, 1915)

Directors: William Christy Cabanne, Raoul Walsh. *Released:* April 15, 1915.
Cast: Raoul Walsh (The outlaw), Irene Hunt (The outlaw's older sister), Teddy Sampson (The outlaw's younger sister), Mae Marsh (The American lover),

Robert Harron (The American lover), Eagle Eye (The outlaw's servant), Walter Long (Federal officer), Spottiswoode Aitken (The soothsayer), W. E. Lawrence (Federal officer).

Note: Filmed in Mexico. A reissue or reedited version of *The Life of Villa.*

A Man for All That (Majestic, 1915)

Director: Raoul Walsh. *Running time:* 2 reels. *Released:* April 17, 1915.

Cast: Elmer Clifton (Young convict), Miriam Cooper (Young boy's sister), Tom Wilson (The warden), Raoul Walsh (Detective), Jennie Lee (Young boy's mother), Paul Willis (Young boy).

The Smuggler (Majestic, 1915)

Director: Raoul Walsh. *Running time:* 1 reel. *Released:* May 11, 1915.

Cast: Raoul Walsh (Connors), Billie West (Betty Sampson), Ralph Lewis (John Sampson), John T. Dillon (Wilson), Elmer Clifton.

11:30 PM (Majestic, 1915)

Director: Raoul Walsh. *Running time:* 2 reels. *Released:* May 23, 1915.

Cast: Sam De Grasse (Lloyd James), Loretta Blake (Muriel Main), Erich von Ritzau, George Walsh, Al W. Filson, Curt Rehfeld.

The Celestial Code (Reliance, 1915)

Director: Raoul Walsh. *Running time:* 2 reels. *Released:* June 5, 1915.

Cast: Irene Hunt, George Walsh, Harry L. Fraser, Dark Cloud, Tote Du Crow, James Warnack, Al W. Filson, Harry Burns.

A Bad Man and Others (Reliance, 1915)

Director: Raoul Walsh. *Running time:* 2 reels. *Released:* June 26, 1915.

Cast: George Walsh, Elmo Lincoln, Violet Wilkey, Daisy Jefferson, W. E. Lowry, Nat G. Deverich.

Regeneration (Fox, 1915)

Director: Raoul Walsh. *Screenplay:* Raoul Walsh, Carl Harbaugh (from a book by Owen Kildare and Walter Hackett). *Running time:* 6 reels. *Released:* September 13, 1915.

Cast: Rockliffe Fellowes, Anna Q. Nilsson, Carl Harbaugh, John McCann, William Sheer, James A. Marcus, Maggie Weston, H. McCoy.

Carmen (Fox, 1915)

Director: Raoul Walsh. *Screenplay:* Raoul Walsh (based on the novel by Prosper Mérimée). *Running time:* 5 reels. *Released:* November 1, 1915.

Cast: Theda Bara (Carmen), Einar Linden (Don Jose), Carl Harbaugh (Escamillo), James A. Marcus (Dancaire), Emil De Varney (Capt. Morales), Elsie MacLeod (Michaela), Fay Tunis (Carlotta).

The Serpent (Fox, 1916)

Producer: William Fox. *Director:* Raoul Walsh. *Screenplay:* Raoul Walsh, George Walsh (based on the story "The Wolf's Claw" by Philip Bartholomae). *Cinematographer:* Georges Benoît. *Running time:* 6 reels. *Released:* January 23, 1916.
Cast: Theda Bara (Vania Lazar), James A. Marcus (Ivan Lazar), Lillian Hathaway (Martsa Lazar), Charles Craig (Grand Duke Valanoff), Carl Harbaugh (Prince Valanoff).

Blue Blood and Red (Fox, 1916)

Producer: Raoul Walsh. *Director:* Raoul Walsh. *Screenplay:* Raoul Walsh. *Cinematographers:* Georges Benoît, Len Powers, George Richter. *Assistant director:* J. Gordon Cooper. *Running time:* 5 reels. *Released:* April 2, 1916.
Cast: George Walsh (Algernon DuPont), Martin Kinney (Peterkin), Doris Pawn, James A. Marcus, Jack Woods, Augustus Carny, Vester Pegg.

Pillars of Society (Triangle, 1916)

Supervising director: D. W. Griffith. *Director:* Raoul Walsh. *Screenplay:* D. W. Griffith (based on the play *Samfundets stotter* by Henrik Ibsen). *Running time:* 5 reels. *Released:* August 27, 1916.
Cast: Henry B. Walthall (Karsten Bernick), Mary Alden (Lona Tonnesen), Juanita Archer (Betty), George Beranger (Johan Tonnesen), Josephine Crowell (Karsten's mother), Olga Grey (Madame Linda Dorf), Raoul Walsh.

The Honor System (Fox, 1917)

Producer: William Fox. *Director:* Raoul Walsh. *Screenplay:* Raoul Walsh (from a story by Henry Christeen Warnack). *Cinematographers:* Georges Benoît, Len Powers, George Richter. *Set designer:* George Grenier. *Assistant director:* J. Gordon Cooper. *Running time:* 10 reels. *Released:* February 12, 1917.
Cast: Milton Sills (Joseph Stanton), Cora Drew (His mother), James A. Marcus (Gov. John Hunter), Arthur Mackley (Steven Holt), Miriam Cooper (Edith), George Walsh (Jack Taylor), Charles Clary (Crales Harrington), Gladys Brockwell (Trixie Bennett), Roy Rice (Three-fingered Louis), Pomeroy Cannon (James Phelan), Johnny Reese (Mugsey). *New York premiere:* Lyric Theatre. *Rereleased:* March 1, 1920.
Note: The rerelease was in 8 reels.

Hearts and Saddles (Fox, 1917)

Director: Raoul Walsh. *Screenplay:* Robert Eddy, Tom Mix. *Running time:* 2 reels. *Released:* March 31, 1917.

Cast: Tom Mix, Victoria Forde, Victor Potel, Sid Jordan, Pat Chrisman.

The Silent Lie (Fox, 1917)

Director: Raoul Walsh. *Screenplay:* Chester B. Clapp (based on the short story "Conahan" by Harry Evans). *Cinematographer:* Dal Clawson. *Running time:* 5 reels. *Released:* May 28, 1917.

Cast: Miriam Cooper (Lady Lou), Ralph Lewis (Hatfield), Charles Clary (Conahan), Monoe Salisbury (The stranger), Henry A. Barrows (The priest), Howard Davies (The fur dealer), William Eagle Shirt (The Indian).

The Innocent Sinner (Fox, 1917)

Director: Raoul Walsh. *Screenplay:* Raoul Walsh (from a short story by Mary Synon). *Cinematographer:* Dal Clawson. *Running time:* 6 reels. *Released:* July 21, 1917.

Cast: Miriam Cooper (Mary Ellen Ellis), Charles Clary (David Graham), Jack Standing (Walter Benton), Jane Novak (Jane Murray), Rosita Marstini (Madame De Coeur), William Parsons (Bull Clark), Johnny Reese (The Weasel), Jennie Lee (Mother Ellis).

Betrayed (Fox, 1917)

Director: Raoul Walsh. *Screenplay:* Chester B. Clapp, Raoul Walsh. *Cinematographer:* Dal Clawson. *Released:* September 2, 1917.

Cast: Miriam Cooper (Carmelita), James A. Marcus (Carpi), Hobart Bosworth (Leopoldo Juares), Monte Blue (Pepo Esparenza), Wheeler Oakman (William Jerome).

The Conqueror (Fox, 1917)

Director: Raoul Walsh. *Screenplay:* Henry Warnack, Raoul Walsh (based on a story by Henry Christeen Warnack). *Cinematographer:* Dal Clawson. *Set designer:* George Grenier. *Running time:* 8 reels. *Released:* September 16, 1917.

Cast: William Farnum (Sam Houston), Jewel Carmen (Eliza Allen), Charles Clary (Sidney Stokes), James A. Marcus (Jumbo), Carrie Clark Ward (Mammy), William Chisholm (Dr. Spencer), Robert Dunbar (Judge Allen), Owen Jones (James Houston), William Eagle Shirt (Indian chief), Chief Birdhead (Indian chief), Little Bear (Indian chief).

This Is the Life (Fox, 1917)

Director: Raoul Walsh. *Screenplay:* Raoul Walsh. *Cinematographer:* Dal Clawson. *Running time:* 5 reels. *Released:* October 21, 1917.

Cast: George Walsh, Wanda Hawley, James A. Marcus, Ralph Lewis, Jack McDonald, William Ryno, Hector Sarno.

The Pride of New York (Fox, 1917)

Director: Raoul Walsh. *Screenplay:* Raoul Walsh (based on a story by Ralph Spence). *Cinematographer:* Dal Clawson. *Running time:* 5 reels. *Released:* December 9, 1917.

Cast: George Walsh (Jim Kelly), James A. Marcus (Pat Kelly), William Bailey (Harold Whitley), Regina Quinn (Mary).

The Lone Cowboy (Fox, 1917)

Director: Raoul Walsh.
Cast: Tom Mix, Mildred Harris, Alan Hale, Crazy Wolf.
Note: Mentioned by Walsh in *Each Man in His Time.*

The Woman and the Law (Fox, 1918)

Producer: William Fox. *Executive producer:* Winfield R. Sheehan. *Director:* Raoul Walsh. *Screenplay:* Raoul Walsh (based on the DeSaulles murder case). *Running time:* 7 reels. *Released:* March 17, 1918.

Cast: Jack Connors (Mr. Jack La Salle), Miriam Cooper (Mrs. Jack La Salle), George Humbert, Peggy Hopkins Joyce (Josie Sabel), Agnes Neilson, Ramsey Wallace.

On the Jump (Fox, 1918)

Director: Raoul Walsh. *Screenplay:* Raoul Walsh (based on a scenario by Ralph Spence). *Cinematographer:* Roy Overbaugh. *Running time:* 6 reels. *Released:* March 31, 1918.

Cast: George Walsh (Jack Bartlett), Frances Burnham (Margaret Desmond), James A. Marcus (William Desmond), Henry Clive (Otto Crumley), Ralph Faulkner (President Woodrow Wilson).

The Prussian Cur (Fox, 1918)

Director: Raoul Walsh. *Screenplay:* Raoul Walsh. *Cinematographer:* Roy Overbaugh. *Running time:* 8 reels. *Released:* September 1, 1918.

Cast: Miriam Cooper (Rosie O'Grady), Sidney Mason (Dick Gregory), H. von der Goltz (Otto Goltz), Leonora Steward (Lillian O'Grady), James A. Marcus (Patrick O'Grady), Pat O'Malley (Jimmie O'Grady), Walter McEwen (Count Johann von Bernstorff), William Black (Wolff von Eidel), Ralph Faulkner

(Woodrow Wilson), Walter Lawrence (Emperor William II), Charles Reynolds (Emperor William I), William Harrison (Crown Prince Frederick), James Hathaway (Field Marshal von Hindenburg), Pat Hartigan (Adm. Von Tirpitz), John E. Franklin (James W. Gerard), John Harbon (U.S. congressman).

Every Mother's Son (Fox, 1918)

Director: Raoul Walsh. *Screenplay:* Raoul Walsh. *Running time:* 5 reels. *Released:* December 1, 1918.

Cast: Charlotte Walker (An American mother), Percy Standing (An American father), Edwin Stanley (Eldest son), Ray Howard (Second son), Gareth Hughes (Third son), Corona Paynter (Daughter of France), Bernard Thornton (Lt. Von Sterbling).

I'll Say So (Fox, 1918)

Director: Raoul Walsh. *Screenplay:* Ralph Spence. *Editor:* Ralph Spence. *Running time:* 5 reels. *Released:* December 22, 1918.

Cast: George Walsh (Bill Durham), Regina Quinn (Barbara Knowles), William Bailey (August Myers), James Black (Carl Vogel), Ed Keeley (Judge).

Evangeline (Fox, 1919)

Producer: Raoul Walsh. *Director:* Raoul Walsh. *Screenplay:* Raoul Walsh (based on the poem by Henry Wadsworth Longfellow). *Cinematographer:* Devereaux Jennings. *Original music:* Fred Fischer, Joseph McCarthy. *Running time:* 5 reels. *Released:* August 19, 1919.

Cast: Miriam Cooper (Evangeline), Alan Roscoe (Gabriel), Spottiswoode Aitken (Benedict Bellefontaine), James A. Marcus (Basil), Paul Weigel (Father Felician), William A. Wellman (British lieutenant).

Should a Husband Forgive? (Fox, 1919)

Director: Raoul Walsh. *Screenplay:* Raoul Walsh. *Cinematographer:* Devereaux Jennings. *Running time:* 7 reels. *Released:* November 1, 1919.

Cast: Miriam Cooper (Ruth Fulton), Beatrice Beckley (Mary Carroll), Eric Mayne (John Carroll), Vincent Coleman (John Carroll Jr.), Lyster Chambers (Rogue), Percy Standing (Rex Burleigh), Charles Craig (A human jackal).

The Strongest (Fox, 1920)

Director: Raoul Walsh. *Screenplay:* Raoul Walsh (based on the novel by Georges Clemenceau). *Cinematographer:* Ben Bail. *Running time:* 5 reels. *Released:* February 1920.

Cast: Renee Adoree (Claudia), Carlo Liten (Henri), Harrison Hunter (Harle), Beatrice Noyes (Betty Macklin), Florence Malone (Claire Harle), Jean Gauthier De Trigny (Visconte), Madame Tressida (Nanette), Georgette

Gauthier De Trigny (Comtesse), James A. Marcus (Curate), C. A. de Lima (Prefect of Police).

Note: Originally released with tinted sequences.

The Deep Purple (Realart, 1920)

Producer: Raoul Walsh. *Director:* Raoul Walsh. *Screenplay:* Earle Browne (from the play by Paul Armstrong and Wilson Mizner). *Cinematographer:* Jacques Bizeul. *Art director:* William Cameron Menzies. *Running time:* 7 reels. *Released:* May 2, 1920.

Cast: Miriam Cooper (Doris Moore), Helen Ware (Kate Fallon), Vincent Serrano (Harry Leland), William J. Ferguson (Pop Clark), Stuart Sage (William Lake), William B. Mack (Gordon Laylock), Lincoln Plumer (Connelly), Ethel Hallor (Flossie), Lorraine Frost (Phyllis Lake), Louis Mackintosh (Mrs. Lake), Amy Ongley (Christine), Walter Lawrence (Finn), J. C. King (Inspector George Bruce), Eddie Sturgis (Skinny), C. A. de Lime (Balke).

Headin' Home (Kessell & Baumann, 1920)

Producers: William Shea, Herbert H. Yudkin. *Supervisor:* Raoul Walsh. *Director:* Lawrence Windom. *Screenplay:* Raoul Walsh (based on story by Earle Browne). *Running time:* 71 minutes. *Released:* September 19, 1920.

Cast: Babe Ruth (Babe), Ruth Taylor (Mildred Tobin), William Sheer (Harry Knight), Margaret Seddon (Babe's Mother), Frances Victory (Pigtails), James A. Marcus (Simon Tobin), Ralf Harolde (John Tobin), Charles Byer (David Talmadge), George Halpin (Doc Hedges), William J. Gross (Eliar Lott), Walter Lawrence (Tony Marino), Ann Brody (Mrs. Tony Marino), Ricca Allen (Almira Worters), Sammy Blum (Jimbo Jones), Ethel Kerwin (Kitty Wilson), Tom Cameron (Deacon Flack), Charles J. Hunt (Reverend David Talmadge).

Note: According to Miriam Cooper, Walsh not only supervised but also directed the film.

From Now On (Fox, 1920)

Director: Raoul Walsh. *Screenplay:* Raoul Walsh (from a story by Frank L. Packard). *Cinematographer:* Joseph Ruttenberg. *Running time:* 7 reels. *Released:* September 26, 1920.

Cast: George Walsh (Dave Henderson), Regina Quinn (Teresa Capriano), Mario Majeroni (Capriano), Paul Everton (Bokky Sharvan), James A. Marcus (Martin Tydeman), Tom Walsh (Detective Barjan), Cesare Gravina (Tony Lomazzi), Robert Byrd (Millman).

Note: Originally shown with tinted sequences.

The Oath (Mayflower, 1921)

Producer: Raoul Walsh. *Director:* Raoul Walsh. *Screenplay:* Ralph Spence (based on the novel *Idols* by William J. Locke). *Cinematographers:* Dal

Clawson, G. O. Post. *Costume designer:* Miriam Cooper. *Running time:* 8 reels. *Released:* April 10, 1921.

Cast: Miriam Cooper (Minna Hart), Robert Fischer (Israel Hart), Conway Tearle (Hugh Coleman), Henry Clive (Gerald Merriam), Ricca Allen (Anna Cassaba), Anna Q. Nilsson (Irene Lansing).

Serenade (R. A. Walsh, 1921)

Director: Raoul Walsh. *Screenplay:* James T. O'Donohoe (from the play *Maria del Carmen* by Jose Feliu i Codina). *Running time:* 7 reels. *Released:* August 21, 1921.

Cast: Miriam Cooper (Maria del Carmen), George Walsh (Pancho), Rosita Marstini (Maria's mother), James A. Marcus (Pepuso), Josef Swickard (Domingo Maticas), Bertram Grassby (Ramon Maticas), Noble Johnson (Capt. Ramirez), Ethelbert Knott (Don Fulgenico), Eagle Eye (Juan), Ardita Milano (The dancer), Peter Vanzuella (Pedro), John Eberts (the secretary), Tom Kennedy (Zambrano).

Kindred of the Dust (R. A. Walsh, 1922)

Producer: Raoul Walsh. *Director:* Raoul Walsh. *Screenplay:* James T. O'Donohoe (based on the novel by Peter B. Kyne). *Cinematographers:* H. Lyman Broening, Charles Van Enger. *Art director:* William Cameron Menzies. *Running time:* 8 reels. *Released:* February 27, 1922.

Cast: Miriam Cooper (Nan of the Sawdust Pile), Ralph Graves (Donald McKaye), Lionel Belmore (The Laird of Tyee), Eugenie Besserer (Mrs. McKaye), Maryland Morne (Jane McKaye), Elizabeth Waters (Elizabeth McKaye), William J. Ferguson (Mr. Daney), Caroline Rankin (Mrs. Daney), Patrick Rooney (Dirty Dann O'Leary), John Herdman (Caleb Brent), Bruce Guerin (Little Donald).

Lost and Found on a South Sea Island (Goldwyn, 1923)

Producer: Samuel Goldwyn. *Director:* Raoul Walsh. *Screenplay:* Paul Bern (from a story by Carey Wilson). *Cinematographers:* Clyde de Vinna, Paul Kerschner. *Editors:* H. H. Caldwell, Katherine Hilliker. *Running time:* 7 reels. *Released:* February 1923.

Cast: House Peters (Capt. Blackbird), Pauline Starke (Lorna), Antonio Moreno (Lloyd Warren), Mary Jane Irving (Baby Madge), Rosemary Theby (Madge), George Siegmann (Faulke), William V. Mong (Skinner), Carl Harbaugh (Waki), David Wing (Kerito).

Rosita (United Artists, 1923)

Producer: Mary Pickford. *Directors:* Ernst Lubitsch, Raoul Walsh (uncredited). *Screenplay:* Edward Knoblock (based on the play *Don Cesar de Bazan* by Adolphe d'Ennery and Philippe Dumanoir). *Cinematographer:* Charles

Rosher. *Music:* Louis F. Gottschalk. *Art directors:* Svend Gade, William Cameron Menzies. *Costume designer:* Mitchell Leisen. *Assistant director:* James Townsend. *Running time:* 90 minutes. *Released:* September 3, 1923.

Cast: Mary Pickford (Rosita), Holbrook Blinn (The King), Irene Rich (The Queen), George Walsh (Don Diego), Charles Belcher (The Prime Minister), Frank Leigh (Prison commandant), Mathilde Comont (Rosita's mother), George Periolat (Rosita's father).

Note: Walsh was brought in as collaborator at Mary Pickford's request.

The Thief of Bagdad (United Artists, 1924)

Producers: Douglas Fairbanks, Theodore Reed. *Director:* Raoul Walsh. *Screenplay:* Achmed Abdullah, Lotta Woods (based on a story by Douglas Fairbanks). *Cinematographer:* Arthur Edeson. *Editor:* William Nolan. *Music:* Carl Davis. *Production designer:* William Cameron Menzies. *Costume designer:* Mitchell Leisen. *Assistant director:* James T. O'Donohoe. *Running time:* 14 reels. *Released:* March 23, 1924.

Cast: Douglas Fairbanks (Ahmed the thief), Snitz Edwards (His evil associate), Charles Belcher (The holy man), Julanne Johnston (The Princess), Sojin (The Mongol Prince), Anna May Wong (The Mongol slave), Brandon Hurst (The Caliph), Tote Du Crow (The Soothsayer), Noble Johnson (The Indian Prince).

East of Suez (Paramount, 1925)

Director: Raoul Walsh. *Screenplay:* Sada Cowan (based on a story by W. Somerset Maugham). *Cinematographer:* Victor Milner. *Running time:* 7 reels. *Released:* January 12, 1925.

Cast: Pola Negri (Daisy Forbes), Edmund Lowe (George Tevis), Rockliffe Fellowes (Harry Anderson), Noah Beery (British Consul), Sojin Kamiyama (Lee Tai), Wong Wing (Amah), Florence Regnart (Sylvia Knox), Charles Requa (Harold Knox), E. H. Calvert (Sidney Forbes).

The Spaniard (Paramount, 1925)

Director: Raoul Walsh. *Screenplay:* James T. O'Donohoe (based on a novel by Juanita Savage). *Cinematographer:* Victor Milner. *Art director:* Lawrence Hitt. *Running time:* 7 reels. *Released:* May 4, 1925.

Cast: Ricardo Cortez (Don Pedro de Barrego), Jetta Goudal (Dolores Annesley), Noah Beery (Gomez), Mathilde Brundage (Senora de la Carta), Renzo De Gardi (Count de Albaveque), Emily Fitzroy (Maria), Bernard Siegel (Manuel), Florence Regnart (Consuelo).

The Wanderer (Paramount, 1926)

Producers: Jesse L. Lasky, Raoul Walsh, Adolph Zukor. *Director:* Raoul Walsh. *Screenplay:* James T. O'Donohoe (based on the play by Maurice V. Samuel).

Cinematographer: Victor Milner. *Music:* Hugo Riesenfeld. *Art director:* Lawrence W. Hitt. *Running time:* 9 reels. *Released:* February 1, 1926.

Cast: Greta Nissen (Tisha), William Collier Jr. (Jether), Ernest Torrence (Tola), Wallace Beery (Pharis), Tyrone Power (Jesse), Kathryn Carver (Naomi), Kathlyn Williams (Huldah), George Regas (Gaal), Holmes Herbert (Prophet), Snitz Edwards (Jeweler), Myrna Loy (Girl at Baccanal [uncredited]).

Note: Originally released with tinted prints.

The Lucky Lady (Paramount, 1926)

Producer: Raoul Walsh. *Director:* Raoul Walsh. *Screenplay:* James T. O'Donohoe (based on a story by Bertram Bloch and Robert Sherwood). *Cinematographer:* Victor Milner. *Released:* April 26, 1926.

Cast: Greta Nissen (Antoinette), Lionel Barrymore (Count Ferranzo), William Collier Jr. (Clarke), Marc McDermott (Franz Garletz), Carrie Daumery (Duchess), Sojin (Secretary to Garletz).

The Lady of the Harem (Paramount, 1926)

Producers: Adolph Zukor, Jesse Lasky. *Director:* Raoul Walsh. *Screenplay:* James T. O'Donohoe (based on the play *Hassan* by James Elroy Flecker). *Running time:* 6 reels. *Released:* November 1, 1926.

Cast: Ernest Torrence (Hassan), William Collier Jr. (Rafi), Greta Nissen (Pervaneh), Louise Fazenda (Yasmin), George Beranger (Selim), Sojin (Sultan), Frank Leigh (Jafar), Noble Johnson (Tax collector), Daniel Makarenko (Chief of Police), Christian Frank (Captain of the military), Snitz Edwards (Abdu), Chester Conklin (Ali), Brandon Hurst (Beggar), Leo White (Beggar).

What Price Glory? (Fox, 1926)

Producer: William Fox. *Director:* Raoul Walsh. *Screenplay:* James T. O'Donohoe (based on the play by Maxwell Anderson and Laurence Stallings). *Cinematographer:* Barney McGill. *Music:* R. H. Bassett, Erno Rapee. *Assistant director:* Daniel Keefe. *Running time:* 116 minutes. *Released:* November 23, 1926.

Cast: Edmund Lowe (1st Sgt. Quirt), Victor McLaglen (Capt. Flagg), Dolores del Rio (Charmaine de la Cognac), William V. Mong (Cognac Pete), Phyllis Haver (Shanghai Mabel), Elena Jurado (Carmen), Leslie Fenton (Lt. Moore), Barry Norton (Pvt. "Mother's Boy" Lewisohn), Sammy Cohen (Pvt. Lipinsky), Ted McNamara (Pvt. Kiper), August Tollaire (French Mayor), Mathilde Comont (Camille), Patrick Rooney (Mulcahy).

Note: Remade by John Ford in 1952.

The Monkey Talks (Fox, 1927)

Producer: Raoul Walsh. *Director:* Raoul Walsh. *Screenplay:* Gordon Rigby (based on the novel by Rene Fauchois). *Cinematographer:* L. William

O'Connell. *Assistant director:* R. L. Hough. *Running time:* 6 reels. *Released:* February 20, 1927.

Cast: Olive Borden (Olivette), Jacques Lerner (Jocko Lerner), Don Alvarado (Sam Wick), Malcolm Waite (Bergerin), Raymond Hitchcock (Lorenzo), Ted McNamara (Firmin), Jane Winton (Maisie), August Tollaire (Mata).

The Loves of Carmen (Fox, 1927)

Producers: William Fox, Raoul Walsh. *Director:* Raoul Walsh. *Screenplay:* Raoul Walsh, Gertrude Orr (based on the novel *Carmen* by Prosper Méri-mée). *Cinematographer:* Lucien N. Andriot. *Editors:* H. H. Caldwell, Kath-erine Hilliker. *Assistant director:* Archibald Buchanan. *Running time:* 9 reels. *Released:* September 4, 1927.

Cast: Dolores del Rio (Carmen), Don Alvarado (Jose), Victor McLaglen (Esca-millo), Nancy Nash (Michaela), Jack Baston (Morales), Mathilde Comont (Emilia), Carmen Costello (Teresa), Fred Kohler (Gypsy Chief), Rafael Val-verde (Miguel).

Sadie Thompson (United Artists, 1928)

Producers: Raoul Walsh, Gloria Swanson (uncredited). *Director:* Raoul Walsh. *Screenplay:* Raoul Walsh (based on the story "Miss Thompson" by W. Som-erset Maugham and the play *Rain* dramatized from it by John Colton and Clemence Randolph). *Cinematographers:* George Barnes, Robert Kurrle, Oliver Marsh. *Editor:* C. Gardner Sullivan. *Art director:* William Cameron Menzies. *Running time:* 9 reels. *Released:* January 7, 1928.

Cast: Gloria Swanson (Sadie Thompson), Lionel Barrymore (Alfred David-son), Blanche Friderici (Mrs. Alfred Davidson), Charles Lane (Dr. Angus McPhail), Florence Midgley (Mrs. Angus McPhail), James A. Marcus (Joe Horn), Sophie Artega (Ameena), Will Stanton (Quartermaster Bates), Raoul Walsh (Sgt. Timothy O'Hara).

Notes: Filmed in Los Angeles and on Santa Catalina Island. Later filmed as *Rain* (1932, Lewis Milestone) and *Miss Sadie Thompson* (1953, Curtis Berhnardt).

Me, Gangster (Fox, 1928)

Producer: William Fox. *Director:* Raoul Walsh. *Screenplay:* Raoul Walsh, Charles Francis Coe (based on a story by Charles Francis Coe). *Cinema-tographer:* Arthur Edeson. *Editor:* Louis R. Loeffler. *Assistant director:* Ar-chibald Buchanan. *Running time:* 70 minutes. *Released:* October 20, 1928.

Cast: June Collyer (Mary Regan), Don Terry (Jimmy Williams), Anders Ran-dolf (Russ Williams), Carole Lombard (Blonde Rosie).

The Red Dance (a.k.a. The Red Dancer of Moscow) (Fox, 1928)

Producer: Raoul Walsh. *Director:* Raoul Walsh. *Screenplay:* James Ashmore Creelman (based on a story by Eleanor Browne, adapted from the novel *The*

Red Dancer of Moscow by H. L. Gates). *Cinematographers:* Charles Clarke, John Marta. *Editor:* Louis R. Loeffler. *Music:* Erno Rapee, S. L. Rothfael. *Assistant director:* Archibald Buchanan. *Running time:* 10 reels. *Released:* December 2, 1928.

Cast: Dolores del Rio (Tasia), Charles Farrell (Grand Duke Eugen), Ivan Linow (Ivan Petroff), Boris Charsky (Agitator), Dorothy Revier (Princess Varvara), Andres de Segurola (Gen. Tanaroff), Demetrius Alexis (Rasputin).

Note: Originally released with sound effects and tinted sequences. Footage was used in Walsh's *The Yellow Ticket.*

In Old Arizona (Fox, 1929)

Directors: Irving Cummings, Raoul Walsh. *Screenplay:* Tom Barry (based on the story "The Caballero's Way" by O. Henry). *Cinematographer:* Arthur Edeson. *Editor:* Louis R. Loeffler. *Sound:* Edmund H. Hansen. *Running time:* 7 reels. *Released:* January 20, 1929.

Cast: Warner Baxter (The Cisco Kid), Edmund Lowe (Sgt. Mickey Dunn), Dorothy Burgess (Tonia Maria).

Notes: Filmed in Zion and Bryce Canyon National Parks, UT, the Mojave Desert, Victorville, and the San Fernando and San Juan Capistrano Missions, CA. Baxter won an Academy Award for best actor playing the role originally intended for Walsh, who had to withdraw when he lost his eye.

The Cock-Eyed World (Fox, 1929)

Producer: William Fox. *Director:* Raoul Walsh. *Screenplay:* Raoul Walsh, with dialogue by William K. Wells (based on a story by Maxwell Anderson and Laurence Stallings). *Cinematographer:* Arthur Edeson. *Editor:* Jack Dennis. *Set decorators:* Ben Carré, David Hall. *Sound:* Edmund H. Hansen. *Assistant director:* Archibald Buchanan. *Running time:* 12 reels. *Released:* October 20, 1929.

Cast: Victor McLaglen (Top Sgt. Flagg), Edmund Lowe (Sgt. Harry Quirt), Lili Damita (Mariana Elenita), Leila Karnelly (Olga), El Brendel (Yump Olson), Bob Burns (Connors), Jeanette Dagna (Katinka), Joe Brown (Brownie), Stuart Erwin (Buckley), Ivan Linow (Sanovich), Jean Laverty (Fanny), Soledad Jimenez (Innkeeper), Curly Dresden (O'Sullivan), Joe Rochay (Jacobs), Willie Keeler (Brawler).

Notes: Filmed at Mare Island Naval Yard, Vallejo, and in San Diego, CA. Released in both sound and silent versions.

Hot for Paris (Fox, 1929)

Producer: William Fox. *Director:* Raoul Walsh. *Screenplay:* Charles J. McGuirk, William K. Wells (based on a story by Raoul Walsh). *Cinematographer:* Charles Van Enger. *Editor:* Jack Dennis. *Art director:* David S. Hall. *Set decorator:* Ben Carré. *Costume designer:* Sophie Wachner. *Sound:*

George Leverett. *Assistant director:* Archibald Buchanan. *Running time:* 7 reels. *Released:* December 22, 1929.

Cast: Victor McLaglen (John Patrick Duke), Fifi D'Orsay (Fifi Dupre), El Brendel (Axel Olson), Polly Moran (Polly), Lennox Pawle (Mr. Pratt), August Tollaire (Papa Gouset), George Fawcett (Chop captain), Charles Judels (Charlott Gouset), Edward Dillon (Ship's Cook), Rosita Marstini (Fifi's mother), Agostino Borgato (Fifi's father), Yola D'Avril (Yola Dupre), Anita Murray (Mimi), Dave Balles (Monsieur Furrier).

The Big Trail (Fox, 1930)

Producer: Winfield R. Sheehan. *Director:* Raoul Walsh. *Screenplay:* Jack Peabody, Marie Boyle, Florence Postal (based on a story by Hal G. Evarts). *Cinematographers:* Lucien N. Andriot (35-mm version), Arthur Edeson (70-mm wide-screen version). *Editor:* Jack Dennis. *Set decorators:* Harold Miles, Fred Sersen. *Production manager:* Archibald Buchanan. *Running time:* 125 minutes (35-mm version), 156 minutes (70-mm wide-screen version). *Released:* November 1, 1930.

Cast: John Wayne (Breck Coleman), Marguerite Churchill (Ruth Cameron), El Brendel (Gus), Tully Marshall (Zeke), Tyrone Power Sr. (Red Flack), David Rollins (Dave Cameron), Frederick Burton (Pa Bascom), Ian Keith (Bill Thorpe), Charles Stevens (Lopez), Louise Carver (Gus's mother-in-law).

Notes: Filmed on location at Jackson Hole and Grand Tetons, WY; Saint George, UT; Yuma, AZ; Moesie, MT; and at Grand Canyon, Sequoia, and Yellowstone National Parks. Five different versions of this film were shot simultaneously: (1) a 70-mm version in the Grandeur process for exhibition in the biggest movie palaces; (2) a standard 35-mm version for general release; (3) a 35-mm alternate French-language version *La piste des géants* (1931); (4) a 35-mm alternate Spanish-language version *La gran jornada* (1931); and (5) a 35-mm alternate German-language version *Die große Fahrt* (1931). The three alternate-language versions were shot with mostly different casts.

The Man Who Came Back (Fox, 1931)

Producers: W. R. Sheehan, Raoul Walsh. *Director:* Raoul Walsh. *Screenplay:* E. J. Burke (based on the play by Jules Eckert Goodman, which is based on a novel by John Fleming Wilson). *Cinematographer:* Arthur Edeson. *Editor:* Harold D. Schuster. *Art director:* Joseph Urban. *Sound:* George Leverett. *Running time:* 74 minutes. *Released:* January 11, 1931.

Cast: Janet Gaynor (Angie Randolph), Charles Farrell (Stephen Randolph), Kenneth MacKenna (Capt. Trevelyan), William Holden (Thomas Randolph), Mary Forbes (Mrs. Gaynes), Ullrich Haupt (Charles Reisling), Willam Worthington (Capt. Gallon), Peter Gawthorne (Griggs), Leslie Fenton (Baron le Duc).

Note: Remake of a 1924 film directed by Emmett Flynn.

Women of All Nations (Fox, 1931)

Director: Raoul Walsh. *Screenplay:* Barry Conners. *Cinematographer:* Lucien N. Andriot. *Editor:* Jack Dennis. *Music:* Carli Elinor. *Art director:* David S. Hall. *Sound:* George Leverett. *Running time:* 72 minutes. *Released:* May 31, 1931.

Cast: Victor McLaglen (Capt. Jim Flagg), Edmund Lowe (Sgt. Harry Quirt), Greta Nissen (Elsa), El Brendel (Olsen), Bela Lugosi (Prince Hassan), Fifi D'Orsay (Fifi), Humphrey Bogart (Stone; scenes deleted).

The Spider (Fox, 1931)

Associate producer: William Sistrom. *Directors:* Kenneth MacKenna, William Cameron Menzies. *Writers:* Lowell Brentano (play), Barry Connors, Philip Klein (screenplay). *Cinematographer:* James Howe (James Wong Howe). *Running time:* 59 minutes. *Released:* September 27, 1931.

Cast: Edmund Lowe (Chatrand), Lois Moran (Beverly), Ed Brendel (Ole).

Note: Walsh directed scenes uncredited.

The Yellow Ticket (Fox, 1931)

Producers: William Fox, Raoul Walsh. *Director:* Raoul Walsh. *Screenplay:* Jules Furthman, Guy Bolton (based on the play by Michael Morton). *Cinematographer:* James Wong Howe. *Editor:* Jack Murray. *Music:* Carli Elinor. *Art director:* William S. Darling. *Sound:* W. D. Flick. *Assistant director:* Don B. Greenwood. *Running time:* 81 minutes. *Released:* October 30, 1931.

Cast: Elissa Landi (Marya Kalish), Lionel Barrymore (Count Andreeff), Laurence Olivier (Julian Rolfe), Walter Byron (Count Nikolai), Arnold Korff (Grandfather Kalish), Mischa Auer (Melchior), Edwin Maxwell (Police Agent Boligoff), Rita La Roy (Fania Rubinstein).

Wild Girl (Fox, 1932)

Producer: William Fox. *Director:* Raoul Walsh. *Screenplay:* Doris Anderson, Edwin Justus Mayer (based on the story "Salomy Jane's Kiss" by Bret Harte). *Cinematographer:* Norbert Brodine. *Editor:* Jack Murray. *Music:* Louis De Francesco. *Set decorator:* Joseph C. Wright. *Costume designer:* Earl Luick. *Running time:* 78 minutes. *Released:* October 9, 1932.

Cast: Charles Farrell (Billy, the Stranger), Joan Bennett (Salomy Jane), Ralph Bellamy (Jack Marbury), Eugene Pallette (Yuba Bill), Irving Pichel (Rufe Waters), Minna Gombell (Millie, the prostitute), Willard Robertson (Red Pete), Sarah Padden (Lize), Morgan Wallace (Phineas Baldwin).

Me and My Gal (Fox, 1932)

Producer: Raoul Walsh. *Director:* Raoul Walsh. *Screenplay:* Arthur Kober (based on the story "Pier 13" by Philip Klein and Barry Conners). *Cinema-*

tographer: Arthur C. Miller. *Editor:* Jack Murray. *Music:* George Lipschul-tz. *Art director:* Gordon Wiles. *Costume designer:* Rita Kaufman. *Sound:* George Leverett. *Running time:* 78 minutes. *Released:* December 4, 1932.

Cast: Spencer Tracy (Danny Dolan), Joan Bennett (Helen Riley), Marion Burns (Kate Riley), George Walsh (Duke), J. Farrell MacDonald (Pop Riley), Noel Madison (Baby Face), Henry B. Walthall (Sarge), Bert Hanlon (Jake), Adrian Morris (Allen), George Chandler (Eddie Collins).

Note: Remade in 1940 by Eugene Ford with the title *Pier 13*.

Sailor's Luck (Fox, 1933)

Director: Raoul Walsh. *Screenplay:* Charlotte Miller, Marguerite Roberts (based on a story by Bert Hanlon). *Cinematographer:* Arthur C. Miller. *Editor:* Jack Murray. *Art director:* Joseph C. Wright. *Costume designer:* William Lambert. *Sound:* George Leverett. *Running time:* 64 minutes. *Released:* March 17, 1933.

Cast: James Dunn (Jimmy Harrigan), Sally Eilers (Sally Brent), Victor Jory (Baron Portola), Sammy Cohen (Barnacle Benny), Frank Moran (Bilge), Esther Muir (Minnie Broadhurst), Will Stanton (J. Felix Hemingway), Armand "Curly" Wright (Angelo), Jerry Mandy (Rico), Lucien Littlefield (Elmer Brown), Buster Phelps (Elmer Brown Jr.), Frank Atkinson (Attendant).

Hello Sister! (Fox, 1933)

Producers: Winfield R. Sheehan, Sol M. Wurtzel. *Director:* Erich von Stroheim, Alfred L. Werker, Alan Crosland. *Screenplay:* Erich von Stroheim, Leonard Spigelglass (based on the play *Walking Down Broadway* by Dawn Powell). *Cinematographer:* James Wong Howe. *Editor:* Frank E. Hull. *Costume designer:* Rita Kaufman. *Sound:* Alfred Bruzlin. *Running time:* 59 minutes. *Released:* April 14, 1933.

Cast: James Dunn (Jimmy), Zasu Pitts (Millie), Boots Mallory (Peggy), Minna Gombell (Mona), Terrance Ray (Mac).

Note: James Wong Howe attributed scenes shot on Coney Island to Walsh.

The Bowery (United Artists/Twentieth Century, 1933)

Producer: Darryl F. Zanuck. *Director:* Raoul Walsh. *Screenplay:* Howard Estabrook, James Gleason (based on the novel *Chuck Connors* by Michael L. Simmons and Bessie Roth Solomon). *Cinematographer:* Barney McGill. *Editor:* Allen McNeil. *Music:* Alfred Newman. *Art director:* Richard Day. *Running time:* 92 minutes. *Released:* October 7, 1933.

Cast: Wallace Beery (Chuck Connors), George Raft (Steve Brodie), Jackie Cooper (Swipes McGurk), Fay Wray (Lucy Calhoun), Pert Kelton (Trixie Odbray), Herman Bing (Max Herman), Oscar Apfel (Ivan Rummel), Ferdinand Munier (Honest Mike), George Walsh (John L. Sullivan), Lillian Harmer (Carrie A. Nation).

Going Hollywood (MGM, 1933)

Producer: Walter Wanger. Director: Raoul Walsh. Screenplay: Donald Ogden Stewart (from a story by Frances Marion). Cinematographer: George J. Folsey. Editor: Frank Sullivan. Music: Nacio Herb Brown, Arthur Freed. Art director: Merrill Pye. Costume designer: Adrian. Sound: Douglas Shearer. Running time: 80 minutes. Released: December 22, 1933.

Cast: Marion Davies (Sylvia Bruce), Bing Crosby (Bill "Billy" Williams), Fifi D'Orsay (Lili Yvonne), Stuart Erwin (Ernest Pratt Baker), Ned Sparks (Mr. Bert Conroy), Patsy Kelly (Jill Barker), Bobby Watson (Jack Thompson), Three Radio Rogues (Group performing imitations).

Operator 13 (MGM, 1934)

Producer: Lucien Hubbard. Director: Richard Boleslawski. Screenplay: Harvey F. Thew, Zelda Spears, Eve Greene (based on stories by Robert W. Chambers). Cinematographer: George J. Folsey. Editor: Frank Sullivan. Art director: Cedric Gibbons. Costume designer: Adrian. Running time: 85 minutes. Released: June 8, 1934.

Cast: Marion Davies (Gail Loveless), Gary Cooper (Cpt. Jack Gailliard), Jean Parker (Eleanor Shackleford), Katharine Alexander (Pauline Cushman), Ted Healy ("Doctor" Hitchcock).

Note: Walsh was replaced by Boleslawski after six days of shooting.

Under Pressure (Fox, 1935)

Producer: Robert Kane. Director: Raoul Walsh. Screenplay: Borden Chase, Lester Cole, Noel Pierce, Billy Wilder (based on the book Sand Hog by Borden Chase and Edward Doherty). Cinematographers: Hal Mohr, L. William O'Connell. Costume designer: William Lambert. Running time: 72 minutes. Released: February 2, 1935.

Cast: Edmund Lowe (Shocker Dugan), Victor McLaglen (Jumbo Smith), Florence Rice (Pat Dodge), Marjorie Rambeau (Amelia "Amy" Hardcastle), Charles Bickford (Nipper Moran), Sig Ruman (Doctor), Roger Imhof (George Breck), Warner Richmond (Weasel), Jack Wallace (The Kid), James Donlan (Corky).

Baby Face Harrington (MGM, 1935)

Producer: Edgar Selwyn. Director: Raoul Walsh. Screenplay: Nunnally Johnson, Edwin H. Knopf, with dialogue by Charles Lederer (based on the play Something to Brag About by Edgar Selywyn and William LeBaron). Cinematographer: Oliver T. Marsh. Editor: William S. Gray. Art director: Cedric Gibbons. Art directors: Howard Campbell, Edwin B. Willis. Sound: Douglas Shearer. Running time: 61 minutes. Released: June 19, 1935.

Cast: Charles Butterworth (Willie Harrington), Una Merkel (Millie Harrington), Harvey Stephens (Ronald Lawford), Eugene Pallette (Uncle Henry

Parker), Nat Pendleton (Rocky Bannister), Ruth Selwyn (Dorothy), Donald Meek (Mr. Skinner), Dorothy Libaire (Edith), Edward J. Nugent (Albert), Robert Livingston (George), Stanley Fields ("Moider" Mullens).

Every Night at Eight (Paramount, 1935)

Producer: Walter Wanger. *Director:* Raoul Walsh. *Screenplay:* Gene Towne, C. Graham Baker (based on the story "Three on a Mike" by Stanley Garvey). *Cinematographer:* James Van Trees. *Editor:* W. Donn Hayes. *Production designer:* Alexander Toluboff. *Costume designer:* Helen Taylor. *Sound:* Hugo Grenzbach. *Running time:* 80 minutes. *Released:* August 2, 1935.

Cast: George Raft ("Tops" Cardona), Alice Faye (Dixie Foley), Patsy Kelly (Daphne O'Connor), Frances Langford (Susan Moore), Walter Catlett (Master of ceremonies), Henry Taylor, Jimmy Hollywood, Eddie Bartell (The Radio Rogues)

Note: Filmed at Coldwater Canyon, Los Angeles. Walsh received $3,000 per week with an eight-week guarantee. Shooting lasted from May 27 through June 29, 1935.

Klondike Annie (Paramount, 1936)

Producer: William LeBaron. *Director:* Raoul Walsh. *Screenplay:* Mae West, Frank Dazey (based on a story by Marion Morgan and George B. Dowell). *Cinematographer:* George T. Clemens. *Editor:* Stuart Heisler. *Music and lyrics:* Sam Coslow, Gene Austin, Jimmie Johnson. *Art directors:* Hans Dreier, Bernard Herzbrun. *Set decorator:* A. E. Freudeman. *Sound:* Harold Lewis, Louis Mesenkop. *Running time:* 80 minutes. *Released:* February 21, 1936.

Cast: Mae West (The Frisco Doll/Rose Carlton/Sister Annie Alden), Victor McLaglen (Bull Brackett), Phillip Reed (Inspector Jack Forrest), Helen Jerome Eddy (Sister Annie Alden), Harry Beresford (Brother Bowser), Harold Huber (Chan Lo), Lucile Gleason (Big Tess), Conway Tearle (Vance Palmer).

Big Brown Eyes (Paramount, 1936)

Producer: Walter Wanger. *Director:* Raoul Walsh. *Screenplay:* Bert Hanlon, Raoul Walsh (based on a story by James Edward Grant). *Cinematographer:* George T. Clemens. *Editor:* Robert L. Simpson. *Art director:* Alexander Toluboff. *Set decorator:* Howard Bristol. *Costume designer:* Helen Taylor. *Sound:* Hugo Grenzbach. *Assistant director:* David MacDonald. *Running time:* 77 minutes. *Released:* April 3, 1936.

Cast: Cary Grant (Det. Sgt. Danny Barr), Joan Bennett (Eve Fallon), Walter Pidgeon (Richard Morey), Lloyd Nolan (Russ Cortig), Alan Baxter (Cary Butler), Marjorie Gateson (Mrs. Chesley Cole), Isabel Jewell (Bessie Blair), Douglas Fowley (Benjamin "Benny" Battle), Henry Brandon (Don Butler).

Note: Filmed in March 1936.

Palm Springs (Paramount, 1936)

Producer: Walter Wanger. *Director:* Aubrey Scotto. *Screenplay:* Joseph Fields, Humphrey Pearson (based on the story "Lady Smith" by Myles Connolly). *Cinematographer:* James Van Trees. *Editor:* Robert L. Simpson. *Production designer:* Alexander Toluboff. *Costume designer:* Helen Taylor. *Running time:* 72 minutes. *Released:* June 5, 1936.

Cast: Frances Langford (Joan Smyth), Guy Standing (Cpt. Smyth), Ernest Cossart (Starkey), Smith Ballew (Slim), Spring Byington (Aunt Letty), David Niven (George Britell).

Note: The film was partially reshot by Walsh at the request of the producer Walter Wanger.

Spendthrift (Paramount, 1936)

Producer: Walter Wanger. *Director:* Raoul Walsh. *Screenplay:* Bert Hanlon, Eric Hatch, Raoul Walsh. *Cinematographer:* Leon Shamroy. *Editor:* Robert L. Simpson. *Art director:* Alexander Toluboff. *Costume designer:* Helen Taylor. *Running time:* 70 minutes. *Released:* July 22, 1936.

Cast: Henry Fonda (Townsend Middleton), Pat Peterson (Valerie "Boots" O'Connell), Mary Brian (Sally Barnaby), George Barbier (Uncle Morton Middleton), Edward Brophy (Bill McGuire), Richard Carle (Popsy).

O.H.M.S. (a.k.a. *You're in the Army Now*) (Gaumont-British, 1937)

Executive producer: Geoffrey Barkas. *Producer:* Sydney Box. *Director:* Raoul Walsh. *Screenplay:* Austin Melford, Bryan Edgar Wallace (after a story by Lesser Samuels and Ralph Gilbert Bettinson). *Cinematographer:* Roy Kellino. *Musical director:* Louis Levy. *Art directors:* Edward Carrick, Ernö Metzner. *Costume designer:* Marianne. *Sound:* Sydney Wiles. *Running time:* 87 minutes. *Released:* April 15, 1937.

Cast: Wallace Ford (Jimmy Tracy), John Mills (Cpl. Bert Dawson), Anna Lee (Sally Briggs), Grace Bradley (Jean Burdett), Frank Cellier (Regimental Sgt.-Maj. Briggs), Peter Croft (student).

Note: Walsh arrived back in Hollywood from England on January 23, 1937, to accumulate cast for *The Killer,* a Criterion picture in England. He wanted to feature Frances Farmer in the lead, but the production never got under way.

Jump for Glory (a.k.a. *When Thief Meets Thief*) (United Artists, 1937)

Producers: Douglas Fairbanks Jr., Marcel Hellman. *Director:* Raoul Walsh. *Screenplay:* Harold French, John Meehan Jr. (based on a novel by Gordon McDonnell). *Cinematographer:* Victor Arménise. *Editor:* Conrad von Molo. *Original music:* Percival Mackey. *Art director:* Edward Carrick. *Costume designers:* Norman Hartnell, Schiaparelli. *Running time:* 90 minutes. *Released:* June 14, 1937.

Cast: Douglas Fairbanks Jr. (Ricky Morgan), Valerie Hobson (Glory Fane), Alan Hale (Jim Diall/"Col. Fane"), Jack Melford (Thompson), Anthony Ireland (Sir Timothy Haddon), Barbara Everest (Mrs. Nolan), Edward Rigby (Sanders), Esme Percy (Robinson).

Artists and Models (Paramount, 1937)

Producers: Adolph Zukor, Lewis E. Gensler. Director: Raoul Walsh. Screenplay: Walter DeLeon, Lewis E. Gensler, Frances Martin (from a story by Eugene Thackeray and Sig Herzig). Cinematographer: Victor Milner. Editor: Ellsworth Hoagland. Music: Ted Koehler, Victor Young, Harold Arlen, Frederick Hollander, Leo Robin. Staging director: Vincente Minnelli. Running time: 97 minutes. Released: August 13, 1937.

Cast: Jack Benny (Mac Brewster), Ida Lupino (Paula Sewell, Paula Monterey), Richard Arlen (Alan Townsend), Gail Patrick (Cynthia Wentworth), Ben Blue (Jupiter Pluvius), Judy Canova (Toots), Cecil Cunningham (Stella), Donald Meek (Dr. Zimmer), Hedda Hopper (Mrs. Townsend).

Hitting a New High (RKO, 1937)

Producer: Jesse L. Lasky. Director: Raoul Walsh. Screenplay: Gertrude Purcell, John Twist (based on a story by Robert Harari and Maxwell Shane). Cinematographer: J. Roy Hunt. Editor: Desmond Marquette. Music: Andre Kostelanetz. Art director: Van Nest Polglase. Costume designer: Edward Stevenson. Running time: 85 minutes. Released: December 24, 1937.

Cast: Lily Pons (Suzette, a.k.a. Oogahunga the Bird Girl), Jack Oakie (Corny Davis), John Howard (Jimmy James), Eric Blore (Cedric Cosmo), Edward Everett Horton (Lucius B. Blynn), Eduardo Ciannelli (Andreas Mazzini), Luis Alberni (Luis Marlo), Vinton Hayworth (Carter Haig), Leonard Carey (Jervons).

College Swing (Paramount, 1938)

Producers: Adolph Zukor, Lewis E. Gensler. Director: Raoul Walsh. Screenplay: Walter DeLeon, Francis Martin (from a story by Frederick Hazlitt Brennan). Cinematographer: Victor Milner. Editor: LeRoy Stone. Musical director: Boris Morros. Art directors: Hans Dreier, Ernst Fegté. Costume designer: Edith Head. Sound: Harold Lewis, Howard Lewis. Running time: 86 minutes. Released: April 29, 1938.

Cast: George Burns (George Jonas), Gracie Allen (Gracie Alden), Martha Raye (Mabel Grady), Bob Hope (Bud Brady), Edward Everett Horton (Hubert Dash), Florence George (Ginna Ashburn), Betty Grable (Betty), Jackie Coogan (Jackie), John Payne (Martin Bates).

St. Louis Blues (Paramount, 1939)

Producer: Jeff Lazarus. Director: Raoul Walsh. Screenplay: Jack Moffitt, Malcolm Stuart Boylan, Virginia Van Upp (based on a story by Eleanore Griffin and William Rankin). *Cinematographer:* Theodor Sparkuhl. *Editor:* William Shea. *Music:* Frank Loesser. *Art director:* Hans Dreier. *Running time:* 87 minutes. *Released:* February 3, 1939.

Cast: Dorothy Lamour (Norma Malone), Lloyd Nolan (Dave Guerney), Tito Guízar (Rafael San Ramos), Jerome Cowan (Ivan DeBrett), Jessie Ralph (Aunt Tibbie), William Frawley (Maj. Martingale), Mary Parker (Punkins).

The Roaring Twenties (Warner Bros., 1939)

Executive producer: Hal B. Wallis. *Director:* Raoul Walsh. *Screenplay:* Jerry Wald, Richard Macaulay, Robert Rossen (based on the story "The World Moves On" by Mark Hellinger). *Cinematographer:* Ernest Haller. *Editor:* Jack Killifer. *Art director:* Max Parker. *Makeup:* Perc Westmore. *Sound:* Everett A. Brown. *Special effects:* Edwin B. DuPar, Byron Haskin. *Running time:* 106 minutes. *Released:* October 23, 1939.

Cast: James Cagney (Eddie Bartlett), Priscilla Lane (Jean Sherman), Humphrey Bogart (George Hally), Gladys George (Panama Smith), Jeffrey Lynn (Lloyd Hart), Frank McHugh (Danny Green), Paul Kelly (Nick Brown).

Dark Command (Republic, 1940)

Producer: Sol C. Siegel. *Director:* Raoul Walsh. *Screenplay:* Grover Jones, Lionel Houser, F. Hugh Herbert (based on the novel by W. R. Burnett). *Cinematographer:* Jack A. Marta. *Editor:* William Morgan. *Music:* Victor Young. *Art director:* John Victor Mackay. *Running time:* 93 minutes. *Released:* April 15, 1940.

Cast: Claire Trevor (Mary McCloud), John Wayne (Bob Seton), Walter Pidgeon (William "Will" Cantrell), Roy Rogers (Fletcher "Fletch" McCloud), George "Gabby" Hayes (Andrew "Doc" Grunch), Porter Hall (Angus McCloud), Marjorie Main (Mrs. Cantrell, a.k.a. Mrs. Adams), Raymond Walburn (Judge Bucker), Joe Sawyer (Bushropp), Helen MacKellar (Mrs. Hale).

They Drive by Night (Warner Bros., 1940)

Executive producer: Hal B. Wallis. *Director:* Raoul Walsh. *Screenplay:* Jerry Wald, Richard Macaulay (based on the novel *Long Haul* by A. I. Bezzerides). *Cinematographer:* Arthur Edeson. *Editor:* Thomas Richards. *Music:* Adolph Deutsch. *Art director:* John Hughes. *Costume designer:* Milo Anderson. *Sound:* Oliver S. Garretson. *Makeup:* Perc Westmore. *Special effects:* Byron Haskin, Hans F. Koenekamp. *Running time:* 95 minutes. *Released:* August 3, 1940.

Cast: George Raft (Joe Fabrini), Ann Sheridan (Cassie Hartley), Ida Lupino (Lana Carlsen), Humphrey Bogart (Paul Fabrini), Gale Page (Pearl Fabrini), Alan Hale (Ed Carlsen), Roscoe Karns (Irish McGurn), John Litel (Harry McNamara), George Tobias (George Rondolos).

High Sierra (Warner Bros. 1941)

Executive producer: Hal B. Wallis. *Director:* Raoul Walsh. *Screenplay:* John
Huston, W. R. Burnett (based on the novel by W. R. Burnett). *Cinematographer:* Tony Gaudio. *Editor:* Jack Killifer. *Music:* Adolph Deutsch. *Art director:* Ted Smith. *Costume designer:* Milo Anderson. *Sound:* Dolph Thomas.
Makeup: Perc Westmore. *Special effects:* Byron Haskin, Hans F. Koenekamp.
Running time: 110 minutes. *Released:* January 25, 1941.

Cast: Ida Lupino (Marie), Humphrey Bogart (Roy Earle), Alan Curtis (Babe),
Arthur Kennedy (Red), Joan Leslie (Velma), Henry Hull ("Doc" Banton),
Henry Travers (Pa), Jerome Cowan (Healy).

Note: Remade twice, as *Colorado Territory* (Walsh, 1949) and *I Died a Thousand Times* (Stuart Heisler, 1955).

The Strawberry Blonde (Warner Bros., 1941)

Producers: Hal B. Wallis, William Cagney. *Director:* Raoul Walsh. *Screenplay:*
Julius J. Epstein, Philip G. Epstein (based on the play *One Sunday Afternoon*
by James Hagan). *Cinematographer:* James Wong Howe. *Editor:* William
Holmes. *Music:* Heinz Roemheld. *Art director:* Robert M. Haas. *Costume
designer:* Orry-Kelly. *Sound:* Robert B. Lee. *Makeup:* Perc Westmore. *Special effects:* Willard Van Enger. *Running time:* 99 minutes. *Released:* February 22, 1941.

Cast: James Cagney (Biff Grimes), Olivia de Havilland (Amy Lind), Rita Hayworth (Virginia Brush), Alan Hale (Old Man Grimes), Jack Carson (Hugo
Barnstead), George Tobias (Nicholas Pappalas), Una O'Connor (Mrs. Mulcahey), George Reeves (Harold).

Manpower (Warner Bros., 1941)

Producers: Hal B. Wallis, Mark Hellinger, Jack Saper. *Director:* Raoul Walsh.
Screenplay: Richard Macaulay, Jerry Wald. *Cinematographer:* Ernest Haller.
Editor: Ralph Dawson. *Music:* Adolph Deutsch. *Art director:* Max Parker.
Costume designer: Milo Anderson. *Sound:* Dolph Thomas. *Makeup:* Perc
Westmore. *Special effects:* Byron Haskin, Hans F. Koenekamp. *Running
time:* 104 minutes. *Released:* August 9, 1941.

Cast: Edward G. Robinson (Hank "Gimpy" McHenry), Marlene Dietrich (Fay
Duval), George Raft (Johnny Marshall), Alan Hale (Jumbo Wells), Frank
McHugh (Omaha), Eve Arden (Dolly), Barton MacLane (Smiley Quinn),
Ward Bond (Eddie Adams).

They Died with Their Boots On (Warner Bros., 1941)

Producers: Hal B. Wallis, Robert Fellows. *Director:* Raoul Walsh. *Screenplay:*
Wally Kline, Aeneas MacKenzie. *Cinematographer:* Bert Glennon. *Editor:*
William Holmes. *Music:* Max Steiner. *Art director:* John Hughes. *Costume*

designer: Milo Anderson. *Sound:* Dolph Thomas. *Makeup:* Perc Westmore. *New York premiere:* December 1941. *Running time:* 140 minutes. *Released:* December 1941 and January 1, 1942.

Cast: Errol Flynn (George Armstrong Custer), Olivia de Havilland (Elizabeth Bacon), Arthur Kennedy (Ned Sharp), Charley Grapewin (California Joe), Gene Lockhart (Samuel Bacon, Esq.), Anthony Quinn (Crazy Horse), Stanley Ridges (Maj. Romulus Taipe), John Litel (Gen. Phil Sheridan), Walter Hampden (William Sharp), Sydney Greenstreet (Lt. Gen. Winfield Scott), Hattie McDaniel (Callie).

Note: Filmed in Pasadena, Calabasas, and Chatsworth, CA.

In This Our Life (Warner Bros., 1942)

Executive producer: Hall Wallis. *Associate producer:* David Lewis. *Director:* John Huston. *Screenplay:* Howard Koch. *Cinematographer:* Ernie Haller. *Editor:* William Holmes. *Music:* Max Steiner. *Art director:* Robert Haas. *Visual effects:* Byron Haskin. *Makeup:* Pere Westmore. *Costume-wardrobe:* Orry-Kelly. *Sound:* Robert B. Lee. *Running time:* 97 minutes. *Released:* May 16, 1942.

Cast: Bette Davis (Stanley Timberlake), Olivia de Havilland (Roy Timberlake), George Brent (Craig Fleming), Dennis Morgan (Peter Kingsmill), Charles Coburn (William Fitzroy), Hattie McDaniel (Minerva Clay), Billie Burke (Lavinia Timberlake), Frank Craven (Asa Timberlake), Ernest Anderson (Parry Clay), Lee Patrick (Betty Wilmoth).

Note: Walsh directed the final sequence of the film. Filmed in Los Angeles and Pasadena, CA.

Desperate Journey (Warner Bros., 1942)

Producers: Hal B. Wallis, Jack Saper. *Director:* Raoul Walsh. *Screenplay:* Arthur T. Horman. *Cinematographer:* Bert Glennon. *Editor:* Rudi Fehr. *Music:* Max Steiner. *Art director:* Carl Jules Weyl. *Costume designer:* Milo Anderson. *Sound:* C. A. Riggs. *Makeup:* Perc Westmore. *Running time:* 107 minutes. *Released:* September 26, 1942.

Cast: Errol Flynn (Flight Lt. Terrence "Terry" Forbes), Ronald Reagan (Flying Officer Johnny Hammond), Nancy Coleman (Kaethe Brahms), Raymond Massey (Maj. Otto Baumeister), Alan Hale (Flight Sgt. Kirk Edwards), Arthur Kennedy (Flying Officer Jed Forrest), Ronald Sinclair (Flight Sgt. Lloyd Hollis).

Gentleman Jim (Warner Bros., 1942)

Producer: Robert Buckner. *Director:* Raoul Walsh. *Screenplay:* Vincent Lawrence, Horace McCoy (based on James J. Corbett's autobiography *The Roar of the Crowd*). *Cinematographer:* Sidney Hickox. *Editor:* Jack Killifer. *Music:* Heinz Roemheld. *Art director:* Ted Smith. *Set decorator:* Clarence

Steensen. *Costume designer:* Milo Anderson. *Sound:* C. A. Riggs. *Makeup:* Perc Westmore. *Running time:* 104 minutes. *Released:* November 25, 1942.

Cast: Errol Flynn (James J. Corbett/Gentleman Jim), Alexis Smith (Victoria Ware), Jack Carson (Walter Lowrie), Alan Hale (Pat Corbett), John Loder (Carlton De Witt), William Frawley (Billy Delaney).

Edge of Darkness (Warner Bros., 1943)

Executive producer: Jack L. Warner. *Producer:* Henry Blanke. *Director:* Lewis Nilestone. *Screenplay:* Robert Rossen. *Cinematographer:* Sid Hickox. *Editor:* David Weisbart. *Music:* Franz Waxman. *Art director:* Robert M. Haas. *Visual Effects:* Don Seigel, James Leicester, Lawrence Butler, Willard Van Enger. *Makeup:* Perc Westmore. *Costume-wardrobe:* Orry-Kelly. *Set decorator:* Julia Heron. *Sound:* Everett A. Brown. *Running time:* 120 minutes. *Released:* April 9, 1943.

Cast: Errol Flynn (Gunnar Brogge), Ann Sheridan (Karen Stensgard), Walter Huston (Dr. Martin Stensgard), Helmet Cantine (Capt. Koenig), Ruth Gordon (Ann Stensgard), Nancy Coleman (Katja), Judith Anderson (Gerd Bjarnesen), John Beal (Johann Stensgard).

Note: Walsh is thought to have supervised some action sequences. Filmed in Del Monte, CA, and in and around Monterey Bay, CA.

Action in the North Atlantic (Warner Bros., 1943)

Executive producer: Jack L. Warner. *Producer:* Jerry Wald. *Director:* Lloyd Bacon. *Screenplay:* John Howard Lawson. *Story:* Guy Gilpatric. *Additional dialogue:* W. R. Burnett, A. I. Bezzerides. *Cinematographer:* Ted McCord. *Editor:* George Amy. *Music:* Adolph Deutsch. *Composer:* Cole Porter. *Art director:* Ted Smith. *Set decorator:* Clarence Steensen. *Montage:* Don Siegel, James Leicester. *Director of special effects:* Edwin B. Du Par. *Sound:* C. A. Riggs. *Makeup:* Perc Westmore. *Running time:* 126 minutes. *Released:* June 12, 1943.

Cast: Humphrey Bogart (Joe Rossi), Raymond Massey (Capt. Steve Jarvis), Alan Hale ("Boats" O'Hara), Dane Clark (johnny Pulaski), Ruth Gordon (Sara Jarvis), Julie Bishop (Pearl O'Neill), Sam Levine ("Chips" Abrahams), Peter Whitney (Whitey Lara).

Note: Lloyd Bacon's contract expired during production. Walsh came in and shot battle sequences until the replacement director, Byron Haskin, took over.

Background to Danger (Warner Bros. 1943)

Executive producer: Jack L. Warner. *Producer:* Jerry Wald. *Director:* Raoul Walsh. *Screenplay:* W. R. Burnett (based on the novel by Eric Ambler). *Cinematographer:* Tony Gaudio. *Editor:* Jack Killifer. *Music:* Friedrich Hollaender. *Art director:* Hugh Reticker. *Set decorator:* Casey Roberts.

Costume designer: Milo Anderson. Sound: Dolph Thomas. Makeup: Perc Westmore. Special effects: Warren Lynch, Willard Van Enger. Running time: 80 minutes. Released: July 3, 1943.

Cast: George Raft (Joe Barton), Brenda Marshall (Tamara Zaleshoff), Sydney Greenstreet (Col. Robinson), Peter Lorre (Nikolai Zaleshoff), Osa Massen (Ana Remzi), Turhab Bey (Hassan).

Northern Pursuit (Warner Bros., 1943)

Executive producer: Jack L. Warner. Producer: Jack Chertok. Director: Raoul Walsh. Screenplay: Frank Gruber, Alvah Bessie (based on the story "5,000 Trojan Horses" by Leslie T. White). Cinematographer: Sidney Hickox. Editor: Jack Killifer. Music: Adolph Deutsch. Art director: Leo K. Kuter. Set decorator: Casey Roberts. Costume designer: Leah Rhodes. Sound: Stanley Jones. Makeup: Perc Westmore. Special effects: Roy Davidson. Running time: 94 minutes. Released: November 13, 1943.

Cast: Errol Flynn (Cpl. Steve Wagner), Julie Bishop (Laura McBain), Helmut Dantine (Col. Hugo von Keller), John Ridgely (Jim Austin), Gene Lockhart (Ernst), Tom Tully (Inspector Barnett).

Note: Filmed in Sun Valley, ID.

Uncertain Glory (Warner Bros., 1944)

Executive producer: Jack L. Warner. Producer: Robert Buckner. Director: Raoul Walsh. Screenplay: László Vadnay, Max Brand (based on a story by Joe May and László Vadnay). Cinematographer: Sidney Hickox. Editor: George Amy. Music: Adolph Deutsch. Art director: Robert M. Haas. Set decorator: Walter Tilford. Sound: Oliver S. Garretson. Makeup: Perc Westmore. Special effects: Roy Davidson. Running time: 102 minutes. Released: April 22, 1944.

Cast: Errol Flynn (Jean Picard), Paul Lukas (Insp. Marcel Bonet), Lucile Watson (Mme Maret), Faye Emerson (Louise), James Flavin (Captain of Mobile Guard), Douglass Dumbrille (Police Commissioner LaFarge), Jean Sullivan (Marianne), Dennis Hoey (Father Le Clerc), Odette Myrtil (Mme Bonet), Sheldon Leonard (Henri Duval), Francis Pierlot (Father La Borde).

Objective, Burma! (Warner Bros., 1945)

Executive producer: Jack L. Warner. Producer: Jerry Wald. Director: Raoul Walsh. Screenplay by Ranald MacDougall, Lester Cole (based on a story by Alvah Bessie). Cinematographer: James Wong Howe. Editor: George Amy. Music: Franz Waxman. Art director: Ted Smith. Set decorator: Jack McConaghy. Sound: C. A. Riggs. Makeup: Perc Westmore. Special effects: Edwin B. DuPar. Running time: 142 minutes. Released: February 17, 1945.

Cast: Errol Flynn (Capt. Nelson), James Brown (Sgt. Treacy), William Prince (Lt. Sid Jacobs), George Tobias (Cpl. Gabby Gordon), Henry Hull (Mark

Williams), Warner Anderson (Col. J. Carter), John Alvin (Hogan), Mark Stevens (Lt. Barker), Richard Erdman (Pvt. Nebraska Hooper).

Salty O'Rourke (Paramount, 1945)

Director: Raoul Walsh. *Screenplay:* Milton Holmes. *Cinematographer:* Theodor Sparkuhl. *Editor:* William Shea. *Music:* Robert Emmett Dolan. *Art directors:* Haldane Douglas, Hans Dreier. *Set decorator:* John MacNeil. *Costume designer:* Dorothy O'Hara. *Sound:* Earl S. Hayman, Walter Oberst. *Makeup:* Wally Westmore. *Assistant director:* Oscar Rudolph. *Running time:* 100 minutes. *Released:* April 25, 1945.

Cast: Alan Ladd (Salty O'Rourke), Gail Russell (Barbara Brooks), William Demarest (Smitty), Stanley Clements (Johnny Cates), Bruce Cabot (Doc Baxter), Spring Byington (Mrs. Brooks).

The Horn Blows at Midnight (Warner Bros., 1945)

Executive producer: Jack L. Warner. *Producer:* Mark Hellinger. *Director:* Raoul Walsh. *Screenplay:* Sam Hellman, James V. Kern (based on a story by Aubrey Wisberg). *Cinematographer:* Sidney Hickox. *Editor:* Irene Morra. *Music:* Franz Waxman. *Art Director:* Hugh Reticker. *Set decorator:* Clarence Steensen. *Costume designer:* Milo Anderson. *Sound:* Gerald W. Alexander, Charles David Forrest, Stanley Jones, Robert G. Wayne. *Makeup:* Perc Westmore. *Running time:* 80 minutes. *Released:* April 28, 1945.

Cast: Jack Benny (Athanael), Alexis Smith (Elizabeth), Dolores Moran (Violinist/Fran Blackstone), Allyn Joslyn (Second Trumpeter/Osidro), Reginald Gardiner (Composer/Archie Dexter), Guy Kibbee (Radio director/the Chief), John Alexander (First trumpeter/Doremus), Franklin Pangborn (Radio engineer/Sloan), Margaret Dumont (Mme Traviata/Miss Rodholder), Robert Blake (Junior Pulplinsky).

The Man I Love (Warner Bros., 1947)

Executive producer: Jack L. Warner. *Producer:* Arnold Albert. *Director:* Raoul Walsh. *Screenplay:* Jo Pagano, Catherine Turney (based on the novel *Night Shift* by Maritta M. Wolff). *Cinematographer:* Sidney Hickox. *Editor:* Owen Marks. *Music:* George Gershwin. *Art director:* Stanley Fleischer. *Set decorator:* Eddie Edwards. *Costume designer:* Milo Anderson. *Sound:* Dolph Thomas, Charles David Forrest. *Makeup:* Perc Westmore. *Special effects:* Harry Barndollar, Edwin B. DuPar. *Running time:* 96 minutes. *Released:* January 11, 1947.

Cast: Ida Lupino (Petey Brown), Robert Alda (Nicky Toresca), Andrea King (Sally Otis), Martha Vickers (Virginia "Ginny" Brown), Bruce Bennett (San Thomas), Alan Hale (Riley), Dolores Moran (Gloria O'Connor).

Pursued (Warner Bros., 1947)

Producer: Milton Sperling. *Director:* Raoul Walsh. *Screenplay:* Niven Busch. *Cinematographer:* James Wong Howe. *Editor:* Christian Nyby. *Music:* Max Steiner. *Art director:* Ted Smith. *Set decorator:* Jack McConaghy. *Sound:* Francis J. Scheid. *Makeup:* Perc Westmore. *Running time:* 101 minutes. *Released:* March 2, 1947.

Cast: Teresa Wright (Thor), Robert Mitchum (Jeb), Judith Anderson (Mrs. Callum), Dean Jagger (Grant), Alan Hale (Jake Dingle), John Rodney (Adam), Harry Carey Jr. (Prentice).

Note: Filmed in Gallup, NM.

Stallion Road (Warner Bros., 1947)

Executive producer: Jack L. Warner. *Producer:* Alex Gottlieb. *Director:* James V. Kern. *Cinematographer:* Arthur Edeson. *Screenplay:* Stephen Longstreet. *Editor:* David Weisbart. *Music:* Frederick Hollander. *Art director:* Stanley Fleischer. *Visual effects:* James Leicester, Willard Van Enger, Roy Davidson. *Makeup:* Perc Westmore. *Costume-wardrobe:* Milo Anderson, Leah Rhodes. *Set decorator:* Clarence Steensen. *Sound:* Stanley Jones. *Running time:* 98 minutes. *Released:* April 12, 1947.

Cast: Ronald Reagan (Larry Hanrahan), Alexis Smith (Rory Teller), Zachary Scott (Stephen Purcell), Peggy Knudson (Daisy Otis), Patti Brady (Chris Teller), Harry Davenport (Dr. Stephen).

Note: Walsh is said to have directed some action scenes.

Cheyenne (Warner Bros., 1947)

Producer: Robert Buckner. *Director:* Raoul Walsh. *Screenplay:* Alan Le May, Thames Williamson (based on a story by Paul Wellman). *Cinematographer:* Sidney Hickox. *Editor:* Christian Nyby. *Music:* Max Steiner. *Art director:* Ted Smith. *Set decorator:* Jack McConaghy. *Costume designer:* Milo Anderson. *Sound:* Oliver S. Garretson. *Makeup:* Perc Westmore. *Assistant director:* Ridgeway Callow. *Special effects:* Hans F. Koenekamp, William McGann. *Running time:* 100 minutes. *Released:* June 6, 1947.

Cast: Dennis Morgan (James Wylie), Jane Wyman (Ann Kincaid), Janis Paige (Emily Carson), Bruce Bennett (Ed Landers), Alan Hale (Fred Durkin), Arthur Kennedy (The Sundance Kid), John Ridgely (Chalkeye), Barton MacLane (Webb Yancey).

Note: Filmed in Arizona.

Silver River (Warner Bros., 1948)

Executive producer: Jack L. Warner. *Producer:* Owen Crump. *Director:* Raoul Walsh. *Screenplay:* Stephen Longstreet, Harriet Frank Jr. (based on a novel by Stephen Longstreet). *Cinematographer:* Sidney Hickox. *Editor:* Alan Crosland Jr. *Music:* Max Steiner. *Art director:* Ted Smith. *Set decorator:* William Wallace. *Costume designer:* Marjorie Best. *Sound:* Francis J. Scheid. *Makeup:* Perc Westmore. *Special effects:* Edwin B. DuPar, William McGann. *Running time:* 110 minutes. *Released:* May 29, 1948.

Cast: Errol Flynn (Mike McComb), Ann Sheridan (Georgia Moore), Thomas Mitchell (John Plato Beck), Bruce Bennett (Stanley Moore), Tom D'Andrea ("Pistol" Porter), Barton MacLane ("Banjo" Sweeney).

Note: Filmed in Bishop, CA.

Fighter Squadron (Warner Bros., 1948)

Producer: Seton I. Miller. *Director:* Raoul Walsh. *Screenplay:* Seton I. Miller, Martin Rackin. *Cinematographers:* Wilfred M. Cline, Sidney Hickox. *Editor:* Christian Nyby. *Music:* Max Steiner. *Art director:* Ted Smith. *Set decorator:* Lyle B. Reifsnider. *Sound:* Leslie G. Hewitt. *Special effects:* Roy Davidson, John Holden, Hans F. Koenekamp. *Assistant director:* Russell Saunders. *Running time:* 96 minutes. *Released:* November 27, 1948.

Cast: Edmond O'Brien (Maj. Ed Hardin), Robert Stack (Capt. Stu Hamilton), John Rodney (Col. Bill Brickley), Tom D'Andrea (Sgt. Dolan), Henry Hull (Maj. Gen. Mike McCready), James Holden (Lt. Tennessee Atkins), Walter Reed (Capt. Duke Chappell), Shepperd Strudwick (Brig. Gen. M. Gilbert), Rock Hudson (uncredited).

Note: Shot at the Oscada Air Base at Lake Huron.

One Sunday Afternoon (Warner Bros., 1948)

Producer: Jerry Wald. *Director:* Raoul Walsh. *Screenplay:* Robert L. Richards (based on the play by James Hagan). *Cinematographers:* Wilfred M. Cline, Sidney Hickox. *Editor:* Christian Nyby. *Music:* Ralph Blane. *Art director:* Anton Grot. *Set decorator:* Fred M. MacLean. *Costume designer:* Leah Rhodes. *Sound:* Leslie G. Hewitt. *Assistant director:* Russell Saunders. *New York premiere:* December 25, 1948. *Running time:* 90 minutes. *Released:* January 1, 1949.

Cast: Dennis Morgan (Timothy "Biff" Grimes), Janis Paige (Virginia Brush), Don DeFore (Hugo Barnstead), Dorothy Malone (Amy Lind), Ben Blue (Nick), Oscar O'Shea (Toby), Alan Hale Jr. (Marty).

Note: Musical version of *The Strawberry Blonde*.

Colorado Territory (Warner Bros., 1949)

Producer: Anthony Veiller. *Director:* Raoul Walsh. *Screenplay:* Edmund H. North, John Twist (based on the novel *High Sierra* by W. R. Burnett [uncredited]). *Cinematographer:* Sidney Hickox. *Editor:* Owen Marks. *Music:* David Buttolph. *Art director:* Ted Smith. *Set decorator:* Fred M. MacLean.

Costume designer: Leah Rhodes. Sound: Leslie G. Hewitt. Makeup: Perc Westmore. Special effects. Hans F. Koenekamp, William C. McGann. Running time: 94 minutes. Released: June 11, 1949.

Cast: Joel McCrea (Wes McQueen), Virginia Mayo (Colorado Carson), Dorothy Malone (Julie Ann Winslow), Henry Hull (Fred Winslow), John Archer (Reno Blake), James Mitchell (Duke Harris).

Note: Filmed in Gallup, NM.

It's a Great Feeling (Warner Bros., 1949)

Producer: Alex Gottlieb. Director: David Butler. Screenplay: Jack Rose, Melville Shavelson (based on a story by I. A. L. Diamond). Cinematographer: Wilfred M. Cline. Editor: Irene Morra. Music: Jule Styne. Art director: Stanley Fleischer. Set decorator: Lyle B. Reifsnider. Costume designer: Milo Anderson. Sound: Charles David Forrest, Dolph Thomas. Makeup: Perc Westmore. Special effects: Hans F. Koenekamp, William C. McGann. Assistant director: Philip Quinn. Running time: 85 minutes. Released: August 1, 1949.

Cast: Doris Day (Judy Adams), Dennis Morgan (himself), Jack Carson (himself), Bill Goodwin (Arthur Trent), Raoul Walsh (himself [uncredited]).

White Heat (Warner Bros., 1949)

Producer: Louis F. Edelman. Director: Raoul Walsh. Screenplay: Ivan Goff, Ben Roberts (based on a story by Virginia Kellogg). Cinematographer: Sidney Hickox. Editor: Owen Marks. Music: Max Steiner. Art director: Edward Carrère. Set decorator: Fred M. MacLean. Sound: Leslie G. Hewitt. Makeup: Perc Westmore. Special effects: Roy Davidson. Running time: 114 minutes. Released: September 2, 1949.

Cast: James Cagney (Arthur "Cody" Jarrett), Virginia Mayo (Verna Jarrett), Edmond O'Brien (Hank Fallon/Vic Pardo), Margaret Wycherly (Ma Jarrett), Steve Cochran (Big Ed Somers), John Archer (Philip Evans), Wally Cassel ("Cotton" Valletti), Fred Clark (Daniel Winston).

The West Point Story (Warner Bros., 1950)

Producer: Louis F. Edelman. Director: Roy Del Ruth. Screenplay: John Monks Jr., Charles Hoffman, Irving Wallace. Story: Irving Wallace. Cinematographer: Sid Hickox. Art director: Charles H. Clarke. Editor: Owen Marks. Set decorator: Armor E. Marlowe. Music director: Ray Heindorf. Sound: Francis J. Scheid. Running time: 107 minutes. Released: November 25, 1950.

Cast: James Cagney (Elwin "Bix" Bixby), Virginia Mayo (Eve Dillon), Doris Day (Jan Wilson), Gordon MacRae (Tom Fletcher), Gene Nelson (Hal Courtland), Alan Hale Jr. (Bull Gilbert).

Note: Walsh is said to have contributed by directing several scenes.

The Enforcer (Warner Bros., 1951)

Producer: Milton Sperling. *Directors:* Bretaigne Windust, Raoul Walsh (uncredited). *Screenplay:* Martin Rackin. *Cinematographer:* Robert Burks. *Editor:* Fred Allen. *Music:* David Buttolph. *Art director:* Charles H. Clarke. *Set decorator:* William L. Kuehl. *Sound:* Dolph Thomas. *Running time:* 87 minutes. *Released:* February 24, 1951.

Cast: Humphrey Bogart (Dist. Atty. Martin Ferguson), Zero Mostel (Big Babe Lazick), Ted de Corsia (Joseph Rico), Everett Sloane (Albert Mendoza), Roy Roberts (Capt. Frank Nelson), Michael Tolan (James "Duke" Malloy).

Note: Walsh replaced Windust after several days of shooting.

Along the Great Divide (Warner Bros., 1951)

Producer: Anthony Veiller. *Director:* Raoul Walsh. *Screenplay:* Walter Doniger, Lewis Meltzer (based on a story by Walter Doniger). *Cinematographer:* Sidney Hickox. *Editor:* Thomas Reilly. *Music:* David Buttolph. *Art director:* Edward Carrere. *Set decorator:* G. W. Berntsen. *Costume designer:* Marjorie Best. *Sound:* Leslie G. Hewitt. *Makeup:* Gordon Bau. *Assistant director:* Oren Haglund. *Running time:* 88 minutes. *Released:* June 2, 1951.

Cast: Kirk Douglas (Marshal Len Merrick), Virginia Mayo (Ann Keith), John Agar (Billy Shear), Walter Brennan (Tim "Pop" Keith), Ray Teal (Deputy Lou Gray), Hugh Sanders (Frank Newcombe), Morris Ankrum (Ed Roden).

Note: Shot at Lone Pine, Mojave Desert, CA.

Captain Horatio Hornblower R.N. (Warner Bros., 1951)

Director: Raoul Walsh. *Screenplay:* Ivan Goff, Ben Roberts, Aeneas MacKenzie. *Cinematographer:* Guy Green. *Editor:* Jack Harris. *Music:* Robert Farnon. *Art director:* Thomas N. Morahan. *Costume designers:* Sheila Graham, Thomas N. Morahan. *Sound:* Harold V. King. *Makeup:* Tony Sforzini. *Special effects:* Harry Barndollar, George Blackwell, Arthur Rhoades, Cliff Richardson. *Running time:* 117 minutes. *Released:* September 13, 1951.

Cast: Gregory Peck (Capt. Horatio Hornblower), Virginia Mayo (Lady Barbara Wellesley), Robert Beatty (Lt. William Bush), Moultrie Kelsall (Lt. Crystal), Terence Morgan (2nd Lt. Gerard).

Distant Drums (Warner Bros., 1951)

Producer: Milton Sperling. *Director:* Raoul Walsh. *Screenplay:* Niven Busch, Martin Rackin (based on a story by Niven Busch). *Cinematographer:* Sidney Hickox. *Editor:* Folmar Blangsted. *Music:* Max Steiner. *Art director:* Douglas Bacon. *Set decorator:* William Wallace. *Sound:* Oliver S. Garretson. *Costume designer:* Marjorie Best. *Makeup:* Gordon Bau. *Running time:* 101 minutes. *Released:* December 29, 1951.

Cast: Gary Cooper (Capt. Quincy Wyatt), Mari Aldon (Judy Beckett), Richard Webb (Lt. Richard Tufts), Ray Teal (Pvt. Mohair), Arthur Hunnicutt (Monk), Robert Barrat (Gen. Zachary Taylor).

Note: Filmed in the Everglades.

Glory Alley (MGM, 1952)

Producer: Nicholas Nayfack. *Director:* Raoul Walsh. *Screenplay:* Art Cohn. *Cinematographer:* William H. Daniels. *Editor:* Gene Ruggiero. *Art directors:* Malcolm Brown, Cedric Gibbons. *Set decorators:* F. Keogh Gleason, Edwin B. Willis. *Sound:* Douglas Shearer. *Costume designer:* Helen Rose. *Special effects:* A. Arnold Gillespie. *Running time:* 79 minutes. *Released:* June 6, 1952.

Cast: Ralph Meeker (Socks Barbarrosa), Leslie Caron (Angela Evans), Kurt Kasznar (Gus "The Judge" Evans), Gilbert Roland (Peppi Donnato), John McIntire (Gabe Jordan/Narrator), Louis Armstrong (Shadow Johnson).

The World in His Arms (Universal, 1952)

Producer: Aaron Rosenberg. *Director:* Raoul Walsh. *Screenplay:* Borden Chase, with dialogue by Horace McCoy (based on the novel by Rex Beach). *Cinematographer:* Russell Metty. *Editor:* Frank Gross. *Music:* Frank Skinner. *Art directors:* Alexander Golitzen, Bernard Herzbrun. *Set decorators:* Russell A. Gausman, Julia Heron. *Costume designer:* Bill Thomas. *Sound:* Leslie I. Carey, Corson Jewett. *Makeup:* Bud Westmore. *Special effects:* David S. Horsley. *Running time:* 104 minutes. *Released:* October 9, 1952.

Cast: Gregory Peck (Capt. Jonathan Clark), Ann Blyth (Countess Marina Selanova), Anthony Quinn (Portugee), John McIntire (Deacon Greathouse), Carl Esmond (Prince Semyon), Andrea King (Mamie), Eugenie Leontovich (Anna Selanova), Sig Ruman (Gen. Ivan Vorashilov).

Blackbeard the Pirate (RKO, 1952)

Producer: Edmund Grainger. *Director:* Raoul Walsh. *Screenplay:* Alan Le May (from a story by DeVallon Scott). *Cinematographer:* William E. Snyder. *Editor:* Ralph Dawson. *Music:* Victor Young. *Art directors:* Albert S. D'Agostino, Jack Oakey. *Set decorators:* Darrell Silvera, John Sturtevant. *Costume designer:* Michael Woulfe. *Sound:* Frank McWhorter, Clem Portman. *Makeup:* Mel Berns. Visual effects: Harold E. Wellmann. *Assistant director:* James E. Casey. *Running time:* 98 minutes. *Released:* December 24, 1952.

Cast: Robert Newton (Edward Teach/Blackbeard), Linda Darnell (Edwina Mansfield), William Bendix (Ben Worley), Keith Andes (Robert Maynard), Torin Thatcher (Sir Henry Morgan), Irene Ryan (Alvina), Alan Mowbray (Noll), Richard Egan (Briggs).

The Lawless Breed (Universal, 1953)

Producer: William Alland. *Director:* Raoul Walsh. *Screenplay:* Bernard Gordon (from a story by William Alland based on the life story of John Wesley Hardin as written by himself). *Cinematographer:* Irving Glassberg. *Editor:* Frank Gross. *Music:* Joseph Gershenson. *Art directors:* Bernard Herzbrun, Richard H. Riedel. *Set decorators:* Oliver Emert, Russell A. Gausman. *Costume designer:* Rosemary Odell. *Sound:* Leslie I. Carey, Corson Jewett. *Makeup:* Bud Westmore. *Assistant director:* William Holland. *Running time:* 83 minutes. *Released:* January 3, 1953.

Cast: Rock Hudson (John Wesley Hardin), Julie Adams (Rosie), Mary Castle (Jane Brown), John McIntire (J. G. Hardin/John Clements), Hugh O'Brian (Ike Hanley), Dennis Weaver (Jim Clements), Forrest Lewis (Zeke Jenkins), Lee Van Cleef (Dick Hanley).

Sea Devils (RKO, 1953)

Producer: David E. Rose. *Director:* Raoul Walsh. *Screenplay:* Borden Chase (based on the novel *Les travailleurs de la mer* by Victor Hugo). *Cinematographer:* Wilkie Cooper. *Editor:* John Seabourne Jr. *Music:* Richard Addinsell. *Production designer:* Wilfred Shingleton. *Art director:* Wilfred Shingleton. *Costume designers:* Elizabeth Agombar, R. St. John Roper. *Sound:* W. H. Lindop. *Makeup:* Jim Hydes. *Assistant director:* Philip Shipway. *Running time:* 91 minutes. *Released:* May 23, 1953.

Cast: Yvonne De Carlo (Droucette), Rock Hudson (Gilliatt), Maxwell Reed (Rantaine), Denis O'Dea (Lethierry), Michael Goodliffe (Ragan), Bryan Forbes (Willie), Jacques B. Brunius (Fouche), Gérard Oury (Napoleon).

Note: Filmed on the Isle of Jersey, in Brittany, and on the Normandy coast.

A Lion Is in the Streets (Warner Bros., 1953)

Producer: William Cagney. *Director:* Raoul Walsh. *Screenplay:* Luther Davis (based on the novel by Adria Locke Langley). *Cinematographer:* Harry Stradling Jr. *Editor:* George Amy. *Music:* Franz Waxman. *Production designer:* Wiard Ihnen. *Art director:* William Kissell. *Set decorators:* Wiard Ihnen, Fred M. MacLean. *Sound:* Larry Gannon, John K. Kean. *Wardrobe:* Kay Nelson. *Makeup:* Otis Malcom. *Special effects:* Roscoe Kline. *Assistant director:* William Kissell. *Running time:* 88 minutes. *Released:* September 23, 1953.

Cast: James Cagney (Hank Martin), Barbara Hale (Verity Wade), Anne Francis (Flamingo McManamee), Warner Anderson (Jules Bolduc), John McIntire (Jeb Brown), Jeanne Cagney (Jennie Brown), Lon Chaney Jr. (Spurge McManamee).

Gun Fury (Columbia, 1953)

Producer: Lewis J. Rachmil. *Director:* Raoul Walsh. *Screenplay:* Irving Wallace, Roy Huggins (based on the novel *Ten against Caesar* by Kathleen B. Geoorge and Robert A. Granger). *Cinematographer:* Lester White. *Editors:* James Sweeney, Jerome Thomas. *Music:* Mischa Bakaleinikoff. *Art director:* Ross Bellah. *Set decorator:* James Crowe. *Sound:* J. S. Westmoreland. *Assistant director:* Jack Corrick. *Running time:* 83 minutes. *Released:* November 11, 1953.

Cast: Rock Hudson (Ben Warren), Donna Reed (Jennifer Ballard), Philip Carey (Frank Slayton), Roberta Haynes (Estella Morales), Leo Gordon (Tom Burgess), Lee Marvin (Blinky).

Note: Filmed in Sedona, AZ.

Saskatchewan (Universal, 1954)

Producer: Aaron Rosenberg. *Director:* Raoul Walsh. *Screenplay:* Gil Doud. *Cinematographer:* John F. Seitz. *Editor:* Frank Goss. *Music:* Joseph Gershenson. *Art directors:* Bernard Herzbrun, Richard H. Riedel. *Set decorators:* John P. Austin, Russell A. Gausman. *Costume designer:* Bill Thomas. *Sound:* Leslie I. Carey. *Makeup:* Bud Westmore. *Assistant director:* Frank Shaw. *Running time:* 87 minutes. *Released:* March 30, 1954.

Cast: Alan Ladd (Thomas O'Rourke), Shelley Winters (Grace Markey), J. Carrol Naish (Batouche), Hugh O'Brian (Carl Smith), Robert Douglas (Benton), George J. Lewis (Lawson), Richard Long (Patrick J. Scanlon), Jay Silverheels (Cajou).

Note: Filmed at Banff National Park, Alberta, Canada.

Battle Cry (Warner Bros., 1955)

Producer: Jack L. Warner (uncredited). *Director:* Raoul Walsh. *Screenplay:* Leon Uris (based on his novel). *Cinematographer:* Sidney Hickox. *Editor:* William Ziegler. *Music:* Max Steiner. *Art director:* John Beckman. *Set decorator:* William Wallace. *Sound:* Francis J. Scheid. *Wardrobe:* Mossy Mabry. *Makeup:* Gordon Bau. *Assistant directors:* William Kissell, Russell Saunders. *Running time:* 149 minutes. *Released:* February 2, 1955.

Cast: Van Heflin (Maj. Sam Huxley), Aldo Ray (Pvt. Andy Hookens), Mona Freeman (Kathy), Nancy Olson (Mrs. Pat Rogers), James Whitmore (Sgt. Mac/Narrator), Raymond Massey (Maj. Gen. Snipes), Tab Hunter (Pvt. Cpl. Danny Forrester), Dorothy Malone (Mrs. Elaine Yarborough), Anne Francis (Rae).

Note: Filmed at Camp Pendleton, CA, and on Vieques Island, Puerto Rico.

The Tall Men (Twentieth Century–Fox, 1955)

Producers: William Bacher, William Hawks. *Director:* Raoul Walsh. *Screenplay:* Sydney Boehm, Frank S. Nugent (based on the novel by Clay Fisher). *Cinematographer:* Leo Tover. *Editor:* Louis R. Loeffler. *Music:* Victor Young. *Art directors:* Mark-Lee Kirk, Lyle R. Wheeler. *Set decorators:*

Chester Bayhi, Walter M. Scott. *Sound:* Harry M. Leonard, John D. Stack. *Costume designer:* Travilla. *Makeup:* Ben Nye. *Special effects:* Ray Kellogg. *Assistant director:* Stanley Hough. *Running time:* 122 minutes. *Released:* September 22, 1955.

Cast: Clark Gable (Col. Ben Allison), Jane Russell (Nella Turner), Robert Ryan (Nathan Stark), Cameron Mitchell (Clint Allison), Juan Garcia (Luis), Harry Shannon (Sam), Emile Meyer (Chickasaw Charlie), Steve Darrell (Col. Norris), Will Wright (Gus).

Note: Filmed in Durango, Mexico, and Sun Valley, ID.

Helen of Troy (Warner Bros., 1956)

Director: Robert Wise. *Screenplay:* Hugh Gray, John Twist (based on the *Iliad* by Homer). *Cinematographer:* Harry Stradling Jr. *Editor:* Thomas Reilly. *Music:* Max Steiner. *Art director:* Edward Carrere. *Sound:* Charles Lang. *Makeup:* Bill Phillips. *Assistant director:* Gus Agosti. *Running time:* 118 minutes. *Released:* February 11, 1956.

Cast: Rossana Podesta (Helen of Troy), Jacques Sernas (Paris), Cedric Hardwicke (Priam), Stanley Baker (Achilles), Niall MacGinniss (Menelaus), Nora Swinburne (Hecuba), Robert Douglas (Agamemnon), Torin Hatcher (Ulysses), Harry Andrews (Hector), Janette Scott (Cassandra), Ronald Lewis (Aeneas), Brigitte Bardot (Andraste).

Note: Walsh was called to Rome to direct additional battle scenes for the film.

The Revolt of Mamie Stover (Twentieth Century–Fox, 1956)

Producer: Buddy Adler. *Director:* Raoul Walsh. *Screenplay:* Sydney Boehm (based on the novel by William Bradford Huie). *Cinematographer:* Leo Tover. *Editor:* Louis R. Loeffler. *Music:* Hugo Friedhofer. *Art directors:* Mark-Lee Kirk, Lyle R. Wheeler. *Costume designer:* Travilla. *Sound:* W. D. Flick, Harry M. Leonard. *Assistant director:* Joseph E. Rickards. *Running time:* 93 minutes. *Released:* May 11, 1956.

Cast: Jane Russell (Mamie Stover), Richard Egan (Jim Blair), Joan Leslie (Annalee Johnson), Agnes Moorehead (Bertha Parchman), Jorja Curtright (Jackie), Michael Pate (Harry Adkins), Richard Coogan (Cpt. Eldon Sumac), Alan Reed (Cpt. Gorecki).

Note: Filmed in Honolulu and elsewhere on Oahu.

The King and Four Queens (United Artists, 1956)

Producer: David Hempstead. *Director:* Raoul Walsh. *Screenplay:* Margaret Fitts, Richard Alan Simmons. *Cinematographer:* Lucien Ballard. *Editor:* Howard Bretherton. *Music:* Alex North. *Production designer:* Wiard Ihnen. *Set decorator:* Victor A. Gangelin. *Costume designer:* Renie. *Sound:* Jack Solomon. *Assistant director:* Tom Connors Jr. *Running time:* 84 minutes. *Released:* December 21, 1956.

Cast: Clark Gable (Dan Kehoe), Eleanor Parker (Sabina McDade), Jean Wiles (Ruby McDade), Barbara Nichols (Birdie McDade), Sara Shane (Oralie McDade), Roy Roberts (Sheriff Tom Larrabee), Arthur Shields (Padre).

Note: Filmed in St. George, UT.

Band of Angels (Warner Bros., 1957)

Director: Raoul Walsh. *Screenplay:* John Twist, Ivan Goff, Ben Roberts (based on the novel by Robert Penn Warren). *Cinematographer:* Lucien Ballard. *Editor:* Folmar Blangsted. *Music:* Max Steiner. *Art director:* Franz Bachelin. *Set decorator:* William Wallace. *Costume designer:* Marjorie Best. *Sound:* Francis E. Stahl. *Makeup:* Gordon Bau. *Assistant directors:* Al Alleborn, Russell Saunders. *Running time:* 126 minutes. *Released:* August 3, 1957.

Cast: Clark Gable (Hamish Bond), Yvonne De Carlo (Amantha Starr), Sidney Poitier (Rau-Ru), Efrem Zimbalist Jr. (Lt. Ethan Sears), Rex Reason (Cpt. Seth Parton), Patric Knowles (Charles de Marigny), Torin Thatcher (Cpt. Canavan), Andrea King (Miss Idell).

Note: Filmed in Baton Rouge, LA.

The Naked and the Dead (RKO, 1958)

Producer: Paul Gregory. *Director:* Raoul Walsh. *Screenplay:* Denis Sanders, Terry Sanders (based on the novel by Norman Mailer). *Cinematographer:* Joseph LaShelle. *Editor:* Arthur P. Schmidt. *Music:* Bernard Herrmann. *Art director:* Ted Haworth. *Set decorator:* William L. Kuehl. *Costume designer:* Oscar Rodriguez. *Sound:* Robert B. Lee. *Makeup:* Allan Snyder. *Assistant director:* Russell Saunders. *Running time:* 135 minutes. *Released:* August 6, 1958.

Cast: Aldo Ray (Sgt. Sam Croft), Cliff Robertson (Lt. Robert Hearn), Raymond Massey (Gen. Cummings), Lil St. Cyr (Willie Mae, a.k.a. Lily), Barbara Nichols (Mildred Croft), William Campbell (Brown), Richard Jaeckel (Gallagher), James Best (Ridges), Joey Bishop (Roth), Jerry Paris (Goldstein).

Note: Filmed in Panama.

The Sheriff of Fractured Jaw (Twentieth Century–Fox, 1958)

Producer: Daniel M. Angel. *Director:* Raoul Walsh. *Screenplay:* Arthur Dales (based on a story by Jacob Hay). *Cinematographer:* Otto Heller. *Editor:* John Shirley. *Music:* Robert Farnon. *Art director:* Bernard Robinson. *Costume designer:* Julie Harris. *Sound:* Dudley Messenger. *Makeup:* George Partleton. *Assistant director:* Jack Causey. *Running time:* 110 minutes. *Released:* October 28, 1958 (in the United Kingdom).

Cast: Kenneth More (Jonathan Tibbs), Jayne Mansfield (Kate), Henry Hull (Maj. Masters), Bruce Cabot (Jack), Ronald Squire (Toynbee), William Campbell (Keeno), Sidney James (The drunk), Reed Rouen (Claybourne), Charles Irwin (Luke).

A *Private's Affair* (Twentieth Century–Fox, 1959)

Producer: David Weisbart. *Director:* Raoul Walsh. *Screenplay:* Winston Miller (from a story by Ray Livingston Murphy). *Cinematographer:* Charles G. Clarke. *Editor:* Dorothy Spencer. *Music:* Cyril J. Mockbridge. *Art directors:* Walter Simonds, Lyle R. Wheeler. *Set decorators:* Stuart A. Reiss, Walter M. Scott. *Costume designer:* Adele Balkan. *Sound:* Bernard Freericks, Harry M. Leonard. *Makeup:* Ben Nye. *Assistant director:* Hal Herman. *Running time:* 92 minutes. *Released:* August 14, 1959.

Cast: Sal Mineo (Luigi Maresi), Christine Carère (Marie), Barry Coe (Jerry Morgan), Barbara Eden (Sgt. Katie Mulligan), Gary Crosby (Mike Conroy), Terry Moore (Louise Wright), Jim Backus (Jim Gordon), Jessie Royce Landis (Elizabeth T. Chapman), Robert Burton (Gen. Hargrave).

Esther and the King (Twentieth Century–Fox, 1960)

Producer: Raoul Walsh. *Director:* Raoul Walsh. *Screenplay:* Raoul Walsh, Michael Elkins. *Cinematographer:* Mario Bava. *Editor:* Jerry Webb. *Art director:* Giorgio Giovannini. *Music:* Angelo Francesco Lavagnino, Roberto Nicolosi. *Makeup:* Euclide Santoli. *Assistant director:* Ottavio Oppo. *Running time:* 110 minutes. *Released:* December 14, 1960.

Cast: Joan Collins (Esther), Richard Egan (King Ahasuerus), Denis O'Dea (Mordecai), Sergio Fantoni (Haman), Rik Battaglia (Simon), Renato Baldini (Klydrathes), Gabriele Tinti (Samual), Rosalba Neri (Keresh), Robert Buchanan (Hegai), Daniela Rocca (Queen Vashti), Folco Lulli (Tobiah).

Note: Filmed at Titanus Appia Studios, Rome, and Lazio, Italy.

Come September (Universal, 1961)

Producers: Robert Arthur, Raoul Walsh (uncredited). *Director:* Robert Mulligan. *Screenplay:* Stanley Shapiro, Maurice Richlin (based on a story by Stanley Roberts and Robert Russell). *Cinematographer:* William H. Daniels. *Editor:* Russell F. Schoengarth. *Music:* Hans J. Salter. *Art director:* Henry Bumstead. *Set decorator:* John P. Austin. *Costume designer:* Morton Haack. *Sound:* Sash Fisher, Waldon O. Watson. *Assistant director:* Joseph E. Kenney. *Running time:* 112 minutes. *Released:* August 9, 1961.

Cast: Rock Hudson (Robert L. Tablot), Gina Lollobrigida (Lisa Helena Fellini), Sandra Dee (Sandy Stevens), Bobby Darin (Tony), Walter Slezak (Maurice Clavell), Brenda De Banzie (Margaret Allison), Rossana Rory (Anna), Ronald Howard (Spencer), Joel Grey (Beagle), Rinne Haran (Sparrow).

Notes: Filmed in Cinque Terre, Rome, and Portofino. Walsh coproduced the film with Seven Pictures Corp.

Marines, Let's Go! (Twentieth Century–Fox, 1961)

Producer: Raoul Walsh. *Director:* Raoul Walsh. *Screenplay:* John Twist (from a story by Raoul Walsh). *Cinematographer:* Lucien Ballard. *Editor:* Robert

L. Simpson. *Music:* Irving Gertz. *Art directors:* Jack Martin Smith, Alfred Ybarra. *Sound:* Warren B. Delaplain, Bernard Freericks. *Makeup:* Ben Nye. *Assistant director:* Milton Carter. *Running time:* 103 minutes. *Released:* August 15, 1961.

Cast: Tom Tryon (Pfc. Skip Roth), David Hedison (Pfc. Dave Chatfield), Tom Reese (Pfc. Desmond "Let's Go" McCaffrey), Linda Hutchings (Grace Blake), William Tyler (Pvt. Russ Waller), Barbara Stuart (Ina Baxter), David Brandon (Pvt. Newt Levels), Steve Baylor (Pvt. Chase).

Note: Filmed in Kyoto, Japan.

A Distant Trumpet (Warner Bros., 1964)

Producer: William H. Wright. *Director:* Raoul Walsh. *Screenplay:* John Twist (based on the novel by Paul Horgan). *Cinematographer:* William Clothier. *Editor:* David Wages. *Music:* Max Steiner. *Art director:* William L. Campbell. *Set decorator:* William L. Kuehl. *Costume designer:* Howard Shoup. *Sound:* Francis E. Stahl. *Makeup:* Gordon Bau. *Assistant directors:* William Kissell, Russell Saunders. *Running time:* 116 minutes. *Released:* May 30, 1964.

Cast: Troy Donahue (2nd Lt. Matthew "Matt" Hazard), Suzanne Pleshette (Kitty Mainwarring), Diane McBain (Laura Frelief), James Gregory (Maj. Gen. Alexander Upton Quaint), William Reynolds (1st Lt. Teddy Mainwarring), Claude Akins (Seely Jones), Kent Smith (Secretary of War), Judson Pratt (Capt. Cedric Gray, MD).

Note: Filmed in Gallup, NM, at Red Rock State Park, NM, and in the Painted Desert, AZ.

Nickelodeon (Columbia, 1976)

Director: Peter Bogdanovich. *Screenplay:* Peter Bogdanovich, W. D. Richter. *Cinematographer:* László Kovács. *Music:* Richard Hazard. *Editor:* William C. Carruth. *Art director:* Richard Berger. *Costume designer:* Theadora Van Runkle. *Running time:* 121 minutes. *Released:* December 21, 1976.

Cast: Ryan O'Neal (Leo Harrigan), Burt Reynolds (Buck Greenway), Tatum O'Neal (Alice Forsyte), Brian Keith (H. H. Cobb), Stella Stevens (Marty Reeves), John Ritter (Franklin Frank).

Note: Walsh, along with Allan Dwan, served as technical consultant on the film.

Erroneous Attributions

The Burned Hand (Majestic, 1915)

Director: Tod Browning. *Running time:* 2 reels.
Cast: Miriam Cooper, William Hinckley, W. E. Lowry, Cora Drew.
Note: Sometimes erroneously attributed to Walsh.

Ghosts (Mutual, 1915)

Producer: D. W. Griffith. *Director:* George Nichols. *Screenplay:* Russell E. Smith, from the play *Gengangere* by Henrik Ibsen. *Running time:* 5 reels. *Released:* June 1915.

Cast: Henry B. Walthall (Capt. Arling), Mary Alden (Helen Arling), Loretta Blake (Regina), Juanita Archer (Johanna).

Note: Sometimes erroneously attributed to Walsh or to John Emerson.

Peer Gynt (Paramount, 1915)

Producer: Oliver Morosco. *Screenplay:* Oscar Apfel (after the play by Henrik Ibsen). *Released:* September 16, 1915.

Cast: Cyril Maude (Peer Gynt), Myrtle Steadman (Solveig), Fanny Stockbridge (Ase), Mary Reubens (Anitra), Mary Ruby (Ingrid).

Note: The American Film Institute attributes this film, often attributed to Walsh, to Oscar Apfel.

Notes

Prologue

1. Raoul Walsh, *Each Man in His Time* (New York: Farrar, Straus, Giroux, 1974), 17.

1. Becoming Raoul Walsh

1. Walsh, *Each Man in His Time*, 3–4.

2. Miriam Cooper, *Dark Lady of the Silents: My Life in Early Hollywood* (New York: Bobbs-Merrill, 1973), 116.

3. George Walsh to Kevin Brownlow, April 20, 1972, courtesy Kevin Brownlow.

4. Walsh, *Each Man in His Time*, 5.

5. George Walsh Jr., personal communication with author, June 2009.

6. Walsh's third wife, Mary, held on to the medal for many years, passing it on to a good friend in 2007.

7. Walsh, *Each Man in His Time*, 10.

8. Ibid., 14.

9. Ibid., 14–15.

10. George Walsh Jr., personal communication with author, June 2009.

11. Walsh, *Each Man in His Time*, 17.

12. Ibid.

13. Raoul Walsh, interview by James Child, *Sight and Sound*, Winter 1972–1973.

14. Cooper, *Dark Lady of the Silents*, 114.

15. Walsh, *Each Man in His Time*, 25.

16. Ibid., 24.

17. Ibid., 28–30.

18. Ibid., 40.

19. Ibid., 56.

20. Ibid., 61.

21. Information sent to author by Kevin Brownlow, who also suggests that the Pathé westerns may not have been as "god awful" as Walsh reported they were. Brownlow further suggests that Georges and Gaston Melies may have been the models for Walsh's story here, as they had a studio, the Star Film

Ranch, in Texas, where they made westerns. Whether Walsh ever met the Melies brothers is unknown.

22. Raoul Walsh, interview by Peter Bogdanovich, in Peter Bogdanovich, *Who the Devil Made It? Conversations with Legendary Film Directors* (New York: Ballantine, 1997), 147.

23. Walsh, *Each Man in His Time*, 67.

2. Griffith and Beyond

Epigraph: Griffith cited in Paula Marantz Cohen, *Silent Film and the Triumph of the American Myth* (Oxford: Oxford University Press, 2001), 2.

1. Mark Twain, *Adventures of Huckleberry Finn*, ed. Gerald Graff and James Phelan (New York: Bedford/St. Martin's, 1995), 27–28.

2. Walsh, *Each Man in His Time*, 69.

3. Ibid., 68–69.

4. See Tom Gunning, *D. W. Griffith and the Origins of American Narrative Film: The Early Years at Biograph* (Champaign: University of Illinois Press, 1993), 86–87.

5. This is suggested in Cohen, *Silent Film and the Triumph of the American Myth*, 5–6.

6. See the thorough discussion of filmic mythmaking in the introduction to Cohen, *Silent Film and the Triumph of the American Myth*, esp. 4–10.

7. Raoul Walsh, interview by Kevin Brownlow, 1972, courtesy Kevin Brownlow.

8. Cooper, *Dark Lady of the Silents*, 33–34.

9. Ibid., 44.

10. Ibid.

11. Information courtesy Kevin Brownlow.

12. Walsh, *Each Man in His Time*, 75.

13. Walsh speaking to students and faculty at Wesleyan University, April 25, 1972. Walsh told a version of this story in *Each Man in His Time;* others appear in Richard Schickel, *The Men Who Made the Movies* (New York: Atheneum, 1975); and Bogdanovich, *Who the Devil Made It?*

14. Raoul Walsh, interview by Kevin Brownlow, 1972, courtesy Kevin Brownlow.

15. Cited in Kingsley Canham, *The Hollywood Professionals*, vol. 1, *Michael Curtiz, Raoul Walsh, Henry Hathaway* (London: Tantivy, 1973), 85.

16. See the documentary filmmaker Gregorio Rochas's *The Lost Reels of Pancho Villa* (2003). Rochas attempts to piece together the footage of Villa and establish his relationship to the movie industry at the time.

17. Raoul Walsh, interview by Kevin Brownlow, April 1967, courtesy Kevin Brownlow.

18. *Reel Life*, 6, no. 10 (May 22, 1915): 212.

19. Miriam Cooper Papers, Library of Congress, Washington, DC.

20. Ibid.

21. Cooper, *The Dark Lady of the Silents*, 91.

22. Kevin Brownlow has suggested that this might be Olga Grey, who appeared in Walsh's *Pillars of Society*.

23. Walsh, *Each Man in His Time*, 91.

3. Leaning Forward at Fox

1. Owen Kildare, *My Mamie Rose: The Story of My Regeneration* (New York: Baker & Taylor, 1903), 14–15.

2. The relationship between the two is somewhat vague. It turns out that Walsh supported Harbaugh's mother, Alice Spraul Harbaugh, from the time he first met Harbaugh until her death. Kevin Brownlow suggests that Harbaugh was Walsh's half brother, even though Walsh's nephew, George Walsh, claims that Carl was only a close friend. It remains unclear why Walsh supported Alice.

3. Cited in Philip Kemp, "Raoul Walsh," in *World Film Directors*, ed. John Wakeman, 2 vols. (New York: Wilson, 1987), 1:1150.

4. Eve Golden, *Vamp: The Rise and Fall of Theda Bara* (Vestal, NY: Empire, 1996), 68.

5. Ibid.

6. *Fort-Worth Star Telegraph*, November 12, 1915.

7. *Anaconda (MT) Standard*, November 16, 1915.

8. *Tulsa World*, October 31, 1915.

9. *Cleveland Plain Dealer*, January 23, 1916.

10. Cooper, *Dark Lady of the Silents*, 101.

11. Miriam Cooper Papers.

12. Ibid.

13. Cooper, *Dark Lady of the Silents*, 113.

14. Walsh, *Each Man in His Time*, 137.

15. *Portland Oregonian*, March 10, 1916.

16. *New Orleans Times-Picayune*, March 27, 1916.

17. *Dallas Morning News*, January 16, 1916.

18. Ibid.

19. Cooper, *Dark Lady of the Silents*, 118.

20. Ibid., 120.

21. Walsh, *Each Man in His Time*, 139.

22. Twentieth Century–Fox Papers, Cinematic Arts Library, University of Southern California.

23. Ibid.

24. Ford's statement has been cited often. See esp. Joseph McBride, *Searching for John Ford: A Life* (New York: St. Martin's, 2001), 185. In this definitive biography, McBride refers to Ford's "whimsically eclectic list," which also includes *Ninotchka, Going My Way, The High and the Mighty*, and Ford's own *3 Godfathers*.

25. All three reviews cited in Kevin Brownlow, *Behind the Mask of Inno-*

cence: Sex, Violence, Prejudice, Crime: Films of Social Conscience in the Silent Era (Berkeley and Los Angeles: University of California Press, 1990), 32.

26. *Motion Picture Weekly,* December 22, 1917.

27. No projectionist dared drop much below sixteen frames per second because the nitrate could easily catch fire. The Griffith studio photographed everything at sixteen frames per second until midway through *Intolerance* (1916), when it increased to eighteen frames per second. Lasky was shooting at twenty-one frames per second, and, by 1920, other companies had increased as well. When MGM was formed in 1924, it shot at twenty-two frames per second. This did away with the habit of "racing" that Walsh objected to—projectionists speeding up films so that they could get home earlier. Kevin Brownlow, personal communication, September 28, 2010.

28. Quoted in Kevin Brownlow, *The War, the West and the Wilderness* (New York: Knopf, 1978), 134.

29. Cooper, *Dark Lady of the Silents,* 155.

30. Both Walsh's and Wellman's comments are in Raoul Walsh, interview by Kevin Brownlow, April 1967.

31. Raoul Walsh, interview by Peter Bogdanovich, 160.

32. Ibid.

4. The Dagger, the Sword, and the Gun

1. Cooper, *Dark Lady of the Silents,* 160.

2. Ibid., 161.

3. Ibid., 174.

4. Miriam Cooper Papers.

5. Walsh may have been unconsciously referencing here his having forgotten his own mother's face after her death.

6. Miriam Cooper Papers.

7. Ibid.

8. Raoul Walsh, interview by Peter Bogdanovich, 162.

9. *Captain Blackbird/Under the Skin,* held in the Samuel Goldwyn Collection, Cinematic Arts Library.

10. Walsh, *Each Man in His Time,* 163.

11. Ibid., 164.

12. Walsh, *Each Man in His Time,* 168.

13. Ibid.

14. Miriam Cooper Papers.

15. This could possibly also refer to getting out of the marriage to Miriam, which he would do soon.

16. Walsh, *Each Man in His Time,* 178–79.

17. *Photoplay,* September 1925. Kevin Brownlow has extant footage long ago removed from *The Wanderer.*

18. Brownlow, *The War, the West and the Wilderness,* 194.

19. Ibid.

20. Victor McLaglen, *Express to Hollywood* (London: Jarrolds, 1935), 264–66.

21. Ibid., 272–73.

22. *Motion Picture Classic,* October 1926, 44.

23. *New York Times,* April 14, 1974.

24. See Leslie Fiedler's seminal study of American literature, *Love and Death in the American Novel* (New York: Stein & Day, 1966). His discussion of Emerson, Thoreau (who was the archetypal male wedded to the woods and to himself), and Fenimore Cooper as prototypes of male bonding veers off to suggest a homosexual theme underlying much of American literature—a feature that Walsh's male characters do not share.

25. *Los Angeles Times,* May 24, 1927.

5. Pre-Code Walsh

1. Raoul Walsh, interview by Kevin Brownlow, April 1967.

2. Ibid.

3. Cited in Julian Fox, "Action All the Way," *Film and Filming,* June 1973, 39.

4. Kevin Brownlow, personal communication, September 28, 2010.

5. Walsh, *Each Man in His Time,* 201.

6. Gloria Swanson, *Swanson on Swanson: An Autobiography* (New York: Random House, 1980), 290.

7. Raoul Walsh, interview by James Child.

8. See the discussion of this form of censorship in Brownlow, *Behind the Mask of Innocence,* 20.

9. Gloria Swanson Papers, Harry Ransom Humanities Research Center, University of Texas at Austin.

10. Raoul Walsh to George Walsh, June 22, 1927, Gloria Swanson Papers.

11. Welford Beaton, "Trying to Delouse Sadie Thompson," *Film Spectator,* December 10, 1927.

12. *Sadie Thompson* was considered lost for many years, the only extant copy held by the Swanson estate. As the writer John Gallagher reported in the late 1980s, after Swanson's death in 1983, Don Krim of Kino International purchased the rights and set Dennis Doros to work on a full restoration of the film. Since the last reel of the print had decomposed, still photographs, the original titles, and footage from the 1932 remake, *Rain* (with Joan Crawford), shot by the same cinematographer, Oliver Marsh, re-created the missing eight minutes of the film. Then, with Doros's two and a half years of restoration and an original score composed and conducted by Joseph Turrin, the film was ready to be seen once again. See John Gallagher, "Raoul Walsh," *Films in Review,* October 1987.

13. The quotation is taken from a copy of the letter given to the author by Walsh's friend Bob Bookman.

14. Alma Whitaker, "Directors Are Doormats," *Los Angeles Times,* October 2, 1927, 17.

15. Raoul Walsh, interview, in Eric Sherman, ed., *Directing the Film: Film Directors on Their Art* (Los Angeles: Acrobat, 1976), 294.

16. See Wilson Mizner, "Wilson Mizner Turns Informer," *Photoplay*, November 1928, 40, 94.

17. Herbert Cruikshank, "He Envies His Actors," quoted in Fox, "Action All the Way," 40.

18. Walsh, *Each Man in His Time*, 221.

19. Ibid., 222.

20. Ibid., 224, 225.

21. The film historian William Everson found *The Red Dance* politically fascinating. When it was released, the art of titling was pretty much being abandoned as part of the "old" Hollywood, Everson writes. Walsh's film "reverted to the methods employed by Griffith in *Intolerance* twelve years earlier," though "with so little stress on the device that it was probably done at the instigation of [Walsh] rather than to impress audiences." Everson notes, "Dialogue titles spoken by, or informational titles relating to, the aristocracy or military of old Russia were placed on a tapestry-like card imprinted with a black Tsarist symbol. Trotsky and other leaders of the Revolution were given titles printed against a rough, rock-like surface. The poor, ignorant peasants, with little to say or do, had to be satisfied with the old, nondescript white lettering against a plain black background." See the extended discussion of this subject in William K. Everson, *American Silent Film* (New York: Da Capo, 1998), 138.

22. See the discussion of Fox Movietone in Donald Crafton, *The Talkies: American Cinema's Transition to Sound, 1926–1931*, History of the American Cinema series (Berkeley and Los Angeles: University of California Press, 1997), 280.

23. Ibid., 282.

24. Walsh, *Each Man in His Time*, 235.

25. *Dallas Morning News*, February 19, 1930.

26. *New York Times*, March 16, 1929.

27. "New York Graphic," *Film Daily*, August 29, 1929, 11.

28. Twentieth Century–Fox Papers.

29. Cited in *Film Daily*, January 30, 1929.

30. "The Screen Rabelais," *New York Times*, November 17, 1929.

31. Hal Evarts, log of *The Big Trail*, 4, Twentieth Century–Fox Papers.

32. Ibid., 7.

33. Ibid.

34. Wayne had been a student at the University of Southern California.

35. Raoul Walsh, interview by Richard Schickel, in Schickel, *The Men Who Made the Movies*, 37.

36. *Hollywood Reporter*, November 10, 2010.

37. Raoul Walsh, interview by Richard Schickel, 37–38.

38. Kevin Brownlow, personal communication with author, September 28, 2010.

39. *Film Daily*, April 20, 1930, 5; August 1, 1930, 11; and August 28, 1930, 9, cited in Crafton, *The Talkies*, 364–65.

40. Cited in "The Making of *The Big Trail*," included in *The Big Trail* (Twentieth Century–Fox Home Entertainment 2-disc DVD release, 2008).

41. Evarts, log of *The Big Trail*, 48.

42. Ibid., 46.

43. See the lively discussion of the making of *The Big Trail* in Robert Parrish, *Growing Up in Hollywood* (New York: Harcourt Brace Jovanovich, 1976), 63–71.

44. Ibid., 64.

45. Ibid., 65.

46. Ibid., 66.

47. Ibid., 69.

48. Jack Warner Papers, Cinematic Arts Library.

49. *Variety*, December 31, 1930.

50. "Widescreen faded out in the early thirties. The Hays office decided the conversion was too expensive for the industry. Widescreen was only practical in theatres seating about 1,500 and exhibitors were not at all keen to install new equipment on top of sound-on-disc and sound-on-film installations—in the teeth of the greatest depression in modern history. In all, fewer than twenty theatres in the whole of the United States were equipped for 63mm, 65mm and 70mm. What's more, nearly all the films were failures at the box office. Could this have had something to do with the way they looked? Most of the widescreen films were projected on 35mm through Magnascope enlarging lenses, which must have upset the cameramen, whose work was shown cropped and made dimmer, grainier and softer by this method. Exactly the opposite of the original idea." Kevin Brownlow, personal communication with author, September 28, 2010.

6. Salt of the Earth

1. *Dallas Morning News*, December 19, 1931.

2. Ralph Bellamy, interview by John Gallagher, *Films in Review*, October 1987.

3. *Dallas Morning News*, May 7, 1933.

4. Walsh, *Each Man in His Time*, 248.

5. Darryl F. Zanuck Papers, Cinematic Arts Library, University of Southern California.

6. Fay Wray, interview by John Gallagher (at the Empire State Building), February 22, 1989, courtesy John Gallagher.

7. George Walsh Jr., personal communication, June 2009.

8. See the fine discussion of the making of *Going Hollywood* in Gary Giddins, *Bing Crosby, A Pocket Full of Miracles: The Early Years, 1903–1940* (Boston: Little, Brown, 2001), 329.

9. Walsh, *Each Man in His Time*, 272.

10. Ibid., 258.

11. Giddins, *A Pocket Full of Miracles*, 331.

12. Ibid., 330.

13. Crosby quoted in ibid., 332. See also Matthew Bernstein, *Walter Wanger, Hollywood Independent* (Minneapolis: University of Minnesota Press, 2000), 89.

14. Giddins, *A Pocket Full of Miracles*, 333.

15. Cited in Fox, "Action All the Way," 34.

16. Walsh, *Each Man in His Time*, 275.

17. William Randolph Hearst Papers, Bancroft Library, University of California, Berkeley.

18. Simon Louvish, *Mae West: It Ain't No Sin* (New York: St. Martin's/Griffin, 2006), 187.

19. *New York Times*, March 12, 1936.

20. *Hollywood Variety*, April 1, 1936.

21. *New York Times*, July 23, 1936.

22. Bryan Forbes, personal communication with author, December 10, 2010.

23. Cited in Susan Courtney, *Hollywood Fantasies of Miscegenation* (Princeton, NJ: Princeton University Press, 2005), 106.

24. Cited in the program for "The Films of Raoul Walsh," British Film Institute, National Film Theatre, London, November 1974.

25. Walsh's few days directing McCrea and Hopkins were confirmed by Broderick Crawford. Broderick Crawford, telephone interview by John Gallagher, August 5, 1983, courtesy John Gallagher.

26. David Nasaw, *The Chief: The Life of William Randolph Hearst* (New York: Mariner, 2001), 563–79.

27. William Randolph Hearst Papers. See also the discussion of Hearst's political views in Nasaw, *The Chief*.

7. Beshert

1. Otto Friedrich, *City of Nets: A Portrait of Hollywood in the 1940s* (Berkeley and Los Angeles: University of California Press, 1997), 154.

2. Raoul Walsh Legal Files, Warner Bros. Archives, University of Southern California.

3. Walsh, *Each Man in His Time*, 298.

4. Raoul Walsh, interview by Patrick McGilligan and Debra Weiner, 1974, in *Film Crazy: Interviews with Hollywood Legends*, ed. Patrick McGilligan (New York: St. Martin's, 2000), 26.

5. Phil Hardy, ed., *Raoul Walsh, Edinburgh Film Festival, 1974* (Colchester: Vineyard, 1974), 42.

6. Ibid.

7. Rudy Behlmer, ed., *Inside Warner Bros., 1935–1951* (New York: Viking, 1985), xxxi.

8. Walsh, *Each Man in His Time*, 298.

9. Raoul Walsh, interview by Hedda Hopper, January 13, 1965, Hedda Hopper Papers, Margaret Herrick Library, Academy of Motion Picture Arts and Sciences, Beverly Hills, CA.

10. Raoul Walsh Legal Files.

11. *The Roaring Twenties* production files, Warner Bros. Archives.

12. Ibid.

13. James Cagney, *Cagney by Cagney* (New York: Doubleday, 1976), 89.

14. *The Roaring Twenties* production files.

15. Ibid.

16. Raoul Walsh, interview by Patrick McGilligan and Debra Weiner, 27.

17. *The Roaring Twenties* production files.

18. *Boxoffice*, October 21, 1939.

19. *Variety*, October 25, 1939.

20. The story also had it that Ford was so angry at Wayne for appearing in Walsh's *The Big Trail*—and that Walsh got Wayne before Ford did—that he refused to hire Wayne for ten years. The historian Kevin Brownlow has posed the question, If Ford wouldn't hire Wayne for those ten years, why didn't Walsh? One answer might be that Walsh hardly directed a western throughout the 1930s and that Wayne was already typecast as a western actor. There might be other explanations, of course.

21. Julian Fox, "Action All the Way," *Films and Filming*, June/July 1973, 38.

22. Claire Trevor, interview by John Gallagher, *Films in Review*, October 1987, 472–79.

23. Cited in Michael Munn, *John Wayne: The Man behind the Myth* (New York: New American Library, 2003), 74.

24. McBride reports Wayne telling Dan Ford (John Ford's son) in 1976, "To this goddam day I don't know why he didn't speak to me for years" (*Searching for John Ford*, 79).

25. Raoul Walsh, interview by Patrick McGilligan and Debra Weiner, 26.

26. Manny Farber, *Negative Space* (New York: Da Capo, 1998), 283.

27. Pierre Rissient, interview by the author, October 2007.

28. Joan Leslie, interview by the author, July 13, 2007.

29. Walsh, *Each Man in His Time*, 313.

30. Pierre Rissient, interview by the author, October 2007.

31. Raoul Walsh Legal Files.

32. Ibid.

8. Out of the Night

1. *They Drive by Night* production files, Warner Bros. Archives.

2. Ibid.

3. Ibid.

4. William Donati, *Ida Lupino: A Biography* (Lexington: University Press of Kentucky, 1996), 63.

5. Walsh, *Each Man in His Time*, 303.

6. *They Drive by Night* production files.

7. Ibid.

8. A. M. Sperber and Eric Lax, *Bogart* (New York: Morrow, 1997), 123.

9. *High Sierra* production files, Warner Bros. Archives.

10. Ibid.

11. Ibid.

12. Ibid.

13. Cited in Sperber and Lax, *Bogart,* 124.

14. W. R. Burnett, interview by Ken Mate and Patrick McGilligan, in Patrick McGilligan, ed., *Backstory 1: Interviews with Screenwriters of Hollywood's Golden Age* (Berkeley: University of California Press, 1986), 49–84.

15. Joan Leslie, interview by the author, July 13, 2007.

16. *High Sierra* production files.

17. Walsh, *Each Man in His Time,* 307–8.

18. *High Sierra* pressbooks, Warner Bros. Archives.

19. W. R. Burnett, *High Sierra* (New York: Zebra, 1940), 7.

20. Ibid., 6–7.

21. *High Sierra* production files.

22. Raoul Walsh, interview by Patrick McGilligan and Debra Weiner, 29.

23. W. R. Burnett, interview by Ken Mate and Patrick McGilligan, 76.

24. *Variety,* December 31, 1940.

25. Walsh himself directed a westernized remake, the 1949 *Colorado Territory.*

26. W. R. Burnett, interview by Ken Mate and Patrick McGilligan, 67–69.

27. *The Strawberry Blonde* production files, Warner Bros. Archives.

28. Ibid.

29. Ibid.

30. Ibid.

31. *Los Angeles Herald Examiner,* August 29, 1940.

32. *The Strawberry Blonde* production files.

33. Rudy Behlmer, interview by the author, July 18, 2007.

34. *The Strawberry Blonde* production files.

35. Olivia de Havilland, interview by the author, June 2007.

36. Julius J. Epstein, interview by Patrick McGilligan, in McGilligan, ed., *Backstory 1,* 170–95.

37. Raoul Walsh, "Leave Me Out of the Literati," *Hollywood Reporter,* December 31, 1940.

38. *Los Angeles Herald Examiner,* March 31, 1941.

39. *Manpower* production files, Warner Bros. Archives.

40. Ibid. The entire Raft-Robinson episode is fully documented in these files.

41. *Life,* August 1941.

42. Olivia de Havilland, interview by the author.

43. "Raoul Walsh, February 16, 1972," in *Conversations with the Great Moviemakers of Hollywood's Golden Age at the American Film Institute,* ed. George Stevens Jr. (New York: Vintage, 2006), 29.

44. *In This Our Life* production files, Warner Bros. Archives.

9. One Thousand and One Nights with Errol Flynn

1. *They Died with Their Boots On* production files, Warner Bros. Archives.

2. Ibid.

3. Ibid.

4. Ibid.

5. Ibid.

6. Ibid.

7. Ibid.

8. Ibid.

9. Olivia de Havilland, interview by the author.

10. Elizabeth Bacon Custer, *Boots and Saddles: Life in Dakota with General Custer* (New York: Harper & Bros., 1885), 265.

11. *They Died with Their Boots On* production files.

12. "Raoul Walsh, February 16, 1972," 20–22.

13. Walsh, *Each Man in His Time*, 311.

14. *New York Times,* November 21, 1941.

15. *Desperate Journey* production files, Warner Bros. Archives.

16. Ibid.

17. Ibid.

18. Ibid.

19. Ibid.

20. Saunders was the assistant director Walsh trusted more than anyone else and was often by his side.

21. *Desperate Journey* production files.

22. Ibid.

23. Ibid.

24. Ibid.

25. Ibid.

26. Ibid.

27. Ibid.

28. Ibid.

29. Pierre Rissient, personal communication, October 2007.

30. *Gentleman Jim* production files, Warner Bros. Archives.

31. Ibid.

32. Ibid.

33. Ibid.

34. *New York Times,* November 26, 1942.

10. In Love and War

1. Ridgeway (Reggie) Callow, interview by Rudy Behlmer, 1976, Oral History Series, American Film Institute (also available through the Margaret Herrick Library).

2. Walsh, *Each Man in His Time*, 335.

3. *Background to Danger* production files, Warner Bros. Archives.

4. See a solid description of the incident in Stephen D. Youngkin, *The Lost One: A Life of Peter Lorre* (Lexington: University Press of Kentucky, 2005), 208.

5. *The Nation,* July 3, 1943, in *Agee on Film,* 2 vols. (New York: Perigee/Putnam, 1958–1960), 1:45.

6. *Northern Pursuit* production files, Warner Bros. Archives.

7. *Variety,* December 31, 1942.

8. Jean Sullivan, interview by John Gallagher, *Films in Review,* October 1987.

9. *Uncertain Glory* production files, Warner Bros. Archives.

10. *Los Angeles Times,* April 20, 1943.

11. Richard Erdman, interview by the author, September 10, 2007.

12. *Variety,* January 1, 1945.

13. Mary Simpson Walsh kept the cigarette case on the Walsh living-room table, where her family keeps it still.

14. Papers documenting the case can be found in the Raoul Walsh Papers, Wesleyan University Cinema Archives, Middletown, CT.

15. Errol Flynn, *My Wicked, Wicked Ways* (New York: Dell, 1959), 338.

16. William Prince, interview by John Gallagher, *Films in Review,* October 1987, 476.

17. *Objective, Burma!* production files, Warner Bros. Archives.

18. Ibid.

19. Ibid.

20. Ibid.

21. Ibid.

22. Richard Erdman, personal communication, September 10, 2007.

23. Ibid.

24. *Dallas Morning News,* May 3, 1945.

25. *Cheyenne* production files, Warner Bros. Archives.

26. None of these titles were ever filmed.

27. Jack Warner Papers.

28. Louise Randall Pierson, one of many Warners contract writers, who also worked briefly on *Mildred Pierce.*

29. Steve Trilling Papers, Cinematic Arts Library.

30. Donati, *Ida Lupino,* 129.

31. *The Man I Love* production files, Warner Bros. Archives.

32. Ibid.

33. Ridgeway (Reggie) Callow, interview by Rudy Behlmer.

34. *The Man I Love* production files.

35. Ibid.

36. *Los Angeles Herald Examiner,* September 11, 1945.

11. Oedipus Wrecked

1. *Cheyenne* production files.

2. Ibid.

3. Ibid.

4. Lee Server, *Robert Mitchum: "Baby, I Don't Care"* (New York: St. Martin's/Griffin, 2002), 112–13.

5. *New York World Telegraph,* September 3, 1946.

6. Mitchum's words are a compilation of various interviews he gave about working with Walsh. For one version especially, see Robert Mitchum, interview by Richard Schickel, in Jerry Roberts, ed., *Mitchum: In His Own Words* (New York: Limelight, 2000), 69.

7. Ibid.

8. Walsh said the same thing to John Wayne when he cast him in *The Big Trail.*

9. Harry Carey Jr., interview by the author, September 12, 2007.

10. *Film Daily,* March 8, 1947.

11. Jack Warner Papers.

12. Ibid.

13. *New York Times,* May 22, 1948.

14. Jack Warner Papers.

15. *One Sunday Afternoon* production files, Warner Bros. Archives.

16. Ibid.

17. Ibid.

18. Billy Grady, *The Irish Peacock* (New Rochelle, NY: Arlington House, 1972), 79–80.

19. Ibid.

20. Ford had changed his name from O'Ferna.

21. Raoul Walsh, interview by Hedda Hopper.

22. Jerry Oppenheimer, *Idol: Rock Hudson* (New York: Bantam, 1987), 24–25.

23. Walsh, interview, in Sherman ed., *Directing the Film,* 36.

24. Virginia Mayo, *The Best Years of My Life* (Chesterfield, MO: Beach House, 2001), 174.

25. Ibid., 176.

26. See chapter 10.

27. Raoul Walsh Papers.

28. *White Heat* production files, Warner Bros. Archives.

29. *White Heat,* ed., and with an introduction by, Patrick McGilligan, Wisconsin/Warner Bros. Screenplay Series (Madison: University of Wisconsin Press, 1984), 15.

30. Ibid., 12.

31. Ibid., 28.

32. Walsh, *Each Man in His Time,* 348.

33. Cagney, *Cagney by Cagney,* 126.

12. By Land and by Sea

1. *Captain Horatio Hornblower* production files, Warner Bros. Archives.

2. I thank Elizabeth Anthony for providing me with this information from Alida Valli's papers.

3. *Los Angeles Herald Examiner,* February 11, 1949.

4. Gary Fishgall, *Gregory Peck: A Biography* (New York: Scribner, 2002), 153–55.

5. *Captain Horatio Hornblower* production files.

6. Ibid.

7. "Raoul Walsh Leaves an Impression in London," *New York Times*, April 23, 1950.

8. *Captain Horatio Hornblower* production files.

9. Ibid.

10. Ibid.

11. Ibid.

12. Ibid.

13. Walsh, *Each Man in His Time*, 354.

14. John Huston Papers, Margaret Herrick Library.

15. *Captain Horatio Hornblower* production files.

16. *Variety,* May 1, 1951.

17. Pierre Rissient, personal communication, October 23, 2007.

18. Walter Doniger, interview by the author, April 24, 2008.

19. Ibid.

20. Kirk Douglas, *The Ragman's Son* (New York: Simon & Schuster, 1998), 181.

21. Kirk Douglas, personal communication, February 2010.

22. Quoted in Fox, "Action All the Way," 34.

23. Raoul Walsh Legal Files.

24. Walsh, *Each Man in His Time*, 356.

25. Cited in Fox, "Action All the Way," 35.

26. *Variety,* January 1, 1952.

27. Raoul Walsh to Marilynn Charlebois, n.d., Raoul Walsh Papers. Walsh rarely dated his letters.

28. Jean-Pierre Coursodon and Bertrand Tavernier, *50 ans de cinema americain* (Paris: Omnibus, Nathan, 1995), 962–74. See also Jean-Pierre Coursodon and Pierre Sauvage, *American Directors,* 2 vols. (New York: McGraw-Hill, 1983), vol. 1.

29. Leslie Caron, *Thank Heaven: A Memoir* (New York: Viking Adult, 2009), 91–92.

30. *Variety,* May 16, 1952.

31. Cited in Fox, "Action All the Way," 36.

32. Production Code files for *The World in His Arms,* Margaret Herrick Library.

33. Bryan Forbes, personal communication, December 10, 2010.

34. Anthony Quinn, with Daniel Paisner, *One Man Tango* (New York: HaperCollins, 1995), 176.

35. Hugh O'Brian, interview by the author, October 1, 2009.

36. *Variety,* December 3, 1952.

37. *Sea Devils* production files, RKO Studios Collection, Cinematic Arts Library, University of Southern California.

38. Bryan Forbes, personal communication, December 10, 2010.

39. Peter Newbrook, interview by the author, June 2009.

40. Ibid.

41. Ibid.

42. *Los Angeles Herald Examiner,* September 17, 1953.

43. Raoul Walsh Papers.

13. Reverie

1. Quoted in George Stevens Jr., dir., *George Stevens: A Filmmaker's Journey* (Castle Hill Productions, 1984).

2. James Cagney, interview by Thomas M. Pryor, *New York Times,* October 19, 1952.

3. *A Lion Is in the Streets* production files, Warner Bros. Archives.

4. Anne Francis, interview by the author, September 2009.

5. Farber, *Negative Space,* 288.

6. Lee Marvin quoted in Gallagher, "Raoul Walsh," 476.

7. Jack Warner Papers.

8. *Daily Variety,* October 27, 1987.

9. *Gun Fury* production files, Warner Bros. Archives.

10. Hugh O'Brian, interview by the author.

11. Ibid.

12. *Saskatchewan* production files, Universal Pictures Collection, Cinematic Arts Library, University of Southern California.

13. Ibid.

14. *Battle Cry* production files, Warner Bros. Archives.

15. Ibid.

16. Cited in Fox, "Action All the Way," 37.

17. *Battle Cry* production files.

18. Ibid.

19. L. Q. Jones, interview by the author, December 21, 2009.

20. *Battle Cry* production files.

21. Ibid.

22. Ibid.

23. L. Q. Jones, interview by the author, December 21, 2009.

24. Tommy Cook, personal communication, January 5, 2011.

25. *Battle Cry* production files.

26. Ibid.

27. See Tab Hunter, with Eddie Muller, *Tab Hunter Confidential: The Making of a Movie Star* (Chapel Hill, NC: Algonquin, 2005), 95.

28. *Battle Cry* production files.

29. L. Q. Jones, interview by the author.

30. *New York Times,* February 3, 1955.

31. Raoul Walsh, interview by Hedda Hopper.

32. Darryl F. Zanuck Papers.

33. *The Tall Men* production files, Twentieth Century–Fox Papers, Cinematic Arts Library, University of Southern California.

34. Ibid.

35. Ibid.

36. Jane Russell, interview by the author, June 2008.

14. His Kind of Women

1. George Walsh's letters to his brother, Raoul Walsh, are collected in the Raoul Walsh Papers.

2. Tag Gallagher, "Raoul Walsh," *Senses of Cinema,* July 2002, http://www.sensesofcinema.com.

3. Cited in Jean-Louis Noames, "Entretien avec Raoul Walsh," *Cahiers du Cinema,* April 1964, 154.

4. *The Revolt of Mamie Stover* production files, Twentieth Century–Fox Papers.

5. Ibid.

6. Jane Russell, *Jane Russell: My Path and My Detours: An Autobiography* (New York: F. Watts, 1985), 167.

7. Christa Fuller (Sam Fuller's widow), interview by the author, January 2009.

8. Mary Walsh Papers, Mary Walsh Estate.

9. Production Code files for *Band of Angels,* Margaret Herrick Library. See also the discussion of *Band of Angels* in Courtney, *Hollywood Fantasies of Miscegenation,* 193–94.

10. Walter Doniger, interview by the author, April 24, 2008.

11. *New Yorker,* July 20, 1957.

12. Raoul Walsh, interview by Patrick McGilligan and Debra Weiner, 49.

13. L. Q. Jones, interview by the author.

14. Ibid.

15. Ibid.

16. *Battle Cry* production files.

17. *New York Times,* August 15, 1959.

15. The Adventure Is Larger Than the Man

1. Mary Walsh Papers.

2. *Esther and the King* production files, Twentieth Century–Fox Papers, Cinematic Arts Library, University of Southern California. A small number of production files are also collected in the Twentieth Century–Fox Papers, Arts Library/Special Collections, University of California, Los Angeles.

3. Ibid.

4. Ibid.

5. Mary Walsh Papers.

6. Cited in Fox, "Action All the Way," 40.

7. *New York Herald Tribune,* April 9, 1961.

8. Hisayo Graham, interview by the author, March 8, 2010.

9. Ibid.

10. Ibid.

11. *Dallas Morning News,* September 21, 1961.

12. Cited in Nicholas J. Cull, "Anatomy of a Shipwreck: Warner Bros., the White House and the Sinking of *PT 109*" (n.d.). Cull generously provided me with a copy of this essay (a chapter in a forthcoming book project), which covers the entire episode (and the fiasco) of the making of *PT 109*.

13. *PT 109* production files, Warner Bros. Archives.

14. Correspondence regarding Walsh's dismissal from the *PT 109* production is to be found both in the Raoul Walsh Legal Files and in the Jack Warner Papers, both at the USC Cinematic Arts Library.

15. Hisayo Graham, interview by the author, March 8, 2010.

16. Hank Kilgore, interview by the author, February 19, 2010.

17. Jack Warner Papers.

18. *A Distant Trumpet* production files, Warner Bros. Archives.

19. William Clothier, interview by John Gallagher, *Films in Review,* October 1987, 474.

20. Ibid.

21. *A Distant Trumpet* production files.

22. See the photograph gallery, especially shot and caption, from *A Distant Trumpet* in Diana Serra Cary, *The Hollywood Posse: The Story of a Gallant Band of Horsemen Who Made Movie History* (New York: Houghton Mifflin, 1975).

23. Pierre Rissient, interview by the author.

24. *Los Angeles Times,* January 19, 1965.

25. Hisayo Graham, personal communication, March 8, 2010.

26. Ibid.

27. Pierre Rissient, interview by the author.

28. Raoul Walsh, interview by Hedda Hopper.

29. Ibid.

30. Pierre Rissient, interview by the author.

31. Ibid.

32. Ibid.

33. Raoul Walsh, interview by Hedda Hopper.

34. Hedda Hopper Papers.

35. Bill Stephens, "Freud Wears a Black Hat in Western Author's Credo," *Los Angeles Times,* 1963, courtesy Bob Bookman.

36. Original manuscript in the private collection of Bob Bookman, courtesy Bob Bookman.

37. Pierre Rissient, personal communication, November 2007.

38. Original manuscript in the private collection of Bob Bookman, courtesy Bob Bookman.

39. Pierre Rissient, personal communication, November 2007.

40. Bob Bookman, interview by the author, March 2010.

41. Courtesy Bob Bookman.

42. Jeanine Basinger, interview by the author, June 2007.

43. Bob Bookman, interview by the author, March 2010.

44. Ibid.

45. Charles Silver, curator, Department of Film, Museum of Modern Art, personal communication, June 2008.

46. Todd McCarthy, *Howard Hawks: The Grey Fox of Hollywood* (New York: Grove, 1997), 464.

47. Peter Bogdanovich, interview by the author, June 2008.

48. Ibid.

49. Ibid.

50. *International Herald Tribune,* July 2, 1972.

51. *New York Times*, April 14, 1974.

52. Courtesy Bob Bookman.

53. Sue Kilgore, personal communication, October 2009.

54. Courtesy Bob Bookman.

55. Courtesy Fred Lombardi, Allan Dwan's biographer.

Epilogue

1. L. Q. Jones, interview by the author.

2. Raoul Walsh Papers (used with the permission of Richard Schickel).

3. L. Q. Jones, interview by the author.

Selected Bibliography

Oral Histories, Seminars, and Retrospectives Pertaining to Walsh

Adamson, Joe. Interview with Byron Haskin. *The Directors Guild of America Oral History Series.* Los Angeles, 1984.

"Seminar with Raoul Walsh." New York Times Oral History. American Film Institute, Los Angeles, 1977.

The Thousand Eyes. "Raoul Walsh." New York, June 1974. Notes from the Raoul Walsh Retrospective at MOMA under the direction of Roger McNiven and Howard Mandelbaum.

Books and Articles Containing Interviews with Walsh

Bogdanovich, Peter. *Who the Devil Made It? Conversations with Legendary Film Directors.* New York: Ballantine, 1997. Interview on 127–69.

Child, James. "Can You Ride the Horse?" *Sight and Sound,* Winter 1972–1973.

Eyquem, Olivier, Michael Henry, and Jacques Saada. "Entretien avec Raoul Walsh." *Positif,* February 1973.

Fox, Julian. "Action All the Way." *Films and Filming,* June–July 1973.

McGilligan, Patrick, ed. *Film Crazy: Interviews with Hollywood Legends.* New York: St. Martin's, 2000. Interview on 9–52.

McGilligan, Patrick, Debra Weiner, and Bruce Dix. "Raoul Walsh Remembers Warners." *Velvet Light Trap,* Autumn 1975.

Montgomery, Patrick. "Raoul Walsh Talks about D. W. Griffith." *Film Heritage,* Spring 1975.

Noames, Jean-Louis. "Entretien avec Raoul Walsh." *Cahiers du Cinema,* April 1964.

Schickel, Richard. *The Men Who Made the Movies.* New York: Atheneum, 1975. Interview on 15–54.

Sherman, Eric, ed. *Directing the Film: Directors on Their Art.* Los Angeles: Acrobat, for the American Film Institute, 1976.

Stevens, George, Jr., ed. *Conversations with the Great Moviemakers of Hollywood's Golden Age—at the American Film Institute.* New York: Vintage, 2006. Interview on 20–32.

Books and Articles Discussing Walsh, His Films, and His Times

Agee, James. *Agee on Film*. 2 vols. New York: Perigee/Putnam, 1958–1960.

Behlmer, Rudy, ed. *Inside Warner Bros., 1935–1951*. New York: Viking, 1985.

Bernstein, Matthew. *Walter Wagner, Hollywood Independent*. Minneapolis: University of Minnesota Press, 2000.

Bessie, Alvah. *Inquisition in Eden*. New York: Macmillan, 1965.

Beylie, Claude. "Meconnaissance de Raoul Walsh." *Cinematext*, May–June 1963.

Biette, Jean-Claude. "Aperçu Raoul Walsh." *Traffic*, Winter 1998.

Bitzer, Billy. *Billy Bitzer, His Story*. New York: Farrar, Straus, Giroux, 1973.

Bleys, Jean-Pierre. "Quelques jalons (peu connus) dans le parcours de Raoul Walsh." *Positif*, July–August 1989.

Bodeen, DeWitt. "Raoul Walsh." *Films in Review*, April 1982.

Brownlow, Kevin. *Behind the Mask of Innocence: Sex, Violence, Prejudice, Crime: Films of Social Conscience in the Silent Era*. Berkeley and Los Angeles: University of California Press, 1990.

———. *The Parade's Gone By*. Berkeley and Los Angeles: University of California Press, 1968.

———. "Raoul Walsh." *Film*, Autumn 1982.

———. *The War, the West and the Wilderness*. New York: Knopf, 1978.

Burnett, W. R. *High Sierra*. New York: Zebra, 1940.

Cagney, James. *Cagney by Cagney*. New York: Doubleday, 1976.

Canham, Kingsley. *The Hollywood Professionals*. Vol. 1, *Michael Curtiz, Raoul Walsh, Henry Hathaway*. London: Tantivy, 1973.

Caron, Leslie. *Thank Heaven: A Memoir*. New York: Viking Adult, 2009.

Cary, Diana Serra. *The Hollywood Posse: The Story of a Gallant Band of Horsemen Who Made Movie History*. New York: Houghton Mifflin, 1975.

Casas, Joaquin. *Raoul Walsh*. Madrid: JC, 1982.

Cohen, Paula Marantz. *Silent Film and the Triumph of the American Myth*. Oxford: Oxford University Press, 2001.

Comuzio, Emmano. *Raoul Walsh*. Florence: La Nuovo Italia, 1974.

Conley, Walter. "Raoul Walsh, His Silent Films." *Silent Picture*, Winter 1970–1971.

Cooper, Miriam. *Dark Lady of the Silents: My Life in Early Hollywood*. New York: Bobbs-Merrill, 1973.

Coursodon, Jean-Pierre, and Bertrand Tavernier. *American Directors*. 2 vols. New York: McGraw-Hill, 1983.

Courtney, Susan. *Hollywood Fantasies of Miscegenation*. Princeton, NJ: Princeton University Press, 2005.

Crafton, Donald. *The Talkies: American Cinema's Transition to Sound, 1926–1931*. Berkeley and Los Angeles: University of California Press, 1997.

Cruikshank, Herbert. "He Envies His Actors; And upon the Least Provocation Raoul Walsh Stops Directing and Joins Them." *Motion Picture Classic*, January 1929.

Custer, Elizabeth Bacon. *Boots and Saddles: Life in Dakota with General Custer.* New York: Harper & Bros., 1885.

D'Angela, Toni. *Raoul Walsh o dell'avventura singolare.* Rome: Bulzone, 2008.

Donati, William. *Ida Lupino: A Biography.* Lexington: University Press of Kentucky, 1996.

Douglas, Kirk. *The Ragman's Son.* New York: Simon & Schuster, 1998.

Everson, William K. *American Silent Film.* New York: Da Capo, 1998.

Farber, Manny. *Negative Space.* New York: Da Capo, 1998.

Fiedler, Leslie. *Love and Death in the American Novel.* New York: Stein & Day, 1966.

"Film Division Names Director Advisors." *Moving Picture World,* July 20, 1918, 363–64.

Fishgall, Gary. *Gregory Peck: A Biography.* New York: Scribner, 2002.

Flynn, Errol. *My Wicked, Wicked Ways.* New York: Dell, 1959.

Forbes, Bryan. "The Last Buccaneer." *Observer Magazine,* December 2, 1979.

———. *Notes for a Life.* London: Collins, 1974.

Fox, Susan, and Donald G. Rosellini. *William Fox: A Story of Early Hollywood.* Baltimore: Midnight Marquee, 2006.

Freedland, Michael. *The Two Lives of Errol Flynn: The Legends and the Truth about a Lovable, Outrageous Rogue.* New York: Morrow, 1978.

Gallagher, John. "Raoul Walsh." *Films in Review,* October 1987, 472–78.

Giddins, Gary. *Bing Crosby: A Pocketful of Miracles: The Early Years, 1903–1940.* Boston: Little, Brown, 2001.

Giuliani, Pierre. *Raoul Walsh.* Filmo no. 14. Paris: Edilig, 1985.

Golden, Eve. *Vamp: The Rise and Fall of Theda Bara.* Vestal, NY: Empire, 1996.

Gomery, Douglas. *The Hollywood Studio System: A History.* London: British Film Institute, 2005.

Grady, Bill. *The Irish Peacock: Confessions of a Legendary Talent Agent.* New Rochelle, NY: Arlington, 1972.

Graham, Cooper, Steve Higgins, Elaine Mancini, and Joao Luiz Viera. *D. W. Griffith and the Biograph Company.* Metuchen, NJ: Scarecrow, 1985.

Gunning, Tom. *D. W. Griffith and the Origins of the American Narrative Film: The Early Years at Biograph.* Champaign: University of Illinois Press, 1993.

Hardy, Phil, ed. *Raoul Walsh, Edinburgh Film Festival, 1974.* Colchester: Vineyard, 1974.

Henry, Michael. "Raoul Walsh, le roman du continent perdu." *Positif,* December 1998.

Higham, Charles. "He Directed Them All." *New York Times,* April 14, 1974.

"His Beard Was Long and His Hair Hung Down, and the Girl of His Heart Was Coming to Town." *Moving Picture World,* October 4, 1919, 66.

Huggins, Roy. "Remembering Raoul Walsh." *Variety,* October 27, 1987.

Hunter, Tab, with Eddie Muller. *Tab Hunter Confidential: The Making of a Movie Star.* Chapel Hill, NC: Algonquin, 2005.

Kemp, Philip. "Raoul Walsh." In *World Film Directors* (2 vols.), ed. John Wakeman, 1:1149–59. New York: Wilson, 1987.

Kildare, Owen. *My Mamie Rose: The Story of My Regeneration.* New York: Baker & Taylor, 1903.

Marmin, Michael, *Raoul Walsh.* Paris: Seghers, 1970.

Mason, Fred. *American Gangster Cinema: From Little Caesar to Pulp Fiction.* New York: Palgrave Macmillan, 2002.

Mayo, Virginia. *The Best Years of My Life.* Chesterfield, MO: Beach House, 2001.

McBride, Joseph. *Searching for John Ford: A Life.* New York: St. Martin's, 2001.

McCarthy, Todd. *Howard Hawks: The Grey Fox of Hollywood.* New York: Grove, 1997.

McGilligan, Patrick, ed. *Backstory 1: Interviews with Screenwriters of Hollywood's Golden Age.* Berkeley: University of California Press, 1986.

———, ed. *White Heat.* Wisconsin/Warner Bros. Screen Play Series. Madison: University of Wisconsin Press, 1984.

McGilligan, Patrick, and Paul Buhle. *Tender Comrades: A Backstory of the Hollywood Blacklist.* New York: St. Martin's, 1997.

McLaglen, Victor. *Express to Hollywood.* London: Jarrolds, 1935.

McNiven, Roger. "Raoul Walsh, 1887–1981 [*sic*]." *Film Comment,* July–August 1981.

———. "The Western Landscape of Raoul Walsh." *Velvet Light Trap,* Autumn 1975.

Mizner, Wilson. "Wilson Mizner Turns Informer." *Photoplay,* November 1928.

"A Motion Picture Director's Problems." *Moving Picture World,* May 4, 1918, 702.

Munn, Michael. *John Wayne: The Man behind the Myth.* New York: New American Library, 2003.

Nasaw, David. *The Chief: The Life of William Randolph Hearst.* New York: Mariner, 2001.

Oppenheimer, Jerry. *Idol: Rock Hudson.* New York: Bantam, 1987.

Parrish, Robert. *Growing Up in Hollywood.* New York: Harcourt Brace Jovanovich, 1976.

Phillip, Claude-Jean. "Un sublime si familiar." *Presence du cinema,* May 1962.

Poitier, Sydney. *This Life.* New York: Knopf, 1980.

Quinn, Anthony, with Daniel Paisner. *One Man Tango.* New York: Harper Collins, 1995.

Ramsaye, Terry. *A Million and One Nights: A History of the Motion Picture Industry through 1925.* New York: Touchstone, 1954.

"Raoul A. Walsh to Direct George Walsh." *Moving Picture World,* September 22, 1917, 1838.

"Raoul A. Walsh to Make Special Stills for Use on Posters." *Moving Picture World,* August 21, 1920, 1055.

"Raoul Walsh Asks Damages of $245,000, Charging Mayflower Violated Contract." *Moving Picture World*, March 12, 1921, 176.

"Raoul Walsh Back to Coast." *Moving Picture World*, February 19, 1916, 1113.

"Raoul Walsh Plays and Directs." *Moving Picture World*, December 17, 1927, 27.

"Raoul Walsh to Direct Gloria." *Moving Picture World*, June 4, 1927, 329.

"Raoul Walsh Will Return to Fox." *Moving Picture World*, September 24, 1927, 223.

Ravanbaz, Raymond. "Le monde de Raoul Walsh est celui de l'aventure." *Radio-Cinema-Television*, February 22, 1959.

Roberts, Jerry, ed. *Mitchum: In His Own Words*. New York: Limelight, 2000.

Robinson, Edward G., and Leonard Spigelgass. *All My Yesterdays*. New York: Hawthorn, 1973.

Russell, Jane. *Jane Russell: My Path and My Detours: An Autobiography*. New York: F. Watts, 1985.

Saada, Jacques. "Un homme ocean." *Presence du cinema*, May 1962.

Saint Johns, Ivan. "The Lion Tamer." *Photoplay*, September 1925.

Schickel, Richard. *D. W. Griffith: An American Life*. New York: Limestone, 1984.

Segond, Jacques. "*Each Man in His Time* and Raoul Walsh." Edited by Phil Hardy. *Positif*, June 1976.

Server, Lee. *Robert Mitchum: "Baby, I Don't Care."* New York: St. Martin's/Griffin, 2002.

———. *Screenwriter, Words Become Pictures*. Pittstown, NJ, 1987. [Interviews with A. I. Bezzerides on *They Drive by Night* and Catherine Turney on *The Man I Love*.]

Sklar, Robert. *City Boys: Cagney, Bogart, Garfield*. Princeton, NJ: Princeton University Press, 1992.

Skorecki, Louis. *Raoul Walsh et moi, suivi de Contre la nouvelle cinephilie*. Paris: Presses Universitaires de France, 2001.

Special issue on Raoul Walsh. *Cahiers du cinema*, April 1964.

Special issue on Raoul Walsh. *Contrechamp*, May 1962.

Special issue on Raoul Walsh. *Film and Filming*, June 1977.

Special issue on Raoul Walsh. *Positif*, February 1973.

Special issue on Raoul Walsh. *Positif*, December 1998.

Special issue on Raoul Walsh. *Positif*, April 2001.

Special issue on Raoul Walsh. *Presence du cinema*, May 1962.

Sperber, A. M., and Eric Lax. *Bogart*. New York: Morrow, 1997.

Swanson, Gloria. *Swanson on Swanson: An Autobiography*. New York: Random House, 1980.

"To Probably Transfer Walsh-Mayflower Suit." *Moving Picture World*, April 23, 1921, 828.

Tornabene, Lyn. *Long Live the King*. New York: Putnam's, 1976.

Vance, Jeffrey, with Tony Maietta. *Douglas Fairbanks*. Berkeley and Los Angeles: University of Californa Press/Academy of Motion Picture Arts and Sciences, 2008.

Villelaur, Anne. "Raoul Walsh." *Dossiers du cinema, Cineastes II*. Casterman, Paris, 1971.

Walsh, Raoul. *La colère des justes* (The wrath of the just ones). Paris: Belford, 1972.

——. *Each Man in His Time*. New York: Farrar, Straus, Giroux, 1974.

——. "Spontaneity in Acting." *New York Times*, April 27, 1924.

"Walsh an Adventurer." *Moving Picture World*, July 4, 1914, 18.

"Walsh Joins Goldwyn." *Moving Picture World*, December 1, 1917, 1301.

"The Walsh's [sic] Are Working Together." *Moving Picture World*, August 17, 1918, 997.

"Walsh Talks about Casting." *Moving Picture World*, January 12, 1918, 57.

"Walsh to Occupy Municipal Studios in Long Island City Now Being Formed." *Moving Picture World*, January 31, 1920, 760.

"Walsh to Remain with Fox." *Moving Picture World*, January 19, 1918, 345.

Warner, Jack. *My First Hundred Years in Hollywood*. New York: Random House, 1965.

Watts, Jill. *Mae West: An Icon in Black and White*. New York: Oxford University Press, 2003.

West, Mae. *Goodness Had Nothing to Do with It*. New York: Manor, 1976.

"What Walsh Found in Goldwyn Studio." *Moving Picture World*, January 5, 1918, 57.

Wills, Garry. *John Wayne's America*. New York: Touchstone, 1998.

Wilson, Michael Henry. *Raoul Walsh; ou, La saga du continent perdu*. Paris: Cinematheque Française, 2001.

Youngkin, Stephen D. *The Lost One: A Life of Peter Lorre*. Lexington: University Press of Kentucky, 2005.

Index